W9-AEO-459

Fodor's

ESSENTIAL
SCOTLAND

Welcome to Scotland

Scotland packs spectacular landscapes, as well as rich history and tradition, into a small country. From the Lowlands to the Highlands, its lush woodlands, windswept moors, and deep lochs will take your breath away. Impressive castles, whisky distilleries, and golf courses entice, and cities such as Edinburgh and Glasgow combine tradition with cutting-edge festivals and vibrant cultural scenes. This book was produced during the COVID-19 pandemic. As you plan your upcoming travels to Scotland, please confirm that places are still open and let us know when we need to make updates by writing to us at editors@fodors.com.

TOP REASONS TO GO

★ **Castles:** Stirling, Glamis, Floors, and others tell tales of a complex, turbulent past.

★ **Cool cities:** Edinburgh's International Festival and Fringe; Glasgow's nightlife.

★ **Islands:** Skye's misty mountains, Islay's seabirds, Orkney's prehistoric remains.

★ **Whisky:** Distillery tours and tastings refine an appreciation for the national drink.

★ **Landscapes:** Crystal-clear lochs and rivers, wooded hills, wide-open moors.

★ **Golf:** The great names here include St. Andrews, Gleneagles, and Western Gailes.

Contents

MAPS

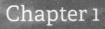

Chapter 1

EXPERIENCE SCOTLAND

25 ULTIMATE EXPERIENCES

Scotland offers terrific experiences that should be on every traveler's list. Here are Fodor's top picks for a memorable trip.

1 Prehistoric Monuments

Around Scotland, haunting structures like the Calanais Standing Stones on the Isle of Lewis provide an intriguing glimpse into the past. Sights are scattered across the landscape but Orkney claims a large concentration. (Ch. 9, 11, 12)

2 Castles

Whether in ruins or full of treasure, castles dating from the medieval period to Victorian times are among Scotland's glories. (Ch. 3–12)

3 Isle of Skye

With the misty Cuillin Mountains and rocky shores, Skye has few rivals among the country's islands for sheer loveliness. (Ch. 11)

4 Glencoe

The wild beauty of Glencoe's craggy peaks and deep valley provided the background for a tragic massacre in 1692, but today the area is popular for outdoor activities. (Ch. 10)

5 Whisky Tours

From Speyside to Islay, whisky distilleries offer tours and tastings of Scotland's signature drink. Their often-spectacular settings are an added bonus. (Ch. 5, 7–12)

6 Scottish Folk Culture

For a true Scottish experience, attend a *ceilidh*, a night of traditional folk dancing, singing, and music. (Ch. 3–12)

7 Glasgow

An urban renaissance has brought great shopping and nightlife to complement the city's rich architectural heritage and museums like the Kelvingrove. (Ch. 4)

8 Iona Abbey

One of Scotland's most spiritual spots, the abbey located on the island of Iona, in the Inner Hebrides, is considered the birthplace of Christianity in Scotland. (Ch. 9)

9 Hiking

Fully immerse yourself into the Scottish landscape by embarking on a hike through the countryside, like on the 93-mile West Highland Way. (Ch. 7)

10 Dundee

Once an industrial powerhouse, this Fife city has become a booming art hub in recent years, with impressive museums like the V&A Dundee and the McManus Galleries. (Ch. 6)

11 Loch Ness

Scotland's most famous loch continues to charm thanks to its alleged longtime resident, Nessie (aka the Loch Ness Monster). (Ch. 10)

12 Loch Lomond and the Trossachs

Its clear water makes Loch Lomond a coveted retreat, while the lakes and hills of the Trossachs are the essence of the Highlands. (Ch. 7)

13 Robert Burns

Visit the birthplace of Scotland's most famous poet (known for writing "Auld Lang Syne") or celebrate his birthday with a Burns Supper via poetry, haggis, and whisky. (Ch. 4)

14 Edinburgh Festival

The Edinburgh Festival is actually a collection of several festivals—including the Fringe, book, and art festivals—all taking place around the same time in August. (Ch. 3)

15 Hogmanay

New Year's Eve, or "Hogmanay," is Edinburgh's biggest night of the year. In fact, Edinburgh's Hogmanay party is one of the world's biggest New Year celebrations. (Ch. 3)

16 Culloden Moor Battlefield

The final Jacobite uprising, in which "Bonnie Prince" Charles Edward Stuart attempted to reclaim the British throne, was decisively and brutally crushed in 1746 at Culloden in the Highlands. (Ch. 10)

17 Cairngorms National Park

Many of Scotland's highest peaks are found in the Great Glen in stunning Cairngorms National Park, where you can also hike, ski, and spot wildlife. (Ch. 10)

18 The Northern Isles

Two remote islands in the north, the beautifully remote Orkney and Shetland have a colorful Scandanavian heritage, notable prehistoric artifacts, and rollicking festivals. (Ch. 12)

19 Cycling

Another popular way to explore the Central Highlands is via bicycle. The Low/Highland Trail stretches over 60 miles through the Trossachs and Loch Katrine. (Ch. 7)

20 Edinburgh

Scotland's capital charms with its Royal Mile and Old Town while the National Museum of Scotland and Edinburgh Castle give history lessons. (Ch. 3)

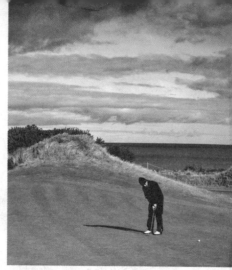

21 Seafood

From salmon to oysters, the superb fish and seafood from the rivers, lakes, and the sea are treats to savor. Delicately smoked fish is a specialty, served hot or cold. (Ch. 3–12)

22 Golf

The home of golf, Scotland claims some of the world's most challenging holes but has courses for all levels, many in beautiful settings by lakes, hills, or the ocean. (Ch. 3–11)

23 Jacobite Steam Train

The famous trip from Fort William to the coast at Mallaig offers spectacular views of mountains and lochs as well as a ride over the 21 arches of the Glenfinnan Viaduct. (Ch. 10)

24 Stirling

One of the best places to explore the country's history is Stirling, with its grand castle and Old Town telling the tales of early Scotland. (Ch. 7)

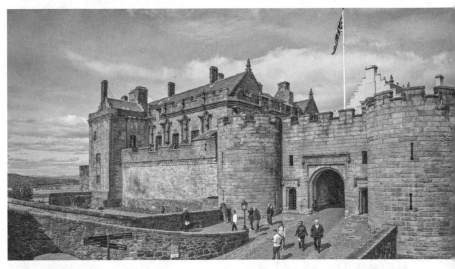

25 Seaside Towns

The country's jagged coastline and many islands create scenic settings for towns such as Tobermory on the Isle of Mull, with its colorfully painted houses. (Ch. 9)

WHAT'S WHERE

1 Edinburgh and the Lothians. Scotland's captivating capital is the country's most popular city, famous for its high-perched castle, Old Town and 18th-century New Town, unusual Parliament building, Georgian and Victorian architecture, superb museums, and the most celebrated arts festival in the world. For fewer crowds, escape to the Lothians and its coastal towns, beaches, and castles.

2 Glasgow. The country's largest city has evolved from prosperous Victorian hub to depressed urban center to thriving modern city with a strong artistic, architectural, and culinary reputation. Museums and galleries such as the Kelvingrove and Gallery of Modern Art (GoMA) are here, along with the Arts and Crafts architecture of Charles Rennie Mackintosh and renowned institutions such as Glasgow University.

3 The Borders and the Southwest. Scotland's southern gateway from England, the Borders is rustic but historically rich. It's known for being the home of Sir Walter Scott and has impressive stately

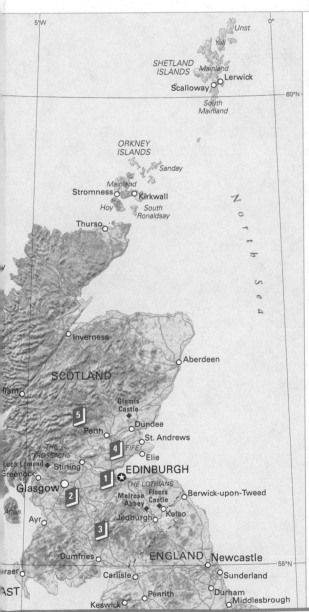

homes such as Floors Castle and ruined abbeys including Melrose. The southwest, or Dumfries and Galloway region, is perfect for scenic drives, castles, and hiking.

4 Fife and Angus. The "kingdom" of Fife is considered the sunniest and driest part of Scotland, with sandy beaches, fishing villages, and stone cottages. St. Andrews has its world-famous golf courses, but this university town is worth a stop even for nongolfers. To the north in Angus are Glamis Castle, the legendary setting of Shakespeare's *Macbeth*, as well as the city of Dundee with its increasing cultural and leisure attractions.

5 Stirling and the Central Highlands. Convenient to both Edinburgh and Glasgow, this area encompasses some of Scotland's most beautiful terrain, with rugged, dark landscapes broken up by lochs and fields. Not to be missed are Loch Lomond and the Trossachs, Scotland's first national park. Perth and Stirling are the main metropolitan hubs and worth a stop; Stirling Castle has epic views that stretch from coast to coast.

WHAT'S WHERE

6 Aberdeen and the Northeast. Malt-whisky buffs can use the prosperous port city of Aberdeen, known for its silvery granite buildings, as a base for exploring the region's distilleries, including those on the Malt Whisky Trail. Aberdeen also makes a good starting point for touring Royal Deeside, with its purple moors and piney hills as well as the notably rich selection of castles built over many centuries, including Balmoral.

7 Argyll and the Isles. Remote and picturesque, this less visited region of the southwestern coastline has excellent gardens, religious sites, and distilleries. If you like whisky, a trip to Islay is a must; if it's mountains you're after, try Jura; if a Christian site strikes a chord, head to Iona. The Isle of Arran is the place to see Scotland's diversity shrunk down to a more intimate size.

8 Inverness and Around the Great Glen. An awe-inspiring valley laced with rivers and streams defines this part of the country. A top spot for hikers, this Highland glen is ringed by tall mountains, including

10°W

SCOTLAND

ATLANTIC OCEAN

Lewis ○ Stornoway
OUTER
HEBRIDES
Harris

North
Uist
Isle
of Skye   Eilean Donan
Castle
South
Uist

Fort William

Coll
Tiree
Iona ◆   Isle
of Mull   Oban
INNER
HEBRIDES   ARGYLL

Jura
Green
Islay   7

Arran

Kintyre

0   50 mi
0   50 km

IRELAND   ○ Londonderry
Donegal ○   NORTHERN   Stranraer
IRELAND
○ Omagh   ✪ BELFAST

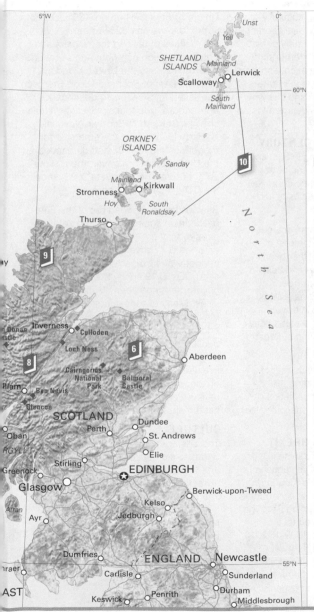

Ben Nevis, Britain's tallest mountain. Rugged Cairngorms National Park lies to the east of this area. Glencoe and Culloden are historic sites not to miss; those who believe in Nessie, Scotland's famous monster, can follow the throngs to Loch Ness.

9 The Northern Highlands and the Western Isles. This rugged land is home to the lore of clans, big moody skies, and wild rolling moors. It's also the place to see one of Scotland's most picturesque castles, Eilean Donan, which you pass on the way to the beautiful, popular Isle of Skye. The stark, remote Outer Hebrides, or Western Isles, offer ruined forts and chapels. This is where you go for real peace and quiet.

10 Orkney and Shetland Islands. Remote and austere, these isles at the northern tip of Scotland require tenacity to reach but have an abundance of prehistoric sites, including standing circles, *brochs* (circular towers), and tombs, as well as wild, open landscapes. The Shetland Isles, with their barren moors and vertical cliffs, are well known for bird-watching and diving opportunities.

Scotland Today

It may have just 5.5 million people, but today Scotland has some big ideas about where it's headed socially, culturally, and economically. International sporting events, the lively (but ultimately defeated) 2014 referendum on whether to become an independent nation, and even First Minister Nicola Sturgeon's state visits to the United States and elsewhere continue to focus worldwide attention on Scotland.

TRAVEL IN THE 21ST CENTURY

The experience of traveling in Scotland has changed markedly for the better in recent years, with wholesale improvements in standards of hospitality and food especially.

Today hotels and restaurants charge prices similar to those in the rest of the United Kingdom. On the other hand, most of Scotland's biggest and best museums and galleries are free. Walk through well-tended gardens, along bustling waterfronts, and in beautifully renovated neighborhoods—a good day out can show you everything but cost nothing at all.

In 2022 Scotland presents its Year of Scotland's Stories, celebrating the country's rich storytelling traditions. Check out ⊕ *www.visitscotland.org* for upcoming themed years.

INDEPENDENCE AND BREXIT

Dominating Scotland's public life in recent years has been the relationship of Scotland with the United Kingdom, Parliament, and the increasingly troubled state of this 300-year-old union. Through devolution, Scotland elected its first parliament in 300 years in 1999. In 2014 the independence referendum saw 55% vote against Scotland becoming an independent country. But that vote by no means resolved the matter, especially given the unpopularity in Scotland of the 2016 U.K. vote to leave the European Union, or Brexit, when only 38% of Scots voted to leave and 62% to remain. With the realities of leaving the single-market European Union contributing to economic turmoil across the United Kingdom, First Minister of Scotland Nicola Sturgeon has called for a second independence referendum, due to a significant material change. Sturgeon's Scottish Nationalist Party (SNP) reset the timetable for triggering "IndyRef 2" and demanded the United Kingdom government allow another referendum in late 2023, should the COVID pandemic permit.

Besides being dragged out of the European Union against the wishes of its people, why are many Scots dissatisfied with the U.K. government? In a time of budget woes exacerbated by the ill-managed COVID-19 crisis, the Westminster government has been slashing public services. Many of these cuts deeply offend the Scots, who are committed to free education and free health care from the publicly owned National Health Service. Many commentators predict that further Brexit-induced economic turmoil and erosions of public services by the largely reviled Prime Minister Boris Johnson will hasten another independence vote.

CULTURE

The arts continue to thrive, a sign of Scotland's creative energy. Edinburgh's arts festivals grow bigger every year, attracting visitors from around the globe. The National Theatre of Scotland has been such a resounding success that productions have made their way to Broadway. Glasgow is renowned for contemporary arts—Glasgow artists often win the Turner Prize, Britain's most prestigious art honor.

In a sign of vitality, culture is not confined only to the large cities. Far to the north, Shetland (already drawing audiences with its folk festivals) has built Mareel, a remarkable live-music venue and cinema. Dundee is the United Kingdom's sole UNESCO City of Design (Detroit represents the United States) and is the location of the first outpost of London's Victoria and Albert Museum, opened in 2018. Perth's renewal will center on the transformation of Perth City Hall into a museum and gallery.

LAND

It's a disturbing fact that just 500 people own half the land in Scotland, many of them wealthy foreigners who have become absentee landlords. Experts say that giving residents a say on what happens to the land they live on is crucial if communities are going to thrive. New models of community ownership and management are being hard won, particularly in the Western Isles. There have been some community buyouts in which farming communities get the government's help to purchase the land where they live and work.

Still the depopulation of rural Scotland continues. The popularity of holiday homes has meant that some villages are fully inhabited for only a few weeks each summer. Those who want to live here permanently find that low wages, a high cost of living, and a lack of affordable housing mean that they are priced out of a home surrounded by such beauty.

WIND POWER

Urged by the government to help the country meet its ambitious targets for renewable energy, Scottish landowners began leasing land to the corporations behind wind farms. Scotland now has many large-scale commercial wind farms—including some of Europe's largest—and hundreds of smaller ones, many in community ownership. This has sparked vociferous debate. The pro-wind lobby argues in favor of emission-free energy that's better for the environment than coal or nuclear plants, while the anti-wind camp decries the environmental damage to ancient peat bogs and bird populations.

Turbines are now being built offshore, which is another cause for dispute. Donald Trump, who ignored environmental activists while building his sprawling golf estate, had a very public fallout with government officials over the "ugly" planned offshore turbine plant that will be visible from his golf course. The former American president continues to withhold the multimillion-dollar investment he promised at the outset.

SCOTLAND, FINALLY WINNING

When it comes to sports, the Scots have reveled in their traditional role as the underdog. But Olympic gold medal–winning cyclist Chris Hoy and tennis Grand Slam winner Andy Murray have shown that this narrative needs rewriting.

As well as regularly hosting major golf tournaments, Scotland has of late proved itself as a worthy and welcoming venue for prestigious international events. After the success of the Glasgow Commonwealth Games in 2014 and with St. Andrews hosting the landmark 150th Open Golf Championship in 2022, pride and participation in Scottish sports is growing.

What to Eat and Drink in Scotland

SHORTBREAD

The traditional Scottish biscuits may seem simple enough (they're typically made from one part white sugar, two parts butter, and three parts oat flour), but there are countless varieties, from big name brands like Walkers to artisan biscuit makers.

FULL SCOTTISH BREAKFAST

The full Scottish is a hearty, filling, and artery-clogging morning staple, which includes some or all of the following: back bacon, sausages, black pudding, haggis, eggs (fried, poached, or scrambled), baked beans, grilled tomatoes, mushrooms, tattie (potato) scones, and toast.

WHISKY

No trip to Scotland is complete without trying a dram or two of Scotland's most famous tipple. There are several distinct Scotch whisky regions, each producing a single malt with its own complex character, from sweeter Speyside whiskies to smokier Islays.

HAGGIS, NEEPS, AND TATTIES

From the offal-heavy list of ingredients (minced heart, liver, and lungs mixed with onions, oatmeal, and spices) and the unconventional cooking method (the mixture is boiled in a sheep's stomach), haggis may not sound like the most appetizing of meals. But there's a very good reason for its status as Scotland's national dish: it's delicious. Travel the country and you'll see haggis all over menus. It's traditionally served with neeps (turnips) and tatties (potatoes), but is also found at breakfast, in sandwiches, and even on nachos.

SMOKED FISH

From Arbroath smokies to Finnan haddie, smoked fish is a staple of Scottish dining tables nationwide. Smokies are haddock, salted and dried overnight, then smoked in a barrel over a hardwood fire, while Finnan haddies are cold-smoked haddock, cooked over green wood and peat. And that's only the start of the many regional variations of smoked fish all over Scotland. Visitors will also find menus featuring smoked herring (kippers), smoked trout, and, of course, smoked salmon.

Smoked fish

REAL ALES

Also known as draught cask ale, real ale is unfiltered, unpasteurized beer that is served directly from a cask. The term was coined in the early 1970s to differentiate traditional English-style beers, containing live yeast and therefore naturally bubbly, from the highly processed, artificially carbonated beers made by big breweries of the time. Today real ales (from IPAs and stouts to golden ales and porters) are served in all good Scottish pubs; look for a traditional hand-pulled pump or for beer being served directly from the cask.

FISH-AND-CHIPS

Usually known as a "fish supper" in Scotland, this British staple comprises battered and deep-fried fish (most commonly cod, haddock, or another white fish) served with a portion of thick-cut potato "chips" (a thicker, greasier version of fries). For a true Scottish experience, ask for it with salt and "chippy sauce," a pungent mix of malt vinegar and brown sauce, which is similar to American steak sauce.

SCOTCH PIE

Once frowned upon by the Church of Scotland for being too decadent, these savory snacks are now embraced by all. The small, double-crust meat pastries are filled with mutton or similar meat and spiced with pepper. You can pick them up from most Scottish bakeries and fish-and-chips shops to eat on the go.

CULLEN SKINK

Cullen skink is a decadently creamy fish soup that's made with hearty smoked haddock, potatoes, onions, and cream. Think American chowder, but thicker, smokier, and served piping hot with bread. You'll find it on the menu in many Scottish pubs and restaurants, especially on the coasts.

What to Buy in Scotland

KILTS

These knee-length pleated skirts, usually made from woolen cloth in a tartan pattern, are the traditional dress of men in the Highlands. While no longer everyday wear for most modern Scots, you'll still see kilts worn on special occasions like weddings.

TUNNOCK'S TEA CAKES

A small shortbread biscuit covered in a marshmallow dome and then dipped in milk chocolate, these small sweet treats are quintessentially Scottish, with the Tunnock's bakery based just outside Glasgow. You will find the cookies in B&B bedrooms, coffee shops, and hipster bars all across the country, and if you want to take a selection home as a taste of Scotland, you can pick up a pack of six in any Scottish supermarket.

ANYTHING TARTAN PRINT

Like the look of tartan but can't see yourself in a kilt? No problem. You'll find plenty of other tartan print products on sale in Scotland, from sweaters and scarves to coats and cushions to backpacks and bow ties. If you want to go the whole hog, order yourself a statement tartan-clad armchair from ANTA in Edinburgh.

SINGLE-MALT WHISKY

It's no surprise that whisky is one of the most popular Scottish souvenirs. After all, nowhere makes single-malt whisky quite like Scotland. If you have a chance to try some drams on a distillery tour, you can then pick up a bottle (or several) to take home. Otherwise, most supermarkets have a good selection of Scottish whiskies. Don't worry if you are low on luggage space; you can pick up a bottle at the airport duty-free.

A SCOTTISH CREST

If you have Scottish heritage or know someone else who does, why not order something decorated with the family crest of a Scottish clan? Whether you are an Armstrong, a McDonald, or a Walker, there are all manner of crest-related gifts available in Scotland, from certificates and cufflinks to embossed hip flasks.

GREYFRIARS BOBBY STUFFED ANIMAL

Every visitor to Edinburgh can recount the tale of Greyfriars Bobby, a Skye Terrier dog who guarded his master's grave for 14 years and who is now immortalized in a popular statue next to Greyfriars Kirk. You will find "cuddly" (stuffed) toys of the city's renowned canine resident for sale all over Edinburgh; it's the perfect gift for a little one.

Quaich

OOR WULLIE COMIC BOOK

A popular Scottish comic character "born" in 1936, Oor Wullie (real name: William Russell) is considered a Scottish institution. In fact, in a 2004 poll, he was voted "Scotland's Favorite Son" ahead of William Wallace, Sean Connery, and Robert Burns. To see the latest strip, simply pick up a copy of the *Sunday Post* from any newsstand, or for a longer read, pick up the latest Oor Wullie Annual from any good bookshop.

QUAICH

An old Highland symbol of kinship and friendship, this shallow drinking vessel was the original whisky tumbler. Its distinctive two-handle design means it can be shared amicably between friends and loved ones (and it's still used to toast the bride at weddings).

Though traditionally made of wood and modestly decorated, modern quaichs are commonly made from pewter and silver to allow for personalized engraving.

HEATHERGEMS JEWELRY

For a truly unique Scottish souvenir or gift, it's hard to beat Heathergems. This unique range of jewelry is made from the stems of natural heather, a plant that grows throughout Scotland and is recognizable for its purple flowers. Choose from elegant silver drop earrings, stylish animal-shaped brooches, and more.

HARRIS TWEED

A traditional cloth handwoven from pure virgin wool by crofters in the Western Isles (not just Lewis and Harris, but also North Uist, Benbecula, South Uist, and Barra), Harris

Tweed is world famous for its warmth, softness, resilience, and breathability. From jackets to scarves to blankets, Harris Tweed items are for sale across the Western Isles but also on the mainland; simply look for the official orb trademark.

IRN-BRU

After whisky, Irn-Bru is the drink most associated with Scotland. The luminous orange carbonated soda even outsells Coca-Cola in these parts. Nobody can quite agree exactly what the flavor is, and it famously isn't to everyone's taste, but you can't say you have truly experienced Scotland without a sip of Irn-Bru. They also make for an inexpensive but distinctly Scottish souvenir.

Best Museums in Scotland

NATIONAL MUSEUM OF SCOTLAND, EDINBURGH
From Dolly the Sheep (the world's first cloned mammal) to the Lewis Chessmen (ivory-carved medieval chess pieces), the National Museum of Scotland has a host of fascinating, family-friendly exhibits. It also has one of Edinburgh's best city views; take the elevator to the rooftop terrace for a stunning panorama of the city.

KELVINGROVE ART GALLERY AND MUSEUM, GLASGOW
One of Scotland's most popular museums, Kelvingrove's collection includes works by Rembrandt, van Gogh, and Dali, an impressive collection of arms and armor, a gigantic concert pipe organ, and much more.

AUCHINDRAIN MUSEUM, ARGYLL
The open-air Auchindrain Museum is a rarity: a real opportunity to step back in time. As one of the last surviving examples of an 18th-century farming community, this fine museum allows you to wander freely around its furnished thatched buildings and learn about the lives of Highland farmers living in the 1700s.

RIVERSIDE MUSEUM, GLASGOW
Set within an eye-catching, Zaha Hadid–designed building on the banks of the Clyde, the award-winning Riverside Museum has an exhaustive collection of transport exhibits, from skateboards to steam trains and everything in between. The Tall Ship *Glenlee* at Riverside, a Victorian cargo ship turned fascinating attraction, is moored outside.

SCOTTISH FISHERIES MUSEUM, FIFE

This fascinating Fife museum brings to life the history and heritage of Scottish fisherfolk through a series of exhibits, including fishing apparatus, paintings, and model ships, while a look out the window reveals a working boatyard. If the fishing-themed exhibits make you hungry, famous Anstruther Fish Bar is next door.

V&A DUNDEE

The V&A Dundee design museum is not only the first V&A outpost outside London but also the country's first design museum; it features permanent exhibits from designers across Scotland, including Charles Rennie Mackintosh.

McMANUS GALLERY, DUNDEE

Another Dundee favorite, the McManus houses one of Scotland's most impressive fine art collections, while the building—a grand Gothic Revival style construction—is a work of art in itself.

ROBERT BURNS BIRTHPLACE MUSEUM, ALLOWAY

Although a little off the beaten track, this interesting little Alloway museum is well worth the journey. As the name suggests, the Robert Burns Birthplace Museum is dedicated to Scotland's national poet, Rabbie Burns, who is perhaps best known for his poem—and now a New Year's Eve staple song—"Auld Lang Syne." Set within the humble cottage where he was born, it houses thousands of his manuscripts and artifacts.

WEST HIGHLAND MUSEUM, FORT WILLIAM

You're unlikely to spend more than a few days in Scotland without hearing the story of Bonnie Prince Charles and the 1745 Jacobite Rebellion (fans of the TV show *Outlander* will be especially familiar with it). This small museum explores this important slice of Scottish history through a host of fascinating and folksy exhibits.

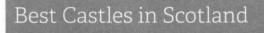

Best Castles in Scotland

STIRLING CASTLE

Magnificent Stirling Castle was at the heart of the Wars of Independence, and the biggest prize for Robert the Bruce's famous victory at Bannockburn. The castle's royal connections lasted for centuries; it was later the childhood home of Mary, Queen of Scots. Today exhibits tell the story of the castle's roles as a battle site, royal palace, and tourism hot spot.

EDINBURGH CASTLE

Scotland's most famous medieval fortress, Edinburgh Castle is the capital's crowning glory, having played host to kings, queens, soldiers, and prisoners for close to a millennium.

DUNNOTTAR CASTLE

The site of these captivating castle ruins, perched on a cliff overlooking the turbulent North Sea, is one of the most dramatic in Scotland. Famed for saving the Scottish crown jewels from the grasp of Oliver Cromwell, Dunnottar Castle now provides a fine sea-air stop on a drive from Dundee to Aberdeen.

DRUMLANRIG CASTLE

Owned by one of the wealthiest families in Britain, pink-sandstone Drumlanrig Castle sits at the heart of an enormous estate and has period features dating back to the 16th century, a world-class art collection, and a host of activities on offer.

CRATHES CASTLE

With a beautiful backdrop of rolling green hills, the impeccably preserved 16th-century Crathes Castle is one of Scotland's lesser-known gems. Situated just outside Aberdeen, it is home to Jacobean rooms with painted ceilings, an impressive collection of portraits, and a vast estate of gardens, fields, and woodland.

FLOORS CASTLE

Built in the 1720s as the seat of the Duke of Roxburghe, the enormous Floors Castle remains the property of the duke to this day. which makes it the largest inhabited castle in Scotland. It has grand rooms decorated with plush furnishings, old portraits, and precious porcelain.

CAERLAVEROCK CASTLE

A true Scottish landmark, 13th-century Caerlaverock Castle is instantly recognizable for its rare triangular design. Although built to control trade, its strategic location on the border of Scotland and England inevitably led to a key role in the Wars of Independence; it subsequently endured cycles of ruin, repair, and rebuilding.

BALMORAL CASTLE

This imposing estate house has been an official residence of the royal family since 1852 and remains the Queen's summer home of choice. Its 19th-century design is faux–Scottish baronial, but its grandiose ballroom, formal grounds, and fascinating exhibits make it a worthwhile stop.

GLAMIS CASTLE

Beautiful Glamis Castle has a long history of royal connections, from Macbeth, King of the Scots (who was the Thane of Glamis, as well as Cawdor) to Princess Margaret (who was born within its four walls). Consequently, for any lovers of Shakespeare or the British royal family, Glamis Castle is a must-see sight.

EILEAN DONAN

The most postcard-perfect castle, Eilean Donan sits pretty on a loch islet en route to the Isle of Skye. Often obscured by rolling fog, the 14th-century fortification—a merry mess of imposing towers, timber-framed roofs, and crooked staircases—connects to the mainland via a stone-arched bridge.

Best *Outlander* Filming Locations

DOUNE CASTLE
A stand-in for the fictional Castle Leoch in the show (the home of dashing warrior Jamie Fraser's uncle, Colum Mackenzie, and his clan), Doune Castle is a medieval stronghold that dates back to the 14th century. In addition to *Outlander*, the castle has featured in *Game of Thrones*, *Ivanhoe*, and *Monty Python and the Holy Grail*.

BLACKNESS CASTLE
Located about eight miles west of South Queensferry on the shores of the Firth of Forth, the mighty fortification of Blackness Castle ably plays the Fort William base of dastardly Black Jack Randall in the show.

PALACE OF HOLYROODHOUSE
The official Scottish residence of the Queen, this is where Bonnie Prince Charlie established his court for six weeks before the Jacobite Uprising; in the show, Claire and Jamie visit the prince here to beg him to abandon his hopeless cause.

GLENCOE
Even if you've never made it beyond the opening credits of *Outlander*, you will still have seen glimpses of Glencoe, as its lush green valleys, snowcapped peaks, and glistening lakes feature in the title sequence. And no wonder, when it is one of Scotland's most attractive locations.

CULLODEN BATTLEFIELD
A popular tourist attraction not far outside Inverness, Culloden Battlefield was the site of the last battle of the Jacobite Uprising. Unusual for this list, this is a real-life attraction that plays itself in the series; it appears in the scene where Jamie and Claire say goodbye before he leaves to fight in the historic battle.

CALANAIS STANDING STONES AND CLAVA CAIRNS
The mysterious, prehistoric Calanais Standing Stones were the main inspiration for Craigh na Dun, the fictional stones that send Claire back in time in *Outlander*. There's also a touch of the Clava Cairns (a Bronze Age burial site) about Craigh na Dun.

HOPETOUN HOUSE
As perhaps Scotland's finest stately home, the turn-of-the-18th-century building houses stunning interiors and a sprawling English garden–style landscape park. It's been used as several locations in the show, standing in for the home of the Duke of Sandringham and the Hawkins Estate.

CULROSS
As a living museum of 17th-century Scottish life, the seaside town of Culross has played the Black Kirk, the village of Cranesmuir, the location of Balriggan Cottage, and has been a backdrop to the Jacobite encampment and makeshift hospital scenes.

LINLITHGOW PALACE
As the birthplace of Mary, Queen of Scots and the seat of Stewart kings, Linlithgow Palace is steeped in real medieval history. But in the fictional world of *Outlander*, the palace stood in as Wentworth Prison, where Jamie is tried and sentenced to hang—though not before being tortured by Black Jack Randall.

CRAIGMILLAR CASTLE
Known to *Outlander* fans as the remote Ardsmuir Prison, the place of Jamie's incarceration in season three, the handsome ruined Craigmillar Castle is in fact situated just a few miles from the center of Edinburgh.

The Best Whisky Distilleries in Scotland

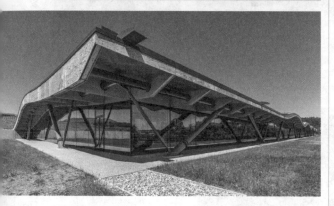

THE GLENLIVET

Founded in 1824, The Glenlivet was the first licensed distillery anywhere in the Highlands, and it's been in operation almost continually since. The 12-year-old distillery's signature smooth, lightly fruity style makes it the biggest selling single malt in the United States, while the full collection features experimental sherry-cask whiskies, light peaty drams, and white oak reserves.

THE MACALLAN

One of the world's most popular single malts, The Macallan has produced whisky here for nigh on two centuries. Its collection is matured in a mix of bourbon oak and oak sherry casks, making for a heady blend of perfumed, spicy, and sweet drams.

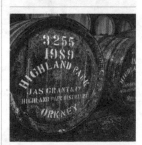

HIGHLAND PARK

It may no longer be Scotland's northernmost distillery, but it remains one of Scotland's finest. The Highland Park distillery was founded in Orkney more than 220 years ago and has since won countless global awards for its peat-heavy, Viking-themed spirits.

GLEN GRANT DISTILLERY

A perennial Speyside favorite, Glen Grant Distillery is renowned for three things: it was the first Scottish distillery to be electrically powered; it's surrounded by beautiful gardens that feature rivers and lily ponds; and it consistently produces excellent whisky.

ISLE OF ARRAN DISTILLERS

Located on the southwestern Isle of Arran, this distillery only began producing whisky in 1995, but it has quickly gained an enviable reputation for its fresh, sweet, and spicy single malts. Choose from a series of distillery tours and whisky tastings.

LAPHROAIG

For lovers of peaty whiskies, the Laphroaig distillery is a place of pilgrimage, as Islay's most distinctive single malt is renowned for its smoky flavor and smooth finish. Take a tour of the distillery, which includes great views of the coast and its iconic pagoda-style chimney.

TOBERMORY DISTILLERY
For an off-the-beaten-path whisky-tasting experience, look no further than Tobermory Distillery. Situated on the Isle of Mull, it has been producing whisky on and off since 1798. Today you can try its signature Ledaig single malt, as well as its unpeated Tobermory whisky, on a visit to its white-walled visitor center.

GLENMORANGIE DISTILLERY

One of the Highlands' best-known distilleries, Glenmorangie makes arguably the archetypal Speyside whisky: light, floral, and sweet. The distillery offers a range of experiences, including in-depth tours and tasting master classes.

BUNNAHABHAIN
A special distillery with an equally special view, Bunnahabhain (pronounced Boon-a-ha-bin) sits on the northeastern shore of Islay looking across the sea to Jura. Along with its setting, the whisky is also one of a kind—less peaty and more citrusy than its neighbors— and you can try it yourself on a distillery tour.

GLENFIDDICH

The world's most popular single malt whisky and one of the most famous stops on the Malt Whisky Trail, Glenfiddich is a bona fide Scotch superstar. As you would expect, it has a visitor center to suit its status. Knowledgeable guides offer a range of tours and tastings.

Playing Golf in Scotland

There are some 550 golf courses in Scotland for just 5.5 million residents, so the country has probably the highest ratio of courses to people anywhere in the world. If you're visiting Scotland, you'll probably want to play the "famous names" sometime in your career.

So by all means, play the championship courses such as the Old Course at St. Andrews, but remember they *are* championship courses. You may enjoy the game itself much more at a less challenging course. Remember, too, that everyone else wants to play the big names, so booking can be a problem at peak times in summer. Reserving three to four months ahead is not too far for the famous courses, although it's possible to get a time up to a month (or even a week) in advance if you are relaxed about your timing. If you're staying in a hotel attached to a course, get the concierge to book a tee time for you.

Happily, golf has always had a peculiar classlessness in Scotland. It's a game for everyone, and for centuries Scottish towns and cities have maintained courses for the enjoyment of their citizens. Admittedly, a few clubs have always been noted for their exclusive air, and some newer golf courses are losing touch with the game's inclusive origins, but these are exceptions to the tradition of recreation for all. Golf here is usually a democratic game, played by ordinary folk as well as the wealthy.

TIPS ON PLAYING

Golf courses are everywhere in Scotland. Most courses welcome visitors with a minimum of formalities, and some at a surprisingly low cost. Other courses are very expensive, but a lot of great golf can be played for between about £30 to £100 a round. Online booking at many courses has made arranging a golf tour easier, too.

Be aware of the topography of a course. Scotland is where the distinction between "links" and "parkland" courses was first made. Links courses are by the sea and are subject to the attendant sea breezes—some quite bracing—and mists, which can make them trickier to play. The natural topography of sand dunes and long, coarse grasses can add to the challenge. A parkland course is in a wooded area and its terrain is more obviously landscaped. A "moorland" course is found in an upland area.

Here are three pieces of advice, particularly for North Americans: (1) in Scotland the game is usually played fairly quickly, so don't dawdle if others are waiting; (2) caddy carts are hand-pulled carts for your clubs and driven golf carts are rarely available; and (3) when they say "rough," they *really* mean "rough."

Unless specified otherwise, hours are generally sunrise to sundown, which in June can be as late as 10 pm. Note that some courses advertise the SSS, "standard scratch score," instead of par (which may be different). This is the score a scratch golfer could achieve under perfect conditions. Rental clubs, balls, and other gear are generally available from clubhouses, except at the most basic municipal courses. Don't get caught by the dress codes enforced at many establishments: in general, untailored shorts, round-neck shirts, jeans, and sneakers are frowned upon.

The prestigious courses may ask for evidence of your golf skills by way of a handicap certificate; check in advance and carry this with you.

COSTS AND COURSES

Many courses lower their rates before and after peak season—at the end of September, for example. It's worth asking about this.

■TIP→ **Some areas offer regional golf passes that save you money. Check with the local tourist board.**

For a complete list of courses, contact local tourist offices or VisitScotland's official and comprehensive golf website, ⊕ *www.visitscotland.com/see-do/active/golf.* It has information about the country's golf courses, special golf trails, regional passes, special events, and tour operators, as well as on conveniently located accommodations. U.K. Golf Guide (⊕ *www.ukgolfguide.com/countries/scotland)* has user-generated reviews.

For information about regional courses, also see individual chapters.

BEST BETS AROUND SCOTLAND

If your idea of heaven is teeing off on a windswept links, then Scotland is for you. Dramatic courses, many of them set on sandy dunes alongside the ocean, are just one of the types you'll encounter. Highland courses that take you through the heather and moorland courses surrounded by craggy mountains have their own challenges.

Boat of Garten Golf Club, Inverness-shire. With the Cairngorm Mountain as a backdrop, this beautiful course has rugged terrain that requires even seasoned players to bring their A game. As an added bonus, a steam railway runs alongside the course.

Carnoustie Golf Links, Angus. Challenging golfers for nearly 500 years, Carnoustie is on many golfers' must-do list. The iconic Championship Course has tested many of the world's top players, while the Burnside and Buddon courses attract budding McIlroys, Spieths, and Koepkas.

Castle Stuart Golf Links, Inverness-shire. A more recent addition to Scotland's world-class courses offers cliff-top hazards, sprawling bunkers, and rolling fairways overlooking the Moray Firth.

Cruden Bay Golf Club, Aberdeenshire. This challenging and enjoyable links course was built by the Great North of Scotland Railway Company in 1894. Its remote location beside a set of towering dunes makes it irresistible.

Dunbar Golf Club, East Lothian. This classic and challenging links course has dramatic weather and scenery, with a backdrop of the Firth of Forth, Bass Rock, and a lighthouse.

Gleneagles, Perthshire. Host of the 2014 Ryder Cup championship, Gleneagles has three 18-hole courses that challenge the pros and a nine-hole course that provides a more laid-back game. It's also home to the PGA National Golf Academy.

Machrihanish Golf Club, Argyll. A dramatic location on the Mull of Kintyre and some exciting match play make these links well worth a journey.

Royal Dornoch Golf Club, Sutherland. Extending across a coastal shelf, Royal Dornoch has fast greens, pristine beaches, and mountain views. In spring yellow gorse sets the green hills ablaze.

St. Andrews Links, Fife. To approach the iconic 18th hole in the place where the game was invented remains the holy grail of golfers worldwide.

Western Gailes Golf Club, near Glasgow. This splendid links course is a final qualifying course for the British Open. Sculpted by Mother Nature, it's the country's finest natural links course.

Film Locations Throughout Scotland

Scotland's dramatic scenery and the character of its people have left impressions on viewers since the birth of the moving image. Today visitors not only seek out the locations seen in blockbuster series such as *Outlander*, *Game of Thrones*, and James Bond films, but also classic and cult movie scenes: from *Local Hero* and *The Wicker Man* to *Shallow Grave* and *Trainspotting*. Here is a selection of some standout film locations:

EDINBURGH AND THE LOTHIANS

Edinburgh and the Lothians' handsome architecture is the backdrop for many productions. In the 1969 adaptation of Muriel Spark's novel *The Prime of Miss Jean Brodie*, Oscar winner Maggie Smith leads her 1930s schoolgirls around Edinburgh Academy on Henderson Row, Greyfriars Churchyard, and the Vennel (Grassmarket), retreating to Cramond. In *Trainspotting's* (1994) opening sequence Renton and pals flee the police down Princes Street and steps toward Calton Street Bridge. *T2*, the 2017 sequel, revisits this iconic chase scene and also includes Commercial Street, Leith, Arthur's Seat, Scottish Parliament, Royal Circus, and Stockbridge. The feel-good musical *Sunshine on Leith* (2013), based on the Proclaimers' rousing tunes, plays out in the Old Town and on the Port of Leith's cobblestone streets. Auld Reekie's magical skyline and atmosphere is captured in the charming animation *The Illusionist* (2010). *Outlander* (2014) season one and two feature Hopetoun House, Blackness Castle, and Linlithgow Palace.

GLASGOW

Glasgow's street grid makes it a good stand-in for U.S. cities including Philadelphia in zombie flick *World War Z* (2013) starring Brad Pitt; while Blythswood Hill resembles San Francisco in *Cloud Atlas* (2012). The grand City Chambers stand in for: belle époque New York mansions in *House of Mirth* (2000); the Vatican in *Heavenly Pursuits* (1986); and the Kremlin in *An Englishman Abroad* (1983). Hutcheson's Hall on Ingram Street appears in *The Wife* (2017), starring Glenn Close. *Mission Impossible's* (2000) railway chase finale is a blur of East Ayrshire countryside and Ballochmyle Viaduct. Brooding landscapes make the Borders and the Southwest ripe for intrigue, murder, and mystery. Hermitage Castle's role in 16th-century regal plotting appears in *Mary Queen of Scots* (1971), starring Vanessa Redgrave and Glenda Jackson; a lavish retelling was filmed in 2017. Chilling cult B-feature *The Wicker Man* centers on a pagan Scottish isle, with many creepy scenes filmed around Newton Stewart, including St. Ninian's Cave, Castle Kennedy, and Logan Botanic Gardens.

FIFE AND ANGUS

Many visitors to Fife and Angus hum Vangelis's *Chariots of Fire* (1984) synthesizer soundtrack, reenacting the slow-motion sprint along St. Andrews West Beach. The Royal and Ancient club and Fife's coastal links also appear in *Tommy's Honour* (2017), telling the story of Old and Young Tom Morris's relationship and golfing history.

CENTRAL HIGHLANDS

Doune Castle in the Central Highlands is synonymous with *Monty Python and the Holy Grail* (1975), the first Winterfell in *Game of Thrones* (2011), and then Castle Leoch for *Outlander*. The Falls of Dochart appear in the *39 Steps* (1959) and *Casino Royale* (1967).

ABERDEEN AND THE NORTHEAST

Fans of the much-loved *Local Hero* (1983) with Burt Lancaster and Peter Reigert make a pilgrimage to Aberdeen and the northeast harbor village Pennan's red telephone box and nearby Banff's Ship Inn. For the fictional west-coast village of Furness's beach and Ben's shack, go west to Camusdarach, Morar. Royal Deeside and Balmoral Estate are at the heart of *The Queen* (2009), *The Crown* (2016), and *Mrs. Brown* (1997).

ARGYLL AND THE ISLES
Duart Castle in Argyll and the Isles has staged real-life kidnap attempts and celluloid dramas including *I Know Where I'm Going* (1945) and *Entrapment* (1999). Mull's Treshnish Peninsula and Oban feature in the spy thriller the *Eye of the Needle* (1981), starring Donald Sutherland.

INVERNESS AND AROUND THE GREAT GLEN
Glen Nevis is clan central in *Braveheart* (1995), while *Rob Roy* (1995) rampages around Glen Coe, Rannoch Moor, Lochs Morar, and Leven, and Eilean Donan Castle. The lochside castle also stars in *Master of Ballatrae* (1953) with Errol Flynn, *Highlander* (1986) with Sean Connery, and *The World Is Not Enough* (1999) as MI6 headquarters Scotland. Another Bond movie, *Skyfall* (2012), has a spectacular A82 driving scene. Billie Wilder's *The Private Life of Sherlock Holmes* (1971) introduces Urquhart Castle for some Loch Ness monster encounters. Glenfinnan Viaduct has become synonymous with the Harry Potter films; Clachaig Gully, Glencoe, Steall Falls in Glen Nevis, and Loch Eilt also appear.

NORTHERN HIGHLANDS AND WESTERN ISLES
Skye's Cuillin mountain outcrops are now so popular with jet-setting fans of *Outlander*, *Macbeth* (2015), *Prometheus* (2012), *Skyfall* (2012), and *Stardust* (2007) that they are best visited in low season. Animation adventure *Brave* (2012) enchants children with its hyper-realistic depictions of Calanais Standing Stones, Glen Affric, and Dunnotar Castle. Dunrobin Castle impersonates a French chateau in Stanley Kubrick's adaptation of William Makepeace Thackeray's novel

Barry Lyndon (1975). *Whisky Galore* (1949) was filmed on Barra, while the 2016 remake barrels around the mainland (see ⊕ *www.visitscotland.com/blog/films/whisky-galore*).

ORKNEY AND SHETLAND ISLANDS
The essence of Scotland's far-flung isles and the evacuation of St. Kilda inspired *The Edge of the World* (1937), filmed on Foula in the Orkney and Shetland Islands. Pioneering filmmakers Jenny Gilbertson and Margaret Tait were stirred by the landscapes and communities on these archipelagos, directing *The Rugged Island* (1934) and *Blue Black Permanent* (1992), respectively. Four seasons of crime drama *Shetland* (2013–) showcase the windswept Nordic scenery, including extinct volcano Eshaness.

SILENT FILMS
Early silent short film reels of the late 1890s and early 1900s focused on Scots history, customs, and events. *Gordon Highlanders* (1899) and *Rothesay Entertainers Trailer* (1918) are among 2000 clips and feature films that can be viewed at the Moving Image Archive, at Kelvingrove, Glasgow, and ⊕ *www.nls.uk/collections/moving-image-archive*. A fascinating selection of the archive appears in the documentary *From Scotland with Love* (2014).

FILM TOURS
Mary's Meanders. Mary's has themed tours including *Outlander* film locations. ☎ *0781/868-7066* ⊕ *www.marysmeanders.co.uk* ✉ *From £80.*

Open Roads Scotland. Open Roads offers James Bond-, Harry Potter-, and *Outlander*–themed tours. ☎ *0141/634–8444* ⊕ *openroadscotland.com.*

What to Watch and Read Before Your Trip

OUTLANDER

If you're traveling to Scotland in the 21st century, chances are you're going to hear about the cultural phenomenon that is *Outlander*. The book series by Diana Gabaldon first captured the attention of the world in 1991, with many readers becoming dedicated fans of the time-traveling series through eight (and counting) novels. But then the television series debuted in 2014 on Starz and it seems the entire world fell in love with the love story between Claire Randall and Jamie Fraser amid a stunning Scottish Highlands backdrop. Both the book and the television show tell the same story: a nurse in 1946 finds herself sent back in time to 1743 Scotland, where she becomes entangled in the Jacobite uprising and falls in love with a Highland warrior. Many scenes are filmed on location, and you will find many a tour eager to take you to filming spots throughout the country.

BRAVEHEART

This 1995 classic starring Mel Gibson was many a filmgoer's introduction to Scottish history and remains one of the most quoted movies ever. It tells a very embellished story of the real 13th-century Scottish warrior, William Wallace, who did lead the Scots in the First War of Scottish Independence against England. While historians will be happy to point out the many historical inaccuracies, the film was nonetheless a commercial and critical success, earning several Academy Awards, including Best Picture.

BRAVE

The first Pixar film directed by a woman (Brenda Chapman) and the first with a female main character, this 2012 animated film tells the story of Merida, the headstrong daughter of a Scottish king and queen who wishes to defy tradition in the name of her independence. Along with a heartwarming tale of mother and daughter love and acceptance, it portrays gorgeous animation of the Scottish Highlands and Highland traditions.

MACBETH BY WILLIAM SHAKESPEARE

Shakespeare may be England's most famous writer, but one of his most famous plays tells a distinctly Scottish tale. The play is based on the lives of actual men who fought for power in 11th-century Scotland although the real life versions of Macbeth, Macduff, and Duncan were quite different. Nevertheless, the fiction that the Bard weaves is one of the most powerful stories of ambition, power, and politics (and witchcraft) ever written.

THE HEART OF MIDLOTHIAN BY SIR WALTER SCOTT

Scotland's other famous literary son is Sir Walter Scott, a late-18th-/early-19th-century poet, historian, and writer who wrote several classics with Scotland as the backdrop, including *Ivanhoe* and *The Lady of the Lake*. But perhaps his most truly Scottish work is this 1818 novel that tells the tale of a woman who wishes to receive a royal pardon for her sister amid the 1736 Porteous riots in Edinburgh.

THE PRIME OF MISS JEAN BRODIE BY MURIEL SPARK

One of Scotland's most popular writers of the 20th century, Muriel Spark was born in Edinburgh and went on to write several novels and essays well known for their satire and wit. In her most famous book, written in 1961, she tells the story of Jean Brodie, a free-spirited teacher at a 1930s school for girls, whose emphasis on art and romance inspires a group of young women.

Chapter 2

TRAVEL SMART

Updated by
Nick Bruno

★ **CAPITAL:**
Edinburgh

♛ **POPULATION:**
5,438,100

💬 **LANGUAGE:**
English

$ **CURRENCY:**
British pound

☎ **COUNTRY CODE:**
44

⚠ **EMERGENCIES:**
999

🚗 **DRIVING:**
On the left

⚡ **ELECTRICITY:**
230V/50 cycles; plugs have
three rectangular blades

🕐 **TIME:**
Five hours ahead of New
York

🌐 **WEB RESOURCES:**
www.visitbritain.com
www.visitscotland.com
www.nts.org.uk

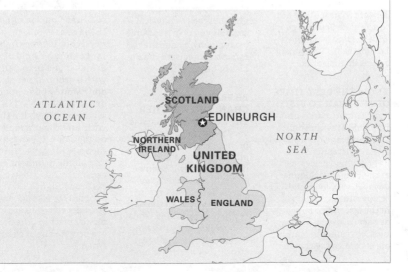

Know Before You Go

Scotland is indeed one of the most accessible places for a traveler to visit, but there are still some key things to keep in mind before your trip. From tipping to understanding the ever-elusive Scottish accent, here's everything you need to know before a trip to Scotland.

DON'T MIX UP YOUR SCOTS WITH YOUR WELSH.

Remember that although Scotland is part of the United Kingdom politically and does share many cultural links with England, Wales, and Northern Island, Scots do not take kindly to their country being called England or being called English (or increasingly even British). In recent years the Scottish have developed a burgeoning pride in their distinctive identity, which has led to a waning sense of being British. So when in conversation, it's best not to associate Scottish people with the much maligned London-based Parliament and its English elite.

KNOW THE BEST TIMES OF THE YEAR TO VISIT.

Peak tourist season runs from mid-May through mid-September. Crowds at main attractions can be heavy, and prices are at their highest. Summer days are very long, and temperatures can linger in the 60s, 70s, or 80s, with dry spells lasting a week or two. November to March marks the low season for travel. Winter sees lots of rain, some snow, and icy winds, not to mention the short days. City museums stay open year-round, but some tourist sites such as castles and historic houses close from November to Easter. You can get some excellent deals in spring (April to mid-May) and fall (mid-September to October); weather is cool and often rainy, but crowds are not as intense.

DON'T HUG A SCOT.

Although many Scots are fantastic talkers, they're less enthusiastic with greetings on the physical front. If you're in less familiar company, a handshake is more appreciated than a kiss or hug.

BE PREPARED FOR CHANGING WEATHER.

The weather in Scotland is very temperamental so be prepared for all possibilities, even in summer (including snow); it can be smart to pack layers and have a decent waterproof jacket on you at all times. If you plan on hiking while here, make sure you have decent outdoor equipment, sturdy footwear, food, and refreshments. If you don't know how to read a map and use a compass, hire an expert hiking guide.

THERE AREN'T REALLY ANY DRESS CODES OR EATING CODES.

When you are visiting houses of worship, modest attire is appreciated, though you will see shorts and even bared midriffs. Photographs are welcome in churches, outside of services. Shorts and other close-fitting attire are allowed just about anywhere else at any time, weather permitting; these days locals tend not to cover up as much as they used to. It's the same with food; Scots eat and drink just about anywhere, and much of the time they do it standing up or even walking.

BUT IT'S STILL GOOD TO KNOW SOME SCOTTISH ETIQUETTE.

In Scotland it's rude to walk away from a conversation, even if it's with someone you don't know. If you're at a pub, keep in mind that it's very important to buy a round of drinks if you're socializing with a group of people. You don't simply buy your own drink; you buy a drink for all the people you're there with, and those people do the same. It can make for a very foggy evening and public drunkenness, especially on Friday and Saturday nights. Conversational topics that are considered taboo are money matters; the Scots are private about their finances.

Driving etiquette is carefully observed, too; be courteous and allow people to pass. Jaywalking isn't rude or illegal, but it's much safer to cross with the lights, especially if traffic is coming from a direction you might not be used to. As for waiting in lines and moving through crowds, put your best foot forward. The Scots are very polite and you'll be noticed (and not in a good way) if you're not.

BE PREPARED TO NOT UNDERSTAND THE SCOTTISH ACCENT.
The Scots language, which borrows from Scandinavian, Dutch, French, and Gaelic, survives in various forms, with each region having its own dialect. In the northeast they speak Doric, while the Shetland and Orkney "tongue" is influenced by the now-extinct Norn. The Gaelic language, the indigenous language of those from the Western Isles and Highlands, has been given a new lease on life. Many primary schools in the region are teaching a new generation of Gaelic speakers. The language has its own TV channel, BBC Alba, and is being promoted in a huge signage campaign. Otherwise, Scots speak English often with a strong accent (which may be hard for nonnative Brits and Americans to understand), but your ear will soon come to terms with it.

BE AWARE IF YOU'RE HERE ON A BANK HOLIDAY.
The following days are public holidays in Scotland; note that the dates for England and Wales are slightly different. Ne'er Day and a day to recover (January 1–2), Good Friday, May Day (first Monday in May), Spring Bank Holiday (last Monday in May), Summer Bank Holiday (first Monday in August), St. Andrew's Day (November 30; for Scots government but optional for businesses), and Christmas (December 25–26). The majority of businesses might be closed on these days, but some museums and other major sights might be more crowded if they are open.

CHECK OUT THE OPTIONS FOR SIGHTSEEING PASSES.
Discounted sightseeing passes are a great way to save money on visits to castles, gardens, and historic houses. Just check what the pass offers against your itinerary to be sure it's worthwhile. The Explorer Pass, available from any staffed Historic Scotland (HS) property as well as from many tourist information centers, allows visits to HS properties for 5 (£33) or 14 (£45) consecutive days. The Scottish Heritage pass gives free access from April through October to over 120 Heritage Scotland–and National Trust for Scotland–run properties.

YES, YOU SHOULD TIP HERE.
Tipping is done in Scotland as in the United States, but at a lower level. Some restaurants include a service charge on the bill; if not, add about 10% to 15%. Taxi drivers, hairdressers, and barbers should also get 10% to 15%.

DON'T UNDERTAKE HIKES LIGHTLY.
Scotland has a stunning array of landscapes that make for some great walks and hikes, including the Great Glen, the Highlands, and more. But the wilderness of Scotland can still be quite a rugged place, so if you're not experienced as a hiker or camper, check to make sure you're undertaking the easiest trails possible. For longer or overnight hikes, consider going with a guide and always take the necessary precautions: bring plenty of food and water and always notify someone of the path you're taking and when you plan to return.

WATCH OUT FOR MIDGES IN THE HIGHLANDS.
If you're traveling in the Highlands and islands in summer, pack some midge repellent and antihistamine cream to reduce swelling: the Highland midge is a force to be reckoned with. Check ⊕ *www.smidgeup. com/midge-forecast* for updates on these biting pests.

Getting Here and Around

Air

Scotland's main hubs are Glasgow, Prestwick (near Glasgow), Edinburgh, Inverness, and Aberdeen. Glasgow and Prestwick are the gateways to the west and southwest, Edinburgh the east and southeast, Aberdeen and Inverness the north. All these cities have excellent bus and train transportation services and well-maintained roads that link them with each other and other cities within Scotland. Taxis are also an efficient and reliable option, but they are three to four times the cost of going by public transport.

Traveling by air is straightforward in Scotland. Security is heavy but efficient. You can often breeze through check-in lines by using your airline's online check-in option or bag drop, but confirm this ahead of time.

Flying time to Glasgow and Aberdeen is 6½ hours from New York, 7½ hours from Chicago, 9½ hours from Dallas, 10 hours from Los Angeles, and 21½ hours from Sydney. Flying time to Edinburgh is 7 hours from New York, 8 hours from Chicago, 10 hours from Dallas, 10½ hours from Los Angeles, and 22 hours from Sydney. Not all airlines offer direct flights to Scotland; many go via London. For those flights allow an extra four to five hours of travel (two to three for the layover in London plus an additional hour or two for the duration of the flight).

AIRPORTS

The major international gateways to Scotland are Glasgow Airport (GLA), about 7 miles outside Glasgow, and Edinburgh Airport (EDI), 7 miles from the city. Both offer connections for dozens of European cities and regular flights to London's Gatwick (LGW) and Heathrow (LHR) airports. Aberdeen Airport (ABZ) has direct flights to most major European cities. Prestwick (PIK) has direct flights to some European cities at discounted rates. Inverness (INV) offers direct flights in and around the United Kingdom.

Airport tax is included in the price of your ticket. Generally the tax for economy tickets within the United Kingdom from European Union countries is £13 while anywhere else is £78. The standard rate for flights from the United Kingdom and European Union is £26; for all other destinations it's £185.

All Scottish airports offer typical modern amenities: restaurants, cafés, shopping, sandwich and salad bars, pubs, pharmacies, bookshops, and newsstands; some even have spas and hair salons. Glasgow and Edinburgh are the most interesting airports when it comes to a delayed flight. Good food and shopping options abound—try Discover Scotland, Scottish Fine Gifts, and Tartan Plus for Scottish-inspired goods.

There are plenty of hotels near all airports, and all airports also have Internet access.

GROUND TRANSPORTATION

The best way to get to and from the airport based on speed and convenience is by taxi. All airport taxi stands are just outside the airport's front doors and are well marked with clear signs. Most taxis have a set price when going to and from the airport to the city center but will turn on the meter at your request. Ask the driver to turn on the meter to confirm the flat-rate price.

If you're traveling with a large party, you can request a people carrier to transport everyone, luggage included. Luggage is included in the taxi fare; you should not be charged extra for it.

If you're traveling alone, a more economical transfer option is public transportation. Buses travel between city centers and Glasgow, Edinburgh, Aberdeen, and

Inverness airports. Trams travel between Edinburgh Airport and the city center; Edinburgh Gateway station links the airport to the tram and rail network; trains go direct to Glasgow Prestwick Airport. All are fast, inexpensive, and reliable.

TRANSFERS BETWEEN AIRPORTS

Scottish airports are relatively close to one another and all are connected by a series of buses and trains. Flights between airports add hours to your journey and are very expensive (between £200 and £400). The best way to travel from one airport to another is by bus, train, car, or taxi. Normally you must take a combination of bus and train, which is easy and—if you travel light—quite enjoyable.

Those wishing to connect to Glasgow from Edinburgh airports who have some time on their hands can take a tram (£6.50) or bus (£4.50) to the Edinburgh city center and then a train to Glasgow city center (£13.50) and a shuttle bus to Glasgow Airport (£8.50). This journey should take you less than two hours. Taxis are fast but costly. The price of a taxi from Edinburgh Airport to Glasgow Airport is around £90, a good choice if you're traveling with a few people. Renting a car would be a good choice if you want to get from Edinburgh to, say, Aberdeen Airport and you're traveling with a group of people. Otherwise, take a train from Edinburgh Gateway.

FLIGHTS

Scotland has a significant air network for a small country. British Airways (or British Airways Express) has flights from London's Heathrow Airport or from Glasgow, Edinburgh, Aberdeen, and Inverness to the farthest corners of the Scottish mainland and to the islands.

Among the low-cost carriers, Virgin has service from Heathrow; and easyJet flies from London Luton/Gatwick/Stansted to and between Glasgow, Edinburgh, Aberdeen, and Inverness, plus to and from Belfast. Flybe has services to Sumburgh (Shetland) and Kirkwall (Orkney) from Aberdeen, Inverness, Glasgow, and Edinburgh, where you can continue on to Bristol, Cardiff, Exeter, Manchester, Newquay, and Southampton. Loganair also runs the Dundee–London City route.

🚲 Bike

Bicycling in Scotland is variable. The best months for cycling are May, June, and September, when the roads are often quieter and the weather is usually better. Because Scotland's main roads are continually being upgraded, bicyclists can easily reach the network of quieter rural roads in southern and much of eastern Scotland, especially Grampian. In a few areas of the Highlands, notably in northwestern Scotland, the rugged terrain and limited population have resulted in the lack of side roads, making it difficult—sometimes impossible—to plan a minor-road route in these areas.

For those sticking to the cities, dozens of electric bike rental stations have appeared across major cities in recent years, with established docks in Dundee, Inverness, and Glasgow.

Several agencies now promote routes for recreational cyclists. These routes are signposted, and agencies have produced maps or leaflets showing where they run. Perhaps best known is the Glasgow–Loch Lomond–Killin Cycleway. VisitScotland has advice on a site dedicated to cycling.

You can take bicycles on car and passenger ferries in Scotland, and it's usually not necessary to book in advance. Arrive early so that your bike can be loaded through the car entrance.

Getting Here and Around

ScotRail strongly advises that you make a train reservation for you and your bike at least one month in advance. On several trains, reservations are mandatory. ScotRail Highland Explorer trains have special carriages dedicated to cyclists on the scenic West Highland Line Glasgow-Oban.

ScotRail has also teamed up with cycle-rental companies to offer various discounts in Mallaig, Blair Atholl, Inverness, Oban, and Fort William.

BIKING ORGANIZATIONS

The Cyclists' Touring Club publishes a members' magazine, route maps, and guides. Sustrans is a nonprofit organization dedicated to providing environmentally friendly routes for cyclists. Active Scotland, part of the national tourism agency, has a great list of bike routes ranked by area and difficulty.

🚢 Boat and Ferry

Because Scotland has so many islands, plus the great Firth of Clyde waterway, ferry services are of paramount importance. Most ferries transport vehicles as well as foot passengers, although a few smaller ones are for passengers only.

It's a good idea to make a reservation ahead of time, although reservations are not absolutely necessary. Most travelers show up on the day of departure and buy their tickets from the stations at the ports. Keep in mind that these are working ferries, not tourist boats. Although journeys are scenic, most people use these ferries as their daily means of public transportation to and from their hometowns.

The main operator is Caledonian MacBrayne, known generally as CalMac. Services extend from the Firth of Clyde in the south, where there's an extensive network, right up to the northwest of Scotland and all the Hebrides. CalMac offers 33 island-hopping itineraries, called Hopscotch, valid for 31 days, which can be combined for tailored exploration. Fares can range from £5 to £8 for a short trip to over £50 for a longer trip with several legs.

The Dunoon–Gourock route on the Clyde is served by Western Ferries (for cars) and CalMac (for passengers and cycles only).

Northlink Ferries operates a car ferry for Orkney between Scrabster, near Thurso, and Stromness, on the main island of Orkney; and between Aberdeen and Kirkwall, which is also on the mainland of Orkney. Northlink also runs an efficient ferry to Lerwick, Shetland, and Kirkwall, Orkney. The journey to Lerwick is overnight, but comfortable cabins are available. These ferries can be busy in summer, so book well in advance.

🚌 Bus

Long-distance buses usually provide the cheapest way to travel between England and Scotland; fares may be as little as a third of the rail fares for comparable trips and are cheaper if you buy in advance. Nevertheless, the trip is not as comfortable as by train (no dining cart, smaller bathrooms, less spacious seats), and travel takes longer. Glasgow to London by nonstop bus takes 8 hours, 45 minutes; by train it takes about 5 hours, 30 minutes. Scotland's bus (short-haul) and coach (long-distance) network is extensive. Bus service is comprehensive in cities, less so in country districts. Express service links main cities and towns, connecting, for example, Glasgow and Edinburgh to Inverness, Aberdeen, Perth, Skye, Ayr, Dumfries, and Carlisle; or Inverness with Aberdeen, Wick, Thurso, and Fort William.

Express service is very fast, and fares are reasonable. Scottish Citylink, National Express, and Megabus are among the main operators; there are about 20 in all. All buses are nonsmoking.

DISCOUNTS AND DEALS

On Scottish Citylink, the Explorer Passes offer complete freedom of travel on all services throughout Scotland. Three permutations give 3 days of travel out of a 5-day period, 5 days of travel out of 10, and 8 days of travel out of 16. They're available from Scottish Citylink offices, and cost £49, £74, and £99 respectively.

National Express offers discounted seats on buses from London to more than 50 cities in the United Kingdom, including Glasgow and Aberdeen. Tickets range from £15 to £70, but only when purchased online. Megabus (order tickets online), a discount service, has similarly competitive prices between major cities throughout Scotland, including Aberdeen, Dundee, Glasgow, Inverness, and Perth.

FARES AND SCHEDULES

Contact Traveline Scotland for information on all public transportation and timetables.

For town, suburban, or short-distance journeys, you buy your ticket on the bus, from a pay box, or from the driver. You need exact change. For longer journeys—for example, Glasgow to Inverness—it's usual (and a good idea; busy routes and times can book up) to reserve a seat online.

🚗 Car

If you plan to stick mostly to the cities, you will not need a car. All cities in Scotland are either so compact that most attractions are within easy walking distance of each other (Aberdeen, Dundee, Edinburgh, Inverness, and Stirling) or are accessible by an excellent local public transport system (Glasgow). And there is often good train or bus service from major cities to nearby day-trip destinations. Bus tours are a good option for day trips.

Once you leave Edinburgh, Glasgow, and the other major cities, a car will make journeys faster and much more enjoyable than trying to work out public-transportation connections to the farther-flung reaches of Scotland (though it is possible, if time-consuming, to see much of the country by public transportation). A car allows you to set your own pace and visit off-the-beaten-path towns and sights most easily.

In Scotland your own driver's license is acceptable. International driving permits (IDPs) are available from the American Automobile Association and, in the United Kingdom, from the Automobile Association and Royal Automobile Club. These international permits, valid only in conjunction with your regular driver's license, are universally recognized; having one may save you a problem with local authorities.

PARKING

On-street parking is a bit of a lottery in Scotland. Depending on the location and time of day, the streets can be packed or empty of cars. In the cities you must pay for your on-street parking by getting a sticker from a parking machine; these machines are clearly marked with a large *P*. Make sure you have the exact change; the cost is around £3 for two hours, but can vary considerably from central to suburban zones, especially in Edinburgh and Glasgow. Put the parking sticker on the inside of your windshield. Parking lots are scattered throughout urban areas and tend to be more or less the same price as on-street parking.

Getting Here and Around

ROAD CONDITIONS

A good network of superhighways, known as motorways, and divided highways, known as dual carriageways, extends throughout Britain. In remote areas of Scotland where the motorway hasn't penetrated, travel is noticeably slower. Motorways shown with the prefix *M* are mainly two or three lanes in each direction, without any right-hand turns. These are the roads to use to cover long distances, though inevitably you'll see less of the countryside. Service areas are at most about an hour apart.

Dual carriageways, usually shown on a map as a thick red line (often with a black line in the center) and the prefix "a" followed by a number perhaps with a bracketed "t" (for example, "a304[t]"), are similar to motorways, except that right turns are sometimes permitted, and you'll find both traffic lights and traffic circles along the way. The vast network of other main roads, which typical maps show as either single red *A* roads, or narrower brown *B* roads, also numbered, are for the most part the old roads originally intended for horses and carriages. Travel along these roads is slower than on motorways, and passing is more difficult. On the other hand, you'll see much more of Scotland. The A9, Perth to Inverness, is a particularly dangerous road with the worst road accident record in Scotland because of the stopping and starting on the dual carriageway.

Minor roads (shown as yellow or white on most maps, unlettered and unnumbered) are the ancient lanes and byways of Britain, roads that are not only living history but a superb way of discovering hidden parts of Scotland. You have to drive slowly and carefully. On single-track (one-lane) roads, found in the north and west of Scotland, there's no room for

From:	To:	Driving Time:
Edinburgh	Glasgow	1 hour
Glasgow	Stirling	¼ hour
Stirling	Dundee	1¼ hours
Dundee	Aberdeen	1½ hours
Aberdeen	Inverness	2¾ hours
Inverness	Glasgow	3½ hours
Edinburgh	Inverness	3¼ hours
Glasgow	Dundee	1¾ hours

two vehicles to pass, and you must use a passing place if you meet an oncoming car or tractor, or if a car behind wishes to overtake you. Never hold up traffic on single-track roads.

RULES OF THE ROAD

The most noticeable difference for most visitors is that when in Britain, you drive on the left and steer the car on the right. Give yourself time to adjust to driving on the left—especially if you pick up your car at the airport. One of the most complicated questions facing visitors to Britain is that of speed limits. In urban areas it's generally 20 mph or 30 mph, but it's 40 mph on some main roads, as indicated by circular red-rimmed signs. In rural areas the official limit is 60 mph on ordinary roads and 70 mph on divided highways and motorways. Traffic police can be hard on speeders, especially in urban areas. Driving while using a cell phone is illegal, and the use of seat belts is mandatory for passengers in front and back seats. Service stations and newsstands sell copies of the Highway Code (£2.50), which lists driving rules and has pictures of signs, or you can download the information or get the mobile app at ⊕ *www. highwaycodeuk.co.uk*

Drunk-driving laws are strictly enforced and penalties are heavy. Be aware that the legal alcohol limit is lower than in the rest of the United Kingdom: just 50 mg in every 100 ml of blood. That equates to just under a pint of beer or glass of wine for an average male, and half a pint or a small glass of wine for a woman. To be safe, avoid any alcohol if you're driving.

CAR RENTALS

You can rent any type of car you desire; however, in Scotland cars tend to be on the smaller side. Many roads are narrow, and a smaller car saves money on gas. Common models are the VW Golf, Ford Focus, and Vauxhall Corsa. Four-wheel-drive vehicles aren't a necessity. Most cars are manual, not automatic, and come with air-conditioning, although you rarely need it in Scotland. If you want an automatic, reserve ahead. Green Motion rents electric, hybrid, and low–carbon dioxide cars with service pick-up points at Edinburgh and Glasgow airports.

When you're returning the car, allow an extra hour to drop it off and sort out any paperwork. If you're traveling to more than one country, make sure your rental contract permits you to take the car across borders and that your insurance policy covers you in every country you visit.

Rates from Edinburgh Airport begin at £230 a week for an economy car with a manual transmission and unlimited mileage. This does not include tax on car rentals, which is 20%. The busiest months are June through August, when rates may go up 30%. During this time, book at least two to four weeks in advance. Online booking is fine.

Companies frequently restrict rentals to people over age 23 and under age 75. If you are over 70, some companies require you to have your own insurance. If you

are under 25, a surcharge of around £25 per day plus V.A.T. will apply.

Cruise

Many of the crossings from North America to Europe are repositioning sailings for ships that cruise the Caribbean in winter and European waters in summer. Sometimes rates are reduced, and fly-cruise packages are usually available. To get the best deal on a cruise, consult a cruise-only travel agency.

The National Trust for Scotland runs a Cultural Cruising program with natural history, literary, and culinary themes. The destinations change each year but may include the west coast or Northern Isles. Hebridean Island Cruises offers 4- to 10-night luxury cruises aboard the MV *Hebridean Princess* around the Scottish islands, including all the Western Isles. Majestic Line runs small-group cruises on converted wooden fishing boats around Argyll and the Hebrides.

Taxi

In Edinburgh, Glasgow, and the larger cities, black hackney taxis—similar to those in London—with their "taxi" sign illuminated can be hailed on the street, or booked by phone (expect to pay an extra 80-pence charge for this service in Edinburgh). If you call a private-hire taxi, expect a regular-looking car to pick you up. The only distinctions are that they have a taxi license and a meter stuck on the dashboard, along with an ID card for the driver. Private-hire taxis are cheaper than black hackney taxis and will pick you up only from a specific location, not off the street.

Getting Here and Around

Scottish taxis are reliable, safe, and metered. In Edinburgh, meters begin at £3 weekdays and increase in 25-pence increments. Beyond the larger cities, most communities of any size have a taxi service; your hotel will be able to supply telephone numbers.

Train

Train service within Scotland is generally run by ScotRail, one of the most efficient of Britain's service providers. Trains are generally modern, clean, and comfortable. Long-distance services carry buffet and refreshment cars. Scotland's rail network extends all the way to Thurso and Wick, the most northerly stations in the British Isles. Lowland services, most of which originate in Glasgow or Edinburgh, are generally fast and reliable. A shuttle makes the 50-minute trip between Glasgow and Edinburgh every 15 minutes. It's a scenic trip with plenty of rolling fields, livestock, and traditional houses along the way. Rail service throughout the country, especially the Highlands, is limited on Sunday.

CLASSES
Most trains have first-class and standard-class coaches. First-class coaches are always less crowded; they have wider seats and are often cleaner and newer than standard-class cars, and they're a lot more expensive. Nevertheless, you can often upgrade from standard to first class for a fee (often £10 to £25)—ask when you book.

FARES AND SCHEDULES
The best way to find out which train to take, which station to catch it at, and what times trains travel to your destination is to call National Rail Enquiries. It's a helpful, comprehensive service that covers all Britain's rail lines. National Rail will help you choose the best train to take, and then connects you with the ticket office for that train company so that you can buy tickets. You can also check schedules and purchase tickets on its website.

Train fares vary according to class of ticket purchased, time (off-peak travel will be much cheaper), and distance traveled. Before you buy your ticket, stop at the Information Office/Travel Centre and request the lowest fare to your destination and information about any special offers. There's sometimes little difference between the cost of a one-way and round-trip ticket, and returns are valid for one month. So if you're planning on departing from and returning to the same destination, buy a round-trip fare upon your departure, rather than purchasing two separate one-way tickets.

It's often much cheaper to buy a ticket in advance than on the day of your trip (except for commuter services); the closer to the date of travel, the more expensive the ticket will be. Try to purchase tickets at least eight weeks in advance during peak-season summer travel to save money and reserve good seats. You must stick to the train you have booked (penalties can be the full price), and you need to keep the seat reservation ticket, which is part of the valid ticket. All the operators now provide the option for a paperless ticket download that can be managed via a smartphone app.

Check train websites, especially ScotRail, for deals. You can also check The Trainline, which sells discounted advance-purchase tickets from all train companies to all destinations in Britain.

TRAIN PASSES
Rail passes may save you money, especially if you're going to log a lot of miles. If you plan to travel by train in Scotland, consider purchasing a BritRail Pass, which also allows travel in England and

Wales. There are Scotland-specific passes, too, for the Highlands, central region, and countrywide travel. All BritRail passes must be purchased in your home country, with an M-Pass option if you wish to use it via a phone app; they're sold by travel agents as well as ACP, The Trainline, or Rail Europe. Rail passes do not guarantee seats on the trains, so be sure to reserve ahead. Remember that Eurail Passes aren't honored in Britain.

The cost of an unlimited BritRail adult pass starts at around $250 for 4 days standard class, rising to $1,000 for a first-class monthly pass.

FROM ENGLAND

There are two main rail routes to Scotland from the south of England. The first, the west-coast main line, runs from London Euston to Glasgow Central; it takes 5½ hours to make the 400-mile trip to central Scotland, and service is frequent and reliable. Useful for daytime travel to the Scottish Highlands is the direct train to Stirling and Aviemore, terminating at Inverness. The east-coast main line from London King's Cross to Edinburgh provides the quickest trip to the Scottish capital. Between 8 am and 6 pm there are usually trains every half hour to Edinburgh; three of them travel directly to Aberdeen. LNER East Coast's limited-stop expresses like the *Flying Scotsman* make the 393-mile London-to-Edinburgh journey in about 4½ hours. Connecting services to most parts of Scotland—particularly the Western Highlands—are often better from Edinburgh than from Glasgow.

Trains from elsewhere in England are good: regular service connects Birmingham, Manchester, Liverpool, and Bristol with Glasgow and Edinburgh.

OVERNIGHT TRAINS

For a restful route, take the overnight *Caledonian Sleeper*, now run by Serco, with its comfortable sleeping carriages. It arrives the next morning after departing London Euston late evening, before splitting into sections heading to different parts of Scotland: one portion stops at Perth, Stirling, Aviemore, and Inverness; another covers the east coast stations Leuchars (for St. Andrews), Dundee, and Aberdeen; and the West Highland route terminates at Fort William. You can choose from the selection of cozy rooms with access to the stylish Club Car serving food and drinks. Classic rooms have a twin bunk and washbasin; Club has en suite and shower while the Caledonian Double has a double bed. Waking up in your berth while rolling through the sunrise-lit West Highlands is particularly stunning.

SCENIC ROUTES

Although many routes in Scotland run through extremely attractive countryside, several stand out: from Glasgow to Oban via Loch Lomond; to Fort William and Mallaig via Rannoch (ferry connection to Skye); from Edinburgh to Inverness via the Forth Bridge and Perth; from Inverness to Kyle of Lochalsh and to Wick; and from Inverness to Aberdeen.

A private train, the *Royal Scotsman*, does all-inclusive scenic tours, with banquets en route. This is a luxury experience: you choose itineraries from two nights (£4,000) to seven nights (£13,000) per person.

Essentials

Dining

Today the traditional Scottish restaurant offers more than fish-and-chips, fried sausage, and black pudding. Instead you'll find the freshest of scallops, organic salmon, wild duck, and Aberdeen Angus beef, as well as locally grown vegetables and fruits. There's also a wide array of international restaurants: Chinese, French, Greek, Indian, Italian, Japanese, and Mexican (to name but a few) can be truly exceptional.

Places like Glasgow, Edinburgh, Dundee, and Aberdeen have sophisticated restaurants at various price levels; of these, the more notable tend to open only in the evening. But fabulous restaurants are popping up in the smaller villages as well. Dining in Scotland can be an experience for all the senses. These meals are rarely cheap, so don't forget your credit card.

Note that most pubs do not have a table service, so go to the bar and order your meal. You're not expected to tip the bartender, but you are expected to tip restaurant waitstaff by leaving 10% to 15% of the tab on the table.

There are a couple of vegetarian options on every menu, and most restaurants, particularly pubs that serve food, welcome families with young children. Smoking is banned from pubs, clubs, and restaurants throughout Britain.

The restaurants we review in this book are the best in each price category. Properties are assigned price categories based on dinner prices.

Prices in the reviews are the average cost of a main course at dinner or, if dinner is not served, at lunch.

DISCOUNTS AND DEALS

Many city restaurants have good pretheater meals from 5 to 7 pm. Lunch deals can also save you money; some main courses can be nearly half the price of dinner entrées. All supermarkets sell a large variety of high-quality sandwiches, wraps, and salads at reasonable prices. If the weather's dry, opt for a midday picnic.

MEALS AND MEALTIMES

To start the day with a full stomach, try a traditional Scottish breakfast of bacon and eggs served with sausage, fried mushrooms, and tomatoes, and usually fried bread or potato scones. Some places also serve kippers (smoked herring). All this is in addition to juice, porridge, cereal, toast, and other bread products.

"All-day" meal places are becoming prevalent. Lunch is usually served 12:30 to 2:30. A few places serve high tea—masses of cakes, bread and butter, and jam—around 2:30 to 4:30. Dinner is fairly early, around 5 to 8.

Restaurant chains are often more expensive than home-cooked meals in local establishments, where large servings of British comfort food—fish-and-chips, stuffed baked potatoes, and sandwiches—are served. In upscale restaurants cutting costs can be as simple as requesting *tap* water; "water" means a bottle of mineral water that could cost up to £5.

Unless otherwise noted, the restaurants listed in this guide are open daily for lunch and dinner.

PAYING

Credit cards are widely accepted at most types of restaurants. Some restaurants exclude service charges from the printed menu (which the law obliges them to display outside), then add 10% to 15% to the check, or else stamp "service not included" along the bottom, in which case you should add the 10% to 15% yourself. Just don't pay twice for service—unscrupulous restaurateurs add a service charge but leave the total on the credit-card slip blank. To make sure your servers get a fair share of tips, it's best to leave them cash.

PUBS

A common misconception among visitors to Scotland is that pubs are cozy bars. But they are also gathering places, conversation zones, even restaurants. Pubs are, generally speaking, where people go to have a drink, meet their friends, and catch up on one another's lives. Traditionally, pubs are open until midnight, with last orders called about 20 minutes before closing time. In the bigger cities pubs can stay open until 1 am or later.

Some pubs are child-friendly, but others have restricted hours for children. If a pub serves food, it will generally allow children in during the day. Some are stricter than others, though, and will not admit anyone younger than 18. If in doubt, ask the bartender. Family-friendly pubs tend to be packed with kids, parents, and all of their accoutrements.

RESERVATIONS AND DRESS

It's a good idea to make a reservation if you can. For popular restaurants, book as far ahead as you can (often 30 days), and reconfirm as soon as you arrive. Large parties should always call ahead to check the reservations policy.

Online reservation services make it easy to book a table before you even leave home. OpenTable has listings in many Scottish cities.

Lodging

Your choices in Scotland range from small, local B&Bs to large, elegant hotels—some of the chain variety. Bed-and-breakfasts tend to be less expensive than large hotels, and are often different from those in the United States: many consist of spare rooms in someone's home, where breakfasts are cooked in the host's kitchen and served at the dining or kitchen table. Proprietors keep costs down, and guests get a more personal, if less private, Scottish touch. Recent economic stagnation, political uncertainty, and the fall in the value of the pound sterling means there are special deals if you look. Furthermore, some lodgings offer discounted rates for stays of two nights or longer.

If you haven't booked ahead, you're not likely to be stranded. Even in the height of the season—July and August—hotel occupancy runs at about 80%. Nevertheless, your choice of accommodations will be extremely limited if you show

Essentials

up somewhere during a festival or golf tournament. Your best bet will be to try for a room in a nearby village.

VisitScotland classifies and grades accommodations using a simple star system. The greater the number of stars, the greater the number of facilities and the more luxurious they are.

The lodgings we list are the best in each price category. When pricing accommodations, always ask what's included. Many hotels and most guesthouses and B&Bs include a breakfast with the basic room rate. Meal-plan information appears at the end of a review.

APARTMENT AND HOUSE RENTALS

Rental houses and flats (apartments) are becoming more popular lodging choices for travelers visiting Scotland, particularly for those staying in one place for more than a few days. Some places may rent only by the week. Prices can be cheaper than a hotel (though perhaps not less than a bed-and-breakfast), and the space and comfort are much better than what you'd find in a typical hotel.

In the country your chances of finding a small house to rent are good; in the city you're more likely to find a flat (apartment) to let (rent). Either way, your best bet for finding these rentals is online. Individuals and large consortiums can own these properties, so it just depends on what you're looking for. Citybase Apartments is a handy resource for finding an apartment, from single studios to large apartments suitable for families and groups. Dreamhouse Apartments has

swanky, serviced flats in Edinburgh, Glasgow, and Aberdeen. The National Trust for Scotland has many unique properties, from island cottages to castles, for rent. Knight Residence has 19 well-appointed, modern apartments in the heart of the Old Town, Edinburgh; it has 16 similarly smart apartments in Inverness, many with spectacular terrace views.

BED-AND-BREAKFASTS

Common throughout Scotland, B&Bs are a special British tradition and the backbone of budget travel. Prices average about £50 to £140 per night, depending on the region and the time of year. They're usually in a family home, occasionally don't have private bathrooms, and usually offer only breakfast. More upscale B&Bs, along the line of American B&Bs or small inns, can be found in Edinburgh and Glasgow especially, but in other parts of Scotland as well. Guesthouses are a slightly larger, somewhat more luxurious version. All provide a glimpse of everyday life. Note that local tourist offices can book a B&B for you; there may be a small charge for this service.

FARMHOUSE AND CROFTING HOLIDAYS

A popular option for families with children is a farmhouse holiday, combining the freedom of B&B accommodations with the hospitality of Scottish family life. You'll need a car if you're staying deep in the country, though. Information is available from VisitBritain or VisitScotland, and from the Farm Stay UK website.

HOTELS

Large hotels vary in style and price. Many lean toward Scottish themes when it comes to decoration, but you can expect the same quality and service from a chain hotel wherever you are in the world. Keep in mind that hotel rooms in Scotland are smaller than what you'd find in the United States. Today hotels of all sizes are trying to be greener, and many newer chains are striving for government environmental awards. Discounted rooms are another trend, as are discounts for room upgrades.

In the countryside some older hotels are former castles or converted country homes. These types of hotels are full of character and charm but can be very expensive, and they may not have elevators. Normally they have all the amenities, if not more, of their urban counterparts. Their locations may be so remote that you must eat on the premises, which may be costly.

Some small regional chains operate in Scotland that are not internationally known. Apex (in Edinburgh, Glasgow, and Dundee) is modish and has Scandinavian-inspired bedrooms; Malmaison (in Aberdeen, Dundee, Edinburgh, and Glasgow) is luxury on a budget; Hotel du Vin (Glasgow, St. Andrews, and Edinburgh), with its chic bistros, sumptuous bedding, and original art, may blow the budget.

✚ Health and Safety

Overall, Scotland is a very safe country to travel in, but be a cautious traveler and keep your cash, passport, credit cards, and tickets close to you or in a hotel safe. Don't agree to carry anything for strangers. It's a good idea to distribute your cash, credit cards, IDs, and other valuables between a deep front pocket, an inside jacket or vest pocket, and a hidden money pouch. Don't reach for the money pouch once you're in public. Use common sense as your guide.

Scotland is largely welcoming to LGBTQ travelers, with big cities like Edinburgh and Glasgow having especially lively LGBTQ scenes; gay marriage has been legal in Scotland since 2014.

COVID-19

Although COVID-19 brought travel to a virtual standstill for most of 2020 and into 2021, vaccinations have made travel possible and safe again. Remaining requirements and restrictions—especially those for non-vaccinated travelers—can, however, vary from one place (or even business) to the next. Check out the websites of the CDC and the U.S. Department of State, both of which have destination-specific, COVID-19 guidance. Also, in case travel is curtailed abruptly again, consider buying trip insurance. Just be sure to read the fine print: not all travel-insurance policies cover pandemic-related cancellations.

2

Travel Smart ESSENTIALS

Essentials

Nightlife

Bars and pubs typically sell two kinds of beer: lager is light in color, very carbonated, and served cold, while ale is dark, less fizzy, and served just below room temperature. You may also come across a pub serving "real ales" or "craft beers," which are very flavorful beers from smaller breweries. Both traditional real ale and innovatively crafted brews have a fervent following; check out the Campaign for Real Ale's website, ⊕ www.camra.org.uk.

You can order Scotland's most famous beverage—whisky (most definitely spelled without an e)—at any local pub. All pubs serve single-malt and blended whiskies. It's also possible to tour numerous distilleries, where you can sample a dram and purchase a bottle. Most distilleries are concentrated in Speyside and Islay, but there are notable ones on Orkney and Skye. In recent years a new breed of craft gin producers have opened stills, many producing small batches of botanically infused tipples and offering tours, tastings, and lessons.

The legal drinking age in Scotland is 18.

🛍 Shopping

Tartans, tweeds, and woolens may be a Scottish cliché, but nevertheless the selection and quality of these goods make them a must-have for many visitors, whether a made-to-measure traditional kilt outfit or a designer sweater from Skye. Particular bargains can be found in Scottish cashmere sweaters; look for Johnstons of Elgin. Glasgow is great for designer wear, although prices may seem high.

Food items are another popular purchase: whether shortbread, smoked salmon, boiled sweets, tablet (a type of hard fudge), marmalade and raspberry jams, Dundee cake, or black bun, it's far too easy to eat your way around Scotland.

Unique jewelry is available all over Scotland, but especially in some of the remote regions where get-away-from-it-all craftspeople have set up shop amid the idyllic scenery.

Scottish antique pottery and table silver make unusual, if sometimes pricey, souvenirs: a WemyssWare pig for the mantelpiece, perhaps, or Edinburgh silver candelabra for the dining table. Antique pebble jewelry is a unique style of jewelry popular in Scotland; several specialized antique jewelry shops can be found in Edinburgh and Glasgow. Antiques shops and one- or two-day antiques fairs held in hotels abound all over Scotland. In general, goods are reasonably priced. Most dealers will drop the price a little if asked "What's your best price?"

Best Tours in Scotland

🛈 General-Interest Tours

Many companies offer fully guided tours in Scotland, from basic to luxury. Most of these are full packages including hotels, all food, and transportation costs in one flat fee. Because each tour company has different specialties, do a bit of research—either on your own or through a travel agent—before booking. You'll want to know about the hotels you'll be staying in, how big your group is likely to be, precisely how your days will be structured, and who the other people are likely to be.

CIE Tours
BUS TOURS | It offers all-inclusive tours of Scotland with various themes, from distillery tours to cruises to Home of Golf and St. Andrews packages. ☎ 800/243–8687 ⊕ www.cietours.com ✉ From $1,125 for a 5-day Taste of Scotland tour.

Globus
BUS TOURS | Covering Scotland and Great Britain, Globus offers many packages including a 7-day Bonnie Scotland tour from Glasgow to Edinburgh, and a 12-day Essential Britain journey. ☎ 866/755–8581 ⊕ www.globusjourneys.com ✉ From $1,719, excluding airfare, for 7-day Bonnie Scotland.

Heart of Scotland Tours
BUS TOURS | Offered here are small-group (16 maximum) minibus tours that aim to take you off the beaten track. ☎ 0131/228–2888 ⊕ www.heartofscotlandtours.co.uk ✉ From £55.

Rabbie's Trail Burners
BUS TOURS | These minibus guided tours include handy day trips for small groups (16 maximum) and depart from Edinburgh and Glasgow. The company has won numerous awards including the Scottish Thistle award for sustainable tourism. ☎ 0131/226–3133 ⊕ www.rabbies.com ✉ From £34 for day trips.

🛈 Special-Interest Tours

You can find tours for many special interests from whisky and vegetarian-friendly to cultural, historic, and wildlife-themed packages.

The Wayfarers
SPECIAL-INTEREST TOURS | Enjoy walking tours through the countryside and scenic towns, exploring natural and historic sights. ☎ 800/249–4620 ⊕ www.thewayfarers.com ✉ From $4,695 per person (double occupancy).

Wild Scotland
SPECIAL-INTEREST TOURS | Inverness-based Wild Scotland acts as a portal to dozens of small operators offering a wealth of outdoors and wildlife-related tours across Scotland. ⊕ www.wild-scotland.org.uk ✉ From £1,995.

◉ Private Guides

Scottish Tourist Guides Association
PRIVATE GUIDES | The association has members throughout Scotland who are fully qualified professional guides able to conduct walking tours in the major cities, half- or full-day tours or extended tours throughout Scotland, driving tours, and special study tours. Fees are negotiable. ☎ 01786/447784 ⊕ www.stga.co.uk.

On the Calendar

Winter

DEC. 29–JAN. 2
Hogmanay. Scotland's ancient, still-thriving New Year's celebration, Hogmanay takes place over several days. In rural areas neighbors "first foot" each other's houses—thereby ensuring the good luck of the household—and toast the new year with a dram. ⊠ *Edinburgh* ⊕ *www. edinburghshogmanay.com.*

JAN. 25
Burns Night. Burns Night dinners and other events are held in memory of poet Robert Burns on his birthday, January 25. Haggis and mashed turnips, whisky, and poetry readings are familiar elements of the supper. ⊕ *www.scotland.org/ whats-on/burns-night.*

LAST TUES. IN JAN.
Up-Helly-Aa. Every year Shetlanders celebrate their Viking heritage and torch a replica Viking longship. The biggest Up-Helly-Aa is in Lerwick on the last Tuesday in January. ⊕ *www.uphellyaa.org.*

JAN.
Celtic Connections. Glasgow's immensely popular celebration of Celtic music, Celtic Connections hosts national and international musicians from mid-January to early February. ⊠ *Glasgow* ⊕ *www. celticconnections.com.*

Spectra: Aberdeen's Festival of Light.
Brightening up four February nights is a light-filled extravaganza staged in prominent city locations featuring international artists and Scots collaborators. ⊕ *www. spectrafestival.co.uk.*

Spring

LATE APR.–EARLY MAY
Shetland Folk Festival. This festival is one of the biggest folk gatherings in Scotland, and musicians from all over the world stay up for four days of fiddle frenzy. It normally falls as April turns to May. ☎ *01595/694757* ⊕ *www.shetlandfolkfestival.com.*

APR. 30
Beltane Fire Festival. This festival celebrates the rites of spring according to the traditional Celtic calendar on April 30. You can witness displays of pyrotechnics and elaborately costumed mythological creatures at Calton Hill in Edinburgh. ⊠ *Edinburgh* ⊕ *www.beltane.org.*

LATE MAY
Orkney Folk Festival. This annual festival brings the folkies back up to the remote far north by the hundreds. Festivities take place over a few days in late May or early June. ⊕ *www.orkneyfolkfestival.com.*

Summer

MAY–SEPT.
Highland Games. Held annually in many Highland towns, the Highland games include athletic and cultural events like hammer throwing, caber tossing, and Highland dancing. The fun takes place from May through September. ⊕ *www. visitscotland.com/see-do/events/ highland-games.*

Dundee Design Festival. Dundee is the United Kingdom's sole UNESCO City of Design and home to the V&A Dundee design museum. In late May and September, the city hosts a series of innovative and collaborative events and workshops exploring the world of design. ⊕ *www.dundeecityofdesign.com.*

JUNE

Edinburgh International Film Festival. Concentrating on new films from all over the world, Edinburgh International Film Festival screenings are held over two weeks in June. ⊠ *Edinburgh* ⊕ *www. edfilmfest.org.uk.*

St. Magnus International Festival. Orkney's weeklong St. Magnus International Festival is a feast of classical and modern music each June, often showcasing new vocal or orchestral compositions. ☏ *01856/871445* ⊕ *www.stmagnusfestival.com.*

JULY

Merchant City Festival. Glasgow's transformed mercantile district–turned–cultural quarter stages a few days of pop-up performances and various artsy gatherings in late July, including comedy, dance, music, markets, fashion and design, family events, tours, heritage walks, and food and drink. ⊠ *Glasgow* ☏ *0141/287–4350* ⊕ *www.merchantcityfestival.com.*

AUG.

Pitenweem Arts Festival. In early August the picturesque Fife fishing village–turned–artists' retreat favorite opens dozens of small home studios and other intimate venues to the public. ⊕ *www. pittenweemartsfestival.co.uk.*

Edinburgh Festival Fringe. The rowdy, unofficial counterpart to the Edinburgh International Festival, the Edinburgh Festival Fringe takes over the city during three weeks in August. ☏ *0131/226–0000* ⊕ *www.edfringe.com.*

Edinburgh International Festival. The world's largest festival of the arts, the Edinburgh International Festival takes place over three weeks in August. ☏ *0131/473–2000* ⊕ *www.eif.co.uk.*

Edinburgh Military Tattoo. A stirring, colorful show of marching bands and military regiments, the Edinburgh Military Tattoo takes place during three weeks in August. ⊠ *Edinburgh* ☏ *0131/225–1188* ⊕ *www.edintattoo.co.uk.*

EARLY SEPT.

Braemar Royal Highland Gathering. Kilted clansmen from all over Scotland get together for the Braemar Royal Highland Gathering on the first Saturday in September. Bagpipe bands, dancers, and athletes join in the fun and games. ☏ *013397/41098* ⊕ *www.braemargathering.org.*

Fall

MID-OCT.

Royal National Mòd. This weeklong Gaelic festival includes speech competitions and theatrical performances, in addition to piping, choir, and Highland dancing exhibitions. The location changes each year, but it's generally held in mid-October. ⊠ *Inverness* ☏ *01463/709705* ⊕ *www.acgmod.org.*

Festival of the Future. In October the University of Dundee hosts a festival of collaborations, performances, and discussions bringing together scientists, artists, and thinkers. ⊕ *www.dundee. ac.uk/festival-future.*

LATE NOV.–DEC.

Glasgow Loves Christmas. From late November through December, George Square in Glasgow is transformed into a winter wonderland: sparkling ornaments and an impressive palace facade tower over a gigantic ice rink. Festive markets and other seasonal events are part of the program, too. ⊠ *Glasgow* ⊕ *www. glasgowloveschristmas.com.*

Great Itineraries

The Best of Scotland in 10 Days

Scotland isn't large, but its most famous cities and most iconic landscapes take time to explore. This itinerary packs in many national icons: Edinburgh's enormous charm and Glasgow's excellent museums; an iconic castle or two; and misty lochs, soaring mountains, and an impossibly-green island.

DAYS 1 AND 2: EDINBURGH

The capital of Scotland is loaded with iconic sights in its Old Town and New Town. Visit **Edinburgh Castle** and the **National Gallery of Scotland,** and take tours of the **National Museum of Scotland** and the modern **Scottish Parliament** building. Walk along Old Town's **Royal Mile** and New Town's **George Street** for some fresh air and retail therapy. Later on, seek out a traditional pub with live music.

Logistics: Fly into Edinburgh Airport if you're flying via London. If you're flying directly into Glasgow from overseas, make your way from Glasgow Airport to Queen Street station via taxi or bus. It takes an hour to travel from Glasgow to Edinburgh by car or bus, about 45 minutes to an hour by train. Explore on foot or by public transportation.

DAY 3: STIRLING TO ST. ANDREWS

Rent a car in Edinburgh and drive to the historic city of **Stirling.** Spend the day visiting **Stirling Castle** and the **National Wallace Monument.** If you're eager to tour a distillery, make time for a stop at the **Glenturret Distillery** in **Crieff.** For your overnight stay, drive to the seaside town of St. Andrews, famous for golf.

Logistics: It's 35 miles or a one-hour drive to Stirling from Edinburgh, and 50 miles and 90 minutes from Stirling to St.

Andrews. You can easily take a train or bus to these destinations.

DAY 4: ST. ANDREWS TO AVIEMORE

Spend the morning exploring **St. Andrews,** known for its castle and the country's oldest university as well as its golf courses. If you've booked well in advance, play a round of golf. After lunch, drive to **Aviemore.** Along the way, either make a detour to **Dundee** and its spectacular V&A Dundee design museum or **Blair Castle** (just off the A9 and 10 miles north of **Pitlochry**). Head to Aviemore, gateway to the Cairngorm Mountains and Britain's largest national park, for two nights. The town is a center for outdoor activities and has many choices for accommodations, dining, and shopping, but you can also consider the more attractive surrounding villages and towns such as **Kingussie** for your stay.

Logistics: It's 120 miles from St. Andrews to Aviemore via the A9, a drive that will take 2½ hours. You can also take a train or bus.

DAY 5: THE CAIRNGORMS

For anyone who enjoys outdoor pursuits or dramatic scenery, the arctic plateau of the Cairngorms is a must. Hiking, biking, and climbing are options (Glenmore Lodge is a renowned outdoor-sports center), but so is visiting attractions such as the **Cairngorm Reindeer Centre** and **Highland Folk Museum.**

DAY 6: THE ISLE OF SKYE

Leave Aviemore early and head to Inverness, which has a busy center suited for a wander. **Inverness Castle** and the **Inverness Museum and Art Gallery** are worth seeing. The drive southwest to Skye is peaceful, full of raw landscapes and big, open horizons. Stop at **Eilean Donan Castle** on the way. Set on an island among three lochs, the castle is the stuff

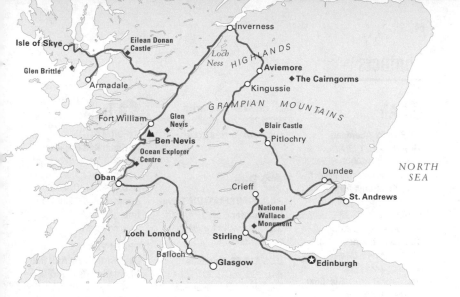

postcards are made of from the outside, although the interiors are comically underwhelming. Explore Skye: **Glen Brittle** is the perfect place to enjoy mountain scenery including the crystal clear **Fairy Pools** at the foot of the Black Cuillins; and **Armadale** is a good place to go crafts shopping. End up in Portree for dinner and the night.

Logistics: It's 30 miles (a 40-minute drive) via the A9 from Aviemore to Inverness, and then it's 80 miles (a two-hour drive) from Inverness to Skye. Public transportation is possible but a car is best.

DAY 7: OBAN VIA BEN NEVIS

Leave Skye no later than 9 am and head for **Fort William** (get up an hour earlier and you can go via **Loch Ness**). The town isn't worth stopping for, but the view of Britain's highest mountain, the 4,406-foot Ben Nevis, is. If time permits, take a hike in **Glen Nevis,** and then continue on to **Oban,** a traditional Scottish resort town on the water, to overnight. Outside Oban, stop by the **Ocean Explorer Centre.** At night, feast on fish-and-chips in a local pub.

Logistics: It's nearly 100 miles from Skye to Oban; the drive is 3½ hours without stopping. Public transportation is challenging.

DAYS 8 AND 9: LOCH LOMOND AND GLASGOW

Enjoy a waterfront stroll in Oban. Midmorning set off for **Glasgow** via **Loch Lomond.** Arrive in Glasgow in time for dinner; take in a play or concert, or just relax in a pub on the first of your two nights in this rejuvenated city. Spend the next day visiting the sights; **Kelvingrove Art Gallery and Museum,** Charles Rennie Mackintosh's iconic buildings, and the **Riverside Museum** are a few highlights.

Logistics: It's 127 miles (a three-hour drive) from Oban to Glasgow via Balloch. Traveling by train is a possibility, but you won't be able to go via Balloch. Return your rental car in Glasgow.

DAY 10: GLASGOW AND HOME

On your final day, stow your suitcases at your hotel and hit Buchanan and Sauchiehall streets for some of Britain's best shopping. Clothes, whisky, and tartan items are good things to look for.

Logistics: It's less than 10 miles (15 minutes) by taxi to Glasgow's international airport in Paisley but more than 30 miles (40 minutes) to the international airport in Prestwick.

Contacts

Air

AIRPORTS Aberdeen Airport. *(ABZ).* ✉ *Aberdeen* ☎ *0344/481–6666* ⊕ *www.aberdeenairport.com.* **Edinburgh Airport.** *(EDI).* ✉ *Edinburgh* ☎ *0131/357–6337* ⊕ *www.edinburghairport.com.* **Glasgow Airport.** *(GLA).* ✉ *Glasgow* ☎ *0344/481–5555* ⊕ *www.glasgowairport.com.* **Glasgow Prestwick Airport.** *(PIK).* ✉ *Prestwick* ☎ *0871/223–0700* ⊕ *www.glasgowprestwick.com.* **Inverness Airport.** *(INV).* ✉ *Dalcross* ☎ *01667/464000* ⊕ *www.invernessairport.co.uk.*

Bicycle

BIKE MAPS AND INFORMATION ActiveScotland. ☎ *0131/472–2222* ⊕ *active.visitscotland.com.* **Cycling UK.** ☎ *01483/238300* ⊕ *www.cyclinguk.org.* **Sustrans.** ☎ *0131/346–1384* ⊕ *www.sustrans.org.uk.*

⊙ Boat and Ferry

INFORMATION Caledonian MacBrayne. ☎ *0800/066–5000* ⊕ *www.calmac.co.uk.* **Northlink Ferries.** ☎ *0800/111–4422* ⊕ *www.northlinkferries.*

co.uk. **Western Ferries.** ☎ *01369/704452* ⊕ *www.western-ferries.co.uk.*

Bus

BUS INFORMATION Traveline Scotland. ☎ *0871/200–2233* ⊕ *www.travelinescotland.com.*

BUS LINES Megabus. ☎ *0900/160–0900* ⊕ *uk.megabus.com.* **National Express.** ☎ *0871/781–8181* ⊕ *www.nationalexpress.com.* **Scottish Citylink.** ☎ *0871/266–3333* ⊕ *www.citylink.co.uk.*

⊙ Car Rental

LOCAL CAR RENTAL AGENCIES Arnold Clark. ☎ *0141/237–4374* ⊕ *www.arnoldclarkrental.com.* **Green Motion.** ☎ *03338/884000 in U.K., 0207/186–4000 rest of the world* ⊕ *www.greenmotion.com.*

MAJOR RENTAL AGENCIES Avis. ☎ *0808/284–0014* ⊕ *www.avis.co.uk.* **Budget.** ☎ *0808/284–4444* ⊕ *www.budget.co.uk.* **Hertz.** ☎ *020/7026–0077* ⊕ *www.hertz.co.uk.* **National Car Rental.** ☎ *0800/121–8303* ⊕ *www.nationalcar.co.uk.*

⊙ Train

INFORMATION National Rail Enquiries. ☎ *03457/484950* ⊕ *www.nationalrail.co.uk.* **ScotRail.** ☎ *0344/811–0141* ⊕ *www.scotrail.co.uk.* **The Trainline.** ☎ *0333/202–2222* ⊕ *www.thetrainline.com.*

TRAIN PASS INFORMATION ACP Rail International. ☎ *866/938–7245* ⊕ *www.acprail.com.* **BritRail Travel.** ⊕ *www.britrail.com.* **Rail Europe.** ⊕ *www.raileurope.com.*

SPECIAL TRAINS LNER. ☎ *03457/225–333* ⊕ *www.lner.co.uk.*

⊙ Sightseeing Passes

DISCOUNT PASSES Historic Environment Scotland. ☎ *0131/668–8600* ⊕ *www.historicenvironment.scot.* **National Trust for Scotland.** ☎ *0131/458–0303* ⊕ *www.nts.org.uk.*

⊙ Visitor Information

CONTACTS IN BRITAIN VisitScotland. ✉ *Edinburgh* ⊕ *www.visitscotland.com.*

EDINBURGH AND THE LOTHIANS

3

Updated by
Joseph Reaney

👁 Sights	🍽 Restaurants	🏨 Hotels	🛍 Shopping	🍸 Nightlife
★★★★★	★★★★★	★★★★★	★★★★★	★★★★★

WELCOME TO
EDINBURGH AND THE LOTHIANS

TOP REASONS
TO GO

★ **Culture:** From floor-stomping *ceilidhs* to avant-garde modern dance, the city's calendar of cultural festivals, including the remarkable Edinburgh Festival Fringe—the world's largest arts festival by a mile—is truly outstanding.

★ **The Royal Mile:** History plays out before your eyes in this centuries-old capital along the Royal Mile. Edinburgh Castle and the Palace of Holyroodhouse were the locations for some of the most important struggles between Scotland and England.

★ **Architecture:** From the Old Town's labyrinthine medieval streets to the neoclassical orderliness of the New Town to imaginative modern developments like the Scottish Parliament, the architecture of Auld Reekie spans the ages.

★ **Food:** The city's ever-expanding restaurant scene attracts celebrity chefs that serve up international dishes and genuine Scottish cuisine, like Cullen skink and haggis with neeps and tatties.

For all its steep roads and hidden alleyways, Edinburgh is not a difficult place to navigate. Most newcomers gravitate to two areas, the Old Town and the New Town. The former funnels down from the castle on either side of High Street, better known as the Royal Mile. Princes Street Gardens and Edinburgh Waverley station separate this side of the city from the stately New Town, known for its neoclassical architecture and verdant gardens. To the north the city sweeps down to the Firth of Forth. It is here you will find the port of Leith, replete with trendy pubs and fine-dining restaurants. The southern and western neighborhoods are mainly residential, but are home to a few attractions, such as Edinburgh Zoo.

1 Old Town. The focal point of Edinburgh for centuries, the Old Town is a picturesque jumble of medieval tenements. Here are prime attractions such as Edinburgh Castle and the newer symbol of power, the Scottish Parliament. You will also find everything from happening bars and nightclubs to ghostly alleyways and vaults.

2 New Town. Built in the 18th and 19th centuries to prevent the wealthier residents of overcrowded Old Town from decamping to London, the neoclassical sweep of the New Town is a masterpiece of city planning. Significant sights include the National Gallery of Scotland and Calton Hill, which offers some of the best views of the city from its summit.

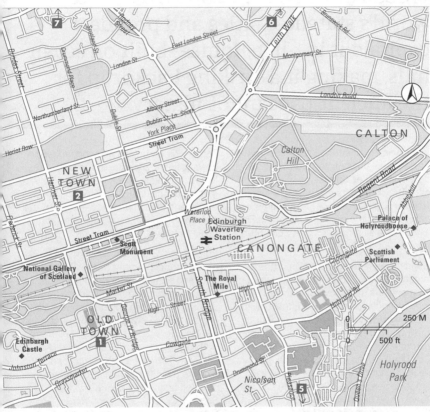

3 Haymarket. West of the Old Town and south of the West End is Haymarket, a district with its own down-to-earth character and well-worn charm. It's close to Edinburgh's second train station.

4 West End. Edinburgh's commercial center has boutiques aplenty as well as the Edinburgh Zoo.

5 South Side. Mostly residential, the South Side makes a good base for budget-conscious travelers. It's where most of the city's students live.

6 Leith. On the southern shore of the Firth of Forth, Edinburgh's port of Leith is where you'll find the now-retired Royal Yacht *Britannia,* along with some of the city's smartest restaurants and bars.

7 West Lothian, the Forth Valley, Midlothian, and East Lothian. Known collectively as the Lothians, the areas of green countryside and seafront villages around Edinburgh are replete with historic houses, castles, museums, and world-renowned golf courses.

Edinburgh is "a city so beautiful it breaks the heart again and again," as Alexander McCall Smith once wrote. One of the world's stateliest cities and proudest capitals, it is—like Rome—built on seven hills, making it a striking backdrop for the ancient pageant of history.

In a skyline of sheer beauty, Edinburgh Castle looks out over the city, frowning down on Princes Street's glamour and glitz. But despite its rich past, the city's famous festivals, excellent museums and galleries, and the modernist Scottish Parliament are all reminders that Edinburgh has its feet firmly in the 21st century.

Nearly everywhere in Edinburgh (the *burgh* is always pronounced *burra* in Scotland) are spectacular buildings, whose Doric, Ionic, and Corinthian pillars add touches of neoclassical grandeur to the largely Presbyterian backdrop. Large gardens are a strong feature of central Edinburgh, while Arthur's Seat, a craggy peak of bright green-and-yellow furze, rears up behind the spires of the Old Town. Even as Edinburgh moves through the 21st century, its tall guardian castle remains the focal point of the city and its venerable history.

Modern Edinburgh has become a cultural capital, staging the Edinburgh International Festival and the Festival Fringe in every possible venue each August. The stunning National Museum of Scotland complements the city's wealth of galleries and artsy hangouts. Add Edinburgh's growing reputation for food and nightlife and you have one of the world's most beguiling cities.

Today, Edinburgh is the second-most-important financial center in the United Kingdom, and is widely renowned for its exceptional (and ever-expanding) dining and nightlife scenes—some of the reasons it regularly ranks near the top of quality-of-life surveys.

Edinburgh's Old Town, which bears a great symbolic weight as the "heart of Scotland's capital," is a boon for lovers of atmosphere and history. In contrast, if you appreciate the unique architectural heritage of the city's Enlightenment, then the New Town's for you. If you belong to both categories, don't worry—the Old and New Towns are only yards apart. Explore the city's main thoroughfares—peopled by the spirits of Mary, Queen of Scots, Sir Walter Scott, and Robert Louis Stevenson—then get lost among the tiny *wynds* and *closes* (old medieval alleys that connect the winding streets). And remember: you haven't earned your porridge until you've climbed Arthur's Seat.

Head out of the city center and you'll find smaller communities with an abundance of charm. Dean Village, with its cobbled streets and 19th-century water mills, has a character all its own. Duddingston, just southeast of Arthur's Seat, has all the bucolic charm of a country village. Then there's Edinburgh's port, Leith, home to some of Scotland's smartest bars and restaurants. Visible beyond them all, across the Firth of Forth, is the patchwork of fields that is the county of Fife—a reminder, like the mountains to the northwest that can be glimpsed from Edinburgh's highest points, that the rest of Scotland lies within easy reach.

Planning

When to Go

Scotland's reliably unreliable weather means that you could visit at the height of summer and be forced to wear a winter coat. Conversely, conditions can be balmy in early spring and late autumn. You may choose to avoid the crowds (and hotel price hikes) of July and August, but you'd also miss some of the greatest festivals on Earth. May, June, and September are probably the most hassle-free months in which to visit, while still offering hope of good weather. Short days and grim conditions make winter less appealing, though there are few better New Year's Eve celebrations than Edinburgh's Hogmanay.

FESTIVALS

Walk around Edinburgh in late July and you'll likely feel the first vibrations of the earthquake that is festival time, which shakes the city throughout August. You may hear reference to an "Edinburgh Festival," but this is really an umbrella term for five separate festivals all taking place around the same time. For an overview, check out ⊕ www.edinburgh-festivalcity.com.

Beltane Fire Festival

FESTIVALS | Held every year on April 30, this flame-filled Calton Hill extravaganza is inspired by an Iron Age Celtic festival, which was held to celebrate the return of summer. Expect drumbeat processions, bonfires, and fireworks, as costumed fire dancers reveal the fates of the May

Queen and the Green Man. ⊠ *Calton Hill, Calton* ⊕ *www.beltane.org.*

★ Edinburgh Festival Fringe

ARTS FESTIVALS | FAMILY | During the world's largest arts festival in August, most of the city center becomes one huge performance area, with fire eaters, sword swallowers, unicyclists, jugglers, string quartets, jazz groups, stand-up comedians, and magicians all thronging into High Street and Princes Street. Every available performance space—church halls, community centers, parks, sports fields, nightclubs, and more—is utilized for every kind of event, with something for all tastes. There are even family-friendly shows. Many events are free; others start at a few pounds and rise to £15 or £20. There's so much happening in the three weeks of the festival that it's possible to arrange your own entertainment program from early morning to after midnight. ■ **TIP→ Be aware that hotels get booked up months in advance during the Fringe and bargains are virtually impossible to come by, so plan your trip as far in advance as possible.** ⊠ *Edinburgh Festival Fringe Office, 180 High St., Old Town* ☎ *0131/226–0026* ⊕ *www.edfringe.com.*

Edinburgh International Book Festival

FESTIVALS | FAMILY | This two-week-long event held every August pulls together a heady mix of authors from around the world, from Nobel laureates to best-selling fiction writers, and gets them talking about their work in a magnificent tent village. There are more than 750 events in total, with the workshops for would-be writers and children proving hugely popular. ⊠ *Edinburgh International Book Festival Admin Office, 5 Charlotte Sq., New Town* ☎ *0131/718–5666* ⊕ *www. edbookfest.co.uk.*

Edinburgh International Festival

ARTS FESTIVALS | FAMILY | Running throughout August, this flagship traditional arts festival attracts international performers and audiences to a celebration of music, dance, theater, opera, and art. Programs,

The Festival Fringe started in 1947 at the same time as the International Festival, when eight companies that were not invited to perform in the latter decided to attend anyway.

tickets, and reservations are available from the Hub, set within the impressive Victorian-Gothic Tolbooth Kirk. Tickets for the festival go on sale in April, and the big events sell out within the month. Nevertheless, you'll still be able to purchase tickets for some events during the festival; prices range from around £4 to £60. ⊠ *The Hub, 348–350 Castlehill, Old Town* ☎ *0131/473–2015* ⊕ *www.eif.co.uk*.

Edinburgh International Film Festival

FESTIVALS | One of Europe's foremost film festivals, promoting the best of global independent cinema since 1947, this event takes place from mid-June to early July each year. It's a great place for a first screening of a new film—movies from *Billy Elliot* to *Little Miss Sunshine* to *The Hurt Locker* have premiered here. ⊠ *Edinburgh Film Festival Office, 88 Lothian Rd., West End* ☎ *0131/228–4051* ⊕ *www. edfilmfest.org.uk*.

Edinburgh Science Festival

FESTIVALS | FAMILY | Held around Easter each year, the Edinburgh Science Festival is one of Europe's largest, and aims to make science accessible, interesting, and fun for kids (and adults) through an extensive program of innovative exhibitions, workshops, performances, and screenings. ⊠ *The Hub, 348–350 Castlehill, Old Town* ☎ *0131/553–0320* ⊕ *www.sciencefestival.co.uk*.

Edinburgh Jazz & Blues Festival

FESTIVALS | Held over a week in late July, the Edinburgh Jazz & Blues Festival attracts world-renowned musicians playing everything from blues-rock to soul music, and brings local enthusiasts out of their living rooms and into the pubs, clubs, and Spiegeltents (pop-up performance spaces) around the city. ⊠ *Edinburgh Jazz & Blues Festival, 89 Giles St., Leith* ☎ *0131/467–5200* ⊕ *www. edinburghjazzfestival.com*.

★ Edinburgh's Hogmanay

FESTIVALS | Nowadays most capital cities put on decent New Year's celebrations, but Edinburgh's three-day-long Hogmanay festivities are on a whole other level. There's a reason this city is famous around the world as the best place to ring in the New Year. Yes, it's winter and yes, it's chilly, but joining a crowd of 80,000 people in a monster street party, complete with big-name rock concerts, torchlight processions, ceilidh dancing, and incredible fireworks, is something you won't forget in a hurry. The headline city center events are ticketed (and can be pricey), but there are free parties happening all over the city. ⊠ *Princes St., Old Town* ⊕ *www.edinburghshogmanay. com* ✉ *From £20.*

The Royal Edinburgh Military Tattoo
FESTIVALS | It may not be art, but The Tattoo (as it's commonly known) is at the very heart of Scottish cultural life. Taking place, like many of the city's festivals, during August, this celebration of martial music features international military bands, gymnastics, and stunt motorcycle teams on the castle esplanade. Each year 22,000 seats are made available, yet it's always a sellout, so book your place early. If you are lucky enough to get tickets, dress warmly for evening shows and always bring a raincoat; the show goes on in all weathers. ⊠ *The Tattoo Box Office, 1–3 Cockburn St., Old Town* ☎ *0131/225–1188* ⊕ *www.edintattoo.co.uk.*

Planning Your Time

One of Edinburgh's greatest virtues is its compact size, which means it's possible to pack a lot into even the briefest of visits. The two main areas of interest are the Old Town and the New Town, where you'll find Edinburgh Castle, the Scottish Parliament, Princes Street Gardens, and the National Gallery of Scotland. You can cover the major attractions in one day, but to give the big sights their due, you should allow at least two. Stay even longer and you'll have time to explore the Palace of Holyroodhouse, the Royal Botanic Garden, and the city's other important muse-ums. You could also head down to leafy, village-like Stockbridge, then immerse yourself in the greenery along the Water

of Leith, visiting the Scottish National Gallery of Modern Art along the way.

Getting out of town is also an option for longer stays. Hop on a bus out to Midlothi-an to see the magnificent Rosslyn Chapel (even if you're not a fan of *The Da Vinci Code,* it's still interesting), and Crichton Castle, parts of which date back to the 14th century. Head west along the Firth of Forth to explore South Queensferry, with its three Forth bridges (including the iconic red railway bridge) and palatial Hopetoun House, or head east for the beautiful beaches, bird-watching, and golf courses in and around North Berwick.

■ **TIP→ Some attractions have special hours during August, due to the large influx of festival-goers. If you want to see some-thing special, be sure to check the hours ahead of time.**

Getting Here and Around

AIR

Edinburgh Airport is 7 miles west of the city center. Flights bound for Edinburgh depart virtually every hour from London's Gatwick, Heathrow, and City airports.

Airlines serving Edinburgh, Scotland's busiest airport, include Air France, Aer Lingus, American Airlines, British Air-ways, Delta Virgin, easyJet, Iberia, Jet2, KLM, Lufthansa, and Ryanair.

Delta flies direct to Edinburgh from New York's JFK airport, while United flies direct from Newark. There are also direct, seasonal flights from Boston (Delta), Chicago and Washington D.C. (United), Philadelphia (American), and Orlando (Virgin Atlantic). Otherwise, your airline is likely to require a change somewhere in Europe. You could also fly into Glasgow Airport, 50 miles away, or the smaller Glasgow Prestwick, another 30 miles south, but these will add about an hour and a half to your journey.

There are no rail links to the city center, so the most efficient way to do the journey on public transport is by tram; the service runs every 8 to 12 minutes and takes about half an hour. Tickets cost £6.50 one-way and £9 for a round-trip. By bus or car you can usually make it to Edinburgh in a half hour, unless you hit the morning (7:30 to 9) or evening (4 to 6) rush hours. Lothian Buses runs an Airlink express service to Waverley railway station via Haymarket that usually takes around half an hour, depending on traffic. Buses run every 15 to 30 minutes; tickets cost £4.50 one way or £7.50 round-trip and can be purchased from the booth beside the bus. Local buses also run between Edinburgh Airport and the city center every 15 minutes or so from 9 to 5, and roughly every hour during off-peak hours; they are far cheaper—just £1.80 one-way—but can take twice as long.

You can arrange for a chauffeur-driven limousine to meet your flight at Edinburgh Airport through Transvercia Chaffeur Drive, Little's, or W L Sleigh Ltd, for upwards of £50.

Taxis are readily available outside the terminal. The trip takes 20 to 30 minutes to the city center, 15 minutes longer during rush hour. The fare is roughly £25. Note that airport taxis picking up fares from the terminal are any color, not the typical black cabs.

AIRPORT INFORMATION Edinburgh Airport. ⊠ Glasgow Rd., Ingliston ☎ 0844/448–8833 ⊕ www.edinburghairport.com.

AIRPORT TRANSFER CONTACTS Little's. ⊠ 1282 Paisley Rd. W, Glasgow ☎ 0131/883–2111 ⊕ www.littles.co.uk. **Transvercia Chaffeur Drive.** ⊠ The Harland Bldg., Unit 6, Suite 19, Pilrig Heights, Leith ☎ 0131/334–5825 ⊕ www.transvercia.co.uk. **W L Sleigh.** ⊠ 1 The Roundal, Edinburgh ☎ 0131/339–9607 ⊕ sleigh.co.uk.

BUS

National Express provides a coach service to and from London and other major towns and cities. The main terminal, Edinburgh Bus Station, is a short walk north of Edinburgh Waverley station, immediately east of St. Andrew Square. Long-distance coaches must be booked in advance online, by phone, or at the terminal. Edinburgh is approximately eight hours by bus from London.

Lothian Buses provides most of the services between Edinburgh and the Lothians and conducts day tours around and beyond the city. First Bus runs additional buses out of Edinburgh into the surrounding area. Megabus offers dirt-cheap fares to selected cities across Scotland.

Lothian Buses is also the main operator within Edinburgh. You can buy tickets from the driver on the bus, though you will need the exact fare (£1.80). A better option is to use a contactless card to pay for single journeys, safe in the knowledge that the price is automatically capped if you pass the threshold for a day (£4.50) or week (£20) ticket. A third option is to buy tickets in advance on your phone through the Lothian Buses M-Tickets app. Note that NightBus services are not included in a day ticket; you will pay £3 for a single journey.

■ TIP→ Buses can be packed on Friday and Saturday nights, so you may want to consider a taxi instead.

BUS CONTACTS First Bus. ☎ 03451/646–0707 ⊕ www.firstbus.co.uk. **Lothian Buses.** ☎ 0131/555–6363 ⊕ www.lothianbuses.com. **Megabus.** ☎ 0900/160–0900 ⊕ uk.megabus.com. **National Express.** ☎ 0371/781–8181 ⊕ www.nationalexpress.com.

CAR

It's not necessary to have a car in Edinburgh, as the city is quite walkable and has an extensive and efficient public transport system. Driving in Edinburgh has its quirks and pitfalls—particularly at the height of festival season. Metered parking in the city center is scarce and expensive, and the local traffic wardens are an unforgiving lot. Note that illegally parked cars are routinely towed away, and getting your car back will be expensive. After 6 pm, the parking situation improves considerably, and you may manage to find a space quite near your hotel, even downtown. If you park on a yellow line or in a resident's parking bay, be prepared to move your car by 8 the following morning. Parking lots are clearly signposted; overnight parking is expensive and not always permitted.

TAXI

Taxi stands can be found throughout the city, mostly in the New Town. The following are the most convenient: the west end of Princes Street, South Street, David Street, and North Street, Andrew Street (both just off St. Andrew Square), Waverley Mall, Waterloo Place, and Lauriston Place. Alternatively, hail any taxi displaying an illuminated "for hire" sign.

TRAIN

Edinburgh's main train hub, Edinburgh Waverley station, is downtown, below Waverley Bridge and around the corner from the unmistakable spire of the Scott Monument. Travel time from Edinburgh to London by train is as little as 4½ hours for the fastest service.

Edinburgh's other main station is Haymarket, about four minutes (by rail) west of Edinburgh Waverley. Most Glasgow and other western and northern services stop here.

TRAIN CONTACTS National Rail Enquiries. ☏ 08457/484950 ⊕ www.nationalrail. co.uk. **ScotRail.** ☏ 0344/811–0141 ⊕ www.scotrail.co.uk.

TRAM

Absent since 1956, trams returned to the streets of Edinburgh in 2014. The 8½-mile stretch of track currently runs between Edinburgh Airport in the west to York Place in the east, although work is under way to extend it all the way to Newhaven (via Leith Walk, The Shore, and Ocean Terminal). This extension is scheduled for completion in early 2023. Useful stops for travelers include Haymarket, Princes Street, and St. Andrew Square (for Edinburgh Waverley station). Tickets are £1.80 for a single journey in the "City Zone" (which is every stop excluding the airport) or £6.50 for a single to/from the airport (£9 return). Day tickets, allowing unlimited travel, cost £4.50 in the City Zone and £10 including the airport.

TRAM CONTACT Edinburgh Trams. ☏ 0131/338–5780 ⊕ www.edin-burghtrams.com.

Restaurants

Edinburgh's eclectic restaurant scene has attracted a brigade of well-known chefs, including the award-winning trio of Martin Wishart, Tom Kitchin, and Paul Kitching, who have abandoned the tried-and-true recipes for more adventurous cuisine. Of course, you can always find traditional fare, which usually means the Scottish-French style that harks back to the historical "Auld Alliance" of the 13th century. The Scottish element is the preference for fresh and local produce; the French supplies the sauces. In Edinburgh you can sample anything from Malaysian *rendang* (a thick, coconut-milk stew) to Kurdish kebabs, while the long-established French, Italian, Chinese, Pakistani, and Indian communities ensure that the majority of the globe's most treasured cuisines are well represented. It's possible to eat well in Edinburgh without spending a fortune. Multicourse prix-fixe options are common, and almost always less expensive than ordering à la carte, while set lunch menus are increasingly widespread. Even at restaurants in the highest price category, you can easily spend less than £40 per person. People tend to eat later in Scotland than in England—around 8 pm on average—and then drink on in leisurely Scottish fashion.

Hotels

From stylish boutique hotels to homey bed-and-breakfasts, Edinburgh has a world-class array of accommodation options to suit every taste. Its status as one of Britain's most attractive and fascinating cities ensures a steady influx of visitors, but the wealth of overnight options means there's no need to compromise on where you stay. Grand old hotels are rightly renowned for their regal bearing and old-world charm, but if your tastes are a little more contemporary, the city's burgeoning contingent of chic design hotels offers an equally alluring alternative. For those on a tighter budget, the town's B&Bs are the most obvious choice—most proprietors provide front-door keys and very few impose curfews.

Space is at a premium in August and September, when the Edinburgh International Festival and the Festival Fringe take place, so reserve your room at least three months in advance. B&Bs may prove trickier to find in the winter months (with the exception of Christmas and New Year), as this is when many owners choose to close up shop and go on vacation themselves.

To save money and see how local residents live, stay in a B&B in one of the areas away from the city center, such as Leith to the north, Murrayfield to the west, or Mayfield to the south. Public buses can whisk you to the city center in 10 to 15 minutes.

Restaurant and hotel reviews have been shortened. For full information, visit Fodors.com. Restaurant prices are the average cost of a main course at dinner or, if dinner is not served, at lunch. Hotel prices are the lowest cost of a standard double room in high season, including 20% V.A.T.

WHAT IT COSTS in Pounds

	$	$$	$$$	$$$$
RESTAURANTS				
	under £15	£15–£19	£20–£25	over £25
HOTELS				
	under £125	£125–£200	£201–£300	over £300

Nightlife

The nightlife scene in Edinburgh is vibrant—whatever you're looking for, you'll find it here. There are traditional pubs, chic modern bars, and cutting-edge clubs. Live music pours out of many watering holes on weekends, particularly folk, blues, and jazz, while well-known artists perform at some of the larger venues.

Edinburgh has hundreds of pubs, and each is a study in itself. In the eastern and northern districts of the city, you can find some grim, inhospitable-looking places that proclaim that drinking is no laughing matter. But throughout Edinburgh, many pubs have deliberately traded in their old spit-and-sawdust vibe for atmospheric revivals of the warm, oak-paneled, leather-chaired *howffs* (meeting places). Most pubs and bars are open weekdays, while on weekends they're open from about 11 am to midnight (some until 2 am on Saturday).

The List and *The Skinny* carry the most up-to-date details about cultural events. *The List* is available at newsstands throughout the city, while *The Skinny* is free and can be picked up at a number of pubs, clubs, and shops around town. *The Herald* and *The Scotsman* newspapers are good for reviews and notices of upcoming events throughout the city and beyond.

Performing Arts

Think Edinburgh's arts scene consists of just the elegiac wail of a bagpipe and the twang of a fiddle? Think again. Edinburgh is one of the world's great performing arts cities. Live events take place throughout the city all year long, but things really come alive in August during the famed Edinburgh Festival Fringe and Edinburgh International Festival, which attract the best in music, dance, theater, circus, stand-up comedy, poetry, painting, and sculpture from all over the globe. *The Scotsman* and *Herald,* Scotland's leading daily newspapers, carry listings and reviews in their arts pages every day, with special editions during the festival. Tickets are generally sold in advance; in some cases they're also available from certain designated travel agents or at the door, although concerts by national orchestras often sell out long before the day of the performance.

Shopping

The New Town is considered Edinburgh's main shopping district yet its **Princes Street** disappoints some visitors with its dull modern architecture, average chain stores, and many fast-food outlets. However, head to its eastern end (on the corner of Leith Street) to find the recently refurbished **St James Quarter**, a vast, state-of-the-art shopping mall.

One block north of Princes Street lies pretty **Rose Street**. Partly pedestrianized, it's a pleasant place to stroll and browse a host of smaller specialty shops. Another block up is bustling **George Street**. The stores here tend to be fairly upscale, with posh London names like Jo Malone, Penhaligons, and Hawes & Curtis prominently featured, though some of the older independent stores continue to do good business.

The streets crossing George Street—Hanover, Frederick, and Castle—are also worth exploring. **Dundas Street,** the northern extension of Hanover Street beyond Queen Street Gardens, has several antiques shops. **Thistle Street,** originally George Street's "back lane," or service area, has several boutiques and even more antiques shops.

Walk to the west end of Princes Street and then along its continuation, Shandwick Place, to reach **Stafford Street** and the intersecting **William Street**. Together, they form a small, upscale shopping area in a gorgeous Georgian setting.

North of Princes Street, on the way to the Royal Botanic Garden Edinburgh, is **Stockbridge,** an oddball shopping area of some charm, particularly on St. Stephen Street. To get here, walk north down Frederick Street and Howe Street, away from Princes Street, then turn left onto North West Circus Place.

Shopping in the Old Town is a little more limited. As may be expected, many shops along the **Royal Mile** sell what may be politely or euphemistically described as "touristware"—think whiskies, tartans, and tweeds. Careful exploration, however, will reveal some worthwhile establishments, including shops that cater to highly specialized interests and hobbies.

A street below the Royal Mile, just off George IV Bridge at the castle end, is **Victoria Street,** which has some popular specialty shops grouped in a small area. Follow the tiny West Bow to **Grassmarket** for more specialty stores.

Halfway down the Royal Mile, and off the other side, is one of Edinburgh's hippest shopping experiences: **The Arches**. Here you'll find a number of glass-fronted independent stores set within Victorian-era archways. It's on East Market Street, just to the southeast of Edinburgh Waverley train station.

Tours

ORIENTATION TOURS

One good way to get oriented in Edinburgh is to take a bus tour. If you want to get to know the area around Edinburgh, Rabbie's leads small groups on several different excursions.

Edinburgh Bus Tours

BUS TOURS | Explore every corner of Edinburgh with this company's range of bus tours. The most popular are the Edinburgh Tour, which mainly covers Old Town sights including Edinburgh Castle, the Royal Mile, and the Palace of Holyroodhouse; and the Majestic Tour, which explores the New Town and farther corners of the city, including the Royal Yacht *Britannia* at Leith and the Royal Botanic Garden. Buses depart from Waverley Bridge, with each tour lasting an hour. ■TIP→ **If you plan more than one bus tour during a weekend, buy a money-saving Grand 48 ticket.** ⊠ *Waverley Bridge, New Town* ☎ *0131/475–0618* ⊕ *www.edinburghtour.com* ✉ *From £8.*

Rabbie's

BUS TOURS | Venture farther afield from Edinburgh on day trips run by this cheerful company. Its minibuses will take you a surprisingly long way and back in a day, with sights including Loch Ness, St. Andrews, Rosslyn Chapel, and Loch Lomond National Park. There are also multi-day trips available. Groups are kept to a guaranteed maximum of 16, giving these a less impersonal feel than some of the big enterprises. ⊠ *6 Waterloo Pl., Old Town* ☎ *0131/226–3133* ⊕ *www.rabbies.com* ✉ *From £34.*

PERSONAL GUIDES

Scottish Tourist Guides Association

PRIVATE GUIDES | This organization can supply guides (in 19 languages) who are fully qualified and will meet clients at any point of entry into the United Kingdom or Scotland. Guides can also tailor tours to your interests. ☎ *01786/447–784* ⊕ *www.stga.co.uk* ✉ *From £150.*

WALKING AND CYCLING TOURS

The Cadies & Witchery Tours

WALKING TOURS | Spooky tours tracing Edinburgh's ghouls, murders, and other grisly happenings start outside the Witchery Restaurant. The Cadies & Witchery Tours has built an award-winning reputation for combining entertainment and historical accuracy in its lively and enthusiastic Murder & Mystery and (in summer only) Ghosts & Gore tours. Both take you through the narrow Old Town lanes and closes, with costumed guides and other theatrical characters popping up along the route. ⊠ *84 West Bow, Old Town* ☎ *0131/225–6745* ⊕ *www.witcherytours.com* ✉ *£10.*

The Edinburgh Literary Pub Tour

WALKING TOURS | Professional actors invoke local literary characters while taking you around some of the city's most hallowed watering holes on these lively and informative tours. The experience is led by "Clart and McBrain"—one a bohemian, the other an intellectual—who regale you with witty tales of the literary past of Edinburgh's Old and New Towns. Tours run daily from May to September, Thursday through Sunday in April and October, Friday through Sunday in January to March, and Fridays in November and December; they meet outside the Beehive Inn. ⊠ *The Beehive Inn, 18–20 Grassmarket, Edinburgh* ☎ *0800/169–7410* ⊕ *www.edinburghliterarypubtour.co.uk* ✉ *£14.*

★ The Tartan Bicycle Company

BICYCLE TOURS | Cycling enthusiast and Edinburgh native Johann offers a range of guided and self-guided bike tours in and around the capital. Each half-day or full-day tour includes hotel pickup and your choice of standard or e-bikes. For a relaxed half-day introduction to Edinburgh, including some lesser-visited neighborhoods, opt for the Sky to Sea tour; it starts at leafy Union Canal, passes by The Meadows and Arthur's Seat, visits Portobello Beach, The Shore, and the Water of Leith, and ends in the New Town. ⊠ *Edinburgh* ☎ *0797/394–0924* ⊕ *www.tartanbiketours.co.uk* ⊠ *From £45.*

Visitor Information

The VisitScotland Edinburgh iCentre, located close to St. Giles' Cathedral on the Royal Mile, offers an accommodation-booking service, along with regular tourist information services.

CONTACT VisitScotland Edinburgh iCentre. ⊠ *249 High St., Old Town* ☎ *0131/473–3820* ⊕ *www.visitscotland.com.*

Activities

FOOTBALL

Like Glasgow, Edinburgh is mad for football (soccer in the United States), and there's an intense rivalry between the city's two professional teams.

Heart of Midlothian Football Club
SOCCER | Better known simply as "Hearts," the Heart of Midlothian Football Club plays in maroon and white and is based at Tynecastle. The club's crest is based on the Heart of Midlothian mosaic on the Royal Mile. ⊠ *Tynecastle Stadium, McLeod St., Edinburgh* ☎ *0333/043–1874* ⊕ *www.heartsfc.co.uk.*

Hibernian Football Club
SOCCER | Known to most as simply "Hibs," the green-and-white-bedecked Hibernian Club was founded in 1875—one year after Hearts—and plays its home matches at Easter Road Stadium in Leith. ⊠ *Easter Road Stadium, 12 Albion Pl., Leith* ☎ *0131/661–2159* ⊕ *www.hibernianfc.co.uk.*

GOLF

Edinburgh is widely considered to be the birthplace of modern golf, as its first official rules were developed at Leith Links. Naturally, there are a number of great courses in the city. For more information, the VisitScotland website has an extensive, searchable guide to Scottish courses.

Braid Hills
GOLF | This golf course is beautifully laid out over a rugged range of small hills in the southern suburbs of Edinburgh. The views in each direction—the Pentland Hills to the south, the city skyline and Firth of Forth to the north—are worth a visit in themselves. The city built this course at the turn of the 20th century after urban development forced golfers out of the city center. There's also a nine-hole "Wee Braids" course for beginners and younger players. Reservations are recommended for weekend play. ⊠ *27 Braids Hill Approach, Edinburgh* ☎ *0131/447–6666* ⊕ *www.edinburghleisure.co.uk* ⊠ *Braids: £29 weekday, £30 weekends; Wee Braids: £14.50* ⅃. *Braids: 18 holes, 5865 yards, par 71; Wee Braids: 9 holes, 2232 yards, par 31.*

Bruntsfield Links
GOLF | The British Seniors and several other championship tournaments are held at this prestigious Willie Park–designed course. It's located 3 miles west of Edinburgh, and should not be confused with Bruntsfield Links park in the city center. The course meanders among 155 acres of mature parkland and has fine views over the Firth of Forth. A strict dress code applies. Bruntsfield takes its name from one of the oldest golf links in Scotland, in the center of Edinburgh, where the club used to play—all that remains there is a nine-hole pitch-and-putt course. ■**TIP**→ **Full-day tickets are available for just £20 more than the cost of a single round on weekends.** ⊠ *32 Barnton Ave., Edinburgh* ☎ *0131/336–1479* ⊕ *www.bruntsfieldlinks.co.uk* ⊠ *£90 weekdays, £110 weekends Apr.–Sept.; £60 weekdays, £80 weekends Oct.; £45 Nov.–Mar.* ⅃. *18 holes, 6437 yards, par 70.*

Duddingston Golf Club

GOLF | Founded in 1895, this excellent public parkland course is 2 miles east of the city. The first hole is located in an idyllic deer park (watch out for four-legged spectators). Braid Burn—a stream that flows across the southern part of Edinburgh—also runs through the course, creating a perilous hazard on many holes. Prices drop sharply in the winter months for those willing to risk strong winds and rain. ⊠ *135 Duddingston Rd. W, Duddingston* ☎ *0131/661–7688* ⊕ *www. duddingstongolfclub.co.uk* ⌑ *£65 May–Sept.; £40 Apr. and Oct.; £35 Mar. and Nov.; £25 Dec.–Feb.* ⅄ *18 holes, 6466 yards, par 72.*

Royal Burgess Golfing Society

GOLF | Edinburgh's other Victorian courses are newcomers when compared to Royal Burgess, which opened in 1735. Its members originally played on Bruntsfield Links; now they and their guests play on elegantly manicured parkland in the city's northwestern suburbs. It's a challenging course with fine, beautifully maintained greens. Be aware that there's a strict, conservative dress code—tailored pants and collared shirts on the course and in the clubhouse (so no denim, T-shirts, or sweaters), and jackets and ties in the Members' Bar. ⊠ *181 Whitehouse Rd., Barnton* ☎ *0131/339–2075* ⊕ *www.royal-burgess.co.uk* ⌑ *£100 for 1 round; £150 day ticket* ⅄ *18 holes, 6511 yards, par 71.*

RUGBY

Edinburgh is the home of Scottish rugby, with national stadium Murrayfield hosting regular international matches. It's also home to several amateur clubs and the professional club Edinburgh Rugby, who compete in the international Pro14 League.

★ Murrayfield Stadium

RUGBY | Home of the Scottish Rugby Union, Murrayfield Stadium hosts rugby matches in early spring and fall, as well as prestigious Six Nations tournament games in February and March. Crowds of good-humored rugby fans from all over the world add greatly to the sense of excitement in the streets of Edinburgh. Stick around after the game as there's often live music, food, and drinks to enjoy in the stadium grounds. Outside of the rugby season, you can still see Murrayfield with a stadium tour; tickets are £12 for adults. ⊠ *Roseburn St., Murrayfield* ☎ *0131/346–5000* ⊕ *www. scottishrugby.org.*

Edinburgh

Old Town

East of Edinburgh Castle, the historic castle esplanade becomes the street known as the Royal Mile, leading down through Old Town to the Palace of Holyroodhouse. The Mile, as it's known locally, is actually made up of one thoroughfare that bears, in consecutive sequence, different names—Castlehill, Lawnmarket, Parliament Square, High Street, and Canongate. This thoroughfare, and the streets and passages that wind off it on both sides, really *were* Edinburgh until the 18th century saw expansions to the south and north. Everybody lived here: the richer folk on the lower floors of houses; the less well-to-do families on the middle floors; and the poor highest up.

Time and progress (of a sort) have swept away some of the narrow closes and tall tenements of the Old Town, but enough survive for you to be able to imagine the original profile of Scotland's capital. There are many guided tours of the area, or you can simply stroll around at your leisure—often a better choice in summer when tourists pack the area and large guided groups have trouble making their way through the crowds.

Sights

Arthur's Seat
VIEWPOINT | The high point of 640-acre Holyrood Park is this famously spectacular viewpoint. You'll have seen it before—countless photos have been snapped from this very spot. The "seat" in question is actually the 822-foot-high plateau of a small mountain. A ruined church—the 15th-century Chapel of St. Anthony—adds to its impossible picturesqueness. There are various starting points for the walk, but one of the most pleasant begins at the Scottish Parliament building. Cross the road from Parliament, skirt around the parking lot, cross a second road, and join the gently rising path to the left (rather than the steeper fork to the right). At a moderate pace, this climb takes around 45 minutes up and 30 minutes down, and is easy so long as you're reasonably fit. Even if you aren't, there are plenty of places to stop for a rest and to admire the views along the way. A faster—though less beautiful—way to reach the summit is to drive to the small parking area at Dunsapie Loch, on Queen's Road, then follow the footpath up the hill; this walk takes about 20 minutes. ⊠ *Queen's Dr., Old Town*.

Camera Obscura and World of Illusions
OBSERVATORY | FAMILY | View Edinburgh like a Victorian at the city's 19th-century camera obscura. Head up Outlook Tower for the headline attraction—an optical instrument that affords live bird's-eye views of the city, illuminated onto a concave table. It's been wowing visitors since 1853, and yet it retains a magical quality that can captivate even the most cynical smartphone-toting teen. After you've seen the camera obscura and enjoyed the rooftop views, head down to explore five more floors of interactive optical illusions. They are guaranteed to keep the kids entertained and educated for an hour or two. ⊠ *549 Castlehill, Old Town* ☎ *0131/226–3709* ⊕ *www.camera-obscura.co.uk* 🎟 *£18.95.*

Canongate
STREET | This section of the Royal Mile takes its name from the canons who once ran the abbey at Holyrood. Canongate—in Scots, *gate* means "street"—was originally an independent town, or *burgh*, another Scottish term used to refer to a community with trading rights granted by the monarch. In this area you'll find **Canongate Kirk** and its graveyard, **Canongate Tolbooth**, as well as the **Museum of Edinburgh.** ⊠ *Royal Mile, between High St. and Abbey Strand, Old Town*.

Canongate Kirk
CEMETERY | This unadorned Church of Scotland building, built in 1688, is best known for its graveyard. It is the final resting place of several notable Scots, including economist Adam Smith (1723–90), author of *The Wealth of Nations* (1776); Dugald Stewart (1753–1828), the leading European philosopher of his time; and the undervalued Scottish poet Robert Fergusson (1750–74). The fact that Fergusson's grave is even distinguishable is due to the far more famous Robert Burns (1759–96), who commissioned a marker to be made. Incidentally, Robert Burns's literary lover Agnes Maclehose (the "Clarinda" to his "Sylvander" as noted in a series of passionate letters) also has a memorial stone here. ⊠ *153 Canongate, Old Town* ☎ *0131/556–3515* ⊕ *canongatekirk.org.uk* ⊗ *Closed Oct.–Apr.*

Canongate Tolbooth and People's Story Museum
HISTORY MUSEUM | Nearly every city and town in Scotland once had a tolbooth. Originally a customhouse, where tolls were gathered, it soon came to mean town hall and later prison, as there were detention cells in the cellar. The building where Canongate's town council once met now has a museum, the People's Story Museum, which focuses on the lives of everyday folk from the 18th century to today. Exhibits describe how Canongate once bustled with the activities of the tradespeople needed to

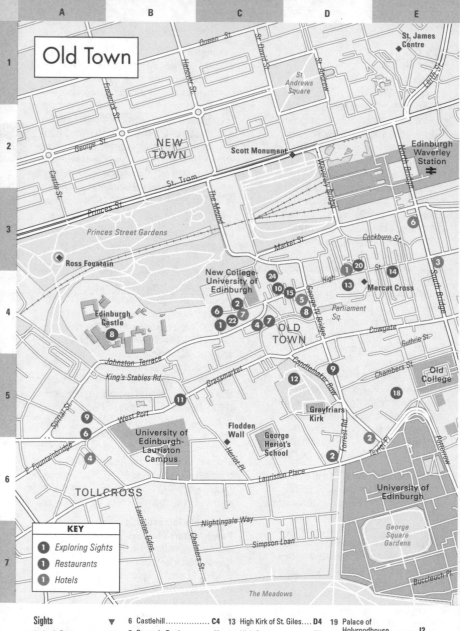

Old Town

KEY

- ● Exploring Sights
- ● Restaurants
- ● Hotels

The History of Edinburgh Castle

Archaeological investigations have established that the rock on which Edinburgh Castle stands was inhabited as far back as 1,000 BC, in the latter part of the Bronze Age. There have been fortifications here since the mysterious tribal Picts first used it as a stronghold in the 3rd and 4th centuries AD. Anglian invaders from northern England dislodged the Picts in AD 452, and for the next 1,300 years the site saw countless battles and skirmishes.

In the castle you'll hear the story of Randolph, Earl of Moray, the nephew of freedom fighter Robert the Bruce. He scaled the heights one dark night in 1313, surprised the English guard, and recaptured the castle for the Scots. During this battle he destroyed every one of the castle's buildings except for St. Margaret's Chapel, dating from around 1076, so that successive Stewart kings had to rebuild the castle bit by bit.

The castle has been held over time by Scots and Englishmen, Catholics and Protestants, soldiers and royalty. In the 16th century Mary, Queen of Scots, gave birth here to the future James VI of Scotland (1566–1625), who was also to rule England as James I. In 1573 it was the last fortress to support Mary's claim as the rightful Catholic queen of Britain, causing the castle to be virtually destroyed by English artillery fire.

supply life's essentials. There are also displays on the politics, health care, and leisure time (such as it was) in days of yore. Other exhibits leap forward in time to show, for example, a typical 1940s kitchen. ⊠ *163 Canongate, Old Town* ☎ *0131/529–4057* ⊕ *www.edinburghmuseums.org.uk.*

Castlehill

STREET | This street, the upper portion of the Royal Mile, was where alleged witches were brought in the 16th century to be burned at the stake. The cannonball embedded in the west gable of Castlehill's Cannonball Restaurant was, according to legend, fired from the castle during the Jacobite Rebellion of 1745, led by Bonnie Prince Charlie (1720–88)—though the truth is probably that it was installed there deliberately in 1681 as a height marker for Edinburgh's first piped water-supply system. Atop the Gothic Tolbooth Kirk, built in 1844 for the General Assembly of the Church of Scotland, stands the tallest spire in the city, at 240 feet. The church now houses the cheery Edinburgh Festival offices and a pleasant café known as the Hub. ⊠ *East of Esplanade and west of Lawnmarket, Old Town.*

Dynamic Earth

HISTORY MUSEUM | **FAMILY** | Using state-of-the-art technology, the 11 theme galleries at this interactive science museum educate and entertain as they explore the wonders of the planet, from polar regions to tropical rain forests. Geological history, from the big bang to the unknown future, is also examined, all topped off with an eye-popping, 360-degree planetarium experience. ⊠ *Holyrood Rd., Old Town* ☎ *0131/550–7800* ⊕ *www.dynamicearth.co.uk* ≡ *£15.95* ⊘ *Closed Mon.–Wed. Nov.–Feb.*

★ Edinburgh Castle

CASTLE/PALACE | **FAMILY** | The crowning glory of the Scottish capital, Edinburgh Castle is popular not only for its pivotal role in Scottish history, but also because of the spectacular views from its battlements: on a clear day the vistas stretch all the way to Fife. You'll need at least three hours to see everything it has to

An emblem of the city's history, the rock where Edinburgh Castle stands has been inhabited as far back as 1,000 BC.

offer (even longer if you're a military history buff), though if you're in a rush, its main highlights can just about be squeezed into an hour and a half.

You enter across the Esplanade, the huge forecourt built in the 18th century as a parade ground. The area comes alive with color and music each August when it's used for the Military Tattoo, a festival of magnificently outfitted marching bands and regiments. Head over the drawbridge and through the gatehouse, past the guards, and you'll find the rough stone walls of the Half-Moon Battery, where the one-o'clock gun is fired every day in an impressively anachronistic ceremony; these curving ramparts give Edinburgh Castle its distinctive silhouette. Climb up through a second gateway and you come to the oldest surviving building in the complex, the tiny 11th-century St. Margaret's Chapel, named in honor of Saxon queen Margaret (circa 1045–93), who persuaded her husband, King Malcolm III (circa 1031–93), to move his court from Dunfermline to Edinburgh.

The story goes that Edinburgh's environs—the Lothians—were occupied by Anglian settlers with whom the queen felt more at home, as opposed to the Celts who surrounded Dunfermline. The Crown Room, a must-see, contains the "Honours of Scotland"—the crown, scepter, and sword that once graced the Scottish monarch—as well as the Stone of Scone, upon which Scottish monarchs once sat to be crowned (it's still a feature of British coronation ceremonies today). In the section now called Queen Mary's Apartments, Mary, Queen of Scots, gave birth to James VI of Scotland. The Great Hall, which held Scottish Parliament meetings until 1840, displays arms and armor under an impressive vaulted, beamed ceiling.

Military features of interest include the Scottish National War Memorial, the Scottish United Services Museum, and the famous 15th-century Belgian-made cannon Mons Meg. This enormous piece of artillery has been silent since 1682, when it exploded while firing a salute

Grassmarket Gallows

Grassmarket's history is long and gory. The cobbled cross at the east end marks the site of the town gallows. Among those hanged here were many 17th-century Covenanters, members of the Church of Scotland who rose up against Charles I's efforts to enforce Anglican or "English" ideologies on the Scottish people. Judges were known to issue the death sentence for these religious reformers with the words, "Let them glorify God in the Grassmarket." Two Grassmarket pubs have names that reference the local hangings: the Last Drop and Maggie Dickson's. The latter references a woman who was hanged and proclaimed dead, but when traveling for her burial, sprang back to life. She lived for another 40 years with the nickname Half-Hangit Maggie.

for the Duke of York; it now stands in an ancient hall behind the Half-Moon Battery. Contrary to what you may hear from locals, it's not Mons Meg but the battery's gun that goes off with a bang every weekday at 1 pm, frightening visitors and reminding Edinburghers to check their watches. ■ TIP→ **Avoid the queues and save some money by buying tickets in advance online. When you arrive, you can pick up your ticket from one of the automated collection points at the entrance.** ✉ *Castle Esplanade and Castlehill, Old Town* ☎ *0131/225–9846* ⊕ *www.edin-burghcastle.scot* 🎟 *£17.50.*

George IV Bridge

BRIDGE | Here's a curiosity—a bridge that most of its users don't ever realize is a bridge. With buildings closely packed on both sides, George IV Bridge can feel to many like a regular Edinburgh street, but for those forewarned, the truth is plain to see. At the corner of the bridge stands one of the most photographed sculptures in Scotland, *Greyfriars Bobby*. This statue pays tribute to the legendarily loyal Skye terrier who kept vigil beside his master's grave for 14 years after he died in 1858. The 1961 Walt Disney film *Greyfriars Bobby* tells a version of the heartrending tale. ✉ *Bank St. and Lawnmarket, Old Town.*

Gladstone's Land

HISTORIC HOME | This narrow, six-story tenement is one of the oldest buildings on the Royal Mile. Start on the third floor and work your way down through the centuries, with each room showcasing different time periods in the life of the building. You'll start in a traditional boarding house (early 1900s), move through a fashionable draper's shop (mid-1700s), and end in a plush apartment with a kitchen and stockroom (early 1600s). All rooms are decorated in authentic period furnishings, with visitors welcome to rummage through drawers, pick up ornaments, and even recline on the four-poster beds—which, incidentally, offer the best views of the magnificent hand-painted ceilings. The ground floor is home to a pleasant little coffeeshop and ice cream parlor. ✉ *477B Lawnmarket, Old Town* ☎ *0131/226–5856* ⊕ *www.nts. org.uk* 🎟 *£7.50.*

Grassmarket

PLAZA/SQUARE | For centuries an agricultural marketplace, Grassmarket is now the site of numerous shops, bars, and restaurants, making it a hive of activity at night. Sections of the Old Town wall can be traced on the north side by a series of steps that ascend from Grassmarket to Johnston Terrace. The best-preserved section of the wall can be found by

The Greyfriars Kirkyard, part of the church Greyfriars Kirk, is allegedly one of the most haunted cemeteries in Europe.

crossing to the south side and climbing the steps of the lane called the Vennel. Here the 16th-century **Flodden Wall** comes in from the east and turns south at Telfer's Wall, a 17th-century extension.

From the northeast corner of the Grassmarket, **Victoria Street,** a 19th-century addition to the Old Town, leads to the George IV Bridge. Shops here sell antiques, designer clothing, and souvenirs. ✉ *Grassmarket, Edinburgh.*

★ Greyfriars Kirkyard

CEMETERY | This sprawling, hillside graveyard, surely one of the most evocative in Europe (particularly at twilight), is a giddy mess of old, tottering tombstones that mark the graves of some of Scotland's most respected heroes and despised villains. Many of these inspired character names in the Harry Potter book series; fans can seek out Potters, McGonagalls, and Moodies, to name a few. Among the larger tombs arranged in avenues and the seemingly random assortment of grave markers, lie two rare surviving *mortsafes*: iron cages erected around graves in the early 1800s to prevent the theft of corpses for sale to medical schools.

At the southern end of the graveyard stands Greyfriars Kirk, the 400-year-old church where the National Covenant—a document declaring the Presbyterian Church in Scotland independent of the monarchy, and so plunging Scotland into decades of civil war—was signed in 1638. Nearby, at the corner of George IV Bridge and Candlemaker Row, stands one of Scotland's most photographed sites: the statue of Greyfriars Bobby, a Skye terrier who supposedly spent 14 years guarding the grave of his departed owner. ✉ *26A Candlemaker Row, Old Town* ☎ *0131/225–1900* ⊕ *www.greyfriarskirk.com/visit/kirkyard.*

High Kirk of St. Giles (*St Giles' Cathedral*)
RELIGIOUS BUILDING | St. Giles, which lies about one-third of the way along the Royal Mile from Edinburgh Castle, is one of the city's principal churches. It may not quite rival Paris's Notre Dame or London's Westminster Abbey—it's more like a large parish church than a

great European cathedral—but it has a long and storied history. There has been a church here since AD 854, although most of the present structure dates from either 1120 or 1829, when the church was restored.

The tower, with its stone crown 161 feet above the ground, was completed between 1495 and 1500. Inside the church stands a life-size statue of the Scot whose spirit still dominates the place—the great religious reformer and preacher John Knox. But the most elaborate feature is the **Chapel of the Order of the Thistle,** built onto the southeast corner of the church in 1911 for the exclusive use of Scotland's only chivalric order, the Most Ancient and Noble Order of the Thistle. It bears the belligerent national motto "*nemo me impune lacessit*" ("No one provokes me with impunity"). Look out for the carved wooden angel playing bagpipes. ⊠ *High St., Old Town* ☎ *0131/226–0677* ⊕ *www.stgilescathedral.org.uk* ✉ *Free, but donations welcome.*

High Street

STREET | The High Street (one of the five streets that make up the Royal Mile) is home to an array of impressive buildings and sights, including some hidden historic relics. Near Parliament Square, look on the west side for a **heart** mosaic set in cobbles. This marks the site of the vanished Old Tolbooth, the center of city life from the 15th century until the building's demolition in 1817. The ancient municipal building was used as a prison and a site of public execution, so you may witness a local spitting on the heart as one walks by—for good luck.

Just outside Parliament House lies the **Mercat Cross** (*mercat* means "market"), a great landmark of Old Town life. It was an old mercantile center, where royal proclamations were—and are still—read. Most of the present cross is comparatively modern, dating from the time of William Gladstone (1809–98), the great

Victorian prime minister and rival of Benjamin Disraeli (1804–81). Across High Street from the High Kirk of St. Giles stands the **City Chambers,** now the seat of local government. Built by John Fergus, who adapted a design of John Adam in 1753, the chambers were originally known as the Royal Exchange and intended to be where merchants and lawyers could conduct business. Note how the building drops 11 stories to Cockburn Street on its north side.

A *tron* is a weigh beam used in public weigh houses, and the **Tron Kirk** was named after a salt tron that used to stand nearby. The *kirk* (church) itself was built after 1633, when St. Giles's became an Episcopal cathedral for a brief time. In 1693 a minister here delivered an often-quoted prayer: "Lord, hae mercy on a' [all] fools and idiots, and particularly on the Magistrates of Edinburgh." ⊠ *Between Lawnmarket and Canongate, Old Town.*

Lawnmarket

STREET | The second uppermost of the streets that make up the Royal Mile, this was formerly the site of the city's produce market, with a once-a-week special sale of wool and linen. Now it's home to historic Gladstone's Land and the Writers' Museum. At various times, the Lawnmarket Courts housed James Boswell, David Hume, and Robert Burns, while in the 1770s this area was home to the infamous Deacon Brodie, pillar of society by day and a murdering gang leader by night. Robert Louis Stevenson (1850–94) may well have used Brodie as the inspiration for his novella *Strange Case of Dr. Jekyll and Mr. Hyde*. ⊠ *Between Castlehill and High St., Old Town.*

Museum of Childhood

CHILDREN'S MUSEUM | FAMILY | Even adults tend to enjoy this cheerfully noisy museum—a cacophony of childhood memorabilia, vintage toys, antique dolls, and fairground games. The museum claims to have been the first in the world devoted

The Grand Gallery of the National Museum of Scotland is reminiscent of a classic Victorian arcade mall.

solely to the history of childhood. ⊠ *42 High St., Old Town* ☎ *0131/529–4142* ⊕ *www.edinburghmuseums.org.uk.*

Museum of Edinburgh

HISTORY MUSEUM | A must-see if you're interested in the details of Old Town life, this bright yellow, 16th-century building is home to a fascinating museum of local history. It houses some of the most important artifacts in Scottish history—including the National Covenant, a document signed by Scotland's Presbyterian leadership in defiance of a reformed liturgy imposed by King Charles I of England that ignited decades of civil war—alongside Scottish pottery, silver, and glassware, as well as curios like Greyfriars Bobby's dog collar. ⊠ *142–146 Canongate, Old Town* ☎ *0131/529–4143* ⊕ *www.edinburghmuseums.org.uk.*

★ National Museum of Scotland

HISTORY MUSEUM | **FAMILY** | This museum traces the country's fascinating story from the oldest fossils to the most recent popular culture, making it a must-see for first-time visitors to Scotland.

Two of the most famous treasures are the Lewis Chessmen, a set of intricately carved 12th-century ivory chess pieces found on one of Scotland's Western Isles, and Dolly the sheep, the world's first cloned mammal and biggest ovine celebrity. A dramatic, cryptlike entrance gives way to the light-filled, birdcage wonders of the Victorian grand hall and the upper galleries. Other exhibition highlights include the hanging hippo and sea creatures of the Wildlife Panorama, beautiful Viking brooches, Pictish stones, and Queen Mary's *clarsach* (harp). Take the elevator to the lovely rooftop terrace for spectacular views of Edinburgh Castle and the city below. ⊠ *Chambers St., Old Town* ☎ *0300/123–6789* ⊕ *www.nms. ac.uk* ✉ *Free.*

★ Palace of Holyroodhouse

CASTLE/PALACE | The one-time haunt of Mary, Queen of Scots, the Palace of Holyroodhouse has a long history of gruesome murders, destructive fires, and power-hungry personalities. Today, it's Queen Elizabeth II's official residence in

The Palace of Holyroodhouse is the Queen's official residence in Scotland.

Scotland. A doughty, impressive palace standing at the foot of the Royal Mile, it's built around a graceful, lawned central court at the end of Canongate. And when royals are not in residence, you can take a tour. There's plenty to see here, so make sure you have at least two hours to tour the palace, gardens, and the ruins of the 12th-century abbey; pick up the free audio guide for the full experience.

Many monarchs, including Charles II, Queen Victoria, and George V, have left their mark on the rooms here, but it's Mary, Queen of Scots whose spirit looms largest. Perhaps the most memorable room is the chamber in which David Rizzio (1533–66), secretary to Mary, was stabbed more than 50 times by the henchmen of her second husband, Lord Darnley. Darnley himself was murdered the next year, clearing the way for the queen's marriage to her lover, the Earl of Bothwell.

The King James Tower is the oldest surviving section of the palace, containing Mary's rooms on the second floor,

and Lord Darnley's rooms below. Though much has been altered, there are fine fireplaces, paneling, tapestries, and 18th- and 19th-century furnishings throughout. At the south end of the palace front, you'll find the Royal Dining Room, and along the south side is the Throne Room, now used for social and ceremonial occasions.

At the back of the palace is the King's Bedchamber. The 150-foot-long Great Picture Gallery, on the north side, displays the portraits of 110 Scottish monarchs. These were commissioned by Charles II, who was eager to demonstrate his Scottish ancestry—but most of the people depicted are entirely fictional, and the likenesses of several others were invented and simply given the names of real people. The Queen's Gallery, in a former church and school at the entrance to the palace, holds rotating exhibits from the Royal Collection. There is a separate admission charge (£7.80).

Holyroodhouse has its origins in an Augustinian monastery founded by David

I (1084–1153) in 1128. In the 15th and 16th centuries, Scottish royalty, preferring the comforts of the abbey to drafty Edinburgh Castle, settled into Holyroodhouse, expanding the buildings until the palace eclipsed the monastery. Nevertheless, you can still walk around some evocative abbey ruins.

After the Union of the Crowns in 1603, when the Scottish royal court packed its bags and decamped to England, the building began to fall into disrepair. It was Charles II (1630–85) who rebuilt Holyrood in the architectural style of Louis XIV (1638–1715), and this is the style you see today. Queen Victoria (1819–1901) and her grandson King George V (1865–1936) renewed interest in the palace, and the buildings were refurbished and again made suitable for royal residence. ⊠ *Canongate, Old Town* ☎ *0131/123–7306* ⊕ *www.rct.uk* ⚏ *£16.50; £21.90 with Queen's Gallery* ⊘ *Closed Tues.-Wed.* ⚞ *Advance booking required.*

The Real Mary King's Close
HISTORIC SIGHT | FAMILY | Buried beneath the City Chambers, this narrow, cobbled close (alleyway) provides a glimpse into a very different Edinburgh. It was once a busy open-air thoroughfare with hundreds of residents and a lively market, but in 1753 it was sealed off when the Royal Exchange (now the City Chambers) was built on top. Today costumed guides take you around the claustrophobic remains of the shops and houses, describing life here for the residents from plague and quarantine to rivers of sewage, as well as the odd murder mystery and ghost story. But for all the (somewhat over-the-top) theatricality, the real highlights here are historical; the sealed-in street is a truly fascinating insight into 17th-century Edinburgh. ⊠ *2 Warriston's Close, off High St., Old Town* ☎ *0131/225–0672* ⊕ *www.realmarykingsclose.com* ⚏ *£18.95.*

The Scottish Parliament
GOVERNMENT BUILDING | Scotland's now-iconic Parliament building is starkly modernist, with irregular curves and angles that mirror the twisting shapes of the surrounding landscape. Stylistically, it is about as far removed from Westminster as can be. Originally conceived by the late Catalan architect Enric Miralles, and completed by his widow Benedetta Tagliabue, the structure's artistry is most apparent when you step inside. The gentle slopes, the forest's worth of oak, the polished concrete and granite, and the walls of glass create an understated magnificence. Take a free guided tour to see the main hall and debating chamber, a committee room, and other areas of the building, or choose a specialist subject for your tour, from art to architecture. All tour reservations must be made online. Call well in advance to get a free ticket to view Parliament in action. ⊠ *Horse Wynd, Old Town* ☎ *0131/348–5000* ⊕ *www. parliament.scot* ⊘ *Closed Sun.*

The Scotch Whisky Experience
OTHER MUSEUM | Transforming malted barley and spring water into one of Scotland's most important exports—that's the subject of this popular Royal Mile attraction. An imaginative approach to the subject has guests riding in low-speed barrel cars and exploring Scotland's diverse whisky regions and their distinct flavors. Sniff the various aromas and decide whether you like fruity, sweet, or smoky, and afterward experts will help you select your perfect dram. Your guide will then take you into a vault containing the world's largest collection of Scotch whiskies. Opt for one of the premium tours (from £32 to £82) for extras ranging from additional tastings to a Scottish dining experience. ⊠ *354 Castlehill, Old Town* ☎ *0131/220–0441* ⊕ *www.scotchwhiskyexperience.co.uk* ⚏ *From £19.*

The Building of Edinburgh

Towering over the city, Edinburgh Castle was actually built over the plug of an ancient volcano. Many millennia ago, an eastward-grinding glacier encountered the tough basalt core of the volcano and swept around it, scouring steep cliffs and leaving a trail of matter. This material formed a ramp gently leading down from the rocky summit. On this *crag* and *tail* would grow the city of Edinburgh and its castle.

Castle, Walled Town, and Holyroodhouse

By the 12th century Edinburgh had become a walled town, still perched on the hill. Its shape was becoming clearer: like a fish with its head at the castle, its backbone running down the ridge, and its ribs leading briefly off on either side. The backbone gradually became the continuous thoroughfare now known as the Royal Mile, and the ribs became the closes (alleyways), some still surviving, that were the scene of many historic incidents.

By the early 15th century, Edinburgh had become the undisputed capital of Scotland. The bitter defeat of Scotland at Flodden in 1513, when Scotland aligned itself with France against England, caused a new defensive city wall to be built. Though the castle escaped destruction, the city was burned by the English Earl of Hertford under orders from King Henry VIII (1491–1547). This was during a time known as the "Rough Wooing," when Henry was trying to coerce the Scots into allowing the young Mary, Queen of Scots (1542–87), to marry his son Edward. The plan failed and Mary married Francis, the Dauphin of France.

By 1561, when Mary returned from France already widowed, the guesthouse of the Abbey of Holyrood had grown to become the Palace of Holyroodhouse, replacing Edinburgh Castle as the main royal residence. Her legacy to the city included the destruction of most of the earliest buildings of Edinburgh Castle.

Enlightenment and the City

In the challenging decades after the union with England in 1707, many influential Scots, both in Edinburgh and elsewhere, went through an identity crisis. Out of the 18th-century difficulties, however, grew the Scottish Enlightenment, during which educated Scots made great strides in medicine, economics, and science.

Changes came to the cityscape, too. By the mid-18th century, it had become the custom for wealthy Scottish landowners to spend the winter in the Old Town of Edinburgh, in town houses huddled between the high Castle Rock and the Royal Palace below. Cross-fertilized in coffeehouses and taverns, intellectual notions flourished among a people determined to remain Scottish despite their Parliament being dissolved. One result was a campaign to expand and beautify the city, to give it a look worthy of its future nickname, the Athens of the North. Thus, the New Town of Edinburgh was built, with broad streets and gracious buildings creating a harmony that even today's throbbing traffic cannot obscure.

★ Scottish Storytelling Centre and John Knox House

ARTS CENTER | The stripped-down, low-fi, traditional art of storytelling has had something of a resurgence in Britain since the turn of the century, and there are few places better than this to experience a master storyteller in full flow. Housed in a modern building that manages to blend seamlessly with the historic structures on either side, the center hosts a year-round program of storytelling, theater, music, and literary events. A great little café serves lunch, tea, and home-baked cakes.

The center's storytellers also hold tours of John Knox House next door. It isn't certain that the religious reformer ever lived here, but there's evidence he died here in 1572. Mementos of his life are on view inside, and the distinctive dwelling gives you a glimpse of what Old Town life was like in the 16th century—projecting upper floors were once commonplace along the Royal Mile. ✉ *43–45 High St., Old Town* ☎ *0131/556–9579* 🌐 *www.scottishstorytellingcentre.com* 🎟 *Storytelling Centre free; John Knox House £6.*

Writers' Museum

ART MUSEUM | Situated down a narrow close off Lawnmarket is Lady Stair's House, a fine example of 17th-century urban architecture. Inside, the Writers' Museum evokes Scotland's literary past with such exhibits as the letters, possessions, and original manuscripts of Sir Walter Scott, Robert Burns, and Robert Louis Stevenson. ✉ *Lady Stair's Close, off Lawnmarket, Old Town* ☎ *0131/529–4901* 🌐 *www.edinburghmuseums.org.uk.*

🍴 Restaurants

The most historic part of the city houses some of its grander restaurants (though, curiously, none of its Michelin stars). It is also home to some of Edinburgh's oldest and most atmospheric pubs, which serve good, informal meals.

★ Cannonball Restaurant

$$$ | ITALIAN | The name refers to one of the most delightful quirks of Edinburgh's Old Town—the cannonball embedded in the wall outside, said to have been fired at the castle while Bonnie Prince Charlie was in residence (not true, but a good story). The atmosphere in this three-story restaurant and whisky bar is casual and relaxed, despite the gorgeous art deco dining room with views of the castle esplanade. **Known for:** bread-crumbed haggis cannonballs; scrumptious Italian-Scottish cuisine; great views of the castle. [$] *Average main: £25* ✉ *356 Castlehill, Old Town* ☎ *0131/225–1550* 🌐 *www.contini.com/cannonball* 🕒 *Closed Sun.-Tues. No lunch Wed.-Fri.*

Civerinos

$ | PIZZA | With its primary color interiors, blaring 1980s hip-hop soundtrack, and brightly dressed waitstaff, this pizza diner may be Edinburgh's most upbeat dining option yet. Luckily, the food is equally joyful: take your pick from a dozen delicious pizza pies, from meaty feasts to vegan delights, or opt for a tasty pasta or salad instead. **Known for:** bingeable garlic crust bites; Edinburgh's best pizza pies; mood-liftingly bright decor. [$] *Average main: £14* ✉ *5 Hunter Sq., Old Town* ☎ *0131/220–0851* 🌐 *www.civerinos.com.*

David Bann

$ | VEGETARIAN | This hip eatery, situated just off the Royal Mile, serves exclusively vegetarian and vegan favorites, and its inventive dishes and modern interior make it a popular place with young locals. The menu changes constantly, but the invariably creative, flavorful dishes often leave carnivores forgetting they're eating vegetarian. **Known for:** lovely setting; superb vegetarian and vegan cuisine; very affordable. [$] *Average main: £14* ✉ *56–58 St. Mary's St., Old Town* ☎ *0131/556–5888* 🌐 *www.davidbann.co.uk.*

Hanam's

$ | MIDDLE EASTERN | Kurdish food may not be as well known as other Middle Eastern cuisines, but dishes like *bayengaan surocrau* (marinated slow-roasted eggplant) and lamb *tashreeb* (a flavorful casserole) are worth checking out. Hanam's proudly promotes Kurdish cuisine, but also serves more familiar and equally delicious Middle Eastern fare, from shish kebabs to falafel. **Known for:** hookah on heated terrace; traditional Kurdish cooking; BYOB policy. $ *Average main: £14* ✉ *3 Johnston Terr., Old Town* ☎ *0131/225–1329* ⊕ *www.hanams.com* ۩ *No lunch Mon.-Thurs.*

La Garrigue

$$$ | FRENCH | Edinburgh is blessed with several excellent French bistros, and this is one of the best. Although the modern decor evokes Paris, the food has the rustic flavor of the southern Languedoc region. **Known for:** colorful crockery; rustic French cuisine; attentive service. $ *Average main: £22* ✉ *31 Jeffrey St., Old Town* ☎ *0131/557–3032* ⊕ *www.lagarrigue. co.uk* ۩ *Closed Sun.-Mon.*

★ Lovecrumbs

$ | CAFÉ | A bakery-café with an inordinately sweet tooth, Lovecrumbs joyously, deliciously, and unashamedly focuses on what *really* matters in life: cake. It serves delectable confections of all kinds, from sumptuous Victoria sponges to heavenly peanut-butter brownies to mouthwatering lemon tarts. **Known for:** large crowds despite unpredictable opening times; extraordinary cakes galore; junk shop-esque decor. $ *Average main: £4* ✉ *155 W. Port, Old Town* ☎ *0131/629–0626* ⊕ *www.lovecrumbs.co.uk.*

★ Oink

$ | BRITISH | For a quick, cheap bite while wandering the Royal Mile, you can't beat Oink—possibly the best hog roast (pulled pork) in Edinburgh. Located on Canongate (there are two other outlets, but this one is the best), it was founded by two farmers in 2008, and their high-quality, hand-reared pork has proved a huge hit ever since. **Known for:** no options for vegetarians; unbelievable pulled pork; great-value lunch. $ *Average main: £6* ✉ *82 Canongate, Old Town* ☎ *07584/637416* ⊕ *www.oinkhogroast.co.uk.*

Ondine

$$$$ | SEAFOOD | This fabulous seafood restaurant just off the Royal Mile makes waves with its expertly prepared dishes from sustainable fishing sources. The menu is populated with Scottish seafood staples, from salmon and sea bream to lobster and langoustines, but these are often served in interesting and surprising ways. **Known for:** delicious fish dishes; lavish decor; best oysters in Edinburgh. $ *Average main: £30* ✉ *2 George IV Bridge, Old Town* ☎ *0131/226–1888* ⊕ *www.ondinerestaurant.co.uk* ۩ *Closed Sun. and Mon.*

★ Timberyard

$$ | BRITISH | There are few restaurants that feel so wonderfully, well, *Edinburgh* as this one. The freshest seasonal ingredients, mostly sourced from small local producers, go into creating delicious, inventive fare. **Known for:** pricey multicourse menus; exciting dishes; hip interior. $ *Average main: £17* ✉ *10 Lady Lawson St., Old Town* ☎ *0131/221–1222* ⊕ *www.timberyard.co* ۩ *Closed Mon.-Wed. No lunch Thurs.*

★ Wedgwood the Restaurant

$$$ | MODERN BRITISH | Rejecting the idea that fine dining should be a stuffy affair, owners Paul Wedgwood and Lisa Channon are in charge at this Royal Mile gem. Local produce and some unusual foraged fronds enliven the taste buds on menus that radically change with the seasons; expect deliciously quirky pairings like scallops in a cauliflower korma or roe deer with buttermilk. **Known for:** great value lunch deals; unfussy fine dining; delicious sticky toffee pudding. $ *Average main: £25* ✉ *267 Canongate, Old Town* ☎ *0131/558–8737* ⊕ *www.wedgwoodtherestaurant.co.uk* ۩ *Closed Mon.-Tues.*

Hotels

The narrow *pends* (alleys), cobbled streets, and steep hills of the Old Town remind you that this is a city with many layers of history. From medieval to modernist, these hotels are within a stone's throw of the action.

★ Cheval Old Town Chambers
$$$ | **APARTMENT** | Just a few steps down from the Royal Mile, Cheval Old Town Chambers offers all the space and flexibility of luxury apartments, but with hotel-style amenities like a 24-hour reception, a concierge desk, and a free on-site gym (with personal trainer). **Pros:** spacious apartments; spectacular three-bedroom penthouse suite; gorgeous artwork by local photographer. **Cons:** no on-site dining; no air-conditioning in older building; lots of steps. [$] *Rooms from: £300* ✉ *329 High St., Old Town* ☎ *0131/510–5499* 🌐 *www.chevalcollection.com* 🛏 *75 rooms* 🍴 *No Meals.*

★ Hotel du Vin
$$ | **HOTEL** | Leave it to one of the United Kingdom's most forward-thinking hotel chains to convert a Victorian-era asylum into this understated luxury property, which combines a real sense of history with contemporary decor and trappings. **Pros:** lively on-site dining and drinking; unique and historic building; trendy design. **Cons:** service can be hit-and-miss; neighborhood can be noisy; quarter-mile walk to nearest parking. [$] *Rooms from: £200* ✉ *11 Bristo Pl., Old Town* ☎ *0131/285–1479* 🌐 *www.hotelduvin.com* 🛏 *47 rooms* 🍴 *Free Breakfast.*

The Inn on the Mile
$$$ | **B&B/INN** | This chic and welcoming boutique inn could hardly be more central—some rooms even overlook the Royal Mile. **Pros:** great design; views of the Royal Mile; excellent on-site bar. **Cons:** nearest parking at a public lot (three-minute walk); sometimes noisy; lots of steps and no elevator. [$] *Rooms from: £270* ✉ *82 High St., Old Town* ☎ *0131/556–9940* 🌐 *www.theinnonthemile.co.uk* 🛏 *9 rooms* 🍴 *Free Breakfast.*

The Knight Residence
$$ | **APARTMENT** | Situated just around the corner from Grassmarket, these spacious serviced apartments offer a great base for exploring the city center by foot. **Pros:** secure parking available (at a cost); ultra-convenient central location; spacious rooms with comfy beds. **Cons:** some areas need refurbishment; lots of street noise when windows are open; Wi-Fi could be stronger. [$] *Rooms from: £200* ✉ *12 Lauriston St., Old Town* ☎ *0800/304–7160* 🌐 *www.bymansley.com* 🛏 *28 apartments* 🍴 *No Meals.*

Radisson Collection Royal Mile Edinburgh
$$$ | **HOTEL** | The bright primary colors, striking stenciled wallpapers, and bold, eclectic furnishings inside this über-trendy design hotel contrast with the Gothic surroundings of the Royal Mile—and yet, somehow, it works. **Pros:** complimentary gin-and-tonic on arrival; perfect location in the heart of the city; bold and fashionable decor. **Cons:** street noise can leak into rooms; expensive during high season; decor a little Austin Powers in places. [$] *Rooms from: £260* ✉ *1 George IV Bridge, Old Town* ☎ *0131/220–6666* 🌐 *www.radissonhotels.com* 🛏 *136 rooms* 🍴 *Free Breakfast.*

The Scotsman
$$$ | **HOTEL** | This magnificent turn-of-the-20th-century building, with its grand marble staircase and its fascinating history (it was once the headquarters of *The Scotsman* newspaper) now houses a modern luxury hotel. **Pros:** ideal Old Town location; gorgeous rooms and public areas; personalized service. **Cons:** not all rooms have air-conditioning; Grand Cafe dining is hit-or-miss; elevators are painfully slow. [$] *Rooms from: £270* ✉ *20 N. Bridge, Old Town* ☎ *0131/556–5565* 🌐 *scotsmanhotel.co.uk* 🛏 *69 rooms* 🍴 *Free Breakfast.*

The Witchery by the Castle

$$$$ | HOTEL | For a giant helping of Gothic romance, you can't beat the indulgent suites at this gorgeously appointed Castlehill hotel. **Pros:** atmospheric dining; unique and truly romantic retreat; plush antique furnishings. **Cons:** very expensive; food is good but not top shelf; extravagant decor not for everybody. $ Rooms from: £695 ⊠ 352 Castlehill, Old Town ☏ 0131/225–5613 ⊕ www.thewitchery. com 🛏 9 suites ⫧ Free Breakfast.

Ⓨ Nightlife

BARS AND PUBS

The Canons' Gait

PUBS | In addition to a fine selection of local real ales and malts, The Canons' Gait has live jazz and blues performances, as well as edgy comedy shows in the cellar bar. ⊠ 232 Canongate, Old Town ☏ 0131/556–4481.

★ The Holyrood 9A

BARS | This warm, wood-paneled hipster hangout has a fine array of craft beers on tap, as well as an impressive whisky collection. It also serves some of Edinburgh's best gourmet burgers. ⊠ 9A Holyrood Rd., Old Town ☏ 0131/556–5044 ⊕ www.theholyrood.co.uk.

The Last Drop

PUBS | There's plenty of atmosphere (and plenty of tourists) amid the nooks and crannies at The Last Drop. The name has a grim double meaning, as it was once the site of public hangings. ⊠ 74–78 Grassmarket, Old Town ☏ 0131/225–4851 ⊕ www.nicholsonspubs.co.uk.

The Three Sisters

PUBS | This pub is a hive of activity during festival season, when the courtyard transforms into a beer garden with food stalls, and is packed wall-to-wall with revelers until the wee hours. Outside of the summer months, it remains a lively local favorite and the best place to watch live sports in Edinburgh. ⊠ 139 Cowgate, Old Town ☏ 0131/622–6802 ⊕ www. thethreesistersbar.co.uk.

Under the Stairs

COCKTAIL LOUNGES | As the name suggests, this shabby-chic cocktail bar-cum-bistro is tucked away below street level. A cozy, low-ceilinged place, full of quirky furniture and hip art exhibits, Under the Stairs serves specialty, seasonal cocktails—as well as superb bar food—to a mostly young crowd. ⊠ 3A Merchant St., Old Town ☏ 0131/466–8550 ⊕ www. underthestairs.org.

★ Whiski Rooms

BARS | This venerable establishment offers one of Old Town's most enjoyable whisky tastings: an informative and interactive experience with an expert guide. The 90-minute Premium Whisky Tasting features five unusual drams you'll almost certainly not have tasted before. When you're finished, either browse the shop stacked high with tempting bottles or head into the bar for another dram. ⊠ 4–7 N. Bank St., Old Town ☏ 0131/225–7224 ⊕ www.whiskirooms.co.uk.

LIVE MUSIC

You can still find folk and jazz musicians performing in pubs and clubs throughout the Old Town.

★ The Jazz Bar

LIVE MUSIC | This basement music venue delivers exactly what the name promises: jazz, in all its many weird and wonderful forms. Blues, funk, acoustic, electric—there's something new to discover every night of the week. There's usually a small cover charge (cash only), but this all goes to musicians, not the venue. ⊠ 1A Chambers St., Old Town ☏ 0131/220–4298 ⊕ www.thejazzbar.co.uk.

The Royal Oak

LIVE MUSIC | With a piano in the corner, this cozy, friendly pub presents excellent live blues and folk music most nights—usually with no cover charge. ⊠ 1 Infirmary St., Old Town ☏ 0131/557–2976 ⊕ www.royal-oak-folk.com.

Hogmanay: Hello, New Year

In Scotland New Year's Eve is called Hogmanay—and to call it a big deal is an understatement. All over Scotland there are huge parties on December 31, and celebrations continue the next day with customs such as "first-footing"—visiting your neighbors with gifts that include whisky to bring good fortune for the year ahead. In fact, Hogmanay is so important that January 2 as well as January 1 are holidays in Scotland, while the rest of the United Kingdom trudges back to work.

What to Expect

Edinburgh's Hogmanay celebrations extend over several days, with music, dance, and theater performances taking place throughout the city. The lineup changes every year, but always includes a number of free events. Festivities featuring fire add a dramatic motif; buildings may open for rare night tours; a ceilidh has everyone dancing outdoors to traditional music; and family concerts and serious discussions during the day round out the agenda. At the heart of Hogmanay, though, is the evening street party on New Year's Eve, with different music stages, food and drink (and people *do* drink), and the cockle-warming sight of glowing fireworks over Edinburgh Castle. And it all ends with communal renditions of "Auld Lang Syne," written by Scotland's own Robert Burns.

Planning Basics

Besides the £30+ you'll pay to get into the street party celebrations, expect to shell out extra for some related events. For example, the torchlight procession on December 30 costs around £15, while the big-name concert in the Princes Street Gardens on 30 will run you at least £70. Book rooms as far ahead as possible. Obvious but essential is warmth: extra fluffy hats and the bundled-up look are de rigueur. Check out ⊕ *www.edinburghshogmanay.com* for full details.

Whistle Binkies

LIVE MUSIC | This atmospheric North Bridge bar, with its main entrance on Niddry Street (as it's *in* the bridge), presents rock, blues, and folk music every night of the week, with as many as six or seven acts on Saturday nights. ⊠ *4–6 South Bridge, Old Town* ☎ *0131/557–5114* ⊕ *whistlebinkies.com.*

NIGHTCLUBS

Cabaret Voltaire

DANCE CLUBS | The vaulted ceilings of this subterranean club reverberate with dance music most nights, with an ever-changing lineup of cutting-edge DJs on the decks. The club also hosts regular live gigs and, during the Fringe, stand-up comedy shows. ⊠ *36–38 Blair St., Old Town* ☎ *0131/247–4704* ⊕ *www.thecabaretvoltaire.com.*

The Liquid Room

DANCE CLUBS | Top indie bands and an eclectic mix of club nights (techno, hip-hop, and alternative, to name a few) have made the Liquid Room a favorite after-dark venue since 1997. ⊠ *9C Victoria St., Old Town* ☎ *0131/225–2564* ⊕ *www.liquidroom.com.*

Performing Arts

Festival Theatre

MUSIC | This popular theater hosts regular pop concerts, as well as musical theater, opera, and ballet productions. ⊠ *13–29 Nicolson St., South Side* ☎ *0131/529–6000* ⊕ *www.capitaltheatres.com.*

The Lyceum

THEATER | Traditional plays and contemporary works, including previews or tours of London West End productions, are presented here. ✉ *30b Grindlay St., West End* ☎ *0131/248–4848* ⊕ *www.lyceum.org.uk.*

Traverse Theatre

THEATER | With its specially designed space, the Traverse Theatre has developed a solid reputation for new, stimulating plays by Scottish dramatists, as well as innovative dance performances. ✉ *10 Cambridge St., West End* ☎ *0131/228–1404* ⊕ *www.traverse.co.uk.*

Usher Hall

MUSIC | Edinburgh's grandest concert venue, Usher Hall hosts a wide range of national and international performers, from Paul Weller and Paloma Faith to the Royal Scottish National Orchestra. ✉ *Lothian Rd., West End* ☎ *0131/228–1155* ⊕ *www.usherhall.co.uk.*

🛍 Shopping

BOOKS AND STATIONERY

Armchair Books

BOOKS | Just a two-minute walk from Grassmarket, Armchair Books is a chaotic but characterful bookshop heaving with secondhand and antiquarian books. ✉ *72–74 W. Port, Old Town* ☎ *0131/229–5927* ⊕ *www.armchairbooks.co.uk.*

Main Point Books

BOOKS | This bibliophile's haven is stacked high with obscure first editions and bargain tomes. It also hosts regular literary events. ✉ *77 Bread St., Old Town* ☎ *0131/228–4837* ⊕ *www.mainpoint-books.co.uk.*

CLOTHING

Bill Baber

MIXED CLOTHING | One of the more imaginative Scottish knitwear designers, Bill Baber's creative and colorful pieces are a long way from the conservative pastel woolies sold at some of the large mill shops. ✉ *66 Grassmarket, Old Town* ☎ *0131/225–3249* ⊕ *www.billbaber.com.*

Herman Brown

MIXED CLOTHING | This secondhand clothing store is where cashmere twinsets and classic luxe labels are sought and found. ✉ *151 W. Port, West End* ☎ *0131/228–2589* ⊕ *www.hermanbrown.co.uk.*

Ragamuffin

MIXED CLOTHING | First established on the Isle of Skye, Ragamuffin's Edinburgh outlet sells some of the funkiest, brightest, and most elegant knitwear produced anywhere in Scotland. ✉ *278 Canongate, Old Town* ☎ *0131/557–6007* ⊕ *www.ragamuffinstore.com.*

JEWELRY

Clarksons of Edinburgh

JEWELRY & WATCHES | A family firm, Clarksons handcrafts a unique collection of jewelry, from Celtic to contemporary styles. The pieces here are made with silver, gold, platinum, and precious gems, with a particular emphasis on diamonds. ✉ *87 W. Bow, Old Town* ☎ *0131/225–8141* ⊕ *www.clarksonsedinburgh.co.uk.*

SCOTTISH SPECIALTIES

★ Cadenhead's Whisky Shop

WINE/SPIRITS | Edinburgh's most iconic Scotch shop, Cadenhead's has an incredible selection of whisky to purchase (including rare bottles from closed distilleries), and also offers tasting sessions. The friendly and knowledgeable staff can help you pick out the perfect whisky to suit your palate. ✉ *172 Canongate, Old Town* ☎ *0131/556–5864* ⊕ *www.cadenhead.scot.*

Geoffrey Tailor Kiltmakers

MEN'S CLOTHING | This shop can clothe you in full Highland dress, with high-quality kilts made in its own workshops. ✉ *57–59 High St., Old Town* ☎ *0131/557–0256* ⊕ *www.geoffreykilts.co.uk.*

New Town

It was not until the Scottish Enlightenment, a civilizing time of expansion in the 1700s, that the city's elite decided to break away from the Royal Mile's craggy slope and narrow closes to create a new neighborhood below the castle. This was to become the New Town, an area of elegant squares, classical facades, wide streets, and harmonious proportions.

Clearly, change had to come. At the dawn of the 18th century, Edinburgh's unsanitary conditions—primarily a result of overcrowded living quarters—were becoming notorious. The well-known Scottish fiddle tune "The Flooers (flowers) of Edinburgh" was only one of many ironic references to the capital's unpleasant environment.

To help remedy this sorry state of affairs, in 1767 James Drummond, the city's lord provost (the Scottish term for mayor), urged the town council to hold a competition to design a new district for Edinburgh. The winner was an unknown young architect named James Craig (1744–95). His plan called for a grid of three main east–west streets, balanced at either end by two grand squares. These streets survive today, though some of the buildings that line them have been altered by later development. Princes Street is the southernmost, with Queen Street to the north and George Street as the axis, punctuated by St. Andrew and Charlotte squares. A look at the map will reveal a geometric symmetry unusual in Britain. Even the Princes Street Gardens are balanced by the Queen Street Gardens, to the north. Princes Street was conceived as an exclusive residential address, with an open vista facing the castle. It has since been altered by the demands of business and shopping, but the vista remains.

The New Town was expanded several times after Craig's death and now covers an area about three times larger than Craig envisioned. Indeed, some of the most elegant facades came later and can be found by strolling north of the Queen Street Gardens. Just north of the New Town lies the strollable shopping quarter of Stockbridge, as well as Inverleith, home to the Royal Botanic Garden Edinburgh.

Sights

Calton Hill

VIEWPOINT | Robert Louis Stevenson's favorite view of his beloved city was from the top of this hill, and it's easy to see why. Located in the heart of the city, Calton Hill offers stunning vistas of the Old and New Towns and out to the Firth of Forth, making it a popular setting for picnicking and watching festival fireworks. Great views aside, the hill is also home to a number of impressive monuments. The most notable is the so-called **National Monument,** also known as "Scotland's Disgrace," which was commissioned in 1822 and intended to mimic Athens's Parthenon. But after just 12 columns had been built, the money ran out, leaving the facade as a monument to high aspirations and poor fundraising. Nearby, the 100-foot-high **Nelson Monument,** completed in 1815 in honor of Britain's greatest naval hero, is topped with a "time ball" that is dropped at 1 pm every day. Other hillside monuments honor notable Scots ranging from mathematician John Playfair to philosopher Dugald Stewart.

The hill is also home to the **City Observatory,** which hosts regular contemporary art exhibitions, as well as upscale restaurant **The Lookout by Gardener's Cottage**. It also plays host to the **Beltane Fire Festival** every April 30. ✉ *Bounded by Leith St. to the west and Regent Rd. to the south, New Town* 🚌 ⊕ *www.edinburgh.gov.uk* 🎫 *Free; Nelson Monument £6.*

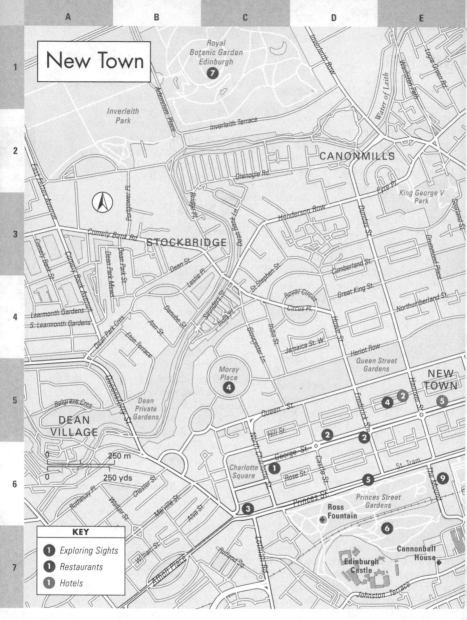

New Town

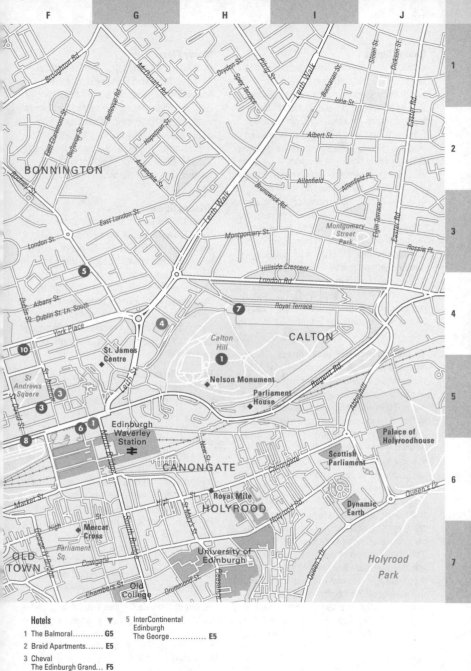

Hotels ▼

George Street

STREET | With its high-end shops, upmarket bistros, and five-star hotels, all with handsome Georgian frontages, George Street is a more pleasant, less crowded thoroughfare for strolling than Princes Street. It also has a couple of points of interest. First, there's the statue of King George IV, at the intersection of George and Hanover streets, which recalls the visit of George IV to Scotland in 1822; he was the first British monarch to do so since King Charles II in the 17th century. Next, the Assembly Rooms, between Hanover and Frederick streets, are where Sir Walter Scott officially acknowledged having written the Waverley novels (the author had hitherto been a mystery, albeit a badly kept one). It's now a popular venue during the Fringe Festival. ⊠ *Between Charlotte Sq. and St. Andrew Sq., New Town.*

★ Johnnie Walker Princes Street

OTHER ATTRACTION | Opened in late 2021, this state-of-the-art, interactive whisky experience is a dizzying sensory experience. The regular 90-minute Journey of Whisky tour uses impressive animation, immersive light and sound effects, and even live actors to tell the tale of Johnnie Walker whisky, from its humble grocer's shop origins to its current status as the world's best-selling Scotch. Visitors will enjoy a whisky highball—matched to their own flavor preferences after a quick quiz—at the start of the tour, as well as two more drams or cocktails at the end. The three drinks alone are worth the £25 admission. Real whisky connoisseurs can also visit the Whisky Makers' Cellar (£95) to taste drams straight from the cast. Not interested in a tour? Head straight up to the 1820 Rooftop Bar for a drink with a view. ⊠ *145 Princes St., New Town* ☎ *0131/376–9494* ⊕ *www.johnniewalker. com* ⌖ *£25.*

Moray Place

PLAZA/SQUARE | With its "pendants" of Ainslie Place and Randolph Crescent, Moray Place was laid out in 1822 by the Earl of Moray. From the start the homes were planned to be of particularly high quality, with lovely curving facades, imposing porticos, and a central secluded garden reserved for residents. ⊠ *Between Charlotte Sq. and Water of Leith, New Town.*

Princes Street

STREET | The south side of this dominant New Town street is occupied by the well-kept Princes Street Gardens, which act as a wide green moat to the castle on its rock. The north side is now one long sequence of chain stores with mostly unappealing modern fronts, with one or two exceptions: most notably the handsome Victorian facade on the corner of South St. David Street. ⊠ *Waterloo Pl. to Lothian Rd., New Town.*

Princes Street Gardens

CITY PARK | These beautifully manicured gardens, directly overlooked by Edinburgh Castle, are just a few steps and yet a whole world away from bustling Princes Street. The 38-acre park, divided into the East and West Gardens, was first laid out in the 1760s, on marshland created by the draining of a (long-since-vanished) loch. It has a host of attractions, including a functioning floral clock on the corner of Princes Street and The Mound, the Ross Fountain, a series of memorials, a children's play park, and a café. The gardens often host free concerts, and have a central role in the city's famed Hogmanay festivities. ⊠ *Princes St., New Town.*

★ Royal Botanic Garden Edinburgh

GARDEN | **FAMILY** | Explore Britain's largest rhododendron and azalea gardens at this beautiful 70-acre botanical garden. Founded in 1670 as a physic garden, it now has a range of natural highlights such as soaring palms in the glass-domed Temperate House and the steamy Tropical Palm House, an extensive Chinese garden, and a pretty rock garden and stream. There's a visitor center with exhibits on biodiversity, a fabulous gift shop selling plants, books, and gifts, and two cafeterias. The handsome 18th-century Inverleith House hosts art exhibitions.

It's free to roam the gardens, though it costs extra for greenhouse admission, and you can splash out even more for guided garden walks and private tours. It takes 20 minutes to walk to the garden from Princes Street, or you can take a bus. ✉ *Arboretum Pl., Inverleith* ☎ *0131/248–2909* 🌐 *www.rbge.org.uk* 🎟 *Free; Glasshouses £7.*

Scott Monument

MONUMENT | What appears to be a Gothic cathedral spire that's been chopped off and planted on Princes Street is in fact Scotland's tribute to one of its most famous sons, Sir Walter Scott. Built in 1844 and soaring to 200 feet, it remains the largest monument to a writer anywhere in the world. Climb the 287 steps to the top for a stunning view of the city and the hills and coast beyond. ✉ *E. Princes St. Gardens, New Town* ☎ *0131/529–4068* 🌐 *www.edinburghmuseums.org.uk* 🎟 *£8 (cash only).*

★ Scottish National Gallery

ART MUSEUM | Opened to the public in 1859, the Scottish National Gallery presents a wide selection of paintings from the Renaissance to the Postimpressionist period within a grand Neoclassical building. Most famous are the Old Master paintings bequeathed by the Duke of Sutherland, including Titian's *Three Ages of Man.* Works by Velázquez, El Greco, Rembrandt, Goya, Poussin, Turner, Degas, Monet, and van Gogh, among others, complement a fine collection of Scottish art, including Sir Henry Raeburn's *Reverend Robert Walker Skating on Duddingston Loch* and other works by Ramsay, Raeburn, and Wilkie. The gallery also has an information center, a quirky gift shop, and the excellent Scottish Cafe and Restaurant.

You can also hop on a shuttle bus (£1 donation requested) from here to the Scottish National Gallery of Modern Art, which has paintings and sculptures by Pablo Picasso, Georges Braque, Henri Matisse, and André Derain, among others. ✉ *The Mound, New Town* ☎ *0131/624–6200* 🌐 *www.nationalgalleries.org.*

Scottish National Portrait Gallery

ART MUSEUM | Set within a magnificent red-sandstone Gothic building from 1889, this gallery is an Edinburgh must-see. Conceived as a gift to the people of Scotland, it divides into five broad themes, from Reformation to Modernity, with special galleries for photography and contemporary art—all centered around the stunning Great Hall. It also plays host to regular temporary exhibitions, including the annual BP Portrait Award. ✉ *1 Queen St., New Town* ☎ *0131/624–6200* 🌐 *www.nationalgalleries.org* 🎟 *Free.*

🍴 Restaurants

The New Town, with its striking street plan, ambitious architecture, and professional crowd, has restaurants where you can get everything from a quick snack to a more formal dinner.

Baba

$$$ | **MIDDLE EASTERN** | Set within the upmarket Kimpton Charlotte Square Hotel, Baba serves tasty Middle Eastern—specifically Levantine—fare in a colorful, shabby-chic setting. Dishes are designed for sharing so take your pick from the mezze and grills menu, where highlights include the baba ganoush (with pomegranate seed and mint) and the beef and bone marrow kofte. **Known for:** costs that quickly add up; inventive takes on Middle Eastern staples; delicious hummus with a *zhug* (Yemeni hot sauce) kick. [$] *Average main: £22* ✉ *130 George St., New Town* ☎ *0131/527–4999* 🌐 *baba.restaurant.*

Contini George Street

$$$ | ITALIAN | Set within a grand former banking hall on George Street, this superb restaurant serves light but satisfying Italian favorites divided into *primi, secondi,* and *dolci,* all within an airy setting of grand Corinthian columns, an open marble-topped bar, intricate wall hangings, and soft gray banquettes. The food choices are strictly seasonal, but regularly appearing favorites include the Scotch beef carpaccio and the homemade ravioli with ricotta and spinach. **Known for:** tasty Scotch beef carpaccio; deliciously light Italian cuisine; grand but relaxed setting. $ *Average main: £20* ⊠ *103 George St., New Town* ☎ *0131/225–1550* ⊕ *www.contini.com/ contini-george-street* ⊗ *Closed Sun.*

Dishoom

$ | INDIAN | The city's most inventive Indian restaurant, Dishoom serves up an all-sensory experience, from the smells that greet you (delicious whiffs of incense mixed with aromatic spices) to the sight and sounds of the interior (the decor is all distressed-wood panels and chandeliers, inspired by Bombay's 1920 Iranian cafés) to the taste of the food itself. A tapas-style menu of deliciously tender meat, seafood, and vegetarian dishes welcomes you, along with delicious desserts. **Known for:** unique Indian breakfast rolls; incredible lamb *salli boti;* great cocktail and mocktail menu. $ *Average main: £10* ⊠ *3a St. Andrew Sq., Edinburgh* ☎ *0131/202–6406* ⊕ *www. dishoom.com.*

Dusit

$$ | THAI | Tucked down narrow Thistle Street, Dusit doesn't register on most travelers' radars, but it has been a local favorite since 2002. An authentic, contemporary Thai restaurant run by Bangkok-born Pom, the menu here delights with deliciously creamy curries, spicy stir-fries, and fragrant seafood specialties, all of which use a mix of fresh local produce and imported Thai vegetables. **Known** **for:** good value lunch menu; award-winning Thai food; local haunt. $ *Average main: £17* ⊠ *49A Thistle St., New Town* ☎ *0131/220–6846* ⊕ *www.dusit.co.uk.*

Fhior

$$$$ | BRITISH | Owner and chef Scott Smith, who previously ran the award-winning Norn, serves up seasonal, Scandinavian-inspired fare here with rare Scottish ingredients, from beremeal (an ancient form of barley) bread to sea buckthorn. Choose from seven to 10 courses for dinner (£65 to £90), with menus arriving sealed in envelopes; you're encouraged to trust the chef and leave them unopened until after dessert. **Known for:** multicourse menu options chosen by the chef; modernist decor; old-school Scottish dishes with a Scandinavian flair. $ *Average main: £35* ⊠ *36 Broughton St., Edinburgh* ☎ *0131/477–5000* ⊕ *www. fhior.com* ⊗ *Closed Mon.–Wed.*

Number One

$$$$ | BRITISH | Clublike but unstuffy, this outstanding basement restaurant, set within the Edwardian splendor of The Balmoral hotel, is made for intimate dining. The food is extraordinary, with a menu that highlights the best of Scottish seafood and meat in inventive fashion— from scallops and sturgeon to lamb and beef. **Known for:** very expensive; wonderfully intimate setting; inventive dishes. $ *Average main: £110* ⊠ *The Balmoral, 1 Princes St., New Town* ☎ *0131/557–6727* ⊕ *www.roccofortehotels.com* ⊗ *Closed Tues. and Wed. No lunch.*

21212

$$$$ | MODERN FRENCH | Paul Kitching is one of Britain's most innovative chefs, and the theatrical dining experience at 21212 delivers surprises galore. Set within a Georgian town house, the fine dining restaurant is sumptuously appointed while, behind a large glass screen, a small army of chefs is busy assembling the delicious and intricate dishes. **Known for:** choice between two starters, two mains, and two desserts (with soup and cheese in between, hence 21212); contemporary Franco-Anglo-Scottish cuisine; atmospheric and romantic. $ Average main: £85 ⊠ 3 Royal Terr., New Town ☎ 0131/523–1030 ⊕ www.21212restaurant.co.uk ☾ Closed Sun.–Tues.

🛏 Hotels

Calton Hill, which offers some of the best views of the city from its summit, is just one of the reasons to base yourself in the New Town. Architecture fans will enjoy the gorgeous 18th- and 19th-century buildings, many of which are now grand accommodation options.

★ The Balmoral

$$$$ | HOTEL | The attention to detail in the elegantly appointed rooms and suites, where colors and patterns echo the country's heathers and moors, and the sheer Edwardian splendor of this grand, former railroad hotel make staying at The Balmoral a special introduction to Edinburgh. **Pros:** top-notch spa, restaurant, and whisky bar; big and beautiful Edwardian building; top-hatted doorman. **Cons:** some rooms are small; spa books up fast; small lap pool. $ Rooms from: £490 ⊠ 1 Princes St., New Town ☎ 0131/556–2414 ⊕ www.roccofortehotels.com ⋗ 187 rooms ⋓ Free Breakfast.

Braid Apartments

$$ | APARTMENT | This collection of chic, comfortable, and spacious self-service apartments is tucked away on quiet Thistle Street, meaning that guests can enjoy being in the heart of the New Town and yet out of sight (and sound) of the crowds. **Pros:** friendly reception staff; good modern facilities; quiet central location. **Cons:** no accessible rooms (elevator starts on mezzanine floor); noisy water pumps; no on-site parking. $ Rooms from: £175 ⊠ 27 Thistle St., New Town ☎ 0800/304–7160 ⊕ www.bymansley.com ⋗ 20 apartments ⋓ No Meals.

Cheval The Edinburgh Grand

$$$$ | APARTMENT | Despite all appearances—the classical Edinburgh exterior, the Corinthian-columned art deco lobby, the friendly and attentive concierges, and the in-house high-end restaurants—the Edinburgh Grand is not a swanky hotel, but rather a collection of grand and luxurious serviced apartments. **Pros:** all amenities included; beautiful apartments with supercomfy beds; ideal location for trams and trains. **Cons:** Register Club food disappointing and overpriced; no doors on some bathrooms; perilously dark corridors. $ Rooms from: £320 ⊠ 42 St. Andrew Sq., New Town ☎ 0131/230–0570 ⊕ www.chevalcollection.com ⋗ 50 apartments ⋓ No Meals.

★ The Glasshouse

$$$ | HOTEL | Glass walls extend from the 19th-century facade of a former church, foreshadowing the daring, modern interior of one of the city's original, and best, boutique hotels. **Pros:** near all the attractions; truly stunning rooftop garden; very modern and stylish. **Cons:** continental breakfast extra (hot breakfast even more); decor a little sterile for some; loud air-conditioning and toilet flushing. $ Rooms from: £265 ⊠ 2 Greenside Pl., New Town ☎ 0131/525–8200 ⊕ www.theglasshousehotel.co.uk ⋗ 77 rooms ⋓ No Meals.

InterContinental Edinburgh The George

$$$ | HOTEL | Built in 1775 for Edinburgh's elite, this row of five Georgian town houses in the heart of the New Town now hosts a luxury hotel. **Pros:** in-room treat boxes with chips and candy; excellent central location; stylish and comfortable bedrooms. **Cons:** breakfast is expensive; floors in older rooms are on a slight slope; regular wedding parties in reception area. $ Rooms from: £250 ⊠ 19–21 George St., New Town ☎ 0131/225–1251 ⊕ edinburgh.intercontinental.com ⋗ 240 rooms ⋓ Free Breakfast.

Ⓨ Nightlife

BARS AND PUBS

The Basement
BARS | This funky, cheerful bar has something of the 1950s jet-setter vibe—which might explain its happy-go-lucky mash-up of cocktails, Mexican food, and Hawaiian-shirted bar staff. ✉ 10A–12A Broughton St., New Town ☎ 0131/557–0097 ⊕ www.basement-bar-edinburgh.co.uk.

Bramble Bar & Lounge
COCKTAIL LOUNGES | This easily walked-by basement bar on Queen Street—take the stairs down to a clothing-alteration shop and you'll see a small sign—is one of Edinburgh's great hidden gems. Expect superb cocktails, eclectic music (DJs spin most nights), young crowds, and lots of nooks and crannies. ✉ 16A Queen St., New Town ☎ 0131/226–6343 ⊕ www.bramblebar.co.uk.

★ Cafe Royal Circle Bar
BARS | Famed for its atmospheric Victorian interiors—think ornate stucco, etched mirrors, tiled murals, stained glass, and leather booths—the Cafe Royal Circle Bar has been drawing a cast of Edinburgh characters since it opened in 1863. Regulars and newcomers alike pack in for the drinks (a host of real ales and malt whiskies) and tasty bar food (everything from bar snacks and sandwiches to elaborate seafood platters). ✉ 19 W. Register St., New Town ☎ 0131/556–1884 ⊕ www.caferoyaledinburgh.co.uk.

Cask and Barrel
PUBS | A spacious, traditional pub on trendy Broughton Street, the Cask and Barrel serves hand-pulled ales from a horseshoe-shaped bar, ringed by a collection of brewery mirrors. ✉ 115 Broughton St., New Town ☎ 0131/556–3132 ⊕ www.caskandbarrelbroughton.co.uk.

★ Guildford Arms
PUBS | Like the Café Royal Circle Bar on the other corner of the same Victorian block, the Guildford Arms has a spectacular interior of intricate plasterwork, elaborate cornices, and wood paneling. The ornate ceiling alone is worth the visit. Stay for the range of excellent Scottish ales on tap. ✉ 1 W. Register St., New Town ☎ 0131/556–4312 ⊕ www.guildfordarms.com.

Joseph Pearce's
BARS | FAMILY | One of eight Swedish bars and restaurants in Edinburgh owned by the Boda group, Joseph Pearce's has a distinctly northern European feel, despite its solidly Edwardian origins. Scandi-themed cocktails are popular here, as are the meatballs, open sandwiches, and other Swedish dishes. There's a children's corner with toys to keep the little ones occupied, and a sunny outdoor space in summer. ✉ 23 Elm Row, New Town ☎ 0131/556–4140 ⊕ www.bodabar.com.

★ Juniper Edinburgh
COCKTAIL LOUNGES | Situated right opposite Edinburgh Waverley Station, Juniper cultivates an air of glamorous fun with its plant-filled interior and postcard-worthy views of the city and the castle. The wine list is good (if a little pricey), but it's the imaginative cocktails that really make this place, from Smoke on the Water (a combo of peaty whisky and peach iced tea) to Late Night Tough Guy Colada (a mix of pineapple rum, coconut, and white chocolate liqueur). ✉ 20 Princes St., New Town ☎ 0131/652–7370 ⊕ www.juniperedinburgh.co.uk.

Kay's Bar
PUBS | Housed in a former Georgian coach house, this diminutive but friendly spot serves 50 single-malt whiskies, a range of guest ales, and decent bottled beers. Check out the cute little wood-paneled library room, with its tiny fireplace and shelves full of books. ✉ 39 Jamaica St., New Town ☎ 0131/225–1858 ⊕ www.kaysbar.co.uk.

★ Panda and Sons

BARS | The very definition of a hidden gem, this Prohibition-style speakeasy is cunningly tucked away behind a barbershop exterior. Venture inside and downstairs to discover a quirky bar serving some seriously refined cocktails. And yes, we're baffled by the fictional bar-owning panda, too. ⊠ *79 Queen St., New Town* ☎ *0131/220–0443* ⊕ *www. pandaandsons.com.*

Tonic

COCKTAIL LOUNGES | This stylish basement bar has bouncy stools, comfy sofas, and a long list of superb, throwback cocktails. Resident DJs play Thursday through Sunday. ⊠ *34A N. Castle St., New Town* ☎ *0131/225–6431* ⊕ *www.bar-tonic.co.uk.*

COMEDY CLUBS

The Stand

COMEDY CLUBS | Laugh until your sides split at The Stand, a legendary basement comedy club that hosts both famous names and up-and-coming acts all throughout the year, though it's particularly popular during the Fringe. Most, but not all, shows are 18+. ⊠ *5 York Pl., New Town* ☎ *0131/558–7272* ⊕ *www. thestand.co.uk.*

LGBTQ BARS

There's a large and ever-expanding LGBTQ scene in Edinburgh, and the city has many predominantly gay clubs, bars, and cafés. Nevertheless, don't expect the scene to be quite as varied as in London, New York, or even Glasgow. *The List* and *The Skinny* have sections that focus on gay and lesbian venues.

CC Blooms

DANCE CLUBS | Modern and colorful, CC Blooms is a club spread over two levels, playing a mix of musical styles and with regular cabaret nights. Open nightly, it's been a mainstay on the gay scene since the early '90s, and can now count several other gay-friendly bars and clubs as neighbors. ⊠ *23–24 Greenside Pl., New Town* ☎ *0131/556–9331* ⊕ *www.ccblooms.co.uk.*

Regent Bar

BARS | Billing itself as "the best real ale gay pub in Edinburgh," this popular drinking hole at the far east end of the New Town is warm, homey, and welcoming— and it's dog-friendly, too. As advertised, the real ales selection is great. ⊠ *2 Montrose Terr., Abbeyhill* ☎ *0131/661–8198* ⊕ *www.theregentbar.co.uk.*

🎭 Performing Arts

Edinburgh Playhouse

THEATER | Big-ticket concerts and musicals, along with the occasional ballet and opera production, are staged at the popular Playhouse, with its enormous 3,000-seat auditorium. ⊠ *18–22 Greenside La., East End* ☎ *0844/871–7615* ⊕ *www. atgtickets.com.*

🛍 Shopping

ANTIQUES

★ Unicorn Antiques

ANTIQUES & COLLECTIBLES | This Victorian basement is crammed with fascinating antiques, including artworks, ornaments, silverware, and other such curios. ⊠ *65 Dundas St., New Town* ☎ *0131/556–7176* ⊕ *www.unicornantiques.co.uk.*

CLOTHING

Elaine's Vintage Clothing

MIXED CLOTHING | This wee boutique in trendy Stockbridge, northwest of the New Town, is crammed full of vintage threads for women and men. The finds span the 20th century, but most are from the '40s to the '70s. The friendly owner is happy to share her knowledge of the many elegant and quirky outfits on her rails. ⊠ *55 St. Stephen St., New Town* ☎ *0131/225–5783.*

DEPARTMENT STORES

Harvey Nichols

DEPARTMENT STORE | Affectionately known as Harvey Nicks, this high-style British fashion chain has its Scottish outpost on St. Andrew Square, carrying the store's chic, upscale style options. Feeling peckish? Enjoy a meal with a view at the excellent Forth Floor Brasserie and Bar. ⊠ *30–34 St. Andrew Sq., New Town* ☎ *0131/524–8388* ⊕ *www.harveynichols.com.*

John Lewis

DEPARTMENT STORE | John Lewis special-izes in furnishings and household goods, but also stocks designer clothes. It's part of the recently refurbished St. James Quarter. ⊠ *St James Quarter, Leith St., New Town* ☎ *0131/556–9121* ⊕ *www.johnlewis.com.*

JEWELRY

Hamilton & Inches

JEWELRY & WATCHES | Established in 1866, this jeweler is worth visiting not only for its gold and silver pieces, but also for its late-Georgian interior. Designed by David Bryce in 1834, it's all columns and elaborate plasterwork. ⊠ *87 George St., New Town* ☎ *0131/225–4898* ⊕ *www.hamiltonandinches.com.*

Joseph Bonnar

JEWELRY & WATCHES | Tucked behind George Street, Joseph Bonnar stocks Scotland's largest collection of antique jewelry, including 19th-century agate jewels. ⊠ *72 Thistle St., New Town* ☎ *0131/226–2811* ⊕ *www.josephbonnar.com.*

★ Sheila Fleet

JEWELRY & WATCHES | As much art gallery as jewelry shop, designer Sheila Fleet's store in Stockbridge displays a variety of stunning jewelry inspired by her native Orkney, from wind and waves to Celtic spirals to island wildlife. ⊠ *18 St. Stephen St., Stockbridge* ☎ *0131/225–5939* ⊕ *www.sheilafleet.com.*

OUTDOOR SPORTS GEAR

Cotswold Outdoor

SPORTING GOODS | This specialist chain store sells outdoor clothing for all weath-er, as well as accessories, maps, guides, and more. The staff are invariably helpful and informed. ⊠ *Hanover Buildings, 72 Rose St., New Town* ☎ *0131/341–2063* ⊕ *www.cotswoldoutdoor.com.*

Haymarket

West of the Old Town and south of the West End is Haymarket, a district with its own down-to-earth character and well-worn charm. It offers varied shopping and dining options that become more upmarket as you inch toward the West End and Leith.

🍴 Restaurants

This area has many good restaurants that tend to be more affordable than those in the center of town.

First Coast

$ | **INTERNATIONAL** | This laid-back bistro, just a few minutes from Haymarket Station, has a loyal following—and for good reason. Its multicultural menu com-bines Scottish classics with everything from Thai sweep potato soup to Italian affogato. **Known for:** relaxing interiors; great international fare with vegetarian options; big on flavor. $ *Average main: £12* ⊠ *97–101 Dalry Rd., Haymarket* ☎ *0131/313–4404* ⊕ *www.first-coast.co.uk* 🕙 *Closed Sun. and Mon.*

🛏 Hotels

Close to one of Edinburgh's two main train stations, Haymarket—beyond the west end of Princes Street—can make a good, affordable base for exploring the city.

★ The Dunstane Houses

$$$ | **HOTEL** | Set within two Victorian town houses that sit across the road from one another, with each offering a selection of beautifully appointed rooms and suites, this hotel is one of Edinburgh's most luxurious boutique options. **Pros:** quiet residential area; beautifully decorated; excellent food and service. **Cons:** some traffic noise from outside; a 20-minute

walk to Princes Street; no elevator (and stairs to climb). [$] *Rooms from: £300* ✉ *4 W. Coates, Haymarket* ☎ *0131/337–6169* 🌐 *www.thedunstane.com* 🛏 *35 rooms* 🍴 *Free Breakfast.*

The Victorian Town House

$$ | B&B/INN | This handsome B&B, situated in a quiet, leafy crescent but within walking distance of Princes Street, offers bright and spacious rooms with a quirky mix of Edwardian and modern furnishings. **Pros:** beautiful Water of Leith at your doorstep; serene surroundings; super friendly owner. **Cons:** a little way from the Old Town; lacking some modern touches like smart TVs; no parking nearby. [$] *Rooms from: £200* ✉ *14A Eglinton Terr., Haymarket* ☎ *0131/337–7088* 🌐 *www.victoriantownhouse.co.uk* 🛏 *2 rooms* 🍴 *Free Breakfast.*

West End

Handsome Georgian town houses give this neighborhood a dignified feel. People head here for the small boutiques and cafés, as well as the wide range of cultural venues.

👁 Sights

Edinburgh Zoo

ZOO | FAMILY | Home to star attractions Tian Tian and Yang Guang, the United Kingdom's only two giant pandas, Edinburgh's Zoo hosts more than 1,000 animals over 80 acres. Don't miss the famous Penguin Parade, which takes place every afternoon (as long as the penguins are willing), or the ever-popular Koala Territory, where you can get up close to the zoo's five koalas—including Kalari, born in 2019. Discounted tickets are available online. ✉ *Royal Zoological Society of Scotland, 134 Corstorphine Rd., Corstorphine* ☎ *0131/334–9171* 🌐 *www.edinburghzoo.org.uk* 🎟 *£19.95.*

★ Dean Village

NEIGHBORHOOD | Founded as a milling community in the 12th century, this pretty residential area offers a pleasant respite from the noise and crowds of the city. Head down cobbled Bells Brae Street and you'll be met by a charming assortment of old mill buildings, stone bridges, and lush greenery, all lining the Water of Leith. Walk two minutes east for a dramatic view of an imposing, 19th-century viaduct (Dean Bridge) or a little farther west to visit the Scottish National Gallery of Modern Art. ✉ *Dean Path, Dean Village* 🌐 *history.business.site.*

★ Edinburgh Gin Distillery

DISTILLERY | Whisky may be Scotland's most famous spirit, but gin also has a long and storied history here. Edinburgh Gin is a small distillery and visitor center just off Princes Street, offering tours and tastings that give a fascinating insight into craft gin production. You'll see two copper stills, Flora and Caledonia, which helped kick-start the now award-winning operation, and are still used to make some of their experimental, small-batch gins. (Note that the main range, including the navy-strength Cannonball Gin and the coastal botanical-infused Seaside Gin, are now produced at a larger facility in Leith). Choose between the Distillery Tasting Experience (£25) and the Gin Making Experience (£100), then head into the Heads & Tales bar to sample some Scottish gin cocktails. ✉ *1A Rutland Pl., West End* ☎ *0131/656–2810* 🌐 *www.edinburghgin.com* 🎟 *£25* ✍ *Tour reservations necessary.*

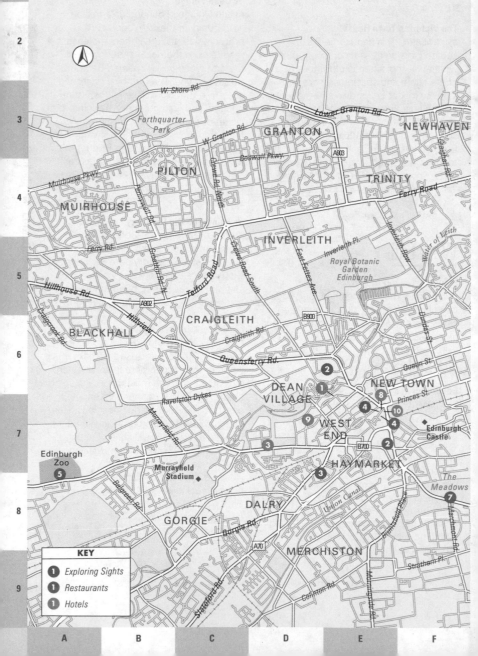

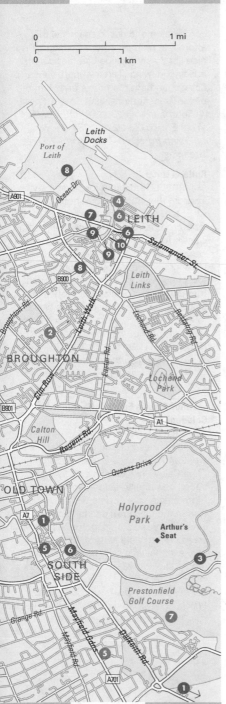

0 | 1 mi
0 | 1 km

Sights ▼

1 Craigmillar Castle.........**I9**
2 Dean Village..............**E6**
3 Duddingston Village......**I7**
4 Edinburgh
  Gin Distillery..............**E7**
5 Edinburgh Zoo...........**A8**
6 Holyrood Distillery......**G8**
7 The Meadows............**F8**
8 The Royal Yacht
  Britannia.................**G3**
9 Water of Leith
  Walkway.................**H4**

Restaurants ▼

1 Bonsai....................**G7**
2 Bread Meats Bread **E7**
3 First Coast **D8**
4 Grazing by
  Mark Greenaway........**E7**
5 Kalpna....................**G8**
6 The King's Wark........**H3**
7 The Kitchin **H3**
8 The Little Chartroom....**H4**
9 Mimi's Bakehouse—
  Leith **H4**
10 Restaurant
  Martin Wishart..........**H4**

Hotels ▼

1 B+B Edinburgh..........**D6**
2 The Conifers.............**G5**
3 The Dunstane
  Houses...................**D7**
4 Fingal.....................**H3**
5 Glenalmond House **H9**
6 Malmaison...............**H3**
7 Prestonfield House **I8**
8 Rutland Hotel............**E7**
9 The Victorian
  Town House **D7**
10 Waldorf Astoria
  Edinburgh—
  The Caledonian **E7**

🍴 Restaurants

Even after business hours, the city's commercial center is a good place to find a variety of international restaurants.

★ Bread Meats Bread

$$ | BURGER | This family-run burger joint has gained a nationwide reputation for its unusual toppings such as beef brisket, pastrami, kimchi, and gochujang mayo. Take a seat inside the chic, reclaimed-wood interior and choose from a menu packed with amped-up burgers as well as chicken, veggie, and halal options. **Known for:** smart and modern interior; the signature Wolf Burger; delicious garlic and parmesan fries. $ *Average main: £15* ✉ *92 Lothian Rd., West End* ☎ *0131/225–3000* ⊕ *www.breadmeatsbread.com.*

Grazing by Mark Greenaway

$$$ | BRITISH | Despite the name and the smattering of shared plates on offer, Grazing is mostly about traditional, hearty bistro fare done brilliantly. Set within a lavish yet unstuffy dining room, the restaurant's menu of seasonal dishes with inventive twists adds a real sense of fun to this consistently excellent dining experience. **Known for:** prices that can add up; fun and inventive dishes; attentive service. $ *Average main: £22* ✉ *Waldorf Astoria Edinburgh—The Caledonian, Rutland St., West End* ☎ *0131/222–8832* ⊕ *www.markgreenaway.com* ⊗ *Closed Mon.-Wed. No lunch Thurs.-Sat.*

🛏 Hotels

With easy access to some of the city's trendiest shops and cafés, the West End has many accommodation options that take advantage of the neighborhood's handsome Georgian-style townhouses.

B+B Edinburgh

$$$ | B&B/INN | FAMILY | Standing out along an elegant and tranquil West End terrace, this excellent B&B is the Scottish outpost of supertrendy B+B Belgravia of London; the imposing Victorian mansion combines grand public spaces with affordable modern accommodation. **Pros:** nice library and lounge bar; fascinating building in tranquil area; superb views. **Cons:** basement rooms are dark; hint of previous institutional use; no night porter. $ *Rooms from: £230* ✉ *3 Rothesay Terr., West End* ☎ *0131/225–5084* ⊕ *www.bb-edinburgh.com* ⌁ *27 rooms* ⫟ *Free Breakfast.*

Rutland Hotel

$$ | HOTEL | Nominated for several style awards, this chic boutique hotel at the west end of Princes Street offers 12 guest rooms with flamboyant fabrics and classic furnishings, as well as nine stylish serviced apartments, a flexible option for a family or two couples traveling together. **Pros:** great bar and restaurant; friendly staff; casual and unpretentious. **Cons:** no free on-site parking; no elevators to apartments; decor too loud and busy for some. $ *Rooms from: £200* ✉ *1–3 Rutland St., West End* ☎ *0131/229–3402* ⊕ *www.therutlandhotel.com* ⌁ *21 rooms* ⫟ *Free Breakfast* Ⓜ *West End-Princes St.*

Waldorf Astoria Edinburgh—The Caledonian

$$$$ | HOTEL | An imposing and ornate red-sandstone building situated at the west end of Princes Street Gardens, "The Caley" has dramatic Victorian decor, beautifully restored interiors, and more castle-view rooms than anywhere else in the city. **Pros:** outstanding and innovative restaurants; gorgeous public areas; impeccable service. **Cons:** gets very expensive in summer; understated rooms lack wow factor; expensive parking (£25 per night). $ *Rooms from: £315* ✉ *Princes St., New Town* ☎ *0131/222–8888* ⊕ *www.hilton.com/en/waldorf-astoria* ⌁ *241 rooms* ⫟ *Free Breakfast.*

Nightlife

BARS AND PUBS
The Hanging Bat
PUBS | A favorite with beer-loving locals, this stylish modern bar of reclaimed wood and exposed brickwork has an extensive, regularly changing selection of craft beers from across the country on tap, from IPAs to saisons to porters. The food, cooked in the in-house smoker, is great, too (try the house-smoked ribs). ⊠ *133 Lothian Rd., West End* ☎ *0131/229–0759* ⊕ *www. thehangingbat.com.*

★ The Jolly Botanist
BARS | Gin lovers are spoiled for choice at this self-proclaimed "liquor emporium." Take a seat amid the quirky period furnishings and flick through a menu of 70-plus gins from around the world, which can be enjoyed with your choice of tonic or as part of an inventive gin cocktail. There's also good bar food available. ⊠ *256–260 Morrison St., West End* ☎ *0131/228–5596* ⊕ *www.thejollybotanist.co.uk.*

Performing Arts

Cameo Picturehouse
FILM | Cameo has one large and two small auditoriums, both of which are extremely comfortable, showing a good mix of mainstream and art-house films. There's also a bar serving snacks late into the evening. ⊠ *38 Home St., Tollcross* ☎ *0871/902– 5747* ⊕ *www.picturehouses.com.*

★ Filmhouse
FILM | Widely considered to be among the best independent cinemas in Britain, the excellent three-screen Filmhouse is the go-to venue for modern, foreign-language, offbeat, and any other less-commercial films. It also holds frequent live events and mini-festivals for the discerning cinephile, and is the main hub for the International Film Festival each summer. The café and bar here are open late on weekends. ⊠ *88 Lothian Rd., West End* ☎ *0131/228– 2688* ⊕ *www.filmhousecinema.com.*

King's Theatre
THEATER | Built in 1906 and adorned with vibrant murals by artist John Byrne, the art nouveau King's Theatre has a great program of contemporary dramatic works. ⊠ *2 Leven St., Tollcross* ☎ *0131/529–6000* ⊕ *www.capitaltheatres.com.*

South Side

This residential district, which includes the suburbs of Morningside, Marchmont, Newington, Mayfield, and Prestonfield (among others), offers a peek at the comings and goings of regular Edinburghers. Cost-conscious visitors can find lots of affordable restaurants and budget B&Bs here.

Sights

Craigmillar Castle
CASTLE/PALACE | This handsome medieval ruin, just 3 miles south of the city center, is the archetypal Scottish fortress: forbidding, powerful, and laden with atmosphere. It is best known for its association with Mary, Queen of Scots: during a stay here in 1563, her courtiers hatched the successful plot to murder her troublesome husband, Henry Stuart (possibly with Mary's approval). Today Craigmillar is one of the most impressive ruined castles in Scotland. Stroll its beautiful courtyard, enter the well-preserved great hall, or climb the 15th-century tower for a superb view across the city. Look out for the unusually ornate defensive arrow slits, shaped like inverted keyholes. ⊠ *Craigmillar Castle Rd., South Side* ☎ *0131/661–4445* ⊕ *www.historicenvironment.scot* ⊠ *£6.*

Duddingston Village
TOWN | Tucked behind Arthur's Seat, and about a 45-minute walk through Holyrood Park, lies this small community, which still has the feel of a country village. The **Duddingston Kirk** has a Norman doorway

and a watchtower that was built to keep body snatchers out of the graveyard; it overlooks **Duddingston Loch,** popular with bird-watchers. Pathways meander down to the lochside **Dr Neil's Garden**, complete with the striking octagonal Thomson's Tower. Nearby, Edinburgh's oldest hostelry, the **Sheep Heid Inn,** serves a wide selection of beers and hearty food. It also has the oldest surviving *skittle* (bowling) alley in Scotland—once frequented (it's said) by Mary, Queen of Scots. ✉ *Duddingston Low Rd., Duddingston.*

★ Holyrood Distillery
DISTILLERY | Despite Edinburgh's long history of whisky production, there hadn't been a single malt distillery in the city for almost a century until this place opened in 2019. Today, Holyrood Distillery's state-of-the-art visitor center, set within an old railway station in the shadow of Salisbury Crags, plays host to entertaining and informative one-hour tours, including tastings of their Height of Arrows gin and new make spirit (the whisky is still busy maturing in barrels). Just a short walk from the Old Town, Holyrood attracts a younger and hipper crowd than most Scottish distilleries. ✉ *19 St Leonard's La., South Side* ☎ *0131/285–8977* 🌐 *www.holyrooddistillery.co.uk* 🎫 *Tour £15.50* 🕒 *Closed Mon.*

★ The Meadows
CITY PARK | FAMILY | Edinburgh's most popular green space, The Meadows is the first port of call for nearby workers, students, and families when the sun is out (or even when it isn't). You'll find people making the most of the grass here: picnicking, barbecuing, playing soccer, throwing frisbees, and flying kites. More formal sports facilities include tennis courts, a small golf putting course, and the biggest kids' play area in Edinburgh. Come during one of the city's many cultural festivals and there's likely to be a show on, too. ✉ *Melville Dr., South Side* ☎ *0131/529–5151* 🌐 *www.themeadowsofedinburgh.co.uk.*

🍴 Restaurants

The presence of university professors and students means restaurants here are both affordable and interesting.

Bonsai
$ | JAPANESE | The owners of Bonsai regularly visit Tokyo to research the casual dining scene, and their expertise is setting a high standard for Japanese cuisine in Edinburgh. The succulent *gyoza* (steamed dumplings) are pliant and tasty, while the wide variety of noodle, teriyaki, and sushi dishes balance sweet and sour deliciously. **Known for:** friendly and informal vibe; authentic sushi; great dragon *gaijin-zushi* (inside-out roll). [$] *Average main: £8* ✉ *46 W. Richmond St., South Side* ☎ *0131/668–3847* 🌐 *www.bonsaibarbistro.co.uk* 🕒 *Closed Mon. and Tues.*

★ Kalpna
$ | INDIAN | Amid an ordinary row of shops, the facade of this vegan and vegetarian Indian restaurant may be unremarkable, but the food is exceptional and great value, too. You'll find south- and west-Indian specialties, including *dum aloo kashmiri* (a medium-spicy potato dish with a sauce made from honey, ginger, and almonds) and *baingan achari* (red-hot marinated eggplants). **Known for:** great lunchtime buffet; authentic veggie Indian fare; lively interior with exotic mosaics. [$] *Average main: £10* ✉ *2–3 St. Patrick Sq., South Side* ☎ *0131/667–9890* 🌐 *www.kalpnarestaurant.com.*

🛏 Hotels

The B&Bs and guesthouses in this residential area offer comfortable, good value stays.

Glenalmond House
$ | B&B/INN | Elegantly furnished rooms, a friendly atmosphere, and a hearty breakfast are three big factors that make this town-house B&B a popular budget stay. **Pros:** delicious breakfasts; friendly and knowledgeable owners; spacious

deluxe rooms with four-poster beds and garden terraces. **Cons:** street noise audible in front-facing rooms; some rooms are small; a 30-minute walk to the Royal Mile. $ *Rooms from: £120* ✉ *25 Mayfield Gardens, South Side* ☎ *0131/668–2392* ⊕ *www.glenalmondhouse.com* ➦ *9 rooms* ⏐◯⏐ *Free Breakfast.*

★ Prestonfield House

$$$$ | **HOTEL** | Baroque opulence reigns in this 1687 mansion, with rich velvet curtains, gold-framed portraits, and alabaster-sculpted busts adorning the grand and eccentric public rooms, and equally plush decorations in the guest rooms. **Pros:** extensive grounds; baroque grandeur; great restaurant. **Cons:** bit pretentious for some; brooding decor can look gloomy; underwhelming showers in some rooms. $ *Rooms from: £375* ✉ *Priestfield Rd., Prestonfield* ☎ *0131/225–7800* ⊕ *www.prestonfield.com* ➦ *23 rooms* ⏐◯⏐ *Free Breakfast.*

▼ Nightlife

BARS AND PUBS

Cloisters

BARS | Set within an old church parsonage, Cloisters now offers a very modern form of sanctuary: real ales, fine whisky, and good food at reasonable prices, with a total absence of music and game machines. ✉ *26 Brougham St., Tollcross* ☎ *0131/221–9997* ⊕ *www.cloistersbar.com.*

★ The Dagda Bar

PUBS | This charming little drinking hole is an interesting mix of the old and new. At first glance, it's a very traditional pub with a dark-wood bar, beautiful embossed ceiling, and beer mats decorating the walls. But look closer and you'll also find a great selection of craft beers, hip shabby-chic decor, and a surprisingly young clientele. ✉ *93–95 Buccleuch St., Newington* ☎ *0131/667–9773* ⊕ *www.facebook.com/thedagdabar.*

Leslie's Bar

BARS | Retaining its original mahogany island bar, the late-Victorian-era Leslie's Bar is renowned for its gorgeous interior and for serving a range of traditional Scottish ales and malt whiskies. ✉ *45–47 Ratcliffe Terr., South Side* ☎ *0131/667–7205.*

CEILIDHS AND SCOTTISH EVENINGS

★ Edinburgh Ceilidh Club

THEMED ENTERTAINMENT | One of Edinburgh's most popular ceilidhs, this traditional Scottish music and dance night is held every Tuesday at Summerhall. It's ideal for beginners, as a caller teaches the dance steps before the live band begins each song. The club also holds irregular nights at Assembly Roxy near South Bridge. ✉ *Summerhall, 1 Summerhall Pl., Newington* ☎ *0131/560–1580* ⊕ *www.edinburghceilidhclub.com.*

☻ Performing Arts

Church Hill Theatre

THEATER | The intimate, 335-seat Church Hill Theatre, managed by the city council, hosts high-quality productions by local amateur dramatic societies. ✉ *Morningside Rd., Morningside* ☎ *0131/220–4348* ⊕ *www.churchhilltheatre.co.uk.*

The Queen's Hall

MUSIC | This intimate venue hosts a range of music events, from indie and rock concerts to jazz and classical music recitals. ✉ *85–89 Clerk St., Newington* ☎ *0131/668–2019* ⊕ *www.thequeenshall.net.*

⬤ Shopping

ANTIQUES

Courtyard Antiques

ANTIQUES & COLLECTIBLES | This lovely shop, tucked down a tiny alleyway, stocks a mixture of high-quality antiques, toys, and militaria. ✉ *108A Causewayside, Sciennes* ☎ *0131/662–9008* ⊕ *www.courtyardantiquesedinburgh.com.*

Leith

Just north of the city is Edinburgh's port, a place brimming with seafaring history and undergoing a supercharged revival after years of postwar neglect. It may not be as pristine as much of modern-day Edinburgh, but there are plenty of cobbled streets, dockside buildings, and bobbing boats to capture your imagination. Here along the lowest reaches of the Water of Leith (the river that flows through town), you'll find an ever-growing array of modish shops, pubs, and restaurants. Leith's major attraction is the Royal Yacht *Britannia*, moored outside the huge Ocean Terminal shopping mall. You can reach Leith from the center by walking down Leith Walk from the east end of Princes Street (20 to 30 minutes)—or, better yet, walk along the beautiful Water of Leith Walkway (a great way to forget you're in a capital city). Alternatively, you can hop on a bus.

◉ Sights

The Royal Yacht *Britannia*
HISTORIC SIGHT | FAMILY | Moored on the waterfront at Leith is the Royal Yacht *Britannia*—launched in Scotland in 1953, retired in 1997, and now returned to her home country. A favorite of Queen Elizabeth II (she is reported to have shed a tear at its decommissioning ceremony), it is now open for the public to explore, from the royal apartments on the upper floors to the more functional engine room, bridge, galleys, and captain's cabin. The visitor center, based within the hulking, onshore Ocean Terminal shopping mall, has a variety of fascinating exhibits and photographs relating to the yacht's history. ✉ *Ocean Terminal, Ocean Dr., Leith* ☎ *0131/555–5566* ⊕ *www.royalyachtbritannia.co.uk* 🎟 *£17.*

★ Water of Leith Walkway
TRAIL | The Water of Leith, Edinburgh's main river, rises in the Pentland Hills, skirts the edges of the city center, then heads out to the port at Leith, where it flows into the Firth of Forth. For a scenic stroll from the West End out to Leith, you can join this waterside walkway at the Scottish National Gallery of Modern Art, follow it through pretty Dean Village and Stockbridge, and continue past the Royal Botanic Garden, before emerging at The Shore. It takes about 90 minutes at a leisurely pace—and with all the tree-lined paths, pretty stone bridges, colorful wildflowers, and stunning birdlife (including herons, kingfishers, and buzzards) to see, we do suggest taking your time. Keep an eye out, too, for Antony Gormley's *6 Times* artwork, a series of life-sized human sculptures dotted along the river. ✉ *Leith* ⊕ *www.waterofleith.org.uk.*

🍴 Restaurants

Seafood lovers are drawn to the old port of Leith to sample the freshest seafood amid the authentic seafaring setting. Some of Scotland's most renowned chefs have made Leith—and more specifically, The Shore, its upmarket waterfront—their home.

The King's Wark
$$ | BRITISH | This gastro-pub at The Shore in Leith combines a beautiful historic setting with great quality food and a wide selection of Scottish gins. At lunchtime, the dark-wood bar does a roaring trade in simple fare such as gourmet burgers, fish cakes, and haggis (traditional or vegetarian), but in the evening, the kitchen ups the ante with a chalkboard menu of locally caught seafood specialties, from hake to monkfish. **Known for:** Leith's best roast dinner; affordable quality cuisine; atmospheric setting. $ *Average main: £16* ✉ *36 The Shore, Leith* ☎ *0131/554–9260* ⊕ *www.thekingswarkpub.com* ⊙ *Closed Mon.–Wed.*

Leith's most famous sight is the moored Royal Yacht *Brittania*, which once carried Queen Elizabeth and is now open to the public to explore.

The Kitchin

$$$$ | **FRENCH** | A perennially popular high-end dining option, Tom Kitchin's Michelin-starred venture packs in the crowds. Kitchin, who trained in France, runs a tight ship, and his passion for using seasonal and locally sourced produce to his own creative ends shows no sign of waning. **Known for:** very expensive dinners; nose-to-tail philosophy; lovely setting. [$] *Average main: £35* ✉ *78 Commercial Quay, Leith* ☎ *0131/555–1755* 🌐 *thekitchin.com* 🕓 *Closed Sun. and Mon.*

★ The Little Chartroom

$$$$ | **BRITISH** | For fine dining with a touch of theater, it's hard to beat this superb open-kitchen restaurant, where you can sit at the bar and watch the skilled chefs prepare and assemble each course. The à la carte menu is small—there's a choice of just three starters, three mains, and three desserts—but it's filled with innovative and exciting dishes, such as dressed crab with curry and smoked almonds or spatchcock partridge with haggis and celeriac. **Known for:** cozy kitchenside seating; unique creations like sweetcorn custard; small but varied menu. [$] *Average main: £30* ✉ *14 Bonnington Rd., Leith* ☎ *0131/556–6600* 🌐 *www.thelittlechartroom.com* 🕓 *Closed Mon.–Wed. No lunch Thurs. and Fri.*

★ Mimi's Bakehouse—Leith

$ | **BAKERY** | **FAMILY** | Despite its large interior with acres of seating, this bakery-café still regularly has lines out the door. The reason is simple: it bakes the best cakes in Edinburgh, using everything from Oreos to Reese's Pieces to strawberries and cream. **Known for:** fun and cheeky decor; delicious and creative cakes; delicious French toast and breakfast rolls. [$] *Average main: £9* ✉ *63 The Shore, Leith* ☎ *0131/555–5908* 🌐 *www.mimisbakehouse.com* 🕓 *No dinner.*

★ Restaurant Martin Wishart

$$$$ | **FRENCH** | Leith's premier dining experience, this high-end restaurant combines imaginative cuisine, luxuriously understated decor, and a lovely waterfront location. Renowned Michelin-starred chef Martin Wishart woos diners with his inspired menu of artistically presented, French-influenced dishes. **Known for:** exceptional vegetarian options; impeccable cuisine; beautiful location and setting. [$] *Average main: £43* ✉ *54 The Shore, Leith* ☎ *0131/553–3557* 🌐 *www.restaurantmartinwishart.co.uk* ⏲ *Closed Sun. and Mon.*

Hotels

Staying in Leith means you'll be away from the main Old and New Town sights, but near to the Royal Yacht *Britannia* and some of the city's best dining and drinking options.

The Conifers

$ | **B&B/INN** | This small family-run guesthouse in a red-sandstone townhouse offers simple, traditionally decorated rooms and warm hospitality. **Pros:** hearty breakfasts; nice mix of old and new; many original fittings. **Cons:** one bathroom not en suite; a bit of a walk to The Shore; a bit of a walk to the city center. [$] *Rooms from: £100* ✉ *56 Pilrig St., Leith* ☎ *0131/554–5162* 🌐 *www.conifersguesthouse.com* 🛏 *4 rooms* 🍴 *Free Breakfast.*

Fingal

$$$ | **HOTEL** | For something completely different, step aboard this floating boutique hotel, permanently moored near the Royal Yacht *Britannia* in Leith. **Pros:** quiet and peaceful; out-of-the-ordinary luxury; close to Leith's best bars and restaurants. **Cons:** a little way out of the center; dinner is underwhelming and overpriced; no room service. [$] *Rooms from: £300* ✉ *Alexandra Dock, Leith* ☎ *0131/357–5000* 🌐 *www.fingal.co.uk* 🛏 *23 rooms* 🍴 *Free Breakfast.*

Malmaison

$$ | **HOTEL** | Once a seamen's hostel, this French-inspired boutique hotel, which is part of a pioneering U.K.-wide chain (there's another in Edinburgh's New Town), draws a refined clientele to its chic shorefront rooms. A dramatic black-and-taupe color scheme prevails in the public areas, while the hip rooms are dominated by tartan designs and shades of heather, with bolder fabrics and brighter features in the suites. **Pros:** great waterfront location; impressive building; elegant interiors. **Cons:** a long way from the center of town; bar sometimes rowdy at night; price fluctuates wildly. [$] *Rooms from: £135* ✉ *1 Tower Pl., Leith* ☎ *0131/285–1478* 🌐 *malmaison.com/edinburgh* 🛏 *100 rooms* 🍴 *Free Breakfast.*

Nightlife

BARS AND PUBS

The Lioness of Leith

PUBS | This historic pub has always been a popular Leith Walk haunt for locals, but recent acclaim for their gourmet, gargantuan Lioness Burgers has brought them wider attention. ✉ *21–25 Duke St., Leith* ☎ *0131/629–0580* 🌐 *www.thelionessofleith.co.uk.*

Malt & Hops

PUBS | First opening its doors in 1749, Malt & Hops has a fine waterfront location and serves microbrewery cask ales—with a selection good enough to be endorsed by CAMRA (the Campaign for Real Ale). It also has a resident ghost. ✉ *45 The Shore, Leith* ☎ *0131/555–0083* 🌐 *www.facebook.com/realaleleith.*

★ Teuchters Landing

PUBS | Tucked away down a side street near The Shore, Teuchters Landing is a perennially popular pub for its wide range of whiskies and beers, its excellent pub food (try the nachos with cheddar and haggis), and its pontoon for sunny days. It's also a great place for watching live sports. If you're feeling lucky, try the Hoop of Destiny game for your chance to land a vintage dram for a fraction of its usual price. ✉ *1c Dock Pl., Leith* ☎ *0131/554–7427* 🌐 *www.teuchtersbar.co.uk.*

🛍 Shopping

SHOPPING CENTERS

Ocean Terminal

MALL | As well as being home to the Royal Yacht *Britannia*, this on-the-water mall also has an impressive range of big-name brand stores and independent craft shops, as well as bars, restaurants, and a cinema. ✉ *74 Ocean Dr., Leith* ☎ *0131/555–8888* ⊕ *www.oceanterminal. com.*

OUTDOOR SPORTS GEAR

Tiso Edinburgh Outdoor Experience

SPORTING GOODS | This sizable store stocks outdoor clothing, boots, and jackets ideal for hiking in the Highlands. It also sells tents and camping accessories for the truly hardy. There's a good little café inside, too. ✉ *41 Commercial St., Leith* ☎ *0131/554–0804* ⊕ *www.tiso.com.*

West Lothian and the Forth Valley

If you stand on an Edinburgh eminence—the castle ramparts, Arthur's Seat, Calton Hill—you can plan a few Lothian excursions without even the aid of a map. The Lothians is the collective name given to the swath of countryside south of the Firth of Forth and surrounding Edinburgh. Many courtly and aristocratic families lived here, and the region still has the castles and mansions to prove it. And with the rich came deer parks, gardens in the French style, and Lothian's fame as a seed plot for Lowland gentility.

West Lothian comprises a good bit of Scotland's central belt. The River Forth snakes across a widening floodplain on its descent from the Highlands, and by the time it reaches the western extremities of Edinburgh, it has already passed below the mighty Forth bridges and become a broad estuary. Castles and historic houses sprout thickly on both sides of the Forth. You can explore a number of them, and the territory north of the River Forth, in a day or two, or you can just pick one excursion for a day trip from Edinburgh.

GETTING HERE AND AROUND

BUS

First Bus and Lothian Buses link most of this area. If you're planning to see more than one sight in this region by bus, it's worth planning an itinerary in advance.

CAR

The Queensferry Road, also known as the A90, is the main thoroughfare connecting Edinburgh to this region. It ends just outside South Queensferry, at which point you can turn west on the A904 and M9 to Linlithgow—passing by Hopetoun House, the House of the Binns, and Blackness Castle—or join the M90 heading north across the Forth Bridge, with branches off to Culross (on the A985) and Dunfermline (on the A823).

TRAIN

Dalmeny (for South Queensferry), Linlithgow, and Dunfermline all have rail stations that can be reached from Edinburgh stations.

South Queensferry

7 miles west of Edinburgh.

This pleasant little waterside community, a former ferry port, is completely dominated by the Forth Bridges, three dramatic structures of contrasting architecture (dating from the 19th, 20th, and 21st centuries) that span the Firth of Forth at this historic crossing point. South Queensferry is also near a number of historic and cultural sights.

GETTING HERE AND AROUND

The Queensferry Road, also known as the A90, is the main artery west from Edinburgh to South Queensferry and around.

Sights

Dalmeny House

HISTORIC HOME | The first of the stately homes clustered on the western edge of Edinburgh, Dalmeny House is the residence of the Earl and Countess of Rosebery. This 1817 Tudor Gothic mansion displays among its sumptuous interiors the best of the family's famous collection of 18th-century French furniture. Highlights include the library, the Napoleon Room, the drawing room (with its tapestries and intricately wrought French furniture), and the Vincennes and Sevres porcelain collections. Admission is by guided tour in June and July only. There's a lovely three-mile shore walk from here to South Queensferry. ✉ *South Queensferry* ☎ *0131/331–1888* 🌐 *www.roseberyestates.co.uk* 🎫 *£10* 🕒 *Closed Aug.–May and Thurs.–Sat. in June and July.*

Forth Bridge

BRIDGE | Opened in 1890, when it was hailed as the eighth wonder of the world, this iconic red cantilevered rail bridge is a UNESCO World Heritage site. The extraordinary, 1½-mile-long crossing expands by another yard or so on a hot summer's day. The famous 19th-century bridge has since been joined by two neighbors; the 20th-century Forth Road Bridge (opened 1964) and the 21st-century Queensferry Crossing (opened 2017). ✉ *South Queensferry* 🌐 *www.theforthbridges.org.*

Hopetoun House

HISTORIC HOME | The palatial premises of Hopetoun House are among Scotland's grandest courtly seats, and are now home to the Marquesses of Linlithgow. The enormous property was started in 1699 to the original plans of Sir William Bruce, then enlarged between 1721 and 1754 by William Adam and his sons Robert and John. The house has decorative work of the highest order and a notable painting collection, plus all the trappings to keep you entertained: a nature trail, a restaurant in the former stables, a farm shop, and a museum. The estate also specializes in clay pigeon shooting; groups of six or more can book an expert-led introductory session, with prices starting at £45 per person. ✉ *South Queensferry* ☎ *0131/331–2451* 🌐 *www.hopetoun.co.uk* 🎫 *£11.50; grounds only £5.50* 🕒 *Closed Oct.–Mar.*

★ Inchcolm Island

ISLAND | Accessible by boat tour from South Queensferry, Inchcolm Island is home to a beautifully preserved 12th-century abbey, a World War I fortress, green cliffs, sandy beaches, and an abundance of wildlife, from playful gray seals to brightly colored puffins. Prepare to be dive-bombed by seagulls if you visit during nesting season. The island is run by Historic Scotland, which levies a landing fee of £6, and it will cost you £16 to get there with either Maid of the Forth or Forth Boat Tours. ✉ *Inchcolm Island, South Queensferry* ☎ *07836/265146* 🌐 *www.historicenvironment.scot* 🎫 *£22 (boat tour plus island landing pass)* 🕒 *Closed Nov.–Mar.*

Restaurants

The Boat House

$$ | **MODERN BRITISH** | Scotland's natural larder is on display at this romantic restaurant on the banks of the Forth. Seafood is the star of the show, and chef Paul Steward is the man behind the imaginative yet unfussy recipes. **Known for:** freshly caught daily specials; spectacular views from the patio; delicious seafood. [$] *Average main: £16* ✉ *22 High St., South Queensferry* ☎ *0131/331–5429* 🌐 *www.theboathouse.online.*

Hotels

★ Parkhead House

$$ | **B&B/INN** | Set within a gorgeous, 300-year-old gamekeeper's cottage on the edge of a deer park, this charming B&B offers large, stylishly appointed

A quick day trip from Edinburgh, one of Inchcolm Island's most interesting sights is its 12th-century abbey.

suites with en suite bedrooms and separate living/dining rooms. **Pros:** overlooking parkland and Firth of Forth; large and beautifully decorated suites; great breakfasts. **Cons:** shower pressure a little low; a short drive into South Queensferry; tricky to find (ask for instructions). [$] *Rooms from: ££170* ✉ *Off Abercorn Rd., South Queensferry* ☎ *0131/331–4348* 🌐 *www.parkhead-house.com* 🛏 *2 rooms* 🍴 *Free Breakfast.*

Jupiter Artland

11 miles southwest of Edinburgh.

For anyone drawn to interesting art and beautiful open spaces, a visit to this open-air collection of sculptures by world-renowned artists is a must.

GETTING HERE AND AROUND

To reach Jupiter Artland from Edinburgh, take the A71 southwest toward Kilmarnock. Just after Wilkieston, turn right onto the B7015. It's also easy to reach by bus: the X27 departs from Edinburgh's Princes Street and takes 30 minutes (get out at "Coxydene").

Sights

★ Jupiter Artland

ART MUSEUM | The beautiful grounds of a Jacobean manor house have been transformed by an art-loving couple, Robert and Nicky Wilson, into an impressive sculpture park. With the aid of a map you can explore the magical landscapes and encounter works by renowned artists including Anish Kapoor, Anya Gallaccio, Nathan Coley, Tania Kovats, and Ian Hamilton Finlay, among many others. A highlight is walking around Charles Jencks's *Cells of Life,* a series of shapely, grass-covered mounds. ✉ *Bonnington House Steadings, Wilkieston, Edinburgh* ☎ *01506/889900* 🌐 *www.jupiterartland.org* 🎟 *£9* 🕒 *Closed Nov.–mid-May.*

Linlithgow

18 miles west of Edinburgh.

Linlithgow is perhaps best known for its impressive palace, once the seat of the Stewart kings. The surrounding area also has some fascinating historical attractions.

GETTING HERE AND AROUND
From Edinburgh, take the A90 westward, continuing onto the A904 and M9, to reach Linlithgow. You can also take a train from Edinburgh Waverley to Linlithgow station, which is just a short walk from the palace.

◉ Sights

Blackness Castle
CASTLE/PALACE | Standing like a grounded ship on the very edge of the Forth, this curious 15th-century structure has had a varied career as a strategic fortress, state prison, powder magazine, and youth hostel. The countryside is gently green and cultivated, and open views extend across the blue Forth to the distant ramparts of the Ochil Hills. ⊠ *Blackness, Linlithgow* ☎ *01506/834807* ⊕ *www.historicenviron-ment.scot* ☎ *£6* ۞ *Closed Fri. and Sat.*

House of the Binns
HISTORIC HOME | The 17th-century general "Bloody" Tam Dalyell (1615–1685) transformed a fortified stronghold into a gracious mansion, the House of the Binns. The name derives from *bynn,* the old Scottish word for hill. The present exterior dates from around 1810 and shows a remodeling into a kind of mock fort with crenellated battlements and turrets. Inside, see magnificent Elizabethan-style plaster ceilings. ⊠ *Off A904, Linlithgow* ☎ *01786/812664* ⊕ *www.nts.org.uk* ☎ *£10.50* ۞ *House closed Jan.–Mar.*

Linlithgow Palace
CASTLE/PALACE | On the edge of Linlithgow Loch stands the splendid ruin of Linlithgow Palace, the birthplace of Mary, Queen of Scots. Burned, perhaps accidentally, by Hanoverian troops during the last Jacobite rebellion in 1746, this impressive shell stands on a site of great antiquity, though an earlier fire in 1424 destroyed any hard evidence of medieval life here. The palace gatehouse was built in the early 16th century, and the central courtyard's elaborate fountain dates from around 1535. The halls and great rooms are cold, echoing stone husks now in the care of Historic Scotland. ⊠ *Kirkgate, Linlithgow* ☎ *01506/842896* ⊕ *www.his-toricenvironment.scot* ☎ *£7.20* ۞ *Closed Sun. and Mon.*

Dunfermline

18 miles northwest of Edinburgh.

Oft-overlooked Dunfermline was once the world center for the production of damask linen, but the town is better known today as the birthplace of millionaire industrialist and philanthropist Andrew Carnegie (1835–1919). Undoubtedly Dunfermline's most famous son, Carnegie endowed the town with a library, fitness center, and, naturally, a Carnegie Hall, still the focus of the town's culture and entertainment.

GETTING HERE AND AROUND
If you're driving, head west on the A90. After it diverts north over the Firth of Forth, you will turn west onto the A823, then follow Queensferry Road into town. You can also reach Dunfermline by train from Edinburgh in about 35 minutes.

◉ Sights

Andrew Carnegie Birthplace Museum
HISTORIC HOME | Scottish-American industrialist and noted philanthropist Andrew Carnegie was born here in 1835. Don't be misled by the simple exterior of this 18th-century weaver's cottage—inside it opens into a larger hall, where documents, photographs, and artifacts relate his fascinating life story, from humble beginnings to the

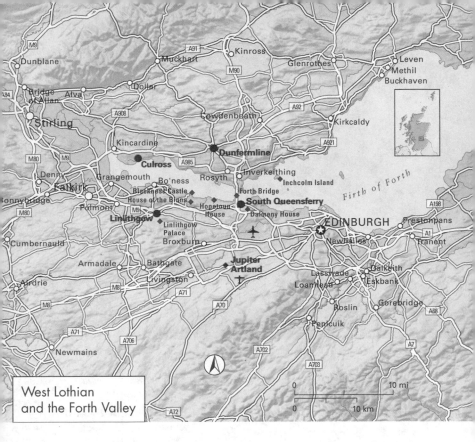

West Lothian
and the Forth Valley

world's richest man. There are also displays on the genus of Jurassic dinosaur named after Carnegie: *Diplodocus carnegii*. ⊠ *Moodie St., Dunfermline* ☎ *01383/724302* ⊕ *www.carnegiebirthplace.com* ☜ *Free.*

★ Dunfermline Abbey and Palace

RELIGIOUS BUILDING | This impressive complex, the literal and metaphorical centerpiece of Dunfermline, was founded in the 11th century as a Benedictine abbey by Queen Margaret, the English wife of Scottish king Malcolm III. The present church is a mishmash of medieval and Norman work, and a decorative brass tomb here is the final resting place of Robert the Bruce (1274–1329). A palace was also part of the complex here, and was the birthplace of Charles I (1600–49); its ruins lie beside the abbey. Dunfermline was the seat of the royal

court of Scotland until the end of the 11th century, and its central role in Scottish affairs is explored by means of display panels dotted around the drafty but hallowed buildings. ⊠ *St. Margaret St., Dunfermline* ☎ *01383/739026* ⊕ *www. historicenvironment.scot* ☜ *£6* ☾ *Closed Thurs. and Fri. Oct.–Mar.*

Pittencrieff Park

CITY PARK | One of Andrew Carnegie's most generous gifts to his hometown was this sprawling green space west of Dunfermline Abbey and Palace. As well as being a lovely place for a stroll or a picnic, it also has historical significance as the original site of **Malcolm's Tower**, named after King Malcolm III (circa 1031–93) and effectively the main seat of royal power in Scotland during the Middle Ages. ⊠ *Dunfermline.*

Due to its role as a living museum, the entire town of Culross is considered a National Trust sight.

Culross

24 miles northwest of Edinburgh.

With its mercat cross, cobbled streets, tolbooth, and narrow *wynds* (alleys), seaside Culross is a picturesque little town. It's also a living museum of 17th-century Scottish life, with preserved historic properties open to the public. Culross once had a thriving industry and export trade in coal and salt (the coal was used in the salt-panning process), but as local coal became exhausted, the impetus of the Industrial Revolution passed Culross by, while other parts of the Forth Valley prospered. Culross became a backwater town, and the merchants' houses of the 17th and 18th centuries were never replaced by Victorian developments or modern architecture.

In the 1930s the National Trust for Scotland started to buy up the decaying properties with a view to preservation. Today ordinary citizens live in many of these properties, but others are available to explore. Walking tours of the town are available from Culross Palace for a small fee.

GETTING HERE AND AROUND

To get here by car from Edinburgh, follow the A90 west then north over the Forth Bridge, before continuing westward on the A985. You can also get here by bus (No. 8) from Dunfermline, which in turn is easily reached by train from Edinburgh.

◉ Sights

★ Culross Palace

MUSEUM VILLAGE | Don't let the name fool you: this 16th-century merchant's house was never a royal residence, and lacks the ostentatious grandeur of a palace. It is, however, a fascinating slice of social history—the owner was a pioneer in local coal mining and salt production—and its interiors of Baltic pine, Durch floor tiles, and Staffordshire pottery was pretty flashy for its time. It was also visited by King James VI in 1617. Today it retains its period charms, including a garden that grows herbs and vegetables typical of

the period. ✉ *Culross Palace, Culross*
☎ *01383/880359* ⊕ *www.nts.org.uk*
💷 *£10.50* 🕙 *Closed Nov.–Mar.*

Midlothian and East Lothian

Stretching east to the sea and south to the Lowlands from Edinburgh, the regions of Midlothian and East Lothian, and their many attractions, are all within an hour's reach of Edinburgh.

Despite its countless tourist draws, including Scotland's finest stone carvings at Rosslyn Chapel, associations with Sir Walter Scott, outstanding castles, and miles of rolling countryside, Midlothian (the area immediately south of Edinburgh) remained off the beaten path for years. Fortunately, things are starting to change, as visitors look beyond the capital and the well-manicured charm of East Lothian to explore the pretty working towns and suburbs of Midlothian.

East Lothian, on the other hand, has been a draw for decades. An upmarket stockbroker belt, East Lothian's biggest draws are its golf courses of world rank, most notably Muirfield, plus a scattering of stately homes and interesting hotels. Its photogenic villages, active fishing harbors, dramatic cliff-side castles, and vistas of pastoral Lowland Scotland seem a world away from bustling Edinburgh—yet excellent transport links mean they're quick and easy to reach.

GETTING HERE AND AROUND
BUS
Buses from Edinburgh serve towns and villages throughout Midlothian and East Lothian. For details of all services, inquire at the Edinburgh Bus Station, immediately northeast of St. Andrew Square in Edinburgh.

CAR
A quick route to the Pentlands follows the A702 directly south. For Rosslyn Chapel, take the at-times parallel A701. For the National Mining Museum Scotland, head southwest on the A7 and continue two miles further for the turning to Crichton Castle. Heading east, the A1 passes Newhailes and Haddington enroute to Dunbar. Or detour onto the coast-hugging A198 to go via Gullane, North Berwick, and Tantallon Castle.

TRAIN
There is very limited train service in Midlothian, but buses will get you close enough to all the main sights. In East Lothian, there are train tracks running east along the coast with regular services to North Berwick and Dunbar. Destinations not served by train, such as Gullane and Haddington, have good bus connections.

The Pentlands

6 miles south of Edinburgh.

These unmistakable hills begin almost in the suburbs of Edinburgh, and they make for a very welcome escape from the city crowds. There are access points to the hills along the A702, but the best two are Snowsports Centre and Flotterstone. At each of these you can find a parking lot, a lovely pub, and quiet walking paths leading up into the hills.

GETTING HERE AND AROUND
The easiest way to reach the Pentlands is by car; simply follow the A702 south. Bus 101 from Edinburgh town center also follows this route. Alternatively, you can cycle into the hills in under an hour.

🍴 Restaurants

The Steading
$ | **BRITISH** | This pleasant pub, set within a converted farm building on the roadside of the A702, serves traditional, freshly

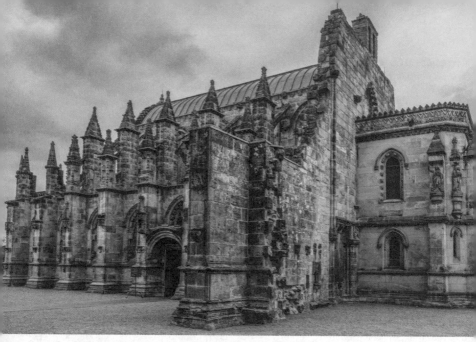

Rosslyn Chapel is one of Scotland's most intact 15th-century churches.

prepared pub food, along with hearty snacks like sandwiches and baked potatoes. It is right by the parking lot for the Snowsports Centre, from which several Pentlands walking trails begin. **Known for:** great location; hearty pub grub; beautiful building. $ *Average main: £10* ✉ *118–120 Biggar Rd., Edinburgh* ☎ *0131/445–1128* ⊕ *www.thesteadingedinburgh.co.uk.*

Roslin

7 miles south of Edinburgh.

It may be best known for its extraordinary chapel, but Roslin itself is a pleasant place to while away some time. There are some lovely walks from the village along the North River Esk.

GETTING HERE AND AROUND

By car take the A701 south from Edinburgh, turning off onto the B7006 just north of the town in Bilston. Lothian Buses also shuttle passengers from Edinburgh: Bus 37 from Princes Street is the most direct way.

◉ Sights

★ Rosslyn Chapel

RELIGIOUS BUILDING | This chapel has always beckoned curious visitors intrigued by the various legends surrounding its magnificent carvings, but today it pulses with tourists as never before. Much of this can be attributed to Dan Brown's best-selling 2003 mystery novel *The Da Vinci Code,* which featured the chapel heavily, claiming it has a secret sign that can lead you to the Holy Grail. Whether you're a fan of the book or not, this Episcopal chapel (services continue to be held here) remains an imperative stop on any traveler's itinerary. Originally conceived by Sir William Sinclair (circa 1404–80) and dedicated to St. Matthew in 1446, the chapel is outstanding for the quality and variety of the carving inside. Covering almost every square inch of stonework are human figures, animals, and plants. The meaning of these remains subject to many theories; some depict symbols from the medieval order of the Knights Templar and from Freemasonry. The chapel's design called for a cruciform structure, but only the choir and parts of the east transept walls were fully completed. Free talks about the building's history are held daily. ⊠ *Chapel Loan, Roslin* ☎ *0131/440–2159* ⊕ *www.rosslynchapel.com* ⊠ *£9.50.*

🍴 Restaurants

The Original Rosslyn Inn

$ | **BRITISH** | This atmospheric inn, on the crossroads in the center of Roslin village, serves tasty and hearty pub grub, from fish-and-chips and burgers to good veggie options. The inn, which also has rooms, is very close to Rosslyn Chapel; walk past the car park for a few minutes and you'll see it on the other side of the main road. **Known for:** convenient location; traditional Scottish pub; great steak-and-ale pie. $ *Average main: £10* ⊠ *2–4 Main St., Roslin, Roslin* ☎ *0131/440–2384* ⊕ *www.theoriginalrosslyninn.co.uk.*

National Mining Museum Scotland

9 miles southeast of Edinburgh.

The museum provides visitors with a sobering look into the lives of coal miners and the difficult conditions they endured down Scotland's mines.

GETTING HERE AND AROUND

To get here by car, head southeast on the A7—the museum is just after Newtongrange. You can also take a train from Edinburgh Waverley to Newtongrange (a six-minute walk away) or come by bus: 29 and X95 stop right outside the museum.

👁 Sights

National Mining Museum Scotland

MUSEUM VILLAGE | Located in Newtongrange, once Scotland's largest mining village, the National Mining Museum Scotland provides a good introduction to the history of the country's coal industry. The main walkaround exhibition is a little dry—expect more on the chemical composition of coal than the social history of Scottish mining—but the guided tours dig (ahem) a little deeper. You'll get to explore a replica coalface, see the colossal mining machinery up close, and hear tales about life deep under ground from the ex-miner guides. In particular, you'll learn about the mining company (and its abusive general manager Mungo Mackay), whose power over workers extended to owning all the houses, shops, and even the local pub. ⊠ *Lady Victoria Colliery, off A7, Newtongrange* ☎ *0131/663–7519* ⊕ *www.nationalminingmuseum.com* ⊠ *£9.50 with guided tour.*

Crichton Castle

14 miles southeast of Edinburgh.

Sitting on a terrace overlooking a beautiful river valley, this 14th-century structure with diamond-faceted facade was home to the Crichtons, and later the earls of Bothwell.

GETTING HERE AND AROUND

From Edinburgh, head east on the A1 and A68, then take the turnoff south onto the B6372 just before Pathhead. You can also come via the National Mining Museum Scotland; continue south on the A7 for 2½ miles, joining the B6732 just after Arniston.

👁 Sights

Crichton Castle

CASTLE/PALACE | Standing amid rolling hills that are interrupted here and there by patches of woodland, Crichton was a Bothwell family castle. Mary, Queen of Scots, attended the wedding here of

Bothwell's sister, Lady Janet Hepburn, to Mary's brother, Lord John Stewart. The curious arcaded range reveals diamond rustication on the courtyard stonework; this particular geometric pattern is unique in Scotland and is thought to have been inspired by the Renaissance styles in Europe, particularly Italy. The oldest part of the structure is the 14th-century keep (square tower). Note that there are no toilets at the castle. ⊠ Off B6372, Pathhead ☎ 01875/320017 ⊕ www.historicenvironment.scot ☜ £6 ⊘ Closed Oct.–Mar.

Newhailes

5½ miles east of Edinburgh.

With sumptuous interiors and relaxing grounds, this neo-Palladian villa a few miles east of Edinburgh hosted many luminaries of the Scottish Enlightenment.

GETTING HERE AND AROUND
To get here from Edinburgh, take the A1 east, then transfer to the A6095. You can also get here by Lothian Bus 30 from Princes Street. Newcraighall train station, with short and direct connections to Edinburgh Waverley, is a 20-minute walk from the villa.

 Sights

Newhailes
CASTLE/PALACE | This fine late-17th-century house was designed by Scottish architect James Smith in 1686 as his own home. He later sold it to Lord Bellendon, and in 1707 it was bought by Sir David Dalrymple, first Baronet of Hailes, who improved and extended the house, adding one of the finest rococo interiors in Scotland. The library here played host to many famous figures from the Scottish Enlightenment, as well as inveterate Scot-basher Dr. Samuel Johnson, who dubbed the library "the most learned room in Europe." Most of the original interiors and furnishings remain intact, and there are beautiful walks around the landscaped grounds and

through the surrounding woodland. ⊠ Off Newhailes. Rd., Musselburgh ☎ 0131/653–5599 ⊕ www.nts.org.uk ☜ £12 ⊘ Closed Dec.–Apr., Mon. and Tues. year-round, and weekdays in Nov.

Haddington

18 miles east of Edinburgh.

One of the best-preserved medieval street plans in the country can be explored in Haddington. Among the many buildings of architectural and historical interest is the Town House, designed by William Adam in 1748 and enlarged in 1830. A wall plaque at the Sidegate recalls the great heights of floods from the River Tyne. Beyond is the medieval Nungate footbridge, with the Church of St. Mary a little way upstream.

GETTING HERE AND AROUND
From Edinburgh, simply drive east on the A1. Alternatively, take the bus: East Coast Buses 104 and X7, as well as Borders Buses 253, will get you there.

Sights

Lennoxlove House
HISTORIC HOME | Majestic Lennoxlove House has been the grand ancestral home of the very grand dukes of Hamilton since 1947 and the Baird family before them. This turreted country house, with parts dating from the 15th century, is a cheerful mix of family life and Scottish history. The beautifully decorated rooms house portraits, furniture, porcelain, and items associated with Mary, Queen of Scots, including her supposed death mask. Sporting activities from falconry to fishing take place on the stunning grounds. Guided tours are available Wednesday, Thursday, and Sunday afternoons. ⊠ Estate Office, Haddington ☎ 01620/823720 ⊕ www.lennoxlove.com ☜ £10 ⊘ Closed Nov.–Apr., Mon., Tues., Fri., and Sat.

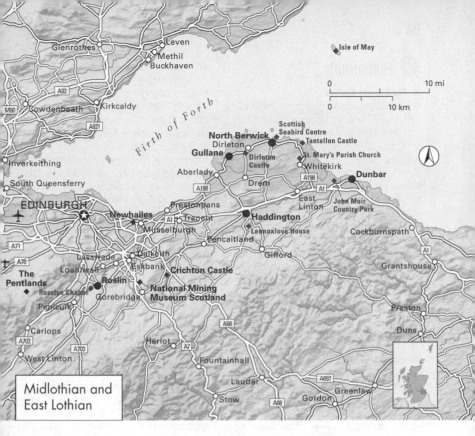

Midlothian and
East Lothian

Gullane

21 miles northeast of Edinburgh.

Follow the coastline on either side of
Gullane and you're faced with golf course
after golf course. Fairways are laid out
wherever there is available links space
along this stretch of East Lothian, with
Muirfield just one of the courses here
replete with players clad in expensive
golfing sweaters. Apart from golf, visitors
can enjoy restful summer-evening strolls
along Gullane's sandy beach.

GETTING HERE AND AROUND

From Edinburgh, drive east on the A1,
then head north along the coast on the
A198. The direct 124 bus leaves to and
from the capital every 30 minutes.

⊙ Sights

Dirleton Castle

CASTLE/PALACE | In the center of tiny
Dirleton, two miles east of Gullane, sits
the impressive-looking 12th-century
Dirleton Castle. It's now a ruin, but its
high outer wall is relatively complete, and
the grounds behind the walls feature a
17th-century bowling green, set in the
shade of yew trees and surrounded by
a herbaceous flower border that blazes
with color in high summer. King Edward
I of England occupied the castle in 1298
as part of his campaign for the continued
subjugation of the unruly Scots. ⊠ *Dirleton
Ave., Off A198, Gullane* ☎ *01620/850330*
⊕ *www.historicenvironment.scot* ⊠ *£6.*

🍴 Restaurants

★ The Bonnie Badger

$$$ | BRITISH | A charming concoction of sandstone walls, raftered roofs, and roaring fireplaces, as well as a lovely garden area, this upmarket inn is the ideal spot for a pub lunch. Owned by star Edinburgh chef Tom Kitchin, the menu at first appears to be fairly by-the-numbers British pub fare—think fish-and-chips, steak pie, and sausage and mash—but with superior local produce and a dash of culinary imagination, classic dishes are transformed into something special. **Known for:** beautiful garden; pigs' ears as a pre-meal snack; delicious desserts. ⓢ *Average main: £22* ✉ *Main St., Gullane* ☎ *01620/621111* ⊕ *www.bonniebadger.com.*

Activities

Gullane Golf Club

GOLF | Often overshadowed by Muirfield, Gullane provides an equally authentic links experience, as well as a far-more-effusive welcome than its slightly snooty neighbor along the road. The three championship courses here crisscross Gullane Hill, and all command outstanding views of the Firth of Forth and particularly the beaches of Aberlady Bay. No. 1 is the toughest, but No. 2 and No. 3 offer up equally compelling sport and for significantly lower green fees. Day tickets can also be purchased, and for No. 3 it's little more than the price of a single round. ✉ *W. Links Rd., Gullane* ☎ *01620/842255* ⊕ *www.gullanegolfclub. co.uk* 🎫 *No. 1: £195 weekdays, £225 weekends; No. 2: £85 weekdays, £95 weekends; No. 3: £49 weekdays, £59 weekends* 🏌 *No. 1 Course: 18 holes, 6583 yards, par 71; No. 2 Course: 18 holes, 6385 yards, par 71; No. 3 Course: 18 holes, 5259 yards, par 68.*

Muirfield

GOLF | Home of the Honourable Company of Edinburgh Golfers and the world's oldest golfing club, Muirfield has a pedigree that few other courses can match. Although this course overlooking the Firth of Forth is considered one of golf's most challenging, players also talk about it being "fair," which means it has no hidden bunkers or sand traps. The club has a well-deserved reputation for being stuffy and traditional; you will be refused entry to the restaurant if you aren't wearing a jacket and tie. In addition, its first female members were only admitted in 2019, 275 years after it first opened (and this was only after threats of losing hosting rights to The Open). Visitors are permitted only on Tuesday and Thursday, and you must apply for a tee time well in advance. ✉ *Duncur Rd., Gullane* ☎ *01620/842123* ⊕ *www.muirfield.org.uk* 🎫 *£310 Apr.–Oct., £110 Nov.–Mar.* 🏌 *18 holes, 7245 yards, par 71.*

North Berwick

24 miles northeast of Edinburgh.

The pleasant little seaside resort of North Berwick manages to retain its small-town charm even when it's crowded with city visitors on warm summer days. Eating ice cream, the city folk stroll on the beach and in the narrow streets or gaze at the sailing craft in the small harbor. The town is near a number of castles and other sights.

GETTING HERE AND AROUND

Travel east on the A1 and join the coast-skirting A198, or take one of the regular trains from Edinburgh Waverley.

👁 Sights

★ Isle of May

ISLAND | This small island in the middle of the Firth of Forth is home to many interesting sights, from the ruins of a medieval priory to a Gothic lighthouse to a wartime signal station. But it's the seabirds that really bring in the visitors. The Isle of May is the largest puffin colony on the east coast of Britain and is home to a quarter of a million birds nesting on the cliffs during late spring and early summer, as well as seals basking on the shore. To visit the island, you'll need to take a 12-seat RIB (rigid inflatable boat) across choppy waters, including a sail by Bass Rock—the world's largest colony of gannets. Tours start from the Scottish Seabird Centre and last four hours, including at least 2½ hours on the island. Book in advance online to avoid disappointment. ✉ *North Berwick* 🌐 *www.seabird.org* 🎟 *Tour £50* ⏲ *Closed Oct.–Mar.*

Scottish Seabird Centre

COLLEGE | FAMILY | An observation deck, exhibits, and films at this excellent family-friendly attraction provide a captivating introduction to the world of the gannets and puffins that nest on the Firth of Forth islands. Live interactive cameras let you take an even closer look at the bird colonies and marine mammals. Kids will enjoy the "Flyway Tunnel," a 3-D multimedia exhibit that simulates walking through an underwater passage, learning all about local nesting birds and sea life along the way. There are plenty of family-focused activities, nature walks, and photography shows, as well as a great on-site café and gift shop. ✉ *The Harbour, North Berwick* ☎ *01620/890202* 🌐 *www.seabird.org* 🎟 *£11.95.*

★ Tantallon Castle

CASTLE/PALACE | Travel east along the flat fields from North Berwick, and the imposing silhouette of Tantallon Castle, a substantial, semiruined medieval fortress, comes dramatically into view. Standing on a headland with the sea on three sides, the red-sandstone walls are being chipped away by time and sea spray, with the earliest surviving stonework dating from the late 14th century. The fortress was besieged in 1529 by the cannons of King James V and again (more damagingly) during the civil war of 1651. Despite significant damage, much of the curtain wall of this former Douglas stronghold survives and is now cared for by Historic Scotland. From the grounds you can see Bass Rock out to sea, which looks gray during winter but bright white in summer. Look through the telescope here and you'll see why. ✉ *Off A198, North Berwick* ☎ *01620/892727* 🌐 *www.historicenvironment.scot* 🎟 *£6.*

🍴 Restaurants

★ The Lobster Shack

$$ | SEAFOOD | North Berwick's most consistently popular dining option isn't a traditional restaurant, or even a restaurant at all—it's a shack. That's testament to the sheer quality of the seafood served at this take-out stand, where freshly caught lobster, crab, haddock, and mussels are cooked before your eyes and served in boxes with double-dipped chips, ready to eat in a fold-up chair, on a harbor wall, or while strolling along the beach. **Known for:** good value; amazing lobster and chips; beautiful harborside location. [$] *Average main: £16* ✉ *North Berwick Harbour, North Berwick* ☎ *07910/620480* 🌐 *www.lobstershack.co.uk* ⏲ *Closed Oct.–Mar.*

🛏 Hotels

The Glebe House

$$ | B&B/INN | This stately 18th-century building was once a *manse* (minister's house), but is now a delightful and luxurious B&B. **Pros:** sociable breakfast around a mahogany table; peaceful atmosphere; interesting antiques. **Cons:** expensive for the area; too precious for some; books up well in advance. [$] *Rooms from: £150* ✉ *Law Rd., North Berwick* ☎ *01620/892608* 🌐 *www.glebehouse-nb.co.uk* 🛏 *4 rooms* 🍽 *Free Breakfast.*

Dunbar

30 miles east of Edinburgh.

In the days before tour companies started offering package deals to the Mediterranean, Dunbar was a popular holiday beach resort. Now a bit faded, the town is still lovely for its spacious

Georgian-style properties, characterized by the astragals, or fan-shaped windows, above the doors; the symmetry of the house fronts; and the parapeted rooflines. Though not the popular seaside playground it once was, Dunbar has an attractive beach and a picturesque harbor. It's also one end of the John Muir Way, a cross-Scotland hiking trail.

GETTING HERE AND AROUND
From Edinburgh, head east on the A1 to get to Dunbar. You can also take a direct train from Edinburgh Waverley.

◉ Sights

John Muir Country Park
NATURE PRESERVE | Set on the estuary of the River Tyne, winding down from the Moorfoot Hills, the John Muir Country Park encompasses varied coastal scenery: rocky shoreline, golden sands, and the mixed woodlands of Tyninghame, teeming with wildlife. Dunbar-born conservationist John Muir (1838–1914), whose family moved to the United States when he was a child, helped found Yosemite and Sequoia national parks in California. ✉ *Off A1087, Dunbar.*

St. Mary's Parish Church
RELIGIOUS BUILDING | In the village of Whitekirk, on the road from Dunbar to North Berwick, lies the unmistakable St. Mary's Parish Church, with its beautiful red-sandstone Norman tower. Occupied since the 6th century, the church was a place of pilgrimage in medieval times because of its healing well. Behind the kirk, in a field, is a tithe barn—the tithe is the portion of a farmer's produce that was given to the local church. Beside this stands a 16th-century tower house, once used to accommodate visiting pilgrims. In the 15th century, the church was visited by a young Italian nobleman, Enea Silvio Bartolomeo Piccolomini, after he was shipwrecked off the East Lothian coast; two decades later, Piccolomini became Pope Pius II. ✉ *A198, Whitekirk* ✈ *Free.*

◉ Activities

GOLF
Dunbar Golf Club
GOLF | There's a lighthouse at the 9th hole of this championship course, first laid out in 1856. It's a good choice for experiencing a typical east coast links, including the unique challenges presented by coastal winds. Within easy reach of Edinburgh, Dunbar Golf Club has stunning views of the Firth of Forth and Bass Rock. The club is currently undergoing an expansion, including the addition of a clubhouse, nine-hole short course, and driving range. ✉ *East Links, Golf House Rd., Dunbar* ☎ *01368/862317* ⊕ *www.dunbargolfclub. com* ✉ *Summer: £90 Mon.–Wed., £105 Fri., £115 weekends; Winter: £50* ⚐ *18 holes, 6597 yards, par 71* ☉ *Closed Thurs. year-round and Fri.–Sun. in Nov.–Feb.*

HIKING
★ John Muir Way
HIKING & WALKING | This much-praised scenic hiking path stretches from Helensburgh, northwest of Glasgow, to Dunbar. The trail's terminus is outside John Muir's birthplace, on the town's High Street. The 130-mile coast-to-coast route passes through some spectacular scenery (especially at the Helensburgh end). It takes about a week to traverse completely, but the official website has maps covering all the various sections. ✉ *The John Muir Way (East End), 125 High St., Dunbar* ⊕ *www.johnmuirway.org.*

Chapter 4

GLASGOW

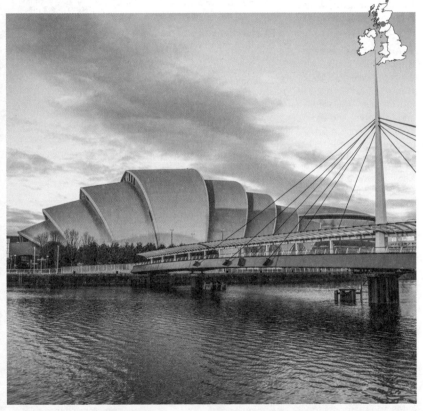

Updated by
Tara Hepburn

◉ Sights	🍴 Restaurants	🛏 Hotels	🛍 Shopping	🍸 Nightlife
★★★★☆	★★★★★	★★★★☆	★★★★★	★★★★★

WELCOME TO GLASGOW

TOP REASONS TO GO

★ **Architecture:** The Victorians left a legacy of striking architecture, and Glasgow's buildings manifest the city's love of grand artistic statements—just remember to look up. The Arts and Crafts buildings by Charles Rennie Mackintosh are reason alone to visit.

★ **Art museums:** Some of Britain's best art galleries are in Glasgow. The Hunterian Art Gallery, the Kelvingrove Art Gallery and Museum, and the Gallery of Modern Art are worth a visit.

★ **Parks and gardens:** From Kelvingrove Park to the Glasgow Botanic Gardens, the city has more parks per square mile than any other in Europe. Stop by the Botanic Gardens for outdoor theatrical productions in summer or Glasgow Green for the annual piping festival.

★ **Food and drink:** Whether you fancy a Guinness in a traditional pub like the Scotia or a Pinot Noir in a fashionable wine bar, there's a place to quench all thirsts. Locals love their cafés and tearooms too.

1 City Centre. From Buchanan Street west to Hope Street and beyond, look up to see grand Victorian and neo-Gothic buildings expressing the confidence of an industrial capital. George Square's City Chambers are worth a visit before you trawl the shops, duck into one of the trendy eateries, or explore the bars and music venues.

2 Merchant City. In the Middle Ages, the city grew up around Glasgow Cathedral. As the city expanded along with the growing transatlantic trade, wealthy tobacco and cotton traders built palatial houses here. They were laid to rest in the glorious tombs of the Necropolis, which overlooks the city. Today the area is busy with restaurants, clubs, and high-end shops.

3 West End. In the quieter, slightly hillier western part of the city is Glasgow University and the more bohemian side of Glasgow. The West End's treasures include the Botanic Gardens, Kelvingrove Park, and the Kelvingrove Art Gallery and Museum. Along Byres Road, there are well-priced restaurants and lively bars that attract weekend revelers from across the city.

4 Finnieston. Once lined with shipyards, the River Clyde has been reborn as a relaxing destination that entrances visitors and locals. The Glasgow Science Centre and the Museum of Transport face each other across the water, while the Scottish Exhibition Centre and the SSE Hydro are major event venues. Argyle Street has been transformed into a fashionable strip of restaurants and bars.

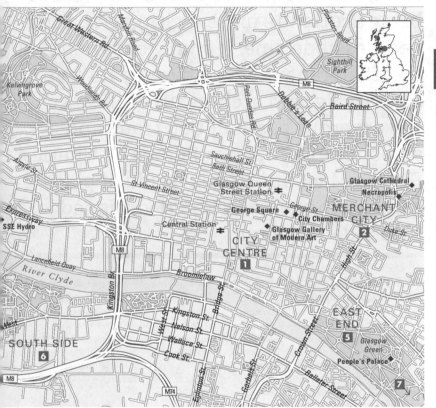

5 East End. What was once the poorest area of Glasgow is being treated to a major face-lift. Glasgow Green's wonderful People's Palace draws visitors throughout the year, and on weekends the nearby Barras market is a reminder of the area's past. Its famous dance hall has also been reborn as a major arts center.

6 South Side. Often overlooked, this less-visited side of the city includes beautiful Pollok Park as well as Pollok House, with its art collection and its elegant gardens. Art-filled Mackintosh's House sits in Bellahouston Park.

7 Side Trips from Glasgow. Just outside Glasgow, you can find Robert Owen's famous community at New Lanark, and in Ayrshire, you'll find many monuments to the life and times of Scottish poet Robert Burns. Alternatively you can follow generations of Glaswegians who took their summer holidays in the coastal resorts of the Clyde Coast.

Trendy stores, a booming cultural life, fascinating architecture, and stylish restaurants reinforce Glasgow's claim to being Scotland's most exciting city. After decades of decline, it finally experienced an urban renaissance uniquely its own. The city's grand architecture reflects a prosperous past built on trade and shipbuilding. Today buildings by Charles Rennie Mackintosh hold pride of place along with the Zaha Hadid–designed Riverside Museum.

Glasgow (the "dear green place," as it was known) was founded some 1,500 years ago. Legend has it that the king of Strathclyde, irate about his wife's infidelity, threw a ring he had given her into the River Clyde. (Apparently she had passed it on to an admirer.) When the king demanded to know where the ring had gone, the distraught queen asked the advice of her confessor, St. Mungo. He suggested fishing for it—and the first salmon to emerge had the ring in its mouth. The moment is commemorated on the city's coat of arms.

The vast profits from American cotton and tobacco built the grand mansions of the Merchant City in the 18th century. The tobacco lords financed the building of wooden ships, and by the 19th century the River Clyde had become the center of a vibrant shipbuilding industry, fed by the city's ironworks and steelworks. The city grew again, but its internal divisions grew at the same time. The West End

harbored the elegant homes of the newly rich shipyard owners. Down by the river, areas like the infamous Gorbals, with its crowded slums, or Govan, sheltered the laborers who built the ships. They came from the Highlands, expelled to make way for sheep, or from Ireland, where the potato famines drove thousands from their homes.

During the 19th century the city's population grew from 80,000 to more than a million. The new prosperity gave Glasgow its grand neoclassical buildings, such as those built by Alexander "Greek" Thomson, as well as the adventurous visionary buildings designed by Charles Rennie Mackintosh and others who produced Glasgow's Arts and Crafts movement.

The decline of shipbuilding and the closure of the factories in the later 20th century led to much speculation as to what direction the city would take. The curious thing is that, at least in part, the past gave the city its new lease on life. It was as if people looked at their city and saw Glasgow's beauty for the first time: its extraordinarily rich architectural heritage, its leafy parks, its artistic heritage, and its complex social history. Today Glasgow is a dynamic cultural center and a commercial hub, as well as a launching pad from which to explore the rest of Scotland, which, as it turns out, is not so far away. In fact, it takes only 40 minutes to reach Loch Lomond, where the other Scotland begins.

As cities go, Glasgow is contained and compact. It's set up on a grid system, so it's easy to navigate and explore, and the best way to tackle it is on foot. In the eastern part of the city, start by exploring Glasgow Cathedral and other highlights of the oldest section of the city, then wander through the rest of the Merchant City. From there you can just continue into the City Centre with its designer shops, art galleries, and eateries. From here you can either walk (it takes a good 45 minutes) or take the subway to the West End. If you walk, head up Sauchiehall Street. Once in the West End, visit the Glasgow Botanic Gardens, Glasgow University, and the Kelvingrove Art Gallery and Museum. A walk through Kelvingrove Park will being you to the fashionable Finnieston area. You can take a taxi to the South Side to experience Pollok House. For Glasgow's East End, walk down High Street from the cathedral to the Tron Cross; from there you can walk to the Barras market, the People's Palace, Glasgow Green, and even farther east to explore the newly trendy Dennistoun area, now regularly included on lists of the world's coolest neighborhoods.

Planning

When to Go

The best times to visit Glasgow are spring and summer and into early fall. Although you may encounter crowds, the weather is more likely to be warm and dry. In summer the days can be long and pleasant—if the rain holds off—and festivals and outdoor events are abundant. Fall can be nice, although cold weather begins to set in after mid-September and the days grow shorter. From November to February it is cold, wet, and dark. Although thousands of people flock to Glasgow for New Year's celebrations, the winter months are relatively quiet in terms of crowds.

Getting Oriented

Glasgow's layout is hard to read at a single glance. The River Clyde, around which Glasgow grew up as a trading city, runs through the center of the city—literally cutting it in two. To the north, the oldest part of Glasgow, the Merchant City, stretches from High Street (the heart of the medieval city) as far as Queen Street, bounded by George Square and Argyle Street to the north and south. Victorian Glasgow, which grew with the shipbuilding boom, extends as far as what is now the M8 motorway and the River Clyde to the south. Beyond the M8 is the West End, originally the wealthy area around Glasgow University. Its main street is Byres Road. Across Kelvingrove Park, what was once a fading and neglected area has sprung back to life; Finnieston is an expensive and trendy neighborhood, with shipbuilding giving way to riverside concerts and exhibition venues. The opposite bank of the river was traditionally the city's poorer quarter, where its workers lived, although that is no longer true. Former residents of the Southern bankside areas such as the Gorbals, Kinning Park, and Cessnock would be surprised at the recent regeneration: large media buildings (such as the BBC's Scottish headquarters), casinos, and penthouse apartments now line the southern banks of the river. Farther into the heart of the city's Southside is the café culture of Shawlands, an area popular with a decidedly young and middle-class crowd. Pollok Park and Pollok House, with its fine collection of art and furniture, can also be found in the city's Southern district.

Planning Your Time

You could quite easily spend five comfortable days here, although in a pinch, two would do. The best strategy for seeing the city is to start at High Street on the east side of Merchant City and work your way west. On the first day explore the city's medieval heritage, taking in Glasgow Cathedral, the Museum of Religious Life, and Provand's Lordship, as well as the Necropolis with its fascinating crumbling monuments. The gentle walk west from here to the Merchant City is also a walk through time, to 17th- and 18th-century Glasgow, and George Square, around which spread the active and crowded shopping areas. For those interested in architect Charles Rennie Mackintosh, the Mackintosh Trail connects the many buildings designed by this outstanding Glasgow designer and architect. Full information on all his buildings can be found online at ⊕ www.crmsociety.com, where you can also purchase tickets, as well as at the individual sites. Another day could be well spent between the Kelvingrove Art Gallery (you can lunch here and listen to the daily concert on its magnificent organ) and the nearby Hunterian Museum and Gallery in the university. From here it's only minutes to lively Byres Road and its shops, pubs, and cafés or to the Finnieston strip along Argyle Street. The redevelopment of the riverside offers another route—to the Transport Museum and the Science Centre.

If you have a few extra days, head out to Robert Burns country and the extraordinary Burns Birthplace Museum in Ayrshire. It's a scenic 45-minute drive from Glasgow. Most destinations on the Clyde Coast are easily accessible from Glasgow. Direct trains from Glasgow Central station take you to Paisley, Irvine, and Lanark in less than an hour. These small towns need no more than a day to explore. To get a flavor of island life, take the hour-long train ride to Wemyss Bay and then the ferry to the Isle of Bute.

FESTIVALS
Aye Write

CULTURAL FESTIVALS | This highly successful literary festival brings together writers from Scotland and the world to discuss their work and exchange ideas. It is held in the Mitchell Library and other venues over one week in July. ⊠ *Mitchell Library, North St., West End* ☎ *0141/287–2999* ⊕ *www.ayewrite.com* Ⓜ *St. George's Cross.*

★ Celtic Connections

FESTIVALS | Continually expanding, this music festival is held throughout the second half of January in venues across the city. Musicians from Scotland, Ireland, and other countries celebrate Celtic music, both traditional and contemporary. There are a series of hands-on workshops and a popular late-night club at the Royal Concert Hall. ⊠ *Glasgow* ☎ *0141/353–8000* ⊕ *www.celticconnections.com.*

Glasgow Jazz Festival

CONCERTS | For five days in late June, Glasgow hosts jazz musicians from around the world in venues throughout the city, though mainly in the City Centre. ⊠ *City Centre* ☎ *0141/552–3552* ⊕ *www.jazzfest.co.uk* Ⓜ *Buchanan St.*

Getting Here and Around

AIR

Airlines flying from Glasgow Airport to the rest of the United Kingdom and to Europe include Aer Lingus, Air Canada, BMI Regional, British Airways, easyJet, Icelandair, Jet 2, and KLM. Several carriers fly from North America, including Air Canada, American Airlines, United, Westjet, and Icelandair (service via Reykjavík).

Ryanair and Vueling offer budget airfares between Prestwick and London and European destinations. Budget-minded easyJet has similar services from Glasgow Airport. Loganair flies to the islands.

Glasgow Airport (GLA) is about 7 miles west of the City Centre on the M8 to Greenock. The airport serves international and domestic flights, and most major European carriers have frequent and convenient connections to many cities on the continent; it closes overnight. There's a frequent shuttle service from London, as well as regular flights from Birmingham, Bristol, East Midlands, Leeds/Bradford, Manchester, Southampton, Isle of Man, and Jersey. There are also flights from Wales (Cardiff) and Ireland (Belfast, Dublin, and Londonderry). Local Scottish connections can be made to Aberdeen, Barra, Benbecula, Campbeltown, Inverness, Islay, Kirkwall, Shetland (Sumburgh), Stornoway, and Tiree.

Prestwick Airport (PIK), on the Ayrshire coast about 30 miles southwest of Glasgow, is known mainly as an airport for budget airlines like Ryanair.

Although there's a railway station about 2 miles from Glasgow Airport (Paisley Gilmour Street), it is not very accessible. Transport to the City Centre is by bus or taxi and takes about 20 minutes. Metered taxis cost around £25. Express buses depart every 15 minutes from Glasgow Airport to Central and Queen Street stations and to the Buchanan Street bus station. The fare is £8.50 one way, £14 open round-trip per person.

The drive from Glasgow Airport into the City Centre via the M8 motorway (Junction 29) is normally quite easy. Most companies that provide chauffeur-driven cars and tours will also do limousine airport transfers. TBR Global Chauffeuring is a worldwide organization offering chauffeur-driven transport in Glasgow and across the United Kingdom.

There's a rapid half-hourly train service (hourly on Sunday) direct from Prestwick Airport's terminal to Glasgow Central. Strathclyde Passenger Transport and ScotRail offer a discount ticket that allows you to travel for half the standard fare; just show a valid airline ticket for a flight to or from Prestwick Airport. An hourly coach service makes the same trip but takes much longer than the train. Travelers arriving after 11 pm can take a late bus (X99); book this online with Dodds of Troon. The fare is £14.

The City Centre is reached by car from Prestwick via the fast M77 in about 40 minutes. Metered taxis are available at the airport. The fare to Glasgow is about £40.

AIRPORTS Glasgow Airport. (*GLA*) ⊠ *Glasgow* ☎ *0344/481–5555* ⊕ *www. glasgowairport.com.* **Prestwick Airport.** ⊠ *A79, Prestwick* ☎ *0871/223–0700* ⊕ *www.glasgowprestwick.com.*

AIRPORT TRANSFER CONTACTS Dodds of Troon. ⊠ *Glasgow* ☎ *01292/288100* ⊕ *www.doddsoftroon.com.* **Little's Chauffeur Drive.** ☎ *0141/883–2111* ⊕ *www. littles.co.uk.* **Strathclyde Passenger Transport Travel Centre.** ⊠ *Buchanan Street Bus Station, Killermont St., City Centre* ☎ *0141/332–6811* ⊕ *www.spt.co.uk* Ⓜ *Buchanan St.* **TBR Global Chauffeuring.** ☎ *0141/280–4800* ⊕ *www.tbrglobal.com.*

BIKE

Increasingly bike-friendly, Glasgow has networks of off-road cycle paths. The city has a public bike-rental operation run by nextbike; ranks of blue cycles at over 30 stations around the city are available for rent. You provide a credit card number and a £10 deposit on the smartphone app, over the phone, or on the on-bike computer, and give the cycle number. You'll be given the number for the combination lock and off you go. It's a great way to see the city, and you can return the bike at any station. Bikes cost £1 per 30 minutes up to 5 hours or £10 for 5–24 hours. The Glasgow Cycle Map available at information centers provides comprehensive route information, or see ⊕ www.glasgow.gov.uk/cycling. Companies like Glasgow Bike Tours also offer tours of the city on bike.

BIKE CONTACTS Glasgow Bike Tours. ☎ 7786/683445 ⊕ www.glasgowbike-tours.co.uk. **nextbike.** ☎ 0208/166–9851 ⊕ www.nextbike.co.uk.

BUS

The main intercity operators are National Express, Scottish Citylink, and Megabus, which serve numerous towns and cities in Scotland, Wales, and England, including London and Edinburgh. Glasgow's bus station is on Buchanan Street, not far from Queen Street station.

When traveling from the City Centre to either the West End or the South Side, it's easy to use the city's integrated network of buses, subways, and trains. Service is reliable and connections are convenient from buses to trains and the subway. Many buses require exact fare, which is usually around £1.75.

Traveline Scotland provides information on schedules, fares, and route planning, as does the Strathclyde Passenger Transport Travel Centre, which has an information center.

BUS CONTACTS Buchanan Street Bus Station. ✉ Killermont St., City Centre ☎ 0141/333–3708 ⊕ www.spt.co.uk Ⓜ Buchanan St. **Megabus.** ☎ 0141/352–4444 ⊕ uk.megabus.com. **National Express.** ☎ 0871/781–8181 ⊕ www.nationalexpress.com. **Scottish Citylink.** ☎ 0871/266–3333 ⊕ www.citylink.co.uk. **Traveline Scotland.** ☎ 0871/200–2233 ⊕ www.travelinescotland.com.

CAR

If you're driving to Glasgow from England and the south of Scotland, you'll approach the city via the M6, M74, and A74. From Edinburgh, the M8 leads to the City Centre. From the north, the A82 from Fort William and the A82/M80 from Stirling join the M8 in the City Centre.

You don't need a car in Glasgow, and you are probably better off without one. In the City Centre meters are expensive, running about £2.40 per hour during the day. In the West End they cost 80 pence per hour. Don't park illegally, as fines are upward of £30. Multistory garages are open 24 hours a day at Anderston Centre, George Street, Waterloo Place, Mitchell Street, Cambridge Street, and Concert Square. Rates run between £1 and £2 per hour. More convenient are the park-and-ride operations at some subway stations (Kelvinbridge, Bridge Street, and Shields Road).

SUBWAY

Glasgow's small subway system—it has 15 stations—is useful for reaching all the City Centre and West End attractions. Stations are signposted by a prominent letter "S." You can choose between a flat fare (£1.55) for one trip and a all-day pass (£4.20) that can be used after 9 am on weekdays and all day on weekends. A Smart Card, which you can get free online or at stations for £3, will give you reduced fares. The distance between many central stops is no more than a 10-minute walk. More information is available from Strathclyde Passenger Transport Travel Centre or its website, including transportation maps.

TAXI

Taxis are a fast and cost-effective way to get around. You'll find metered taxis (usually black and of the London sedan type) at stands all over the City Centre. Most have radio dispatch. Some have also been adapted to take wheelchairs. You can hail a cab on the street if its "for hire" sign is illuminated. A typical ride from the City Centre to the West End or the South Side costs around £7. Uber is also available in Glasgow.

TAXI CONTACT Glasgow Taxis.
☏ *0141/429–7070* ⊕ *www.glasgowtaxis. co.uk.*

TRAIN

Glasgow has two main rail stations: Central and Queen Street. Central serves Virgin trains from London's Euston station (five hours). Trains for Ayr and to the south of Glasgow also depart from Central. East Coast trains run from London's Kings Cross (via Edinburgh) to Glasgow's Queen Street station. For details, contact National Rail. All routes heading north from Glasgow depart from Queen Street.

A regular bus service links the Queen Street and Central stations (although you can easily walk if you aren't too encumbered with bags). Queen Street is near the Buchanan Street subway station, and Central is close to St. Enoch. Taxis are available at both stations.

The Glasgow area has an extensive network of suburban railway services. Locals still call them the Blue Trains, even though most are now painted maroon and cream. For more information and a free map, contact the Strathclyde Passenger Transport Travel Centre or National Rail.

TRAIN CONTACTS National Rail.
☏ *08457/484950* ⊕ *www.nationalrail. co.uk.* **Trainline.** ⊕ *www.thetrainline.com.*

Restaurants

Glasgow's vibrant restaurant culture is constantly renewing itself. More recently, the city has responded enthusiastically to the small-plate and sharing-platter trends, but there are still plenty of fine-dining options on the one hand, and steak houses and burger places on the other. The city continues to present the best that Scotland has to offer: grass-fed beef, free-range chicken, wild seafood, venison, duck, and goose, not to mention superb street food and plenty of vegan and vegetarian options.

The growing emphasis on ethical food production is reflected on menus that increasingly provide detailed information about the source of their ingredients. Around the city, an explosion of coffee shops offer artisanal macchiatos and flat whites. And brunch is becoming an increasingly popular option, with many high-end and casual restaurants offering short but assured brunch selections.

You can eat your way around the world in Glasgow. A new generation of Italian restaurants serves updated versions of classic Italian dishes. Chinese, Indian, and Pakistani foods, longtime favorites, are now more varied and sophisticated, and Thai, Japanese, and Korean restaurants have become popular. Spanish-style tapas are now quite common, and the small-plate trend has extended to every kind of restaurant. Seafood restaurants have moved well beyond the fish-and-chips wrapped in newspaper that were always a Glasgow staple, as langoustines, scallops, and monkfish appear on menus with ever more unusual accompaniments. And Glasgow has an especially good reputation for its vegan and vegetarian restaurants.

Eating in Glasgow can be casual or lavish. For inexpensive dining, consider the benefit of lunch or pretheater set menus. Beer and spirits cost much the same as they would in a bar, but wine is relatively expensive in restaurants. Increasing numbers of pubs offer food, but their kitchens usually close early.

Some restaurants allow you to bring your own bottle of wine, charging just a small corkage fee. It's worth the effort.

Hotels

Glasgow has a whole range of hotel options, from revamped grand hotels to basic budget options to stylish boutique properties. Glasgow's City Centre never sleeps, so downtown hotels may be noisier than those in the leafy and genteel West End. Downtown hotels are within walking distance of all the main sights, while West End lodgings are more convenient for museums and art galleries.

Although big hotels are spread out all around the city, B&Bs are definitely a more popular, personal, and cheaper option. For country-house luxury you should look beyond the city—try Mar Hall, near Paisley. Regardless of the neighborhood, hotels are about the same in price. Some B&Bs as well as the smaller properties may also offer discounts for longer stays. Make your reservations in advance, especially when there's a big concert, sporting event, or holiday (New Year's Eve is popular). Glasgow is busiest in summer, but it can fill up when something special is going on. If you arrive in town without a place to stay, contact the Glasgow Tourist Information Centre.

It is always worthwhile to inquire about special deals or rates, especially if you book online and in advance. Another money-saving option is to rent an apartment. B&Bs are the best-priced short-term lodging option, and you're sure to get breakfast.

Most smaller hotels and all guesthouses include breakfast in the room rate. Larger hotels usually charge extra for breakfast.

Also note that the most expensive hotels often exclude V.A.T. (Value-Added Tax, the sales tax) in the initial price quote but budget places include it.

Restaurant and hotel reviews have been shortened. For full information, visit Fodors.com. Restaurant prices are the average cost of a main course at dinner or, if dinner is not served, at lunch. Hotel prices are the lowest cost of a standard double room in high season, including 20% V.A.T.

WHAT IT COSTS in Pounds

	$	$$	$$$	$$$$
RESTAURANTS				
	under £15	£15–£19	£20–£25	over £25
HOTELS				
	under £125	£125–£200	£201–£300	over £300

Nightlife

Glasgow's music scene is vibrant and creative, and many successful artists began their music careers in its pubs and clubs. When it comes to nightlife, the City Centre and the West End are alive with pubs and clubs offering an eclectic mix of everything from bagpipes and salsa to punk and LGTBQ clubs.

But you haven't really had a night out in Glasgow until you've had one on the City Centre's Sauchiehall Street. There are plenty of great music bars to check out new artists, and the street itself is always busy, with lots of takeaway shops and nightclubs.

The monthly magazines *The List* and *The Skinny,* both available at newsstands and many cafés and arts centers throughout the city, are indispensable guides to Glasgow's bars and clubs.

Performing Arts

Because the Royal Scottish Conservatoire is in Glasgow, a pool of impressive young talent is always pressing the city's artistic boundaries in theater, music, and film. The city has a well-deserved reputation for its theater, with everything from cutting-edge plays to over-the-top pantomimes. The Tron Theatre is one of Europe's leading companies, often showcasing new talent and provocative productions. The Kings and the Theatre Royal play host to touring productions, including musicals from London's West End.

TICKETS
Scottish Music Centre
MUSIC | As well as a library, the Scottish Music Centre serves as the main ticket office for all music events at venues like the Royal Concert Hall and for annual events like the Glasgow Jazz Festival. ⊠ *Candleriggs, City Centre* ☎ *0141/353–8000* ⊕ *www.scottishmusiccentre.com* Ⓜ *Buchanan St.*

Ticketmaster
ARTS CENTERS | Tickets for theatrical performances can be purchased at theater box offices or online through Ticketmaster. ⊕ *www.ticketmaster.co.uk.*

Shopping

You'll find the mark of the fashion industry on Glasgow's hottest shopping streets. In the Merchant City, Ingram Street is lined on either side by high-fashion and designer outlets like Gucci and Ralph Lauren. Buchanan Street, in the City Centre, is home to many chains geared toward younger people, including Urban Outfitters, All Saints, and Zara, as well as malls like the elegant Princes Square and Buchanan Galleries. The adjacent Argyle Street Arcade is filled with jewelry stores. Antiques tend be found on and around West Regent Street in the City Centre. The West End has a number of small shops selling crafts, records, books, vintage clothing, and trendier fashions punctuated by innumerable cafés and restaurants. The university dominates the area around West End, and many shops there cater to students.

Tours

BOAT TOURS
Both Sweeney's and Cruise Loch Lomond offer a range of tours. For cruises along the River Clyde, contact Glasgow Tourist Information Centre for details.

Cruise Loch Lomond
BOAT TOURS | Based in Tarbet on Loch Lomond's western shore, this company offers tours that include the picturesque village of Luss to the west and journeys towards the eastern shore at Inversnaid and Balmaha, sailing around the island of Inchcailloch. ☎ *1301/702356* ⊕ *www.cruiselochlomond.co.uk* ⌦ *From £13.*

Sweeney's Cruise Co. Loch Lomond
BOAT TOURS | This company offers a range of cruises on Loch Lomond, departing from Balloch Pier at the southern end of the loch. Tours sail toward the two main islands, Inchmurrin and Inchcailloch, with views of Ben Lomond. ☎ *1389/752376* ⊕ *www.sweeneyscruiseco.com* ⌦ *From £12.*

BUS TOURS
The Glasgow Tourist Information Centre can give information about city tours and about longer tours northward to the Highlands and islands.

City Sightseeing
BUS TOURS | Daily hop-on, hop-off bus tours of Glasgow in open-topped double-decker buses are offered by City Sightseeing. The full tour lasts just under two hours, with an English-speaking guide aboard and a multilingual commentary. Tours begin at George Square. ⊠ *City Centre* ☎ *0141/204–0444* ⊕ *www.citysightseeingglasgow.co.uk* ⌦ *From £16.*

Rabbie's

BUS TOURS | Choose from a range of well-regarded one-, two-, and three-day minibus tours with guides to Loch Lomond, Loch Ness, Stirling, and the Highlands. There is also a one-day *Outlander* tour from Glasgow. Glasgow-based tours depart from George Street beside the City Chambers, near George Square. ☎ *0131/226–3133* ⊕ *www.rabbies.com.*

PRIVATE GUIDES
Glasgow Taxis

PRIVATE GUIDES | Few people know the city better than taxi drivers. Glasgow Taxis will organize a guided Mackintosh tour around Glasgow, a Burns tour to Ayrshire, or a trip to Loch Lomond, including pickup and drop-off at your place of choice. These black cabs carry up to five passengers. ✉ *City Centre* ☎ *0141/429–7070* ⊕ *www.glasgowtaxis.co.uk* 🚖 *From £45 per taxi.*

Little's Chauffeur Drive

PRIVATE GUIDES | You can arrange personally tailored car-and-driver tours, both locally and throughout Scotland. ☎ *0141/883–2111* ⊕ *www.littles.co.uk.*

Scottish Tourist Guides Association

PRIVATE GUIDES | The association provides qualified and accredited Blue Badge Guides with specific areas of expertise; guides also speak a range of languages. Tours start at half a day, and driver guides are available. Book online in advance. ✉ *Glasgow* ☎ *01786/451953* ⊕ *www.stga. co.uk* 🚖 *From £150 for half-day tours.*

WALKING TOURS

The Glasgow Tourist Information Centre can provide information on a whole range of self-guided walks around the city.

Glasgow Street Art Tour

WALKING TOURS | An hour-and-a-half walking tour takes you around Glasgow to view its diverse and often surprising street art. Tours occur daily at 2 pm. ✉ *81 Mitchell St.* ⊕ *www.walkingtoursin.com* 🚖 *From £12* Ⓜ *Buchanan Street.*

Visitor Information

The Glasgow Tourist Information Centre provides information about different types of tours and has an accommodations-booking service. Books, maps, and souvenirs are also available. There's a branch at Glasgow Airport as well. You can also find helpful information online at ⊕ *www.peoplemakeglasgow.com.*

CONTACT Visit Scotland icentre Glasgow. ✉ *156a/158 Buchanan Street, City Centre* ☎ *0141/566–4083* ⊕ *www.visitscotland. com/glasgow.*

Activities

You can't go far these days in Glasgow without seeing a runner or cyclist; numerous parks provide plenty of opportunities, and the nextbike (⊕ *www.next-bike.co.uk*) public bike-rental program has been a boon to cyclists. It rains a lot in Glasgow, but don't let the weather stop you. It doesn't deter the locals who play soccer, tennis, hike, bike, run, swim, and walk in the rain.

FOOTBALL
Celtic

SOCCER | This famous football club wears white-and-green hoops and plays in the East End of the city at Celtic Park, or Parkhead as it is known locally. Daily stadium tours must be booked ahead, and the Celtic Museum is also in the stadium. To get here, take a taxi from central Glasgow or a train from Central station to Dalmarnock or Bridgeton (10-minute walk from station). Match tickets start at £20. ✉ *Celtic Park, 18 Kerrydale St., East End* ☎ *0871/226–1888* ⊕ *www.celticfc.net* 🚖 *Stadium tours £15.*

Partick Thistle

SOCCER | Football in Glasgow isn't just blue or green, nor is it dominated by international players and big money. Partick Thistle Football Club, known as the Jags, wears red and yellow, and their football stadium is Firhill Park. Partick Thistle is also home to one of the most iconic mascots in world football: Kingsley the unibrowed sun. Designed by Turner prize-winning artist David Shrigley, Kingsley was unveiled in 2015; he's a loud yellow sun with harsh eyebrows, and truly a sight to behold. ⊠ *80 Firhill Rd., West End* ☎ *0141/579–1971* ⊕ *www.ptfc. co.uk* Ⓜ *St. George's Cross.*

Rangers
SOCCER | The Rangers wear blue and play at Ibrox, on the south side of the Clyde. Stadium tours are on Friday, Saturday, and Sunday; booking ahead is essential. ⊠ *150 Edmiston Dr., South Side* ☎ *0871/702–1972* ⊕ *www.rangers.co.uk* ⊠ *Stadium tours £8* Ⓜ *Ibrox.*

GOLF
Alexandra Park Golf Course
GOLF | Located on the grounds of a large city park, the Alexandra Park course is an inviting 9-hole course set in trendy Dennistoun. ⊠ *Alexandra Park, Alexandra Parade, Glasgow* ☎ *0141/276–0600* ⊕ *www.glasgowlife.sportsuite.co.uk/ directory/alexandra-golf-course* ⊠ *£7.50* Ⓜ *Alexandra Parade.*

Carrick at Loch Lomond
GOLF | Located on the banks of legendary Loch Lomond, this imaginatively designed course pays homage to the surrounding landscapes. It's truly a beautiful place to tee off, with a luxury clubhouse to relax in after a round. ⊠ *Alexandria* ☎ *0141/276–0810* ⊕ *www.glasgowlife. org.uk* ⊠ *£25–£80* ⚑ *18 holes, 7082 yards, par 71.*

Douglas Park Golf Club
GOLF | A charming parkland course at Milngavie, on the western outskirts of Glasgow, this attractive and varied course is set among lush rhododendron bushes and birch and pine trees. Each hole is highly individual, and though shorter than many courses it tests the careful, accurate golfer rather than the big swing. The Campsie Fells form a pleasant backdrop. ⊠ *Milngavie Rd., Hillfoot, Bearsden* ☎ *0141/942–0985* ⊕ *www. douglasparkgolfclub.co.uk* ⊠ *Apr.–Oct., £44 weekdays, £55 weekends; Nov.– Mar., £15 weekdays, £20 weekends* ⚑ *18 holes, 5981 yards, par 69.*

City Centre

Some of the city's most important historical buildings are found in the City Centre close to George Square, many of them converted to very different purposes now. Along the streets of this neighborhood are some of the best examples of the architectural confidence and vitality that so characterized the burgeoning Glasgow of the turn of the 20th century. There are also plenty of shops, trendy eateries, and pubs for all budgets and tastes.

GETTING HERE AND AROUND
Every form of public transportation can bring you here, from bus to train to subway. Head to George Square and walk from there.

⊙ Sights

Central Station
TRAIN/TRAIN STATION | It was the railways that first brought hordes of Victorian tourists to Scotland, and the great station hotels were places of luxury for those wealthier Victorian travelers; Central Station and its accompanying hotel are excellent examples of this. The Grand Central Hotel (once the Station Hotel) demonstrates how important this building was to the city. It remains a busy active train station from which to travel south to England or west to the Ayrshire coast and Prestwick Airport. The Champagne Bar in the Grand Central Hotel is a good vantage point for watching the station concourse and its comings and goings. The railway bridge across Argyll Street behind the station is known as the Highlandman's Umbrella because immigrants from the

north once gathered there to look for work in the early 20th century.

Tours of Central Station are an entertaining way to learn not only about the rich history of the station but also of Glasgow itself. Among one of the most popular tourist activities the city has to offer, even locals could learn a lot from the station's fantastic tour guides. ✉ *Gordon St., bounded by Gordon, Union, Argyle, Jamaica, Clyde, Oswald, and Hope Sts., City Centre* ☎ *03457/114141* ⊕ *www. glasgowcentraltours.co.uk* 🎟 *Tours £13.*

★ **City Chambers**

GOVERNMENT BUILDING | Dominating the east side of George Square, this exuberant expression of Victorian confidence, built by William Young in Italian Renaissance style, was opened by Queen Victoria in 1888. Among the interior's outstanding features are the entrance hall's vaulted ceiling, sustained by granite columns topped with marble, the marble-and-alabaster staircases, and Venetian mosaics. The enormous banqueting hall has murals illustrating Glasgow's history. Free guided tours lasting about an hour depart weekdays at 2:30pm; tours are very popular, so pick up a ticket beforehand from the reception desk. The building is closed to visitors during civic functions. ✉ *80 George Sq., City Centre* ☎ *0141/287–2000* ⊕ *www.glasgow.gov. uk* 🎟 *Free* ⊗ *Closed weekends* Ⓜ *Buchanan St.*

Compass Gallery

ART GALLERY | The gallery is something of an institution, having opened in 1969 to provide space for young and unknown artists—a role it continues. It shares space with Cyril Gerber Fine Arts, which specializes in British paintings from 1880 to the present. ✉ *178 W. Regent St., City Centre* ☎ *0141/221–6370* ⊕ *www.compassgallery.co.uk* 🎟 *Free* Ⓜ *Cowcaddens.*

Glasgow School of Art

COLLEGE | Scotland's only public art school's main claim to fame used to be the iconic architecture of its main building, designed by architect Charles Rennie Mackintosh; sadly, the building was badly damaged by fires in 2014 and 2018. Glaswegians mourned its destruction, but plans are in place to rebuild it, although officials have admitted that its restoration will be a long and complicated process. Fortunately, there are other wonderful Mackintosh buildings in and around the city. Stephen Holl's newer interpretation of the Reid Building, directly opposite the original, is a spectacular modern homage to it. ✉ *164 Renfrew St., City Centre* ☎ *0141/353–4526* ⊕ *www.gsa.ac.uk/ tours* Ⓜ *Cowcaddens.*

The Lighthouse

NOTABLE BUILDING | Charles Rennie Mackintosh designed these former offices of the *Glasgow Herald* newspaper, with the emblematic Mackintosh Tower, in 1893. On the third floor, the Mackintosh Interpretation Centre is a great place to start exploring this groundbreaking architect's work, which is illustrated in a glass wall with alcoves containing models of his buildings. From here you can climb the more than 130 steps up the tower and, once you have caught your breath, look out over Glasgow. (Alternatively, a viewing platform on the sixth floor can be reached by elevator.) Today the Lighthouse serves as Scotland's Centre for Architecture, Design and the City, celebrating all facets of architecture and design. There are a number of popular bars at the foot of the lighthouse, which offer a nice spot to take a break from sightseeing. ✉ *11 Mitchell La., City Centre* ☎ *0141/271–5365* ⊕ *www.thelighthouse.co.uk* 🎟 *Free* Ⓜ *St. Enoch.*

Glasgow City Chambers is most charming lit up at night over George Square.

Mackintosh at the Willow

NOTABLE BUILDING | One of Charles Rennie Mackintosh's most admired commissions was the tearooms he designed in 1903 for Miss Cranston, whose tearooms across the city were a magnet for Glasgow's middle class. She commissioned the young Mackintosh for several projects; the Willow Tea Rooms were among the best known. The tearooms have now been restored to their 1903 state, with furniture to match Makintosh's design. You'll find other beautiful examples of his work in the building, too, including the Billiard Room, the Board Room, and the aptly named Salon de Luxe. An interactive exhibition focuses on the great artist in his time and place, together with his contemporaries, including the Glasgow Girls. ⊠ *215-217 Sauchiehall St.* ☎ *141/204–1903* ⊕ *www.mackintoshatthewillow.com* Ⓜ *Buchanan Street.*

Regimental Museum of the Royal Highland Fusiliers

HISTORY MUSEUM | Exhibits of medals, badges, and uniforms relate the history of a famous, much-honored regiment and the men who served in it. ⊠ *518 Sauchiehall St., City Centre* ☎ *0141/332–5639* ⊕ *www.rhf.org.uk* ✉ *Free* ☉ *Closed weekends* Ⓜ *Cowcaddens.*

St. Vincent's Street Church

CHURCH | This 1859 church, the work of Alexander Thomson, stands high above the street. The building exemplifies his Greek Revival style, replete with Ionic columns, sphinxlike heads, and rich interior color. Owned by Glasgow City Council, it is currently used by the Free Church of Scotland. You can see the interior by attending a service Sunday at 11 am or 6 pm or by appointment. ⊠ *265 St. Vincent St., City Centre* ⊕ *www.glasgowcityfreechurch.org* ✉ *Free* ☉ *Closed Mon.–Sat. except by appointment* Ⓜ *Buchanan St.*

The streets of Glasgow are filled with terrace houses like these.

★ Tenement House

HISTORIC HOME | This ordinary first-floor apartment is anything but ordinary inside: it was occupied from 1937 to 1982 by Agnes Toward (and before that by her mother), both of whom seem never to have thrown anything away. Agnes was a dressmaker, and her legacy is this fascinating time capsule, painstakingly preserved with her everyday furniture and belongings. A small museum explores the life and times of its careful occupant. The red-sandstone building dates from 1892 and is in the Garnethill area near the Glasgow School of Art. ⊠ *145 Buccleuch St., City Centre* ☎ *0141/333–0183* ⊕ *www.nts.org.uk* ✉ *£8.50* ☾ *Closed Jan.–Jun.* Ⓜ *Cowcaddens.*

🍴 Restaurants

The City Centre has restaurants catering to the 9-to-5 crowd, meaning there are a lot of fine-dining establishments as well as good restaurants catching people as they leave work, drawing them in with pre-theater menus. Whatever type of food you're interested in, this neighborhood is sure to have something to satisfy you.

Anchor Line

$$$ | STEAKHOUSE | Occupying the former headquarters of the Anchor Line, whose ships sailed from Scotland to America, this bar and restaurant near George Square has been impressively refurbished to create the sense of fine dining aboard a luxury ocean liner. The menu reflects the voyage, too, including Scottish seafood and lamb, and a full range of steaks and their sauces to represent America. **Known for:** steak of all kinds; high-end cocktails; luxurious fine dining. Ⓢ *Average main: £20* ⊠ *12 St. Vincent Pl., City Centre* ☎ *0141/248–1434* ⊕ *www. theanchorline.co.uk* Ⓜ *Buchanan St.*

The Butterfly and the Pig

$ | BRITISH | Down an innocuous-looking flight of stairs, this intimate restaurant is the type of place young locals love: flickering candles, mix-and-match crockery, and inventive, inexpensive food that offers new twists on the familiar. The menu reads like a comedic narrative, with descriptions like "traditional fish-and-chips, battered to death" or "Supreme Commander chicken." Vegetarians are not as well catered to, but they can at least can try the popular portobello-mushroom burgers with extra-thick potato chips. **Known for:** tea shop upstairs; shabby-chic atmosphere; quirky takes on familiar dishes. $ *Average main: £14* ⊠ *153 Bath St., City Centre* ☎ *0141/221–7711* ⊕ *www.thebutterfly-andthepig.com* Ⓜ *Buchanan St.*

★ Chaophraya
$ | **THAI** | You can experience dining at its most sumptuous and elegant for a good price in the grand surroundings of what was the Glasgow Conservatoire, where today golden Buddhas sit comfortably beside busts of great composers. The delicate flavors of Thai cooking are at their finest here in the chef's wonderful signature Massaman lamb (and beef) curry, flavorsome Fisherman's Soup, and fusion dishes like scallops with black pudding. **Known for:** extensive menu of Thai classics; Massaman lamb curry; luxurious surroundings. $ *Average main: £14* ⊠ *The Town House, Nelson Mandela Pl., City Centre* ☎ *0141/332–0041* ⊕ *www.chaophraya.co.uk* Ⓜ *Buchanan St.*

Halloumi
$$ | **GREEK** | Greek cuisine was not well represented in Glasgow until Halloumi arrived to fill the gap. Its large windows onto the street invite you in to a simply decorated interior with white walls and wooden tables, where you will find a reassuringly familiar menu of small plates, or meze. **Known for:** good lunch deal; shared small plates of traditional Greek meze; excellent moussaka. $ *Average main: £17* ⊠ *161 Hope St., City Centre* ⚎ *Near Central station* ☎ *0141/204–1616* ⊕ *www.halloumiglasgow.co.uk* Ⓜ *Buchanan St.*

Las Iguanas
$$ | **SOUTH AMERICAN** | The bright interior of this restaurant, part of a popular chain, echoes the Latin American–themed menu in its vibrant colors and decoration. The extensive menu features items like Argentine steak, Brazilian *Xinxim* (a type of curry stew), and classics like tapas and burritos. **Known for:** equally colorful decor; Xinxim, a stew of chicken and crayfish in a coconut sauce; colorful cocktails. $ *Average main: £15* ⊠ *15–20 W. Nile St., City Centre* ☎ *0141/248–5705* ⊕ *www.iguanas.co.uk* Ⓜ *Buchanan St.*

Loon Fung
$$ | **CANTONESE** | **FAMILY** | The friendly staff at this huge, popular Cantonese eatery guide you through the dishes here, including barbecued duck, deep-fried wontons with prawns, and more challenging dishes like pork with jellyfish or king prawn with salted egg. On most days you will see local Chinese families seated at the huge round tables enjoying the dim sum for which the restaurant is rightly famous. **Known for:** lively family atmosphere; Glasgow's best dim sum; authentic Cantonese cuisine. $ *Average main: £16* ⊠ *417–419 Sauchiehall St., City Centre* ☎ *0141/332–1240* ⊕ *www.loonfungglasgow.com/* Ⓜ *Cowcaddens.*

★ Mackintosh at the Willow
$ | **BRITISH** | Miss Cranston's Willow Tea Rooms were the ultimate place to be seen in Glasgow in 1903, not only for the tasty tea but for the beautiful art nouveau decor and furniture designed by a young architect by the name of Charles Rennie Mackintosh. The original tearooms have now been fully restored here, and you can lunch on traditional Scottish cuisine or take an elegant high tea in the exquisite surroundings of the Salon de Luxe. **Known for:** great steak pie and haggis; traditional high tea in a stunning location; historic Mackintosh furniture. $ *Average main: £12* ⊠ *215–217 Sauchiehall St., City Centre* ☎ *0141/204–1903* ⊕ *www.mackintoshatthewillow.com* ⊘ *No dinner* Ⓜ *Buchanan St.*

Sights ▼

1 Central Station **D5**
2 City Chambers **F5**
3 Compass Gallery **C3**
4 Gallery of
   Modern Art **E5**
5 George Square **F4**
6 Glasgow Cathedral **I4**
7 Glasgow School of Art . **C2**
8 The Lighthouse **E5**
9 Mackintosh at the
   Willow **C3**
10 Necropolis **J4**
11 Provand's Lordship **I4**
12 Regimental Museum
   of the Royal Highland
   Fusiliers **A2**
13 St. Mungo Museum of
   Religious Life and Art.... **I4**
14 St. Vincent's
   Street Church **C5**
15 Tenement House **B2**

Restaurants ▼

1 Anchor Line **E4**
2 Babbity Bowster **G6**
3 The Butterfly and
   the Pig **C3**
4 Café Gandolfi **G6**
5 Chaophraya **E4**
6 Corinthian Club **F5**
7 Halloumi **D4**
8 Kool Ba **G5**
9 Las Iguanas **E5**
10 Loon Fung **B2**
11 Mackintosh
   at the Willow **C3**
12 Opium **D4**

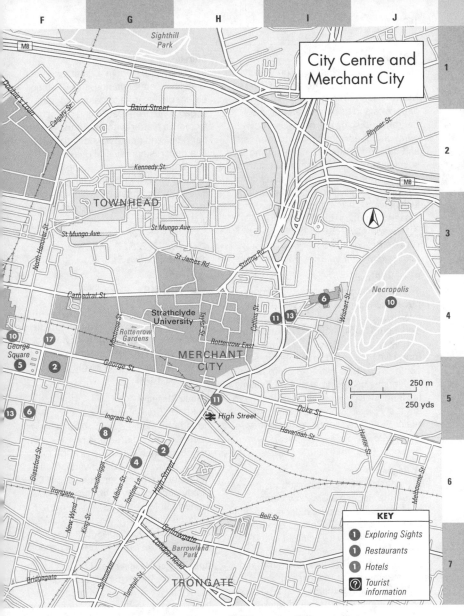

City Centre and Merchant City

KEY

- Exploring Sights
- Restaurants
- Hotels
- Tourist information

0 — 250 m
0 — 250 yds

★ Opium

$$ | **ASIAN** | This eatery has completely rethought Asian cuisine, taking Chinese, Malaysian, and Thai cooking in new directions and using sauces that are fragrant and spicy but never overpowering. Subdued lighting, neutral tones, and dark wood create a calm setting for specialties including superb dim sum and crisp wontons filled with delicious combinations of crab, shrimp, and chicken. **Known for:** excellent dim sum; creative Asian-fusion food; great cocktails. [$] *Average main: £17* ✉ *191 Hope St., City Centre* ☎ *0141/332–6668* 🌐 *www.opiumrestaurant.co.uk* [M] *Buchanan St.*

Paesano Pizza

$ | **PIZZA** | This casual and unassuming pizza place holds a special place in the hearts of Glaswegians and visitors alike. Serving up Naples-style pizzas with large bubbly crusts, the short but confident menu (you choose from a rotating selection of 8 pizzas) is extremely affordable, with prices beginning at just £7. **Known for:** long lines on weekend nights; cheap but tasty pizzas; trendy locals. [$] *Average main: £8* ✉ *94 Miller St., City Centre* ☎ *0141/258-5565* 🌐 *www.paesanopizza.co.uk.*

★ Rogano

$$ | **MODERN EUROPEAN** | Two things have made the Rogano a Glasgow institution: its beautiful art deco decor, which echoes the luxury Clyde-built oceanliners of the thirties, and its seafood menu, which has held its own despite the competition of the city's new generation of restaurants. The main restaurant is a formal affair, but the downstairs Café Rogano is more intimate and relaxed, serving oysters and a signature fish soup among many other options. **Known for:** exquisite cocktails; gorgeous art deco bar; excellent old-school seafood options, including famed fish soup. [$] *Average main: £19* ✉ *11 Exchange Pl., City Centre* ☎ *0141/248–4055* 🌐 *www.roganoglasgow.com* [M] *Buchanan St.*

Stereo

$ | **VEGETARIAN** | Down a quiet lane near Glasgow Central station, this ultracool eatery dishes up a fantastic range of vegan food, from paella and gnocchi to a colorful platter with hummus, red-pepper pâté, and home-baked flatbread. The decor is homey and relaxed, and someone always seems to be nearby reading or writing. **Known for:** perfect side dish of roasted sweet potato chips; imaginative vegan food; hipster vibe with good art and music. [$] *Average main: £10* ✉ *20–28 Renfield La., City Centre* ☎ *0141/222–2254* 🌐 *www.stereocafebar.com* [M] *Buchanan St.*

Hotels

Here you'll be close to everything—the main sights, shops, theaters, restaurants, and bars—the pulse of the city. You don't have to worry about transportation in the center of town, but it can get noisy on weekend nights.

ABode Glasgow

$ | **HOTEL** | Stylish and modern, this boutique hotel in an Edwardian building was once the grand home of a prime minister, hence the high ceilings and huge windows. **Pros:** echoes of Edwardian grandeur; stylish rooms; great location. **Cons:** pricey parking; some front rooms noisy; limited public areas. [$] *Rooms from: £70* ✉ *129 Bath St., City Centre* ☎ *0141/221–6789* 🌐 *www.abodeglasgow.co.uk* 🛏 *59 rooms* 🍴 *Free Breakfast* [M] *Buchanan St.*

Apex City of Glasgow Hotel

$$$ | **HOTEL** | The extraordinary floor-to-ceiling windows here set this modern chain hotel apart, providing a panoramic view over Glasgow and beyond from the upper floors (sixth and seventh). **Pros:** awesome city views from higher floors; bright rooms; central location. **Cons:** corridors quite cramped; no parking facility and nearby lot closes at night; lower-floor rooms overlook other buildings. [$] *Rooms from: £239* ✉ *110 Bath St., City Centre*

☎ 0141/375–3333 🌐 *www.apexhotels.co.uk* 🛏 *106 rooms* 🍴 *Free Breakfast* [M] *Buchanan St.*

Carlton George

$$ | **HOTEL** | A narrow revolving doorway, a step back from busy West George Street, creates the illusion of a secret passageway leading into this lavish boutique hotel. **Pros:** great value; near City Centre attractions and beside Queen Street station; nice resturant with stunning views. **Cons:** parking at nearby paid car park; area sometimes noisy at night; entrance very small and often crowded. [$] *Rooms from: £138* ✉ *44 W. George St., City Centre* ☎ *0141/353–6373* 🌐 *www.carlton.nl/george* 🛏 *64 rooms* 🍴 *Free Breakfast* [M] *Buchanan St.*

★ citizenM Glasgow

$$ | **HOTEL** | There's no lobby at the futuristic citizenM—no reception area at all, because you can only book online—but there are chic "living spaces" with ultramodern furnishings where guests can congregate and streamlined rooms that are smartly designed. **Pros:** free Wi-Fi; wonderful and creative design; central location. **Cons:** the absence of reception staff can be confusing; breakfast costs more if you don't book ahead; not for the claustrophobic. [$] *Rooms from: £139* ✉ *60 Renfrew St., corner of Hope St., City Centre* ☎ *01782/488–3490* 🌐 *www.citizenm.com* 🛏 *198 rooms* 🍴 *No Meals* [M] *Buchanan St.*

★ Dakota Deluxe Glasgow

$$$ | **HOTEL** | At this extremely stylish addition to Glasgow's hotel scene, the textured, neutral decor creates a restful, subdued atmosphere. **Pros:** lovely bathrooms; relaxing public rooms; spacious, well-appointed bedrooms. **Cons:** slightly corporate feel; not right in the middle of the action; unexciting views from hotel. [$] *Rooms from: £290* ✉ *179 W. Regent St., City Centre* ☎ *0141/404–3680* 🌐 *glasgow.dakotahotels.co.uk* 🛏 *83 rooms* 🍴 *Free Breakfast* [M] *Cowcaddens.*

★ voco Grand Central Hotel

$$ | **HOTEL** | One of Europe's great Victorian hotels built when train travel was a luxury, this hotel located within Glasgow's historic train station deserves its name, as everything about it, from the magnificent marble-floor Champagne bar to the ballroom fully restored to its original glory, is grand. **Pros:** great Champagne bar for lingering; a real air of luxury; generally spacious rooms. **Cons:** some small rooms; parking a couple of blocks away; occasional noise from street. [$] *Rooms from: £175* ✉ *99 Gordon St., City Centre* ☎ *0141/240–3700* 🌐 *www.ihg.com/voco/hotels/us/en/glasgow/glags/hoteldetail* 🛏 *233 rooms* 🍴 *Free Breakfast* [M] *Buchanan St.*

Grasshoppers Hotel Glasgow

$ | **HOTEL** | Not visible from the street, this hotel occupies a sixth floor above Central station; guest rooms are on the small side but have expansive windows overlooking the glass roof of the station on one side and across the rooftops of Glasgow on the other. **Pros:** quiet despite its central location; bright and clean; complimentary cakes and ice cream. **Cons:** no parking at hotel; rooms are quite small; no lobby. [$] *Rooms from: £118* ✉ *87 Union St., City Centre* ✥ *Door marked "Caledonian Chambers" leads to elevator* ☎ *0141/222–2666* 🌐 *www.grasshoppersglasgow.com* 🛏 *30 rooms* 🍴 *Free Breakfast* [M] *St. Enoch.*

Hotel Indigo Glasgow

$$ | **HOTEL** | In the center of the city, the fashionable Indigo is awash with bold colors and modern designs that emphasize comfort and calm. **Pros:** good on-site dining; well-designed rooms; vivid colors, patterns, and lighting. **Cons:** restaurant has an anonymous, corporate feel; only showers in the bathrooms; narrow corridors. [$] *Rooms from: £145* ✉ *75 Waterloo St., City Centre* ☎ *0141/226–7700* 🌐 *www.hinglasgow.co.uk* 🛏 *94 rooms* 🍴 *No Meals* [M] *St. Enoch.*

★ **Kimpton Blythswood Square**

$$ | HOTEL | History and luxury come together at this smart conversion of the former headquarters of the Royal Automobile Club of Scotland, which occupies a classical building on peaceful Blythswood Square. **Pros:** great spa, restaurant, and bar; airy and luxurious; glorious bathrooms. **Cons:** the square itself is in need of some care and attention; some street noise; room lighting may be too dim for some. $ Rooms from: £185 ✉ 11 Blythswood Sq., City Centre ☎ 0141/248–8888 ⊕ www.kimptonblythswoodsquare.com ⇆ 113 rooms ⦿ Free Breakfast Ⓜ Cowcaddens.

Malmaison Glasgow

$$ | HOTEL | Housed in a converted church, this modern boutique hotel prides itself on personal service and outstanding amenities like plasma televisions and high-end stereo systems. **Pros:** five-minute walk to Sauchiehall Street; stunning lobby; attention to detail. **Cons:** no on-site parking; dark hallways; bland views. $ Rooms from: £129 ✉ 278 W. George St., City Centre ☎ 0141/572–1000 ⊕ www.malmaison.com ⇆ 72 rooms ⦿ Free Breakfast Ⓜ Cowcaddens.

Premier Inn Glasgow City Centre Buchanan Galleries

$ | HOTEL | The City Centre branch of this popular budget hotel chain is located on Renfield Street, and so it's worth seeking out for its winning location just around the corner from the pedestrian precinct in Sauchiehall Street. **Pros:** modern rooms; great location; bargain rates. **Cons:** no parking facilities; entrance easily missed at street level; some front rooms a bit noisy. $ Rooms from: £90 ✉ Buchanan Galleries, 141 W. Nile St., City Centre ☎ 0871/527–9360 ⊕ www.premierinn.com ⇆ 220 rooms ⦿ No Meals Ⓜ Buchanan St.

Radisson Blu Hotel, Glasgow

$ | HOTEL | You can't miss this eye-catching edifice behind Central station: its glass facade makes the interior, particularly the lounge, seem as though it were part of the street. **Pros:** free Wi-Fi and other amenities; charming kilted doorman; access to gym and pool. **Cons:** no on-site parking; most rooms have poor views; neighborhood is very busy. $ Rooms from: £99 ✉ 301 Argyle St., City Centre ☎ 0141/204–3333 ⊕ www.radissonblu.com ⇆ 250 rooms ⦿ Free Breakfast Ⓜ St. Enoch.

Victorian House

$ | B&B/INN | This unpretentious and affordable hotel sits on a quiet residential area above Sauchiehall Street but still close to Glasgow's Chinatown on one side and the arty streets of Garnethill on the other. **Pros:** close to bars and restaurants; appealing and quiet location; basement rooms very spacious. **Cons:** on-street parking sometimes difficult to find; no elevator; not all rooms are en suite. $ Rooms from: £70 ✉ 212 Renfrew St., City Centre ☎ 0141/332–0129 ⊕ www.thevictorian.co.uk ⇆ 56 rooms ⦿ Free Breakfast Ⓜ Cowcaddens.

YOTEL Glasgow

$ | HOTEL | This shiny and fashionable hotel is the latest big arrival on the Glasgow hotel scene. **Pros:** central location; amazing views; cool decor and public areas (including neon bowling alley). **Cons:** small rooms; restaurant and bar can get quite crowded and book up early; not in a quiet location. $ Rooms from: £89 ✉ 260 Argyle St., City Centre ☎ 0141/428–4490 ⊕ www.yotel.com/en/hotels/yotel-glasgow ⇆ 257 rooms ⦿ Free Breakfast.

ⓨ Nightlife

BARS AND PUBS

Bloc+

BARS | Step behind a curious version of the Iron Curtain where burgers and Tex-Mex diner food mix with an eclectic musical mash of DJs and live rock and folk bands. ✉ *117 Bath St., City Centre* ☎ *0141/574–6066* ⊕ *www.bloc.ru* Ⓜ *Cowcaddens.*

★ The Horseshoe Bar

BARS | This iconic Glasgow boozer is tucked away on a hidden alleyway not far from Central Station. The wood-paneled traditional pub is a lively and upbeat Glasgow institution. If you're feeling brave, head upstairs and participate in their legendary public karaoke on the weekends. ✉ *17-19 Drury St., City Centre* ☎ *0141/248–6368* ⊕ *www.thehorseshoe-barglasgow.co.uk.*

King Tut's Wah Wah Hut

LIVE MUSIC | An intimate venue showcasing up-and-coming independent bands since 1990, King Tut's Wah Wah Hut was the venue where the U.K. britpop band Oasis was discovered. Indeed, the list of those who have played here reads like a catalog of indie music history. It's a favorite with students and hosts live music most nights, but the cozy and traditional pub setting draws people of all ages, and the refurbished bar is a pleasant and comfortable place for a drink or a meal. ✉ *227A St. Vincent St., City Centre* ☎ *0141/221–5279* ⊕ *www.kingtuts.co.uk* Ⓜ *Cowcaddens.*

La Cheetah

LIVE MUSIC | A tiny club in the basement of Max's Bar, La Cheetah is popular precisely because it's small and intimate. It plays a variety of dance and electronic music, with some surprising well-known guests who just like the atmosphere. ✉ *73 Queen St., City Centre* ☎ *0141/221–1379* ⊕ *www.maxsbar. co.uk* Ⓜ *Buchanan St.*

Nice N Sleazy

BARS | A classic dive bar on Sauchiehall Street, drinks here are reasonably priced, and their tiny downstairs gig space has played host to many terrific bands and DJs over the years. It's popular with an eclectic crowd of musicians and artists, so if you head in after attending a show, there's a high chance the band you saw that night will be drinking there too. ✉ *421 Sauchiehall St., City Centre* ☎ *0414/333–0900* ⊕ *www.nicensleazy.com.*

The Pot Still

BARS | This traditional pub has the biggest whisky library in the city, with over 700 libations to choose from. It's popular with locals and tourists alike, and a must for whisky fans. ✉ *154 Hope St., City Centre* ☎ *0141/333–0980* ⊕ *www.thepotstill. co.uk.*

★ Sloans

PUBS | One of Glasgow's oldest and most iconic pubs, the wood-paneled Sloans is always lively and welcoming; it serves traditional pub food like fish-and-chips throughout the day. The upstairs ballroom is a magnificent mirrored affair, and on the floor above there's dancing and a *ceilidh*—traditional music and dancing— every Friday night (booking essential). The pub has a good selection of beers and spirits, and the outdoor area is always lively when the weather cooperates. ✉ *108 Argyle St., City Centre* ⊹ *Entrance during the day is through the Argyll Arcade, otherwise from a nearby alley off Argyle St. when the Argyll Arcade is closed.* ☎ *0141/221–8886* ⊕ *www.sloans-glasgow.com* Ⓜ *St. Enoch.*

The Spiritualist

COCKTAIL LOUNGES | This high-end luxury cocktail bar is hidden away on a surprisingly peaceful alley just minutes from George Square. Creative mixologists can make the drink of your dreams. ✉ *62 Miller St., City Centre* ☎ *0141/248–4165* ⊕ *www.thespiritualistglasgow.com.*

CLUBS

Delmonicas

DANCE CLUBS | Known as "Dels" by locals, this is a lively and upbeat LGBTQ bar and club in the heart of the city's gay quarter. Karaoke, DJs, quiz nights, and an always busy dance floor set the tone for a place where the drinks are cheap and the crowd is warm and friendly. ⊠ *68 Virginia St., Merchant City* ⊕ *www.delmonicas. co.uk.*

Stereo

DANCE CLUBS | The small downstairs music venue gets crowded quickly when bands play Sunday to Thursday night, but that only adds to the electric atmosphere at Stereo. There's also a hopping nightclub where DJs spin on Friday and Saturday nights until the wee hours of the morning. Upstairs, the café-bar serves tasty vegan food and organic drinks. ⊠ *20–28 Renfield La., City Centre* ☎ *0141/222–2254* ⊕ *www.stereocafebar. com* Ⓜ *Buchanan St.*

Sub Club

DANCE CLUBS | This atmospheric underground venue has staged cutting-edge music events since its jazz club days in the '50s. Legendary favorites like Saturday's SubCulture (House) and Sunday's Optimo (a truly eclectic mix for musical hedonists) pack in friendly and sweaty crowds on its large dance floor. Open since the 1980s as a nightclub, it is the longest running underground dance club in the world. ⊠ *22 Jamaica St., City Centre* ☎ *0141/248–4600* ⊕ *www.subclub. co.uk* Ⓜ *St. Enoch.*

Swing

LIVE MUSIC | Hidden behind a narrow doorway on Hope Street, Swing comes as a surprise. It is an art deco bar that has survived the city's changes, and jazz bands play here three times a week. Blues and soul are heard other nights. Cocktails enhance the atmosphere, so go ahead and ask for a Manhattan. ⊠ *183A Hope St., City Centre* ☎ *0141/332–2147* ⊕ *www.swingltd.co.uk* Ⓜ *Buchanan St.*

🎭 Performing Arts

Centre for Contemporary Arts

ARTS CENTERS | The center hosts regular major art exhibitions and other arts events and regularly screens classic, independent, and children's films. It also has a restaurant, the Saramago, which serves vegan dishes; an upstairs bar; and a very good small independent bookshop. ⊠ *350 Sauchiehall St., City Centre* ☎ *0141/352–4900* ⊕ *www.cca-glasgow. com* Ⓜ *Cowcaddens.*

Cineworld Glasgow

FILM | An 18-screen facility, this is Glasgow's busiest movie multiplex. A glass-walled elevator whisks you to the top of the 170-foot-tall building, which is also the world's tallest cinema. ■ **TIP→ Book your tickets online and collect them from machines at the venue to avoid the often very long queues.** ⊠ *7 Renfrew St., City Centre* ☎ *0871/200–2000* ⊕ *www.cineworld.co.uk* Ⓜ *Cowcaddens.*

★ Glasgow Film Theatre

FILM | An independent operation, the three-screen Glasgow Film Theatre shows the best new releases, documentaries, and classic films. It has several programs for young people and hosts the annual Glasgow Film Festival. ⊠ *12 Rose St., City Centre* ☎ *0141/332–6535* ⊕ *www.glasgowfilm.org* Ⓜ *Cowcaddens.*

Glasgow Royal Concert Hall

CONCERTS | The 2,500-seat Glasgow Royal Concert Hall is the venue for a wide range of concerts, from classical to pop. It also hosts the very popular late-night club during the annual Celtic Connections music festival. ⊠ *2 Sauchiehall St., City Centre* ☎ *0141/353–8000* ⊕ *www.glasgowconcerthalls.com* Ⓜ *Buchanan St.*

King's Theatre

THEATER | Dramas, variety shows, and musicals are staged at the King's Theatre, open since 1904. It hosts many touring productions of musicals from London's West End. Check ticket websites to see what's on. ✉ *297 Bath St., City Centre* ☎ *0141/240–1111* ⊕ *www.atgtickets.com* Ⓜ *Cowcaddens.*

Pavilion Theatre

THEATER | FAMILY | This traditional variety theater hosts family-friendly entertainment, some plays, the occasional hypnotist, and concerts, most with a very strong Glasgow flavor. ✉ *121 Renfield St., City Centre* ☎ *0141/332–1846* ⊕ *www.paviliontheatre.co.uk* Ⓜ *Cowcaddens.*

Royal Scottish Conservatoire

CONCERTS | An important venue for music and drama, the Royal Scottish Conservatoire hosts regular concerts by well-known performers, as well as by its own students. The lunchtime concert series is popular. ✉ *100 Renfrew St., City Centre* ☎ *0141/332–4101* ⊕ *www.rcs.ac.uk* Ⓜ *Cowcaddens.*

Theatre Royal

OPERA | Glasgow is home to the Scottish Opera and Scottish Ballet and plays hosts to a range of events throughout the year by visiting dance and theater companies. ✉ *282 Hope St., City Centre* ☎ *844/871–7647* ⊕ *www.atgtickets.com* Ⓜ *Cowcaddens.*

🛍 Shopping

ARCADES AND SHOPPING CENTERS

Argyll Arcade

JEWELRY & WATCHES | An interesting diversion off Argyle Street is the covered Argyll Arcade, the region's largest collection of jewelers under one roof. The L-shaped edifice, built in 1827, houses several locally based jewelers and a few shops specializing in antique jewelry, as well as the famed Sloans pub. ✉ *Buchanan St., City Centre* ⊕ *www.argyll-arcade.com* Ⓜ *St. Enoch.*

Buchanan Galleries

SHOPPING CENTER | Next to the Glasgow Royal Concert Hall, Buchanan Galleries houses the John Lewis department store and more than 80 high-quality shops. ✉ *220 Buchanan St., City Centre* ☎ *0141/333–9898* ⊕ *www.buchanangalleries.co.uk* Ⓜ *Buchanan St.*

★ Princes Square

SHOPPING CENTER | The city's best shopping center is the art nouveau Princes Square, a lovely space filled with impressive shops and pleasant cafés and restaurants. A stunning glass dome was fitted over the original building, which dates back to 1841. ✉ *48 Buchanan St., City Centre* ☎ *0141/221–0324* ⊕ *www.princessquare.co.uk* Ⓜ *St. Enoch.*

St. Enoch's Shopping Centre

SHOPPING CENTER | Eye-catching if not especially pleasing, this modern glass building resembles an overgrown greenhouse. It has dozens of stores, including Hamley's toy store. ✉ *55 St. Enoch Sq., City Centre* ☎ *0141/204–3900* ⊕ *www.st-enoch.com* Ⓜ *St. Enoch.*

BOOKS, PAPER, AND MUSIC

Cass Art Glasgow

CRAFTS | One of the country's largest suppliers of art and craft materials operates this store near the Glasgow Gallery of Modern Art. There's plenty to inspire your creativity, and good choices for kids as well. ✉ *63–67 Queen St., City Centre* ☎ *0141/248–5899* ⊕ *www.cassart.co.uk* Ⓜ *Buchanan St.*

Monorail Music

MUSIC | For the latest on the city's ever-thriving music scene, try this independent record store located within a café-bar called Mono, that is also an occasional music venue. The shop specializes in indie music and has a large collection of vinyl with everything from rock to jazz. ✉ *12 Kings Ct., City Centre* ✛ *Close to the Tron Theatre* ☎ *0141/552–9458* ⊕ *www.monorailmusic.com* Ⓜ *St. Enoch.*

Paperchase

STATIONERY | For everything that stationery has to offer—cards, notebooks, books—Paperchase is the place. And there's a café where you can ponder which notebook you want to buy. ✉ 185–221 Buchanan St., City Centre ☎ 0141/353–3491 ⊕ www.paperchase. co.uk Ⓜ Buchanan St.

Waterstones

BOOKS | In an age of online sales, bookstores seem to be becoming scarcer. Waterstones remains the city's main bookshop, and it has an excellent selection throughout its four floors. There's also a good basement café. ✉ 153–57 Sauchiehall St., City Centre ☎ 0141/248–4814 ⊕ www.waterstones. com Ⓜ Buchanan St.

CLOTHING
Mr. Ben

MIXED CLOTHING | Here you'll find a large, funky selection of vintage and retro clothing for men and women. ✉ 6 King's Ct., City Centre ☎ 0141/553–1936 ⊕ mrbenretroclothing.com Ⓜ St. Enoch.

DEPARTMENT STORES
★ **House of Fraser**

DEPARTMENT STORE | A Glasgow institution, the House of Fraser stocks wares that reflect the city's material aspirations, including European designer clothing. There are also more locally produced articles, such as tweeds, tartans, glass, and ceramics. The magnificent interior is set off by a grand staircase rising to various floors and balconies. ✉ 21–45 Buchanan St., City Centre ☎ 0343/909–2025 ⊕ www.houseoffraser.co.uk Ⓜ St. Enoch.

John Lewis

DEPARTMENT STORE | This store is a favorite for its stylish mix of clothing, household items, electronics, and practically everything else. John Lewis claims to have "never been knowingly undersold" and prides itself on its customer service. It also has an elegant second-floor balcony café. ✉ Buchanan Galleries, 220 Buchanan St., City Centre ☎ 0141/353–6677 ⊕ www.johnlewis.com/glasgow Ⓜ Buchanan St.

Marks & Spencer

DEPARTMENT STORE | Selling sturdy, practical clothing and accessories at moderate prices, Marks & Spencer also offers gourmet foods and household goods. There's a second location at 172 Sauchiehall Street. ✉ 2–12 Argyle St., City Centre ☎ 0141/552–4546 ⊕ www. marksandspencer.com Ⓜ St. Enoch.

SCOTTISH SPECIALTIES
Hector Russell Kiltmakers

OTHER SPECIALTY STORE | Primarily for men, this shop specializes in Highlands outfits, wool, and cashmere clothing. ✉ 110 Buchanan St., City Centre ☎ 0141/221–0217 ⊕ www.hector-russell. com Ⓜ Buchanan St.

Slanj Kilts

OTHER SPECIALTY STORE | For kilts, trews, and all things tartan, this shop offers a nice variety of traditional Scottish clothing to rent and for sale. ✉ 49 Bath St., City Centre ☎ 0333/320–1977 ⊕ www. slanjkilts.com Ⓜ Buchanan St.

SHOPPING DISTRICTS
Argyle Street

NEIGHBORHOODS | On the often-crowded pedestrian area of Argyle Street you'll find some of the more popular and less expensive chains like Gap, Next, and Schuh as well as Primark and H&M. ✉ City Centre Ⓜ St. Enoch.

Buchanan Street

NEIGHBORHOODS | This pedestrian-only street has become increasingly upmarket, with Monsoon, Topshop, Burberry, Jaeger, Pretty Green, and All Saints as well as House of Fraser and other chain stores along its length. Always crowded with shoppers, it has also become a mecca for the growing community of buskers in Glasgow's streets, playing every kind of music. ✉ City Centre Ⓜ Buchanan St.

OUTDOOR GEAR

Tiso Glasgow Outdoor Experience

SPORTING GOODS | You'll find good-quality gear and outerwear at Tiso Glasgow Outdoor Experience, handy if you're planning some Highlands walks or just need protection from the weather. ⊠ *129 Buchanan St., City Centre* ☎ *0141/248–4877* ⊕ *www.tiso.com* Ⓜ *Buchanan St.*

Merchant City

Near the remnants of medieval Glasgow, around Glasgow Cathedral, is the Merchant City, with some of the city's most important 18th-century buildings. Many of them, like the great mansions along Ingram Street, were built by tobacco merchants with profits from the tobacco trade. Today those palatial homes hold restaurants and designer stores; one especially grand example houses the Gallery of Modern Art. Many of Glasgow's young and upwardly mobile have made their home here, in converted buildings ranging from warehouses to the old Sheriff's Court.

GETTING HERE AND AROUND

Buchanan Street is the handiest subway station when you want to explore the Merchant City, as it puts you directly on George Square. You can also easily walk from Central station or the St. Enoch subway station.

◉ Sights

Gallery of Modern Art (*GoMA*)

ART MUSEUM | One of Glasgow's boldest, most innovative galleries occupies the neoclassical former Royal Exchange building. The modern art, craft, and design collections include works by Scottish conceptual artists such as David Mach, and also paintings and sculptures from around the world, including Papua New Guinea, Ethiopia, and Mexico. Each floor of the gallery reflects one of the elements—air, fire, earth, and water—which creates some unexpected juxtapositions and also allows for various interactive exhibits. In the basement is a café, a tourist information center, and an extensive library. The building, designed by David Hamilton (1768–1843) and finished in 1829, was first a meeting place for merchants and traders; later it became Stirling's Library. It also incorporates the mansion built in 1780 by William Cunninghame, one of the city's wealthiest tobacco lords. Standing proudly in front of the gallery is the now-iconic Duke of Wellington statue, rarely seen without a traffic cone (or two) on his head, a playful reflection of the Glaswegian sense of humor. ⊠ *Queen St., Merchant City* ☎ *0141/287–3050* ⊕ *www.glasgowlife. org.uk* 🎟 *Free* Ⓜ *Buchanan St.*

George Square

PLAZA/SQUARE | The focal point of Glasgow is lined with an impressive collection of statues: Queen Victoria; Scotland's national poet, Robert Burns (1759–96); the inventor and developer of the steam engine, James Watt (1736–1819); Prime Minister William Gladstone (1809–98); and, towering above them all atop a column, Scotland's great historical novelist, Sir Walter Scott (1771–1832). That column was originally intended for George III (1738–1820), after whom the square is named, but when he was found to be insane toward the end of his reign, a statue of him was never erected. On the square's east side stands the magnificent Italian Renaissance–style City Chambers; the handsome Merchants' House fills the corner of West George Street, crowned by a globe and a sailing ship. The fine old Post Office building, now converted into flats, occupies the northern side. There are plenty of benches in the center of the square where you can pause and contemplate. Glasgow's Queen Street Station is on the western corner. ⊠ *Merchant City* 🎟 *Free* Ⓜ *Buchanan St.*

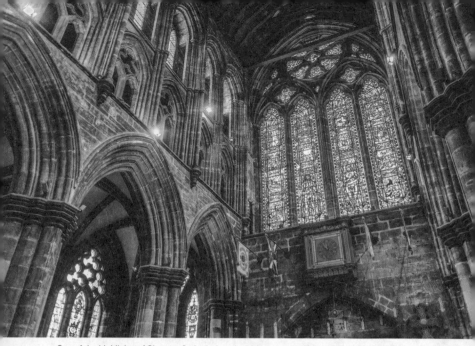
One of the highlights of Glasgow Cathedral are its 20th-century stained glass windows.

★ Glasgow Cathedral

CHURCH | The most complete of Scotland's cathedrals (it would have been more complete had 19th-century vandals not pulled down its two rugged towers), this is an unusual double church, one above the other, dedicated to Glasgow's patron saint, St. Mungo. Consecrated in 1136 and completed about 300 years later, it was spared the ravages of the Reformation—which destroyed so many of Scotland's medieval churches—mainly because Glasgow's trade guilds defended it. A late-medieval open-timber roof in the nave and lovely 20th-century stained glass are notable features.

In the lower church is the splendid crypt of St. Mungo, who was originally known as St. Kentigern (*kentigern* means "chief word"), but who was nicknamed St. Mungo (meaning "dear one") by his early followers. The site of the tomb has been revered since the 6th century, when St. Mungo founded a church here. Mungo features prominently in local legends; one such legend is about a pet bird that

he nursed back to life, and another tells of a bush or tree, the branches of which he used to miraculously relight a fire. The bird, the tree, and the salmon with a ring in its mouth (from another story) are all found on the city's coat of arms, together with a bell that Mungo brought from Rome. ✉ *Cathedral St., Merchant City* ☎ *0141/552–6891* ⊕ *www.glasgowcathedral.org* 🎫 *Free* Ⓜ *Buchanan St.*

★ Necropolis

CEMETERY | A burial ground since the beginning of recorded history, the large Necropolis, modeled on the famous Père-Lachaise Cemetery in Paris, contains some extraordinarily elaborate Victorian tombs. A great place to take it all in is from the monument of John Knox (1514–72), the leader of Scotland's Reformation, which stands at the top of the hill at the heart of the Necropolis. Around it are grand tombs that resemble classical palaces, Egyptian tombs, or even the Chapel of the Templars in Jerusalem. You'll also find a smattering of urns and broken columns, the Roman symbol of a great life cut short. The Necropolis was designed as a place for meditation, which is why it is much more than just a graveyard. The main gates are behind the St. Mungo Museum of Religious Life and Art. The Friends of the Necropolis run regular and informative tours, but booking ahead is essential; the tours are free but donations are welcome. ✉ *2 Castle St., Merchant City* ☎ *0141/287–3961* 🌐 *glasgownecropolis.org* 🎫 *Free* [M] *Buchanan St.*

Provand's Lordship

HISTORIC HOME | Glasgow's oldest house, one of only four medieval buildings surviving in the city, was built in 1471 by Bishop Andrew Muirhead. Before it was rescued by the Glasgow City Council, this building had been a pub, a sweetshop, and a soft drinks factory. It is now a museum that shows the house as it might have looked when it was occupied by officers of the church. The furniture is 17th century, and the top floor is a gallery with prints and paintings depicting the characters who might have lived in the surrounding streets. Behind the house is a medicinal herb garden, and the cloisters house and its rather disturbing carved stone heads. ✉ *3 Castle St., Merchant City* ☎ *0141/276–1625* 🌐 *www.glasgowlife.org.uk* 🎫 *Free* 🕒 *Closed Mon.* [M] *Buchanan St.*

St. Mungo Museum of Religious Life and Art

HISTORY MUSEUM | An outstanding collection of artifacts, including Celtic crosses and statuettes of Hindu gods, reflects the many religious groups that have settled throughout the centuries in Glasgow and the west of Scotland. A Zen garden creates a peaceful setting for rest and contemplation, and elsewhere stained-glass windows include a depiction of St. Mungo himself. Pause to look at the beautiful Chilkat Blanketwofven, made from cedar bark and wool by the Tlingit people of North America. ✉ *2 Castle St., Merchant City* ☎ *0141/276–1625* 🌐 *www.glasgowlife.org.uk* 🎫 *Free* 🕒 *Closed Mon.* [M] *Buchanan St.*

🍴 Restaurants

Despite covering a relatively small area, the Merchant City has a wide variety of restaurants. The selection of cafés and eateries includes many budget-friendly options that cater to the working population.

★ Babbity Bowster

$$ | MODERN EUROPEAN | This warm and welcoming old merchant's house in the heart of the Merchant City offers excellent Scottish food, a barbecue menu, and a lively charming bar area. On Wednesday or Saturday traditional musicians gather for an impromptu session in the bar; the rest of the time there is just conversation. **Known for:** convivial bar atmosphere; classy Scottish pub with rooms upstairs to stay the night; traditional Scottish food with a French twist including saddle of Highland deer. [$] *Average main: £18* ✉ *16–18 Blackfriars St., Merchant City* ☎ *0141/552–5055* 🌐 *www.babbitybowster.com* [M] *Buchanan Street.*

Café Gandolfi

$$ | MODERN BRITISH | Occupying what was once the tea market, this trendy café draws a style-conscious crowd and can justly claim to have launched the dining renaissance of the Merchant City. The café opens early, serving its wonderful signature breakfasts, and the main menu is varied but resolutely Scottish; don't miss the scorched mackerel, the roast rack of Dornoch lamb, or the smoked haddie and Stornaway black pudding. **Known for:** intimate second-floor bar offering the same menu; Stornaway black pudding with mushrooms; unique, locally made furniture. [$] *Average main: £18* ✉ *64 Albion St., Merchant City* ☎ *0141/552–6813* 🌐 *www.cafegandolfi.com* [M] *Buchanan St.*

Corinthian Club

$$ | **MODERN BRITISH** | Inside what was once the mansion of tobacco merchant George Buchanan, the Corinthian Club includes two bars, a nightclub, and a casino in its maze of rooms. At the heart of the building, the main restaurant, the steak-and-seafood-focused Brasserie makes a dramatic first impression with its glass dome and statues. **Known for:** spectacular columns under the roof; extravagant central restaurant; range of menus and spaces. [$] *Average main: £19* ✉ *191 Ingram St., Merchant City* ☎ *0141/552–1101* 🌐 *www.thecorinthianclub.co.uk* [M] *Buchanan St.*

★ Kool Ba

$$ | **ASIAN FUSION** | Thick wooden tables, tapestries, and soft candlelight make you feel at home in the comfortable dining room of this atmospheric haven serving an intriguing mix of Indian and Persian fare. A family-owned restaurant, it's all about healthy, flavorful cooking; chicken tikka masala in a yogurt sauce or lamb korma with coconut cream and fruit or the Persian shashlik are good picks. **Known for:** weekend reservations a must; Indian-Persian fusion cuisine; wide-ranging menu. [$] *Average main: £16* ✉ *109–113 Candleriggs, Merchant City* ☎ *0141/552–2777* 🌐 *www.koolba.com* 🕒 *Closed Mon.* [M] *Buchanan St.*

Hotels

The hotels in the Merchant City are best for those who plan to spend most of their time out and about. In general, this busy area is not the place to come if you want peace and quiet, but rather a place to enjoy the very heart of the city.

Millennium Hotel Glasgow

$ | **HOTEL** | This huge hotel behind an original Georgian facade occupies almost a whole side of George Square and stretches almost as high as the rail station next door. **Pros:** competitive prices; central location; ample comfortable public areas. **Cons:** can feel very anonymous; views of the square only from some (more expensive) rooms; very long corridors. [$] *Rooms from: £90* ✉ *40 George Sq., City Centre* ☎ *0141/332–6711* 🌐 *www.millenniumhotels.co.uk* 🛏 *116 rooms* 🍴 *Free Breakfast* [M] *Buchanan St.*

Moxy Merchant City Hotel

$ | **HOTEL** | With a youthful, defiantly anti-institutional vibe, the Moxy is perfect for those looking to capture Glasgow's lively energy. **Pros:** fun bar great for meeting new people; simple but comfortable rooms; relaxed informal environment. **Cons:** grab-and-go food options a little sparse; surrounding area is a little shabby; can get a little rowdy on weekends. [$] *Rooms from: £90* ✉ *210 High St., Merchant City* ☎ *0141/846–0256* 🌐 *moxy-hotels.marriott.com/en/hotels/glasgow-merchant-city* 🛏 *81 rooms* 🍴 *Free Breakfast* [M] *Buchanan Street.*

The Z Hotel Glasgow

$ | **HOTEL** | Just a few yards from George Square, this good-value modern hotel is one of the newer additions to Merchant City's accommodation options. **Pros:** central location close to Queen Street Station; good beds and bedding; great value. **Cons:** no restaurant; no parking facilities; internal rooms have small (or no) windows. [$] *Rooms from: £85* ✉ *36 N. Frederick St., Merchant City* ☎ *0141/212–4550* 🌐 *www.thezhotels.com* 🛏 *104 rooms* 🍴 *No Meals.*

Nightlife

BARS AND PUBS

Arta

WINE BARS | Built on the site of Glasgow's traditional cheese market, Arta has transformed the place into what feels and looks like a Spanish hacienda. It is a labyrinth of different spaces and unexpected rooms on the ground and basement levels, where a live DJ, a salsa night, or a live band might be in action. You can also stay with the cocktails and tapas on the ground floor. ⊠ *62 Albion St., Merchant City* ☎ *0141/552–2101* ⊕ *www.arta.co.uk* Ⓜ *Buchanan St.*

Boteco do Brasil

BARS | Glasgow's only Brazilian bar-restaurant-club has salsa nights Wednesdays and Latin music to dance to on weekends until 3 am. ⊠ *62 Trongate, Merchant City* ☎ *0141/548–1330* ⊕ *www.botecodobrasil.com* Ⓜ *St. Enoch.*

Old Fruitmarket

LIVE MUSIC | A wonderful venue for almost every type of music, this was once the city's fruit and vegetable market. The first-floor balcony, with its intricate iron railings, still carries some of the original merchants' names. It's adjacent to City Halls in the heart of the Merchant City. ⊠ *Candleriggs, Merchant City* ☎ *0141/353–8000* ⊕ *www.glasgowconcerthalls.com* Ⓜ *Buchanan St.*

★ Scotia Bar

PUBS | This place is a survivor of a different, older city, but it offers a taste of an authentic Glasgow pub, with traditional folk music performances happening regularly. Dark wood, a wood-beamed ceiling, and a classic L-shaped bar set the mood. ⊠ *112 Stockwell St., Merchant City* ☎ *0141/552–8681* ⊕ *www.scotiabar-glasgow.co.uk* Ⓜ *St. Enoch.*

CLUBS

Polo Lounge

DANCE CLUBS | Oozing with Edwardian style, the Polo Lounge is Glasgow's largest gay club. Upstairs is a bar that resembles an old-fashioned gentlemen's club. On the two dance floors downstairs, the DJs spin something for everyone. ⊠ *84 Wilson St., Merchant City* ☎ *0141/553–1221* ⊕ *www.pologlasgow.co.uk* Ⓜ *Buchanan St.*

⊙ Performing Arts

City Halls

CONCERTS | One of the top music venues in the Merchant City, the stone-fronted City Halls hosts orchestral, jazz, and folk concerts. ⊠ *Candleriggs, Merchant City* ☎ *0141/353–8000* ⊕ *www.glasgowconcerthalls.com* Ⓜ *Buchanan St.*

★ Sharmanka Kinetic Theatre

THEATER | FAMILY | A unique spectacle, Sharmanka Kinetic Theatre is the brainchild of Eduard Bersudsky, who came to Glasgow from Russia in 1989 to continue making the mechanical sculptures that are his stock in trade. They are witty and sometimes disturbing, perhaps because they are constructed from scrap materials. They move in a kind of ballet to haunting, specially composed music punctuated by a light show. The shows are 45 or 70 minutes. ⊠ *103 Trongate, Merchant City* ☎ *0141/552–7080* ⊕ *www.sharmanka.com* ⊠ *£10* Ⓜ *St. Enoch.*

Trongate 103

ARTS CENTERS | This vibrant contemporary arts center, housed in a converted Edwardian warehouse, is home base for diverse groups producing film, photography, paintings, and prints. It contains the Russian Cultural Centre and the Sharmanka Kinetic Theatre, as well as the Glasgow Print Studio, a well-established outlet for Glasgow artists; Street Level Photoworks, which aims at making photography more accessible; and the Transmission Gallery, a key exhibition space supporting nonconceptual art in the city. ⊠ *103 Trongate, Merchant City* ☎ *0141/276–8380* Ⓜ *St. Enoch.*

Tron Theatre

THEATER | Come here for contemporary theater from Scotland and around the world; there are three performance spaces. The theater often plays host to works from young Scottish playwrights, and is unafraid to showcase work with provocative and contemporary themes. ✉ *63 Trongate, Merchant City* ☎ *0141/552–4267* ⊕ *www.tron.co.uk* Ⓜ *St. Enoch.*

🛍 Shopping

Many of Glasgow's young and upwardly mobile types make their home in Merchant City. Shopping here is expensive, but the area is worth visiting if you're seeking designer stores.

ANTIQUES AND FINE ART
★ **Glasgow Print Studio**
ART GALLERIES | Essentially an artists' cooperative, the Glasgow Print Studio's facilities launched a generation of outstanding painters, printers, and designers. The work of members past and present can be seen (and bought) at the Print Studio Gallery on King Street. ✉ *103 Trongate, Merchant City* ☎ *0141/552–0704* ⊕ *www.gpsart.co.uk* Ⓜ *St. Enoch.*

CLOTHING
Cruise
MIXED CLOTHING | As one of the first haute couture stores in central Glasgow, Cruise can claim to have launched a new commercial era in the city. It now has two stores in the Merchant City, where its high-fashion clothes and accessories for men and women are beautifully and characteristically displayed to those who can stretch their budgets to its levels. ✉ *180 Ingram St., Merchant City* ☎ *0141/332–5797* ⊕ *www.cruisefashion. com* Ⓜ *Buchanan St.*

West End

Glasgow University dominates the West End, creating a vibrant neighborhood. Founded in 1451, the university is the third oldest in Scotland, after St. Andrews and Aberdeen. The industrialists and merchants who built their grand homes on Great Western Road and adjacent streets endowed museums and art galleries and commissioned artists to decorate and design their homes, as a stroll will quickly reveal. In summer the Glasgow Botanic Gardens, with the iconic glasshouse that is the Kibble Palace, becomes a stage for new and unusual versions of Shakespeare's plays. A fun way to save money is to picnic in the park; you can buy sandwiches, salads, and other portable items at shops on Byres Road. Alternatively, stroll past the university and down Gibson Street and Woodlands Road with their cafés and pubs.

GETTING HERE AND AROUND
The best way to get to the West End from the City Centre is by subway; get off at the Hillhead station. A taxi is another option.

👁 Sights

★ **Botanic Gardens**
GARDEN | FAMILY | It is a minor Glasgow miracle how as soon as the sun appears, the Botanics (as they're known to locals) fill with people. Beautiful flower displays and extensive lawns create the feeling that this is a large back garden for the inhabitants of the West End's mainly apartment homes. At the heart of the gardens is the spectacular circular greenhouse, the Kibble Palace, a favorite haunt of Glaswegian families. Originally built in 1873, it was the conservatory of a Victorian eccentric. Kibble Palace and the other greenhouses contain tree ferns, palm trees, and the Tropicarium, where you can experience the lushness of a rain forest or see its world-famous collection of orchids. There is a tearoom, and in June and July the gardens host presentations of Shakespeare's plays (⊕ *www. bardinthebotanics.co.uk*). ✉ *730 Great Western Rd., West End* ☎ *0141/276–1614* ⊕ *www.glasgowbotanicgardens.com* 🎫 *Free* ☉ *Closed dusk–7 am* Ⓜ *Hillhead.*

Locals head to the Botanic Gardens and its Victorian greenhouse on sunny days.

Glasgow University

COLLEGE | Gorgeous grounds and great views of the city are among the many reasons to visit this university. The Gilbert Scott Building, the university's main edifice, is a lovely example of the Gothic Revival style. Glasgow University Visitor Centre, near the main gate on University Avenue, has exhibits on the university and a small coffee bar; one-hour guided walking tours of the campus (Thursday–Sunday at 2) start here. A self-guided tour starts at the visitor center and takes in the east and west quadrangles, the cloisters, Professor's Square, Pearce Lodge, and the not-to-be-missed University Chapel. The university's Hunterian Museum and Art Gallery are also well worth a visit. ⊠ University Ave., West End ☎ 0141/330–2000 ⊕ www.glasgow. ac.uk ☜ Free Ⓜ Hillhead.

★ Hunterian Art Gallery

ART MUSEUM | Opposite Glasgow University's main gate, this gallery houses William Hunter's (1718–83) collection of paintings. You'll also find prints, drawings, and sculptures by Tintoretto, Rembrandt, and Auguste Rodin, as well as a major collection of paintings by James McNeill Whistler, who had a great affection for the city that bought one of his earliest paintings. Also in the gallery is a replica of Charles Rennie Mackintosh's town house. Between 1906 and 1914, famed architect Mackintosh and his wife Margaret Macdonald lived at 78 Southpark Avenue, just one street away from where their house has been faithfully rebuilt as part of the gallery. Its stunning rooms contain Mackintosh's art nouveau chairs, tables, beds, and cupboards. The upstairs sitting room, with its famous desk, echoes the Japanese motifs so popular with his generation. Free guided

Charles Rennie Mackintosh

Not so long ago, the furniture of innovative Glasgow-born architect Charles Rennie Mackintosh (1868–1928) was broken up for firewood. Today art books are devoted to his distinctive, astonishingly elegant Arts and Crafts—and art nouveau—influenced interiors, and artisans around the world look to his theory that "decoration should not be constructed, rather construction should be decorated" as holy law. Mackintosh's stripped-down designs ushered in the modern age.

An Architect's Career

Mackintosh trained in architecture at the Glasgow School of Art and was apprenticed to the Glasgow firm of John Hutchison at the age of 16. Early influences on his work included the Pre-Raphaelites, James McNeill Whistler (1834–1903), Aubrey Beardsley (1872–98), and Japanese art. But by the 1890s a distinct Glasgow style developed.

The building for the *Glasgow Herald* newspaper, which he designed in 1893, is now the Lighthouse Centre for Architecture, Design, and the City. Other major buildings followed: the Martyrs Public School in Glasgow; Hill House, in Helensburgh, now owned by the National Trust for Scotland; and Queen's Cross Church, completed in 1899 and now the headquarters of the Charles Rennie Mackintosh Society (⊕ www.crmsociety.com). In 1897 Mackintosh began work on a new home for the Glasgow School of Art, recognized as one of his major achievements.

Mackintosh married Margaret Macdonald in 1900, and in later years her decorative work enhanced the buildings' interiors. It was she who inspired the Glasgow Girls group of women artists. In 1904 Mackintosh became a partner in Honeyman and Keppie, and in the same year he designed what is now the Scotland Street School Museum. Until 1913, when he moved to England, Mackintosh's projects included buildings over much of Scotland, and their interiors were always part of his overall design.

Commissions in England after 1913 included design challenges not confined to buildings, such as fabrics, furniture, and even bookbindings. After 1904 architectural taste turned against Mackintosh's style, however, his work was seen as strange. Mackintosh could not conform to the times; he lost commissions, drank heavily, and ended up poor and sick. He died in London in 1928. Mackintosh's reputation revived only in the 1950s and has continued to grow over time. It seems fitting that his unique style has become so emblematic of his home city.

How to See His Work

Glasgow is the best place to admire Mackintosh's work. In addition to the buildings mentioned above, most of which can be visited, the Hunterian Art Gallery contains magnificent reconstructions of the Mackintoshes' home at 78 Southpark Avenue, along with original drawings, documents, and records. The Kelvingrove Art Gallery and Museum also has displays of his work in several galleries. His iconic Glasgow School of Art building is currently being reconstructed after a fire.

tours are available. ⊠ *Hillhead St., West End* ☎ *0141/330–5431* ⊕ *www.gla.ac.uk/ hunterian* ☞ *Free; Macintosh House £6* ⊗ *Closed Mon.* Ⓜ *Hillhead.*

Hunterian Museum

HISTORY MUSEUM | Set within Glasgow University, this museum, dating from 1807, showcases part of the collections of William Hunter, an 18th-century Glasgow doctor who assembled a staggering quantity of valuable material. Check out Hunter's hoards of coins, manuscripts, scientific instruments, and archaeological artifacts in this striking Gothic building. A permanent exhibit chronicles the building of the Antonine Wall, the Romans' northernmost defense. ⊠ *University Ave., West End* ☎ *0141/330–4221* ⊕ *www.gla. ac.uk/hunterian* ☞ *Free* ⊗ *Closed Mon.* Ⓜ *Hillhead.*

★ Kelvingrove Art Gallery and Museum

ART MUSEUM | **FAMILY** | Worthy of its world-class reputation, the Kelvingrove Art Gallery and Museum attracts local families as well as international visitors. This combination of cathedral and castle was designed in the Renaissance style and built between 1891 and 1901. The stunning red-sandstone edifice is an appropriate home for works by Botticelli, Rembrandt, Monet, and others, not to mention the collection of arms and armor. The Glasgow Room houses extraordinary works by local artists. Whether the subject is Scottish culture, design, or storytelling, every room entices you to look deeper; labels are thought-provoking and sometimes witty. You could spend a weekend here, but in a pinch three hours would do one level justice—there are three. Leave time to visit the gift shop and the attractive basement restaurant. Daily free recitals on the magnificent organ (usually at 1) are well worth the trip. ⊠ *Argyle St., West End* ☎ *0141/276–9599* ⊕ *www.glasgowlife. org.uk* ☞ *Free (some special exhibitions require admission)* Ⓜ *Kelvinhall.*

Kelvingrove Park

CITY PARK | **FAMILY** | Both a peaceful retreat and a well-used playground, the park was purchased by the city in 1852. The River Kelvin flows through its green spaces. The park's numerous statues of prominent Glaswegians include one of Lord Kelvin (1824–1907), the Scottish mathematician and physicist remembered for his pioneering work in electricity. The shady park has a massive fountain commemorating a lord provost of Glasgow from the 1870s, a duck pond, two children's playgrounds, and a skateboard park. The An Clachan café beside the children's play area is an excellent daytime eatery and a boon to parents looking for a refuge. Public bowling and croquet greens are free, as are the tennis courts. The Bandstand, a 2,300-seat open-air theater, hosts major concerts in summer. ⊠ *Bounded by Sauchiehall St., Woodlands Rd., and Kelvin Way, West End* ⊕ *www.glasgowlife.org.uk* ☞ *Free* Ⓜ *Kelvinhall.*

Queen's Cross Church

CHURCH | The only church Mackintosh designed houses the Charles Rennie Mackintosh (CRM) Society Headquarters and is the ideal place to learn more about the famous Glasgow-born architect and designer. The church has beautiful stained-glass windows and a light-enhancing, carved-wood interior. The center's library and shop provide further insight into Glasgow's other Mackintosh-designed buildings. A taxi is probably the best way to get here, but you can also take a bus toward Queen's Cross from stops along Hope Street or walk up Maryhill Road from the St. George's Cross subway station. ⊠ *870 Garscube Rd., West End* ☎ *0141/946–6600* ⊕ *www. crmsociety.com* ☞ *£10, includes coffee or tea* ⊗ *Closed weekends year-round and Tues. and Thurs. Nov.–Mar.* Ⓜ *St. George's Cross.*

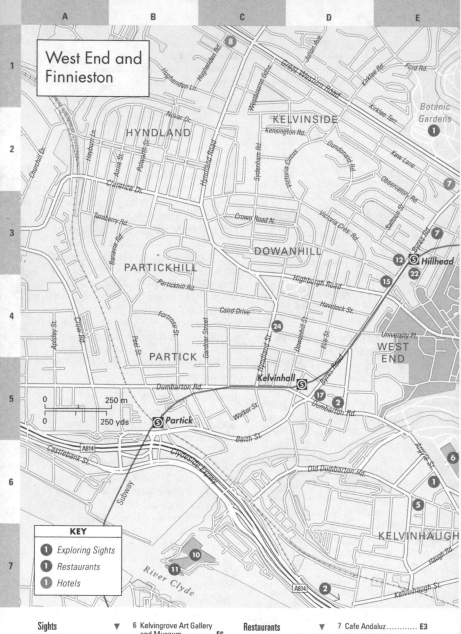

West End and Finnieston

KEY

- **1** *Exploring Sights*
- **1** *Restaurants*
- **1** *Hotels*

🍴 Restaurants

Because of Glasgow University, the eateries in this area were once just the domain of students and professors. In recent years this elegant residential area has also attracted fine restaurants that appeal to a wide range of visitors.

Balbir's

$$ | INDIAN | Don't let the tinted windows discourage you: this place is a temple for pure, healthy Indian food that's impressive in taste and presentation. Try the chicken tikka *chasni* (with mango chutney, lemon juice, and mint), lamb korma, or the traditional celebration dish of Goanese fish curry. **Known for:** everything on a grand scale; healthy but delicious Indian food; multiple spice (and heat) combinations. $ *Average main: £17* ⊠ *7 Church St., West End* ☎ *0141/339-7711* ⊕ *www.balbirs.co.uk* ⊗ *Closed Mon. No lunch* Ⓜ *Kelvinhall*.

Bay Tree

$ | MIDDLE EASTERN | This popular small café in the university area is unpretentious and quite cheap. It serves wonderful Middle Eastern food—mostly vegetarian dishes, but there are a few lamb and chicken creations as well. **Known for:** BYOB-policy (and a great wine store nearby); wide variety of meze; Turkish and Lebanese dishes. $ *Average main: £11* ⊠ *403 Great Western Rd., West End* ☎ *0141/334-5898* ⊕ *www.thebaytree-westend.co.uk* ⊗ *Closed Mon.-Tues.* Ⓜ *Kelvinbridge*.

Bread Meats Bread

$ | BURGER | One of a new breed of burger joints that has emerged in the city, this casual spot with long wooden tables, stools, and benches is also a meeting place for coffee or a drink. The many creatively stuffed burgers and sauces are accompanied by different poutines and cheese toasties, a variation on the British classic known as rarebit. **Known for:** cheerful sociable vibe; creative and delicious burgers; best poutines outside of Canada. $ *Average main: £10* ⊠ *701 Great Western Rd., West End* ☎ *0141/648-0399* ⊕ *www.breadmeats-bread.com* Ⓜ *Hillhead*.

Cafe Andaluz

$$ | TAPAS | With Iberian flair, this lively basement eatery located on the cobbles of Cresswell Lane is beautifully decorated using Spanish tiles throughout. The first tapas place to make an impact in Glasgow, it has been followed by others (and has opened a second location in the City Centre) but remains one of the most successful. **Known for:** delicious paella; nice Spanish wine selection; lively but intimate atmosphere. $ *Average main: £15* ⊠ *2 Cresswell La., West End* ☎ *0141/339-1111* ⊕ *www.cafeandaluz.com* Ⓜ *Hillhead*.

★ Cail Bruich

$$$$ | BRITISH | A Gaelic phrase that means "to eat well", the restaurant known as Cali Bruich certainly lives up to its name as evidenced by its many awards, including a coveted Michelin star (currently the only eatery in Glasgow with one). Run by two brothers, the ambitious and innovative menu makes use of local, high-quality Scottish ingredients, but it's really the delicate and clever cooking style that takes the menu to higher heights. **Known for:** Glasgow's only Michelin star; multi-course chef's table experience; elevated Scottish cuisine. $ *Average main: £55* ⊠ *725 Great Western Rd., West End* ☎ *0141/334-6265* ⊕ *www.cailbruich.co.uk* ⊗ *Closed Sun.-Tues. No lunch Wed.*

Hanoi Bike Shop

$$ | VIETNAMESE | Glasgow's first Vietnamese canteen offers a different style of dining, which is apparent from the moment you walk through the door and see the rustic setting, low tables, and stools. This is classic street food (all cooked on the premises and arriving when it is ready) and choices include blood sausage with razor clam salad, hot-and-sour fish soup, and plenty of pho, the fragrant

Vietnamese soup with noodles and sliced meat. **Known for:** organic tofu options; excellent pho; street food in small plates. $ *Average main: £15* ✉ *8 Ruthven La., West End* ✛ *Down the alley opposite Hillhead subway station* ☎ *0141/334–7165* ⊕ *hanoibikeshop.co.uk* ⊗ *No dinner Mon. and Tues.* Ⓜ *Hillhead.*

Ka Pao

$$ | **ASIAN** | A welcome addition to the West End dining scene, this trendy and accomplished restaurant has a thorough menu of Southeast Asian small plates that allow diners to mix and match different dishes. Founded by the team behind Finniston's popular Ox and Finch restaurant, Ka Pao opened its doors to high expectations from local foodies and absolutely did not disappoint. **Known for:** high quality local ingredients; fried whole fish; spicy and inventive flavors. $ *Average main: £18* ✉ *26 Vinicombe St., West End* ☎ *0141/483–6990* ⊕ *www.ka-pao.com.*

The Left Bank

$$ | **ECLECTIC** | Close to Glasgow University, this popular bar and restaurant attracts a more mature student crowd. It's an airy spot with high ceilings, leather sofas, and wood floors, and the specialty is good, eclectic international food at reasonable prices. **Known for:** tasty brunch; delicious small plates of varied cuisine; casual atmosphere. $ *Average main: £15* ✉ *33–35 Gibson St., West End* ☎ *0141/339–5969* ⊕ *www.theleftbank.co.uk* Ⓜ *Kelvinbridge.*

Little Italy

$ | **ITALIAN** | **FAMILY** | Offering all things Italian, this constantly busy, noisy, and extremely friendly café sits in the heart of the West End. Its pizzas, made on the premises while you wait with a coffee or a glass of Italian wine, are probably the best around, and the house-made pastas are just as consistently good. **Known for:** perfect tiramisu for dessert; simple unassuming surroundings; wide variety of Italian wines. $ *Average main: £10* ✉ *205 Byres Rd., West End* ☎ *0141/339–6287* ⊕ *littleitalyglasgow.com* Ⓜ *Hillhead.*

Number Sixteen

$$ | **BRITISH** | This tiny, intimate restaurant serves only the freshest ingredients, superbly prepared, on a constantly changing menu. Halibut is served with choucroute and a passion-fruit dressing—a typically unpredictable meeting of flavors. **Known for:** cozy interior, so reservations are a good idea; excellent set menus; surprising flavor combinations. $ *Average main: £18* ✉ *16 Byres Rd., West End* ☎ *0141/339–2544* ⊕ *www.number16.co.uk* Ⓜ *Kelvin Hall.*

★ Stravaigin

$$$ | **ECLECTIC** | For many years Stravaigin has maintained the highest quality of cooking, creating adventurous dishes that often combine Asian and local flavors and unusual marriages of ingredients. You can try the *piri piri* quail (the seasoning is used in Africa) or the restaurant's famous haggis and neeps (turnips), symbolizing its commitment to local produce. **Known for:** daily-changing curry option; buzzy bar with a quieter restaurant downstairs; classic haggis and neeps. $ *Average main: £20* ✉ *28 Gibson St., West End* ☎ *0141/334–2665* ⊕ *www.stravaigin.co.uk* Ⓜ *Kelvinbridge.*

Ubiquitous Chip

$$$ | **MODERN BRITISH** | Occupying a converted stable behind the Hillhead subway station on busy Ashton Lane, this restaurant is a Glasgow institution, with an untarnished reputation for creative Scottish cooking. Its street-level restaurant is a beautiful courtyard protected by a glass roof, and the more informal brasserie upstairs also serves less expensive dishes like haggis with neeps and tatties or a plate of mussels. **Known for:** lovely courtyard; creative Scottish cuisine like venison haggis; popular upstairs bar great for socializing. $ *Average main: £24* ✉ *12 Ashton La., West End* ☎ *0141/334–5007* ⊕ *www.ubiquitouschip.co.uk* Ⓜ *Hillhead.*

Wudon

$ | **JAPANESE** | Pleasant and relaxed, this Japanese restaurant with white walls, simple furniture, subdued lighting, and a large window onto the street offers beautifully prepared food presented with great charm by the staff. Whether your taste is for hearty broths, just-made sushi, or savory rice and noodle dishes, the chef will combine the elements to your taste. **Known for:** reasonable prices, including a great weekday lunch special; noodle broth bowls; huge sushi menu. $ *Average main: £11* ⊠ *535 Great Western Rd., West End* ☎ *0141/357–3033* ⊕ *www. wudon-noodlebar.co.uk* Ⓜ *Kelvinbridge.*

Zique's

$$ | **BRITISH** | This small but inviting café has a vibrant, bustling atmosphere while remaining unhurried. Its changing breakfast and lunch menus of British fare are always fresh and exciting. **Known for:** vibrant atmosphere; wonderful breakfasts; tasty sobrasada (a chorizo·spread). $ *Average main: £15* ⊠ *66 Hyndland St., West End* ☎ *0141/339–7180* ⊕ *www. ziques.com* ☾ *No dinner* Ⓜ *Hillhead.*

🛏 Hotels

Many lodgings are on quieter Great Western Road, set apart from busy Byres Road.

Ambassador Hotel

$ | **HOTEL** | **FAMILY** | Opposite the West End's peaceful Glasgow Botanic Gardens, this hotel is within minutes of busy Byres Road yet well away from its noisy weekend activity. **Pros:** five-minute walk to public transportation and West End amenities; views of Botanic Gardens; great for families with kids. **Cons:** on the corner of a fairly busy road; on-street parking difficult after 6 pm; no elevator. $ *Rooms from: £100* ⊠ *7 Kelvin Dr., West End* ☎ *0141/946–1018* ⊕ *www. ambassador-hotel.net* ➪ *26 rooms* ⦿ *Free Breakfast* Ⓜ *Hillhead.*

Clifton Hotel

$ | **HOTEL** | Occupying two of the grand houses along a collection of town houses above Great Western Road, this popular hotel offers wallet-friendly rates and simply furnished rooms done up in cheerful shades. **Pros:** good budget option; conveniently located; free Wi-Fi. **Cons:** some rooms have a shared bathroom; no elevator; basic amenities. $ *Rooms from: £59* ⊠ *26–27 Buckingham Terr., West End* ☎ *0141/334–8080* ⊕ *www.clifton-hotelglasgow.co.uk* ➪ *26 rooms* ⦿ *Free Breakfast* Ⓜ *Hillhead.*

Heritage Hotel

$ | **HOTEL** | This small, unpretentious, but well-established hotel in a very central West End location has cozy, simply decorated rooms. **Pros:** on a quiet street; very good location; lovely breakfast. **Cons:** main road can get noisy; no parking spaces and on-street parking is expensive; rooms quite small. $ *Rooms from: £80* ⊠ *4/5 Albert Terr., West End* ✛ *Entrance by Hillhead St.* ☎ *0141/339–6955* ⊕ *www. theheritagehotel.net* ➪ *27 rooms* ⦿ *Free Breakfast* Ⓜ *Hillhead.*

Hilton Glasgow Grosvenor

$ | **HOTEL** | Behind a row of grand terrace houses, this modern hotel overlooks the Glasgow Botanic Gardens. **Pros:** tasty restaurant; close to Byres Road; some rooms have good views. **Cons:** Wi-Fi in guest rooms costs extra; a rather institutional feel; rooms at the back overlook a parking lot. $ *Rooms from: £111* ⊠ *1–9 Grosvenor Terr., West End* ☎ *0141/339–8811* ⊕ *hiltongrosvenor.com-glasgow. com* ➪ *96 rooms* ⦿ *Free Breakfast* Ⓜ *Hillhead.*

★ Hotel du Vin Glasgow

$$ | **HOTEL** | Consisting of a group of Victorian houses on a tree-lined street, well away from the bustle of Byres Road, this hotel is all about elegance, from the sophisticated drawing room to the individually decorated guest rooms with flowing draperies, Egyptian linens, and mahogany furnishings like four-poster

beds. **Pros:** complimentary whisky on arrival; stunning Scottish-style rooms; understated luxury. **Cons:** a little too much tartan in the decor; on-street parking can be difficult after 6 pm; no elevator. [$] *Rooms from: £146* ✉ *1 Devonshire Gardens, West End* ☎ *0330/016–0390* 🌐 *www.hotelduvin.com* 🛏 *49 rooms* 🍴 *Free Breakfast* [M] *Hillhead.*

Nightlife

BARS AND PUBS

Dram!

BARS | With mismatched furnishings and the odd stag's head on the wall, the four large rooms here are decorated in a style that can only be described as "ultra eclectic." It's no place for a quiet, intimate evening, but Dram feels like a traditional bar while being brashly youthful and up-to-the-minute. There's a wide range of beers, and the place takes special pride in the 75 whiskies. On Thursday and Sunday, musicians gather in an informal jam session. Food is served every night until 9. ✉ *232–246 Woodlands Rd., West End* ☎ *0141/332–1622* 🌐 *www.dramglasgow.co.uk* [M] *Kelvinbridge.*

Inn Deep

BARS | A bit of a hidden gem in the West End bar scene, Inn Deep doesn't look like much from its street entrance on Great Western Road, built into the arches of the Great Western Bridge (also known as Kelvinbridge). But inside, craft beers, regular live music, and the friendly staff make this place popular with locals of all ages. The quirky, cool pub also has a terrific beer garden on the banks of the River Kelvin, which means it's always busy during the summer. ✉ *445 Great Western Rd., West End* ☎ *0141/264–2777* 🌐 *www.inndeep.com* [M] *Kelvinbridge.*

Òran Mór

BARS | At the top of Byres Road, Òran Mór has estabished itself as the heart of West End nightlife. Located in what was once a church, it still has beautiful stained-glass windows and a lovely nave gloriously decorated by outstanding Glasgow artist Alasdair Gray. The bar fills with different types of people at different times of day, but its late license means crowds surge Friday and Saturday nights. In the basement, the hugely successful lunchtime theater series "A Play, a Pie, and a Pint" plays to capacity crowds. It also houses a busy bistro, a brasserie, and an evening music venue, as well as a late-night club. The small beer garden fills up quickly in good weather. ✉ *731 Great Western Rd., West End* ☎ *0141/357–6200* 🌐 *www.oran-mor.co.uk* [M] *Hillhead.*

Tennents

PUBS | A spacious corner bar, Tennents is a typical Glaswegian pub that prides itself on its comprehensive selection of beers. You can expect lively conversation, as there's a refreshing lack of loud music. ✉ *191 Byres Rd., West End* ☎ *0141/341–1021* 🌐 *www.thetennentsbarglasgow.co.uk* [M] *Hillhead.*

COMEDY CLUBS

Stand Comedy Club

COMEDY CLUBS | In the basement of a former school, the Stand Comedy Club has live shows every night of the week and is most popular on Thursday and Friday. Prices vary according to who is appearing, and the doors open at 7:30. ✉ *333 Woodlands Rd., at Park Rd., West End* ☎ *0141/212–3389* 🌐 *www.thestand.co.uk* [M] *Kelvingrove.*

Performing Arts

Grosvenor Cinema

FILM | This popular, compact cinema has two screens and extremely comfortable leather seats (some of them big enough for two). It's part of a small complex in the always busy Ashton Lane, immediately behind the subway station, that also includes bars, cafés, and restaurants. ✉ *Ashton La., West End* ☎ *0845/339–8444* 🌐 *www.grosvenorcafe.co.uk* [M] *Hillhead.*

★ A Play, a Pie, and a Pint

THEATER | In a former church, Glasgow's hugely successful lunchtime theater series called "A Play, a Pie, and a Pint" (and you do get all three) showcases new writing from Scotland and elsewhere. ■ TIP→ **Performances sell out quickly, particularly late in the week, so book well in advance on the website.** Doors open at 12:15 pm and shows begin at 1 pm Monday through Saturday. ✉ Òran Mór, 731 Great Western Rd., Byres Rd. and Great Western Rd., West End ☎ 0141/357–6200 ⊕ www.playpiepint.com Ⓜ Hillhead.

👜 Shopping

BOOKS, PAPER, AND MUSIC
Caledonia Books

BOOKS | This well-organized and well-stocked secondhand bookstore fills the gap left by the departure of other bookstores. The owners are knowledgeable and willing to search for even the most obscure volumes. ✉ 483 Great Western Rd., West End ☎ 0141/334–9663 ⊕ www.caledoniabooks.co.uk Ⓜ Kelvinbridge.

★ Mixed Up Records

RECORDS | This small independent record store is tucked away on Otago Lane. Selling a combination of secondhand and brand-new vinyl, it remains one of the only surviving music shops in the area. It also has a terrific selection of jazz, reggae, and R&B. ✉ 18 Otago La., West End ☎ 0141/357–5737 ⊕ www.mixeduprecords.com.

CLOTHING
Glasgow Vintage Co.

SECOND-HAND | You can find plenty of genuine bargains here for upmarket vintage clothes at down-market prices. There are choices for men, women, and children from the 1950s to the 1980s. ✉ 453 Great Western Rd., West End ☎ 0141/338–6633 ⊕ www.glasgowvintage.co.uk.

Strawberry Fields

CHILDREN'S CLOTHING | Designer clothing for children is the specialty of Strawberry Fields. ✉ 517 Great Western Rd., West End ☎ 0141/339–1121 Ⓜ Kelvinbridge.

FOOD
Demijohn

FOOD | Specializing in infused wines, spirits, oils, and vinegars, Demijohn calls itself a "liquid deli." ✉ 382 Byres Rd., West End ☎ 0141/337–3600 ⊕ www.demijohn.co.uk Ⓜ Hillhead.

Iain Mellis Cheesemonger

FOOD | This shop has a superb, seemingly endless selection of fine Scottish cheeses, in addition to others from England and across Europe, as well as bread and olives. ✉ 492 Great Western Rd., West End ☎ 0141/339–8998 ⊕ www.mellischeese.net Ⓜ Kelvinbridge.

HOME FURNISHINGS AND TEXTILES
Nancy Smillie

HOUSEWARES | Local to the floorboards, Nancy Smillie is a one-of-a-kind boutique that sells unique glassware, jewelry, and furnishings. It also runs a jewelry boutique at 425 Great Western Road. ✉ 53 Cresswell St., West End ☎ 0141/334–0055 ⊕ www.nancysmillieshop.com Ⓜ Hillhead.

Time and Tide

HOUSEWARES | Loosely described as a household goods store, Time and Tide sells an eclectic mix of lamps and candleholders and cushions and things you never realized you needed until you see them. ✉ 398 Byres Rd., West End ☎ 0141/357–4548 ⊕ www.timeandtidestores.co.uk Ⓜ Hillhead.

Finnieston

The River Clyde has long been the city's main artery, bearing Clyde-built ships, from warships to ocean liners, to the sea. Few of the yards remain open, and the Finnieston Crane, which once moved locomotives onto ships, is no longer active. But the area around it, bounded by the river on one side and Sauchiehall Street on the other, has undergone a great transformation since the 1990s. The riverside has been reborn, with Zaha Hadid's Transport Museum and the Tall Ship, as well as the Scottish Event Campus (SEC) occupying pride of place on the Finnieston bank and the Science Museum on the opposite side. The SSE Hydro, an ultramodern concert arena, has generated a new fashionable strip of bars and restaurants along Argyle Street as well as several new hotels.

GETTING HERE AND AROUND

From the Partick subway station it's a 10-minute walk to the Riverside Museum. From that museum it's a short stroll along the river (and across a bridge) to the Glasgow Science Centre. Argyle Street is a short walk from Kelvin Hall subway station or across Kelvingrove Park from Glasgow University.

◉ Sights

Glasgow Science Centre

SCIENCE MUSEUM | FAMILY | Fun and engaging, this museum for children has three floors packed with games, experiments, and hands-on machines from pendulums to small-scale whirlpools, soundscapes to optical illusions. Its space-age home on the south side of the Clyde has a whole wall of glass looking out onto the river. The *BodyWorks* exhibition explores every aspect of our physical selves—you can even try and reconstruct a brain. There are daily events and science shows, a lovely play area for under-sevens, a planetarium, an IMAX theater, and the spectacular Glasgow Tower, 400 feet high, where you can survey the whole city from the river to the surrounding hills. All carry an additional charge. Always inquire whether the tower is open—even moderate winds will close it down. ■ TIP→ **Admission is expensive, but the tower and planetarium cost less if you buy all the tickets at the same time.** ⌂ *50 Pacific Quay, Finnieston* ☎ *0141/420–5000* ⊕ *www.glasgowsciencecentre. org* ⌂ *£12; planetarium £3 with museum admission; Glasgow Tower £3.50 with museum admission; Tower only £6.50* ⊙ *Closed Mon., Tues., and Thurs. Nov.– Mar.* Ⓜ *Cessnock.*

Mitchell Library

LIBRARY | The largest public reference library in Europe houses more than a million items, including what is claimed to be the world's largest collection about Robert Burns. The Mitchell also houses the remarkable private collection of outstanding puppeteer John Blundell. Minerva, goddess of wisdom, looks down from the library's dome, encouraging the library's users and frowning at the drivers thundering along the nearby motorway. This is a genuinely public library with open access to all its materials, nearly 100 computers for public use, and a comfortable on-site café. A bust in the entrance hall commemorates the library's founder, Stephen Mitchell, who died in 1874. The Aye Write Literature Festival takes place here every March, as do many other events celebrating Glasgow's history. ⌂ *North St., West End* ☎ *0141/287–2999* ⊕ *www.glasgowlife. org.uk* ⌂ *Free* ⊙ *Closed Sun.* Ⓜ *St. George's Cross.*

★ Riverside Museum: Scotland's Museum of Transport and Travel

HISTORY MUSEUM | FAMILY | Designed by Zaha Hadid to celebrate the area's industrial heritage, this huge metal structure with curving walls echoes the covered yards where ships were built on the Clyde. Glasgow's shipbuilding history is remembered with a world-famous collection of ship models. Locomotives built at the nearby St. Rollox yards are also on display, as are cars from every age and many countries. You can wander down Main Street, circa 1930, without leaving the building: the pawnbroker, funeral parlor, and Italian restaurant are all frozen in time. Relax with a coffee in the café, wander out onto the expansive riverside walk, or board the Tall Ship that is moored permanently behind the museum. Take Bus 100 from the City Centre, or walk from Partick subway station. ⊠ 100 Poundhouse Pl., Finnieston ☎ 0141/287–2720 ⊕ www.glasgowlife. org.uk ⊿ Free Ⓜ Partick.

Tall Ship at Riverside

NAUTICAL SIGHT | FAMILY | Built in 1896, this fine tall sailing ship now sits on the River Clyde immediately behind the Riverside Museum. The Glenlee once belonged to the Spanish Navy (under a different name), but carried cargo all over the world in her day. She returned to Glasgow and the River Clyde in 1993, and now forms part of the museum. You can wander throughout this surprisingly large cargo ship with or without an audio guide, peer into cabins and holds, and stand on the forecastle as you gaze down the river (but bring your own binoculars). Bus 100 from George Square brings you here, or you can walk from the Partick subway station in 10 minutes. ⊠ 150 Pointhouse Pl., Finnieston ☎ 0141/357–3699 ⊕ www.thetallship.com ⊿ Free Ⓜ Partick.

🍴 Restaurants

A small strip of Argyle has been transformed in recent years into an exciting new restaurant area, dominated by seafood restaurants, hip steak houses, old pubs transformed into trendy cocktail bars, and small-plate innovators. It caters to the visitors brought in by the music arena and the riverside development.

Baffo

$ | ITALIAN | There has been something of an explosion of new pizzerias in Glasgow, many of them newer chains, but Baffo has made its mark and won approval from a demanding audience. Not only are the pizzas beautifully crispy and varied, they are also very large: if you need a half-meter of pizza (about 1½ feet), it's available as an economical choice. **Known for:** famous half-meter pizza; busy but friendly atmosphere; good pasta at decent prices. $ Average main: £10 ⊠ 1377 Argyle St., Finnieston ☎ 0141/583–0000 ⊕ www.baffo.co.uk Ⓜ Kelvin Hall.

The Brunch Club

$ | CAFÉ | The name says it all: this pleasant, airy café pays homage to all things brunch. There are eggs in every combination, decadent waffles and French toast, and a delicious array of classic brunch cocktails from Bloody Marys to mimosas. **Known for:** relaxing vibe; best brunch in Glasgow; great cocktails. $ Average main: £9 ⊠ 67 Old Dumbarton Rd., Finnieston ☎ 0141/237–7374 ⊕ www.the-brunchclub.co ⊙ No dinner Ⓜ Kelvin Hall.

Butchershop Bar and Grill

$$ | STEAKHOUSE | An early arrival in the redeveloping Finnieston area, Butchershop occupies what was once a pub and overlooks the bowling greens in Kelvingrove Park. Modern, open, and airy, it preserves the sociable atmosphere of its predecessor, though it is now a quality steak house offering a range of cuts from rump to T-bone. **Known for:** publike atmosphere; steaks of every variety; good value fixed-price menus. $ Average main: £19 ⊠ 1055 Sauchiehall St., Finnieston ☎ 0141/339–2999 ⊕ www.butchershop-glasgow.com Ⓜ Kelvin Hall.

★ Crabshakk

$$ | SEAFOOD | Anything but a shack, this intimate dining room has heavy wooden tables and chairs, an elegantly ornate ceiling, and a bar so shiny and inviting that it seems to almost insist you have

a drink. The food comes from the sea—oysters, lobster, and squid—and you can have your choice served iced, grilled, roasted, or battered. **Known for:** reservations essential; local and sustainably sourced Scottish seafood; art deco decor. [$] *Average main: £15* ✉ *1114 Argyle St., Finnieston* ☎ *0141/334–6127* 🌐 *www.crabshakk.com* [M] *Kelvin Hall.*

★ The Finnieston

$$ | SEAFOOD | A 19th-century inn turned into an elegant restaurant, the Finnieston retains the dark wood and narrow cubicles of earlier times, but today it is one of the new high-quality seafood restaurants that have transformed the faded Finnieston area into a fashionable district. The menu allows you to choose the fish and how it is prepared, the sauce, and salad or vegetable sides. **Known for:** comfy wooden booths; impressive seafood cuisine; stunning array of cocktails. [$] *Average main: £18* ✉ *1125 Argyle St., Finnieston* ☎ *0141/222–2884* 🌐 *www.thefinniestonbar.com* [M] *Kelvin Hall.*

The Gannet

$$$$ | MODERN EUROPEAN | One of the early occupants of the new Finnieston, the Gannet has maintained its stellar reputation. Its comfortable wood-and-brick interior denotes the emphasis on the natural provenance and unencumbered presentation of their food. **Known for:** local produce; varied seafood menu; tasting menus for both carnivores and vegetarians. [$] *Average main: £55* ✉ *1155 Argyle St., Finnieston* ☎ *0141/204–2081* 🌐 *www.thegannetgla.com* 🕓 *Closed Mon.–Wed. No lunch Thurs.* [M] *Kelvin Hall.*

★ Mother India

$$ | INDIAN | The brand known as Mother India really covers four adjacent restaurants rather than just one location, all highlighting small plates of impressive Indian cuisine. What makes this place across from Kelvingrove Art Gallery so popular is the combination of high-quality cooking and an extensive range of tastes, from the vegetarian dal to spicy ginger chicken. **Known for:** BYOB policy; casual small-plate Indian food; no reservations, which means there are crowds and usually some wait. [$] *Average main: £15* ✉ *1355 Argyle St., Clyde* ☎ *0141/339–9145* 🌐 *www.motherindiaglasgow.co.uk* [M] *Kelvin Hall.*

★ Ox and Finch

$$$ | ECLECTIC | This immensely popular restaurant shines at every level—service, presentation, and taste. The stripped-back, rustic decor encourages chatter and the sharing of the eclectic small plates that are its specialty. **Known for:** huge wine list; small-plates dining with a wide variety of options; relaxed and buzzy atmosphere. [$] *Average main: £22* ✉ *920 Sauchiehall St., Finnieston* ☎ *0141/339–8627* 🌐 *www.oxandfinch.com* [M] *Kelvin Hall.*

Rioja

$$ | SPANISH | This spot belongs to the second generation of tapas restaurants, combining classic small plates with new and innovative interpretations. Here the *patatas riojanas* go a stage beyond *patatas bravas,* adding pork and chorizo, while the spring lamb with almond crust adds new flavors. **Known for:** late-night dining; contemporary take on tapas; good Spanish wines. [$] *Average main: £15* ✉ *1116 Argyle St., Clyde* ☎ *0141/334–0761* 🌐 *www.riojafinnieston.co.uk* [M] *Kelvin Hall.*

Six by Nico

$$$ | BRITISH | In a street of adventurous eateries, Six by Nico adds a new dimension of fun and wit. The concept at this intimate, modern restaurant with black tile, wood floors and tables, and black chairs is a six-course tasting menu linked to a theme that changes every six weeks, whether it's fish-and-chips or Route 66, with dishes that deconstruct and reconstruct the familiar. **Known for:** reservations essential; highly original approach to a tasting menu; imaginative dishes (with wine-pairing option).

$ Average main: £25 ✉ 1132 Argyle St., Finnieston ☎ 0141/334–5661 ⊕ www.sixbynico.co.uk ⊙ Closed Mon. Ⓜ Kelvin Hall.

Hotels

Besides a handful of interesting museums and a popular cluster of busy bars and restaurants, this hip area near the river also has a few lodgings, mostly on Sauchiehall Street.

Argyll Guest House
$ | B&B/INN | In this budget-minded annex to the Argyll Hotel, across the road on Sauchiehall Street, the rooms are plainly furnished but scrupulously clean. **Pros:** bargain prices; close to Kelvingrove Park and public transportation; tasty breakfast. **Cons:** basic amenities; no elevator; front rooms noisy on weekends. *$ Rooms from: £65 ✉ 966–970 Sauchiehall St., Finnieston ☎ 0141/357–5155 ⊕ www.argyllhotelglasgow.co.uk ⇌ 20 rooms ⏐◎⏐ Free Breakfast Ⓜ Kelvin Hall.*

Argyll Hotel
$ | HOTEL | The tartan in the reception area reflects the clan theme throughout the hotel; each room is named after a clan, but each is also very different from the next. **Pros:** reasonable prices; centrally located; comfortable rooms. **Cons:** downstairs breakfast area and bar need refurbishing; metered parking on the street; street can get noisy on weekends. *$ Rooms from: £79 ✉ 973 Sauchiehall St., Finnieston ☎ 0141/337–3313 ⊕ www.argyllhotelglasgow.co.uk ⇌ 38 rooms ⏐◎⏐ Free Breakfast Ⓜ Kelvin Hall.*

Hilton Garden Inn Glasgow City Centre
$ | HOTEL | Overlooking the Clyde, this hotel is within sight of the SSE Hydro entertainment arena and a short walk along the water from the Riverside Museum, and a slightly longer walk from Argyle Street in Finnieston. **Pros:** some great views; convenient location; lovely terrace. **Cons:** prices rise if there is a performance at the Hydro; no nearby metro; isolated from the rest of the city. *$ Rooms from: £87 ✉ Finnieston Quay, Finnieston ☎ 0141/240–1002 ⊕ www3.hilton.com ⇌ 164 rooms ⏐◎⏐ Free Breakfast.*

Radisson Red
$ | HOTEL | Located within the increasingly busy Finnieston Quay area, the stylish rooms here (with hand-drawn artwork from local comic book artist Frank Quietly) have large windows that take full advantage of the river view, which can be more fully enjoyed from the ninth-floor rooftop bar. **Pros:** riverside rooms have lovely views; close to all riverside amenities; fun rooftop bar overlooking the river. **Cons:** not the easiest area to get to by public transport; reception area can be confusing; not all rooms have riverside views. *$ Rooms from: £108 ✉ Finnieston Quay, 25 Tunnel St., Finnieston ☎ 0141/471–1700 ⊕ www.radissonhotels.com/en-us/hotels/radisson-red-glasgow ⇌ 174 rooms ⏐◎⏐ No Meals.*

The Sandyford
$ | HOTEL | The Victorian exterior of this hotel anticipates the colorful decor you'll find inside, where the large windows in the reception area let in lots of light. **Pros:** very competitive prices; extremely well located; minutes from several good restaurants. **Cons:** parking on the street is metered; no elevator; front rooms can get late-night noise. *$ Rooms from: £54 ✉ 904 Sauchiehall St., Finnieston ☎ 0141/334–0000 ⊕ www.sandyfordhotelglasgow.com ⇌ 55 rooms ⏐◎⏐ Free Breakfast Ⓜ Kelvin Hall.*

ⓨ Nightlife

BARS AND PUBS
Ben Nevis
PUBS | A traditional pub still holding its own on the trendy Finnieston strip, this eccentric spot is full of Highland artifacts. There are more than 180 whiskies from which to choose and traditional live music on Wednesday, Thursday, and

Nelson Column towers over Glasgow Green, the city's oldest park.

Sunday. ✉ *1147 Argyle St., Finnieston* ☎ *0141/576–5204* ⊕ *www.thebennevis. co.uk* Ⓜ *Kelvinhall.*

★ Kelvingrove Cafe

COCKTAIL LOUNGES | At this very inventive cocktail bar in the heart of Finniston, the chic vintage interior feels a bit like a Gatsby party, attracting a well-heeled crowd. ✉ *1161 Argyle St., Finnieston* ☎ *0141/221–8988* ⊕ *www.kelvingroveca-fe.com.*

The 78

BARS | Enjoy cozy sofas, a real coal fire, and tasty vegan food throughout the day here. There's live music every night, with jazz on Sunday. ✉ *10–14 Kelvinhaugh St., Finnieston* ☎ *0141/576–5018* ⊕ *www. the78cafebar.com* Ⓜ *Kelvinhall.*

 Performing Arts

SEC Armadillo

CONCERTS | The 3,000-seat riverside SEC is known as the Armadillo for its distinctive, curved design by Norman Foster. It hosts large-scale pop concerts and other events. ✉ *Exhibition Way, Finnieston* ⊹ *Train to Exhibition Centre station from Glasgow Central Low Level station* ☎ *0141/248–3000* ⊕ *www.sec.co.uk.*

SSE Hydro

CONCERTS | This dramatic addition to the banks of the Clyde is a 12,000-seat arena under a silver dome. Built for the 2014 Commonwealth Games, it has proved enormously popular as a music and event venue. ✉ *SEC Exhibition Way, Finnieston* ☎ *0844/395–4000* ⊕ *www.thessehydro. com.*

East End

Glasgow Green has always been the heart of Glasgow's East End, a formerly down-at-heel neighborhood that has seen many changes over time. One of the top attractions is the People's Palace, which tells the story of daily life in the city. On Sunday head to the nearby Barras market to hunt for bargains.

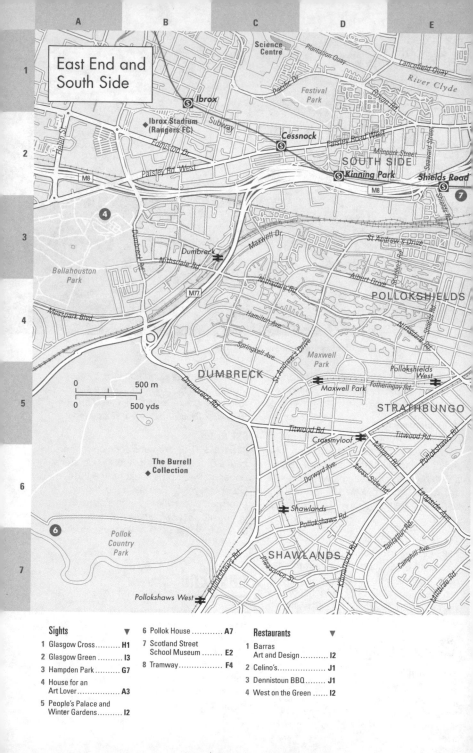

East End and South Side

Sights ▼

1 Glasgow Cross........... **H1**
2 Glasgow Green **I3**
3 Hampden Park **G7**
4 House for an
  Art Lover................. **A3**
5 People's Palace and
  Winter Gardens........... **I2**
6 Pollok House **A7**
7 Scotland Street
  School Museum **E2**
8 Tramway................. **F4**

Restaurants ▼

1 Barras
  Art and Design **I2**
2 Celino's................... **J1**
3 Dennistoun BBQ......... **J1**
4 West on the Green **I2**

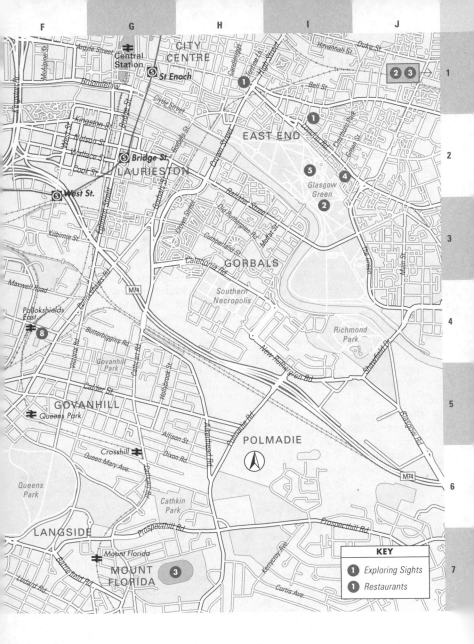

KEY

- ❶ Exploring Sights
- ❶ Restaurants

GETTING HERE AND AROUND

To get to the East End, take the subway to the St. Enoch station and walk along Argyle Street to the Tron Cross. From there, London Road takes you to Glasgow Green. Walking even farther along the road will lead you to the increasingly hip and trendy area of Dennistoun.

◉ Sights

Glasgow Cross

HISTORIC SIGHT | This crossroads was the center of the medieval city. The Mercat Cross (*mercat* means "market"), topped by a unicorn, marks the spot where merchants met, where the market was held, and where criminals were executed. Here, too, was the *tron*, or weigh beam, installed in 1491 and used by merchants to check weights. The Tolbooth Steeple dates from 1626 and served as the civic center and the place where travelers paid tolls. ✉ *Intersection of Saltmarket, Trongate, Gallowgate, and London Rds., East End* Ⓜ *St. Enoch.*

Glasgow Green

CITY PARK | FAMILY | Glasgow's oldest park has a long history as a favorite spot for public recreation and political demonstrations. Note the Nelson Column, erected long before London's; the McLennan Arch, originally part of the facade of the old Assembly Halls in Ingram Street; and the Templeton Business Centre, a former carpet factory built in the late 19th century in the style of the Doge's Palace in Venice. There is an adventure playground for kids and a small cycle track beside it, with children's bikes for rent. Don't miss the **People's Palace** and the Doulton Fountain that faces it. The Green also hosts the World Piping Championship in summer and a major firework display for Guy Fawkes night (November 5). ✉ *East End* ✛ *North side of River Clyde between ?een St. and Saltmarket St.*

People's Palace and Winter Gardens

HISTORY MUSEUM | FAMILY | The excited conversations among local visitors are the evidence that this museum tells the story of everyday lives in Glasgow. There is always something that sparks a memory: a photo, an object, a sound. Inside you'll find the writing desk of John McLean (1879–1923), the famous "Red Clydeside" political activist, and the banana boots worn onstage by Glasgow-born comedian Billy Connolly. On the top floor a sequence of fine murals by Glasgow artist Ken Currie tells the story of the city's working-class citizens. In contrast, the Doulton Fountain opposite the entrance celebrates the British empire. The museum is housed in a Victorian red-sandstone building at the heart of Glasgow Green, and behind it are the restored Winter Gardens (a Victorian conservatory) and a popular café. To get here from the St. Enoch subway station, walk along Argyle Street past Glasgow Cross. ✉ *Glasgow Green, Monteith Row, East End* ☎ *0141/276–0788* ⊕ *www. glasgowlife.org.uk* ✉ *Free* ☉ *Closed Mon.* Ⓜ *St. Enoch.*

🍴 Restaurants

The East End has developed an increasingly impressive culinary scene in recent years, particularly in the up-and-coming Dennistoun neighborhood, now popular with artistic young professionals. There are also a few gems in the Gallowgate area, just a stone's throw from the famous Barras market.

Barras Art and Design (*BAaD*)

$$ | ECLECTIC | A welcome addition for East End diners, BAaD occupies a sprawling campus of spaces, including a stylish glass-roofed courtyard, a large beer garden split over two levels, several refurbished shipping containers, and a central courtyard space within the heart of Glasgow's original flea market, the Barras. The fashionable space hosts a series of pop-up kitchens, bringing various street food options to a crowd of trendy East

End residents and visitors alike. **Known for:** excellent pop-up kitchens; stylish design; good selection of beers. $ *Average main: £16* ✉ *Barras Architecture and Design Centre, 54 Calton Entry, East End* ☎ *0141/552–4931* ⊕ *www.baadglasgow. com* ⊗ *Closed Mon. and Tues.*

Celino's

$$ | ITALIAN | This amazing Italian delicatessen and restaurant is located on Alexandra Parade, one of the East End's busiest thoroughfares. The beloved spot has been family-run since 1982, when it first opened in the heart of Dennistoun. **Known for:** brilliant selection of meats and cheeses; delicious Sunday lunches; lots of crowds. $ *Average main: £15* ✉ *620 Alexandra Parade, East End* ☎ *0141/554–0523* ⊕ *www.celinos.com.*

Dennistoun BBQ

$ | BURGER | An iconic burger restaurant on Duke Street in Dennistoun, this independent spot has quickly become a cult favorite in the area, with tables filling up most nights of the week. The no-frills burger joint serves huge topped burgers (with vegan and vegetarian options too) and delicious ribs. **Known for:** flame-grilled burgers; good vegan options; imported sodas. $ *Average main: £13* ✉ *585 Duke St., East End* ☎ *0141/237–7200* ⊕ *www.dennistounbbq. com* ⊗ *Closed Mon. and Tues. No lunch Wed. and Thurs.* Ⓜ *Duke Street.*

West on the Green

$$ | GERMAN | This microbrewery serves beer brewed "according to German purity laws of 1516"—in other words, no additives to muddy the flavor. The German theme is continued with the slightly cavernous dining space dotted with large wooden tables, and the food, which includes wursts, Wiener schnitzel, and goulash. **Known for:** weekend brewery tours with tasting; classic German cuisine like wurst and potato salad; variety of its own beer served in a popular beer garden. $ *Average main: £15* ✉ *Templeton Bldg., Templeton St., East End* ☎ *0141/550–0135* ⊕ *www.westbeer.com* Ⓜ *St. Enoch.*

🛍 Shopping

★ Barras

MARKET | Scotland's largest indoor market—named for the barrows, or pushcarts, formerly used by the stallholders—prides itself on selling everything "from a needle to an anchor" and is a must-see for anyone addicted to searching through piles of junk for bargains. Open on weekends only, the atmosphere is always good-natured, and you can find just about anything here, in any condition, from dusty model railroads to antique jewelry. Haggling is mandatory. You can reach the Barras by walking along Argyle Street from the St. Enoch subway station. The Barrowland Ballroom, which forms part of the market, was once where Glaswegians went to dance; today it is a venue for concerts of every kind. **■TIP→ Across the road is one of Glasgow's oldest pubs, the Saracen's Head; enter with caution—ghosts are said to abound.** ✉ *Gallowgate, East End* ⊕ *www.theglasgowbarras.com.*

South Side

Just southwest of the City Centre in the South Side are two of Glasgow's dear green spaces—Bellahouston Park and Pollok Country Park—which have important art collections: Charles Rennie Mackintosh's House for an Art Lover in Bellahouston, and Pollok House in Pollok Country Park. A respite from the buzz of the city can also be found in the parks, where you can have a picnic or ramble through greenery and gardens.

GETTING HERE AND AROUND

Both parks are off Pollokshaws Road, about 3 miles southwest of City Centre. You can take a taxi or car, city bus, or a train from Glasgow Central station to Pollokshaws West station or Dumbreck.

👁 Sights

Hampden Park

SPORTS VENUE | **FAMILY** | A mecca for soccer enthusiasts who come from far and near to tread the famous turf, the home field for the country's national team was the largest stadium in the world when it was built in 1903. There are stadium tours on non-match days at 11, 12:30, 2, and 3. You can then visit the Scottish Football Museum, which traces the history of the game; the museum may close on game days. ✉ *Letherby Dr., East End* ✛ *Nearest rail stations are Mount Florida and Kings Park. Buses from City Centre* ☎ *0141/616–6139* ⊕ *www.hampdenpark. co.uk* 🎫 *Stadium tour £8, museum entrance £8, combined ticket £13.*

House for an Art Lover

HISTORIC HOME | Within Bellahouston Park is a "new" Mackintosh house, based on a competition entry Charles Rennie Mackintosh submitted to a German magazine in 1901. The house was never built in his lifetime, but took shape between 1989 and 1996. It is home to Glasgow School of Art's postgraduate study center, and displays show designs for the various rooms and decorative pieces by Mackintosh and his wife, Margaret. The main lounge is spectacular. There's also a café and shop filled with art. Buses 9, 53, and 54 from Union Street will get you here. Call ahead, as opening times can vary. ✉ *Bellahouston Park, 10 Dumbreck Rd., South Side* ☎ *0141/353–4770* ⊕ *www.houseforanartlover.co.uk* 🎫 *£6* ⊙ *Closed weekdays Oct.–Mar.* Ⓜ *Ibrox.*

Pollok House

HISTORIC HOME | This classic Georgian house, dating from the mid-1700s, sits amid landscaped gardens and avenues of trees that are now part of Pollok Country Park. It still has the tranquil air of a wealthy but unpretentious country house. The Stirling Maxwell Collection includes paintings by Blake and a strong grouping of Spanish works by El Greco, Murillo, and Goya. Lovely examples of 18th- and early-19th-century furniture, silver, glass, and porcelain are also on display. The house has beautiful gardens that overlook the White Cart River. The downstairs servants' quarters include the kitchen, which is now a café-restaurant. The closest train station is Pollokshaws West, from Glasgow Central station; or you can take Buses 45, 47, or 57 to the gate of Pollok County Park. ✉ *Pollok County Park, 2060 Pollokshaws Rd., South Side* ☎ *0141/616–6410* ⊕ *www. nts.org.uk* 🎫 *£7.50.*

Scotland Street School Museum

OTHER MUSEUM | **FAMILY** | A former school designed by Charles Rennie Mackintosh, this building houses a fascinating museum of education. Classrooms re-create school life in Scotland during Victorian times and World War II, and a cookery room recounts a time when education for Scottish girls consisted of little more than learning how to become a housewife. There's also an exhibition space and a café. The building sits opposite Shields Road subway station. ✉ *225 Scotland St., South Side* ☎ *0141/287–0513* ⊕ *www. glasgowlife.org.uk* 🎫 *Free* ⊙ *Closed Mon.* Ⓜ *Shields Rd.*

Tramway

ARTS CENTER | **FAMILY** | South of the City Centre, this innovative arts center is well worth seeking out. It hosts regular exhibitions in its two galleries, and plays—often of a very experimental nature—in its flexible theater space. The city's famed Citizens Theatre Company also currently performs here while its permanent space undergoes a major renovation. Tramway has a café and a more formal restaurant on the first floor. Don't miss the Hidden Garden, which has transformed an empty lot behind the building into a sculpture park. To get here, take the train from Glasgow Central station to Pollokshields East (one stop).

It is also home to the fantastic Scottish Ballet, who train upstairs. Often if you

Ayrshire, Clyde Coast, and Robert Burns Country

ask nicely you can even pop upstairs and watch their training sessions. ✉ *25 Albert Dr., South Side* ☎ *0845/330–3501* 🌐 *www.tramway.org.*

Ayrshire, Clyde Coast, and Robert Burns Country

The jigsaw puzzle of firths and straits and interlocking islands that you see as you fly into Glasgow Airport harbors numerous tempting one-day excursion destinations. You can travel south to visit the fertile farmlands of Ayrshire or west to the Firth of Clyde. Besides the spots related to celebrated Scottish poet Robert Burns, key treasures in this

area include Culzean Castle, as famous for its Robert Adam (1728–92) design as it is for its spectacular seaside setting and grounds.

For many people a highlight of this region is Robert Burns country, a 40-minute drive from Glasgow. The poet was born in Alloway, beside Ayr, and the towns and villages where he lived and loved make for an interesting day out. English children learn that Burns (1759–96) is a good minor poet, but Scottish children know that he's Shakespeare, Dante, Rabelais, Mozart, and Karl Marx rolled into one. As time goes by, it seems that the Scots have it more nearly right, as Burns increases in stature both as a poet and humanist. When you plunge into Burns country, don't forget that he's held in extreme reverence by Scots across the board. They may argue about Sir Walter Scott and Bonnie Prince Charlie, but there's no disputing the merits of the author of "Auld Lang Syne" and "A Man's a Man for A' That."

GETTING HERE AND AROUND

From Glasgow you can take the bus or train (from Glasgow Central station) to Ayr for the Burns Heritage Trail; and Troon, Prestwick, and Ayr to play golf. Bus companies also operate one-day guided excursions; for details, contact the tourist information center in Glasgow or the Strathclyde Passenger Transport Travel Centre. Traveline Scotland has helpful information.

If you're driving from Glasgow, there are two main routes to Ayr. The quickest is to take the M77 to the A77, which takes you to Ayr, where Alloway is well signposted. The alternative and much slower but more scenic route is the coast road; take the M8 to Greenock and continue down the coast on the A78 until you meet the A77 and continue on into Burns Country.

Paisley

7 miles west of Glasgow.

The industrial prosperity of Paisley came from textiles and, in particular, from the woolen paisley shawl. The internationally recognized paisley pattern is based on the shape of a palm shoot, an ancient Babylonian fertility symbol brought from Kashmir. Today you can explore this history at several attractions in town.

GETTING HERE AND AROUND

Paisley-bound buses depart from the Buchanan Street bus station in Glasgow. Trains to Paisley's Gilour Street depart daily every 5 to 10 minutes from Glasgow Central station. If you're driving, take the M8 westbound and turn off at Junction 27, which is clearly signposted to Paisley.

👁 Sights

Paisley Abbey

RELIGIOUS BUILDING | Paisley's 12th-century abbey dominates the town center. Founded as a Cluniac monastery and almost completely destroyed by the English in 1307, the abbey was not totally restored until the early 20th century. It's associated with Walter Fitzallan, the high steward of Scotland, who gave his name to the Stewart monarchs of Scotland (Stewart is a corruption of "steward"). Outstanding features include the vaulted stone roof and stained glass of the choir. ✉ *13 High St., Paisley* ☎ *0141/889–7654* 🌐 *www.paisleyabbey.org.uk* 🎟 *Free.*

Sma' Shot Cottages

HISTORIC HOME | To get an idea of the life led by textile industry workers, visit the Sma' Shot Cottages. These re-creations of mill workers' houses contain displays of linen, lace, and paisley shawls. Two typical cottages, built 150 years apart, are open to visitors. ✉ *11–17 George Pl., Paisley* ☎ *0141/889–1708* 🌐 *www.smashotcottages.co.uk* 🎟 *Free* 🕒 *Closed Oct.–Mar. and Sun.–Tues. and Thurs. in Apr.–Sept.*

🛏 Hotels

Mar Hall

$$$ | **HOTEL** | This imposing baronial house, now a luxurious golf and spa resort, sits amid formal gardens and overlooks the River Clyde and verdant woodlands. **Pros:** wonderful country setting but also near airport; spacious rooms; fantastic pool. **Cons:** not ideal for families; very expensive; quite remote. [$] *Rooms from: £220* ✉ *Earl of Mar Estate, Mar Hall Dr., Bishopton* ☎ *0141/812–9999* 🌐 *www.marhall.com* 🛏 *53 rooms* 🍴 *Free Breakfast.*

Irvine

24 miles south of Glasgow.

Beyond Irvine's cobbled streets and grand Victorian buildings, look for a peaceful crescent-shaped harbor and fishermen's cottages huddled in solidarity against the Atlantic winds. The Scottish Maritime Museum pays homage to the town's seafaring past. Scotland's national poet, Robert Burns, lived here in 1781. Golf clubs Western Gailes and nearby Royal Troon make the area popular with golfers.

GETTING HERE AND AROUND

By car, take the M8 from Glasgow, then the A726 and the A736 to Irvine. By rail, direct trains leave regularly from Glasgow Central station; it's a 40-minute journey.

Sights

★ Scottish Maritime Museum

HISTORY MUSEUM | FAMILY | On the waterfront in the coastal town of Irvine, this museum brings together ships and boats—both models and the real thing—to tell the tale of Scotland's maritime history, as well as chronicle the lives of its boatbuilders, fishermen, and sailors. The atmospheric Linthouse Engine Building, part of a former shipyard, hosts most of the displays. The museum also includes a shipyard worker's tenement home that you can explore. In Dumbarton, 35 miles to the north, you can visit the Denny Tank (part of the museum), where ship designs were tested. **■ TIP→ Children are admitted free.** ✉ *6 Gottries Rd., Irvine* ☎ *01294/278283* 🌐 *www.scottishmaritimemuseum.org* 🎫 *£8.50.*

Hotels

Piersland House Hotel

$$ | HOTEL | Formerly the home of a whisky magnate, this late-Victorian mansion on the southern edge of town is now a country-house hotel. **Pros:** near Prestwick Airport; gorgeous gardens and grounds; close to golf courses. **Cons:** not much nearby besides golf courses; can get crowded with private functions; helps to have a car to get around. [$] *Rooms from: £130* ✉ *15 Craigend Rd., Troon* ✣ *7 miles south of Irvine via the A78* ☎ *01292/314747* 🌐 *www.piersland.co.uk* 🛏 *37 rooms* 🍴 *Free Breakfast.*

Activities

★ Royal Troon Golf Club

GOLF | Of the two courses at Royal Troon, it's the Old or Championship Course—a traditional links course with superb sea views frequently used for the British Open—that is renowned among golfers. The second, Portland, shares the challenges of strong sea breezes and the gorse beside the fairways. Advance payment and a deposit are required, as is a handicap certificate. It is a good idea to check the tournament calendar before you go. ✉ *Craigend Rd., Troon* ✣ *9 miles south of Irvine via the A78* ☎ *01292/311555* 🌐 *www.royaltroon.com* 🎫 *Old Course, £250; Portland Course, £85; both courses £290 total in Sept.* ⛳ *Old Course: 18 holes, 7208 yards, par 71; Portland Course: 18 holes, 6349 yards, par 72* ☞ *Closed for visitors Nov.–mid-Apr.*

★ Western Gailes Golf Club

GOLF | Known as the finest natural links course in Scotland, Western Gailes is entirely nature-made, and the greens are kept in truly magnificent condition. This is the final qualifying course when the British Open is held at Royal Troon or Trump Turnberry. Tom Watson lists the par-5 6th hole as one of his favorites. Visitors can play during restricted hours through the week; reserve online. ✉ *Gailes Rd., Irvine* ☎ *01294/311649* 🌐 *www.westerngailes.com* 🎫 *Nov.–Feb £70 per round; Mar. £100 per round; Apr. and Oct. £140 per round; May–Sept. £175 per round* ⛳ *18 holes, 6640 yards, par 71.*

Ayr and Alloway

10 miles south of Irvine, 34 miles south of Glasgow.

The commercial port of Ayr is Ayrshire's chief town, a peaceful and elegant place with an air of prosperity. Poet Robert Burns was baptized in the Auld Kirk (Old Church) here and wrote a humorous poem about the Twa Brigs (Two Bridges) that cross the river nearby. Burns described Ayr as a town unsurpassed "for honest men and bonny lasses."

If you're on the Robert Burns trail, head for Alloway, on B7024 in Ayr's southern suburbs. A number of sights here are part of the Burns National Heritage Park, including the magnificent Robert Burns Birthplace Museum.

GETTING HERE AND AROUND

From Glasgow you can take the bus or train to Ayr; travel time is about an hour (a bit less by train). Drivers can use the A78 and A77 near the coast; a car would provide more flexibility to see the Burns sites around Alloway.

◉ Sights

Auld Kirk Alloway

CHURCH | This small ruined church is famous for its role in Burns's epic poem, "Tam o' Shanter," which many Scots know by heart and is often recited at Burns Suppers. In the poem, the kirk is where a rather drunk Tam o' Shanter unluckily passed a witches' revel—with Old Nick himself playing the bagpipes—on his unsteady way home. In flight from the witches, Tam managed to cross the medieval Brig o' Doon (*brig* is Scots for *bridge*; you can still see the bridge) just in time. His gray mare, Meg, however, lost her tail to the closest witch. (Any resident of Ayr will tell you that witches cannot cross running water.) ✉ *Murdoch's Alloway* 🎟 *Free.*

Remembering Mr. Burns ◉

Born in Ayrshire, poet and balladeer Robert Burns (1759–96) is one of Scotland's treasures. His most famous song, "Auld Lang Syne," is heard everywhere on New Year's Day. Burns's talent, charisma, and good looks made him an icon to both the upper and lower classes (and made him quite popular with the ladies). Today his birthday (January 25) is considered a national holiday; on "Burns Night" young and old alike get together for Burns Suppers and recite his work over neeps, tatties, and drams of the country's finest whisky.

Burns Cottage

HISTORIC HOME | In the delightful Burns Heritage Park, this thatched cottage is where Scotland's national poet lived for his first seven years. It has a living room, a kitchen, and a stable, one behind the other. The life and times of Burns, born in 1759, are beautifully and creatively illustrated in the fly-on-the-wall videos of daily life in the 18th century. The garden is lush with the types of vegetables the poet's father might have grown. From the cottage, take the Poet's Path through the village to the Robert Burns Birthplace Museum, the spooky churchyard where Tam o' Shanter faced fearsome ghosts, and the Brig o' Doon, all included in the museum entry ticket. ✉ *Greenfield Ave., Alloway* 🕿 *0844/493-2601* ⊕ *www.burnsmuseum.org.uk* 🎟 *£11.50, includes Burns Monument and Robert Burns Birthplace Museum.*

Burns Monument

MONUMENT | This neoclassical structure, built in 1823, overlooks the Brig o' Doon. You can climb to the top (with some care!). Entrance is included in the Burns Museum ticket. ✉ *Murdoch's Lone, Alloway* 🕿

⊕ *www.burnsmuseum.org.uk* ✉ *Free; also included in ticket to Burns Cottage and Robert Burns Birthplace Museum.*

Dumfries House

HISTORIC HOME | Built in the 1750s by the Adam brothers, Dumfries House has preserved the living conditions of the landed aristocracy of the time. The restored house contains a large collection of furniture by Chippendale that is original to the property, as well as pieces by other great designers of the period. Run by a charity headed by Prince Charles, the surrounding 2,000-acre estate is currently in development as a site for an eco-village and centers practicing historic crafts. Entry is by guided tour only; booking ahead is essential. There are 22 guest rooms, some cottages, and a restaurant on the property as well. ✉ *Cumnock* ✛ *From Ayr, take the A70 to Cumnock; it's about 10 miles* ☎ *01290/421742* ⊕ *www.dumfries-house.org.uk* ✉ *Guided tour £12; extended tour £16* ⊙ *Closed weekdays Nov.–Mar.*

★ Robert Burns Birthplace Museum

MUSEUM VILLAGE | Besides being a poet of delicacy and depth, Robert Burns was also a rebel, a thinker, a lover, a good companion, and a man of the countryside. This wonderful museum explains why the Scots so admire this complex "man o' pairts." The imaginative displays present each of his poems in context, with commentaries sensitively written in a modern version of the Scots language in which he spoke and wrote. Headsets let you hear the poems sung or spoken. The exhibits are vibrant and interactive, with touch screens that allow you to debate his views on politics, love, taxation, revolution, and Scottishness. An elegant café offers a place to pause, while the kids can play in the adjoining garden. Included in the ticket are the Burns Cottage, a few minutes' walk down a Burns-themed walkway, and the Burns Monument. ✉ *Murdoch's Lone, Alloway* ☎ *01292/443700* ⊕ *www.burnsmuseum.*

org.uk ✉ *£11.50, includes Burns Cottage and Burns Monument.*

Restaurants

Brig o' Doon House

$$ | BRITISH | Originally built in 1827, this attractive hotel restaurant often has a piper by the door to greet hungry travelers ready for a Scottish setting and some Scottish fare. Tartan carpets, dark-wood paneling, and buck heads mounted on the walls set the mood, and the bar is a shrine to Robert Burns. **Known for:** great venison casserole; riverside location; Scottish food and decor. $ *Average main: £15* ✉ *High Maybole Rd., Alloway* ☎ *01292/442466* ⊕ *www.brigodoonhouse.com.*

Cafe Le Monde

$ | ITALIAN | This Italian-style café with alfresco seating for good weather serves lunch and smaller bites to a mainly day-visitor crowd. The ciabattas and soups are well made and substantial, if not enormously adventurous, and the staff is attentive. **Known for:** outdoor seating; tasty soups and toasted cheese sandwiches; good coffee. $ *Average main: £12* ✉ *36 Newmarket St., Ayr* ☎ *01292/611219* ⊙ *No dinner.*

Activities

GOLF

Prestwick Golf Club

GOLF | Tom Morris helped design this challenging Ayrshire coastal links course, which saw the birth of the British Open Championship in 1860. The first hole is reputed to be among the most challenging in Scotland, since the railway line runs along the length of the hole. But it doesn't get any easier after that. Some of its bunkers are especially threatening, and the bumps at the 5th are high enough to be called the Himalayas. Prestwick has excellent, fast rail links with Glasgow. There are a limited number of tee times on Saturday afternoon. ✉ *2 Links Rd., Prestwick* ✛ *4 miles south*

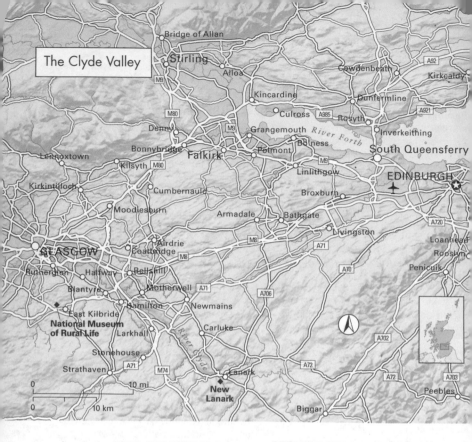

The Clyde Valley

Ayr via the A79 ☎ 01292/477404 ⊕ www.
prestwickgc.co.uk ✉ Apr. and Oct., £180
weekdays, £230 weekends; May–Sept.,
weekdays £220, weekends £250; Nov.–
Mar. Mon.–Sat. £105, Sun. £120 🎏 18
holes, 6544 yards, par 71.

Culzean Castle and Country Park

*12 miles south of Ayr, 50 miles south of
Glasgow.*

There's plenty to do at this popular spot
between visiting the Robert Adam–
designed house and touring the extensive grounds.

GETTING HERE AND AROUND

Stagecoach buses run from Ayr to the
park entrance; the nearest train station
from Glasgow is at Maybole, 4 miles to
the east, but there is Stagecoach bus
service to the park entrance from there.

Note that the park entrance is a mile
walk from the castle visitor center.

◉ Sights

★ Culzean Castle and Country Park

CASTLE/PALACE | **FAMILY** | The dramatic cliff-
top castle of Culzean (pronounced ku-*lain*)
is quite a long drive from Glasgow, but
it's the National Trust for Scotland's most
popular property. Robert Adam designed
the neoclassical mansion, complete with
a walled garden, in 1777. The grounds are
enormous and beautifully kept, combining
parkland, forests, and a beach looking out

To experience life in an 18th-century industrial community, visit New Lanark.

over the Atlantic Ocean; the surprisingly lush shrubberies reflect the warm currents that explain the mild climate. There are caves in the cliffs; tours are occasionally available. In the castle itself you can visit the armory, luxuriously appointed salons and bedchambers, and a nursery with its lovely cradle in a boat. Adam's grand double spiral staircase is the high point of its design. There's a free audio tour, and guided tours are available daily at 11 and 2:30. A short walk through the woods brings you to the visitor center with shops and a restaurant. ⊠ *Culzean Castle, A719, Maybole* ☎ *01655/884455* ⊕ *www.nts.org. uk* 🎫 *£6.50* ☺ *Castle closed Jan.–Apr.*

The Clyde Valley

The River Clyde is (or certainly was) famous for its shipbuilding, yet its upper reaches flow through some of Scotland's most fertile farmlands, rich with crops of tomatoes and fruit. It's an interesting area with some museums, most notably at New Lanark, that tell the story of the growth of manufacturing.

GETTING HERE AND AROUND

If you're driving from Glasgow, head south on the M74 and turn on to the A72. This is the main road through the Clyde Valley, ending at Lanark. Train service runs from Glasgow Central station to Lanark; for details check National Rail.

National Museum of Rural Life

9 miles south of Glasgow.

The effect of farming on the land and on people's lives is the focus of this museum near Glasgow.

GETTING HERE AND AROUND

From Glasgow, take the M77 and then the A726 at Junction 4 to East Kilbride, or the A725 from Blantyre to East Kilbride; it's a 20-minute drive. You can take the train from Glasgow Central station to East Kilbride, then taxi or bus. By bus take First Bus 31 from St. Enoch Centre in Glasgow.

Sights

★ National Museum of Rural Life

OTHER MUSEUM | FAMILY | Set in a rural area, this lovely museum exploring every aspect of the country's agricultural heritage is slightly off the beaten track but well worth the trip. It is a whole day out. In a modern building resembling a huge barn you learn about how farming transformed the land, experience the life and hardships of those who worked it, and see displays of tools and machines from across the ages. Take a tractor ride to a fully functioning 1950s farmhouse. There are also some great exhibits geared toward children and a range of summer events. ✉ *Wester Kittochside, Philipshill Rd., East Kilbride* ☎ *0300/123-6789* 🌐 *www.nms.ac.uk/rural* 🎟 *£8.*

New Lanark

25 miles southeast east of Glasgow.

Set in pleasing, rolling countryside, New Lanark was a model workers' community that is now a museum and World Heritage site. It's about a mile to the south of the old Scottish town of Lanark.

GETTING HERE AND AROUND

If you're driving, take the M74 to the A72. The train from Glasgow Central station to Lanark takes 50 minutes or so; then take a taxi or bus. New Lanark is signposted from Lanark; you drive to the parking lot and walk down into New Lanark.

Sights

★ New Lanark

MUSEUM VILLAGE | FAMILY | Now a UNESCO World Heritage site, New Lanark was home to a social experiment at the beginning of the Industrial Revolution. Robert Owen (1771–1858), together with his father-in-law, David Dale (1739–1806), set out to create a model industrial community with well-designed worker homes, a school, and public buildings. Owen went on to establish other communities on similar principles, both in Britain and in the United States. Robert Owen's son, Robert Dale Owen (1801–77), went on to help found the Smithsonian Institution.

After many changes of fortune, the mills eventually closed. One of the buildings has been converted into a visitor center that tells the story of this brave social experiment. You can also explore Robert Owen's house, the school, and a mill worker's house, and enjoy the Annie McLeod Experience, a fairground ride that takes you through the story of one mill worker's life. Other restored structures hold various shops and eateries; one has a rooftop garden with impressive views of the entire site. Another now houses the New Lanark Mill Hotel. **■ TIP→ It's a good idea to book your ticket ahead in summer to avoid lines.**

The River Clyde powers its way through a beautiful wooded gorge here, and its waters were once harnessed to drive textile-mill machinery. Upstream it flows through some of the finest river scenery anywhere in Lowland Scotland, with woods and waterfalls. ✉ *New Lanark Rd., New Lanark* ☎ *01555/661345* 🌐 *www.newlanark.org* 🎟 *£12.50.*

Hotels

New Lanark Mill Hotel

$$ | HOTEL | Housed in a converted cotton mill by the river in the 18th-century village of New Lanark, this hotel is decorated in a spare, understated style that allows the impressive architecture of barrel-vaulted ceilings and elegant Georgian windows to speak for itself. **Pros:** impressive spa; beautiful river views; large rooms. **Cons:** restaurant is the only one in the vicinity; some rooms can get cold; bland bar. [$] *Rooms from: £135* ✉ *New Lanark Rd., New Lanark* ☎ *01555/667200* 🌐 *www.newlanarkmillhotel.co.uk* 🛏 *38 rooms* 🍴 *Free Breakfast.*

Chapter 5

THE BORDERS AND THE SOUTHWEST

Updated by
Mike Gonzalez

👁 **Sights**
★★☆☆☆

🍴 **Restaurants**
★★☆☆☆

🛏 **Hotels**
★☆☆☆☆

🛍 **Shopping**
★☆☆☆☆

🍸 **Nightlife**
★☆☆☆☆

WELCOME TO
THE BORDERS AND THE SOUTHWEST

TOP REASONS TO GO

★ **Ancient abbeys:** The great abbeys of the Border regions and the wonderful Sweetheart Abbey in the Southwest are mainly in ruins, but they retain an air of their former grandeur.

★ **Outdoor activities:** You can walk, bicycle, or even ride horses across Galloway or through the Borders. Abandoned railway tracks make good paths, and there are forests and moorlands if you prefer wilder country.

★ **Stately homes and castles:** Some of the landed aristocracy still lives in these grand mansions, and most of the homes are open to visitors, like Floors Castle, Threave, Drumlanrig, and the magical Caerlaverock Castle near Dumfries.

★ **Literary Scotland:** The Borders region has enough monuments dedicated to Sir Walter Scott to make him the focus of a visit. The poet Robert Burns spent much of his working life in Dumfries, and the Moat Brae Centre in Dumfries was where J. M. Barrie first came up with Peter Pan.

1 Jedburgh. A pretty town dominated by a glorious abbey.

2 Kelso. A charming market town close to imposing Floors Castle.

3 Melrose. Home to a ruined abbey and the house once belonging to Sir Walter Scott.

4 Galashiels. An old mill town now home to the Great Tapestry of Scotland.

5 Selkirk. Another small town with Sir Walter Scott history.

6 Hawick. A larger Borders town central to the region's wool industry.

7 Innerleithen. A former industrial boomtown of wool mills now popular for its outdoor activities.

8 Peebles. A busy market town with great shopping.

9 Gretna Green. A town right on the Scottish-English border with a quirky reputation as a haven for engaged couples.

10 Dumfries. A tranquil market town that was once home to Robert Burns and J. M. Barrie.

11 North of Dumfries. Where you'll find Drumlanrig Castle, *Crawick Multiverse*, and the Museum of Lead Mining.

12 Solway Firth. One of the area's best-kept secrets with an extraordinary population of wildlife and plants centered around Caerlaverock Castle.

13 Castle Douglas. A pleasant town specializing in local food products and home to Threave Castle.

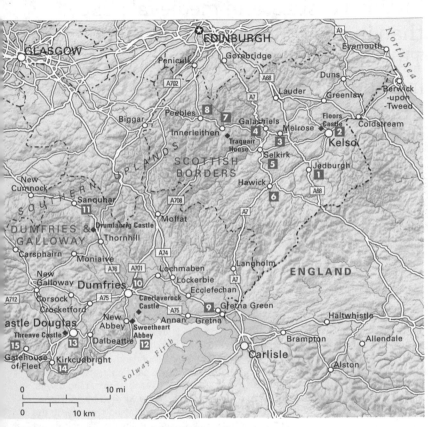

14 Kirkcudbright. A lovely harbor town once a haven for artists, including one of the "Glasgow Boys."

15 Gatehouse of Fleet. A peaceful small town with a traditional Scottish castle.

16 Newton Stewart. The gateway to Galloway Forest Park.

17 Whithorn. Home to the historic early Christian settlement of Whithorn Abbey.

18 Stranraer. Once the main ferry port for Ireland and now in the midst of redevelopment.

19 Portpatrick. A lovely village with dramatic cliff walks.

In the Borders region, south of Edinburgh, are more stately homes, fortified castles, and medieval abbeys than in any other part of Scotland. This is also Sir Walter Scott territory, including his pseudo-baronial home at Abbotsford.

The area embraces the whole 90-mile course of one of Scotland's great rivers, the Tweed. Passing woodlands luxuriant with game birds, the river flows in rushing torrents through this fertile land. To the west of the Borders is Dumfries and Galloway, an area of gentle coasts, forests, and lush hills, ideal country for walkers and cyclists.

For centuries the Borders was a battlefield, where English and Scottish troops remained locked in a struggle for its possession. At different times, parts of the region have been in English hands, just as slices of northern England (Berwick-upon-Tweed, for example) have been under Scottish control. The castles and fortified houses as well as the abbeys across the Borders are the surviving witnesses to those times. After the Union of 1707, fortified houses gradually gave way to the luxurious country mansions that pepper the area. And by the 19th century they had become grand country houses like Mellerstain House, built by fashionable architects.

All the main routes between London and Edinburgh traverse the Borders, whose interland of undulating pastures, woods, and valleys is enclosed within three lone-groups of hills: the Cheviots, the Moor- and the Lammermuirs. Hamlets sperous country towns dot the land, giving valley slopes a lived-in look, yet the total population is still sparse. The sheep that are the basis of the region's prosperous textile industry outnumber human beings by 14 to 1.

To the west is the region of Dumfries and Galloway, on the shores of the Solway Firth. It might appear to be an extension of the Borders, but the southwest has a history all its own. From its ports ships sailed to the Americas, carrying country dwellers driven from their land to make room for sheep. Inland, the earth rises toward high hills, forest, and bleak but captivating moorland, whereas nearer the coast you can find pretty farmlands, small villages, and unassuming towns. The shoreline is washed by the North Atlantic Drift (Scotland's answer to the Gulf Stream), and first-time visitors are always surprised to see palm trees and exotic plants thriving in gardens and parks along the coast.

At the heart of the region is Dumfries, the "Queen o' the South." Once a major port and commercial center, its glamour is now slightly faded. But the memory of poet Robert Burns, who spent several years living and working here and who is buried in the town, remains very much alive. In addition, Moat Brae can claim to be the location of Neverland, the imaginary world of *Peter Pan*, which was written there.

MAJOR REGIONS

The Borders. Borders towns cluster around and between two rivers—the Tweed and its tributary, the Teviot. Borders folk take great pride in the region's fame as Scotland's main woolen-goods manufacturing area. Its main towns—Jedburgh, Hawick, Selkirk, Peebles, Kelso, and Melrose—retain an air of prosperity and confidence with their solid stone houses and elegant town squares. Although many mills have closed since the 1980s, the pride in local identity is still evident in the fiercely contested Melrose Sevens rugby competition in April and the annual Common Ridings—local events commemorating the time when towns needed to patrol their borders—throughout June and July. A visit to at least one of the region's four great ruined abbeys makes the quintessential Borders experience. The monks in these powerful, long-abandoned religious communities were the first to work the fleeces of their sheep flocks, thus laying the groundwork for what is still the area's main manufacturing industry.

Although the Borders has many attractions, it's most famous for being the home base for Sir Walter Scott (1771–1832), the early-19th-century poet, novelist, and creator of *Ivanhoe*. Scott single-handedly transformed Scotland's image from that of a land of brutal savages to one of romantic and stirring deeds and magnificent landscapes. The novels of Scott are not read much nowadays—frankly, some of them are difficult to wade through—but the mystique that he created, the aura of historical romance, has outlasted his books. The ruined abbeys, historical houses, and grand vistas of the Borders provide a perfect backdrop.

Dumfries and Galloway. Galloway covers the southwestern portion of Scotland, west of the main town of Dumfries; it's a quiet and less-visited region of Scotland, in general. Here a gentle coastline gives

way to farmland and then breezy uplands that gradually merge with coniferous forests. The region now claims two extraordinary public art projects—Charles Jencks's *Crawick Multiverse* and Andy Goldsworthy's *Striding Arches*. The Solway Firth is a vast nature preserve, and the climate of the west sustains the surprising tropical plants at the Logan Botanic Gardens and the gardens at Threave Castle. Even farther west, Galloway draws active visitors to its forests to hike or cycle.

Planning

When to Go

Because many lodgings and some sights are privately owned and shut down from early autumn until early April, the area is less suited to off-season touring than some other parts of Scotland. The best time to visit is between Easter and late September. The region does look magnificent in autumn, especially along the wooded river valleys of the Borders. Late spring is the time to see the rhododendrons in the gardens of Dumfries and Galloway.

FESTIVALS
Common Ridings

FESTIVALS | More than 10 Borders communities have reestablished their identities through the annual summer gatherings known as the Common Ridings. In medieval times it was essential that each town be able to defend its area by "riding the marches," or patrolling the boundaries. The Common Ridings that celebrate this history are more authentic than the Highland Games concocted by the Victorians. Although this is above a celebration for native Borderers, y will be welcome to share the exci of clattering hooves and banners displayed. ⊠ *Galashiels* ⊕ *www theridings.co.uk*.

Dumfries & Galloway Arts Festival

FESTIVALS | Celebrated every year since 1979, this festival with music, theater, dance, and other events is usually held at the end of May at several venues throughout the region. ⊠ *Dumfries* ☎ *01387/260447* ⊕ *www.dgartsfestival. org.uk.*

Getting Oriented

What was for centuries a battleground region separating Scotland and England, today the Borders area is a bridge between the two countries. This is a place of upland moors and hills, farmland, and forested river valleys. Yet it also embraces the rugged coastline between Edinburgh and Berwick. It's rustic and peaceful, with textile mills, abbeys, castles, and gardens. The area is a big draw for hikers and walking enthusiasts, especially thanks to the lovely Tweed Valley Forest Park in the east and the Galloway Forest Park in the west. The Borders region is steeped in history, with Mary, Queen of Scots a powerful presence despite the relatively short time she spent here. Galashiels is now home to the magnificent Tapestry of Scotland, a history of the region woven in thread while the moorlands of the Southwest feature dramatic art projects like the *Striding Arches* and *Crawick Multiverse* as well as peaceful seascapes like the Solway Firth and wilder ones on the Galloway coast.

Planning Your Time

The Borders Railway has opened the route between Edinburgh and the Borders, running from Edinburgh's Waverley Station Tweedbank, in the heart of the Borders. mile journey passes through els (for connections to Traquair nd ends at Tweedbank, which is se and Walter Scott's home at Beyond the Borders Railway,

it is still more convenient to explore by car. If you're driving north along the A1 toward Edinburgh, it's easy to take a tour around the prosperous Borders towns. Turn onto the A698 at Berwick-upon-Tweed, which will take you along the Scottish–English border toward Kelso, Jedburgh, Dryburgh, and Melrose. It's 36 miles from Jedburgh to Peebles, a good place to stay overnight. Another day might begin with a visit to Walter Scott's lovely Abbotsford House, and then some shopping in any of these prosperous towns.

To the west, Dumfries and Galloway beckon. If you're traveling north toward Glasgow on the M6/A74, take the A70 west toward Dumfries. From the A1, on the east coast, travel west on the A708 to Moffat and pick up the A70 there. From Glasgow take the A74 south to Beattock and pick up the A701 there. Two days would give you time to explore Burns sites and more in Dumfries. From Dumfries you can visit Sweetheart Abbey (8 miles away), Caerlaverock Castle (9 miles away), and Threave Castle and Gardens (20 miles away). Castle Douglas is a good place to stop for lunch. The A710 and A711 take you along the dramatic coastline of the Solway Firth. Farther west along the A75 are the towns of Newton Stewart and Portpatrick, and on the A714, Glen Trool. The region does not have good rail links but there is good bus service, and by car it is a charming and compact region.

Getting Here and Around

AIR

The nearest Scottish airports are at Edinburgh, Glasgow, and Prestwick (outside Glasgow).

BOAT AND FERRY

P&O European Ferries and Stena Line operate from Larne, in Northern Ireland, to Cairnryan, near Stranraer, several times daily. The crossing takes one hour on the Superstar Express, two hours on other ferries.

BOAT AND FERRY CONTACTS P&O
European Ferries. ☎ *0800/130–0030*
⊕ *www.poferries.com.* **Stena Line.**
☎ *08447/707070* ⊕ *www.stenaline.co.uk.*

BUS

If you're approaching from the south,
check with Scottish Citylink, National
Express, or First about buses from Edinburgh and Glasgow. In the Borders, First-
borders and Borders Buses offer service
within the region. Stagecoach Western is
the main bus company serving Dumfries
and Galloway.

BUS CONTACTS Borders Buses.
☎ *01896/754350* ⊕ *www.bordersbuses.*
co.uk.

CAR

Traveling by car is the best and easiest
way to explore the area, especially if
you get off the main, and often crowded, arterial roads and use the little back
roads. The main route into both the
Borders and Galloway from the south
is the M6, which becomes the M74 at
the border. You can then take the scenic
and leisurely A7 northwestward through
Hawick toward Edinburgh, or the A75
and other parallel routes westward into
Dumfries, Galloway, and the former ferry
ports of Stranraer (nearby Cairnryan is an
active ferry port) and Portpatrick.

There are several other possible routes:
starting from the east, the A1 brings you
from the English city of Newcastle to the
border in about an hour. Moving west,
the A697, which leaves the A1 north of
Morpeth (in England) and crosses the
border at Coldstream, is a leisurely back-
road option. The A68 is probably the most
scenic route to Scotland: after climbing to
Carter Bar, it reveals a view of the Borders
hills and windy skies before dropping into
the ancient town of Jedburgh.

TRAIN

Apart from the main London–Edinburgh
line, the Borders had no train service
until 2015, when the rail link from Edinburgh to Tweedbank began service. The
Borders Railway website has information
about using it to explore the area. In the
Southwest, trains headed from London's
Euston to Glasgow stop at Carlisle, just
south of the border, and some also stop
at Lockerbie. Trains between Glasgow
and Carlisle stop at Gretna Green, Annan,
and Dumfries. From Glasgow there is
service on the coastal route to Stranraer.

First Bus provides connections between
Hawick, Selkirk, and Galashiels and
train service at Carlisle, Edinburgh, and
Berwick.

TRAIN CONTACTS Borders Railway.
☎ *0344/811–0141* ⊕ *www.scotrail.co.uk.*
National Rail. ☎ *03457/484950* ⊕ *www.*
nationalrail.co.uk. **ScotRail.** ☎ *0344/811–*
0141 ⊕ *www.scotrail.co.uk.* **Trainline.**
☎ *0871/244–1545* ⊕ *www.thetrainline.*
com.

Restaurants

Most good restaurants in the region used
to be located in hotels, but today things
are changing. Good independent eateries
are popping up in small (and sometimes
unlikely) towns and villages, and many
new establishments specialize in fresh
local ingredients. Seasonal menus are
now popular. It is important to remember
that restaurants here usually serve lunch
between noon and 2 and dinner until
8:30 only.

Hotels

From top-quality, full-service hotels to
quaint 18th-century drovers' inns to cozy
bed-and-breakfasts, the Borders has
all manner of lodging options. Choices
in Dumfries and Galloway may be a
little less expensive than in the Borders
(with the same full range of services).
These days many establishments are
willing to lower their rates depending on
availability.

Restaurant and hotel reviews have been shortened. For full reviews, see Fodors. com. Restaurant prices are the average cost of a main course at dinner or, if dinner is not served, at lunch. Hotel prices are the lowest cost of a standard double room in high season, including 20% V.A.T.

WHAT IT COSTS in Pounds			
$	$$	$$$	$$$$
RESTAURANTS			
under £15	£15–£19	£20–£25	over £25
HOTELS			
under £125	£125–£200	£201–£300	over £300

Visitor Information

Visit Scottish Borders has offices in Jedburgh, Hawick, and Peebles. The Dumfries & Galloway Tourist Board can be found in Dumfries and Stranraer. Seasonal information centers are at Castle Douglas, Eyemouth, Galashiels, Gretna Green, Kelso, Kirkcudbright, Langholm, Moffat, Sanquhar, and Selkirk. Liveborders provides online information on cultural and sporting activities in the Borders.

CONTACTS VisitScotland Dumfries iCentre. ⊠ *64 Whitesands, Dumfries* ☎ *01387/253862* ⊕ *www.visitscotland.com.* **Liveborders.** ⊠ *Melrose Rd., Galashiels* ☎ *01896/661166* ⊕ *www.liveborders.org.uk.* **VisitScotland Jedburgh iCentre.** ⊠ *Murray's Green, Jedburgh* ☎ *01835/863170* ⊕ *www.visitscotland.com.*

Activities

Rugby Sevens
RUGBY | The Borders invented the fast-and-furious, cut-down version of rugby in 1883, though it has now spread worldwide. Teams are made up of 7 players rather than 15, and the matches are shorter. Although the population of the Borders is about 100,000, the region boasts a total of 17 clubs and some of Scotland's best players. Each spring, 10 teams compete for the Kings of the Sevens title. ⊠ *Melrose* ⊕ *www.k7s.co.uk.*

7stanes Mountain Biking
BIKING | Both the Borders and the Dumfries and Galloway regions are something of meccas for mountain bikers, offering trails and routes of every level of difficulty in beautiful and varying landscapes. This outfitter offers full equipment rental, skills training, advice, and local route maps organized by degree of difficulty. You can bring your own bike or rent one to ride gentle forest routes or tough hill climbs. There are eight centers across the regions; the most popular is Glentress located near Peebles. Each center has showers and changing facilities, as well as good cafés. Specific information on each is available on the comprehensive website. ⊠ *Campbell House, Crichton Business Park, Bankend Rd., Dumfries* ☎ *01721/721180* ⊕ *www.7stanesmountainbiking.com.*

Jedburgh

50 miles south of Edinburgh, 95 miles southeast of Glasgow.

The town of Jedburgh (*burgh* is always pronounced *burra* in Scots) was for centuries the first major Scottish target of invading English armies. In more peaceful times it developed textile mills, most of which have since languished. The large landscaped area around the town's tourist information center was once a mill but now provides an encampment for the armies of modern tourists. The past still clings to this little town, however. The ruined abbey dominates the skyline, a reminder of the formerly strong governing role of the Borders abbeys.

GETTING HERE AND AROUND

By car from Edinburgh, you can take the A68 (about 45 minutes) or the A7 (about an hour). From Glasgow take the M8, then the A68 direct to Jedburgh (about two hours).

There are fairly good bus connections from all major Scottish cities to Jedburgh. From Edinburgh direct routes to Melrose take about two hours. From Glasgow it takes 3½ hours to reach Melrose. From Melrose it's just 20 minutes to Jedburgh.

The Borders Railway runs between Edinburgh and Tweedbank, about 15 miles northwest of Jedburgh.

ESSENTIALS
VISITOR INFORMATION VisitScotland Jedburgh iCentre. ⊠ *Murray's Green, Jedburgh* ☎ *01835/863170* ⊕ *www. visitscotland.com.*

👁 Sights

Harestanes Countryside Visitor Centre
VISITOR CENTER | FAMILY | Housed in a former farmhouse 4 miles north of Jedburgh, this visitor center portrays life in the Scottish Borders through art exhibitions and natural history displays. Crafts such as woodworking and tile making are taught here, and finished projects are often on display. Outside are meandering paths, quiet roads for bike rides, and the biggest children's play area in the Borders. There's plenty for children, including a fascinating puzzle gallery full of sturdy wooden games. It is also on one of the best-known walking routes in the Borders, the St. Cuthbert's Path. ⊠ *Junction of A68 and B6400, 4 miles north of Jedburgh* ☎ *01835/830306* ⊕ *www.liveborders.org.uk* 🖃 *Free* 🕙 *Closed Nov.–Mar.*

Hermitage Castle
CASTLE/PALACE | To appreciate the famous 20-mile ride of Mary, Queen of Scots, in 1566—she rushed to the side of her wounded lover, the Earl of Bothwell—travel southwest from Jedburgh to this, the most complete remaining example of the bare and grim medieval border castles. Restored in the early 19th century, it was built in the 13th century to guard what was at the time one of the important routes from England into Scotland. Local folklore maintains that the 14th-century Lord Soulis, a descendant of the original owner and notorious for diabolical excess, was captured by the local populace, who wrapped him in lead and boiled him in a cauldron—a much better story than the reality, which is that he died in Dumbarton Jail. ⊠ *Hawick* ✛ *2 miles west of B6399, about 21 miles south of Jedburgh* ☎ *01387/376222* ⊕ *www.historicenvironment.scot* 🖃 *£6* 🕙 *Closed Oct.–Mar.*

★ Jedburgh Abbey
RELIGIOUS BUILDING | The most impressive of the Borders abbeys towers above Jedburgh. Built by David I, king of Scots in the 12th century, the abbey was nearly destroyed by the English Earl of Hertford's forces in 1544–45, during the destructive time known as the Rough Wooing. This was English king Henry VIII's (1491–1547) armed attempt to persuade the Scots that it was a good idea to unite the kingdoms by the marriage of his young son to the infant Mary, Queen of Scots (1542–87); the Scots disagreed and sent Mary to France instead. The story is explained in vivid detail at the visitor center, which also has information about the ruins and an audio tour. The arched abbey walls, the nave, and the cloisters still give a sense of the power these buildings represented. ⊠ *High St., Jedburgh* ☎ *01835/863925* ⊕ *www. historicenvironment.scot* 🖃 *£3.*

Jedburgh Castle Jail and Museum
JAIL/PRISON | FAMILY | This building might look like a castle, but it's actually a prison that sits where a castle once stood. Named for the prison reformer John Howard, who campaigned for improved prison conditions, today you can inspect

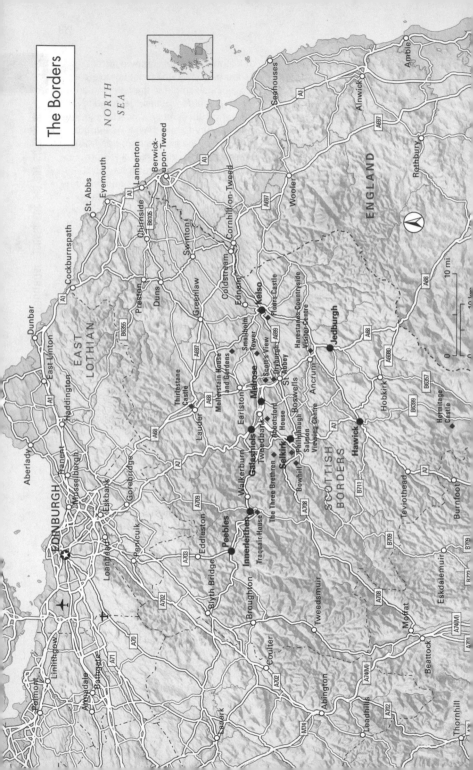

The Borders

prison cells, rooms with period furnishings, and costumed figures. The audio guide, which recounts the history of the prison and the town, is useful. In what was once the prison governor's house, you'll now find an exhibition about the town of Jedburgh. While admission is free, tickets for entry are timed so booking ahead is essential. ✉ *Castlegate, Jedburgh* ☎ *01835/864750* 🌐 *www.scotborders.gov.uk/museums* 🎟 *Free* 🕓 *Closed Tues.–Thurs. and Nov.–Mar.*

Mary, Queen of Scots Visitor Centre
HISTORIC HOME | This *bastel* (from the French *bastille*) was the fortified town house in which, as the story goes, Mary stayed before embarking on her famous 20-mile ride to Hermitage Castle to visit her wounded lover, the Earl of Bothwell (circa 1535–78) in 1566. Displays relate the tale and other episodes in her life, including her questionable choices of lovers and husbands and her own reflections on her life. Still, Mary's death mask suggests that she was serene at the end. There are tapestries and furniture of the period, and the house's ornamental garden has pear trees leading down to the river. ✉ *Queen St., Jedburgh* ☎ *01835/863331* 🌐 *www.scotborders.gov.uk* 🎟 *Free* 🕓 *Closed Tues, Wed., and Dec.–Feb.*

🍴 Restaurants

Born in Scotland
$ | **BRITISH** | **FAMILY** | This family-friendly complex is built around a café and brewery producing Born in the Borders beer. The café serves breakfast and lunch while a shop sells the on-site brewed beer as well as gin from its "ginnery," where visitors can learn about how gin is made and sample a gin-and-tonic after a tour (£5). **Known for:** remote location; craft beer and gin; classic café cuisine. [$] *Average main: £10* ✉ *Lanton Mill, Jedburgh* ✣ *Off the A78 near Jedburgh* ☎ *01835/830495* 🌐 *www.bornintheborders.com* 🕓 *No dinner.*

The Caddy Mann Restaurant
$$ | **BRITISH** | The talented chef at this unpretentious restaurant has built its menu around what local suppliers can offer. This range of ingredients creates options like the wood pigeon starter and the occasional squirrel dish, which is very popular. **Known for:** famous Sunday roasts; dishes focusing on wild game, including the surprisingly popular squirrel; expansive vegetarian menu. [$] *Average main: £18* ✉ *Mounthooly, Jedburgh* ✣ *On the A698, 2 miles outside Jedburgh* ☎ *01835/850787* 🌐 *www.caddymann.com* 🕓 *Closed Mon. and Tues. No dinner Sun.–Thurs.*

The Capon Tree Town House
$$ | **BRITISH** | The interiors of this traditional red-sandstone house in central Jedburgh are quite conservative, but the fine-dining menu is creative. Food presentation is artistic, and the taste of what is always local produce confirms the artistry. **Known for:** great cheese board; venison three ways; Thursday steak nights. [$] *Average main: £19* ✉ *61 High St., Jedburgh* ☎ *01835/869596* 🌐 *www.thecapontree.com* 🕓 *Closed Sun. and Mon.*

🛏 Hotels

Hundalee House
$ | **B&B/INN** | **FAMILY** | The richly decorated Victorian-style rooms of this 18th-century stone manor house have nice touches such as four-poster beds and cozy fireplaces; 15 acres of gardens and woods surround the B&B. **Pros:** lovely views; fantastic views of apple orchards; hearty breakfasts. **Cons:** small rooms; far from shops and restaurants; farm aromas. [$] *Rooms from: £82* ✉ *Off A68, Jedburgh* ✣ *1 mile south of Jedburgh* ☎ *01835/863011* 🌐 *www.accommodation-scotland.org* 🕓 *Closed Jan.–Mar* 🛏 *5 rooms* 🍽 *Free Breakfast.*

Meadhon House

$ | **B&B/INN** | On a row of medieval buildings in the heart of town, Meadhon House is a charming 17th-century house with a history to match; rooms are bright and clean, with views onto the street or over the large and fragrant garden behind the house. **Pros:** welcoming atmosphere; central location; pleasant rooms. **Cons:** garden not open to guests; some street noise; rooms on the small side. [$] *Rooms from: £80* ✉ *48 Castlegate, Jedburgh* ☎ *01835/862504* 🌐 *www.meadhon.co.uk* 🛏 *5 rooms* 🍴 *Free Breakfast.*

Shopping

Edinburgh Woollen Mill

KNITTING | The shelves at this shop burst with sweaters, kilts, tartan knitwear, and scarves. It's a good place to stock up on gifts. ✉ *Bankend North, Edinburgh Rd., Jedburgh* ☎ *01835/863773* 🌐 *www.ewm.co.uk.*

Kelso

12 miles northeast of Jedburgh.

One of the most charming Borders burghs, Kelso is often described as having a Continental flavor—some people think its broad, paved square makes it resemble a Belgian market town. The community also has some fine examples of Georgian and Victorian Scots town architecture.

GETTING HERE AND AROUND

There are direct bus routes from Jedburgh to Kelso. Edinburgh has direct buses to Jedburgh; buses from Glasgow aren't direct. Your best option is to travel by car. From Jedburgh to Kelso take the A698, which is 12 miles, or about 20 minutes. Alternatively, the A699 is a scenic half-hour drive.

ESSENTIALS

VISITOR INFORMATION Kelso Tourist Information Centre. ✉ *Town House, The Square, Kelso* ☎ *01573/221119* 🌐 *www.kelso.bordernet.co.uk.*

Sights

★ Floors Castle

CASTLE/PALACE | The palatial Floors Castle, the largest inhabited castle in Scotland, is an architectural extravagance bristling with pepper-mill turrets. Not so much a castle as the ancestral seat of a wealthy and powerful landowning family, the Roxburghes, it stands on the "floors," or flat terrain, on the banks of the River Tweed. The enormous home was built in 1721 by William Adam (1689–1748) and modified by William Playfair (1789–1857), who added the turrets and towers in the 1840s. Rooms are crowded with valuable furniture, paintings, porcelain, and an eerie circular room full of stuffed birds; each room has a knowledgeable guide at the ready. The surrounding 56,000-acre estate is home to more than 40 farms. Although the castle itself is closed to visitors in winter, the grounds and café are open year-round. ✉ *A6089, Kelso* ☎ *01573/223333* 🌐 *www.floorscastle.com* 🎟 *Castle and grounds £11.50, gardens only £3* 🕒 *Castle closed Nov.–Mar. and weekdays.*

Kelso Abbey

RELIGIOUS BUILDING | The least intact ruin of the four great abbeys, Kelso Abbey is just a bleak fragment of what was once the largest of the group. It was here in 1460 that the nine-year-old James III was crowned king of Scotland. On a main invasion route, the abbey was burned three times in the 1540s alone, on the last occasion by the English Earl of Hertford's forces in 1545, when the 100 men and 12 monks of the garrison were butchered and the structure all but destroyed. The abbey itself is currently not considered structurally sound enough for visitors, but you can admire it from afar. ✉ *Bridge St., Kelso* ☎ *0131/668-8600* 🌐 *www.historicenvironment.scot.*

Mellerstain House and Gardens

HISTORIC HOME | One fine example of the Borders area's ornate country homes is Mellerstain House, begun in the 1720s and finished in the 1770s by Robert Adam (1728–92); it is considered one of his finest creations. Sumptuous plasterwork covers almost all interior surfaces, and there are outstanding examples of 18th-century furnishings, porcelain and china, paintings, and embroidery. The beautiful terraced gardens (open an hour before the house itself) are as renowned as the house. ✉ *Off A6089, Gordon* ✣ *7 miles northwest of Kelso* ☎ *01573/410636* 🌐 *www.mellerstain.com* 🎫 *Gardens £6, house and gardens £10* 🕒 *Closed Tues.–Thurs. and Oct.–Mar.*

The River Tweed Salmon Fishing Museum

OTHER MUSEUM | In Kelso's main square, you'll find this small museum that is both a history of salmon fishing in the area and of the River Tweed itself, exploring the significance of fishing on the local economy and its decline. Historic maps and collections of fishing gear show the evolution of life (and fishing) on the river. There are even replicas of the biggest fish reportedly ever caught and the disputes each one provoked. ✉ *The Square, Kelso* 🌐 *www.salmonfishingmuseum.com* 🎫 *Free.*

★ Smailholm Tower

HISTORIC SIGHT | Standing uncompromisingly on top of a barren, rocky ridge in the hills south of Mellerstain, this 16th-century peel tower, characteristic of the Borders, was built solely for defense, and its unadorned stones contrast with the luxury of Mellerstain House. If you let your imagination wander at this windy spot, you can almost see the rising dust of an advancing raiding party. Sir Walter Scott found this spot inspiring, and he visited the tower often during his childhood. Anne Carrick's tableaux in the tower illustrate some of Scott's Borders ballads, and the ticket includes an audio tour of the building. ✉ *Kelso* ✣ *Off B6404, 4½ miles south of Mellerstain House* ☎ *01573/460365* 🌐 *www.historicenvironment.scot* 🎫 *£6* 🕒 *Closed Oct.–Mar.*

🍴 Restaurants

The Cobbles

$$ | **BRITISH** | Just off the town's cobbled square, this well-established pub and restaurant with wooden tables and a bustling, cheerful atmosphere seems to be permanently busy. Its extensive menu combines generously sized burgers, steaks, and meat pies with the ever-popular fish-and-chips. **Known for:** generous portions of classic Scottish cuisine; housemade desserts; craft beer menu. [$] *Average main: £16* ✉ *7 Bowmont St., Kelso* ☎ *01573/223548* 🌐 *cobbleskelso.co.uk* 🕒 *Closed Mon. and Tues.*

🛏 Hotels

★ Ednam House Hotel

$$ | **HOTEL** | This rather grand building on the banks of the River Tweed is close to Kelso's great abbey and sprawling market square. **Pros:** impressive restaurant; great outdoor activities; atmospheric lobby. **Cons:** rooms with a river view cost more; popular for weddings and other events, so can be crowded; some rooms need a makeover. [$] *Rooms from: £183* ✉ *Bridge St., Kelso* ☎ *01573/224168* 🌐 *www.ednamhouse.com* 🕒 *Closed late Dec.–early Jan.* 🔑 *32 rooms* 🍴 *Free Breakfast.*

Melrose

15 miles west of Kelso.

Though it's small, there is nevertheless a bustle about Melrose, the perfect example of a prosperous Scottish market town and one of the loveliest in the Borders. It's set around a square lined with 18th- and 19th-century buildings housing myriad small shops and cafés. Despite its proximity to the much larger Galashiels, Melrose has rejected industrialization.

You'll likely hear local residents greet each other by first name in the square.

GETTING HERE AND AROUND

Buses do go to Melrose, and the Borders Railway ends at Tweedbank, just 2 miles to the northwest. Driving remains the easiest way to get here from the south or east. From Galashiels, take the A6091 (10 minutes).

Sights

★ Abbotsford House

HISTORIC HOME | In this great house overlooking the Tweed, Sir Walter Scott lived, worked, and received the great and the good in luxurious salons. In 1811 the writer bought a farm on this site named Cartleyhole, which was a euphemism for the real name, Clartyhole (*clarty* is Scots for "muddy" or "dirty"). The romantic Scott renamed the property after a ford in the nearby Tweed used by the abbot of Melrose. Scott eventually had the house entirely rebuilt in the Scottish baronial style. It was an expensive project, and Scott wrote feverishly to keep his creditors at bay. John Ruskin, the art critic, disapproved, calling it an "incongruous pile," but most contemporary visitors find it fascinating, particularly because of its expansive views and delightful gardens.

A free audio tour guides you around the salon, the circular study, and the library with its 9,000 leather-bound volumes. Perhaps more than anyone else, Scott redefined Scotland as a place of mystery and romance, and awoke the English, who read him avidly, to its natural beauty and its past—or at least a heavily dramatized version of it. The visitor center houses displays about Scott's life, a gift shop, and a restaurant serving lunch. To get here, take the A6091 from Melrose and follow the signs for Abbotsford. Entry is by timed ticket and advance reservations are essential. ⊠ *B6360, Melrose* ✛ *Between Melrose and Tweedbank* ☎ *01896/752043* ⊕ *www.*

scottsabbotsford.co.uk ✉ *House and gardens £11.70; gardens only £5.90* ⊙ *Mar–Nov. Open 10–4 daily. House closed Dec.–Feb.* ⚃ *Booking by timed slots essential.*

Dryburgh Abbey

RELIGIOUS BUILDING | The final resting place of Sir Walter Scott and his wife, and the most peaceful and secluded of the Borders abbeys, the "gentle ruins" of Dryburgh Abbey sit on parkland in a loop of the Tweed. The abbey, founded in 1150, suffered from English raids until, like Melrose, it was abandoned in 1544. The style is transitional, a mingling of rounded Romanesque and pointed early English. The north transept, where the Haig and Scott families lie buried, is lofty and pillared, and once formed part of the abbey church. ⊠ *St. Boswell's, B6404, Melrose* ☎ *01835/822381* ⊕ *www.historicenvironment.scot* ✉ *£6.*

★ Melrose Abbey

RELIGIOUS BUILDING | Just off Melrose's town square sit the ruins of Melrose Abbey, one of the four Borders abbeys: "If thou would'st view fair Melrose aright, go visit it in the pale moonlight," wrote Scott in *The Lay of the Last Minstrel.* So many of his fans took the advice literally that a custodian begged him to rewrite the lines. Today the abbey is still impressive: a red-sandstone shell with slender windows, delicate tracery, and carved capitals, all carefully maintained. Among the carvings high on the roof is one of a bagpipe-playing pig. An audio tour is included in the admission price. The heart of 14th-century national hero Robert the Bruce is rumored to be buried here. You can tour the on-site museum and its historical artifacts for free in July and August, but be sure to book in advance. ⊠ *Abbey St., Melrose* ☎ *01896/822562* ⊕ *www.historicenvironment.scot* ✉ *£6.*

Priorwood Garden and Harmony Garden

GARDEN | The National Trust for Scotland's Priorwood Garden, next to Melrose

The grand Abbotsford House was once home to Sir Walter Scott.

Abbey, specializes in flowers for drying, and dried flowers are on sale in the shop. Next to the gardens is an orchard with some old apple varieties and other fruit trees. The walled Harmony Garden, belonging to the lovely Georgian house at its heart, sits nearby opposite the abbey. ⊠ *Abbey St., Melrose* ☎ *01896/822493* ⊕ *www.nts.org.uk* ▦ *Free* ⊙ *Closed Nov.–Mar.*

Scott's View

VIEWPOINT | This is possibly the most photographed rural view in the south of Scotland. (It's almost as iconic as Eilean Donan Castle, far to the north.) The sinuous curve of the River Tweed and the gentle landscape unfolding to the triple peaks of the Eildons and then rolling out into the shadows beyond are certainly worth seeking out. ⊠ *B6356, Dryburgh* ✛ *3 miles east of Melrose* ▦ *Free.*

Thirlestane Castle

CASTLE/PALACE | This large, turreted, and castellated house, part of which was built in the 13th century and part in the 16th century, looks for all the world like a French château, and it brims with history. The former home of the Duke of Lauderdale (1616–82), one of Charles II's advisers, Thirlestane is said to be haunted by the duke's ghost. Exquisite 17th-century plaster ceilings and rich collections of paintings, porcelain, and furniture fill the rooms. In the nursery, children are invited to play with Victorian-style toys and to dress up in masks and costumes. Guided tours are available 11 to 2. ⊠ *Off A68 at Lauder, Lauder* ✛ *11 miles north of Melrose* ☎ *01578/722430* ⊕ *www.thirlestanecastle.co.uk* ▦ *Castle and grounds £9.50; grounds only £4* ⊙ *Closed Fri., Sat., and Nov.–Apr.*

Trimontium Museum and Three Hills Roman Heritage Centre

HISTORY MUSEUM | Its Roman occupation may be one of the least known periods of Scottish history, but this exciting museum, focused on the excavation of the site of the Roman settlement of Trimontium in nearby Newstead, brings it to life. Interactive displays illustrate the lives lived in the fort during its 100-year occupation, not just with displays of weaponry and military dress, but also with the everyday objects discovered at the site and used by the families of troops. There is a Roman-themed shop, and guided walks around the site itself are available on Thursdays and Saturdays. ✉ *The Ormiston, Market Sq., Melrose* ☎ *01896/822651* 🌐 *www.trimontium.org.uk* 🎫 *Museum £5, site tour £7.50* ⏲ *Closed Dec.–Feb. and Mon. and Tues. in Nov. and Mar.*

Restaurants

Burts Hotel

$$ | BRITISH | This charming 18th century building in Melrose's central square offers an interesting bar menu that includes Camembert croquettes and Kofta kebabs. The main supper menu is ambitious, with choices like monkfish tail and salmon with prawn risotto. **Known for:** garden dining in nice weather; lively bar; imaginative menu. $ *Average main: £18* ✉ *Market Sq., Melrose* ☎ *01896/822285* 🌐 *www.burtshotel.co.uk.*

★ Hoebridge Inn

$$ | BRITISH | Whitewashed walls, oak-beamed ceilings, and an open fire welcome you into this converted 19th-century bobbin mill just across the river in Gattonside. The cuisine is a blend of British and Mediterranean styles with occasional Asian influences. **Known for:** intimate atmosphere; excellent pork belly; impressive cocktail list. $ *Average main: £25* ✉ *B6360, Gattonside* ☎ *01896/823082* 🌐 *www.thehoebridge.com* ⏲ *Closed Jan. and Mon.–Wed. No lunch Thurs.–Sat. No dinner Sun.*

Seasons

$$$ | BRITISH | A family-run restaurant in an appealing village setting, Seasons has a reputation for using local produce consistently well in imaginative ways. White walls and wooden tables create an uncluttered setting for the elegant and creative dishes offered. **Known for:** on-site garden provides herbs and vegetables; fresh local ingredients; delicious bread. $ *Average main: £25* ✉ *Main St., Gattonside* ☎ *01896/823217* 🌐 *www.seasonsborders.co.uk* ⏲ *Closed Mon.–Thurs. No lunch Fri. and Sat.*

Hotels

Burts Hotel

$$ | HOTEL | Dating from the 18th century, this charming whitewashed building in the center of Melrose has individually decorated rooms filled with floral pastels. **Pros:** central location; walking distance to restaurants and pubs; good on-site restaurant. **Cons:** bar can get noisy; slightly overpriced for some rooms; rooms can be tiny. $ *Rooms from: £148* ✉ *Market Sq., Melrose* ☎ *01896/822285* 🌐 *www.burtshotel.co.uk* *20 rooms* 🍽 *Free Breakfast.*

Dryburgh Abbey Hotel

$ | HOTEL | Mature woodlands and verdant lawns surround this imposing, 19th-century mansion-turned-hotel, which is adjacent to the ruins of Dryburgh Abbey on a sweeping bend of the River Tweed. **Pros:** swimming pool, a rarity in this part of the country; beautiful grounds; romantic setting. **Cons:** some (but not all) rooms look out onto the grounds; service can be on the slow side; some rooms need to be freshened up. $ *Rooms from: £90* ✉ *Off B6404, St. Boswells* ☎ *01835/822261* 🌐 *www.dryburgh.co.uk* *38 rooms* 🍽 *Free Breakfast.*

Shopping

The Main Street Trading Company

BOOKS | This bookshop in the village of St. Boswells has a wide range of publications organized in well-defined thematic areas. The stock is impressive and the space lends itself to comfortable browsing. The café-bakery within the bookshop serves delicious home-cooked items that change daily. ✉ *Main St., St. Boswells* ☎ *01835/824087* 🌐 *www.mainstreetbooks.co.uk.*

Galashiels

5 miles northwest of Melrose.

A busy gray-stone Borders town, Galashiels is still active with textile mills and knitwear factories. It is also now home to the much-celebrated Tapestry of Scotland.

GETTING HERE AND AROUND
There is regular bus service from Melrose to Galashiels (20 minutes). You can also drive; from Melrose, take the B6374 or the A6091 (both 10 minutes).

◉ Sights

★ The Great Tapestry of Scotland
ART MUSEUM | This purpose-built museum at the end of Galashiels High Street houses the 160 panels of the stunning Tapestry of Scotland, which showcases major moments in Scotland's history and culture in stitched panels created by 1000 needles. The handcrafted nature of the visual narratives gives them a kind of warmth and intimacy, as well as an element of wit. The museum itself is extremely user-friendly: the panels are set out in a series of spaces fanning out from the center, with each corresponding to a historical period, but you can follow them by topic or by region using the accessible guides found throughout. You can also grab a magnifying glass or an iPad to examine them more closely. You can even go down to the Makers Space and try stitching yourself. In each space is a central panel that includes interviews with the stitchers. There is ample seating to spend time with the tapestry and an on-site café to relax over coffee and a cake before you continue your visit. ⊠ *14–20 High St., Galashiels* ☎ *01986/809354* ⊕ *www.greattapestryofscotland.com* ⊠ *£10.50* ⊗ *Closed Tues.–Wed.*

Selkirk

6 miles south of Galashiels.

Selkirk is a hilly outpost with a smattering of antiques shops and an assortment of bakers selling Selkirk bannock (fruited sweet bread) and other cakes. It is the site of one of Scotland's iconic battles, Flodden Field, commemorated here with a statue in the town. Sir Walter Scott was sheriff (judge) of Selkirkshire from 1800 until his death in 1832, and his statue stands in Market Place. Selkirk is also near Bowhill, a stately home.

The town claims its Common Riding (⊕ *returntoheridings.co.uk*) is the largest mounted gathering anywhere in Europe. More than 400 riders take part in the event in June. It's also the oldest Borders festival, with roots back to the Battle of Flodden in 1513.

GETTING HERE AND AROUND
If you're driving, take the A7 south to Galashiels. The scenic journey is less than 7 miles and takes around 10 minutes. First Edinburgh Bus offers a regular service between Galashiels and Selkirk.

◉ Sights

Bowhill
HISTORIC HOME | Home of the Duke of Buccleuch, Bowhill dates from the 19th century and houses an outstanding collection of works by Gainsborough, Van Dyck, Canaletto, Reynolds, and Raeburn, as well as porcelain and period furniture. The grounds include an excellent adventure playground and are mostly accessible from April through August. Access to the house is only by guided tours on specific days in the summer; check the website for exact dates. All tickets must be booked ahead of time online. There is a 57-mile country ride for those who prefer horseback riding. A local stable rents horses. ⊠ *Off A708, Selkirk, miles west of Selkirk* ☎ *01750/*

⊕ www.bowhillhouse.co.uk ✉ Grounds £6, house and grounds £12 ⊙ Closed Sept.–Mar.

Halliwell's House Museum

HISTORY MUSEUM | Tucked off the main square, Halliwell's House Museum was once an ironmonger's shop, which is now re-created downstairs. Upstairs, an exhibit tells the town's story, illustrates the working lives of its inhabitants, and provides useful background information on the Common Ridings. ✉ Halliwell's Close, Market Pl., Selkirk ☎ 01750/726456 ⊕ www.scotborders. gov.uk ✉ Free ⊙ Closed Nov.–Mar.

Lochcarron Mill Tour

FACTORY | You can take an informative guided tour of this world-renowned working textile mill and also purchase some of the best woolen goods on offer, from knitwear to tartans and tweeds. The shop also sells Scottish jewelry. ✉ Dinsdale Rd., Selkirk ☎ 01750/726100 ⊕ www. lochcarron.com ✉ Tour £12 ⊙ Closed Fri.–Sun. and Nov.–Feb.

Philiphaugh Salmon Viewing Centre

NATURE PRESERVE | On the site of a famous battle in 1645 in which the Scottish Covenanters drove off the pro-English armies under the Earl of Montrose, the Philiphaugh Salmon Viewing Centre is devoted to more peaceful pursuits: watching salmon. Its viewing platforms and underwater cameras allow you to follow the life cycle of the salmon. There are also country walks and cycling routes to follow, and an on-site restaurant, the Water Wheel, good for lunch or afternoon tea. The website has a self-guided audio tour of the battlefield. ✉ A708, Selkirk ✛ 1 mile outside Selkirk ☎ 01750/21766 ⊕ www. salmonviewingcentre.com ✉ Free.

Walter Scott's Courtroom

HISTORIC SIGHT | The historic courtroom where Sir Walter Scott presided as sheriff from 1804 to 1832 contains a display covering his life, writings, and time on the bench. It uses models to re-create the atmosphere of a 19th-century Scottish court and includes an audiovisual presentation. A statue of the famous writer overlooks the comings and goings outside the court. ✉ Market Sq., Selkirk ☎ 01750/720761 ⊕ www.scotborders. gov.uk ✉ Free ⊙ Closed Nov.–Feb.

The Three Brethren

VIEWPOINT | These three identical cairns, 9 feet high and 6 feet around at the base, are the end point of a fairly strenuous 11-mile walk that begins 4 miles north of Selkirk on the A707. The view from the Three Brethren is spectacular and embraces the whole of the Borders. Park at the car park at Philipburn on the A707, 4 miles from Selkirk. The path is signposted from there. ✉ A707, Selkirk ✉ Free.

🛏 Hotels

Best Western Philipburn House Hotel

$$ | **HOTEL** | West of Selkirk, this Alpine-style hotel enjoys a lovely setting among the woods and hills. **Pros:** on-site parking; pleasant rural setting; bright rooms. **Cons:** breakfast is extra; restaurant closes rather early; no elevator. ⑤ Rooms from: £143 ✉ Linglie Rd., Selkirk ✛ Opposite Salmon Viewing Centre ☎ 01750/720747 ⊕ www.bw-philipburnhousehotel.co.uk ⇨ 24 rooms ❍ No Meals.

Hawick

10 miles south of Selkirk.

Hawick (pronounced *hoyk*) is a busy town at the center of the region's textile industry, commemorated in the interesting Borders Textile Towerhouse. The Victorian buildings along its High Street recall the town's heyday. The largest community in the Borders, it's a good place to buy the delicate cashmere and woolen goods that made the region famous. Hawick's Common Riding festival, held each June, draws onlookers from all over Scotland while the Hawick Museum tells the story of the town.

GETTING HERE AND AROUND

Driving here from Selkirk or Jedburgh is no trouble—it's a straight shot on major roads. There is also bus service from many of the other Borders towns.

◉ Sights

Borders Textile Towerhouse

VISITOR CENTER | FAMILY | In the former Drumlanrig Tower, this museum includes a good exhibition about the textile industry, once the lifeblood of the Borders. Plenty of interactive elements make it interesting for children as well. One room commemorates the demonstrations by textile workers who were demanding the right to vote in the 1880s. On the upper floor are up-to-the-minute fabrics that define the 21st century. Check out the shop, too. ⊠ 1 Tower Knowe, Hawick ☎ 01450/377615 ⊕ www.liveborders.org.uk ☜ Free ⊗ Closed Tues., Wed., Sun., and Nov.–Mar.

Hawick Museum

HISTORY MUSEUM | FAMILY | Located in a historic house on the town's attractive Wilton Lodge Park, the Hawick Museum is a comprehensive look at local history, with changing art exhibitions in its two first floor galleries. The War Room tells the story of local men who fought in World War I as well as memorabilia from the POW camps in the area and copies of a newspaper produced by German prisoners in the town. A moving metal sculpture outside the museum commemorates the battle of Passchendaele. One of Hawick's favorite sons, Jimmy Guthrie, a world champion motorcyclist, has his own exhibition that draws motorcycle enthusiasts from around the world. ⊠ Wilton Lodge Park, Hawick ☎ 01896/661166 ⊕ www.liveborders.org.uk ☜ Free ⊗ Closed Mon.–Wed. and Dec.–Feb.

🍴 Restaurants

★ Damascus Drum

$ | CAFÉ | Decorated in muted colors, this lovely little café and bookshop named for a traditional folktale (you can find it on the tables) provides a tranquil refuge in the town center. It's a perfect spot for a light lunch; choose from a limited menu that includes soup, delicious meze, and burgers with or without meat. **Known for:** lovely bookstore that is regularly host to readings and book launches; vegetarian burgers; quiet atmosphere. Ⓢ Average main: £10 ⊠ 2 Silver St., Hawick ☎ 07707/856123 ⊕ www.damascusdrum.co.uk ⊗ Closed Sun. No dinner.

🎭 Performing Arts

Heart of Hawick

ARTS CENTERS | Located in the heart of the town near the Drumlanrig Bridge, this arts and entertainment complex has a cinema and a performance space that regularly hosts cultural events. Book tickets through the website. ⊠ Kirstile, Hawick ☎ 01450/360680 ⊕ www.liveborders.org.uk/heart-of-hawick.

🛍 Shopping

Johnstons of Elgin

MIXED CLOTHING | This shop specializes in fine cashmere and merino clothing. ⊠ Eastfield Mills, Mansfield Rd., Hawick ☎ 01450/360549 ⊕ www.johnstonsofelgin.com.

Innerleithen

17 miles northwest of Hawick.

Innerleithen is one of the larger Borders towns; you'll feel that you've entered a hub of activity when you arrive. It's also dramatically beautiful. Surrounded by hills and glens, the town is where the Tweed and Leithen rivers join, then separate. Historically, Innerleithen dates back to pre-Roman times, and there are artifacts all around for you to see. Once a booming industrial town of wool mills, today it's a great destination for outdoor activities including hiking, biking, and fly-fishing.

GETTING HERE AND AROUND

To drive to Innerleithen, take the A7 north from Hawick and then the A707 northwest from Selkirk. There are no trains between the two towns.

Sights

Robert Smail's Printing Works

FACTORY | FAMILY | Try your hand at printing the way it used to be done: painstakingly setting each letter by hand. Robert Smail's print shop, founded in 1866 to produce materials for nearby factories, boat tickets, theater posters, and the local newspaper, is still a working print shop as well as a museum. Two great waterwheels once powered the presses, and they are still running. The guided tour, which includes making your own bookmark, takes 90 minutes. ✉ *7–9 High St., Innerleithen* ☎ *01896/830206* 🌐 *www.nts.org.uk* 🎫 *£7* 🕒 *Closed Nov.–Mar. and Tues.–Thurs.*

★ Traquair House

HISTORIC HOME | Said to be the oldest continually occupied home in Scotland (since 1107), Traquair House has secret stairways and passages, a library with more than 3,000 books, and a bed said to be used by Mary, Queen of Scots in 1566. You can walk freely through the rooms, and each has an explanatory leaflet as well as helpful guides dressed in period costume. The top floor of the house is an interesting small museum. Outside is a reasonably scary maze, an adventure playground, and some lovely woodland walks as well as pigs, goats, and chickens. The 18th-century brew house still makes highly recommended ale, and there's a café on the grounds near the beautiful walled garden. The Traquair Fair in August is the nearest you are likely to get to a medieval fair, and well worth the visit. You may even spend the night, if you wish. ✉ *B709, Innerleithen* ✥ *From the A70 some 6 miles south of Peebles, take the B709 for 7 miles; the car entrance into the house is in the village* ☎ *01896/830323* 🌐 *www.traquair.co.uk* 🎫 *Grounds £6, house and grounds £12, guided tours £10* 🕒 *Closed Dec.–Mar. and weekdays in Nov.*

Hotels

Traquair House

$$ | B&B/INN | Staying in one of the guest rooms in the 12th-century wing of Traquair House is to experience a slice of Scottish history. **Pros:** great breakfast; stunning grounds; spacious rooms. **Cons:** parking can be difficult in summer months; rooms fill up quickly in summer; nearly 2 miles to restaurants and shops. [$] *Rooms from: £200* ✉ *B709, Innerleithen* ☎ *01896/830323* 🌐 *www.traquair.co.uk* 🛏 *3 rooms* 🍴 *Free Breakfast.*

Windlestraw Lodge

$$$ | HOTEL | This elegant bed-and-breakfast and restaurant occupies a grand Edwardian country home surrounded by extensive gardens. **Pros:** lovely location; beautifully designed rooms; excellent restaurant. **Cons:** restaurant is pricey; not all rooms have Tweed views; expensive for what you get. [$] *Rooms from: £209* ✉ *9 Galashiels Rd., Walkerburn, Innerleithen* ✥ *On the A72 between Galashiels and Innerleithen* ☎ *01896/870636* 🌐 *www.windlestraw.co.uk* 🛏 *6 rooms* 🍴 *Free Breakfast.*

Peebles

6 miles west of Innerleithen.

Thanks to its excellent though pricey shopping, Peebles gives the impression of catering primarily to leisured country gentlefolk. Architecturally, the town is nothing out of the ordinary, just a very pleasant burgh. Don't miss the splendid dolphins ornamenting the bridge crossing the River Tweed.

GETTING HERE AND AROUND

Because of its size and location, direct buses run from both Edinburgh and Glasgow to Peebles. There are also buses here from Innerleithen, though driving from here is more direct. (Take the A72; it's about a 10-minute drive.)

ESSENTIALS

VISITOR INFORMATION Peebles Visitor Information Centre. ✉ *23 High St., Peebles* ☎ *01721/728095* 🌐 *www.visitscotland.com.*

Sights

Peebles War Memorial

MONUMENT | The exotic, almost Moorish mosaics of the Peebles War Memorial are unique in Scotland, although most towns have a memorial to honor those killed in service. It's a remarkable tribute to the 225 Peebleans killed in World War II. ✉ *Chambers Quadrangle, High St., Peebles* 🎟 *Free.*

Restaurants

Adam Room

$ | BRITISH | FAMILY | With a minstrels' gallery, crystal chandeliers, and tall windows with views over the Tweed, the dining room at the Tontine Hotel has a grand feel. It's a bit surprising, therefore, that it also serves good home cooking for the family at reasonable prices. **Known for:** luxurious dining room with river views; solid wine list; traditional home cooking. [$] *Average main: £14* ✉ *Tontine Hotel, High St., Peebles* ☎ *01721/720892* 🌐 *www.tontinehotel.com.*

Coltman's Delicatessen and Kitchen

$$$ | SANDWICHES | The pleasant white-walled, modern dining room of this bright, airy eatery sits behind the tempting deli counter, and its windows overlook the Tweed. All-day options include salads, platters, and sandwiches as well as heartier choices such as cod with curried cauliflower and a rump of lamb with salsa verde and lemon. **Known for:** well-balanced menu; tasty deli lunches; tempting desserts. [$] *Average main: £24* ✉ *71–73 High St., Peebles* ☎ *01721/720405* 🌐 *www.coltmans.co.uk* 🕒 *No dinner Sun.–Wed.*

Horseshoe Inn

$$ | BRITISH | A country hotel that recalls an old coaching inn, the opulent dining room at the Horseshoe Inn has large gold-framed mirrors and heavy drapes to emphasize its grand style. The dinner menu combines well-established favorites with fine dining, from fish-and-chips to roast lamb and baked cod. **Known for:** luxurious surroundings; Scottish fine dining; Sunday roast menu. [$] *Average main: £18* ✉ *Horsehoe Inn, Eddleston, Peebles* ✥ *3 miles outside Peebles on the A72 to Glasgow* ☎ *01721/730225* 🌐 *www.horseshoeinn.co.uk.*

Osso

$$ | BRITISH | The atmosphere in this popular restaurant near the Eastgate Theatre on Peebles's main street is relaxed and cheerful; there is a buzz of conversation and an informality that reflects the shared plates that are the basis of the menu. These small plates make dining a creative experience as the dishes reflect and combine several culinary traditions. **Known for:** adventurous flavor combinations; lunch menu with pub favorites; fun ambience. [$] *Average main: £20* ✉ *1 Innerleithen Rd., Peebles* ☎ *01721/724477* 🌐 *www.ossorestaurant.com* 🕒 *Closed Sun.–Tues.*

Hotels

Cringletie House

$$$ | HOTEL | With medieval-style turrets and crow-step gables, this small-scale, peaceful retreat has been restored to

its luxurious Victorian past, though with modern facilities like flat-screen TVs. **Pros:** decadent dining; elegant bedrooms; cozy fireplaces. **Cons:** some public rooms a little faded; atmosphere can be almost too quiet; some bedrooms have low ceilings. [$] *Rooms from: £265* ✉ *Edinburgh Rd., Peebles* ✣ *Off the A703, 2 miles north of Peebles* ☎ *01721/725750* 🌐 *www.cringletie.com* 🕒 *Closed Nov.–Feb.* 🛏 *13 rooms* 🍴 *Free Breakfast.*

Peebles Hydro

$$ | HOTEL | FAMILY | One of the great "hydro hotels" built in the 19th century for those anxious to "take the waters," the family-friendly Peebles Hydro has comfortable if rather old-fashioned rooms that are slowly but surely being renovated. **Pros:** delicious breakfast; plenty of activities available, including a gin school and archery; interesting history. **Cons:** still an air of faded glory despite renovations; some rooms have bland decor; can feel impersonal. [$] *Rooms from: £125* ✉ *Innerleithen Rd., Peebles* ☎ *01721/720602* 🌐 *www.peebleshydro.co.uk* 🛏 *132 rooms* 🍴 *Free Breakfast.*

Tontine Hotel

$ | HOTEL | A small and charming facade hides a spacious, lovingly refurbished hotel that stretches back from Peebles High Street and has lovely views of the Tweed River in the back. **Pros:** good restaurant on-site; centrally located; pleasant rooms. **Cons:** no elevator; old-fashioned decor in some areas; some small rear rooms. [$] *Rooms from: £120* ✉ *High St., Peebles* ☎ *01721/729732* 🌐 *www.tontinehotel.com* 🛏 *36 rooms* 🍴 *Free Breakfast.*

Performing Arts

Eastgate Theatre

CONCERTS | A year-round program of films, concerts, and theater as well as community activities for adults and children are on offer here. The theater also has a very pleasant café, which is open throughout the day. ✉ *1 School Brae, Peebles* ☎ *01721/725777* 🌐 *www.eastgatearts.com.*

Shopping

Be prepared for temptations at every turn as you browse the shops on High Street and in the courts and side streets leading off it.

Brevity

WOMEN'S CLOTHING | Although it's tiny, this fashion boutique seems to cram an enormous amount of imaginative clothing into a small space. Younger designers, especially Italian ones, have their work on sale here at very reasonable prices; everything is presented with enormous enthusiasm by the owner. ✉ *50 High St., Peebles* ☎ *01721/724323* 🌐 *www.brevitypeebles.co.uk.*

Caledonia

MIXED CLOTHING | For anything and everything Scottish, from kilts to dirks and jams to tablecloths and fine cashmere, look no further than Caledonia. You can also rent kilts here. ✉ *57 High St., Peebles* ☎ *01721/722343* 🌐 *caledonialifestyle.com.*

Head to Toe

JEWELRY & WATCHES | The shop stocks natural beauty products, handmade pine furniture, and handsome linens—from patchwork quilts to silk flowers. ✉ *43 High St., Peebles* ☎ *01721/722752* 🌐 *www.headtotoepeebles.co.uk.*

Keith Walter

JEWELRY & WATCHES | Among the many jewelers on High Street, Keith Walter is a master of gold and silver who makes his creations on the premises. He also stocks jewelry made by other local designers. ✉ *28 High St., Peebles* ☎ *01721/720650* 🌐 *www.keithwalterjeweller.co.uk.*

Activities

Glentress Bike Shop

BIKING | Located just outside Peebles, the 7stanes mountain biking center at Glentress is widely regarded as one of the best in Europe. Its trails take cyclists and hikers through forestry commission lands; the trail lengths vary between 2 and 18 miles long and from fairly basic to extremely difficult. On-site, there's also an information center, a bike shop with rentals (from £25), and an excellent café as well as changing rooms and showers. Entry is free, but all-day parking costs £3.50. ⊠ *On A68, Peebles* ⊹ *2 miles outside Peebles* ☎ *01721/724522* ⊕ *www. tiso.com/shops/glentress.*

Go Ape Glentress

ZIP-LINING | In the forests of Glentress, Go Ape is made for those who prefer treetop adventures to cycling or walking. With a combination of climbing and zip lines, you'll explore the treetops of Glentress; your adventure lasts between two and three hours (and the Glentress Cycling Centre café is nearby for post-treetop relaxation). ⊠ *Glentres Forest, Falla Brae, Peebles* ☎ *01721/722361* ⊕ *www.goape.co.uk* 🎫 *From £25.*

Gretna Green

40 miles southwest of Hawick.

The first town across the English–Scottish border, Gretna Green (not to be confused with nearby Gretna) was historically where runaway couples went to be married by the local blacksmith under Scotland's more lenient laws. No one could accuse the town of failing to exploit its reputation as the place to tie the knot. Although it is highly commercialized, it is still a favorite venue for weddings, even though the original reasons for going have long since changed.

GETTING HERE AND AROUND

From Glasgow you can reach Gretna Green via the M74 and A74; it's an hour-and-a-half drive. From Edinburgh take the A74 (about two hours). Buses and trains travel daily to Gretna Green from Glasgow and Edinburgh.

ESSENTIALS

VISITOR INFORMATION Gretna Green Tourist Information Centre. ⊠ *Gretna Gateway Outlet Village, Glasgow Rd., Gretna* ☎ *01461/337834* ⊕ *www.gretnagreen. com.*

Sights

Blacksmith's Shop

OTHER ATTRACTION | Today the 18th-century house of the village blacksmith, known as the "anvil priest," contains a collection of blacksmithing tools, as well as the anvil over which many weddings may have been conducted to symbolize the forging of the link between two people. The village was on the new coaching road from London to Edinburgh when the marriage laws in England became more restrictive than Scotland's, where, for a time at least, boys and girls in their early teens could marry without parental permission. Gretna Green was the first place in Scotland runaway couples reached after crossing the border, hence its fame and the fact that over 1,000 couples a year still go there to marry. Today it also contains a shop, restaurant, and museum, as well as the Courtship Maze, which couples enter separately in the hope of finding each other. ⊠ *Headless Cross* ☎ *01461/338441* ⊕ *www. gretnagreen.com* 🎫 *Museum £4.20.*

Activities

Powfoot Golf Club

GOLF | A pleasant mix of links and parkland holes, this course looks out across the Solway Firth. Its roughs and the tough thorny whins (local bushes with yellow flowers) make the course quite challenging, especially when the wind blows off the firth in summer, but it is the views from here that make it memorable and a pleasure to play. Powfoot is included in the Gateway to Golf Pass. The club is 14 miles west of Gretna Green via the A75. ⌧ *Off B724, Cummertrees, Annan* ☎ *01461/204100* ⊕ *www.powfootgolf-club.com* ✉ *Mid-Mar.–Sept., £50 weekdays, £55 weekends; Oct.–early Mar., £27* 🏌 *18 holes, 6250 yards, par 71.*

Dumfries

24 miles west of Gretna Green.

The River Nith meanders through Dumfries, and the pedestrian-only center of this town of 31,000 makes wandering and shopping a pleasure. Author J. M. Barrie (1860–1937) spent his childhood in Dumfries, and the garden of Moat Brae House is said to have inspired his boyish dreams in *Peter Pan*. But the town also has a justified claim to Robert Burns, who lived and worked here for several years. His house and his favorite *howff* (pub), The Globe Inn, are here, too, as is his final resting place in St. Michael's Churchyard.

The Dumfries & Galloway Tourist Board has a lodging service and also sells golf passes for the region at £70 for three rounds.

GETTING HERE AND AROUND

Public transportation is a good option for reaching Dumfries—there's a good train station here, and most major Scottish cities have regular daily bus routes to the town. If you're driving from Gretna Green, take the A75; it's a 35-minute drive. From Glasgow take the M74 to the A701. From Edinburgh take the A701.

ESSENTIALS

VISITOR INFORMATION Dumfries & Galloway Tourist Board. ⌧ *64 Whitesands, Dumfries* ☎ *01387/253862* ⊕ *www.visitscotland.com.*

◉ Sights

Dumfries Museum and Camera Obscura
HISTORY MUSEUM | A camera obscura is essentially a huge reflecting mirror that projects an extraordinarily clear panoramic view of the surrounding countryside onto an internal wall. The one at the Dumfries Museum, which claims to be the oldest in the world, is housed in the old Windmill Tower, built in 1836. The museum itself covers the culture and daily life of the people living in the Dumfries and Galloway region from the earliest times. ⌧ *Rotchell Rd., Dumfries* ☎ *01387/253374* ⊕ *www.dumgal.gov.uk/artsandmuseums* ✉ *Museum free; Camera Obscura £3.60* ☉ *Closed Nov.–Mar.*

Globe Inn
HISTORIC SIGHT | Poet Robert Burns spent quite a lot of time at the Globe Inn, where he frequently fell asleep in the tack room beside the stables; today it's still an active pub where you can eat and drink. Burns later graduated to the upstairs bedroom where he slept with Anna Park, and scratched some lines of poetry on the window. The room is preserved (or at least partly re-created), and there are now organized tours of the room that leave from the pub on Wednesday through Saturday at 4 pm. Just beware, if you choose to sit in Burns's chair in the bar, tradition has it that you have to buy a round for the whole pub. ⌧ *56 High St., Dumfries* ☎ *01387/223010* ⊕ *www.globeinndumfries.co.uk* ✉ *Tours £5* ☉ *Closed Sun.–Tues.*

Gracefield Arts Centre
ART GALLERY | With galleries hosting changing exhibits of Scottish art mostly from the 1840s to today, Gracefield Arts Centre also has a well-stocked crafts shop. A café serves lunch and snacks. ⌧ *28 Edinburgh Rd., Dumfries* ☎ *01387/262084* ⊕ *www.exploreart.co.uk* ✉ *Free* ☉ *Closed Sun. and Mon.*

Dumfries and Galloway

John Paul Jones Museum

HISTORY MUSEUM | The little community of Kirkbean is the backdrop for the bright-green landscape of the Arbigland Estate; in a cottage here, now the John Paul Jones Museum, John Paul (1747–92), the son of an estate gardener, was born. He eventually left Scotland, added "Jones" to his name, and became the founder of the U.S. Navy. The cottage where he was born is furnished as it would have been when he was a boy. There is an informative video, which you watch in a reconstruction of his captain's cabin. Jones returned to raid the coastline of his native country in 1778, an exploit recounted in an adjoining visitor center. ⊠ *Off A710, Kirkbean ✦ 12 miles south of Dumfries on the A710* ☎ *01387/880613* ⊕ *www.johnpauljonesmuseum.com* ▣ *£4.50* ☉ *Closed Sun., Mon., and Oct.–Mar.*

Moat Brae and the Neverland Garden

HISTORIC HOME | FAMILY | Writer J.M. Barrie was a regular visitor to the Gordon family's grand Edwardian home at Moat Brae. The stories he told their children would eventually go on to become the tale of *Peter Pan*, and the house's garden was the inspiration for Neverland. Today the garden has a replica of Captain Hook's ship, where kids can play. After coming perilously close to demolition, the house was saved and restored to its original state over several years, and the on-site center has been conceived as a National Storytelling Centre rather than simply a historical museum. It's meant to be a place where today's children can exercise their own imaginations. In the children's bedroom, Tinker Bell flies around the walls, and you can try to catch her. ⊠ *101 George St., Dumfries* ☎ *01387/255549* ⊕ *www.peterpanmoatbrae.org* ▣ *£7* ☉ *Closed Sun. and Mon. Sept.–Apr.*

Robert Burns Centre

HISTORY MUSEUM | Not surprisingly, Dumfries has its own Robert Burns Centre, housed in a sturdy 18th-century former mill overlooking the River Nith.

The extensive yet compact exhibition commemorates Burns's last years in Dumfries. The center has an audiovisual program; it also houses Dumfries's only cinema. Tours of the center are available, but should be booked in advance. ⊠ *Mill Rd., Dumfries* ☎ *01387/264808* ⊕ *www.dumgal.gov.uk/artsandmuseums* ▣ *Free* ☉ *Closed Sun. and Mon.*

Robert Burns House

HISTORIC HOME | Poet Robert Burns (1759–96) lived here, on what was then called Mill Street, for the last three years of his life, when his salary from the customs service allowed him to improve his living standards. Many distinguished writers of the day visited him here, including William Wordsworth. The house contains some of his writings and letters, a few pieces of furniture, and some family memorabilia. ⊠ *Burns St., Dumfries* ☎ *01387/255297* ⊕ *www.dumgal.gov.uk/artsandmuseums* ▣ *Free* ☉ *Closed Sun. and Mon.*

St. Michael's Churchyard

CEMETERY | When he died in 1796, Robert Burns was buried in a modest grave in St. Michael's Churchyard. English poet William Wordsworth, visiting a few years later, was horrified by the small gravestone and raised money to build the much grander monument that stands there today. ⊠ *39 Cardiness St., Dumfries* ☎ *01387/253849* ⊕ *www.dumgal.gov.uk/artsandmuseums* ▣ *Free.*

Sweetheart Abbey

RELIGIOUS BUILDING | At the center of the village of New Abbey are the impressive red-tinted, roofless remains of Sweetheart Abbey, founded in 1273 by the Lady of Galloway Devorgilla (1210-90), who, it is said, kept her dead husband's heart in a tiny casket she carried everywhere. After she died, she was laid to rest in the Abbey with the casket resting on her breast. The couple's son John Balliol (1249–1315) was the puppet king installed in Scotland by Edward of England when the latter claimed sovereignty over Scotland. After

John's appointment the Scots gave him a scathing nickname that would stay with him for the rest of his life: Toom Tabard (Empty Shirt). Currently the abbey is closed for restoration, but you can still view it from afar. ⊠ *A710, New Abbey* ⊹ *7 miles south of Dumfries* ☎ *01387/253849* ⊕ *www.historic-scotland.gov.uk.*

🍴 Restaurants

Cavens Arms

$ | BRITISH | This lively, welcoming traditional pub in the center of town has a separate bar and dining area, comfortable seating, and a large selection of beers. It's a magnet for locals at dinnertime and always seems to be busy, a testimony to the quality of its food as well as the large portions. **Known for:** vibrant atmosphere; local beers; good food in generous pub portions. $ *Average main: £13* ⊠ *20 Buccleuch St., Dumfries* ☎ *01387/252896* ⊕ *www.cavensarms.com.*

★ Home Restaurant

$$ | MEDITERRANEAN | The arrival of this tiny family-run restaurant has lifted Dumfries's status in the culinary world. The menu is small and changes regularly but is always creative and adventurous with clear Mediterranean influences. **Known for:** reservations a must; fine cooking with local ingredients; excellent slow beef with polenta. $ *Average main: £16* ⊠ *Whitesands, Dumfries* ⊹ *Above the Coach and Horses pub* ☎ *01387/262296* ⊕ *www.facebook.com/homedumfries* ⊗ *Closed Sun.–Wed. No lunch.*

The Stove Cafe

$ | CAFÉ | A vibrant community arts project in the very center of Dumfries, the Stove is best known for its café that offers wholesome breakfasts, sandwiches, and cakes. You can enjoy your coffee surrounded by the work of local artists. **Known for:** popular breakfasts and brunches; good coffee; relaxed atmosphere good for hanging out. $ *Average main: £10* ⊠ *100 High St., Dumfries*

☎ *03787/252435* ⊕ *www.thestove.org* ⊗ *Closed Sun.*

🛏 Hotels

Cairndale Hotel

$$ | HOTEL | Centrally located, the Cairndale has a Victorian Gothic appearance and spacious and comfortable rooms. **Pros:** pool, sauna, and gym; central location; comfortable rooms. **Cons:** small lobby; can get very crowded; generally old-fashioned feel. $ *Rooms from: £149* ⊠ *132–6 English St., Dumfries* ☎ *01387/354111* ⊕ *www.cairndalehotel. co.uk* ⇒ *91 rooms* ⭐ *Free Breakfast.*

Holiday Inn

$ | HOTEL | With the secluded feel of a country hotel, this modern and very comfortable Holiday Inn is less than 2 miles from the center of Dumfries. **Pros:** easy access to Dumfries; beautiful setting; very different from your standard Holiday Inn. **Cons:** frequently used for weddings and large events; a little remote from the town; slightly institutional feel. $ *Rooms from: £80* ⊠ *Bankend Rd., Crichton* ☎ *01387/272410* ⊕ *www.hidumfries. co.uk* ⇒ *71 rooms* ⭐ *Free Breakfast.*

🛍 Shopping

Dumfries is the main shopping center for the region, with all the big-name chain stores as well as specialty shops.

★ Loch Arthur Creamery and Farm Shop

FOOD | Found by Rudolf Steiner, the Camphill farm community is built on shared experience and joint work, and its shop and café are an expression of those values. Loch Arthur sells a cornucopia of vegetables grown on the farm and the bakery offers its own bread, cakes, and high-quality cheeses and cold meats. The café building itself has large windows opening directly on to the fields beyond; on a nice day, you can eat outside. ⊠ *On A711, Beeswing* ⊹ *6 miles south of Dumfries* ☎ *01387/259669* ⊕ *www.locharthur.org.uk.*

⚡ Activities

G&G Cycle Centre

BIKING | You can rent bicycles here, and the staff gives good advice on route options. ⊠ *10–12 Academy St., Dumfries* ☎ *01387/259483* ⊕ *www.cycle-centre. co.uk.*

North of Dumfries

18 miles northwest of Dumfries.

Travel north along the A70 from Dumfries for a short trip through time at some very different attractions. Drumlanrig Castle is one of Scotland's grandest houses, set amid hills, moorland, and forest. In contrast, the world of lead miners, explored at the Museum of Lead Mining, was a great deal harsher. A spectacular modern addition to the area, the land artwork the *Crawick Multiverse,* transforms the landscape into a mirror of the heavens. Sculptor Andy Goldsworthy's *Striding Arches* frame a natural space and invite the walker to explore them.

GETTING HERE AND AROUND

Trains run from Dumfries to Sanquhar, near *Crawick Multiverse.* You can get a bus from Dumfries to Drumlanrig and Sanquhar along the A701. For Ledhills and the mining museum, it's best to drive. The same is true for *Striding Arches*: Take the A76 from Dumfried to Thornhill, and then the A702 toward Monaive.

👁 Sights

★ Crawick Multiverse

PUBLIC ART | The extraordinary 2015 land artwork by Charles Jencks, 45 minutes north of Dumfries near the village of Sanquhar, must surely become a focus for visitors to the region for years to come. Jencks has transformed a 55-acre site, once an open-pit mine, into a beautiful and inspiring created landscape, at the heart of which are two grass spiral mounds that represent the Milky Way and the Andromeda Constellation. But they are simply the heart of a site where woodland, moor, mountain, and desert meet. Local rocks have been lifted to form avenues and labyrinths across the site. As you look across from its highest point, it is as if you were looking in a mirror in which the skies were reflected on the earth. Set aside two or three hours at least for the experience. ⊠ *Crawick, Off B740, by Sanquhar* ⊹ *Take the A75 toward Kirkconnel from Sanquhar, then turn on to the B740 (signposted Crawfordjohn)* ☎ *01659/50242* ⊕ *www. crawickmultiverse.co.uk* 🖾 *£5.*

★ Drumlanrig Castle

CASTLE/PALACE | **FAMILY** | A spectacular estate, Drumlanrig Castle is as close as Scotland gets to the treasure houses of England—which is not surprising, since it's owned by the dukes of Buccleuch, one of the wealthiest British peerages. Resplendent with romantic turrets, this pink-sandstone palace was constructed between 1679 and 1691 by the first Duke of Queensbury, who, after nearly bankrupting himself building the place, stayed one night and never returned. The Buccleuchs inherited the palace and filled the richly decorated rooms with paintings by Holbein, Rembrandt, and Murillo, among others. Because of the theft of a Leonardo da Vinci painting in 2003, all visits are now conducted by guided tour. There is also a playground, a gift shop, and a tearoom. The grounds are varied and good for walking and mountain biking; bikes can be rented at the castle. ⊠ *Off A76, Thornhill* ⊹ *18 miles northwest of Dumfries* ☎ *01848/600283* ⊕ *www. drumlanrig.com* 🖾 *Park £6, castle and park £12* 🕑 *Closed Oct.–Mar.*

Museum of Lead Mining

HISTORY MUSEUM | The Lochnell Mine was abandoned in 1861, after 150 years of operation, and the mine and miners' homes now form part of this museum re-creating their lives. The isolated village of Wanlockhead, where the mine is located, has not changed a great deal since then—there was little alternative employment for the miners and their families. In the visitor center, housed in the old smithy, there are tableaux depicting the work of the miners and explanations of the nature of the ore from which the lead was taken. A visit consists of a tour of the miners' library, followed by a walk through the long gallery of the mine itself as well as some of the miners' houses. Hard hats are included, but it is still wise to keep your head down. The nearby Leadhills and Wanlockhead Narrow Gauge Railway runs on weekends throughout the summer and costs £4, with a 10% reduction for a joint ticket with the museum. There is also a pleasant tearoom and shop in the visitor center. ⊠ *Off B797, Wanlockhead* ✛ *32 miles north of Dumfries* ☎ *01659/74387* ⊕ *www.leadminingmuseum.co.uk* ⌸ *£22* ⊘ *Closed Oct.–Mar.*

Striding Arches
PUBLIC ART | British sculptor Andy Goldsworthy's extraordinary piece of public landscape art enriches the great natural amphitheater at Cairnhead in the southern uplands of Dumfries and Galloway. His three red-sandstone arches stand 13 feet high and mark out the area, "striding" across the landscape and symbolizing all those who have left the area and migrated in search of work or better lives. ⊠ *Cairnhead Forest, near Moniaive* ✛ *Take the A702 (off the A76 at Thornhill) to Moniaive, then the road to Benbuie until you reach The Byre. From there it is a walk to the viewpoint* ☎ *07801/232229* ⊕ *www.stridingarches.com* ⌸ *Free.*

Solway Firth

10 miles south of Dumfries.

Mostly undiscovered by travelers, the Solway Firth is a must for walkers, cyclists, and bird-watchers. This lovely and protected inlet, guarded by beautiful Caerlaverock Castle, is a haven for a great variety of seabirds. You can see them at the nature reserve behind the castle. Cycling or on foot, you can stroll gentle coastal paths beside the firth that link the villages of Sandyhills, Rockcliffe, and Kippford.

GETTING HERE AND AROUND
There is a bus from Dumfries to Kippford (one hour), but a car is best for visiting this area. Take the A710 from Dumfries and then the A711.

⊙ Sights

★ Caerlaverock Castle
CASTLE/PALACE | The stunningly beautiful moated Caerlaverock Castle stands in splendid isolation amid the surrounding wetlands. Built in a unique triangular design, this 13th-century fortress has solid-sandstone masonry and an imposing double-tower gatehouse. King Edward I of England (1239–1307) besieged the castle in 1300, when his forces occupied much of Scotland at the start of the Wars of Independence. A splendid residence was built inside in the 1600s. Now largely in ruins, the interior is still atmospheric, and the siege engines on the grounds give some sense of what medieval warfare was like. The castle has a pleasant café for coffee, cakes, or lunch. ⊠ *Off B725, Ruthwell* ✛ *10 miles south of Dumfries* ☎ *01387/770244* ⊕ *www.historicenvironment.scot* ⌸ *£6.*

★ Caerlaverock Wildfowl and Wetlands Centre
NATURE PRESERVE | This wild and beautiful wetland provides a stunning backdrop to Caerlaverock Castle. Here you can observe wintering wildfowl, including migrating geese, spy ducks, swans, and raptors. In summer, ospreys patrol the waters of this northernmost outpost of the Wildfowl and Wetlands Trust. The triops, the tadpole shrimp that is one of the oldest known species, lives in

the aquarium here. There are bats and badgers, sparrows, and natterjack toads as well. Free guided walks are available in the afternoons throughout the year. ✉ *Eastpark Farm, Off B725, Dumfries* ✥ *9 miles southeast of Dumfries off the A75* ☎ *01387/770200* 🌐 *www.wwt.org.uk* 🎫 *£8.27.*

Hotels

Clonyard House Hotel

$ | HOTEL | A modest hotel occuping a stone house, most of the comfortable rooms look out on a well-tended, pleasant garden. **Pros:** beautiful setting; good location; hearty breakfasts. **Cons:** limited access to public transport; lounge bar rather small; not all rooms look onto the garden. [$] *Rooms from: £80* ✉ *Colvend, Dalbeattie, Kippford* ☎ *01556/630732* 🌐 *www.clonyardhotel.co.uk* 🛏 *4 rooms* 🍴 *Free Breakfast.*

Castle Douglas

18 miles southwest of Dumfries, 25 miles west of Caerlaverock Castle.

A quaint town that sits beside Carlingwark Loch, Castle Douglas is a popular base for exploring the surrounding countryside. The loch sets off the town perfectly, reflecting its dramatic architecture of sharp spires and soft sandstone arches. Its main thoroughfare, King Street, has unique shops and a number of eateries.

GETTING HERE AND AROUND

There's no train station in Castle Douglas, and buses from Dumfries make several stops along the way. The best way to get here is by car. From Dalbeattie take the A711/A745 (10 minutes). From Glasgow take the A713 (just under two hours). From Edinburgh take the A70 (a little over 2 hours).

BICYCLING TOURS

Galloway Cycling Holidays

BICYCLE TOURS | For a slower-paced look at the sights in the region, take a bike tour that begins in Castle Douglas. This small outfit is run by local residents and offers tours, self-guided or otherwise, varying from weekend packages to week-long explorations of the region for castle seekers, nature watchers, and passionate cyclists. ✉ *Threve Rd., Castle Douglas* ☎ *01556/502979* 🌐 *www.gallowaycycling.com.*

Sights

★ Threave Castle

CASTLE/PALACE | Once home to the Black Douglases, earls of Nithsdale and lords of Galloway, Threave's imposing towers reflect well the Lord of Galloway who built it in the 14th century, Archibald the Grim. Not to be confused with the mansion in Threave Gardens, the castle was dismantled in the religious wars of the mid-17th century, though enough of it remained to have housed prisoners from the Napoleonic Wars two centuries later. It's a few minutes from Castle Douglas by car and is signposted from the main road. To get here, leave your car in a farmyard and make your way down to the edge of the river. Ring the bell (loudly) and, rather romantically, a boatman will come to ferry you across to the great stone tower looming from a marshy island in the river. ✉ *A75, Castle Douglas* ✥ *3 miles west of Castle Douglas* ☎ *07711/223101* 🌐 *www.historicenvironment.scot* 🎫 *£6 including ferry; buy tickets online or from the NTS Osprey Centre on the site (cash only)* ⏲ *Closed Nov.–Mar.*

Threave Garden and Estate

GARDEN | The National Trust for Scotland cares for the gently sloping parkland and gardens around an 1867 mansion built by William Gordon, a Liverpool businessman. The house, fully restored in the 1930s, gives a glimpse into the daily life

To get to moody Threave Castle, you must be ferried across the River Dee by boat.

of a prosperous 19th-century family. The grounds demand an army of gardeners, and today many of them are students at the National Trust's School of Heritage Gardening, which has developed the variety of gardens here. Bats, ospreys, and other birds and animals share the space. Entry to the house is by timed guided tour, and it's wise to book ahead. There's an on-site restaurant. ✉ *South of A75, Castle Douglas* ✥ *1 mile west of Castle Douglas* ☎ *01556/502575* 🌐 *www.nts.org.uk/Visits* 🎟 *Gardens £9, house and gardens £15, nature reserve free* 🕓 *Gardens closed Dec.–Feb., house closed Nov.–Apr.*

🍴 Restaurants

The Café at Designs Gallery

$ | CAFÉ | For a good balance of art and food, look no further than this café at a contemporary art and crafts gallery in the town center. You'll find the freshest ingredients here, from soup to salads, sandwiches to quiches; everything is made on-site, including the bread, and it's all organic. **Known for:** lovely garden; good lunch menu; house-made soups. [$] *Average main: £10* ✉ *179 King St., Castle Douglas* ☎ *01556/504552* 🌐 *www.designsgallery.co.uk* 🕓 *Closed Sun. No dinner.*

🛍 Shopping

Galloway Gems and Craft Centre and Outback Yarns

CRAFTS | In this glittery shop you can purchase mineral specimens, polished stone slices, and a range of Celtic- and Nordic-inspired jewelry, as well as craft materials of every kind. For fiber artists and sewers, it's a real find. ✉ *130–132 King St., Castle Douglas* ☎ *01556/503254* 🌐 *www.outbackyarns.co.uk.*

Tessera

HOUSEWARES | At this stylish interiors shop on Castle Douglass main street, you can shop for a wide range of gifts, cards, and jewelry. ✉ *58 King St., Castle Douglas* ☎ *01556/503003* 🌐 *tesserahomeinteriors.co.uk.*

🏃 Activities

BICYCLING

Castle Douglas Cycle Centre

BIKING | You can rent bicycles for everyone in the family from Castle Douglas Cycle Centre. It also handles repairs and service. ⊠ *11 Church St., Castle Douglas* ☎ *01556/504542* ⊕ *www.cdbikes.co.uk.*

BOATING

Galloway Activity Centre

WATER SPORTS | With dinghies, kayaks, and canoes for rent, the Galloway Activity Centre on the banks of Loch Ken specializes in water sports. "Dry" sports include mountain biking, archery, and rock climbing. ⊠ *Shirmers Bridge, Loch Ken, Castle Douglas* ✛ *10 miles northwest of Castle Douglas off A713* ☎ *01556/502011* ⊕ *www.lochken.co.uk.*

GOLF

Southerness Golf Club

GOLF | Mackenzie Ross designed this course, the first built in Scotland after World War II. Southerness is a long course, played over extensive links with fine views southward over the Solway Firth. The greens are hard and fast, and the frequent winds make for some testing golf. Thursday is reserved for women. ⊠ *Southerness St., Southerness* ✛ *19 miles west of Castle Douglas via the A745 and B793* ☎ *01387/880677* ⊕ *www. southernessgolfclub.com* 🖾 *Apr.–Sept. £60 weekdays, £70 weekends; Oct.–Mar. £35 weekdays, £40 weekends* 🏌 *18 holes, 6110 yards, par 69.*

Kirkcudbright

9 miles southwest of Castle Douglas.

Kirkcudbright (pronounced kir-*coo*-bray) is an 18th-century town of Georgian and Victorian houses, some of them washed in pastel shades and roofed with the blue slate of the district. It sits on an inlet from the Solway Firth. In the early 20th century the town and its lovely harbor became a haven for artists, and today its L-shaped main street is full of crafts and antiques shops.

GETTING HERE AND AROUND

Driving is your best and only real option. From Castle Douglas take the A711 (15 minutes). From Glasgow take the A713 (about two hours). From Edinburgh take the A701 (about 2½ hours).

ESSENTIALS

VISITOR INFORMATION VisitScotland Kirkcudbright iCentre. ⊠ *Harbour Sq., Kirkcudbright* ☎ *01557/330494* ⊕ *www. visitscotland.com.*

👁 Sights

★ Broughton House

HISTORIC HOME | The 18th-century Broughton House was the home of the artist E. A. Hornel from 1901 until his death in 1933 and remains largely as it was in his time. Hornel was a member of the school of painters called the "Glasgow Boys," who were influenced by the Vienna Secession and art nouveau. You can see many of his paintings in the gallery Hornel built onto the house to impress the guests and buyers who came to see his work. His use and love of color is obvious in the beautiful garden, which combines lawns, ponds, and formal and wildflower beds. The knowledgeable guides will gladly provide information about the life and work of the painter. Tickets for entry are timed so be sure to reserve in advance online. ⊠ *12 High St., Kirkcudbright* ☎ *01557/330437* ⊕ *www. nts.org.uk* 🖾 *£8* 🕙 *Closed Nov.–Apr.*

Dark Space Planetarium

SCIENCE MUSEUM | **FAMILY** | At this fascinating interactive museum, both the young and the not-so young can test their scientific knowledge and travel into the solar system via the planetarium. You can even try on astronaut gloves to get an idea of how hard it is to use your hands in space. It seems especially appropriate since Dumfries and Galloway both have expansive areas of dark sky for great star-gazing within Galloway Forest. ⊠ *St. Mary St., Kirkcudbright* ☎ *01557/337213* ⊕ *www.darkspaceplanetarium.org* ⊠ *£15* ⊘ *Closed Mon.–Wed.*

MacLellan's Castle

CASTLE/PALACE | Conspicuous in the center of town are the stone walls of MacLellan's Castle, a once-elaborate castellated mansion dating from the 16th century. You can walk around the interior, still atmospheric even though the rooms are bare. The "Lairds Lug," behind the fireplace, allowed the *laird* (lord) to listen in to what his guests were saying about him. You can also get a glimpse of life below stairs in the kitchen vaults beneath the main staircase. The mansion has lovely views over the town. ⊠ *Off High St., Kirkcudbright* ☎ *01557/331856* ⊕ *www.historicenvironment.scot* ⊠ *£4.80* ⊘ *Closed Oct.–Mar.*

Stewartry Museum

HISTORY MUSEUM | Stuffed with all manner of local paraphernalia, the delightfully old-fashioned Stewartry Museum allows you to putter and absorb as much or as little as takes your interest in the display cases. Stewartry is the former name of Kirkcudbright. ⊠ *St. Mary St., Kirkcudbright* ☎ *01557/331643* ⊕ *www.dumgal. gov.uk* ⊠ *Free* ⊘ *Closed Sun.*

Tolbooth Arts Centre

ART GALLERY | In the 17th-century tolbooth (a combination town hall–courthouse–prison), the Tolbooth Arts Centre describes how the town attracted famous artists, among them E. A. Hornel, Jessie King, and Charles Oppenheimer. Some of their paintings are on display, as are works by contemporary artists. There is also a shop on the ground floor. ⊠ *High St., Kirkcudbright* ☎ *01557/331556* ⊕ *www.dumgal.gov.uk* ⊠ *Free* ⊘ *Closed Sun. Oct.–May.*

🍴 Restaurants

★ Artistas at the Selkirk Arms

$$ | MODERN BRITISH | Paintings of Scotland, starched white tablecloths, and giant windows overlooking the well-kept garden beckon you into this highly praised eatery. Locals love that the food on the bar and regular menus is locally sourced and full of imagination. **Known for:** charming location in town; local produce; both familiar and more exotic dishes. $ *Average main: £16* ⊠ *Selkirk Arms, High St., Kirkcudbright* ☎ *01557/330402* ⊕ *www.selkirkarmshotel.co.uk.*

🛏 Hotels

★ Selkirk Arms

$ | HOTEL | Bursting with charm, this · elegant 18th-century hotel has a lot going for it, including spacious guest rooms that are individually decorated with cozy beds, contemporary wood furniture, and soft lighting. **Pros:** lively traditional pub; free Wi-Fi; massive breakfast. **Cons:** some rooms are small; bar gets crowded during sporting events; rooms closest to restaurant can be noisy. $ *Rooms from: £120* ⊠ *High St., Kirkcudbright* ☎ *01557/330402* ⊕ *www.selkirkarmshotel.co.uk* ⇱ *16 rooms* ⏸ *Free Breakfast.*

Gatehouse of Fleet

9 miles west of Kirkcudbright.

A peaceful, pleasant, backwoods sort of place, Gatehouse of Fleet has a castle guarding its southern approach.

GETTING HERE AND AROUND

There's no train station in Gatehouse of Fleet. Local buses are available, but you may need to make several transfers. Driving is your best option. From Kirkcudbright take the A755/B727 (15 minutes). From Glasgow take the A713 (about two hours). From Edinburgh take the A7 (about 2½ hours).

Sights

Cardoness Castle
CASTLE/PALACE | The castle was a typical Scottish tower house, severe and uncompromising. The 15th-century structure once was the home of the McCullochs of Galloway, then the Gordons—two of the area's important and occasionally infamous families. Though ruined, it is well preserved with fireplaces and some carvings intact. ✉ *A75, Gatehouse of Fleet* ✥ *1 mile southwest of Gatehouse of Fleet* ☎ *01557/814427* 🌐 *www.historic-scotland.gov.uk/places* 🎟 *£6* ⏲ *Closed Oct.-Mar.*

Mill on the Fleet
HISTORY MUSEUM | This converted mill is a reminder that this tranquil town was for more than a hundred years the center of the region's cotton industry. You can learn more inside, where arts and crafts are also on display. The tearoom serves light lunches and delicious home-baked goods. The building also houses the town's tourist information center. ✉ *High St., Gatehouse of Fleet* ☎ *01557/814099* 🌐 *www.millonthefleet.co.uk* 🎟 *Free* ⏲ *Closed Nov.-Mar.*

Hotels

Cally Palace
$$$ | **HOTEL** | Many of the public rooms in this Georgian hotel, built in 1763 as a private mansion, retain their original grandeur, with elaborate plaster ceilings and marble fireplaces. **Pros:** piano music at dinner; beautiful views from balconies; impressive setting. **Cons:** slightly isolated from other sights; atmosphere can feel old-fashioned; decor is a bit bland. [$] *Rooms from: £209* ✉ *Off A75, Gatehouse of Fleet* ✥ *About 1 mile south of Gatehouse of Fleet* ☎ *01557/814341* *www.mcmillanhotels.co.uk* ⏲ *Closed and Feb.* 🛏 *56 rooms* 🍴 *Free fast.*

Shopping

Galloway Lodge Preserves
FOOD | This family-run shop sells marmalades, mustards, chutneys, jams, and jellies, all made in the village. You can also pick up some Scottish pottery and eat at the café. ✉ *24–28 High St., Gatehouse of Fleet* ☎ *01557/814001* 🌐 *www.gallowaylodge.co.uk.*

Newton Stewart

18 miles northwest of Kirkcudbright.

The bustling town of Newton Stewart is the place to stop when touring the western region of Galloway. It is the gateway to the Galloway Forest and Glen Trool.

GETTING HERE AND AROUND

Newton Stewart does not have a train station, but the town is served by regular buses from Glasgow and Edinburgh as well as local buses from neighboring towns. By car from Glasgow, take the A77 (about two hours). From Edinburgh take the A702 (about 2¾ hours).

Sights

Creetown Gem Rock Museum
OTHER MUSEUM | In the village of Creetown seven miles outside Newton Stewart, this museum has an eclectic mineral collection, a dinosaur egg, an erupting volcano, and a crystal cave. There's also an Internet café, a tearoom, and a shop selling stones and crystals—both loose and in settings. Entry is good for two weeks. ✉ *Chain Rd., Creetown* ✥ *Off A75* ☎ *01671/820357* 🌐 *www.gemrock.net* 🎟 *£5* ⏲ *Closed Dec. and Jan.*

★ **Galloway Forest Park**
FOREST | The expansive facilities in Galloway Forest Park are evidence of the growing enthusiasm for active vacations in Scotland; it offers chances for cycling, walking, kayaking on the rivers, bird-watching, and mountain-biking.

You can walk or bicycle along the paths through moorland and forests, by lochs and over hills—all contained within the 300 square miles of the forest. The Forestry Commission, which manages the forest, has three visitor centers at Glen Trool, Kirroughtree, and Clatteringshaws and also offers exhibits about the region's wildlife, a reconstructed Iron Age dwelling, and 7stanes mountain-biking centers. The forest is designated as a Dark Sky Park; the low light pollution here ensures exceptional stargazing. ✉ *A712, Newton Stewart* ✥ *7 miles northeast of Newton Stewart* ☎ *01671/402420* 🌐 *www.gallowayforestpark.com* 🎫 *Free.*

Glen Trool

FOREST | With high purple-and-green hilltops shorn rock-bare by glaciers, and with a dark, winding loch and thickets of birch trees sounding with birdcalls, Glen Trool's setting almost looks more highland than the real Highlands. Note **Bruce's Stone,** just above the parking lot, marking the site where in 1307 Scotland's champion Robert the Bruce (King Robert I, 1274–1329) won his first victory in the Scottish Wars of Independence. A little road off the A714 leads through increasingly wild woodland scenery to a parking lot. The visitor center is open daily. Only after you have climbed for a few minutes onto a heathery knoll does the full, rugged panorama become apparent. Driving is really the only way to get to Glen Trool, which is part of Galloway Forest Park. From Glasgow take the A77 (about 2¼ hours). From Edinburgh take the A702 (about three hours). ✉ *Off A714, Bargrennan* ✥ *A714 north from Newton Stewart for about 15 mins; turn right at the signpost for Glen Trool* ☎ *01671/840302* 🌐 *www.forestry.gov.uk* 🎫 *Free.*

Wood of Cree Nature Reserve

NATURE PRESERVE | Birders love the Wood of Cree Nature Reserve, managed by the Royal Society for the Protection of Birds. In the reserve you can see such species as the redstart, pied flycatcher, and wood warbler. You might also spot otters and roe deer. To get there, take the minor road that travels north from Newton Stewart alongside the River Cree east of the A714. The entrance is next to a small parking area at the side of the road. ✉ *Off A714, Newton Stewart* ✥ *4 miles north of Newton Stewart* ☎ *01988/402130* 🌐 *www.rspb.org.uk* 🎫 *Donations accepted.*

🛏 Hotels

Creebridge House Hotel

$ | **HOTEL** | Close to the River Cree and set among gardens and woodland, the Creebridge places the emphasis on comfort and quiet rural surroundings. **Pros:** within easy reach of Newton Stewart; practical center for exploring the area; comfort in a rural setting. **Cons:** gets busy and noisy with weddings; not easy to reach without a car; slightly conservative feel. [$] *Rooms from: £89* ✉ *Minigaff, Off B7079, Newton Stewart* ☎ *01671/402121* 🌐 *www.creebridge.co.uk* 🛏 *18 rooms* 🍴 *Free Breakfast.*

Whithorn

17 miles south of Newton Stewart.

Known for its early Christian settlement, Whithorn is full of history. The main street is notably wide, with pretty pastel buildings nestled up against each other, their low doorways and small windows creating images of years long past. It's still mainly a farming community but is fast becoming a popular tourist destination. Several scenes from the original *Wicker Man* (1973) were shot in and around the area. During the summer months, it's a popular place for festivals. The Isle of Whithorn, just beyond the town, is not an island at all but a fishing village of great charm.

GETTING HERE AND AROUND

There's no train station in Whithorn, and most of the buses are local (getting to main Scottish cities from Whithorn takes careful planning and several transfers). To drive from Newton Stewart, take the A714 and then A746. From Glasgow take the A77 (about 2½ hours). From Edinburgh take the A702 (about three hours).

Sights

St. Ninian's Chapel

RELIGIOUS BUILDING | The Isle of Whithorn (a fishing village on the mainland) holds the ruins of the 14th-century St. Ninian's Chapel, where pilgrims who came by sea prayed before traveling inland to Whithorn Priory. Some people claim that this, and not Whithorn Priory, is the site of the Candida Casa, a 4th-century church. The structure seems to have been erected on top of a much older chapel built around 1100. It's 4 miles south of Whithorn. ✉ *Isle of Whithorn* ✥ *Take A746 and B7004 from Whithorn* ☎ *01998/500508* 🌐 *www.whithorn.com* 🎟 *Free.*

Whithorn Trust Visitor Centre

RELIGIOUS BUILDING | The road that is now the A746 was a pilgrims' path that led to the royal burgh of Whithorn, where sat Whithorn Priory, one of Scotland's great medieval cathedrals, now an empty shell. It was built in the 12th century and is said to occupy the site of a former stone church, the Candida Casa, built by St. Ninian in the 4th century. As the story goes, the church housed a shrine to Ninian, the earliest of Scotland's saints, and kings and barons tried to visit the shrine at least once in their lives. As you approach the priory, observe the royal arms of pre-1707 Scotland—that is, Scotland before the Union Act with England—carved and painted above the *pend* (covered walkway). The museum houses restored stonework from the period, including crosses and a reconstructed Celtic circular home. ✉ *45-47 George St., Whithorn* ☎ *01988/500508* 🌐 *www.whithorn.com* 🎟 *£6 (includes the Whithorn Story and Visitor Centre)* 🕓 *Closed Sat. and Nov.–Mar.*

Restaurants

★ Steam Packet Inn

$$ | BRITISH | FAMILY | Lovely and old-fashioned, this white-washed inn is always full, mainly because of its good beer and hearty, well-cooked food including steak and ale pie. Located directly on the harbor, it has few local rivals, but customers come from far and wide to eat here and walk the headland behind the pub to the rocky shore of the Solway Firth. **Known for:** garden dining in nice weather; superior pub food; outstanding desserts. [$] *Average main: £15* ✉ *Harbour Row, Isle of Whithorn* ☎ *01988/500334* 🌐 *www.thesteampacketinn.biz.*

Stranraer

31 miles northwest of Whithorn.

Stranraer was for more than a century the main ferry port between Scotland and Northern Ireland. Its closure, and the transfer of ferry traffic to nearby Cairnryan, continues to bring changes to the town. The city center has had a major face-lift, and there are plans to redevelop the harbor as a leisure center and transportation hub. Stranraer has a lovely garden.

GETTING HERE AND AROUND

Stranraer's train station is directly accessible from Glasgow; bus services are also good (with many connections to smaller towns). If you're driving, take the A747 from Whithorn (about 45 minutes). From Glasgow take the M77/A77 (two hours), and from Edinburgh take the A77 (three hours).

◉ Sights

★ **Castle Kennedy Gardens**

GARDEN | The lovely Castle Kennedy Gardens surround the shell of the original Castle Kennedy, which burned down in 1716. Parks scattered around the property were built by the second Earl of Stair in 1733. The earl was a field marshal and used his soldiers to help with the heavy work of constructing banks, ponds, and other major landscape features. When the rhododendrons are in bloom (April through July, depending on the variety), the effect is kaleidoscopic. There's also a pleasant tearoom. ⊠ *Sheuchan, Stranraer* ✛ *3 miles east of Stranraer on the A875* ☎ *01776/702024* ⊕ *www.castlekenne-dygardens.co.uk* ⌦ *£6* ⊘ *Closed Nov.–Jan. and weekdays in Feb. and Mar.*

Glenwhan Gardens

GARDEN | Like its neighbor Castle Kennedy, this wonderful garden, created some 40 years ago, benefits from the warm gulf stream that flows along the area's coasts, allowing tropical plants to grow. Rare trees and shrubs grow here beside ferns, wild grasses, and a variety of wildflowers. It is also an arboretum with a tree trail. Paths and walks crisscross the garden, leading out into the surrounding moorland, where you can enjoy the views across to the Mull of Galloway. ⊠ *Dunragit, Stranraer* ☎ *015811/400222* ⊕ *www.glenwhangardens.co.uk* ⌦ *£6.50.*

Portpatrick

8 miles southwest of Stranraer.

The holiday town of Portpatrick lies across the Rhinns of Galloway from Stranraer. Once an Irish ferry port, Portpatrick's harbor eventually proved too small for larger vessels.

GETTING HERE AND AROUND

Direct buses travel between Portpatrick to Stranraer and some of the neighboring towns, but travel to and from the larger Scottish cities can prove more difficult. There is no train station in Portpatrick (though there is one in nearby Stranraer). Driving is probably your best bet. From Stranraer take the A77; it's about a 15-minute journey. Take the M77/A77 from Glasgow (just over two hours) and the M8/A77 from Edinburgh (about three hours).

◉ Sights

Logan Botanic Garden

GARDEN | One of the four major sites belonging to the Edinburgh-based National Botanic Gardens of Scotland, the spectacular Logan Botanic Garden is a must-see for garden lovers. Displayed here are plants that enjoy the prevailing mild climate, especially tree ferns, cabbage palms, and other Southern Hemisphere exotica. There are free guided walks every second Tuesday of the month at 10:30 am; at other times there is a free audio guide. ⊠ *Port Logan, Port Logan* ✛ *On B7065, 16 miles south of Portpatrick* ☎ *01776/860231* ⊕ *www.rbge.org.uk* ⌦ *£6.50* ⊘ *Closed Jan. and weekdays in Feb.*

Mull of Galloway

SCENIC DRIVE | If you wish to visit the southern tip of the Rhinns of Galloway, called the Mull of Galloway, follow the B7065/B7041 until you run out of land. The cliffs and seascapes here are rugged, and there's a lighthouse and the Mull of Galloway bird reserve. ⊕ *www.rspb.org.uk* ⊘ *Reserve closed Nov.–mid-Mar.*

Southern Upland Way
TRAIL | The village of Portpatrick is the starting point for Scotland's longest official long-distance footpath, the Southern Upland Way, which runs a switchback course for 212 miles to Cockburnspath, on the east side of the Borders. The path begins on the cliffs just north of the town and follows the coastline for 1½ miles before turning inland. 🌐 *www.dgtrails.org* 🎟 *Free.*

Hotels

Crown Hotel Portpatrick
$$ | **HOTEL** | From the terrace of this simple small hotel in a working fishing village, you can look out across the sea to Ireland while eating some delicious seafood. **Pros:** base for lots of outdoor activities; beautiful location; very good restaurant. **Cons:** extra cost for sea-view rooms; rooms are fairly basic; fairly remote town. [$] *Rooms from: £135* ✉ *9 N. Crescent, Portpatrick* ☎ *01776/810261* 🌐 *www.crownportpatrick.com* 🛏 *12 rooms* 🍴 *Free Breakfast.*

Portpatrick Hotel
$ | **B&B/INN** | From its vantage point in splendid isolation on the top of a cliff, the Portpatrick Hotel has wonderful views across the Mull of Galloway. **Pros:** good restaurant; beautiful location; gorgeous views. **Cons:** can feel quite isolated; not every room has a sea view; some rooms are small. [$] *Rooms from: £89* ✉ *Heugh Rd., Portpatrick* ☎ *08444/4999357* 🌐 *bespokehotels.com/portpatrick-hotel* 🛏 *55 rooms* 🍴 *Free Breakfast.*

Chapter 6

FIFE AND
ANGUS

Updated by
Nick Bruno

⊙ Sights	🍴 Restaurants	🛏 Hotels	🛍 Shopping	🍸 Nightlife
★★★★☆	★★★☆☆	★★★☆☆	★★☆☆☆	★★★☆☆

WELCOME TO FIFE AND ANGUS

TOP REASONS TO GO

★ **St. Andrews:** With its medieval streets, ruined cathedral and castle, and peculiarly posh atmosphere, St. Andrews is one of the most incongruous yet beguiling places in Scotland—even without its famous golf course.

★ **East Neuk:** As you take in crowstep-gabled fishermen's cottages, winding cobbled lanes, seaside harbor scenes, and lovely beaches, you can almost imagine the harsh lives of the hardworking Fifers who lived in tiny hamlets such as Crail, Anstruther, Pittenweem, and Elie. Today artists and visitors make it all pleasantly picturesque.

★ **Dundee:** This former industrial city is becoming better known for its vibrant arts, music, theater, restaurant, and nightlife scenes.

★ **The Angus Glens:** These long glens (such as Glen Clova) that run into the wild Grampian Mountains are magical places beloved by outdoors enthusiasts and those just wanting to rediscover nature.

1 St. Andrews. A university town famed for golfing.

2 Crail. An East Neuk fishing village.

3 Anstruther. A working port.

4 Pittenweem and St. Monans. Harbor villages with impressive art.

5 Elie. A Victorian resort.

6 Falkland. A royal burgh.

7 Cupar. A busy market town.

8 Dundee. One of Scotland's most vibrant cities.

9 Arbroath. Famed for its smoked fish.

10 Montrose. A charming town by an estuary.

11 Brechin. A market village.

12 The Angus Glens. Rolling glens that cut into the Cairngorms.

13 Kirriemuir. Peter Pan's hometown.

14 Forfar. Farming and ancient stone carvings.

15 Glamis. Home to a grand castle.

16 Meigle. Notable Pictish stones.

17 Alyth. A rural market town.

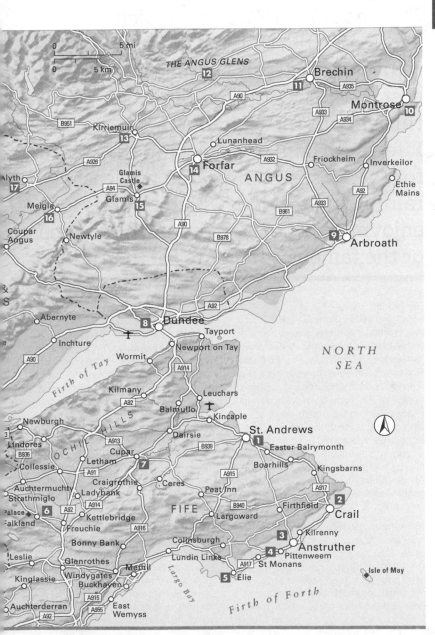

Breezy cliff-top walkways, fishing villages, and open beaches characterize Fife and Angus. They sandwich Scotland's fourth-largest city, the rejuvenated city of Dundee. Scotland's east coast has only light rainfall throughout the year; northeastern Fife, in particular, may claim the record for the most sunshine and the least rainfall in Scotland, which all adds to the enjoyment when you're touring the coast or the famous golf center of St. Andrews.

Fife proudly styles itself as a "kingdom," and its long history—which really began when the Romans went home in the 4th century and the Picts moved in—lends some substance to the boast. From medieval times its earls were first among Scotland's nobility and crowned her kings. For many, however, the most historic event in the region was the birth of golf, in the 15th century, which, legend has it, occurred in St. Andrews, an ancient university town with stone houses and seaside ruins. The Royal & Ancient Golf Club, the ruling body of the game worldwide, still has its headquarters here.

Not surprisingly, fishing and seafaring have also played a role in the history of the East Neuk coastal region. From the 16th through the 19th century a large population lived and worked in the small ports and harbors that form a chain around Fife's coast, which James V once called "a beggar's mantle fringed with gold." When the sun shines, this golden fringe—particularly at Tentsmuir, St. Andrews, and Elie—gleams like the beaches of Normandy. Indeed, the houses of the East Neuk villages have a similar character, with color-washed fronts, fishy weather vanes, outdoor stone stairways to upper floors, and crude carvings of anchors and lobsters on their lintels. All the houses are crowded on steep *wynds* (narrow streets), hugging pint-size harbors that in the golden era supported village fleets of 100 ships apiece.

North, across the Firth of Tay, lies the region of Angus, whose charm is its variety: in addition to its seacoast and pleasant Lowland market centers, there's also a hinterland of lonely rounded hills with long glens running into the typical Grampian Highland scenery beyond. One of Angus's interesting features, which it shares with the eastern Lowland edge of Perthshire, is its fruit-growing industry, which includes raspberries.

Known as the "City of Discovery" (after the RRS *Discovery,* a polar exploration vessel that set sail from this port in 1901), and as the United Kingdom's UNESCO City of Design, Dundee has a sophisticated arts and cultural scene and some beguiling sights. The ongoing regeneration of the city's waterfront has created a buzz, with the cliff-shaped V&A Dundee design museum making a bold statement beside the Tay. Today's Dundee makes a superb base for a cultural stay and from which to launch a number of day trips.

MAJOR REGIONS

St. Andrews and East Neuk. In its western parts Fife still bears the scars of heavy industry, especially coal mining, but these signs are less evident as you move east. Northeastern Fife, around the town of St. Andrews, seems to have played no part in the Industrial Revolution; instead, its residents earned a living from the grain fields or from the sea. Fishing has been a major industry, and in the past a string of Fife ports traded across the North Sea. Today the legacy of Dutch-influenced architecture, such as crowstepped gables (the stepped effect on the ends of the roofs)—gives these East Neuk villages a distinctive character. St. Andrews is unlike any other Scottish town. Once Scotland's most powerful ecclesiastical center as well as the seat of the country's oldest university and then, much later, the very symbol and spiritual home of golf, the town has a comfortable, well-groomed air, sitting almost smugly apart from the rest of Scotland. Its latest cachet is being the place where the riveting 21st-century royal romance between Prince William and Kate Middleton began, which boosted university applications from around the world.

Dundee and Angus. The small, friendly city of Dundee sits near the mouth of the River Tay surrounded by the farms and glens of rural Angus and the coastal grassy banks and golf courses of northeastern Fife. A vibrant, industrious, and cultural city, it's undergoing a postindustrial renaissance of sorts, with the V&A museum as the centerpiece of the emerging waterfront regeneration. The first outpost of London's world-famous Victoria and Albert Museum, a repository of the decorative arts and design, is housed in a sculptural building jutting into Britain's most powerful river. Dundee is the United Kingdom's sole UNESCO City of Design, with a large student population, a lively arts and nightlife scene, and several historical and nautical sights. The tree-lined country roads of the Angus heartlands roll through strawberry and raspberry fields to busy market towns, wee villages, and Glamis Castle. Angus combines coastal agriculture on rich, red soils with dramatic inland glens that pierce their way into the foothills of the Grampian mountain range to the northwest.

■**TIP→ The main road from Dundee to Aberdeen—the A90—requires special care with its mix of fast cars and unexpectedly slow farm traffic.**

Planning

When to Go

Spring in the Angus glens can be quite captivating, with the hills along Angus's northernmost boundary still covered in snow. Similarly, the moorland colors of autumn are appealing. But Fife and Angus are really summer destinations, when most of the sights are open to visitors. Note that during the summer, St. Andrews hosts several international golf tournaments that effectively take over the town. Nongolfers may become incredibly frustrated when searching for accommodations or places to eat during these times, so check ahead.

Getting Oriented

Fife lies north of the Lothians, across the iconic bridges of the Firth of Forth. A headland, Fife's northeastern coast (or East Neuk) is fringed with golden sands, rocky shores, fishermen's cottages, and, of course, the splendor of St. Andrews, home of golf. Northwest of Fife and across the glorious Firth of Tay, the city of Dundee is undergoing a postindustrial reinvention. Its rural hinterland, Angus, hugs the city, which, stretching north toward the foothills of the Grampian Mountains, houses agricultural and fishing communities, and Glamis, one of Scotland's best-loved castles.

Planning Your Time

St. Andrews, 52 miles from Edinburgh, is not to be missed, for its history and atmosphere as much as for the golf; allot an overnight stop and at least a whole day if you can. The nearby East Neuk of Fife has some of Scotland's finest coastline, now becoming gentrified by the Edinburgh second-home set but still evoking Fife's past. A day's drive along A917 (allow for exploring and stops for ice cream and fish) will take you through the fishing villages of Elie, Pittenweem, Anstruther, and Crail. Dundee, with its rich maritime history, stunning riverside setting, and grand museums, is an ideal base for a drive round the Angus towns of Arbroath, Kirriemuir, and Alyth; if you make a three-hour stop at Glamis Castle, this trip will take about a day.

Getting Here and Around

AIR
There are handy flight options via Edinburgh and the small Dundee airport. For international flights, Edinburgh Airport is the easiest gateway into the region. The Dundee airport has twice daily connections with London Stansted.

CONTACTS Dundee Airport. ✉ *Dundee* ☎ *01382/662200* ⊕ *www.hial.co.uk/dundee-airport.* **Edinburgh Airport.** ✉ *Edinburgh* ☎ *0131/357–6337* ⊕ *www.edinburghairport.com.*

BUS
Among the various bus operators that serve much of the region, Stagecoach (www.stagecoachbus.com) has the most coverage through Angus and Fife. Xplore Dundee (⊕ *www.nxbus.co.uk/dundee*) serves the city and runs the airport transfer bus to and from Edinburgh Airport. Visit ⊕ www.travelinescotland.com to plan any bus or train journey through the region.

CAR
For seeing the most of Fife and Angus, car travel is basically essential, although there are some public transport alternatives. The major roads that span the region are not big motorways, but second-tier A roads; many of these roads are single-lane only, so be especially cautious when driving in this region.

TRAIN
The East Coast Main Line makes stops at Cupar, Leuchars (for St. Andrews), Dundee, Arbroath, and Montrose.

CONTACTS East Coast Main Line. ⊕ *www.scotrail.co.uk.*

Restaurants

With an affluent population, St. Andrews supports several stylish hotel restaurants. Because it's a university town and popular tourist destination, there are also many good cafés and bistro-style restaurants. Bar lunches are the rule in large and small hotels throughout the region, and in seaside places the carry-*oot* (to-go) meal of fish-and-chips is an enduring tradition.

Hotels

If you're staying in Fife, the obvious choice for a base is St. Andrews, with ample accommodations of all kinds. Dundee and its hinterlands have a number of diverse accommodations, including an influx of smart city center hotels, many of which offer good value.

Restaurant and hotel reviews have been shortened. For full information, visit Fodors.com. Restaurant prices are the average cost of a main course at dinner or, if dinner is not served, at lunch. Hotel prices are the lowest cost of a standard double room in high season, including 20% V.A.T.

WHAT IT COSTS in Pounds			
$	$$	$$$	$$$$
RESTAURANTS			
under £15	£15–£19	£20–£25	over £25
HOTELS			
under £125	£125–£200	£201–£300	over £300

Visitor Information

The Dundee and St. Andrews tourist offices are open year-round. Smaller tourist information centers operate seasonally in Arbroath, Crail, Forfar, Kirriemuir, and Montrose.

St. Andrews

52 miles northeast of Edinburgh, 83 miles northeast of Glasgow.

It may have a ruined cathedral and a grand university—the oldest in Scotland—but the modern claim to fame for St. Andrews is mainly its status as the home of golf. Forget that Scottish kings were crowned here, or that John Knox preached here and that Reformation reformers were burned at the stake here. Thousands flock to St. Andrews to play at the Old Course, home of the Royal & Ancient Club, and to follow in the footsteps of Hagen, Sarazen, Jones, and Hogan.

The layout is pure Middle Ages: its three main streets—North, Market, and South—converge on the city's earliest religious site, near the cathedral. Like most of the ancient monuments, the cathedral ruins are impressive in their desolation—but this town is no dusty museum. The streets are busy, the shops are stylish, the gray houses sparkle in the sun, and the scene is particularly brightened during the academic year by bicycling students in scarlet gowns.

GETTING HERE AND AROUND

If you arrive by car, be prepared for an endless drive round the town as you look for a parking space. The parking lots around Rose Park (behind the bus station and a short walk from the town center) are your best bet. If you arrive by local or national bus, the bus station is a five-minute walk from town. The nearest train station, Leuchars, is 10 minutes away by taxi (£15) or bus (£3.50), both of which can be found outside the station. St. Andrews can be fully enjoyed on foot without too much exertion.

ESSENTIALS

VISITOR INFORMATION St. Andrews.
✉ *70 Market St., St. Andrews* ☎ *01334/472021* ⊕ *www.visitscotland.com/destinations-maps/st-andrews.*

◉ Sights

★ Bell Pettigrew Museum of Natural History

HISTORY MUSEUM | Founded by Elsie Bell Pettigrew in memory of her husband, James, a former professor of medicine, this fascinating collection of zoological specimens takes you from sea to jungle, mountain to sky. The antiquated manner of their presentation reminds you of their significance in an age when most of these creatures were still unknown to most people. In the handsome 16th-century St. Mary's Quadrangle, home to the St. Andrews University's divinity and psychology departments, you'll find an impressive holm oak and a thorn tree supposedly planted by Mary, Queen of Scots. ⊠ *Bute Medical Bldg., Queens Gardens, off South St., St. Andrews* ☎ *01334/461660* ⊕ *www.st-andrews. ac.uk/museums/visit-us/bell-pettigrew* 🖾 *Free* ⊗ *Closed weekends.*

R&A World Golf Museum

HISTORY MUSEUM | Just opposite the Royal & Ancient Golf Club, this museum explores the centuries-old relationship between St. Andrews and golf and displays golf memorabilia from the 18th century to the 21st century. ⊠ *Bruce Embankment, St. Andrews* ☎ *01334/460046* ⊕ *www.worldgolfmuseum.com* 🖾 *£12.*

Royal & Ancient Golf Club of St. Andrews

HISTORIC SIGHT | The ruling house of golf worldwide is the spiritual home of all who play or follow the game. Founded in 1754, its clubhouse on the dunes—open to members only, including women since September 2014—is a mix of classical, Victorian, and neoclassical styles; it's adjacent to the famous Old Course. ⊠ *The Scores, St. Andrews* ⊕ *www. randa.org.*

★ St. Andrews Botanic Garden

GARDEN | FAMILY | Immerse yourself in these verdant botanics, replete with 2,000 square feet of heated greenhouses, woodland, rock gardens, allotments, and an enchanting butterfly house. It's just 15 minutes out of town via the Lade Braes footpath. ■ TIP→ **Bring a picnic or enjoy the on-site tearoom. There are picnic tables around the gardens plus a plant nursery and gift shop.** ⊠ *Canongate, St. Andrews* ☎ *01334/461200* ⊕ *www. standrewsbotanic.org* 🖾 *£6.*

St. Andrews Castle

RUINS | On the shore north of the cathedral stands ruined St. Andrews Castle, begun at the end of the 13th century. The remains include a rare example of a cold and gruesome bottle-shaped dungeon, in which many prisoners spent their last hours. Even more atmospheric is the castle's mine and countermine. The former was a tunnel dug by besieging forces in the 16th century; the latter, a tunnel dug by castle defenders in order to meet and wage battle belowground. You can stoop and crawl into this narrow passageway—an eerie experience, despite the addition of electric light. The visitor center has a good audiovisual presentation on the castle's history. In summer the beach below is popular with sunbathers and tide-pool investigators, weather permitting. ⊠ *N. Castle St., St. Andrews* ☎ *01334/472–563* ⊕ *www.historicenvironment.scot* 🖾 *£9.*

★ St. Andrews Cathedral

CHURCH | These are the poignant remains of what was once the largest and most magnificent church in Scotland. Work on it began in 1160, and after several delays it was finally consecrated in 1318. The church was subsequently damaged by fire and repaired but fell into decay during the Reformation. Only ruined gables, parts of the nave's south wall, and other fragments survive. The on-site museum helps you interpret the remains and gives a sense of what the cathedral must once have been like. ⊠ *Off Pends Rd., St. Andrews* ☎ *01334/472563* ⊕ *www. historicenvironment.scot* 🖾 *£6, includes St. Rule's Tower.*

★ St. Andrews Preservation Trust Museum and Garden

HISTORY MUSEUM | Housed in a stone 17th-century house and former fisherfolk dwelling, this charming museum run by friendly volunteers contains furniture, shop fittings, curious objects, and displays relating to St. Andrews's history. The real draw though—especially in bonnie weather—is the flower-filled

Although it is considered to be in ruins, St. Andrews Castle is still one of the city's prettiest sites.

garden and curious outbuildings including a laundry and twin-bowled privy. ⊠ *12 North St., St. Andrews* ☎ *01334/477629* ⊕ *archive.standrewspreservationtrust. co.uk* ✉ *Free (donations welcome)* ⊗ *Closed Oct.–late Apr.*

St. Rule's Tower
VIEWPOINT | Local legend has it that St. Andrews was founded by St. Regulus, or Rule, who, acting under divine guidance, carried relics of St. Andrew by sea from Patras in Greece. He was shipwrecked on this Fife headland and founded a church. The holy man's name survives in the cylindrical tower, consecrated in 1126 and the oldest surviving building in St. Andrews. Enjoy dizzying views of town from the top of the 108-foot high tower, reached via a steep staircase. ⊠ *Off Pends Rd., St. Andrews* ☎ *01334/472563* ⊕ *www.historicenvironment.scot* ✉ *£6, includes St. Andrews Cathedral.*

★ Tentsmuir Forest and Beach
FOREST | **FAMILY** | Ten miles north of St. Andrews, this wonderful 50-square-mile nature reserve contains a Scots and Corsican pine forest and the birdlife-rich Morton Lochs, fringing dynamic sand dunes and the long, sandy Kinshaldy Beach. Popular with families, beach-combers, and naturalists, the beach is 5 miles long and has enough space for everyone. If you don't bring a picnic, the Crepe Shack at the car park is a decent food-and-drink option. ⊠ *B945, Leuchars* ⊕ *www.tentsmuir.org* ✉ *Parking £2.*

University of St. Andrews
COLLEGE | Scotland's oldest university is the alma mater of John Knox (Protestant reformer), King James II of Scotland, the Duke and Duchess of Cambridge (William and Kate), and Chris Hoy, Scotland's Olympic cyclist. Founded in 1411, the university's buildings pepper the town. For the quintessential University of St. Andrews experience, St. Salvator's Quadrangle reveals the magnificence of this historic institution. Looking out onto this impressive college green is the striking St. Salvator's Chapel, founded in 1450. It bears the marks of a turbulent past: the initials PH, carved into the paving stones

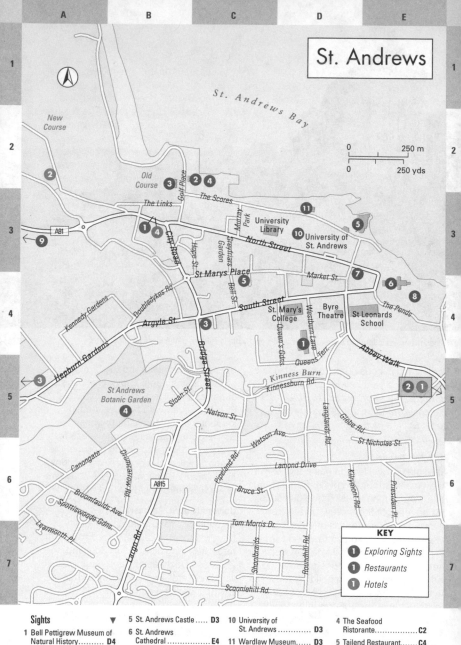

St. Andrews

St. Andrews Bay

0 — 250 m
0 — 250 yds

KEY

1 Exploring Sights
1 Restaurants
1 Hotels

under the bell tower, are those of Patrick Hamilton, who was burned alive outside the chapel for his Protestant beliefs. ✉ *St. Mary's Pl., St. Andrews* 🌐 *www.st-andrews.ac.uk.*

★ Wardlaw Museum

HISTORY MUSEUM | **FAMILY** | With four intimate thematic galleries, this museum tells engaging stories about St. Andrews University, the world, and the universe through its wonderful collections. It also showcases groundbreaking research. You'll find ecumenical regalia, decorative arts, and early scientific instruments, including Humphrey Cole's astrolabe of 1575. It also has sweeping views over St. Andrews Bay. ✉ *7A the Scores, St. Andrews* ☎ *01334/461660* 🌐 *www.st-andrews.ac.uk/musa* 🎟 *Free.*

🍴 Restaurants

★ 18 at Rusacks

$$$$ | **MODERN BRITISH** | Set in the Rusacks Hotel's sophisticated yet relaxed brasserie-style rooftop venue, 18 delivers an exquisite dining experience along with attentive service and a quality Scottish produce-heavy seasonal menu by top chef Derek Johnstone. The freshest seafood, including Orkney scallops and halibut, are accompanied by zesty but not overpowering flavors and tasty al dente vegetable sides, while the impressive selection of dry-aged Aberdeen Angus cuts on display as you enter are expertly cut, flame-licked, and seared to perfection. **Known for:** golf course and beach balcony views; excellent dessserts including raspberry Cranachan soufflé; impressive dry-aged steaks. [$] *Average main: £28* ✉ *Rusacks, Pilmour Links, St. Andrews* ☎ *01865/256604* 🌐 *www.18standrews.co.uk* 🕓 *No lunch Mon.–Sat. No dinner Sun.–Tues.*

★ The Grange Inn

$$$$ | **CONTEMPORARY** | Fife foodies flock to this beautifully converted 17th-century farmhouse surrounded by verdant fields just 10 minutes outside town. The prix-fixe menus offer exquisitely crafted dishes using the best seasonal Scots produce such as beef, pork, mackerel, and wild sea trout. **Known for:** superb service; stunning location; great lunch deals. [$] *Average main: £30* ✉ *Grange Rd., St. Andrews* ☎ *01334/472675* 🌐 *www.thegrangeinn.com* 🕓 *Closed Mon. and Tues.*

The Saint

$ | **MODERN BRITISH** | **FAMILY** | Once local favorite the Westport, this reliable lunch and brunch stop has been revamped with swanky contemporary interiors complimented by a relaxed vibe, tasty cocktails, and excellent pub food. The reasonably priced menu offers everything from chunky gourmet sandwiches to seared scallops to heaped salads—all are best enjoyed in the flowery garden on sunny afternoons. **Known for:** friendly youthful staff; gorgeous sun-draped beer garden; first-rate food from breakfast until late night. [$] *Average main: £14* ✉ *170 South St., St. Andrews* ☎ *01334/473186* 🌐 *www.the-saint-bar.co.uk.*

The Seafood Ristorante

$$$$ | **SEAFOOD** | The striking glass-walled venue perched above the West Sands consistently delivers the freshest and most refined seafood dishes in St. Andrews. Scottish-Italian owner Stefano keeps the emphasis on prime Scots seafood while adding *il bel paese* flourishes and menu staples like risotto, agnolotti (stuffed pasta pockets), and *cicchetti* (Venetian-style tapas). **Known for:** halibut straight off a Pittenweem boat; sea or car-park views (ask for the bay-watching tables); seasonal Scots delights like hand-dived Orkney scallops. [$] *Average main: £32* ✉ *Bruce Embankment, St. Andrews* ☎ *01334/479475* 🌐 *www.theseafoodrestaurant.com.*

Tailend Restaurant

$ | SEAFOOD | FAMILY | The line of customers outside might be a bit off-putting, but just focus on the sweet smell of fish-and-chips from St. Andrews's best chipper. There's a busy light-filled dining room and modish seating area, or you can carry out and eat on the university grounds (though be wary of the dive-bombing gulls). **Known for:** fabulous starters and desserts; the best fish-and-chips in St. Andrews; Arbroath smokies. *Average main: £14* *130 Market St., St. Andrews* *01334/474070* *www.thetailend.co.uk.*

Hotels

Fairmont St Andrews

$$$ | HOTEL | Two miles from St. Andrews, this modern hotel has spectacular views of the bay and two superb golf courses. **Pros:** golf at your doorstep; spacious feel; excellent spa. **Cons:** patchy service; feels a bit impersonal and corporate; the huge atrium feels like a shopping center. *Rooms from: £250* *A917, St. Andrews* *01334/837000* *www.fairmont.com/st-andrews-scotland* *209 rooms* *Free Breakfast.*

Old Course Hotel

$$$ | HOTEL | Regularly hosting international golf stars and jet-setters, the Old Course Hotel has much-coveted guest room fairway views, grand public spaces, and fabulous facilities including a swanky spa. **Pros:** golfer's heaven; fabulous location and lovely views; unpretentious service. **Cons:** expensive; standard rooms are small; all the golf talk might bore nongolfers. *Rooms from: £285* *Old Station Rd., St. Andrews* *01334/474371* *www.oldcoursehotel.co.uk* *175 rooms* *Free Breakfast.*

★ Rufflets St. Andrews

$$$ | HOTEL | Ten acres of formal and informal gardens surround this vine-covered country house with individually designed rooms, a wonderful restaurant, and a cozy lounge-bar with a handsome fireplace and terrace. **Pros:** family-friendly lodges; attractive gardens; cozy drawing room. **Cons:** no elevator in the main house; primarily venue for those celebrating, so can get noisy; too far to walk to St. Andrews. *Rooms from: £247* *Strathkinness Low Rd., St. Andrews* *01334/472594* *www.rufflets.co.uk* *26 rooms* *Free Breakfast.*

★ Rusacks St Andrews

$$$$ | HOTEL | Occupying a handsome 17th-century building with a swanky modern extension overlooking the 18th hole and West Sands, Rusacks offers stylish Caledonian luxury, top-notch dining, and friendly service. **Pros:** sumptuous large beds and Old World Scotia design details; best location and views in town; fabulous dining options including 18's rooftop fine-dining. **Cons:** bar is sometimes understaffed; no spa; golf-related decor not to everyone's tastes. *Rooms from: £431* *Pilmour Links, St. Andrews* *01334/474321* *www.marineandlawn.com* *123 rooms* *Free Breakfast.*

Nightlife

Central Bar

BARS | There are still some old-fashioned pubs to be found among the cocktail bars of St. Andrews, and this wood-and-leather-furnished haunt is a good bet for a friendly mingle with a pint in hand. You'll find a good range of beers (bottled and on tap) and decent pub food. *77 Market St., St. Andrews* *01334/478296.*

Performing Arts

Byre Theatre

THEATER | Experimental plays, small-scale operatic performances, contemporary dance, musical performances, and film screenings are on the bill at the Byre. There's also coffee and comfy seating in the revamped Byre Living Room. *Abbey St., St. Andrews* *01334/475000* *byretheatre.com.*

New Picture House Cinema

FILM | FAMILY | A lovely old cinema shows a well-chosen mix of Hollywood and independent films. ⊠ *117 North St., St. Andrews* ☎ *01334/474902* ⊕ *showtimes. nphcinema.co.uk.*

🛍 Shopping

Artery

CRAFTS | This well-curated shop sells work by local, Scottish, and British artists, including jewelry, ceramics, paintings, and intriguing handmade clocks. ⊠ *183 South St., St. Andrews* ☎ *01334/473153* ⊕ *arterygifts.com.*

Balgove Larder

FOOD | Here you'll discover a huge selection of Scottish items, from spurtles (for stirring your porridge) to tablet (sugary toffee) to big, thick sausages made in its butchery. Foodies should check out the Farm Shop and monthly Night Market, while carnivores can follow their noses to the Steak Barn, where platters piled with huge hunks of beef and sausages are combined with twice-fried chips and onion rings. ⊠ *A91, St. Andrews* ☎ *01334/898145* ⊕ *www.balgove.com.*

Mellis

FOOD | This heady-smelling store is truly a cheese lover's mecca. Look for a soft, crumbly, and citrusy cheese (called Anster) made thanks to a local herd of Holstein-Friesians. ⊠ *149 South St., St. Andrews* ☎ *01334/471410* ⊕ *www. mellischeese.net.*

★ Topping and Company Booksellers

BOOKS | This is a bibliophile's dream haunt, with high ceilings and alcoves lined with over 45,000 titles, knowledgeable staff, and frequent readings and literary events. ⊠ *7 Greyfriars Garden, St. Andrews* ☎ *01334/585111* ⊕ *www. toppingbooks.co.uk.*

🏃 Activities

GOLF

What serious golfer doesn't dream of playing at world-famous St. Andrews? Seven St. Andrews courses, all part of the St. Andrews Trust, are open to visitors, and more than 40 other courses in the region offer golf by the round or by the day.

Balgove Course

GOLF | At the beginner-friendly Balgove Course you can turn up and tee off without prior reservation. ⊠ *West Sands Rd., A91, St. Andrews* ⊕ *www.standrews. com* ⊠ *£8–£15* ⅄ *9 holes, 1520 yards, par 30.*

Castle Course

GOLF | Designed by David McLay Kidd in 2008, the Castle Course hugs the rugged coastline and has jaw-dropping views. It's 2 miles from the town center. ⊠ *A917, St. Andrews* ⊕ *www.standrews.com* ⊠ *£60– £125* ⅄ *18 holes, 6759 yards, par 71.*

Eden Course

GOLF | The aptly named Eden Course, designed in 1914 by Harry S. Colt, winds through inland fields bordered with lovely foliage. It's a bit more forgiving compared to other St. Andrews courses. ⊠ *West Sands Rd., St. Andrews* ⊕ *www.standrews.com* ⊠ *£28–£55* ⅄ *18 holes, 6250 yards, par 70.*

★ Jubilee Course

GOLF | This windswept course offers quite a challenge even for experienced golfers. When it opened in 1897 it was intended for beginners, but the popularity of its seaside location encouraged the powers that be to convert it into a championship course. Many golfers say the 15th hole is one of the best in the sport. ⊠ *West Sands Rd., St. Andrews* ⊕ *www.standrews.com* ⊠ *£43–£90* ⅄ *18 holes, 6742 yards, par 72.*

The Evolution of Golf

The matter of who invented golf has been long debated, but there's no doubt that its development into one of the most popular games in the world stems from Scotland. The first written reference to golf, variously spelled as *gowf* or *goff*, was in 1457, when James II (1430–60) of Scotland declared that both golf and football (soccer) should be "*utterly cryit doune and nocht usit*" (publicly criticized and prohibited) because they distracted his subjects from archery practice. Mary, Queen of Scots (1542–87) was fond of golf. When in Edinburgh in 1567, she played on Leith Links and on Bruntsfield Links. When in Fife she played at Falkland and at St. Andrews itself.

Golf Expands

Golf clubs (i.e., organizations) arose in the middle of the 18th century. The Honourable Company of Edinburgh Golfers, now residing at Muirfield, was founded in 1744. From then on, clubs sprang up all over Scotland: Royal Aberdeen (1780), Crail Golfing Society (1786), Dunbar (1794), and the Royal Perth Golfing Society (1824).

As for the town of St. Andrews, which now prospers on golf, golf schools, and golf equipment (the manufacture of golf balls is a local industry), locals say that the game was first played here with a piece of driftwood, a shore pebble, and a rabbit hole on the sandy, coastal turf. Residents were playing golf on the town links as far back as the 15th century. Rich golfers eventually formed exclusive clubs. The Royal & Ancient Golf Club of St. Andrews was founded in 1754.

By the early 19th century, clubs had been set up in England, and the game was being carried all over the world by enthusiastic Scots. These golf missionaries spread their knowledge not only of the sport but also of the courses. Large parts of the Scottish coast are natural golf courses; indeed, the origins of bunkers and the word *links* (courses) are found in the sand dunes of Scotland's shores. Willie Park of Musselburgh, James Braid, and C. K. Hutchison are some of the best known of Scotland's golf-course architects.

Changes in the Game

The original balls, called *featheries*, were leather bags stuffed with boiled feathers and often lasted only one round. In 1848 the gutta-percha ball, called a *guttie*, was introduced. It was in general use until the invention of the rubber-core ball in 1901. Clubs were made of wood with shafts of ash (later hickory), and heads of thorn, apple, or pear. Heads were spliced, then bound to the shaft with twine. Later in the 19th century, manufacturers began to experiment with metal in clubfaces and shafts. The technology of golf continues to change, but its addictive qualities are timeless.

New Course

GOLF | Not exactly new—it opened in 1895—the New Course is rather over-shadowed by the Old Course, but it has a firm following of golfers who appreciate the loop design. ⊠ *West Sands Rd., St. Andrews* ⊕ *www.standrews.com* ☎ *£43–£90* ⚑ *18 holes, 6625 yards, par 71.*

★ Old Course

GOLF | Believed to be the oldest golf course in the world, the Old Course was first played in the 15th century. Each year, more than 44,000 rounds are teed off, and no doubt most get stuck in one of its 112 bunkers. A handicap certificate and some very early morning waits for a possible tee-off are required. ⊠ *West Sands Rd., St. Andrews* ⊕ *www.standrews.com* ☎ *£98–£195* ⅃. *18 holes, 6721 yards, par 72.*

Strathtyrum Course

GOLF | Those with a high handicap will enjoy this course, opened in 1993, without the worry or embarrassment of holding up more experienced golfers. ⊠ *West Sands Rd., A91, St. Andrews* ⊕ *www.standrews.com* ☎ *£17–£35* ⅃. *18 holes, 5620 yards, par 69.*

Crail

10 miles south of St. Andrews.

The oldest and most aristocratic of East Neuk burghs, pretty Crail is where many fish merchants retired and built cottages. The town landmark is a picturesque Dutch-influenced town house, or *tolbooth*, which contains the oldest bell in Fife, cast in Holland in 1520. Crail may now be full of artists, but it remains a working harbor; take time to walk the streets and beaches and to sample fish by the harbor.

■ TIP→ As you head into East Neuk from this tiny port, look about for market crosses, merchant houses, and little doocots (dovecotes, where pigeons were kept)—typical picturesque touches of this region.

GETTING HERE AND AROUND

Stagecoach bus No. 95 operates between Crail and St. Andrews. This service also takes you on to Anstruther, Pittenweem, St. Monans, and Lower Largo. Crail is about 15 minutes from St. Andrews by car via A917.

◉ Sights

Crail Museum and Heritage Centre

HISTORY MUSEUM | The story of this trading and fishing town can be found in the delightfully crammed Crail Museum and Heritage Centre, entirely run by local volunteers. There is a small tourist information desk within the center and fascinating guided walks start here Wednesday and Sunday from June through October. ⊠ *62–64 Marketgate, Crail* ☎ *01333/450869* ⊕ *www.crailmuseum.uk* ☎ *Free* ⊗ *Closed Oct.–Mar. Limited hrs Apr. and May.*

🍴 Restaurants

★ Reilly Shellfish Lobster Hut

$$ | SEAFOOD | This hut on the pier, a hidden gem, sells beautifully cooked lobsters for £12–£20 each (depending on size) and other items at times, including lobster rolls and dressed crab. They'll crack the lobster for you to allow for easy eating on a nearby bench; there is no seating, but the lobster is wonderful. **Known for:** varying, sometimes random hours; freshest seafood; casual alfresco eating in a beach and harbor setting. $ *Average main: £15* ⊠ *34 Shoregate, Crail* ☎ *01333/450476* ⊗ *Closed Oct.–Easter and Mon. No dinner.*

🛏 Hotels

The Hazelton

$ | B&B/INN | Beautifully polished wood, exquisitely restored period features, and gentle hues put the Hazelton head and shoulders above the typical seaside B&B. **Pros:** decent breakfast; handsome building; central location near pub and harbor. **Cons:** intermittent traffic noise; unreliable communication via email; a couple of rooms on the small side. $ *Rooms from: £105* ⊠ *29 Marketgate N, Crail* ☎ *01333/450250* ⊕ *www.thehazelton.co.uk* ⊗ *Closed Jan* ⤳ *3 rooms* ⦿ *Free Breakfast.*

Anstruther

4 miles southwest of Crail.

Anstruther, locally called Ainster, has a lovely waterfront with a few shops brightly festooned with children's pails and shovels, a gesture to summer vacationers.

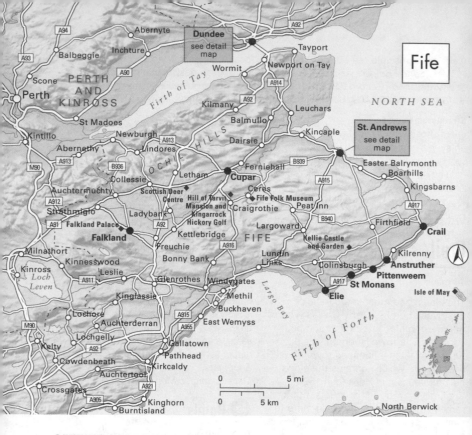

GETTING HERE AND AROUND

Stagecoach bus No. 95 operates between St. Andrews, Crail, Anstruther, Pittenweem, St. Monans, and Lower Largo. By car Anstruther is 5 to 10 minutes from Crail via A917.

⊙ Sights

Isle of May

ISLAND | Take to the waves (April through September) on the compact *Max Princess* for a round-trip to the Isle of May, a rocky bird reserve near the mouth of the Forth. Measuring just under a mile long and a third of a mile wide, it harbors 14 species of breeding birds including arctic terns, guillemots, and puffins. The round-trip takes five hours, with three hours on shore to explore the island's history, the monastery remains, and the breathtaking sights, sounds, and smells of the avian multitudes. ✉ *Middle Pier, Anstruther Harbour* ☎ *07957/585200* ⊕ *www.isleofmayferry.com* ✉ *£34.*

★ Scottish Fisheries Museum

OTHER MUSEUM | FAMILY | Facing Anstruther Harbor, the Scottish Fisheries Museum is inside a colorful cluster of buildings, the earliest of which dates from the 16th century. A charming trail around the various buildings and odd spaces illustrates the life of Scottish fisherfolk; you can spend a couple of hours examining the many documents, artifacts, model ships, paintings, and displays (complete with the reek of tarred rope and net). There are floating exhibits at the quayside and a window onto a working boatyard. ✉ *Harbourhead, Anstruther* ☎ *01333/310628* ⊕ *www.scotfishmuseum.org* ✉ *£9* ⊗ *Closed Mon.–Wed.*

🍴 Restaurants

★ Anstruther Fish Bar and Restaurant
$ | SEAFOOD | FAMILY | Next door to the Scottish Fisheries Museum, this popular fish-and-chips shop has a functional space to eat, but most people order takeout. Try local specialties including Pittenweem prawns in batter or the catch of the day, which could be mackerel (line caught by the owners), hake, or local crab. **Known for:** ice-cream counter with novel flavors; consistently excellent fish-and-chips; friendly staff. $ *Average main: £12* ✉ *42–44 Shore St., Anstruther* ☎ *01333/310518* ⊕ *www.anstrutherfish-bar.co.uk.*

The Cellar
$$$$ | EUROPEAN | Entered through a cobbled courtyard, this unpretentious, atmospheric restaurant is run by talented head chef Billy Boyter and family. The three-course prix-fixe meals feature locally sourced seafood and meat such as crab, hake, mussels, beef, lamb, and quail. **Known for:** wine-pairing option; elegant yet informal dining; exquisite produce. $ *Average main: £70* ✉ *24 E. Green, Anstruther* ☎ *01333/310378* ⊕ *www.thecellaranstruther.co.uk* ⊘ *Closed Mon. and Tues. No lunch Wed.*

🍸 Nightlife

★ Dreel Tavern
PUBS | A 16th-century coaching inn, the Dreel Tavern was resurrected and refurbished in 2017 by two young sisters who have built on the characterful stone building and added some tasteful improvements including an à la carte menu and a Mexican-inspired street food hut, the Shack. Alongside the draft beers, the food showcases local produce such as lobster and smoked fish. The low-ceilinged wood-beamed bar makes for a lively atmosphere, especially during low-key musical gigs and gourmet events. A pretty beer garden overlooks the Dreel Burn and the family garden where much

Fife Coastal Path ◉

Fife's green and undulating landscape includes the Lomond Hills, which are easy to climb and offer fabulous views of both the Tay and Forth estuaries. The Fife Coastal Path (⊕ *fifecoastand-countrysidetrust.co.uk*) can be a bracing epic or a wandering amble. The 7-mile stretch between East Wemyss and Lower Largo is the easiest going, with some of it along the beaches of Elie. The 8-mile route between Pittenweem and Fifeness (four to six hours) can be rougher in patches, but takes you through Anstruther and Crail.

of the produce on the menu grows. ✉ *16 High St., Anstruther* ☎ *01333/279238* ⊕ *www.dreeltavern.co.uk.*

🏃 Activities

East Neuk Outdoors
KAYAKING | FAMILY | This company runs a host of outdoor activities including archery, bushcraft, paddle-boarding, kayaking, and canoeing. ✉ *Cellardyke Park, Anstruther* ☎ *01333/310370* ⊕ *www.eastneukoutdoors.co.uk.*

Pittenweem and St. Monans

1½ and 3 miles southwest of Anstruther.

These neighboring harbors are places to wander among lobster creels, fishing nets, and rocks, discovering quirky local artworks and architectural features. Many examples of East Neuk architecture serve as the backdrop for the working harbor at Pittenweem. Look for the crow-stepped gables, white *harling* (the rough mortar finish on walls), and red *pantiles* (roof tiles with an S-shaped profile). The *weem* part of the town's name comes from the Gaelic *uaime*, meaning cave. Nearby St. Monans has an attractive working fishing harbor, small pebbly beach, and a trio of free sights: pop in first to the wonderful, volunteer-run heritage center by the harbor and curious Wellington boot garden; nearby to the west is the parish church dating from 1265; nearly a mile east along the coastal path is St. Monans Windmill (collect keys from the post office), where Fife salt production is explained.

GETTING HERE AND AROUND

Stagecoach bus No. 95 operates between St. Andrews, Crail, Anstruther, Pittenweem, St. Monans, and Lower Largo. Pittenweem is about five minutes from Anstruther by car via A917.

👁 Sights

★ ART@47 and Pittenweem Arts Festival

ART GALLERY | There is nothing quite like August's Pittenweem Arts Festival. Exhibitions, which involve hundreds of local and international artists, take place in the town's public buildings and in private homes and gardens. Even outside this week of events, you are likely to encounter local art and artists by visiting the festival headquarters, gallery ART@47. ✉ *47 High St., Pittenweem* ☎ *01333/313109* 🌐 *www.pittenweemartsfestival.co.uk.*

Kellie Castle and Garden

CASTLE/PALACE | Dating from the 16th to 17th century and restored in Victorian times, Kellie Castle stands among the grain fields and woodlands of northeastern Fife. Four acres of pretty gardens surround the castle, which is in the care of the National Trust for Scotland. In summer you can buy berries grown in the walled garden, and baked goods are sold in the tearoom. The garden and estate are open year-round, even when the castle itself is closed. ✉ *B9171, Pittenweem* ✣ *3 miles northwest of Pittenweem* ☎ *01337/720271* 🌐 *www.nts.org.uk* 🎫 *£10.50* ⏲ *Garden closed Tues. and Wed; castle closed Mon.–Thurs.*

St. Fillan's Cave

CAVE | This town's cavern, St. Fillan's Cave, contains the shrine of St. Fillan, a 6th-century hermit who lived here. It's up a *pend* (alleyway) behind the waterfront. If the cave isn't open, ask at the Cocoa Tree on High Street. Those who can are asked to make a donation of £1 to cover the upkeep of the spooky, spiritual site. ✉ *Cove Wynd, Pittenweem* 🎫 *Free* ⏲ *Closed Sun.*

🍴 Restaurants

Craig Millar @ 16 West End

$$$$ | **SEAFOOD** | This eatery overlooking the harbor run by Dundonian chef Craig Millar put St. Monans on Scotland's culinary map. The fixed-price menu has vegetarian and meat options, but with salty fruits of the North Sea on the Fife quayside—such as crab, cod, hake, and mackerel—it's all about Craig's expertise with seafood. **Known for:** attentive service; elegant seafood dining; gorgeous terrace with sea views. [$] *Average main: £55* ✉ *16 West End, St. Monans* ✣ *2 miles west of Pittenweem* ☎ *01333/730327* 🌐 *www.16westend.com* ⏲ *Closed Mon. and Tues. No dinner Sun.*

East Pier Smokehouse

$ | **SEAFOOD** | Painted powder-blue, this long harborside building-turned-eatery and foodie shop is the place to pick up freshly netted and smoked local seafood. After ordering at the shop counter, head up the stairs round the back to feast on lobster, langoustine, and crab accompanied by salads and chips. **Known for:** great views from the rooftop terrace; fresh seafood; imaginative salads. [$] *Average main: £13* ✉ *East Shore, St. Monans, Pittenweem* ☎ *01333/405030* 🌐 *www.eastpier.co.uk* ⏲ *Closed Nov.–Mar., weekdays in Apr. and Oct., and Mon. and Tues. in May–Sept. No dinner.*

Shopping

★ Pittenweem Chocolate Company
FOOD | Open daily, this place stocks the most imaginative and comprehensive range of fine chocolates you'll find in this part of the world. Its lovely Cocoa Tree Café serves cakes, drinks, light meals, and, of course, handmade chocolates from the Pittenweem Chocolate Company. ✉ *9 High St., Pittenweem* ☎ *01333/311495* 🌐 *www.pittenweem-chocolate.co.uk.*

Elie

5 miles south of Pittenweem.

To give it its full name, the Royal Burgh of Elie and Earlsferry is an old trading port with a handsome harbor that loops around one of the most glorious stretches of sand in the British Isles. Since Victorian times, when a railway (sadly defunct since the 1960s) linked it with the capital, Elie has been a weekend and summer retreat for the great and the good of Edinburgh. The beach to the south of the harbor is a mile long and has clean sands, clear waters, and tide pools to interest young and old.

Restaurants

★ Ship Inn
$$ | **BRITISH** | **FAMILY** | Overlooking Elie's sandy beach, the Ship Inn combines a nautically themed pub-restaurant serving superb Scottish cuisine with six pristine, tastefully white-shuttered rooms, four with stunning views of the sea. The relaxed atmosphere and views—with the comedy of a cricketing contest on shifting sands a bonus—make for an afternoon you'll never forget, especially if the weather is nice. **Known for:** excellent seafood; buzzy, stylish community hub; dining with sea views. $ *Average main: £18* ✉ *The Toft, Elie* ☎ *01333/330246* 🌐 *www.shipinn.scot.*

Activities

GOLF

Leven Links
GOLF | A fine Fife course that has been used as a British Open qualifier, Leven Links has a whiff of the more famous St. Andrews, with a hummocky terrain and a tang of salt in the air. The 1st and 18th holes share the same fairway, and the 18th green has a creek running beside it. Saturday play must be booked at least a week in advance. ✉ *The Promenade, Leven* ☎ *01333/421390* 🌐 *www.leven-links.com* 🎫 *£40–£85* ⛳ *18 holes, 6551 yards, par 71.*

Falkland

24 miles northwest of Pittenweem, 15 miles northwest of Elie.

One of the loveliest communities in Scotland, Falkland is a royal burgh of twisting streets and crooked stone houses.

GETTING HERE AND AROUND

Stagecoach bus No. 64 is the only direct service connecting Falkland to St. Andrews as well as Cupar and Ladybank (both of which are train stations on the Edinburgh to Dundee line). Falkland is about 15 minutes from Cupar and a half hour from St. Andrews by car via A91 and A912, or A91 to A914 to A912.

Sights

Falkland Palace
CASTLE/PALACE | **FAMILY** | A former hunting lodge of the Stewart monarchs, Falkland Palace dominates the town and is one of the country's earliest and finest examples of the French Renaissance style. Overlooking the main street is the palace's most impressive feature, the walls and chambers on its south side, all rich with buttresses and stone medallions, built by French masons in the 1530s for King James V (1512–42). He died here,

and the palace was a favorite resort of his daughter, Mary, Queen of Scots (1542–87). The beautiful gardens behind Falkland Palace contain a rare survivor: a royal tennis court, built in 1539. In the gardens, overlooked by the palace turret windows, you may easily imagine yourself back at the solemn hour when James on his deathbed pronounced the doom of the house of Stewart: "It cam' wi' a lass and it'll gang wi a lass." ⊠ *Main St., Falkland* ☎ *01337/857397* ⊕ *www.nts.org.uk* ⊠ *£13* ⊙ *Closed Nov.–Feb.*

🍴 Restaurants

★ Pillars of Hercules

$ | VEGETARIAN | FAMILY | Head down a country lane to this organic farm and café-bistro for a tasty vegetarian meal made of produce grown in the wonderful gardens. On a sunny day take your crepe or heaped salad to a bench outside by the nursery, or grab some take-out deli foods from the shop. **Known for:** beautiful grounds; organic produce grown on-site; inventive dishes. $ *Average main: £9* ⊠ *A912, Falkland* ✛ *1 mile northwest of Falkland* ☎ *01337/857749* ⊕ *pillars.co.uk* ⊙ *No dinner.*

Cupar

21 miles northwest of Loch Leven, 10 miles west of St. Andrews.

Cupar is a busy, if tad-neglected, market town with some interesting architecture and sites, including a museum about Fife.

GETTING HERE AND AROUND

Cupar has a train station on the Edinburgh–Aberdeen line (which passes through Dundee), and there are trains almost every hour. Stagecoach buses serve the town as well. By car you can reach Cupar from Loch Leven via M90 and A91; take A91 if you're traveling from St. Andrews.

⊙ Sights

★ Fife Folk Museum

HISTORY MUSEUM | To learn more about the history and culture of rural Fife, visit the wonderful Fife Folk Museum in the attractive nearby village of Ceres. The life of local rural communities is reflected in fascinating artifacts and documents housed in a former weigh house and adjoining weavers' cottages. Refreshments and food are served in the Weigh House Tearoom with views of Ceres Burn. The museum is 3 miles southeast of Cupar via A916 and B939. Next door is the wonderfully peaceful St. John's Garden with a meadow labyrinth, beehives, kitchen garden, pond, and mysterious vaults (it's private but welcomes respectful visitors Thursdays or by appointment via emailing ✉ stjohns-gardenceres@gmail.com). ⊠ *High St., Ceres* ☎ *01334/828180* ⊕ *www.fifefolk-museum.org* ⊠ *Free (donations welcome)* ⊙ *Closed Mon., Tues., and Nov.–Mar.*

Hill of Tarvit Mansion and Kingarrock Hickory Golf

HISTORIC HOME | On rising ground near Cupar stands the National Trust for Scotland's Hill of Tarvit House, a 17th-century mansion that was altered in the high-Edwardian style in the late 1890s and early 1900s by the Scottish architect Sir Robert Lorimer (1864–1929). The extensive wood and parklands offer an enjoyable place for a picnic or stroll, and the house itself is well worth a visit. Golfers will also want to play a round on the old Lorimer family course, the Hickory, which was brought back to life in 2008 after being ploughed up for agricultural use during World War II. ⊠ *Off A916, Cupar* ✛ *2 miles south of Cupar* ☎ *01334/653127* ⊕ *www.nts. org.uk* ⊠ *£10.50; golf £30–£60* ⊙ *Closed Nov.–Mar.*

Scottish Deer Centre

ZOO | FAMILY | At the Scottish Deer Centre, many types of deer can be seen at close quarters or on ranger-guided tours. There are falconry displays every two hours, woodland walks, and a café. The zoolike center, west of Cupar, is one of the few places you can spot the red squirrel, as well as wolves, lynx, wildcat, and European brown bear. ⊠ *A91, Cupar* ☎ *01337/810391* ⊕ *www.tsdc.co.uk* 🖅 *£11.50.*

🍴 Restaurants

Ostlers Close Restaurant

$$$$ | **BRITISH** | Tucked away in an alley off the main street, this cottage-style restaurant has earned a well-deserved reputation for top-quality cuisine that is imaginative without trying to be showy. Elegantly presented in the warm-hued, smart dining room, dishes show off the locally sourced meat and fish, as well as homegrown and foraged produce to best advantage. **Known for:** intimate atmosphere that can get crowded; fine produce; daily menus including vegetarian options. 🖅 *Average main: £28* ⊠ *25 Bonnygate, Cupar* ☎ *01334/655574* ⊕ *www.ostlersclose.co.uk* 🕙 *Closed Sun.–Tues.*

🛏 Hotels

★ The Peat Inn

$$$ | **B&B/INN** | With eight bright and contemporary two-room suites, this popular "restaurant with rooms" is perhaps best known for its outstanding, modern, Scottish-style restaurant. **Pros:** verdant gardens and views; exceptional restaurant; supercomfy and large beds. **Cons:** hard to get a restaurant reservation; you need a car to get here; books up quickly. 🖅 *Rooms from: £295* ⊠ *B941, at intersection of B940, Cupar* ☎ *01334/840206* ⊕ *www.thepeatinn.co.uk* 🕙 *Closed Sun. and Mon* 🛏 *8 suites* 🍴 *Free Breakfast.*

Activities

Ladybank Golf Club

GOLF | Fife is known for its coastal courses, but this one provides an interesting inland layout. Although Ladybank, designed by Tom Morris in 1876, is on fairly level ground, the fir and birch trees and heathery rough give it a Highland flavor among the gentle Lowland fields. Qualifying rounds of the British Open are played here when the main championship is played at St. Andrews. ⊠ *A92, Annsmuir, Ladybank* ☎ *01337/830814* ⊕ *www.ladybankgolf.co.uk* 🖅 *£36–£95* ⛳ *18 holes, 6821 yards, par 71.*

Dundee

14 miles northwest of St. Andrews, 58 miles north of Edinburgh, 79 miles northeast of Glasgow.

Dundee makes an excellent base for a cultural stay and Fife and Angus exploration at any time of year. The Dundee Contemporary Arts center gave the city a much-needed boost in 1999; today artsy and foodie hangouts and a vibrant mix of student and creative life make it a beguiling stop. As you explore the streets and waterfront, including Slessor Gardens's green havens and sleek urban beach, you may glimpse contrasting bold lines of the 2018 V&A Dundee museum of design, 1966 Tay Road Bridge, and 1888 Tay Rail Bridge. Those ever-changing views of the Tay led actor and wordsmith Stephen Fry to describe Dundee's setting as "ludicrously ideal." Heading southwest down cobbled Roseangle you reach Magdalen Green, where landscape artist James McIntosh Patrick (1907–98) found inspiration from the river and skyscapes. Dundonians' deadpan humor was distilled in the popular comic strips *The Beano* and *The Dandy,* first published here in the 1930s; statues by Scottish sculptors Tony and Susie Morrow depicting characters Desperate Dan, Dawg, and a catapult-wielding Minnie the Minx are in City Square.

GETTING HERE AND AROUND

The East Coast train line runs through the city, linking it to Edinburgh (and beyond, to London), Glasgow (and the West Coast of England), and Aberdeen, with trains to all every hour or half hour at peak times. Cheaper bus service is available to all these locations, as well as St. Andrews and several other towns in Fife and Angus.

If you're traveling by car, the A92 will take you north from Fife to Abroath and the Angus coast towns. The A90, from Perth, heads north to Aberdeen.

Most of the sights in Dundee are clustered together, so you can easily walk around the city. If the weather is bad or your legs are heavy, hail one of the many cabs on the easy-to-find taxi ranks for little more than a few pounds.

ESSENTIALS
VISITOR INFORMATION VisitScotland Dundee iCentre. ⊠ *Welcome Desk, V&A Dundee, 1 Riverside Esplanade, Dundee* ☎ *01382/527527* ⊕ *www.dundee.com.*

 Sights

Broughty Castle
CASTLE/PALACE | FAMILY | Originally built to guard the Tay Estuary, Broughty Castle is now a museum focusing on fishing, ferries, and the history of the area's whaling industry. The cannons and ramparts make for fine photo opportunities, and inside (up a very narrow stairway) are four floors of displays, including some of the lovely art collection of the Victorian inventor and engineer Sir James Orchar. To the north of the castle lies beautiful Broughty Ferry Beach, which, even in midwinter, is enjoyed by the locals; there is regular bus service from Dundee's city center. ⊠ *Castle Approach, Broughty Ferry* ✛ *4 miles east of city center* ☎ *01382/436916* ⊕ *www.leisureandculturedundee.com/broughty-castle* 🎫 *Free* ☼ *Closed Mon. Oct.–Mar.*

Dundee Botanic Garden
GARDEN | FAMILY | This renowned botanical garden contains an extensive collection of native and exotic plants outdoors and in tropical and temperate greenhouses. There are some beautiful areas for picnicking, as well as a visitor center, an art gallery, and a coffee shop. ⊠ *Riverside Dr., Dundee* ☎ *01382/381190* ⊕ *www.dundee.ac.uk/botanic* 🎫 *£5.*

★ Dundee Contemporary Arts
ART MUSEUM | Between a 17th-century mansion and a cathedral, this strikingly modern building houses one of Britain's most exciting artistic venues. The two galleries house changing shows by internationally acclaimed contemporary artists. There are children's and adult's workshops, special events, and meet-the-artist events throughout the year. Two movie theaters screen mainly independent, revival, and children's films. There's also a craft shop and a buzzing café-bar that's open until midnight. ⊠ *152 Nethergate, Dundee* ☎ *01382/432444* ⊕ *www.dca.org.uk* 🎫 *Free.*

The Law
VIEWPOINT | For sweeping views of the city, the Angus Glens to the north, and Fife's coastline to the south, head up to Dundee's very own extinct volcano. This 1,640-feet-above-sea-level hill (*law* means hill in Scots) has a World War II memorial, parking lot, and seating area. ⊠ *Law Rd., Dundee.*

★ McManus Galleries
ART MUSEUM | Dundee's principal museum and art gallery, housed in a striking Gothic Revival–style building, has an engaging collection of artifacts that document the city's history and the working, social, and cultural lives of Dundonians throughout the Victorian period and the 20th century. Its varied fine art collection includes paintings by Rossetti, Raeburn, and Peploe as well as thought-provoking yet accessible contemporary works and visiting exhibitions. ⊠ *Albert Sq., Dundee* ☎ *01382/307200* ⊕ *www.mcmanus.co.uk* 🎫 *Free.*

The McManus Galleries are home to many artifacts on local history and culture from the 19th and 20th centuries.

Mills Observatory

OBSERVATORY | FAMILY | At the top of a thickly forested hill, Mills Observatory is the only full-time public observatory in Britain. There are displays on astronomy, space exploration, scientific instruments, and a 12-inch refracting telescope for night viewing of the stars and planets. ■**TIP➜ Dundonians flock here when there's a solar or lunar event. If one happens during your visit, don't miss this universally happy experience.** ✉ *Balgay Hill, Dundee* ✛ *2 miles west of city center* ☎ *01382/435967* ⊕ *www.leisureandculturedundee.com/mills* ✉ *Free* ⊙ *Closed Sun.–Tues., Thurs., and Fri. in Apr.–Aug.*

Newport-on-Tay

PROMENADE | Across the Tay River, this charming shoreline suburb has spectacular river views, handsome Victorian architecture, and an interesting collection of independent shops and restaurants, plus some beguiling walks. Once just a small village with cottages, Newport was transformed and renamed "New Dundee" when the city's Victorian jute barons

and middle classes made it a fashionable enclave. Dundee's mill workers folllowed suit, traveling on the *Fifie* steam ferries to escape the cachaphonous and polluted city; you can follow in their brogues and barefoot soles by walking along the Braes Riverside Park. Although the Victorian bathing establishments once there have gone, the ornate 1878 ferry port has been partly restored. You'd be brave to take a dip even on a warm Tayside day, so opt for a sunset sit-down here instead. ■**TIP➜ Head here by bus from Dundee midafternoon to walk the Braes, landscaped gardens, and woodland of nearby Tayfield Estate (aka Berry's Den). Then head to the Boat Brae for refreshments while watching the sunset over the Tay.** ✉ *Boat Brae, Dundee* ✛ *Take bus 77 or X54 from Dundee.*

North Carr Lightship

NAUTICAL SIGHT | Moored next to the *Unicorn*, you'll see a strange rusting red ship, the *North Carr Lightship*. After playing a significant role in World War II, Scotland's only remaining lightship was wrecked on the Fife shore during a storm

The acclaimed V&A Dundee features exhibits from designers across Scotland, including local legend Charles Rennie Mackintosh.

in 1959; seven crew members were lost. ■ TIP➔ The ship is sadly closed awaiting funds for refurbishment but is worth a look from the dock. Donations for restoration welcomed by the Taymara charity, which also runs boat trips. ⊠ Broughty Ferry Harbour, Beach Crescent, Dundee ☎ 01382/542516 ⊕ www.taymara.org.

★ RRS Discovery

NAUTICAL SIGHT | FAMILY | Dundee's urban-renewal program—the city is determined to celebrate its industrial past—was motivated in part by the arrival of the RRS (Royal Research Ship) Discovery, the vessel used by Captain Robert F. Scott (1868–1912) on his polar explorations. The steamer was originally built and launched in Dundee; now it's a permanent resident, sitting by the suitably clifflike V&A museum. At Discovery Point, under the handsome cupola, the story of the ship and its famous expedition unfold; you can even feel the Antarctic chill as if you were there. The ship, berthed outside, is the star: wander the deck, then explore the quarters to see

the daily existence endured by the ship's crew and captain. ⊠ Discovery Quay, Riverside Dr., Dundee ☎ 01382/309060 ⊕ www.rrsdiscovery.com ⊠ £11.50, £18.65 includes Verdant Works.

Tay River Trips

NATURE SIGHT | FAMILY | Taymara, the nonprofit group that looks after the North Carr Lightship, runs exhilarating dolphin-watching trips on the vessel Missel Thrush. Hour-long excursions leave from Broughty Ferry Harbour (weekdays) and Tayport Harbour (weekends), and take you around the mouth of the delta, where dolphins jump and play. Booking in advance is essential. ⊠ Broughty Ferry Harbour, Beach Crescent, Dundee ☎ 01382/542516 ⊕ www.taymara.org ⊠ £16.

Unicorn

NAUTICAL SIGHT | FAMILY | It's easy to spot this 46-gun wood warship, as it's fronted by a figurehead of a white unicorn. This frigate has the distinction of being the oldest British-built warship afloat, having been launched in 1824 at Chatham,

England. You can clamber right down into the hold, or see the models and displays about the Royal Navy's history. Live events like jazz concerts and theater performances are staged onboard. ✉ *Victoria Dock, Dundee* ✥ *East of Tay Rd. bridge* 🌐 *www.frigateunicorn.org* 🎟 *£7.25* ⏲ *Closed Mon. year-round and Tues. and Wed. Nov.–Mar.*

★ V&A Dundee

ART MUSEUM | Opened to worldwide acclaim in 2018, the first outpost of the Victoria and Albert Museum of London is housed in an arresting riverside building by Japanese architect Kengo Kuma. Scotland's first-ever design museum contains seminal works and inspiring displays by Scots and international designers. The Scottish Design Galleries present the past, present, and future through the V&A collections and loans from around the world. Among the many highlights is Charles Rennie Mackintosh's Oak Room, unveiled for the first time in 50 years. Stellar shows, exclusively created for the new V&A galleries, spark inspiration among young and old. This "living room for the city," as Kuma described his design, is worth a visit for the building and setting alone: the vistas in and around its sea-cliff-like edges and perches provide places to linger, mingle, and reflect. If the weather is bad, the Living Room Café here is a great place to linger, refuel, and admire the views of the architecture and river, plus the gift shop has a wealth of quirky design gift ideas. ✉ *Discovery Quay, Dundee* ☎ *01382/411611* 🌐 *www.vam.ac.uk/dundee* 🎟 *Free for permament collection; £12 for temporary shows.*

Verdant Works

HISTORY MUSEUM | **FAMILY** | In a former jute mill, Verdant Works houses a multifaceted exhibit on the story of jute and the town's involvement in the jute trade. Restored machinery, audiovisual displays, and tableaux all bring to life the hard, noisy life of the jute worker. A light and airy café serves Dundee cakes. ✉ *W. Hendersons Wynd, Dundee* ☎ *01382/309060* 🌐 *www.verdantworks.com* 🎟 *£11.75, £18.65 includes RRS Discovery* ⏲ *Closed Mon. and Tues. Nov.–Mar.*

🍴 Restaurants

Boat Brae

$$ | **BRITISH** | Located within Newport's handsome former Victorian ferry terminal, this is a stunning spot to dine casually while spellbound by views of the Tay River and the Dundee skyline across the water. A versatile menu includes seafood shared platters and maritime mains, Scots steaks and lamb, and plenty of vegetarian options. **Known for:** huge west-facing windows for sunset dining; historic building associated with the Thomas Telford-desgned pier; excellent breakfasts, sandwiches, and a cozy wood-filled bar. [$] *Average main: £19* ✉ *2–14 Boat Brae, Dundee* ✥ *In Newport across the Tay; take bus 77 or X54* ☎ *01382/540540* 🌐 *www.boatbrae.com.*

★ Jute

$$ | **BRITISH** | Downstairs at Dundee Contemporary Arts, this lively eatery serves breakfast at the bar, cocktails and snacks on the terrace in fine weather, or dinner in the open-plan dining area with huge windows that offer views of artists at work in the printmakers studio. There are plenty of handsomely presented dishes featuring quality Scottish meat, fish, and vegetables. **Known for:** busy on weekends; open-plan dining in artsy atmosphere; good for lunch and bar snacks. [$] *Average main: £16* ✉ *152 Nethergate, Dundee* ☎ *01382/909246* 🌐 *www.jutecafebar.co.uk.*

Manchurian Chinese Restaurant

$ | **CHINESE** | This family-run restaurant above a Chinese supermarket will not win any style awards (it feels a little like a hotel conference suite), but thanks to its food it has won a loyal following.

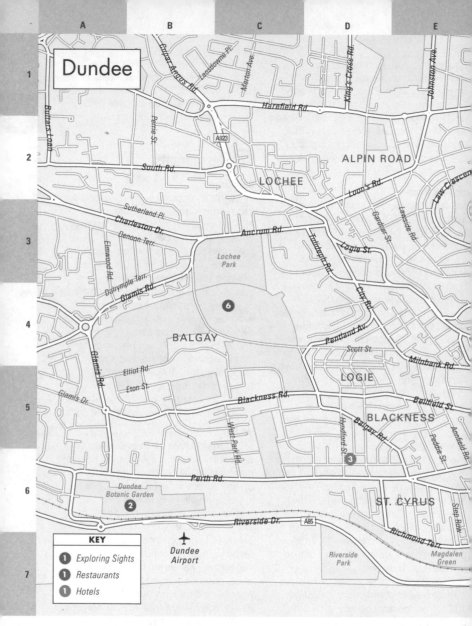

Dundee

A1 Cupar Angus Rd., Lansdowne Pl.
B1 Perrie St.
C1 Merton Ave., Harefield Rd.
D1 King's Cross Rd.
E1 Johnston Ave.

A923

C2 ALPIN ROAD, LOCHEE
D2 Loon's Rd., Gardner St., Lawside Rd.
E2 Lane Crescent

A2 South Rd.
A3 Sutherland Pl., Charleston Dr., Denoon Terr., Elmwood Rd.
C3 Ancrum Rd.
D3 Tullideph Rd., Logie St., City Rd.

A3 Dalrymple Terr., Glamis Rd.

Lochee Park

6

BALGAY

D4 Pentland Av., Scott St.
E4 Milnbank Rd.

A4 Glamis Rd.
A5 Glamis Dr.
B5 Elliot Rd., Eton St.
C5 Blackness Rd.
D5 LOGIE, BLACKNESS, Hyndford St., Balgay Rd.
E5 Belfield St., Peddie St., Annfield Rd.

3

B5 West Park Rd.
B6 Perth Rd.

Dundee Botanic Garden **2**

D6 ST. CYRUS
E6 Step Row

KEY

1 Exploring Sights
1 Restaurants
1 Hotels

✈ Dundee Airport

A85 Riverside Dr.

Riverside Park

E6 Richmond Terr., Magdalen Green

Sights ▼

1 Broughty Castle.......... **J4**
2 Dundee
  Botanic Garden.......... **B6**
3 Dundee
  Contemporary Arts..... **G6**
4 The Law.................. **F3**
5 McManus Galleries.... **H4**

6 Mills Observatory....... **C4**
7 Newport-on-Tay......... **J7**
8 *North Carr Lightship*..... **I5**
9 RRS *Discovery*.......... **H6**
10 Tay River Trips........... **J4**
11 *Unicorn*.................. **I5**
12 V&A Dundee............ **H5**
13 Verdant Works.......... **F5**

Restaurants ▼

1 Boat Brae................ **J7**
2 Jute...................... **G6**
3 Manchurian
  Chinese Restaurant.... **H5**
4 Piccolo................... **F6**
5 Sol y Sombra
  Tapas Bar................ **J4**

Hotels ▼

1 Apex City Quay........... **I5**
2 Malmaison............... **H5**
3 Shaftesbury Lodge..... **D6**

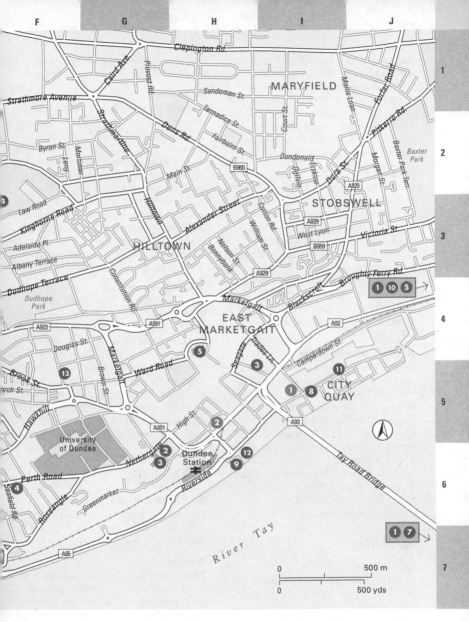

Dishes are fresh and light, from plump and fragrant dim sum to more unusual offerings. **Known for:** handy takeout service; authentic Chinese with modern twist; Chinese supermarket downstairs. $ *Average main: £14* ⊠ *15a Gellatly St., Dundee* ☎ *01382/228822* ⊕ *www.man-churiandundee.com* ⊙ *Closed Wed.*

Piccolo

$$ | **ITALIAN** | This small basement eatery on Perth Road, with wooden tables and chairs and a quirky staff, attracts a diverse clientele. It serves well-crafted pasta dishes and mains that show-case fresh Scottish ingredients. **Known for:** Italian pancakes with ice cream; candlelit intimacy; reservations needed on weekends. $ *Average main: £19* ⊠ *21 Perth Rd., Dundee* ☎ *01382/201419* ⊕ *www.piccolodundee.co.uk* ⊙ *Closed Sun.–Tues.*

★ Sol y Sombra Tapas Bar

$$$ | **TAPAS** | It looks like an old Scottish pub, and it is, but the vibrant ceramics, tapas, and sangria are so authentic they'll make you feel as if you're in España. Choose from the set menus, like a £20 lunch or £28 dinner, and you'll be served a steady stream of cracking little dishes. **Known for:** occasional live music; boisterous atmosphere; revelatory tapas. $ *Average main: £25* ⊠ *27 Gray St., Broughty Ferry* ☎ *01382/776941* ⊕ *www. solysombratapasbar.co.uk.*

🛏 Hotels

Apex City Quay

$ | **HOTEL** | Scandinavian-style rooms with easy chairs, plump bedding, and flat-screen TVs help you unwind at this contemporary quayside hotel. **Pros:** dockside location and riverside walks; stylish rooms; lively, especially on week-ends. **Cons:** conference venue feel; the bar is often mobbed; outside is popular with seagulls, too. $ *Rooms from: £118* ⊠ *1 W. Victoria Dock Rd., Dundee*

☎ *01382/202404* ⊕ *www.apexhotels. co.uk* ⮑ *151 rooms* ⦙◉⦙ *Free Breakfast.*

Malmaison

$$ | **HOTEL** | British brand Malmaison has brought life and a dash of panache to a dilapidated but much-loved Dundee landmark near the new waterfront. **Pros:** central location; beautifully restored old building; stylish rooms. **Cons:** busy location, so there's traffic and other noise; some bathrooms need a refresh; pricey restaurant and bar. $ *Rooms from: £150* ⊠ *44 Whitehall Crescent, Dundee* ☎ *0330/016–0380* ⊕ *www.malmaison. com/locations/dundee* ⮑ *91 rooms* ⦙◉⦙ *Free Breakfast.*

Shaftesbury Lodge

$ | **HOTEL** | Just off Perth Road, this Victorian-era villa set among well-tend-ed shrubs is a find for those who like smaller, more intimate hotels. **Pros:** close, but not too close, to the city; first-rate service; handsome Victorian details. **Cons:** decor a tad dated; 15-minute walk into town; some bathrooms are small. $ *Rooms from: £90* ⊠ *1 Hyndford St., Dundee* ☎ *01382/669216* ⊕ *www.shaft-esburylodge.co.uk* ⮑ *12 rooms* ⦙◉⦙ *Free Breakfast.*

🌙 Nightlife

BARS AND PUBS

Dundee's pub scene, centered around Perth Road and City Centre, is one of the liveliest in Scotland.

Draffens

BARS | Secreted down a *wynd* (alley), this small speakeasy has stylish, exposed-brick interiors, with decorative nods to the defunct Draffens department store and plenty of cocktail shaking going on. ⊠ *Couttie's Wynd, Nethergate, Dundee.*

Fisherman's Tavern

PUBS | If you find yourself in Broughty Ferry, you can't leave without a tipple in what the locals call The Fisherman's. It's a great place to mingle with locals and catch some folk music. ✉ *10–16 Fort St., Broughty Ferry* ☎ *01382/775941* ⊕ *www.fishermanstavern-broughtyferry.co.uk.*

Jute
BARS | Better known as the bar at Dundee Contemporary Arts, this café-bar attracts film fans (the art-house cinema's entrance is next door), students, and the well-heeled for European beers, wine, cocktails, or coffee. It serves tasty bar snacks every night and hosts events related to the arts and cinema. ✉ *152 Nethergate, Dundee* ☎ *01382/909246* ⊕ *www.jutecafebar.co.uk.*

Ship Inn
PUBS | Right on Broughty Ferry's promenade, this bright and breezy pub has a friendly atmosphere and decent bar food. ✉ *121 Fisher St., Broughty Ferry* ☎ *01382/779176* ⊕ *www.theship-inn-broughtyferry.co.uk.*

★ Speedwell Bar
PUBS | Called Mennie's by locals, the Speedwell Bar is in a mahogany-paneled building brimming with Dundonian characters and architectural features. It's renowned for its superb cask beers, choice of malts, and Edwardian interior. ✉ *165–168 Perth Rd., Dundee* ☎ *01382/667783.*

 **Performing Arts**

Caird Hall
MUSIC | One of Scotland's finest concert halls, Caird Hall stages a wide range of music and events. ✉ *City Sq., Dundee* ☎ *01382/434940* ⊕ *www.leisureandculturedundee.com/culture/caird-hall.*

★ Dundee Repertory Theatre
THEATER | This is home to the award-winning Dundee Rep Ensemble and to Scotland's preeminent contemporary-dance group, Scottish Dance Theatre. Popular with locals, the restaurant and bar welcome late-night comedy shows and jazz bands. ✉ *Tay Sq., Dundee* ☎ *01382/223530* ⊕ *www.dundeerep.co.uk.*

Shopping

COFFEE AND TEA
J. Allan Braithwaite
OTHER FOOD & DRINK | Established in 1868 and in its current home since 1932, this enticingly aromatic emporium has large old vats of many freshly roasted coffee blends and tea that you can pop into one of the quaint teapots you'll find here. ✉ *6 Castle St., Dundee* ☎ *01382/322693.*

JEWELRY
DCA
JEWELRY & WATCHES | Just as you enter Dundee Contemporary Arts, the shop on the left sells artist-made jewelry, housewares, books, prints, and gifts. ✉ *DCA, 152 Nethergate, Dundee* ☎ *01382/432456* ⊕ *dca.org.uk.*

Gallery Q
JEWELRY & WATCHES | A compelling selection of jewelry, ceramics, textiles, sculptures, prints, and paintings by Scottish artists awaits at Gallery Q. ✉ *160 Nethergate, Dundee* ☎ *01382/220600* ⊕ *www.galleryq.co.uk.*

MUSIC
Thirteen Records
MUSIC | Rising from the ashes of legendary record shop Groucho's, former staffers Frank, Moog, and Lee keep the tunes spinning at this cheery, yellow-festooned shop. Browse its well-curated racks and sample the day's soundtrack with musos, crate diggers, and the curious. Secondhand and new vinyl of all genres can be found, from rare Northern Soul 45s to the latest releases. There's also a good selection of CDs, DVDs, cassettes, posters, and cool merch. It's a fab place for a chat and to discover the sounds of the local scene. ✉ *13 Union St., Dundee* ☎ *01382/227887* ⊕ *www.facebook.com/ThirteenRecordsDundee.*

Beautiful Beaches

Scotland's east coast enjoys many hours of sunshine, compared with its west coast, and is blessed with lots of sandy beaches under the ever-changing backdrop of the sky. Take time to explore the beaches and walk along the coast for a change of pace whatever the time of year.

In Fife, Tentsmuir's Beach near St. Andrews is popular with kite flyers and horseback riders, and the famous and lovely West Sands in St. Andrews is where the running sequences in the movie *Chariots of Fire* were filmed.

The small cove beach at Elie, south of Crail, hosts cricket matches in summer.

In Angus the beach at Broughty Ferry, near the city of Dundee, fills with families and children on weekends and during school holidays—even on the most blustery of days.

North of Arbroath lies Auchmithie Beach, more shingly (pebbly) than the others and offering a bracing breath of North Sea air. And finally, near the Montrose Basin you can discover the enchanting crescent of Lunan Bay, home to many species of seabirds.

 Activities

GOLF
East of Perthshire, near the city of Dundee, lies a string of demanding courses along the shores of the North Sea and inland into the foothills of the Grampian Mountains. Golfers who excel in windy conditions particularly enjoy the breezes blowing westward from the sea.

★ Carnoustie Golf Links
GOLF | The venue for the British Open in 1999, 2007, and 2018, the coastal links around Carnoustie have challenged golfers since at least 1527. Winners here have included many of the sport's biggest names: Armour, Hogan, Cotton, Player, and Watson. There are three courses, the most famous of which is the breathtaking Championship Course, ranked among the very best in the world. The choice Burnside course is full of historical interest and local color, as well as being tough and interesting. The Buddon course, designed by Peter Allis and Dave Thomas, is recommended for links novices. ⊠ *20 Links Parade, Carnoustie* ☎ *01241/802270* ⊕ *www.carnoustie-olflinks.co.uk* 🏌 *Championship, £275;*

Buddon, £75; Burnside, £75 🏌. *Championship Course: 18 holes, 6948 yards, par 72; Buddon Course: 18 holes, 5921 yards, par 68; Burnside Course: 18 holes, 6028 yards, par 68.*

Panmure Golf Club
GOLF | Down the road from the famous Carnoustie Golf Links, this traditional course offers an excellent challenge with its seaside setting, undulating greens, and sometimes excruciating—but always entertaining—burrows. The signature 6th is named after British Open Championship winner Ben Hogan, who practiced here prior to his triumphant tournament at Carnoustie in 1953. ⊠ *Burnside Rd., off Station Rd., Carnoustie* ☎ *01241/855120* ⊕ *www.panmuregolfclub.co.uk* 🏌 *£90– £145* 🏌. *18 holes, 6551 yards, par 70.*

Arbroath

15 miles north of Dundee.

You can find traditional boatbuilding in the fishing town of Arbroath. It has several small curers and processors as well, and shops sell the town's most famous delicacy, Arbroath smokies—whole haddock gutted and lightly smoked. The town is also known for its association with the Declaration of Arbroath, a key document in Scotland's history. A few miles north along the coast is the old fishing village of Auchmithie, with a beautiful little beach that you can walk to via a short path. The jagged, reddish cliffs and caves are home to a flourishing seabird population.

GETTING HERE AND AROUND

The East Coast train line stops at Arbroath. The Abbey and Signal Tower are all within walking distance, but you'll need a car to get to Auchmithie. If you're driving from Dundee, take A92.

ESSENTIALS

VISITOR INFORMATION Arbroath Tourist Information. ✉ *Fish Market Quay, A92, Arbroath* ☎ *01241/872609* 🌐 *www.visitscotland.com, www.visitangus.com.*

Sights

Arbroath Abbey

RUINS | Founded in 1178 and linked to the famous Declaration of Arbroath, Arbroath Abbey is an unmistakable presence in the town center; it seems to straddle whole streets, as if the town were simply ignoring the red-stone ruin in its midst. Surviving today are remains of the church, as well as one of the most complete examples in existence of an abbot's residence. From here in 1320 a passionate plea was sent by King Robert the Bruce (1274–1329) and the Scottish Church to Pope John XXII (circa 1249–1334) in far-off Rome. The pope had until then sided with the English kings, who adamantly refused to acknowledge Scottish independence. The Declaration of Arbroath stated firmly, "It is in truth not for glory, nor riches, nor honours that we are fighting, but for freedom—for that alone, which no honest man gives up but with life itself." Some historians describe this plea, originally drafted in Latin, as the single most important document in Scottish history. The pope advised English king Edward II (1284–1327) to make peace, but warfare was to break out along the border from time to time for the next 200 years. The excellent visitor center recounts this history in well-planned displays. ✉ *Abbey St., Arbroath* ☎ *01241/878756* 🌐 *www.historicenvironment.scot* 🎟 *£4.50.*

Signal Tower Museum

HISTORY MUSEUM | In the early 19th century, Arbroath was the base for the construction of the Bell Rock lighthouse on a treacherous, barely exposed rock in the Forth of Tay. A signal tower was built to facilitate communication with the builders working far from shore. That structure now houses the Signal Tower Museum, which tells the story of the lighthouse, built by Robert Stevenson (1772–1850) in 1811. The museum also houses a collection of items related to the history of the town, its customs, and the local fishing industry: look out for the 1813 Book of Signals and the witch's eye, a blue-glass buoy hung from the window to ward off evil spirits. ✉ *Ladyloan, Arbroath* ✣ *West of harbor* ☎ *01241/464554* 🌐 *www.angusalive.scot* 🎟 *Free* 🕐 *Closed Sun.–Wed.*

Restaurants

Bellrock

$ | **FAST FOOD** | You can't go to Arbroath and not sample some fish-and-chips. Just across the road from the Signal Museum and painted in nautical white and blue, this local favorite has outside benches for warmer days. You'll find all the classics—breaded or battered—but if you are in the mood for something a little different, the spicy fish (in a spiced batter) has certainly won over discerning locals. **Known for:** extensive menu that also includes pizza and burgers; great fish suppers; weekday buffet. [$] *Average main: £10* ✉ *33 Ladyloan, Arbroath* ☎ *01241/873656* 🌐 *www.thebellrock.com.*

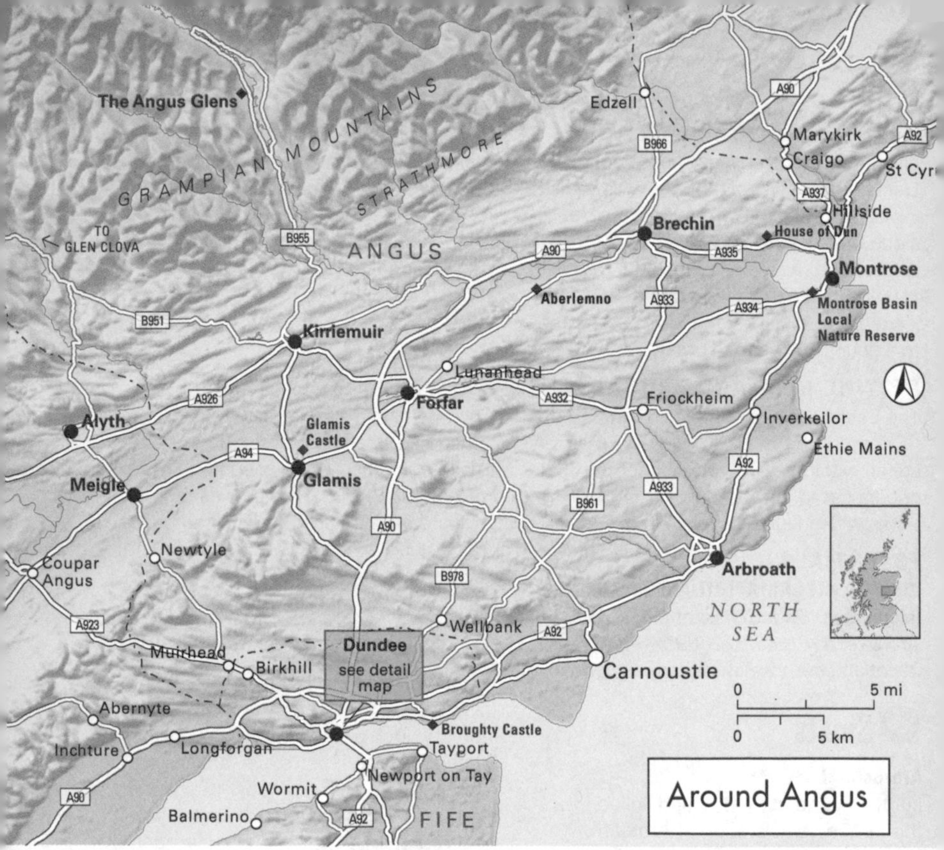
The Angus Glens
GRAMPIAN MOUNTAINS
STRATHMORE
TO GLEN CLOVA
ANGUS
Edzell
A90
B966
Marykirk
Craigo
A92
St Cyr
A937
Hillside
Brechin
House of Dun
A935
Montrose
B955
A90
Aberlemno
A933
A934
Montrose Basin Local Nature Reserve
B951
Kirriemuir
Lunanhead
Forfar
A926
A932
Friockheim
Inverkeilor
Alyth
Glamis Castle
Ethie Mains
A94
Glamis
A92
Meigle
A933
B961
A90
Newtyle
Coupar Angus
Arbroath
B978
NORTH SEA
A923
Wellbank
A92
Dundee
see detail map
Muirhead
Birkhill
Carnoustie
0
5 mi
0
5 km
Abernyte
Broughty Castle
Inchture
Longforgan
Tayport
Newport on Tay
Wormit
A90
Balmerino
A92
FIFE

Around Angus

★ **But 'n' Ben**

$$ | **BRITISH** | This homey restaurant serves lunches and dinners that offer a taste of quality Scottish home cooking, including Arbroath smokie pancakes, mince and tatties, venison with rowan jelly, and rich moist gingerbread, all at reasonable prices. It's next to Auchmithie's lovely shingle beach; a stroll here is the perfect way to work up an appetite or work off overindulgence. **Known for:** Sunday high tea; low-ceilinged crofthouse surroundings; traditional Scottish fare. [$] *Average main: £18* ✉ *Ethie St., Auchmithie* ✣ *3 miles off A92* ☎ *01241/877223* 🌐 *www.thebutnben.com* 🕒 *Closed Tues. No dinner Mon.*

Hotels

Brucefield Boutique

$$ | **B&B/INN** | This old manor house, set among well-tended grounds, offers luxurious rooms for very reasonable rates. **Pros:** tranquil gardens; all the touches you'd expect in a five-star hotel; quality bedding. **Cons:** books up quickly; a 20-minute walk to the city center; two-night minimum in high season. [$] *Rooms from: £125* ✉ *Cliffburn Rd., Arbroath* ☎ *01241/875393* 🌐 *www.brucefieldbandb.com* 🛏 *4 rooms* 🍴 *Free Breakfast.*

Harbour Nights

$ | **B&B/INN** | An excellent and somewhat plush budget option, this B&B is right on the harbor, affording you the most authentic Arbroath stay possible. **Pros:** thoughtful decor; splendid seafront location; delicious breakfasts. **Cons:** some may find it cluttered; you must book far in advance; only one room with a private bathroom. $ *Rooms from: £100* ✉ *4 Shore, Arbroath* ☎ *01241/551629* ⊕ *www.harbournights.co.uk* 🛏 *4 rooms* ⦿ *Free Breakfast.*

Montrose

14 miles north of Arbroath.

An unpretentious and attractive town with some charming museums and a selection of shops, Montrose sits beside a wide estuary known as the Montrose Basin.

GETTING HERE AND AROUND
On the main East Coast train line, the town is easily accessed by public transportation. Nevertheless, you'll need a car to get to attractions outside town.

ESSENTIALS
VISITOR INFORMATION Montrose Tourist Information Point. ✉ *Montrose Museum, Panmure Pl., Montrose* ☎ *01674/907447* ⊕ *www.visitangus.com.*

👁 Sights

★ House of Dun
HISTORIC HOME | The National Trust for Scotland's leading attraction in this area is the stunning House of Dun, which overlooks the Montrose Basin. The mansion was built in the 1730s for lawyer David Erskine, otherwise known as Lord Dun (1670–1755). Designed by architect William Adam (1689–1748), the house is particularly noted for its magnificently ornate plasterwork and curious Masonic masonry. Showing everything from Lady Dun's collection of embroidery to the working kitchens, this house tells the story of the Seat of Dun and the eminent family's history. The sprawling grounds have a restored hand-loom weaving workshop, plus an enchanting walled Victorian garden and wooded den. ✉ *A935, Montrose* ✣ *4 miles west of Montrose*

☎ *01674/810264* ⊕ *www.nts.org.uk* 🎟 *£13.50* ⊗ *House closed Jan.–June.*

Montrose Basin Local Nature Reserve
NATURE PRESERVE | Run by the Scottish Wildlife Trust, the Montrose Basin Local Nature Reserve hosts migrating geese, ducks, and swans. Several nature trails can take you up close to the reserve's residents if you're quiet. In October, at least 20,000 pink-footed geese arrive: come in the morning and the evening to see them fill the sky. ✉ *Rossie Braes, Montrose* ☎ *01674/676336* ⊕ *www.montrosebasin. org.uk* 🎟 *£4.50* ⊗ *Closed Tues.–Thurs.*

Montrose Museum
HISTORY MUSEUM | The town's museum—housed in a neoclassical building that also contains the tourist information center—exhibits some fascinating bequests by the local gentry, including an early-19th-century ship carved from bone by French prisoners in the Napoleonic Wars. ✉ *Panmure Pl., Montrose* ☎ *01674/907447* ⊕ *www.angusalive.scot* 🎟 *Free* ⊗ *Closed Sun.–Wed.*

★ William Lamb Studio
ART MUSEUM | A visit to the studio of renowned Montrosian artist and sculptor William Lamb (1893–1951) provides a glimpse into his intriguing life, travels, and obsessions. In the intimate studio you can walk among the heads of 20th-century royalty, society figures, and everyday Montrose folk. The museum is open only in July and August and by appointment; ask the lovely staff at the Montrose Museum. ✉ *24 Market St., Montrose* ☎ *01674/662660* ⊕ *www. friendswilliamlambstudio.uk* 🎟 *Free* ⊗ *Closed Sept.–June.*

Restaurants

★ The Pavilion Cafe
$ | **CAFÉ** | Bringing new purpose to an old bowling pavilion, this café's owner freshly painted its clapboard, spruced up the delightful color-glazed fanlights, and gently restored many of the unusual features

of this late-Victorian beauty. Expect light meals, breakfasts, salads, buttermilk pancakes, and superfresh home bakes: the seasonal fruit-festooned cream sponges are a treat. **Known for:** quirky setting; bowling-green-scene jollity; scrumptious cakes. $ *Average main: £10* ⊠ *Melville Gardens, Montrose* ☎ *01674/958188* ⊗ *Closed Sun. and Mon.*

🎭 Performing Arts

★ Montrose Playhouse

ARTS CENTERS | This alluring multipurpose cinema and arts center was built from a dilapidated 1950s swimming pool. Along with its three cinema screens, Montrose's community hub hosts events, talks, and workshops. Pop into the fab Reel Café Bar to refuel and see what's coming up. ⊠ *The Mall, Montrose* ☎ *7395/071636* ⊕ *montroseplayhouse.co.uk.*

Brechin

10 miles northwest of Montrose.

The small market town of Brechin has a cathedral that was founded around 1200 and contains an interesting selection of antiquities, including the Mary Stone, a Pictish relic.

GETTING HERE AND AROUND

Brechin is not on the East Coast train line but can be reached by bus from Montrose or Arbroath (Stagecoach Strathtay No. 30). It's on the A935, just off the main A90 road between Dundee and Aberdeen.

👁 Sights

Brechin Cathedral and Round Tower

CHURCH | The town's 13th-century Brechin Cathedral and Round Tower is on the site of a former Celtic monastery (priory of the Culdee monks) and has some unusual examples of medieval sculpture. The tower is one of only two on mainland

Scotland. This type of structure is more frequently found in Ireland. ⊠ *6 Church St., Brechin* ☎ *01356/629360* ⊕ *brechin-cathedral.org.uk* ⊠ *Free.*

Brechin Town House Museum

HISTORY MUSEUM | Located in the old courtroom that had cells in its cellars, the Brechin Town House Museum houses a small but interesting collection of objects from inhabitants of the area: from Bronze Age jewelry to a Jacobite sporran to a letter from a World War I soldier. There is a small tourist information desk within the museum. ⊠ *28 High St., Brechin* ☎ *01356/237227* ⊕ *www.angusalive.scot* ⊠ *Free* ⊗ *Closed Sun. and Mon.*

🍴 Restaurants

Brechin Castle Garden Centre

$ | **CAFÉ** | **FAMILY** | Just off the A90, this small country park has lots of children's activities, including a giant sand pit, go-karts, a barrel train, and a wooden maze. Most essentially, there's an excellent café, serving door-stop-size sandwiches, full breakfasts, tasty soups, meringues, and warm scones. **Known for:** vegan options; hearty food; family-friendly dining. $ *Average main: £9* ⊠ *Haughmuir, Brechin* ☎ *01356/626813* ⊕ *www.brechincastlecentre.co.uk* ⊗ *No dinner.*

The Angus Glens

25 miles northwest of Brechin.

You can rejoin the hurly-burly of the A90 for the return journey south from Montrose or Brechin; the more pleasant route, however, leads southwesterly on minor roads (there are several options) that travel along the face of the Grampians, following the fault line that separates Highlands and Lowlands. The Angus Glens extend north from points on A90. Known individually as the glens of Isla, Prosen, Clova, and Esk, these long valleys run into the high hills of the Grampians and some clearly marked walking routes. Those in Glen Clova are especially appealing.

Be aware that Thursday is a half-day in Angus; many shops and attractions close at lunch.

GETTING HERE AND AROUND
You really need a car to reach the Angus Glens and enjoy the gentle (and not so gentle) inclines here. Glamis and Kirriemuir are both on the A928 (just off the A90), and the B955—which loops round at Glen Clova—is one of the loveliest Scottish roads to drive along, especially when the heather is blooming in late summer.

🛏 Hotels

Glen Clova Hotel
$$ | HOTEL | Since the 1850s, the hospitality of this hotel has lifted the spirits of many a bone-tired hill walker, and it remains as comfortable a spot as ever today. **Pros:** spacious accommodations; stunning location; great base for outdoor pursuits. **Cons:** poor email communication; bar and live-music nights may be noisy; lack of decent public transportation. ⓢ *Rooms from: £125* ⊠ *B955, Glen Clova* ☎ *01575/550350* ⊕ *www.clova. com* ⇨ *10 rooms* ⃭◯⃤ *Free Breakfast.*

Kirriemuir

15 miles southwest of Brechin.

Kirriemuir stands at the heart of Angus's red-sandstone countryside and was the birthplace of the writer J. M. Barrie (1860–1937), best known abroad as the author of *Peter Pan* (a statue of whom you can see in the town's square). *Kirrie,* as it's known here, salutes favorite son Bon Scott (1946–80)—the rasping AC/DC vocalist—in a bronze-and-Caithness-rock memorial statue at Bellies Brae. Metal pilgrims gather each springtime for Bonfest.

GETTING HERE AND AROUND
A number of roads lead to Kirriemuir, but A928 (off A90), which also passes Glamis Castle, is one of the loveliest. Stagecoach Strathtay runs buses to this area; Nos. 20 and 22 from Dundee are the most regular.

👁 Sights

Camera Obscura
VIEWPOINT | FAMILY | J. M. Barrie donated this Camera Obscura to the town; located within a cricket pavilion, it magically projects an image of the wonderful landscape views onto the opposite wall. It is one of only four in the country and run by lovely volunteers. ⊠ *Kirrie Hill, Kirriemuir* ☎ *01575/575885* ⊕ *www.kirriemuircameraobscura.com* ⃬ *Free (donations welcome)* ⊗ *Closed Nov.–Mar. and Tues.–Fri.*

J.M. Barrie's Birthplace
HISTORIC HOME | At J. M. Barrie's Birthplace, the National Trust pays tribute to the man who sought to preserve the magic of childhood more than any other writer of his age. The house's upper floors are furnished as they might have been in Barrie's time, complete with domestic necessities, while downstairs is his study, replete with manuscripts and personal mementos. The outside washhouse is said to have served as Barrie's first theater. ⊠ *9 Brechin Rd., Kirriemuir* ☎ *01575/572646* ⊕ *www.nts.org. uk/Property/J-M-Barries-Birthplace* ⃬ *£8* ⊗ *Closed Nov.–Mar. and weekdays.*

Kirriemuir Gateway to the Glens Museum
HISTORY MUSEUM | As is the style in Angus, the local museum doubles as the visitor center, meaning you can get all the information you need and admire a few stuffed birds and artifacts at the same time. Rock fans will appreciate the exhibit celebrating local lad made good (or rather bad), the late Bon Scott, original lead singer of the rock band AC/DC. ⊠ *32 High St., Kirriemuir* ☎ *01575/526006* ⊕ *www.angusalive.scot* ⃬ *Free* ⊗ *Closed Sun. and Mon.*

Restaurants

88 Degrees

$ | CAFÉ | FAMILY | If you're not in a rush, take time to savor excellent coffee, inventive sandwiches, pizzettes, cakes, and handmade chocolates at this appealing café and shop selling quality fare. If you're in a hurry, buy delicious cheese or chocolates to go or pick up a cheese and apple scone. **Known for:** cash-only policy; creative house-baking including sourdough bread; handmade chocolates and truffles. $ *Average main: £8* ⊠ *17 High St., Kirriemuir* ☎ *07449/345089* ▭ *No credit cards* ◷ *Closed Mon. and Tues. No dinner.*

Forfar

7 miles east of Kirriemuir.

Forfar goes about its business of being the center of a farming hinterland without being preoccupied with (or even that interested in) tourism.

GETTING HERE AND AROUND

Buses are slow here. The quickest route is by car: take the A90 north, then the A926 turnoff. Alternatively, the A932/ A933 route from Arbroath takes you through farmland and Angus villages.

Sights

Aberlemno

RUINS | You can see excellent examples of Pictish stone carvings about 5 miles northeast of Forfar alongside the B9134. Carvings of crosses, angels, serpents, and other animals adorn the stones, which date from the 7th to the early 9th century. Note the stone in the nearby churchyard—one side is carved with a cross and the other side depicts the only known battle scene in Pictish art, complete with horsemen and foot soldiers. During the winter months, the stones are covered to protect them from the elements. ⊠ *Forfar* ⊕ *www.historicenvironment.scot.*

Meffan Museum and Art Gallery

HISTORY MUSEUM | The high point of a visit to Fofar is the Meffan Museum and Art Gallery, which displays an interesting collection of Pictish carved stones, a recreation of Forfar's cobbled street The Vennel, and artifacts from the dark days of burning witches. Two galleries host frequently changing exhibitions by leading local and Scottish artists. The museum also houses a tourist information desk. ⊠ *20 W. High St., Forfar* ☎ *01307/491771* ⊕ *www.angusalive.scot* ⊠ *Free* ◷ *Closed Sun.–Wed.*

Glamis

5 miles southwest of Forfar, 6 miles south of Kirriemuir.

Set in rolling countryside is the little village of Glamis (pronounced *glahms*), the highlight of which is nearby famous Glamis Castle.

GETTING HERE AND AROUND

The drive to Glamis Castle, along beech- and yew-lined roads, is as majestic as the castle itself. Take the A90 north from Dundee, then off onto the A928. The village of Glamis can be reached by the Stagecoach Strathtay No. 22, but service is rather infrequent.

Sights

★ Glamis Castle

CASTLE/PALACE | One of Scotland's best known and most beautiful castles, Glamis Castle connects Britain's royalty through 10 centuries, from Macbeth (Thane of Glamis) to the late Queen Mother and her daughter, the late Princess Margaret, born here in 1930 (the first royal princess born in Scotland in 300 years). The property of the earls of Strathmore and Kinghorne since 1372, the castle was largely reconstructed in the late 17th century; the original keep, which is much older, is still intact. One of the most famous rooms in

Majestic Glamis Castle and its Duncan's Hall is also the setting for Shakespeare's Macbeth.

the castle is Duncan's Hall, the legendary setting for Shakespeare's *Macbeth*. Guided tours allow you to see fine collections of china, tapestries, and furniture. Within the castle is the delightful Castle Kitchen restaurant; the grounds contain a huge gift shop, a shop selling local produce, and a pleasant picnic area. ■ TIP → If you are looking to hear the pipes and see some Highland dancing and games of strength, the Strathmore Highland Games are held here around the second weekend of June. See ⊕ *www.strathmorehighlandgames.co.uk* for more information. ✉ *A94, Glamis* ✛ *1 mile north of Glamis* ☎ *01307/840393* ⊕ *www. glamis-castle.co.uk* ☞ *£15.50* ⊘ *Closed Mon.–Wed. Nov.–Feb.*

Meigle

7 miles southwest of Glamis, 11 miles northwest of Dundee.

The historic village of Meigle, nestled in the rich agricultural land of the Strathmore Valley, is well known to those with an interest in Pictish stones. Said to be built on an 11th-century Pictish monastery, the village has a number of elaborate Victorian buildings.

GETTING HERE AND AROUND

Meigle is an easy and pleasant drive from Glamis on the A94 (or from Dundee on the B954). The hourly Stagecoach Strathtay from Dundee (No. 57) stops here.

◉ Sights

Meigle Sculptured Stone Museum

HISTORY MUSEUM | The town of Meigle, in the wide swathe of Strathmore, has one of the most notable collections of sculpted stones in western Europe, housed at the Meigle Sculptured Stone Museum. It consists of some 25 monuments from the Celtic Christian period (8th to 11th century), nearly all of which were found in or around the local churchyard. The large 9th-century prayer cross-slab known as Meigle 2 shows Daniel in the lions' den. Local legend holds the slab marked the grave of Guinevere, wife of King Arthur; in the story, Arthur sentences her to death by being torn apart by wild animals. ✉ *A94, Meigle* ☎ *01828/640612* 🌐 *www.historicenvironment.scot* 🎟 *£6* 🕐 *Closed Oct.–Mar.*

Alyth

4 miles north of Meigle, 15 miles northwest of Dundee.

Dating back to the Dark Ages, this market town just over the county line in Perth and Kinross was completely transformed by the Industrial Revolution, which lined its streets with mills and factories. The 20th century saw the closing of most of these companies, but the town had never forgotten its agricultural heritage, retaining a rural allure today.

GETTING HERE AND AROUND

Just 4 miles farther along the B954 from Meigle, Alyth is also served by Stagecoach Strathtay No. 57.

👁 Sights

Alyth Museum

HISTORY MUSEUM | This small but intriguing local-history museum has a collection of old photos and an engaging audio Story Box mining tales of local legend, history, and today's community, as well as nearly every type of tool used by the resourceful Alyth folk. ✉ *Commercial St., Alyth* ☎ *01828/633474* 🎟 *Free* 🕐 *Closed Mon.–Thurs. and Oct.–Apr.*

🍴 Restaurants

Little's

$$ | MODERN BRITISH | Seek out this fabulous seafood restaurant in nearby Blairgowrie for its beautifully cooked catch of the day specials served amid the beautiful converted church interiors and towering stained glass windows. The daily specials, such as the chunky flatfish megrim, are cooked in almond-flaked nutty butter and served with sautéed potatoes. **Known for:** incredibly fresh fish; atmospheric church surroundings; intimate adjoining bar. [$] *Average main: £20* ✉ *1 Riverside Rd., Blairgowrie* ☎ *01250/875358* 🌐 *www.littlesrestaurant.com* 🕐 *Closed Sun. and Mon.*

🛏 Hotels

Tigh Na Leigh

$ | B&B/INN | This grand house turned classy B&B, originally built by the Earl of Airlie, is a relaxing place with spacious, elegant rooms. **Pros:** evening meals made with local produce; lovingly restored building; charming rooms. **Cons:** a car needed to explore the area; books up quickly; away from the action. [$] *Rooms from: £120* ✉ *22–24 Airlie St., Alyth* ☎ *01828/632372* 🌐 *www.tighnaleigh.com* 🔑 *6 rooms* 🍽 *Free Breakfast.*

Chapter 7

STIRLING AND THE CENTRAL HIGHLANDS

Updated by
Mike Gonzalez

7

◉ Sights	🍴 Restaurants	🛏 Hotels	🛍 Shopping	🍸 Nightlife
★★★★☆	★★☆☆☆	★★☆☆☆	★★☆☆☆	★★☆☆☆

WELCOME TO STIRLING AND THE CENTRAL HIGHLANDS

TOP REASONS TO GO

★ **Loch Lomond:** You can see the sparkling waters of Scotland's largest loch by car, by boat, or on foot. A popular option is the network of bicycle tracks that creep around Loch Lomond and the Trossachs National Park, offering every conceivable terrain.

★ **Castles:** Choosing among Scotland's most splendid fortresses and mansions is a challenge. Among the highlights are Stirling Castle, Scone Palace, and Doune Castle.

★ **Great hikes:** The best way to experience the Central Highlands is to head out on foot. The less-demanding wood-land paths and gentle rambles of the Trossachs will stir even the least adventurous rambler.

★ **Whisky tours and tastes:** The Scots love their whisky, and what bet-ter way to participate in Scottish life and culture than to learn about the land's finest? There are some exceptional distill-eries in this region, from the Edradour Distillery to Glenturret in Crieff.

1 Stirling. A historic town dominated by its castle.

2 Falkirk. A key medieval city and historic industrial center.

3 Dunblane. A small town with a 12th-century cathedral.

4 Callander. The gateway to the Trossachs.

5 The Trossachs. A national park with every kind of landscape.

6 Aberfoyle. Easy access to Queen Elizabeth Forest Park and the eastern banks of Loch Lomond.

7 Loch Lomond. Scotland's largest and perhaps most famous loch.

8 Perth. Once Scotland's capital and now a gateway to the Highlands.

9 Dunkeld. The land of Beatrix Potter.

10 Pitlochry. An old Victorian spa town.

11 Blair Atholl. Home to Blair Castle, one of Scotland's great houses.

12 Aberfeldy. A town with a unique bridge and a popular distillery.

13 Crieff. Home to a glass-making community.

14 Auchterarder. A small Highland town dominated by a famous golf course.

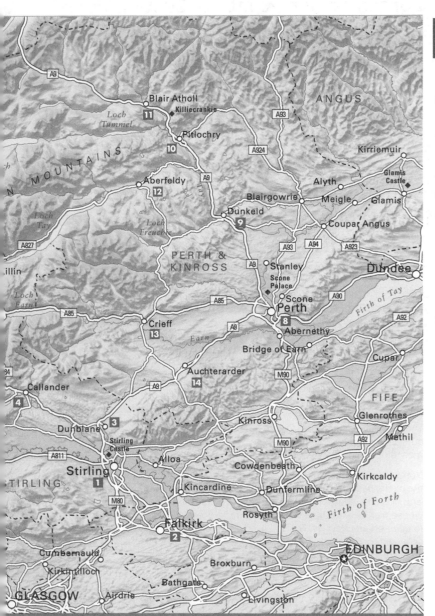

The Central Highlands are home to superb castles, moody mountains, and gorgeous glens that are best explored at a leisurely pace. The waters of Loch Lomond reflect the crags and dark woods that surround it, and attract those in search of a more romantic and nostalgic Scotland enshrined in the verses of the famous song that bears its name. When you finish a day of exploring, celebrate with a glass of one of the region's top-notch whiskies.

The Carse of Stirling, the wide plain guarded by Stirling Castle, was the scene of many important moments in Scotland's history—from the Roman invasion commemorated by the Antonine Wall to the castles that mark the site of medieval kingdoms and the battles to preserve them. Look up at Stirling Castle from the valley and you can see why so many battles were fought over its possession. The Battle of Bannockburn Centre, just outside Stirling, commemorates the most emblematic battle of them all.

North from Stirling, past Dunblane, are the birch-, oak-, and pine-covered Highland hills and valleys of the Trossachs, whose high peaks attract walkers and a tougher breed of cyclist. From Callander, a neat tourist town, the hills stretch westward to the "bonnie, bonnie banks" of Loch Lomond. The Victorians were drawn here by the lyrical descriptions of the area by romantic poets like Sir Walter Scott (1771–1832), who set his dramatic verse narrative of 1810, "The Lady of the Lake," in the landscape of the Trossachs. From the peaks of the Trossachs, on a good day, you can see Edinburgh Castle to the east and the tower blocks of Glasgow's housing projects to the west.

Farther north is Perth, once Scotland's capital; its wealthy mansions reflect the prosperous agricultural land that surrounds the city, and it is still an important market town today. Overlooking the River Tay, the city can reasonably claim to be the gateway to the Highlands, sitting as it does on the Highland Fault that divides Lowlands from Highlands. From Perth the landscape begins to change on the road to Pitlochry and the high, rough country of Rannoch Moor.

The region is full of reminders of heroic struggles, particularly against the English, from the monument to William Wallace to Bannockburn, where Robert the Bruce took on the invader. In Balquhidder near

Callander, Rob Roy MacGregor, the Scottish Robin Hood, lived (and looted and terrorized) his way into the storybooks.

MAJOR REGIONS

Stirling. Famous for its castle and vibrant with history, Stirling has a small Old Town on the hill that is worth covering on foot. Look down from the Stirling Castle crag that dominates the plains below and you can see the stages of the city's growth descending from the hill. The town is a good center from which to explore the changing landscape of central Scotland.

The Trossachs and Loch Lomond. Immortalized by Wordsworth and Sir Walter Scott, the Trossachs (the name means "bristly country") contains some of Scotland's loveliest forest, hills, and glens, well justifying the area's designation as a national park. The area has a special charm, combining the wildness of the Highlands with the prolific vegetation of an old Lowland forest. Its open ground is a dense mat of bracken and heather, and its woodland is of silver birch, dwarf oak, and hazel—trees that fasten their roots into the crevices of rocks and stop short on the very brink of lochs. There are also many small towns to visit along the way, some with their roots in a medieval world; others sprang up and expanded in the wake of the first tourists who came to Scotland in the late 19th century in search of wild country or healing waters. Dunblane has a magnificent cathedral; Doune's castle will make you stare in awe. This area is small but incredibly varied—from dramatic mountain peaks that attract walkers and climbers, to the gentler slopes and forests that stretch from Perth westward to Aberfoyle and the shores of Loch Lomond. The glens and streams that pepper the region create a romantic landscape that is a perfect habitat for the figure of Rob Roy McGregor—Robin Hood or bandit according to taste, but undeniably Scottish. Loch Lomond's western side is more accessible, if

busier, than the east, but the views across the loch are spectacular.

The most colorful season is fall, particularly October, a lovely time when most visitors have departed, and the hares, deer, and game birds have taken over. Even in rainy weather the Trossachs of "darksome glens and gleaming lochs" are memorable: the water filtering through the rocks by Loch Lomond comes out so pure and clear that the loch is like a sheet of glass. The best way to explore this area is by car, by bike, or on foot; the latter two depend, of course, on the weather. Keep in mind that roads in this region of the country are narrow and winding, which can make for dangerous conditions in all types of weather.

Perthshire. The prosperous air of Perth, once the capital of Scotland, testifies to its importance as a port exporting wool, salmon, and whisky to the world. Scone Palace serves as a monument to that era. If Perthshire's castles invoke memories of past conflicts, the grand houses and spa towns here are testimony to the continued presence of a wealthy landed gentry. This is also a place for walking, cycling, and water sports. In some ways Perthshire is a crossing point where Lowlands and Highlands, two Scottish landscapes and two histories, meet. Perthshire itself is rural, agricultural Scotland, fertile and prosperous. Its woodlands, rivers, and glens (and agreeable climate and strategic position) drew the Romans and later the Celtic missionaries. In fact, the motto of the capital city, Perth, is "the perfect center." The route northward leads across the Highland Boundary and into the changing landscapes beyond Pitlochry to Rannoch Moor, where the wind sweeps across the hardy heather.

7

Stirling and the Central Highlands

Planning

When to Go

The Trossachs and Loch Lomond are in some ways a miniature Scotland, from the tranquil east shore of Loch Lomond to the hills and glens of the Trossachs and the mountains to the west—and all within a few hours' drive. In spring and summer, despite the erratic weather, the area is always crowded; this is a good time to go. Nevertheless, the landscape is notably dramatic when the trees are turning red and brown in autumn, and evening skies are spectacular. Scotland in winter has a different kind of beauty, especially for skiers and climbers.

■ TIP→ **Pack clothes for wet and dry weather, and carry both types on hikes, as the weather can change quickly. Summer evenings attract midges; bring some repellent.**

Planning Your Time

Scotland's beautiful interior is excellent touring country, though the cities of Stirling and Perth are worth your time, too; Stirling is a good starting point, and exploring its castle can take a half day. Two (slightly rushed) days would be enough to explore the Trossachs loop, to gaze into the waters of Loch Venachar and Loch Achray. The glens, in some places, run parallel to the lochs, including those along Lochs Earn, Tay, and Rannoch, making for satisfying loops and round-trips. Loch Lomond is easily accessible from either Glasgow or Stirling, and is well worth exploring. Don't miss the opportunity to take a boat trip on a loch, especially on Loch Lomond or on Loch Katrine.

Getting Here and Around

AIR
Perth and Stirling can be reached easily from the Edinburgh, Dundee, and Glasgow airports by train, car, or bus.

BUS
A good network of buses connects with this area via Edinburgh and Glasgow. For more information contact Scottish Citylink or National Express. The Perth and Kinross Council supplies a map (available in tourist information centers) showing all public transport routes in Perthshire, marked with nearby attractions.

First, Scottish Citylink, and Stagecoach organize reliable local service on routes throughout the Central Highlands.

BUS CONTACTS First Bus. ☎ *0345/646–0707* ⊕ *www.firstbus.co.uk.* **National Express.** ☎ *0871/781–8181* ⊕ *www. nationalexpress.com.* **Scottish Citylink.** ☎ *0141/352–4444* ⊕ *www.citylink.co.uk.* **Stagecoach.** ☎ *0843/810–1000* ⊕ *www. stagecoachbus.com.*

CAR
It's easy to access the area from the central belt of Scotland via the motorway network. The M80 connects Glasgow to Stirling, and then briefly joins the M9 from Edinburgh, which runs within sight of the walls of Stirling Castle. From there the A9 runs from Stirling to Perth, and onward to Pitlochry; it is a good road but a little too fast (so take care). Perth can also be reached via the M90 over the Forth Bridge from Edinburgh. Three signed touring routes are useful: the Perthshire Tourist Route, the Deeside Tourist Route, and the Pitlochry Tourist Route, a beautiful and unexpected trip via Crieff and Loch Tay. Local tourist information centers can supply maps of these routes, or you can check online (⊕ *www.visitscotland.com*). Once you leave the major motorways, roads become narrower and slower, with many following the

contours of the lochs. Be prepared for your journey to take longer than distances might suggest.

TRAIN

The Central Highlands are linked to Edinburgh and Glasgow by rail, with through routes to England (some direct-service routes from London take fewer than five hours). Several discount ticket options are available, although in some cases on the ScotRail system a discount card must be purchased before your arrival in the United Kingdom. Note that families with children and travelers younger than 26 or older than 60 are eligible for significant discounts. Contact Trainline, Traveline Scotland, National Rail, or ScotRail for details.

The West Highland Line runs through the western portion of the area. Services also run to Stirling, Dunblane, Perth, and Gleneagles; stops on the Inverness–Perth line include Dunkeld, Pitlochry, and Blair Atholl.

TRAIN CONTACTS National Rail Enquiries. ☎ 03457/484950 ⊕ www.nationalrail. co.uk. **ScotRail.** ☎ 0344/811–0141 ⊕ www.scotrail.co.uk. **Trainline.** ☎ 0871/244–1545 ⊕ www.thetrainline. com. **Traveline Scotland.** ☎ 0871/200–2233 ⊕ www.travelinescotland.com.

Restaurants

Regional country delicacies—loch trout, river salmon, lamb, and venison—appear regularly on even modest menus in Central Highlands restaurants. In all the towns and villages in the area, you will find simple pubs, often crowded and noisy, many of them serving substantial food at lunchtime and in the evening until about 9 (eaten balanced on your knee, perhaps, or at a shared table). The more luxurious restaurants tend to be in upscale hotels, with prices to match. It can be difficult to find a place to eat later in the evening (after 9 pm).

Hotels

A wide selection of accommodations is available throughout the region, especially in Stirling, Bridge of Allan, Callander, and Pitlochry. They range from bed-and-breakfasts to private houses with a small number of rooms to rural accommodations (often on farms). The grand houses of the past—family homes to the landed aristocracy—have for the most part become country-house hotels. Their settings, often on ample grounds, offer an experience of grand living—but the area also has modern hotels, for those who prefer 21st-century amenities.

Restaurant and hotel reviews have been shortened. For full information, visit Fodors.com. Restaurant prices are the average cost of a main course at dinner or, if dinner is not served, at lunch, excluding tax. Hotel prices are the lowest cost of a standard double room in high season, including 20% V.A.T.

WHAT IT COSTS in Pounds			
$	$$	$$$	$$$$
RESTAURANTS			
under £15	£15–£19	£20–£25	over £25
HOTELS			
under £125	£125–£200	£201–£300	over £300

Visitor Information

The tourist offices in Stirling and Perth are open year-round, as are offices in larger towns; others are seasonal (generally from April to October).

Activities

This area of the country is ideal for outdoor enthusiasts. Hiking and bicycling are especially popular, and there are routes that cater to one or the other of these sports, including long paths that traverse the Lowlands and the Highlands, covering multiple towns. The town of Callander in particular has several hiking paths. Information on trails throughout Scotland is supplied on the country's main tourism website (⊕ *www.visitscotland.com/see-do/active/walking/routes-trails* or ⊕ *www.visitscotland.com/see-do/active/cycling/national-routes*).

Lowland-Highland Trail

HIKING & WALKING | The region's big attraction for cyclists is the Lowland-Highland Trail, which stretches more than 60 miles and passes through Drymen, Aberfoyle, the Trossachs, Callander, Lochearnhead, and Killin. This route runs along former railroad-track beds, as well as private and minor roads, to reach well into the Central Highlands. Another almost completely traffic-free option is the roadway around Loch Katrine. Almost every town along the route has cycle-hire shops. ⊠ *Aberfoyle.*

★ The Rob Roy Way

HIKING & WALKING | Want a weeklong walk? The Rob Roy Way is a 79-mile footpath from Drymen to Pitlochry. The route takes you past Loch Venachar and Loch Lubnaig, perfect examples of the beauties of the region. And you may be following in the footsteps of famous Jacobite warrior Rob Roy MacGregor, who for a time was a fugitive from justice. Want to add in some inclines? Along the way are Ben Lawers and Ben Ledi, popular hills for those who prefer climbs. Details of the route are on the website. ⊠ *Callander* ⊕ *www.robroyway.com.*

★ West Highland Way

HIKING & WALKING | The long-distance walkers' route, the West Highland Way, begins at Milngavie, outside Glasgow, running 96 miles from the Lowlands of central Scotland to the Highlands at Fort William. Along its course the landscape changes as you walk from the banks of Loch Lomond into the hills beyond, through the dramatic Glencoe, across Ranooch Moor and beyond it to Fort William and the heart of the Central Highlands. Nearly 50,000 people discover the glens each year, climbing the hills and listening to birds singing in the tree canopy. For the most part, this is not an especially difficult walk, although it can be demanding at moments, but keep Scotland's ever-changing weather in mind and go properly prepared. ⊠ *Bearsden* ⊕ *www.west-highland-way.co.uk.*

Stirling

26 miles northeast of Glasgow, 36 miles northwest of Edinburgh.

Stirling is one of Britain's great historic towns. An impressive proportion of the Old Town walls can be seen from Dumbarton Road, a cobbled street leading to Stirling Castle, built on a steep-sided plug of rock. From its esplanade there is a commanding view of the surrounding Carse of Stirling. The guns on the castle battlements are a reminder of the military advantage to be gained from its position.

GETTING HERE AND AROUND

Stirling's central position in the area makes it ideal for travel to and from Glasgow and Edinburgh (or north to Perth and the Highlands) by rail or bus. The town itself is compact and easily walkable, though a shuttle bus travels to and from the town center up the steep road to Stirling Castle every 20 minutes. You can stroll the Back Walk on a circuit around the base of the castle walls—set aside at least 30 minutes for a leisurely walk. The National Wallace Monument (2 miles away) is on the outskirts of the town and can be reached by taxi or on foot.

ESSENTIALS
VISITOR INFORMATION VisitScotland Stirling iCentre. ⊠ Old Town Jail, St. John St., Stirling ☎ 01786/475019 ⊕ my.stirling. gov.uk/tourism-visitors.

👁 Sights

★ Battle of Bannockburn Visitor Centre
VISITOR CENTER | FAMILY | You can almost hear the trotting of horses' hooves and the zip of arrows in this 21st-century re-creation of the battle that changed the course of Scotland's history in 1314. Robert the Bruce's defeat of the armies of the English king, despite a 2-to-1 disadvantage, is the stuff of legend. Using 3-D technology, the visitor center allows you to see a battle raging across screens that ring the central hall. Participants on both sides speak directly to you, courtesy of holograms. Later you can play a role in a Bannockburn battle game (reservations essential; age seven and older only). Bruce pursued the Scottish crown, ruthlessly sweeping aside enemies; but his victory here was masterful, as he drew the English horses into marshy land (now the area around the new center), where they sank in the mud. A circular monument commemorates the battlefield. ■ TIP➔ Book ahead; tickets are for timed entry. ⊠ Glasgow Road, Stirling ☎ 01786/812664 ⊕ www.nts.org.uk/visit/ places/bannockburn ⊠ £7.50.

Church of the Holy Rude
CHURCH | The nave of this handsome church survives from the 15th century, and a portion of the original medieval timber roof can also be seen. This is the only Scottish church still in use to have witnessed the coronation of a Scottish monarch—James VI (1566–1625) in 1567.

The origin of the name Holy Rude (similar to Holyrood in Edinburgh) is Holy Cross. ■ TIP➔ October through April, the building is often open only during service time on Sunday morning (10 am January through June, 11:30 am July through December). ⊠ Top of St. John's St., Stirling ⊕ www. holyrude.org.

National Wallace Monument
MONUMENT | This Victorian-era shrine to William Wallace (circa 1270–1305), the Scottish freedom fighter reborn as "Braveheart" in Mel Gibson's 1995 film of the same name, was built between 1856 and 1869. It sits on Abbey Craig, from which Wallace watched the English armies struggle across the old Stirling Bridge before attacking them and winning a major victory in 1297. A steep stone spiral staircase leads to the roof gallery, with views of the bridge and the whole Carse of Stirling. A less flamboyant version of Wallace's life is told in an exhibition and audiovisual presentation on the second floor. To reach the monument, follow the Bridge of Allan signs (A9) northward, crossing the River Forth by the New Bridge of 1832, next to the old one. The monument is signposted at the next traffic circle. From the car park a free shuttle will take you to the monument, or you can walk (15 minutes). ⊠ Abbey Craig, Hillfoot Rd., Stirling ☎ 01786/472140 ⊕ www.nationalwallace-monument.com ⊠ £10.75.

Old Town Jail
JAIL/PRISON | FAMILY | Though an improvement on the original jail across the road at the Tolbooth, this newer county jail was still a pretty grim place as a visit to its cells and corridors will show. The ticket price includes an audio guide, and in the summer months costumed actors recount in gory detail what went on here. There's also now an Escape Room, where you work as a team to solve some shady activities in the jail. Be sure to book tickets and reserve a time slot in advance, especially in summer.

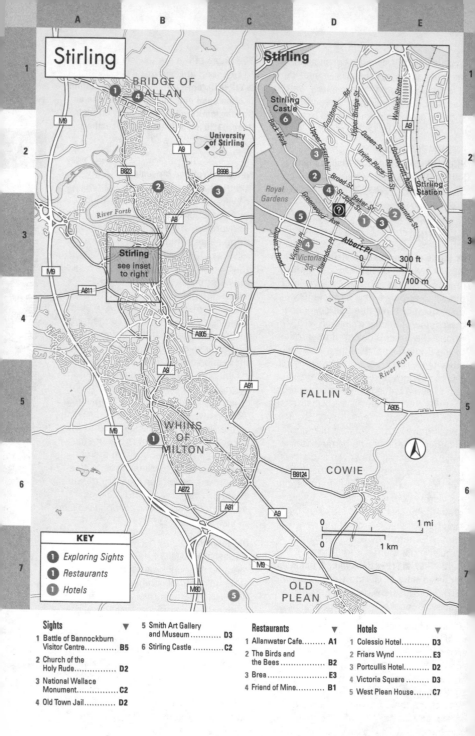

Stirling

Stirling (inset)

Stirling Castle
Royal Gardens

Back Walk
Footroad
Upper Castlehill
Broad St
St John St
Baker St
Greenwood Ave
Albert Pl
Victoria Pl
Victoria Sq
Clarendon Pl
Queen's Road

Upper Bridge St
Queen St
Irvine Place
Spittal St
Barnton St
Wallace Street
A9
Rosemount Place
Stirling Station

0   300 ft
0   100 m

BRIDGE OF ALLAN

University of Stirling

River Forth

Stirling
see inset to right

WHINS OF MILTON

FALLIN

COWIE

OLD PLEAN

M9, A9, B823, B998, A905, A91, A811, A872, B9124, M80, A905

0   1 mi
0   1 km

KEY

1 *Exploring Sights*
1 *Restaurants*
1 *Hotels*

Sights ▼

1 Battle of Bannockburn Visitor Centre............ **B5**

2 Church of the Holy Rude................. **D2**

3 National Wallace Monument................. **C2**

4 Old Town Jail............. **D2**

5 Smith Art Gallery and Museum **D3**

6 Stirling Castle **C2**

Restaurants ▼

1 Allanwater Cafe.......... **A1**

2 The Birds and the Bees **B2**

3 Brea...................... **E3**

4 Friend of Mine........... **B1**

Hotels ▼

1 Colessio Hotel............ **D3**

2 Friars Wynd **E3**

3 Portcullis Hotel.......... **D2**

4 Victoria Square **D3**

5 West Plean House........ **C7**

✉ *St. John St., Stirling* ☎ *01786/595024* ⊕ *www.oldtownjail.co.uk* 🎫 *£8.50, Escape Room £10* 🕑 *Closed Jan. and weekdays Nov. and Dec.*

Smith Art Gallery and Museum

HISTORY MUSEUM | FAMILY | This small but intriguing museum in a neoclassical building, founded in 1874, houses *The Stirling Story*, a comprehensive social history of the town. It holds the oldest (reputedly) football in the world, as well as the charming 16th-century portraits of the Five Stirling Sybils. Closer to the present are banners and memorabilia from the great miners' strike of 1984–85. The chiming clocks remind us, on the hour, of the present. The museum also holds regular temporary art and historical exhibitions and has a pleasant café. ✉ *Dumbarton Road, Stirling* ✛ *A few minutes' walk along Albert Place from the town center* ☎ *01786/471917* ⊕ *www. smithartgalleryandmuseum.co.uk* 🎫 *Free* 🕑 *Closed Mon.–Wed.*

★ Stirling Castle

CASTLE/PALACE | FAMILY | Its magnificent strategic position on a steep-sided crag made Stirling Castle the grandest prize in the Scots Wars of Independence during the late 13th and early 14th centuries. Robert the Bruce's victory at Bannockburn won both the castle and freedom from English subjugation for almost four centuries. Take time to visit the Castle Exhibition beyond the lower gate to get an overview of its evolution as a stronghold and palace.

The daughter of King Robert I (Robert the Bruce), Marjory, married Walter Fitzallan, the high steward of Scotland. Their descendants included the Stewart dynasty of Scottish monarchs (Mary, Queen of Scots, was a Stewart, though she preferred the French spelling, Stuart). The Stewarts were responsible for many of the works that survive within the castle walls. They made Stirling Castle their court and power base, creating fine Renaissance-style buildings within

the walls that were never completely destroyed, despite reconstruction for military purposes.

Today, you enter the castle through its outer defenses, which consist of a great curtained wall and batteries from 1708. From this lower square the most conspicuous feature is the Palace, built by King James V (1512–42) between 1538 and 1542. The decorative figures festooning the ornate outer walls show the influence of French masons. An orientation center in the basement, designed especially for children, lets you try out the clothes and musical instruments of the time. Across a terrace are the Royal Apartments, which re-create the furnishings and tapestries found here during the reign of James V and his French queen, Mary of Guise. The queen's bedchamber contains copies of the beautiful tapestries in which the hunt for the white unicorn is clearly an allegory for the persecution of Christ. Overlooking the upper courtyard is the Great Hall, built on the orders of King James IV (1473–1513) in 1503 and used for extravagant banquets. Before the Union of Parliaments in 1707, when the Scottish aristocracy sold out to England, the building had also been used as one of the seats of the Scottish Parliament.

Among the later works built for regiments stationed here, the Regimental Museum stands out; it's a 19th-century baronial revival on the site of an earlier building. Nearby, the Chapel Royal is unfurnished. The oldest building on the site is the Mint, or Coonzie Hoose, perhaps dating as far back as the 14th century. Below it is an arched passageway leading to the westernmost ramparts, the Nether Bailey, with a view of the *carselands* (valley plain) of the Forth Valley.

To the castle's south lies the hump of the Touch and the Gargunnock Hills, which diverted potential direct routes from Glasgow and the south. For centuries all roads into the Highlands across the narrow waist of Scotland led through Stirling.

If you look carefully northward, you can still see the Old Stirling Bridge, the site of William Wallace's most famous victory.

When visiting, it's smart to book your tickets—and accompanying timeslot—online before you arrive. ✉ *Castlehill, Stirling* ☎ *01786/450000* 🌐 *www.stirling-castle.gov.uk* 🎫 *£16.*

Restaurants

Allanwater Cafe

$ | **BRITISH** | **FAMILY** | Run by the Bechelli family for four generations, this casual, light, and airy café in Bridge of Allan, just a couple of miles from Stirling, is a popular spot with locals. It is a well-tried Scottish combination of fish-and-chip restaurant and ice-cream parlor. **Known for:** quick service; popular "fish tea" (fish-and-chips served with tea or coffee); Italian ice cream. [$] *Average main: £12* ✉ *15 Henderson St., Bridge of Allan* ☎ *01786/833060* 🌐 *www.allanwatercafe.co.uk.*

★ The Birds and the Bees

$$ | **BRITISH** | **FAMILY** | This lively pub in a converted whitewashed farmhouse is a little hard to find but worth the effort for the extensive menu—from burgers and steaks to jambalaya, curry, and haggis "draped" in a whisky-and-mustard sauce. This is all good home cooking without pretensions, and the servings are more than generous. **Known for:** lovely location; hearty home-style cooking; delicious desserts. [$] *Average main: £15* ✉ *Easter Cornton Road, Causewayhead, Stirling* ✥ *From the Wallace Monument head southeast on Hillfoots Road/B998 (if walking, you can take the Logie Road/B998 shortcut), then take the A9 toward Stirling. Make a right at Easter Cornton Road and follow it about one-half mile.* ☎ *01786/473663* 🌐 *www.thebirdsandthe-bees-stirling.com.*

Brea

$$ | **BRITISH** | This unpretentious and popular place with wooden tables and chairs has a menu that celebrates Scottish food, though well-made burgers and steaks are also permanent features. The food offers some new takes on traditional favorites such as the rolled haddock with salmon, the Cullen skink soup, and haggis in various guises. **Known for:** house-made desserts; excellent burgers; good seafood. [$] *Average main: £18* ✉ *5 Baker St., Stirling* ✥ *Down the hill from Stirling Castle* ☎ *01786/446277* 🌐 *www.brea-stirling.co.uk.*

Friend of Mine

$ | **BRITISH** | At this very popular addition to the dining scene in Stirling/Bridge of Allan, you'll find an adventurous menu that includes Chinese bao buns and a cheerful use of spices (the sriracha chicken burger is a delight). The brunch menu features flavors from around the world too, and there are excellent choices for vegetarians such as cauliflower steak and jack fruit tacos. **Known for:** good food in a relaxed atmosphere; nice cocktail menu; lovely pavement terrace. [$] *Average main: £13* ✉ *45 Henderson St., Bridge of Allan* ☎ *001786/831386* 🌐 *www.friend-ofmine.co.uk.*

Hotels

Colessio Hotel

$ | **HOTEL** | Occupying a large stone landmark neoclassical building in the center of town and near the castle, this is a modern hotel in the grand style, with 21st-century amenities. **Pros:** comfortable bedrooms; great central location; modern facilities. **Cons:** limited views in some rooms; black-and-white decor may overpower; difficult parking, though there is a parking lot behind the hotel. [$] *Rooms from: £113* ✉ *33 Spittal St., Stirling* ☎ *01786/448880* 🌐 *www.hotelcolessio.com* 🛏 *40 rooms* 🍴 *Free Breakfast.*

Friars Wynd

$ | HOTEL | This small boutique hotel in a restored townhouse is situated in the heart of Stirling. **Pros:** reasonably priced; pleasant and relaxing atmosphere; tasteful decor. **Cons:** limited social space; no parking; rooms are quite basic. $ *Rooms from: £80* ⊠ *17 Friars St., Stirling* ☎ *01786/447501* ⊕ *www.friarswynd.co.uk* ⇌ *8 rooms* ⦿ *Free Breakfast.*

Portcullis Hotel

$$ | B&B/INN | This small hotel with a lively traditional pub scores above all on location: it is just outside the walls of Stirling Castle, and the views are spectacular, especially from the upper floors where the guest rooms are located. **Pros:** lively atmosphere in the bar; excellent location close to the castle; fine views. **Cons:** not cheap in high season; snug rooms; can get noisy. $ *Rooms from: £135* ⊠ *Castle Wynd, Stirling* ☎ *01786/472290* ⊕ *www.theportcullishotel.com* ⇌ *4 rooms* ⦿ *Free Breakfast.*

Victoria Square

$$ | HOTEL | Looking out over a pleasant grassy square, this rather grand and completely modernized Victorian house has a conveniently central location within walking distance of Stirling Castle. **Pros:** quiet spot (first-floor rooms are the loudest); big and bright rooms; sumptuous decor. **Cons:** rooms are on the expensive side; Orangery restaurant is pricey; atmosphere a bit stuffy. $ *Rooms from: £158* ⊠ *12 Victoria Sq., Stirling* ☎ *01786/473920* ⊕ *www.victoriasquareguesthouse.com* ⇌ *7 rooms* ⦿ *Free Breakfast* ☞ *No children under 12.*

West Plean House

$ | B&B/INN | Dating from 1803, this handsome, rambling B&B with spacious rooms is part of a working farm. **Pros:** huge and hearty breakfast; beautiful gardens; plenty of peace and quiet. **Cons:** occasional noise from the farm; a 3-mile walk to Stirling; a little off the beaten track. $ *Rooms from: £100* ⊠ *Denny Road, Stirling* ☎ *01786/812208* ⊕ *www.westpleanhouse.com* ⊗ *Closed Dec.* ⇌ *4 rooms* ⦿ *Free Breakfast.*

ⓘ Performing Arts

Macrobert Arts Centre

ARTS CENTERS | On the campus of the University of Stirling, this arts center has a theater, gallery, and cinema with programs that range from films to pantomime. It's off the A9 as you're heading toward Bridge of Allan. ⊠ *University of Stirling, West Link Road, Stirling* ☎ *01786/466666* ⊕ *www.macrobert.org.*

Tolbooth

MUSIC | Built in 1705, the Tolbooth has been many things: courthouse, jail, meeting place. At one time the city's money was kept here. Today it serves as an entertainment venue, an art gallery, and a 200-seat theater for concerts and performances of all kinds. The bar is open for performances. ■**TIP**➔ **It has retained its traditional Scottish steeple and gilded weathercock, and a newer tower lets you survey the surrounding country.** ⊠ *Broad St., Stirling* ☎ *01786/274000* ⊕ *stirlingevents.org/tolbooth-event.*

ⓘ Shopping

CLOTHING

House of Henderson

MIXED CLOTHING | An old-school Highland outfitter, House of Henderson sells tartans, woolens, and accessories, and offers a made-to-measure kilt service. ⊠ *6–8 Friars St., Stirling* ☎ *01786/473681* ⊕ *www.houseofhenderson.co.uk.*

GIFTS

Fotheringham Gallery

JEWELRY & WATCHES | This upscale gallery in Bridge of Allan, just outside Stirling, specializes in contemporary Scottish art as well as striking modern jewelry by Leigh Fortheringham. ⊠ *78 Henderson St., Bridge of Allan* ☎ *01786/832861* ⊕ *www.fotheringhamgallery.co.uk.*

Made in Stirling

CRAFTS | This arts-and-crafts gallery in the center of Stirling sells a whole range of creative arts—jewelry, paintings, woodwork, stained glass, cards, and gifts—mostly by local artists. It also offers courses and workshops for locals and visitors. ⊠ *44 King St., Stirling* ☎ *01786/357550* ⊕ *www.madeinstirling-store.com.*

Stirling Bagpipes

MUSIC | This small shop sells bagpipes of every type and at every price, including antiques by legendary craftspeople that are displayed in glass cases. The owner, Alan Waldron, who tunes the chanters and drones in a room behind the shop, has been known to take time to walk shoppers through the history of these wonderful instruments, upon request. ⊠ *8 Broad St., Stirling* ☎ *01786/448886* ⊕ *www.stirlingbagpipes.com.*

Falkirk

14 miles southeast of Stirling.

Falkirk has a fascinating history and some striking attractions. It was here, at the impressive Antonine Wall, that the Roman occupiers drove back the warlike Picts. You can visit parts of the wall and imagine the fierce battles between the Romans and early Scottish natives over this strategic location.

In the late 18th century, Falkirk became an important industrial town thanks to the growth of its iron and steel plants and its location at the center of a network of canals linking Glasgow and Edinburgh; these were the main links between the two cities until the arrival of the railways. Today, the canals have been brought back to life with the Millennium Link Project, which has revived the waterways with the spectacular Falkirk Wheel, a boat lift that has become a major visitor draw, and the Kelpies Country Park. The restored canal side towpaths are now

a network of cycle paths and walking routes; you can rent a bike at the Wheel and cycle to the Kelpies.

GETTING HERE AND AROUND

The M9 from Stirling to Falkirk follows the widening estuary of the River Forth, the view dominated by the huge Grangemouth oil refinery in the distance.

ESSENTIALS

VISITOR INFORMATION Falkirk Council/ Falkirk Community Trust. ⊠ *The Falkirk Stadium, 4 Stadium Way, Unit 2A, Falkirk* ⊕ *www.visitfalkirk.com.*

◉ Sights

Antonine Wall

RUINS | West of Falkirk, Bonnybridge is home to the most extensive remains of the Antonine Wall, a 37-mile-long Roman earthwork fortification that marked the northernmost limit of the Roman Empire. Built around AD 140 as a defense against the warlike Picts of the north, it was abandoned some 20 years later. A UNESCO World Heritage site, the wall was the site of a famous battle in 1298, when William Wallace was defeated by the English. Notable sections of the wall can also be seen in other towns, including Tamfourhill, Callendar Park, Kinneil Estate, and Bridgeness. To get to the Bonnybridge section from Falkirk, take the A803 west. You can download a walking map of the wall from *www. visitfalkirk.com.* ⊠ *Off A803, Bonnybridge* ⊹ *2 miles west of Falkirk off the A803* ⊕ *www.historicenvironment.scot* ⊠ *Free.*

Callendar House

HISTORIC HOME | FAMILY | Near the town center, this grand country house gives you a glimpse of a wealthy family's daily life in the early 1800s. In the kitchen, local guides explain cooking in the early 19th century and may even offer you a sample. Entry is through an impressive wooden hallway, and the first-floor morning and drawing rooms are the grandest in the region. There are exhibits

The Kelpies, located just outside of Falkirk, are the largest works of art in all of Scotland.

on the Romans and the Antonine Wall, as well as on the history of Falkirk. The second floor is a gallery space and houses the town's archives. You can relax in the grand tearoom before you move on to the beautiful grounds of Callendar Park, which has activities year-round. The house is something of a secret, but it's well worth a visit. ⊠ *Callendar Park, off Callendar Road, Falkirk* ☎ *013244/503770* ⊕ *www.falkirkcommunitytrust.org* 🎫 *Free* ☉ *Closed Tues.*

★ Falkirk Wheel

TRANSPORTATION | FAMILY | The only rotating boat lift in the world, the Falkirk Wheel links two major waterways, the Forth and Clyde Canal and the Union Canal, between Edinburgh and Glasgow. Opened in 2001, this extraordinary engineering achievement lifts and lowers boats using four giant wheels shaped like Celtic axes; it can transport eight or more boats at a time from one canal to the other in about 45 minutes. The Falkirk Wheel replaced 11 locks. You can take a 50-minute trip as the wheel turns, and you're transported up or down to the other canal. The site offers children's play areas, as well as children's canoes and bicycle rentals. An on-site office has information on canal boat cruises. There are also several canal path walkways and cycleways. The excellent Heritage Centre provides plenty of information and has a good café and gift shop. There are a number of activities available around the site too, including archery and paddle boats. ■ **TIP→ Booking your ride on the wheel ahead of time is essential in summer.** ⊠ *Lime Road, Tamfourhill* ✛ *Signposted off the A803* ☎ *8700/500208* ⊕ *www. thefalkirkwheel.co.uk* 🎫 *£13.50.*

★ The Kelpies at the Helix

PUBLIC ART | FAMILY | The Helix, a country park on the edges of Falkirk with cycle and walking paths, play areas, and a wetland, is home to sculptor Andy Scott's extraordinary *The Kelpies*, two horse heads forged in steel, 85 and 98 feet high respectively. The largest works of art in Scotland, they sit at the center of the park, their beautiful heads framed against the Ochil Hills behind. The sculptures pay homage to Falkirk's industrial past; the heads are modeled on Clydesdales, the huge draft horses that hauled barges along the canals before the advent of the railways. A special guided tour (book online for convenience) gives you an insight into the area's past and takes you inside the sculptures. There's also a visitor center with a café and gift shop. ⊠ *The Helix, A9 and Falkirk Road, Falkirk* ☎ *01324/590600* ⊕ *www.thehelix.co.uk* ⌑ *Park free; sculpture tour £7.50.*

Dunblane

6 miles north of Stirling.

The small, quiet town of Dunblane has long been an important religious center; it is dominated by its cathedral, which dates mainly from the 13th century. The town also boasts one of Scotland's most impressive libraries, the Leighton Library, as well as a nearby castle that may seem familiar to you, especially if you're an *Outlander* fan.

GETTING HERE AND AROUND
Dunblane station is on the main line to Perth and Inverness, and regular bus service links the town to Stirling. For drivers it is easily reached along the main A9 artery.

◉ Sights

Blair Drummond Safari and Adventure Park
ZOO | FAMILY | As unlikely as it might seem in this gentle valley, the Blair Drummond Safari and Adventure Park is the place to see sea lions bobbing their heads above the water or monkeys swinging from the branches. Take a footbridge to Lemur Land or watch hawks and falcons in the *Birds of Prey* exhibit. Beware the llamas, who are more bad-tempered than they may appear. The spacious drive-through enclosure brings you close to rhinos, antelopes, camels, and lions. Look out for the monkeys there too (might be best to keep your windows closed). There are also rides, slides, and an adventure playground for the kids, as well as some fairground rides that cost extra. ⊠ *Blair Drummond, Doune* ✛ *Off the A84, between Dunblane and Callander* ☎ *01786/841456* ⊕ *www.blairdrummond. com* ⌑ *£16.50* ⊙ *Closed Nov.–Feb.*

Doune Castle
CASTLE/PALACE | This medieval castle may seem eerily familiar because it is a favorite with filmmakers: *Monty Python and the Holy Grail* was filmed here, and more recently it was used in the *Game of Thrones* and *Outlander* series (and the admission price has risen since *Outlander* aired). In 1361 the castle became the seat of Robert Stewart, the Duke of Albany and Governor of Scotland, who embarked on various building projects. The semi-ruined Doune is grim and high-walled, with a daunting central keep and echoing, drafty stairways up to the curtain-wall walk. Climb the wall; the views over the countryside will make it worthwhile. Monty Python's Terry Jones narrates a good audio guide. The best place to photograph this squat, walled fort is from the bridge, a little way upstream. ⊠ *Castle Road, Doune* ✛ *5 miles west of Dunblane* ☎ *01786/841742* ⊕ *www.historicenvironment.scot* ⌑ *£9.*

Dunblane Cathedral
CHURCH | The oldest part of Dunblane—with its narrow winding streets—huddles around this church's square. Bishop Clement built the cathedral in the early 13th century on the site of St. Blane's tiny 8th-century cell; with the Reformation of the 16th century, it ceased to be a cathedral. In 1996 it was the scene of a moving memorial service for the 15 children and one teacher killed in the local school by Thomas Hamilton. There are free guided tours on Sunday afternoons. Be sure to view the medieval carvings in the choir stalls. ⊠ *The Cross, Dunblane* ☎ *01667/460232* ⊕ *www.dunblanecathedral.org.uk* ⌑ *Free.*

Leighton Library

LIBRARY | A 17th-century bishop of Dunblane, and later an archbishop of Glasgow, Robert Leighton donated his collection of roughly 1,400 books for clergy to use, along with funds to build this library to store them. Today the library—which is no longer a lending library but operates like a museum of books—owns more than 4,500 books, and you can view an assortment of old and interesting maps and books here. Donations are encouraged. ✉ *13 Buccleuch Court, Dunblane* ☎ *01786/822034 Library custodian* 🌐 *www.leightonlibrary.org.uk* 🎫 *Free* 🕓 *Closed Sun. and Oct.–Apr.*

🍴 Restaurants

Mason Belles Kitchen

$ | **BRITISH** | Occupying the Old Churches House, this restaurant offers reassuringly familiar dishes with some unusual accompaniments, such as pork belly with broccoli, chicken with spring greens, and the ever reliable fish-and-chips with mushy peas. The decor is bright and comfortable, with a relaxed atmosphere. **Known for:** local ingredients; traditional afternoon tea; tranquil atmosphere. [$] *Average main: £14* ✉ *Kirk St., Dunblane* ☎ *01786/825142* 🌐 *www.masonbelleskitchen.co.uk.*

🛏 Hotels

★ Cromlix House

$$$ | **HOTEL** | A grand refurbished Victorian country house set amid beautiful grounds, Cromlix House is owned by Scottish tennis champion Andy Murray, and you might notice the sound of ball on racket from the tennis court. **Pros:** comfortable beds; luxurious facilities; lovely grounds for walking. **Cons:** an expensive indulgence; a little hard to find; not much for children. [$] *Rooms from: £279* ✉ *Off B8033, beyond the village of Kinbuck, Kinbuck* ✥ *Keep looking for the entrance, 4½ miles north of Dunblane* ☎ *01786/822125* 🌐 *www.cromlix.com* 🛏 *16 rooms* 🍴 *Free Breakfast.*

DoubleTree by Hilton Dunblane Hydro

$$ | **HOTEL** | One of the grandes dames where Victorians would come to "take the waters," this hotel on sprawling grounds has retained elements of its original building with plenty of modern updates. **Pros:** leisure center included in the rates; fine views; lovely grounds. **Cons:** charge for Wi-Fi; some rooms are small; slightly old-fashioned feel. [$] *Rooms from: £129* ✉ *Perth Rd., Dunblane* ☎ *01786/822551* 🌐 *www.doubletreedunblane.com* 🛏 *200 rooms* 🍴 *Free Breakfast.*

Old Churches House

$ | **HOTEL** | In a row of 18th-century houses overlooking the Cathedral Square, this comfortable and unpretentious hotel has a quiet, restful air. **Pros:** traditional and modern Scottish dishes at on-site restaurant; quiet location; all rooms (but one) look out onto the square. **Cons:** parking not on-site, but nearby (and free); slightly distant from major sights; could be too quiet. [$] *Rooms from: £60* ✉ *1–7 Kirk St., Dunblane* ☎ *01786/823663* 🌐 *www.oldchurcheshouse.com* 🛏 *11 rooms* 🍴 *Free Breakfast.*

Callander

8 miles northwest of Doune.

A traditional Highland-edge resort, the little town of Callander bustles throughout the year, largely with visitors and coach parties from Glasgow and Edinburgh. It is a gateway to the beauty of Loch Lomond and the Trossachs National Park, yet never too far from the cities of the central belt. There's plenty of window-shopping here, plus lively pubs and a selection of mainly bed-and-breakfast accommodations.

GETTING HERE AND AROUND

You can access Callander by bus from Stirling, Glasgow, or Edinburgh. If you're traveling by car from Stirling, take the M8 to Dunblane, then the A820 (which becomes the A84) to Callander. If you are coming from Glasgow, take the A81 through Aberfoyle to Callander; an alternative route (longer but more picturesque) is to take the A821 around Loch Venachar, then the A84 east to Callander.

ESSENTIALS

VISITOR INFORMATION Callander Visitor Information Centre. ✉ *55 Main St., Callander* ☎ *01877/330342* 🌐 *incallander.co.uk/visitorcentre.*

Sights

Balquhidder Glen

NATURE SIGHT | A 20-minute drive from Callander, through the Pass of Leny and beyond Strathyre, the lovely Balquhidder Glen (pronounced *bal*-kwidd-*er*) is a typical Highland glen, with a flat-bottom, U-shaped profile, indicating it was formed by prehistoric glaciers. This was MacGregor country, the most famous of whom was Rob Roy MacGregor, the Jacobite hero who is buried in the churchyard here. It is also walkers country, and several walkers routes pass through here. Gentler walks will take you to Kirkton Glen, past Monachyle Mhor, after the road ends. From there the view opens toward the mountain country around Ben More, where the hardier, well-equipped hillwalker may prefer to go. ✉ *Balquhidder* ✣ *From Callander take the A84 and turn left at Kingshouse; the road ends in the glen.*

Hamilton Toy Museum

OTHER MUSEUM | **FAMILY** | This is one of those eccentric museums born of one person's (or one family's) passionate obsession. The small, crowded house and shop on Callander's main street contains one of the most extensive toy collections in Britain. The rooms throughout the house are crammed with everything from Corgi cars and an enormous number of toy soldiers, carefully organized by regiment, to Amanda Jane dolls and Beatles memorabilia. The collection of model railways has extended into tracks in the back garden. The museum is jammed and quirky, but full of reminders of everyone's childhood. ✉ *111 Main St., Callander* ☎ *01877/330004* 🌐 *www.thehamiltontoycollection.co.uk* 🎫 *£3* 🕒 *Closed Nov.–Mar.*

Restaurants

Deli Ecosse

$ | **CAFÉ** | Don't miss it: in one corner of the square, off Callander's main street, a narrow door opens into a high-ceilinged old church hall crowded with good things to eat there or take away. You can order tasty soups, house-made cakes, and plump sandwiches from the counter, or try the excellent coffee or a glass of wine. **Known for:** inexpensive lunch; house-made cakes; excellent breakfast. [$] *Average main: £8* ✉ *10 Ancaster Sq., Callander* ☎ *01877/331220* 🌐 *deliecosse.co.uk* 🕒 *No dinner. Closed Wed.*

Mhor Bread and Tearoom

$ | **BRITISH** | **FAMILY** | Retaining the feel of an old-fashioned bakery, Mhor Bread delights with not only its homemade sourdough and other delicious breads, but also doughnuts, shortbread, and more. The café/tearoom is open for breakfast and lunch, with menu items such as fine sandwiches, soups, and desserts, including an amazing array of pies with different fillings. **Known for:** good breakfasts; house-made bread; fine pies of every variety. [$] *Average main: £10* ✉ *8 Main St., Callander* ☎ *01877/339518* 🌐 *www.mhorbread.net* 🕒 *No dinner.*

MHOR Fish

$ | **SEAFOOD** | Simple white walls and black-and-white floors provide the backdrop for great fish at this very superior, and nicely busy, "chippy" (fish-and-chips shop) and fish restaurant. The fish is fresh and sustainable, so it might be pollock or coley rather than cod or haddock. **Known for:** homemade bread; sustainable fish; great chips (fried in beef fat). [$] *Average main: £12* ✉ *7577 Main St., Callander* ☎ *01877/330213* 🌐 *monachylemhor.net.*

★ Venachar Lochside

$$ | **MODERN BRITISH** | All you see from the road is what seems to be a large shed, but inside is a busy restaurant with excellent views—the restaurant's glass wall affords a lovely panorama of the water and surrounding hills. The menu lives up to its surroundings, with an emphasis on fish—mussels, scallops, the excellent smoked-fish selection to start, and the trout with roast chorizo. **Known for:** lochside dining; gorgeous views; fine seafood. [$] *Average main: £15* ✉ *Loch Venachar, Callander* ✣ *On the A821 about 6 miles from Callander, at Brig o' Turk* ☎ *01877/330011* 🌐 *www.venachar-lochside.co.uk* ⏲ *No dinner.*

Hotels

The Crags Hotel

$ | **HOTEL** | A traditional establishment on Callander's main street, the Crags Hotel has a restrained, elegant style. **Pros:** reasonably priced; friendly staff and atmosphere; appealing restaurant on-site. **Cons:** rooms are quite small; small reception area and bar; some rooms facing the street may be noisy. [$] *Rooms from: £75* ✉ *101 Main St., Callander* ☎ *01877/330257* 🌐 *www.cragshotel.co.uk* 🛏 *8 rooms* 🍴 *Free Breakfast.*

MHOR 84

$ | **B&B/INN** | **FAMILY** | Balquhidder Glen is the perfect place for walkers and cyclists, and this modest but casually chic hotel has been designed with them in mind. **Pros:** good food; beautiful setting; great quality for the price. **Cons:** used above all by walkers (thus not for intimate retreats); breakfast costs extra; a rather isolated spot. [$] *Rooms from: £120* ✉ *Balquhidder, Lochearnhead* ✣ *Off the A84 from Callander to Crianlarich, turn at Kingshouse; 11 miles north of Callender* ☎ *01877/384646* 🌐 *www.mhor84.net* 🛏 *7 rooms* 🍴 *No Meals.*

★ Monachyle MHOR

$$$ | **HOTEL** | Splendidly isolated in Balquhidder Glen, this beautiful converted farmhouse with contemporary interiors is set amid forests and moorland, looking out onto Lochs Voil and Doine. **Pros:** complimentary salmon and trout fishing; stunning scenery; delicious food. **Cons:** bar can get very crowded; rooms are on the small side; remote location. [$] *Rooms from: £250* ✉ *Off A84, Balquhidder* ✣ *From Callander, drive northwest 17 miles (40 minutes)* ☎ *01877/384622* 🌐 *www.mhor.net* 🛏 *14 rooms* 🍴 *All-Inclusive.*

★ Roman Camp

$$ | **HOTEL** | You could easily pass by this beautiful hotel without noticing, though it is just off Callander's main street; look for an unpretentious pink arch on the main street and there you'll find the 17th-century hunting lodge hidden among ornate gardens. **Pros:** close to everything in town; beautiful grounds; luxurious rooms. **Cons:** much sought after for weddings, so could be busy; no Internet in rooms; restaurant is expensive. [$] *Rooms from: £130* ✉ *Off Main Street, Callander* ☎ *01877/330003* 🌐 *www.romancamphotel.co.uk* 🛏 *15 rooms* 🍴 *Free Breakfast.*

Shopping

Trossachs Woollen Mill

MIXED CLOTHING | The Edinburgh Woollen Mill Group owns this mill shop in Kilmahog, a mile west of Callander. It has a vast selection of woolens on display, including luxurious cashmere and striking tartan throws, and will provide overseas mailing and tax-free shopping. The shop has a small café and a couple of resident animals. ✉ *Main St., Kilmahog* ☎ *01877/330178* 🌐 *www.ewm.co.uk.*

⚡ Activities

BICYCLING

Wheels

BIKING | You can rent bikes of every sort by the hour, the half day, or the day from this friendly firm. Most popular are the mountain bikes, which go for £20 per day. The staff can also help you find the best mountain-bike routes around the Trossachs. ⊠ *Invertrossachs Road, Callander* ☎ *01877/331100* ⊕ *www. wheelscyclingcentre.com.*

GOLF

Callander Golf Club

GOLF | Designed by Tom Morris in 1890 and extended to 18 holes in 1913 by Willie Fernie, Callander has a scenic upland feel in a town well prepared for visitors. Pine and birch woods and hilly fairways afford fine views, especially toward Ben Ledi, and the tricky moorland layout demands accurate hitting off the tee. The challenging 15th is one of Scotland's most famous holes. ⊠ *Aveland Road, Callander* ☎ *01877/330090* ⊕ *www. callandergolfclub.co.uk* ⊠ *£24 weekdays, £45 weekends* ⛳ *18 holes, 5208 yards, par 66.*

HIKING

Bracklinn Falls

HIKING & WALKING | A walk is signposted from the car park at the east end of Callander's main street to the Bracklinn Falls, over whose lip Sir Walter Scott once rode a pony to win a bet. It's a fairly gentle 3-mile round trip.

Callander Crags

HIKING & WALKING | It's a 1½-mile walk through the woods up to the Callander Crags, with views of the Lowlands as far as the Pentland Hills behind Edinburgh. The walk begins at the west end of Callander's main street; access is signposted. ⊠ *Callander.*

Pass of Leny

HIKING & WALKING | Just north of Callander, the mountains squeeze both the road and rocky river into the narrow Pass of Leny. An abandoned railway—now a pleasant walking or biking path—also goes through the pass, past Ben Ledi and Loch Lubnaig. ⊠ *Brig o'Turk.*

The Trossachs

10 miles west of Callander.

The Trossachs has been a popular touring region since the late 18th century, at the dawn of the age of the romantic poets. Influenced by the writings of Sir Walter Scott, early visitors who strayed into the Highlands from the central belt of Scotland admired this as the first "wild" part of Scotland they encountered. Perhaps because the Trossachs represent the very essence of what the Highlands are supposed to be, the whole of this area, including Loch Lomond, is now protected as a national park. Here you can find birch and pine forests, vistas down lochs where the woods creep right to the water's edge, and, in the background, peaks that rise high enough to be called mountains, though they're not as high as those to the north and west.

GETTING HERE AND AROUND

To reach the Trossachs, take the A84 from Callander through the Pass of Leny, then on to Crianlarich on the A85; from here you can continue down the western shore of Loch Lomond or carry on toward Fort William. Alternately, turn onto the A821 outside Callander and travel past Loch Katrine through the Duke's Pass to Aberfoyle. Alternatively, the area is just an 1-hour drive from both Glasgow and Edinburgh.

Did You Know?

In 1810, Scottish writer Sir Walter Scott was inspired to write his famous poem after a visit to Loch Katrine.

Sights

Loch Achray

BODY OF WATER | Between Loch Katrine and Loch Venachar, this small and calm man-made lake is popular for fishing. Hikers climb nearby Ben A'an for the views. ✉ *Off A821, Aberfoyle ✛ 11 km (6.8 miles) west of Callander.*

★ Loch Katrine

BODY OF WATER | **FAMILY** | This loch, the setting for Sir Walter Scott's famous poem "The Lady of the Lake", once drew crowds of Victorian visitors in search of the magical mysterious places that Scott described. The thickly wooded and wild banks of the loch have remained an attraction for generations since. Since 1859, it's also been the source of Glasgow's freshwater. Cruises depart from the Trossachs Pier at the eastern end of the loch, where you can find shops, a restaurant, and bike hires. The iconic steamship *Sir Walter Scott* is currently undergoing repairs, but the *Rob Roy III* and the *Lady of the Lake* offer regular 45-minute cruises. You can also make the round-trip journey around the loch or get off at Stronachlachar at the western end of the loch to break for a coffee and admire the pier's beauty; you can return on foot or by bicycle via the lochside road. Reservations are required if you're taking a bike on the boat, so book ahead. Sailings are year-round, but are reduced in number between October and May. ✉ *Trossachs Pier, Aberfoyle ✛ Off A821* ☎ *01877/376315* ⊕ *www.lochkatrine.com* ⛴ *45-minute cruise £13; 2-hour round-trip £22; one-way to or from Stronachlachar £17.*

Loch Venachar

BODY OF WATER | The A821 runs west together with the first and gentlest of the Trossachs lochs, Loch Venachar. A sturdy gray-stone building, with a small dam at the Callander end, controls the water that feeds into the River Teith (and, hence, into the Forth). ✉ *A821, Brig o'Turk.*

★ Trossachs National Park

NATIONAL PARK | Scotland's first national park, designated in 2002, the Trossachs were first discovered and developed as an area for Victorian tourists and visitors. It was Queen Victoria's fascination with the novels of Sir Walter Scott that stimulated an interest in the brooding glens and lochs of the area, as well as the healing qualities of its waters. The park sits on a geological fault that divides the fertile lowlands from the highlands and its hills and mountains, 21 of which are more than 3,000 feet (and known as "Munros"). For hikers there are woodland valleys for pleasant and leisurely walks, long-distance footpaths like the West Highland and Rob Roy Ways for more determined walkers, and mountains like the demanding Cobbler and Ben Lomond, as well as shorter hikes on hills surrounding scenic lochs. For cyclists there are exciting routes, and for the nature lover there are many varieties of birds and animals in this protected habitat—capercaillie, golden eagles, red deer, and beavers among them. As the number of visitors has grown, lochside diners and charming country hotels have also multiplied. ⊕ *www.lochlomond-trossachs.org.*

Aberfoyle

11 miles south of Loch Katrine, in the Trossachs.

This small tourist-oriented town has a rather faded air, but the surrounding hills (some snowcapped) and the green slopes visible from the town are the reason so many people pause here before continuing up to Duke's Pass or on to Inversnaid on Loch Lomond. Access to nearby Queen Elizabeth Forest Park and the Lodge Forest Centre is another reason to visit.

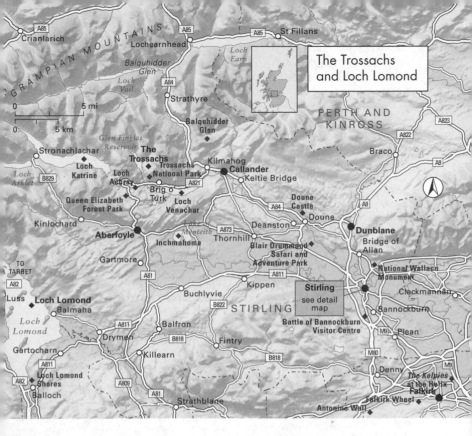

GETTING HERE AND AROUND

The main route out of Glasgow, the A81, takes you through Aberfoyle and on to Callander and Stirling. There are regular buses from Stirling and Glasgow to Aberfoyle.

ESSENTIALS

VISITOR INFORMATION VisitScotland Aberfoyle iCentre. ☒ *Trossachs Discovery Centre, Main Street, Aberfoyle* ☎ *01877/381221.*

 Sights

★ Inchmahome

ISLAND | The 13th-century ruined priory on the tiny island of Inchmahome, on the Lake of Menteith, is a lovely place for a picnic after you explore the building's chapter house and other remains. It was a place of refuge in 1547 for the young Mary, Queen of Scots. In season, a seven-minute ferry takes passengers to the island, now owned by the National Trust for Scotland. The ferry jetty is just past the Port of Menteith (a village) off the A81 shortly before Aberfoyle. ☒ *Off A81, Aberfoyle* ⊹ *Take the A81 to the B8034; it's 4 miles east of Aberfoyle* ☎ *01786/385294* ⊕ *www.historicenvironment.scot* ☒ *Ferry £9* ☉ *Closed Nov.–Mar.*

★ Queen Elizabeth Forest Park

FOREST | For exquisite nature, drive north from Aberfoyle on the A821 and turn right at signposts to Queen Elizabeth Forest Park. Along the way you'll be heading toward higher moorland blanketed with conifers. The conifers hem in the views of Ben Ledi and Ben Venue, which can be seen over the spiky green waves of trees as the road snakes around heathery knolls and hummocks. There's another viewing area, and a small parking lot, at the highest point of the road. Soon the road swoops off the Highland edge and leads downhill.

At the heart of the Queen Elizabeth Forest Park, the Lodge Forest Visitor Centre leads to four forest walks, marked by quirky sculptures, a family-friendly bicycle route, and the 7-mile 3 Lochs Forest Drive, open April to October. Or you can sit on the terrace of the Bluebell Cafe and scan the forests and hills of the Trossachs. The visitor center has a wildlife-watch room, where you can follow the activities of everything from ospreys to water voles. ✉ *Off A821, Aberfoyle* ✣ *1 mile north of Aberfoyle* ☎ *01877/382383* 🌐 *forestryandland.gov.scot/visit/forest-parks/queen-elizabeth-forest-park* 🎟 *Free, but parking costs £3 for the day.*

Scottish Wool Centre
STORE/MALL | FAMILY | Besides selling a vast range of woolen garments and knitwear, the Scottish Wool Centre has a small café and some activities. Three times a day from April to September it presents an interactive "gathering" during which dogs herd sheep and ducks in the large amphitheater, with a little help from the public. ✉ *Off Main Street, Aberfoyle* ☎ *01877/382850* 🌐 *www.ewm.co.uk* 🎟 *Free.*

🍴 Restaurants

Pier Café
$ | BRITISH | At the historic Stronachlachar Pier, this light-filled coffee shop has a satisfying lunch menu (burgers and sandwiches) and a deck with expansive views over Loch Katrine. Cakes, scones, and soups are made on the premises. **Known for:** loch views; on-site baking; good coffee. [$] *Average main: £10* ✉ *B829, Stronachlachar* ☎ *01877/386374* 🌐 *www.thepiercafe.com* 🕒 *No dinner Sun.–Thur.*

🛏 Hotels

★ Lake of Menteith Hotel
$$ | HOTEL | At this beautifully located hotel overlooking the Lake of Menteith, muted colors and simple but elegant rooms create a restful atmosphere, enhanced, perhaps, by the silent hills that surround the hotel and the tranquil lake. **Pros:** lakeside seating at restaurant; elegant, unpretentious bedrooms; beautiful setting. **Cons:** no elevator; not all rooms have lake views and those that do are more expensive; not well signposted. [$] *Rooms from: £150* ✉ *Off A81, Aberfoyle* ☎ *01877/385258* 🌐 *www.lake-hotel.com* 🛏 *17 rooms* 🍴 *Free Breakfast.*

Macdonald Forest Hills Hotel
$$$ | HOTEL | This is a traditional Scottish country resort hotel for families and those who simply want to take it easy, though it also offers numerous sporting and fitness activities. **Pros:** good children's programs; stunning views; 20-plus acres of grounds to explore. **Cons:** feels slightly anonymous; a great deal of tartan; slightly distant from other sights. [$] *Rooms from: £200* ✉ *B829, Kinlochard* ✣ *4 miles west of Aberfoyle* ☎ *08448/799057* 🌐 *www.macdonaldhotels.co.uk/foresthills* 🛏 *55 rooms* 🍴 *No Meals.*

🏃 Activities

GOLF

Aberfoyle Golf Club
GOLF | Queen Elizabeth Forest Park provides the backdrop for this hilly course. One of the area's many James Braid–designed parkland courses, it dates back to 1890. There are views of Ben Lomond and Stirling Castle from different points on the course, which is relatively short but varied and challenging even for quite experienced players, with several uphill shots and undulating ground. ✉ *Braeval, Aberfoyle* ✣ *Off A821* ☎ *01877/382493* 🌐 *www.aberfoylegolf.co.uk* 🎟 *£25 weekdays, £30 weekends* 🏌 *18 holes, 5158 yards, par 66.*

HIKING

★ Ben A'an

HIKING & WALKING | The climb up the steep, heathery Ben A'an requires a couple of hours and good lungs, but it's a worthwhile trip, providing you with some of the best Trossachs views, including those of Loch Achray and Loch Katrine. ⊠ *Off A821, Aberfoyle* ✛ *Access the beginning of the path near the Loch Achray parking lot.*

ZIP-LINING

Go Ape High Wire Forest Adventure
ZIP-LINING | **FAMILY** | Near the Lodge Forest Visitor Centre in the Queen Elizabeth Forest Park, this is an exhilarating experience for thrill seekers age 10 and over. After a short orientation course, you can travel 40 feet above the forest via zip lines and rope ladders on a sort of midair assault course. ⊠ *Queen Elizabeth Forest Park, A821, Aberfoyle* ✛ *1 mile north of Aberfoyle* ☎ *0845/094–9032* ⊕ *www. goape.com* ✉ *The Treetop Challenge (approx. 2.5 hours) £25; zip line trip £20* ⊘ *Closed weekdays in Nov., Feb., and Mar.*

Loch Lomond

14 miles west of Aberfoyle.

The waters of Scotland's largest loch, which also happens to be one of its most beautiful, create a perfect reflection of the surrounding hills. You can cruise among its small islands or take the low road towards to the west to the beginning of the Highlands.

GETTING HERE AND AROUND

To reach Loch Lomond from Aberfoyle, take the A81 toward Glasgow, then the A811 to Drymen and then the B837 as far as it will take you. From Glasgow take the A82 to the Balloch roundabout, and either go right through Balloch for Drymen and the eastern shore, or continue along the A82 as it hugs the west bank all the way to Crianlarich.

You can drive, cycle, or walk along the 32 miles of Loch Lomond along its western shores, and watch the changing face of the loch as you go, or look up toward the shifting slopes of Ben Lomond.

ESSENTIALS

VISITOR INFORMATION Loch Lomond and the Trossachs National Park Headquarters. ⊠ *Carrochan Road, Balloch* ☎ *01389/722600* ⊕ *www.lochlomond-trossachs.org.*

◉ Sights

★ Loch Lomond

BODY OF WATER | Known for its "bonnie, bonnie banks," Loch Lomond is Scotland's most well-known loch and its largest in terms of surface area. Its waters reflect the crags that surround it.

On the western side of the loch, the A82 follows the shore for 24 miles, continuing a farther 7 miles to Crianlarich, passing picturesque Luss, which has a pier where you can hop aboard boats cruising along the loch, and Tarbert, the starting point for the *Maid of the Loch.* On the eastern side of the loch, take the A81 to Drymen, and from there the B837 signposted toward Balmaha, where you can hire a boat or take the ferry to the island of Inchcailloch. Once you're there, a short walk takes you to the top of the hill and a spectacular view of the loch. Equally spectacular, but not as wet, is the view from Conic Hill behind Balmaha, a short but exhilarating climb. The hill marks the fault that divides the Lowlands and Highlands. If you continue along the B837 beyond Rowardennan to where it ends at a car park, you can join the walkers at the beginning of the path up Ben Lomond. Don't underestimate this innocent-looking hill; go equipped for sudden changes in the weather. Hikers can also try part of the 96-mile West Highland Way (⊕ *www.west-highland-way.co.uk*) that runs along the shore of Loch Lomond on its way north.

Loch Lomond Shores

STORE/MALL | This lakeside shopping complex contains restaurants, pubs, and a visitor center. Some cruises set sail from here and there are occasional events, but its most attractive quality is the beautiful view of Loch Lomond. ✉ *Ben Lomond Way, Balloch* ☎ *01389/751031* 🌐 *www.lochlomondshores.com.*

🍴 Restaurants

★ Coach House Coffee Shop

$ | **BRITISH** | With its over-the-top Scottishness, this lively restaurant and café serving Scottish classics fits perfectly into its surroundings. Long wooden tables, a large chimney with an open fire in the winter months, and a cabinet full of mouthwatering cakes baked by the owner create a cheerful atmosphere. **Known for:** very Scottish atmosphere; collection of unique teapots for sale; classic Scottish stovies. [$] *Average main: £12* ✉ *Church Road, Luss* ✣ *Off A82* ☎ *01436/860341* ⏲ *No dinner.*

Drovers Inn

$ | **BRITISH** | Knowing its clientele, this quirky, noisy inn serves huge, hearty portions that are what you need after a day's walking on the nearby West Highland Way. Scottish staples like sausage and mash, minced beef, and haggis jostle for a place beside occasionally more adventurous dishes. **Known for:** good bar with a range of whiskies; big portions; old-school Scottish decor like mounted animals. [$] *Average main: £12* ✉ *On A82 toward Crianlarich, Balloch* ✣ *North of Ardlui, just north of Loch Lomond* ☎ *01301/704234* 🌐 *www.thedroversinn.co.uk.*

🛏 Hotels

Balloch House

$ | **HOTEL** | Cute, cozy, and very Scottish, this small hotel offers simple but clean rooms along with tasty breakfasts and good, hearty pub meals like fish-and-chips and local smoked salmon for reasonable prices. **Pros:** near shopping; beautiful building; peat fires. **Cons:** pub is very busy; not all rooms have views; noisy pinball machine next to bar. [$] *Rooms from: £100* ✉ *Balloch Road, Balloch* ☎ *01389/752579* 🌐 *www.vintage-inn.co.uk* 🛏 *12 rooms* 🍽 *Free Breakfast.*

The Lodge on Loch Lomond

$$ | **HOTEL** | Known for its views, this hotel overlooking Loch Lomond sits beside the picturesque village of Luss. **Pros:** excellent restaurant with full loch views; wonderful setting; big and comfortable rooms. **Cons:** beach area is small and gets crowded in summer; can be busy with weddings and conferences; not all rooms overlook the loch. [$] *Rooms from: £179* ✉ *Luss, Alexandria* ☎ *01436/860201* 🌐 *www.loch-lomond.co.uk* 🛏 *48 rooms* 🍽 *Free Breakfast.*

🏃 Activities

BOATING

Cruise Loch Lomond

BOATING | FAMILY | You can take scenic boat tours of Loch Lomond year-round with this company. What you see on your journey depends on where you embark. From April to October boats depart from various ports around the loch, including Tarbet, Luss, Balmaha, and Inversnaid, while from November to March the boats operate on demand. During the warmer months there is also a Two-Loch Tour taking in Loch Lomond and Loch Katrine. ✉ *Tarbet* ✣ *Off A82* ☎ *01301/702356* 🌐 *www.cruiselochlomond.co.uk* 🎟 *From £15.*

Macfarlane and Son

BOATING | Based in the boathouse in Balmaha on the eastern shore of Loch Lomond, this longtime favorite rents boats with outboard motors for £20 per hour or £50 per day. Rowboats rent for £10 per hour or £30 per day. From Balmaha, it is a short trip to the lovely island of Incailloch. Macfarlane's also runs a ferry to the island for £5 per person. ✉ *Balmaha Boatyard, B837, Balmaha* ✣ *From*

Drymen take the B837 ☎ 01360/870214 ⊕ www.balmahaboatyard.co.uk.

Sweeney's Cruises

BOAT TOURS | This operator runs trips and tours on Loch Lomond from Balloch, Luss, and Tarbert. ✉ *Riverside, Balloch Road, Balloch* ☎ *01389/752376* ⊕ *www.sweeneyscruiseco.com* ⌖ *From £10.50.*

Perth

36 miles northeast of Stirling.

For many years Perth was Scotland's capital, and central to its history. One king (James I) was killed here, and the Protestant reformer John Knox preached in St. John's Kirk, where his rhetoric moved crowds to burn down several local monasteries and helped launch the Reformation. Perth's local whisky trade and the productive agriculture that surrounds the town have sustained it through the centuries. Its grand buildings, especially on the banks of the River Tay, testify to its continued wealth. The open parkland within the city (the Inches) gives the place a restful air, and shops range from small crafts boutiques to department stores. Impressive Scone Palace is nearby.

GETTING HERE AND AROUND

Perth is served by the main railway line to Inverness, and regular and frequent buses run here from Glasgow, Edinburgh, and Stirling. The central artery, the A9, passes through the city en route to Pitlochry and Inverness, while a network of roads opens the way to the glens and hills around Glen Lyon, or the road to Loch Lomond (the A85) via Crianlarich. The train station and bus terminal are both about a 10-minute walk from the city center.

ESSENTIALS

VISITOR INFORMATION VisitScotland Perth iCentre. ✉ *45 High St., Perth* ☎ *01738/450600* ⊕ *www.visitscotland.com/info/services/perth-icentre-p234431.*

⊙ Sights

Elcho Castle

CASTLE/PALACE | Built around 1560 on the River Tay, the castle marks a transition period when these structures began to be built as grand houses rather than fortresses, and it's easy to see that Elcho was built for both comfort and defense. The well-preserved but uncluttered rooms let you imagine how life might have been here in the 17th century. The staircases still give access to all floors, and a flashlight is provided for the darker corners. From the battlements of the castle you can see the river stretching east and west. ✉ *Off A912, Perth ⊹ Close to Rhynd* ☎ *01738/639998* ⊕ *www.historicenvironment.scot/visit-a-place/places/elcho-castle* ⌖ *£6* ⊗ *Closed Oct.–Mar.*

Fergusson Gallery

ART MUSEUM | Originally a waterworks, this gallery with a magnificent dome and rotunda shelters a collection of 6,000 works—paintings, drawings, and prints—by the Scottish artist J. D. Fergusson (1874–1961) and his wife, Margaret Morris, an artist in her own right and a pioneer of modern dance. Fergusson was the longest-lived member of the group called the Scottish Colourists, who took their inspiration from the French impressionist painters in their use of color and light. ✉ *Marshall Place, Perth* ☎ *01738/783425* ⊕ *www.culturepk.org.uk* ⌖ *Free* ⊗ *Closed Tues. and Wed. and Nov.–Mar.*

Perth Art Gallery and Museum

ART MUSEUM | This museum has a wide-ranging collection, including exhibits on natural history, local history, archaeology, and art, as well as an important glass collection. It also includes work by the great painter of animals Sir Edwin Landseer and some botanical studies of fungi by Beatrix Potter. ✉ *78 George St., Perth* ☎ *01738/632488* ⊕ *www.culturepk.org.uk* ⌖ *Free* ⊗ *Closed Tues. and Wed.*

Regimental Museum of the Black Watch

HISTORY MUSEUM | Some will tell you the Black Watch was a Scottish regiment whose name is a reference to the color of its tartan. An equally plausible explanation, however, is that the regiment was established to keep an undercover watch on rebellious Jacobites. The Gaelic word for black is *dubh,* meaning, in this case, "hidden" or "covert." A wide range of uniforms, weaponry, and marching banners are displayed in this museum in Balhousie Castle, and there's a very good café and shop. ⊠ *Balhousie Castle, Hay Street, Perth* ☎ *01738/638152* ⊕ *www. theblackwatch.co.uk* ⊠ *£9, guided tour (book ahead) £16.*

★ Scone Palace

CASTLE/PALACE | FAMILY | The current residence of the Earl of Mansfield, Scone Palace (pronounced *skoon*) is much more cheerful than the city's other castles. Although it incorporates various earlier works, the palace today has mainly a 19th-century theme, with mock castellations that were fashionable at the time. There's plenty to see if you're interested in the acquisitions of an aristocratic Scottish family: magnificent porcelain, some sumptuous furniture, a fine collection of ivory, clocks, and 16th-century needlework. Each room has a guide who will happily talk you through its contents and their associations. In one bedroom hangs a portrait of Dido Elizabeth Belle, a young Black woman who was born into slavery in the British West Indies, then taken to England by her white British father and raised by the Mansfield family; while her father only officially granted her freedom upon his death, she was raised as a free gentlewoman and became a well-known society beauty in the 1760s. (The 2013 film *Belle* is based on her life). A coffee shop, restaurant, gift shop, and play area are on-site. The palace has its own mausoleum nearby, on the site of a long-gone abbey on Moot Hill, the ancient coronation place of the Scottish kings. To be crowned, they sat on the Stone of Scone, which was seized in 1296 by Edward I of England, Scotland's greatest enemy, and placed in the coronation chair at Westminster Abbey, in London. The stone was returned to Scotland in November 1996 and is now on view in Edinburgh Castle. There is a maze and a children's playground on the grounds too. You can only see the palace on a timed guided tour, which you should book in advance. ✉ *Braemar Road, Perth* ✣ *2 miles north of Perth* ☎ *01738/552300* 🌐 *www.scone-palace.co.uk* 🎫 *Guided tours of palace £20, gardens only £10* 🕒 *House closed Nov.–Mar. Grounds closed Mon.–Thurs. Nov.–Mar.*

St. John's Kirk

RELIGIOUS BUILDING | In this impressive cruciform-plan church dating from the 12th century, religious reformer John Knox preached a fiery sermon in May 1559 against idolatry. An enraged crowd stripped the church and poured into the street to attack the wealthy religious institutions; this helped start the Reformation in Scotland. The interior was divided into three parts at the Reformation, but in the 1920s Sir Robert Lorimer restored it to something closer to its medieval state. ✉ *St. John Street, Perth* ☎ *01738/633192* 🌐 *www.st-johns-kirk.co.uk* 🎫 *Free* 🕒 *Closed Oct.–Apr. except for services.*

🍴 Restaurants

Breizh

$$ | FRENCH | Pronounced "*bresh*", this spot on Perth's High Street is the perfect place to experience Breton cuisine, namely dishes that originated on the Brittany coast of France. The decor is muted to focus attention on menu, which includes *galettes* (savory buckwheat crepes), pizzas, mussels, and a mouth-watering steak selection. **Known for:** classic French dishes like bouillabaisse; build-your-own galettes; wood-fired pizzas. [$] *Average main: £18* ✉ *28-30 High St., Perth* ☎ *01738/444427* 🌐 *www.breizhrestaurant.com.*

Deans Restaurant

$$ | BRITISH | The varied clientele here reflects the broad appeal of noted chef Willie Deans's imaginative and satisfying cuisine, including a dinner menu with starters such as tempura prawns, truffled celeriac, and cheese souffle, and delicious Orkney steak and butternut squash, spinach, and feta pastilla among the main courses. The atmosphere is airy and pleasant, merging warm colors and light woods with comfortable sofas perfect for enjoying one of the appealing cocktails. **Known for:** good cocktail menu; delicious sea bream; affordable pre-theater menu. [$] *Average main: £18* ✉ *77–79 Kinnoull St., Perth* ☎ *01738/643377* 🌐 *www.letseatperth.co.uk.*

★ Effie's of Perth

$ | BRITISH | For over 20 years, restaurant namesake Effie baked her glorious cakes and scones here and her family continues the tradition, using her same recipes. The charming, traditional tearoom is hugely popular, with paintings and photographs emphasizing its long history, but what keeps the customers coming back is the superb baking, rich homemade soups, and creative breakfast menu. **Known for:** superior carrot cake; great breakfasts; family-friendly afternoon tea. [$] *Average main: £10* ✉ *202 High St., Perth* ☎ *010173838/634770* 🌐 *www.effiesofperth.co.uk* 🕒 *No dinner.*

★ 63 Tay Street

$$$ | BRITISH | Dine looking out onto the River Tay in this elegant but relaxed restaurant with tall windows, gray-and-white walls, and wooden tables. Chef Graeme Pallister has earned a reputation for imaginative fare with an emphasis on seasonal and local produce in adventurous combinations. **Known for:** good wine list; imaginative use of seasonal ingredients; excellent tasting menu. $ *Average main: £24* ✉ *63 Tay St., Perth* ☎ *01738/441451* ⊕ *www.63taystreet.com.*

🛏 Hotels

Leonardo Boutique Hotel Huntingtower Perth

$$ | **HOTEL** | Less than 5 miles from Perth, this tranquil, traditional country hotel with an air of understated elegance has a spacious garden and trees that make it feel more rural than it really is. **Pros:** dining room overlooks gardens; restful setting; amply sized rooms. **Cons:** no air-conditioning; perhaps a slight excess of tartan; no elevator. $ *Rooms from: £161* ✉ *Crieff Road, Perth* ☎ *01738/583771* ⊕ *www.leonardo-boutique-hotel-huntingtower-perth* ⇄ *34 rooms* ⦿ *Free Breakfast.*

Sunbank House Hotel

$ | **B&B/INN** | This handsome early-Victorian gray-stone mansion near Perth's Branklyn Gardens overlooks the River Tay and the city of Perth. **Pros:** delicious local cuisine; reasonably priced; friendly staff. **Cons:** 15 minutes' walk to town center; some traffic noise from the main road; some rooms are very small. $ *Rooms from: £85* ✉ *50 Dundee Rd., Perth* ☎ *01738/624882* ⊕ *www.sunbankhouse.com* ⇄ *9 rooms* ⦿ *Free Breakfast.*

🎭 Performing Arts

Perth Concert Hall

CONCERTS | The city's main concert venue hosts musical performances of all types. ✉ *Mill Street, Perth* ☎ *01738/621031* ⊕ *www.horsecross.co.uk.*

Perth Theatre

THEATER | Receiving a major face-lift of its Edwardian building in 2017, this respected repertory theater presents a varied theatrical program as well as musical events. ✉ *185 High St., Perth* ☎ *01738/621031* ⊕ *www.horsecross.co.uk.*

🛍 Shopping

Cairncross of Perth

JEWELRY & WATCHES | The Romans coveted freshwater pearls from the River Tay. If you do, too, then head to Cairncross of Perth, where you can admire a display of some of the more unusual shapes and colors. Some of the delicate settings take their theme from Scottish flowers. ✉ *18 St. John's St., Perth* ☎ *01738/624367* ⊕ *www.cairncrossofperth.co.uk.*

Whispers of the Past

ANTIQUES & COLLECTIBLES | This lovely shop has a collection of jewelry, china, and other gift items, some vintage and some new. ✉ *15 George St., Perth* ☎ *01738/635472* ⊕ *whispers-of-the-past.weebly.com.*

Dunkeld

14 miles north of Perth.

The historic town of Dunkeld remains intact and beautifully preserved with its rows of white houses around the town square. The original village was destroyed in 1689 in a ferocious battle during the Jacobite Rebellion and was eventually rebuilt by the Atholl family. Today it survives as part of the National Trust for Scotland's Little Houses Project, which helps maintain the houses. The town is overlooked by the grand but semiruined 12th-century cathedral (still used for services). Atholl Street, leading down to the River Tay, has several crafts shops and a hotel.

The bridge across the River Tay takes you to Birnam Wood, where Shakespeare's Macbeth met the three witches who issued the prophecy about his death. Witty wooden notices lead you to the right tree, a gnarled hollow oak.

GETTING HERE AND AROUND

Dunkeld is on the A9 between Perth and Pitlochry. The town is also on the main train line to Inverness.

Sights

Beatrix Potter Exhibition and Garden

GARDEN | FAMILY | The interactive exhibition, specifically designed for children, celebrates the life and work of this much-beloved children's writer who, for many years, spent her family holidays in the area. You're free to walk around the enchanting garden where you can peep into the homes of Peter Rabbit and Mrs. Tiggy-Winkle, her best-known characters. The visitors center has a well-stocked shop and a small café serving breakfast, lunch, and coffee and cake. The garden is a mile south of Dunkeld, in Birnam. ✉ *Birnam Arts Centre, Station Road, Birnam* ☎ *01350/727674* 🌐 *www.birnamarts.com* 🎫 *£3 exhibition, garden free.*

Birnam Wood

NATURE SIGHT | In Shakespeare's *Macbeth*, the future king meets three witches who prophesy his downfall "when Birnam Wood comes to Dunsinane." They were right. The trees of the once dense wood camouflaged the besieging armies approaching Macbeth's castle at Dunsinane. The Birnam Oak (now sustained by crutches) and the Birnam Sycamore are all that remain of the once great wood, though perhaps not as Macbeth knew it in the 11th century. ✉ *The Birnam Oak, Birnam, Dunkeld* ✣ *Signposted opposite the Birnam Arts Centre* 🎫 *Free.*

Hermitage

FOREST | On the outskirts of Dunkeld, the Hermitage is a 1½-mile woodland walk that follows the River Braan. In the 18th century, the dukes of Atholl constructed two follies (fantasy buildings) here, **Ossian's Cave** and the awesomely decorated **Ossian's Hall,** above a spectacular—and noisy—waterfall. (Ossian was a fictional Celtic poet invented by James MacPherson in the 18th century for an era fascinated by the "primitive" past.) You'll also be in the presence of Britain's tallest tree, a Douglas fir rising to 214 feet. ✉ *Hermitage Car Park, Off A9, Dunkeld* ✣ *2 miles west of Dunkeld* 🌐 *www.nts.org.uk* 🎫 *Free, parking lot £3.*

Loch of the Lowes

NATURE SIGHT | FAMILY | From the lochside hides at this Scottish Wildlife Trust reserve near Dunkeld, you can observe the area's rich birdlife through a powerful telescope. The main attractions are always the ospreys, one of Scotland's conservation success stories, which can be observed between April and August. But there is much to see throughout the year, like the great crested grebe at feeding stations. The enthusiastic staff will willingly describe what is happening around the center. ✉ *Off A923, Dunkeld* ✣ *About 2 miles northeast of Dunkeld off the A9* ☎ *01350/727337* 🌐 *scottishwildlifetrust.org.uk* 🎫 *£4.90* ⏲ *Closed Tues., Wed., and Nov.–Feb.*

Restaurants

The Taybank

$$$ | BRITISH | This lovely spot overlooking the River Tay continues a tradition as a musical meeting place once owned by Scottish singer and composer Dougie MacLean. The restaurant places emphasis on Scottish fare, but there are burgers and pizza in the bar as well as an extremely popular beer garden right by the river. **Known for:** bustling beer garden; traditional Scottish fare; frequent live music. [$] *Average main: £22* ✉ *Tay Terrace, Dunkeld* ☎ *01350/677123* 🌐 *www.thetaybank.co.uk.*

Shopping

Jeremy Law of Scotland

LEATHER GOODS | At this family-owned business you can purchase deerskin shoes and moccasins, as well as leather items including jackets, gloves, shoes, and wallets. ⊠ *City Hall, Atholl Street, Dunkeld* ☎ *0800/146780* ⊕ *www.moccasin.co.uk.*

Pitlochry

15 miles north of Dunkeld.

In the late 19th century Pitlochry was an elegant Victorian spa town, famous for its mild microclimate and beautiful setting. Today it is a busy tourist town, with wall-to-wall gift shops, cafés, B&Bs, large hotels, and a huge golf course. The town itself is oddly nondescript, but it's a convenient base from which to explore the surrounding hills and valleys.

GETTING HERE AND AROUND

The main route through central Scotland, the A9, passes through Pitlochry, as does the main railway line from Glasgow/Edinburgh to Inverness. From here the B8019 connects to the B846 west to Rannoch Moor or south to Aberfeldy.

ESSENTIALS

VISITOR INFORMATION VisitScotland Pitlochry iCentre. ⊠ *22 Atholl Rd., Pitlochry* ☎ *01796/472215* ⊕ *www. visitscotland.com/info/services/ pitlochry-icentre-p234421.*

◉ Sights

★ Loch Rannoch

BODY OF WATER | With its shoreline of birch trees framed by dark pines, Loch Rannoch is the quintessential Highland loch, stretching more than 9 miles from west to east. Fans of Robert Louis Stevenson (1850–94), especially of *Kidnapped* (1886), will not want to miss the last, lonely section of road. Stevenson describes the setting: "The mist rose and died away, and showed us that country lying as waste as the sea, only the moorfowl and the peewees crying upon it, and far over to the east a herd of deer, moving like dots." ⊠ *B846, Pitlochry* ✛ *20 miles west of Pitlochry.*

Pass of Killiecrankie Visitor Centre

VISITOR CENTER | Set among the oak woods and above a rocky river just north of Pilochry, the Pass of Killiecrankie was the site of a famous battle won by the Jacobites in 1689. The battle was notable for the death of the central Jacobite leader, John Graham of Claverhouse (1649–89), also known as Bonnie Dundee, who was hit by a stray bullet. One English soldier is reputed to have escaped the Jacobite troops by jumping into the river at a point still known as "Soldier's Leap." After Dundee's death the rebellion petered out. The National Trust for Scotland's visitor center at Killiecrankie explains the significance of this battle, which was the first attempt to restore the Stewart monarchy. ⊠ *B8079, Pitlochry* ✛ *3 miles north of Pitlochry* ☎ *01796/473233* ⊕ *www.nts.org.uk* 🎟 *Free* ⏱ *Closed Nov.–Apr.*

🍴 Restaurants

Fern Cottage Restaurant

$$ | BRITISH | The stone-built cottage set in pleasant surroundings aims to merge Scottish and Mediterranean cuisine, continuing the work of its previous Turkish chef-owner. The restaurant has now passed to new owners, but the signature kebabs are still on the menu, as are the tabbulleh salad and halloumi. **Known for:** traditional Middle Eastern salads; excellent kebabs; halloumi burger. 💲 *Average main: £15* ⊠ *Ferry Road, Pitlochry* ☎ *01796/473840* ⊕ *www.ferncottagepitlochry.co.uk.*

Moulin Inn and Hotel

$$ | BRITISH | The small and often crowded bar in the Moulin is the best place to try the ales produced in Scotland's first microbrewery, which you can visit in the afternoon after enjoying the good, hearty pub food to be had here. The restaurant features standard Scottish fare in generous quantities, including venison, scallops, and mussels. **Known for:** choice of lively or quiet dining; classic Scottish cuisine; ales made on-site. $ *Average main: £18* ✉ *11–30 Kirkmichael Rd., Pitlochry* ✣ *Between Pitlochry and Edradour* ☎ *01796/472196* 🌐 *www.moulinhotel.co.uk.*

Hotels

Claymore Guest House

$ | **B&B/INN** | One of the large Victorian houses set back from the main road, this B&B is a quiet refuge with spacious, updated rooms with large windows. **Pros:** welcoming and attentive proprietors; large, well-lit rooms with comfortable seating areas; dog-friendly. **Cons:** no elevator; slightly old-fashioned feel; no children allowed. $ *Rooms from: £115* ✉ *162 Atholl Rd., Pitlochry* ☎ *01796/472888* 🌐 *www.claymorehotel.com* 🛏 *10 rooms* 🍴 *Free Breakfast.*

★ **Green Park Hotel**

$$ | **HOTEL** | Set among woods and on the shores of Loch Faskally, Green Park is a genuinely luxurious country-house hotel. **Pros:** country-house comfort; great location; very attentive staff. **Cons:** not as suitable for younger visitors; very popular, thus fills up far in advance; a slightly conservative feel. $ *Rooms from: £130* ✉ *Clunie Bridge Road, Pitlochry* ✣ *5 mins north of Pitlochry center on A924* ☎ *01796/473248* 🌐 *www.thegreenpark.co.uk* 🛏 *51 rooms* 🍴 *All-Inclusive.*

McKays Hotel

$ | **B&B/INN** | A lively hotel and pub in the heart of Pitlochry, you'll find spacious and elegant rooms here. **Pros:** friendly atmosphere; pleasant and bright rooms; central location. **Cons:** live music on weekends can mean noise; no on-site parking; no elevator. $ *Rooms from: £109* ✉ *138 Atholl Rd., Pitlochry* ☎ *0808/506–5543* 🌐 *www.mckayshotel.co.uk* 🛏 *26 rooms* 🍴 *Free Breakfast.*

The Old Mill Inn

$$ | **B&B/INN** | With an old mill wheel the only reminder of its past, the Old Mill Inn features unpretentious rooms with splashes of color and Edwardian-style fabrics. **Pros:** central location; good restaurant and lively beer garden; tasteful decor. **Cons:** not all rooms have nice views; beer garden gets busy; can be noisy in summer months. $ *Rooms from: £179* ✉ *Mill Lane, Pitlochry* ☎ *01796/474020* 🌐 *www.theoldmill-pitlochry.co.uk* 🛏 *13 rooms* 🍴 *Free Breakfast.*

Saorsa 1875 Vegan Hotel

$$ | **HOTEL** | As the name suggests, there are no animal products used anywhere in this hotel, located in a large Victorian house overlooking the town with views across the Tummel Valley; that means no leather or even feathers in the pillows. **Pros:** tranquil retreat; sustainable and ethical ethos; innovative cuisine. **Cons:** no elevator; larger rooms are not cheap; no televisions in rooms. $ *Rooms from: £170* ✉ *2 East Moulin Rd., Pitlochry* ☎ *01796/475217* 🌐 *saorsahotel.com* 🛏 *11 rooms* 🍴 *Free Breakfast.*

Performing Arts

Pitlochry Festival Theatre

THEATER | This theater regularly hosts exciting and innovative programs, including Sunday concerts and art exhibitions. It has a café and restaurant overlooking the River Tummel. ✉ *Port Na Craig, Pitlochry* ☎ *01796/484626* 🌐 *pitlochryfestivaltheatre.com.*

Activities

BUNGEE JUMPING

Highland Fling Bungee Jumping

ZIP LINING | Based at the National Trust's Visitor Centre at Killiecrankie, this addition to the local adventure-sports scene has proved very popular for some. The Killiecrankie Gorge was once famous for the historic Soldier's Leap, where an English soldier escaped Jacobite forces by reputedly leaping 18 feet across the river Garry. The gorge now offers a different kind of jump—140 feet from the nearby Garry Bridge attached to an elastic rope, or bungee. Also on offer are organized rafting and canyoning trips. The nearby Zip Park offers equally challenging activities for the adventurous. All activities must be booked in advance, and there are age and weight limits. ⊠ *Killiecrankie Visitor Centre, Off A94* ✛ *4 miles north of Pitlochry* ☎ *0345/366–5844* ⊕ *www.bungeejumpscotland.co.uk* ✎ *£79 per jump; zip lines £35 (for 1.5 hours)* ☞ *Closed Mon. and Tues. Nov.–Mar.*

GOLF

Blairgowrie Golf Club

GOLF | Well known to area golfers looking for a challenge, the Blairgowrie Golf Club's Rosemount Course is laid out on rolling land in the pine, birch, and fir woods, which bring a wild air to the scene. There are, however, wide fairways and at least some large greens. If Rosemount is hosting a tournament, you can play on Lansdowne, another 18-hole course, or Wee, a 9-hole course. ⊠ *Golf Course Road, Blairgowrie* ☎ *01250/872622* ⊕ *www.theblairgowriegolfclub.co.uk* ✎ *Rosemount/Lansdowne, May–Sept. £95, Apr. and Oct. £70, Nov.–Mar. £25; Wee, May–Sept. £20, Apr. and Oct. £17.50, Nov.–Mar. £7.50* 🏌 *Rosemount: 18 holes, 6630 yards, par 72; Lansdowne: 18 holes, 6886 yards, par 72; Wee: 9 holes, 2327 yards, par 32.*

Pitlochry Golf Course

GOLF | A decent degree of stamina is needed for the first three holes at Pitlochry, where steep climbs are involved. The reward is magnificent Highland scenery. Despite its relatively short length, this beautiful course has more than its fair share of surprises. The course offers golf with food packages. ⊠ *Golf Course Road, Pitlochry* ☎ *01796/472792* ⊕ *www.pitlochrygolf.co.uk* ✎ *Apr. and Oct. £45; May–Sept. £55; Nov.–Mar. £25* 🏌 *18 holes, 5681 yards, par 69.*

Blair Atholl

10 miles north of Pitlochry.

Located where the Tilt and Garry rivers flow together, this small town sits in the middle of the Grampian Mountains and is home to Blair Castle, one of the grandest of Scotland's grand houses.

GETTING HERE AND AROUND

Popular Blair Castle is just off the A9 Pitlochry-to-Inverness road, beyond the village of Blair Atholl. The village has a railway station that is on the main Inverness line.

◉ Sights

★ Blair Castle

CASTLE/PALACE | Its setting among woodlands and gardens, together with its war-torn past, make Blair Castle one of Scotland's most highly rated sights. The turreted white castle was home to successive dukes of Atholl and their families, the Murrays, one of the most powerful in the land. During the Jacobite Rebellion of 1745, the loyalties of the Atholls were divided—a preserved piece of floor shows the marks of red-hot shot fired when the castle was under siege. In the end the supporters of the English king held off the rebels and were well rewarded for it. The dukes were allowed to retain a private army, the Atholl Highlanders. The castle entrance hall presents some of the dukes' collections of weapons, while a rich collection of furniture, china, and paintings occupies the family rooms. The grounds contain a 9-acre walled garden, an 18th-century folly, and a play area for children. ⊠ *Off B8079, Blair Atholl* ☎ *01796/481207* ⊕ *www.blair-castle.co.uk* ✎ *Castle and gardens £15, grounds only £7.70* ⊙ *Closed Mon., Tues., and Nov.–Mar.*

House of Bruar

STORE/MALL | An upscale shopping complex, the House of Bruar has a heavy emphasis on traditional tweeds and cashmeres. A large supermarket sells local produce and food, and a restaurant serves breakfast and lunch. When you're done shopping, take a walk up the path that crosses Bruar Falls, behind the complex. The complex is also a popular stop for coach tours. ⊠ *Off A9, Blair Atholl* ⊹ *3 miles west of Blair Castle* ☏ *01796/483236* ⊕ *www.houseofbruar.com.*

Aberfeldy

15 miles southwest of Pitlochry, 25 miles southwest of Blair Castle.

The most dramatic thing about Aberfeldy is the high humpbacked bridge into the town, built by William Adam in 1733 and commissioned by General Wade, who marched through Scotland suppressing local resistance after the Jacobite Rebellion. The town itself is rather sleepy, but this is a popular base for exploring the region. There's also a whisky distillery and plenty of local golf courses.

GETTING HERE AND AROUND
To get here from Pitlochry, take the A9 and then the A827. You can also reach Aberfeldy from Dunkeld via the A9 and the A827. A longer but very pretty route is the A85 from Crieff, then through Killin on the A827. Aberfeldy is served by regular buses from Perth and Pitlochry.

ESSENTIALS
VISITOR INFORMATION Aberfeldy Tourist Information Centre. ⊠ *The Square, Aberfeldy* ☏ *01887/820276* ⊕ *www.visitscotland.com/aberfedy.*

Sights

Castle Menzies
CASTLE/PALACE | A 16th-century fortified tower house, Castle Menzies contains the **Clan Menzies Museum,** which displays many relics of the clan's history. The rooms have been carefully restored, including the bedroom where Bonnie Prince Charlie once took refuge. The

castle stands west of Aberfeldy, on the opposite bank of the River Tay. A walled garden is nearby. ∎**TIP**➔ **The castle has a tearoom that is open on some Saturdays and Sundays.** ⊠ *Aberfeldy Road, Weem* ⊹ *Off the B846* ☏ *01887/820982* ⊕ *www.castlemenzies.org* ⊠ *£8* ⊙ *Closed Nov.–Mar.*

Dewar's Aberfeldy Distillery
DISTILLERY | This established distillery offers tours that demonstrate how Aberfeldy single-malt whisky is made (with a tasting at the end, of course); audio guides and interactive screens add to the appeal. There's also a worthwhile Heritage Center and a pleasant restaurant. The basic tours are £9, but there are more expensive tours for whisky experts, including cask tastings. Dewar's also makes blended whiskies. ⊠ *A827, Aberfeldy* ☏ *01887/822010* ⊕ *www.dewars.com* ⊠ *Basic tour £9; cask tasting tour £16.50* ⊙ *Closed Sun. Nov.–Mar.*

Glen Lyon
NATURE SIGHT | One of central Scotland's most attractive glens, 34-mile-long Glen Lyon is also one of its longest. It has a rushing river, thick forests, and the typical big house hidden on private grounds. There's a dam at the head of the loch, a reminder that little of Scotland's scenic beauty is unadulterated. The winding road lends itself to an unrushed, leisurely drive, past the visitor center at the access to Ben Lawers, a popular climb. ⊠ *A827, Aberfeldy* ⊹ *15 miles west of Aberfeldy* ⊠ *Free.*

★ Scottish Crannog Centre
HISTORIC SIGHT | **FAMILY** | Here's your chance to travel back 2,500 years to a time when this region's inhabitants lived in circular homesteads known as crannogs. Standing on stilts in the middle of lochs, these dwellings were approachable only by narrow bridges that could be easily defended from intruders. This center reveals the strength of these surprisingly comfortable communal homes that were built entirely of wood, right down to the nails. Visits are by guided

tour, beginning with an interesting exhibit on construction methods, followed by some fun with Neolithic lathes and tips on lighting a fire without matches. You can also reserve ahead to paddle a dugout canoe onto beautiful Loch Tay. It has limited hours of operation in November, February, and March, but there are special events throughout the year. ✉ Off A827, Aberfeldy ✛ 6 miles west of Aberfeldy ☎ 01887/830583 ⊕ www.crannog. co.uk 🎟 £5 ⊘ Closed Dec. and Jan.

🍴 Restaurants

Habitat Cafe

$ | CAFÉ | This café with handmade wooden tables and windows overlooking the main town square offers excellent coffee and tea, sandwiches and burgers, platters, and soup in the central square of Aberfeldy. Habitat takes great pride in its coffee making and has awards to prove it; it works closely with sustainable farmers. **Known for:** lunch platters; local ingredients; excellent coffee. $ Average main: £10 ✉ The Square, Aberfeldy ☎ 01877/822944 ⊕ www.habitatcafe. co.uk ⊘ No dinner.

🛍 Shopping

John A. Lacey

CRAFTS | Carver John Lacey has worked at this house on the road between Killin and Aberfeldy since 1984. Its front room is a treasure trove of horn carving, from a full-masted galleon to knives in their sheaths. He also has deerskins for sale. Lacey says the egg spoons are the most popular items. ✉ A827, Aberfeldy ✛ 15 miles west of Aberfeldy on north side of Loch Tay ☎ 01567/820561 ⊕ www. horncarver.co.uk.

The Watermill

BOOKS | At this converted mill you can visit an excellent independent bookshop with a large children's section. The mill also has a gallery with frequently changing exhibitions, a home-goods store

(called Homer), and a café. ✉ Mill Street, Aberfeldy ☎ 01887/822896 ⊕ www. aberfeldywatermill.com.

🏃 Activities

Highland Safaris

WILDLIFE-WATCHING | FAMILY | This center just outside Aberfeldy offers a full range of outdoor activities, from encounters with the red deer in the neighboring field to off-road driving, fishing, bike rental, and "safaris" into the nearby hills in Land Rovers or on foot. Activities come in a range of prices and lengths, or you can create your own experience. There is a shop and café on the site. ✉ Aberfeldy ✛ 2½ miles west of Aberfeldy on B846 ☎ 01887/820071 ⊕ www.highlandsafaris. net 🎟 Mountain Safari £47.50.

Crieff

24 miles south of Aberfeldy.

Crieff retains the prosperous air of its Victorian heyday as a place to "take the waters." Its central square, where local farmers may once have gathered to trade, is still a lively focus. For a different view of the town, you could climb Knock Hill, which is signposted from the town center.

GETTING HERE AND AROUND

Crieff once prospered because of the arrival of the railway. No station exists here today, but there are regular buses from Stirling and Glasgow. By car take the A85 from Perth, or the A9 from Stirling, turning onto the A822 after Dunblane. From Aberfeldy take the A826 and A822 for a direct route, or explore the longer, scenic A827/A85 route.

ESSENTIALS

VISITOR INFORMATION Crieff Visitor Information Centre. ✉ Muthill Road, Crieff ☎ 01764/654065 ⊕ www.crieff.co.uk.

Some of Scotland's most impressive formal gardens, the Drummond Castle Gardens were first laid-out in the 1630s.

👁 Sights

★ Drummond Castle Gardens

GARDEN | These formal Victorian gardens, regarded as some of the finest of their kind in Europe, celebrate family and Scottish heraldry. Combining the formal French and more relaxed Italian styles, the flower beds are planted and trimmed in the shapes of various heraldic symbols, such as a lion rampant and a checkerboard, associated with the coat of arms of the family that owns the castle. The gardens were on display in the filming of *Outlander*. The house itself is not open to the public. ✉ *Off A822, Crieff* ✛ *6 miles southwest of Crieff* ☎ *01764/681433* ⊕ *www.drummondcastlegardens.co.uk* 💷 *£10* ☉ *Closed Nov.–Apr.*

Glenturret Distillery

DISTILLERY | To discover the delights of whisky distilling, sign up for the Distillery Tour at the Glenturret Distillery, which claims to be Scotland's oldest. Here you learn how whisky is made and why time, water, soil, and air are so important to the taste. A guide takes you through the distillery and to the bar where you can have a glass of Glenturret's famous single malt and try your skill at "nosing." You might cap your tour with lunch in the Wild Thyme café and restaurant. Signs lead to the distillery on the west side of the town. ✉ *The Hosh, Comrie Road, Crieff* ☎ *01764/656565* ⊕ *www.theglenturret. com* 💷 *Tour £11; Fudge Tour £30.*

🛏 Hotels

Crieff Hydro

$$ | **HOTEL** | **FAMILY** | One of Scotland's great Victorian hydropathy centers (treating illnesses using water), this grand resort hotel on 900 acres has been owned by the same family for more than 100 years. **Pros:** wonderful spa; extensive grounds; variety of activities. **Cons:** can feel a little impersonal; some activities are quite expensive; some rooms are rather dull. 💲 *Rooms from: £185* ✉ *Off A85, Crieff* ☎ *01764/655555* ⊕ *www.crieffhy-dro.com* 🛏 *220 rooms* ⦿ *Free Breakfast.*

🛍 Shopping

Caithness Glass at Crieff Visitor Centre
GLASSWARE | Crieff was once best known for its glass. You can watch the glassblowing process (weekdays only) and then browse the sales gallery here for paperweights and other gift items. There's also a garden center and a restaurant. ⊠ *Muthill Road, Crieff* ☎ *01764/654014* ⊕ *www.crieff.co.uk.*

Auchterarder

11 miles southeast of Crieff.

Famous for the Gleneagles Hotel (including its restaurant by Andrew Fairlie) and nearby golf courses, Auchterarder also has a flock of tiny antiques shops to amuse Gleneagles's golf widows and widowers.

GETTING HERE AND AROUND
Gleneagles station is on the main Inverness line, while the A9 gives direct access to Gleneagles and Auchterarder via the A823.

🍴 Restaurants

★ **Andrew Fairlie at Gleneagles**
$$$$ | BRITISH | The late chef Andrew Fairlie established his restaurant in the Gleneagles Hotel in 2001, winning two Michelin stars for his elegant and restrained dishes, and setting in motion a food revolution that changed Scottish cooking. Fairlie's training was in classical French kitchens, and though his restaurant menus were firmly embedded in local Scottish produce, like pheasant and lobster, his style remained classic and detailed. **Known for:** a commitment to local produce; two Michelin stars; cuisine marrying France and Scotland. $ *Average main: £115* ⊠ *Gleneagles Hotel, Off A823, Auchterarder, Auchterarder* ☎ *01764/694267* ⊕ *www.andrewfairlie. co.uk* ☉ *Closed Sun.*

🛏 Hotels

★ **Gleneagles Hotel**
$$$$ | HOTEL | One of Britain's most famous hotels, Gleneagles is the very essence of modern grandeur, a vast palace that stands hidden in breathtaking countryside amid its world-famous golf courses. **Pros:** the three courses are a golfer's paradise; luxurious rooms; famous Andrew Fairlie restaurant. **Cons:** such luxury comes at a price; restaurants get very crowded; quite conservative decor. $ *Rooms from: £435* ⊠ *Off A823, Auchterarder* ☎ *01764/662231* ⊕ *www.gleneagles.com* ⇆ *258 rooms* �'❍❙ *Free Breakfast.*

🚴 Activities

GOLF
★ **Gleneagles**
GOLF | Its superb courses have made Gleneagles a part of golfing history. The 18 holes of the King's Course, designed by James Braid in 1919, have quirky names, such as the Warslin' Lea (Wrestling Ground)—the tough 17th hole that many golfers have grappled with. The Queen's Course mixes varied terrain, including woods and moors. Jack Nicklaus designed the PGA Centenary Course (host of the 2014 Ryder Cup), which sweeps into the Ochil Hills and has views of the Grampians. The 9-hole Wee Course provides challenges for beginners and pros. Gleneagles is also home to the PGA National Academy, a good place to improve your skills. ⊠ *A823, Auchterarder* ☎ *01764/662231* ⊕ *www.gleneagles.com* ⛳ *King's, Queen's, and PGA Centenary courses: May and early Oct. £140, June £160, July–Sept. £200, late Oct. £85, Nov. and Dec. £75. Wee course: May–mid-Oct. £37.50, mid-Oct–Dec. £20* ⚘ *King's: 18 holes, 6790 yards, par 71; Queen's: 18 holes, 6790 yards, par 68; PGA Centenary: 18 holes, 6815 yards, par 72; Wee Course: 9 holes, 1418 yards, par 27.*

Chapter 8

ABERDEEN AND THE NORTHEAST

8

Updated by
Robin Gauldie

● Sights	♨ Restaurants	🛏 Hotels	🛍 Shopping	♉ Nightlife
★★★☆☆	★★★☆☆	★★☆☆☆	★☆☆☆☆	★★☆☆☆

WELCOME TO ABERDEEN AND THE NORTHEAST

TOP REASONS TO GO

★ **Castles:** With more than 75 castles, some Victorian and others dating back to the 13th century, this area has everything from ravaged ruins like Dunnottar to opulent Fyvie Castle.

★ **Distilleries:** The valley of the River Spey is famous for its single-malt distilleries, including those connected by the signposted Malt Whisky Trail.

★ **Seaside cities and towns:** The fishing industry may be in decline, but the big-city port of Aberdeen and the colorful smaller fishing towns of Stonehaven and Cullen in the northeast are great (and very different) places to soak up the seagoing atmosphere—and some seafood.

★ **Walking:** There are all types of walking for all kinds of walkers, from the bracing but spectacular inclines of the Grampian Mountains to the wooded gardens and grounds of Balmoral and Haddo House.

★ **Golf:** The northeast has more than 50 golf clubs, some of which have championship courses.

Aberdeen, on the North Sea in the eastern part of the region, is Scotland's third-largest city; many people start a trip here. Once you have spent time in the city, you may be inclined to venture west into rural Deeside, with its royal connections and looming mountain backdrop. To the north of Deeside is Castle Country, with many ancient fortresses. Speyside and the Whisky Trail lie at the western edge of the region and are equally accessible from Inverness. From Speyside you might travel back east along the pristine coastline at Scotland's northeastern tip.

1 Aberdeen. The gateway to the northeast.

2 Stonehaven. A seaside town with an iconic castle nearby.

3 Banchory. A popular stop on the way to Deeside.

4 Ballater. A handsome riverside town with royal connections.

5 Braemar. Home of the original Highland Games.

6 Corgarff Castle. A lodge that became a redcoat garrison.

7 Alford. An unassuming village next to mighty Castle Fraser.

8 Dufftown. Speyside's whisky capital.

9 Craigellachie. An angler's delight located beside the River Spey.

10 Aberlour. A charming small town surrounded by distilleries.

11 Elgin. A seaside town with a splendid ruined cathedral.

12 Fochabers. A charming market town.

13 Cullen. Harbor village famed for seafood and white sands.

14 Banff. A fishing haven surrounded by Georgian houses.

15 Fyvie Castle. Grand Edwardian retreat with a superb art collection.

16 Ellon. A pretty suburb with magnificent gardens.

Here, in this granite shoulder of Grampian, are some of Scotland's most enduring travel icons: Royal Deeside, the countryside that Queen Victoria made her own; the Castle Country route, where fortresses stand hard against the hills; and the Malt Whisky Trail, where peaty streams embrace the country's greatest concentration of distilleries.

The region's gateway is the city of Aberdeen. Once a prosperous merchant port, it became a boomtown in the 1970s with the discovery of oil beneath the North Sea, but as oil and gas reserves dwindle, the city is looking in new directions for its wealth.

More than 125 miles north of the central belt of Glasgow and Edinburgh, Aberdeen has historically been a fairly autonomous place. Even now it's perceived by many U.K. inhabitants as lying almost out of reach in the northeast. In reality it's a 90-minute flight from London or a little more than two hours by car from Edinburgh. Its 18th- and early-19th-century city center amply rewards exploration. Yet even if this popular base for travelers vanished from the map, an extensive portion of the northeast would still remain at the top of many travelers' wish lists.

Balmoral, the Scottish baronial–style house built for Queen Victoria as a retreat, is merely the most famous castle in the area, and certainly not the oldest. There are so many others that in one part of the region a Castle Trail has been established. In later structures, such as Castle Fraser, you can trace the changing styles and tastes of each of their owners over the centuries. Grand mansions such as 18th-century Haddo House, with its symmetrical facade and elegant interior, surrender any defensive role entirely.

A trail leading to a more ephemeral kind of pleasure can be found south of Elgin and Banff, where the glens embrace Scotland's greatest concentration of malt-whisky distilleries. With so many in Morayshire, where the distilling is centered on the valley of the River Spey and its tributaries, there's now a Malt Whisky Trail. Follow it, and visit other distilleries as well, to experience a surprising wealth of flavors.

The northeast's chief topographical attraction lies in the gradual transition from high mountain plateau—by a series of gentle steps through hill, forest, and farmland—to the Moray Firth and North Sea coast, where the word *unadulterated* is redefined. Here you'll find some of the United Kingdom's most perfect wild shorelines, both sandy and sheer cliff, and breezy fishing villages like Cullen on the Banffshire coast and Stonehaven, south of Aberdeen. The Grampian Mountains, to the west, contain some of the highest ground in the nation, in the area of the Cairngorms.

MAJOR REGIONS

Aberdeen. Family connections or Royal Deeside often take travelers to this part of Scotland, but many are surprised by how grand and rich in history Aberdeen is. The august granite-turreted buildings and rose-lined roads make this a surprisingly pleasant city to explore; don't miss Old Aberdeen in particular.

Royal Deeside and Castle Country. Deeside, the valley running west from Aberdeen down which the River Dee flows, earned its "royal" appellation when Prince Albert designed Balmoral Castle for Queen Victoria, and so began the royal family's love affair with Deeside—and Deeside's love affair with it. To this day, where royalty goes, lesser aristocracy and freshly minted millionaires follow. Many still aspire to own a grand shooting estate in Deeside, and you may appreciate this yearning when you see the piney hills, purple moors, and blue river intermingling. As you travel deeper into the Grampian Mountains, Royal Deeside's gradual scenic change adds a growing sense of excitement. This area has long been the retreat or the fortress of distinguished families, as the clutter of castles throughout the region shows. There are castles along the Dee as well as to the north in Castle Country, a region that illustrates the gradual geological change in the northeast: uplands lapped by a tide of farms. All the Donside and Deeside castles are picturesquely sited, with most fitted out with tall, slender turrets, winding stairs, and crooked chambers that epitomize Scottish baronial style. All have tales of ghosts and bloodshed, siege and torture. Many were tidied up and "domesticated" during the 19th century. Although best toured by car, much of this area is accessible either by public transportation or on tours from Aberdeen. The majesty of the countryside also guarantees a superlative stop for everyone interested in history and romance.

The Northeast and the Malt Whisky Trail. North of Deeside another popular area of this region lies inland, toward Speyside— the valley, or strath, of the River Spey—famed for its whisky distilleries, some of which it promotes in another signposted trail. Distilling Scotch is not an intrinsically spectacular process. It involves pure water, malted barley, and sometimes peat smoke, then a lot of bubbling and fermentation, all of which cause a number of odd smells. The result is a prestigious product with a fascinating range of flavors that you may either enjoy immensely or not at all. Unique in their architecture, their ingredients, and the end product, the distilleries of Speyside are keen to share with you their passion for "the water of life." This region also has rolling hills and, to the north, the beautiful, wild coastline of the North Sea. Instead of closely following the Malt Whisky Trail, dip into it and blend visits to distilleries with some other aspects of the county of Moray, particularly its coastline. Whisky notwithstanding, Moray's scenic qualities, low rainfall, and other reassuring weather statistics are worth remembering. You can also sample the northeastern seaboard, including some of the best but least-known coastal scenery in Scotland.

Planning

When to Go

May and June are probably the loveliest times to visit, but many travelers arrive from late spring to early fall. The National Trust for Scotland tends to close its properties in winter, so many of the northeast's castles are not open for off-season travel, though you can always see them from the outside. Many distilleries are open much of the year, but some close during winter months, so check before visiting.

Planning Your Time

How you allocate your time may depend on your special interests—castles or whisky, for example. But even if you can manage only a morning or an afternoon, do not miss a walk around the granite streets of Old Aberdeen, and take in St. Nicholas Kirk and a pint in the Prince of Wales pub. A trip southward to the fishing town of Stonehaven and the breathtaking cliff-top fortress of Dunnottar makes a rewarding afternoon. Royal Deeside, with a good sprinkling of castles and grandeur, needs a good two days; even this might be tight for those who want to lap up every moment of majesty at Balmoral, Crathes, Fraser, and Fyvie, the best of the bunch. A visit to malt-whisky country should include tours of Glenfiddich, Glenfarclas, Glenlivet, and Glen Grant distilleries, and although it's not technically a maker of malt whisky, Strathisla. Real enthusiasts should allot two days for the distilleries, and they shouldn't pass up a visit to Speyside Cooperage, one of the few remaining cooperages in Scotland. Cullen and Duff House gallery in Banff, on the coast, can be done in a day before returning to Aberdeen.

Getting Here and Around

AIR
The city is easy to reach from other parts of the United Kingdom as well as Europe. British Airways, EasyJet, Loganair, and Ryanair are some of the airlines with service to other parts of Britain. Aberdeen Airport—serving both international and domestic flights—is in Dyce, 7 miles west of the city center on the A96 (Inverness). The drive to the center of Aberdeen is easy via the A96 (which can be busy during rush hour).

CONTACTS Aberdeen Airport. ⊠ Dyce Dr., Dyce ☎ 0344/481–6666 ⊕ www.aberdeenairport.com.

BOAT AND FERRY
Northlink Ferries has service between Aberdeen, Lerwick (Shetland), and Kirkwall (Orkney).

CONTACTS Northlink Ferries. ⊠ Jamieson's Quay, Aberdeen ☎ 0800/1114422 ⊕ www.northlinkferries.co.uk.

BUS
Long-distance buses run to Aberdeen from most parts of Scotland, England, and Wales. Contact Megabus, National Express, and Scottish Citylink for bus connections with English and Scottish towns. There's a network of local buses throughout the northeast run by Stagecoach, but they can take a long time and connections are not always well timed.

CONTACTS Megabus. ☎ 0900/160–0900 ⊕ uk.megabus.com. **National Express.** ☎ 08717/818181 ⊕ www.nationalexpress.com. **Scottish Citylink.** ☎ ⊕ www.citylink.co.uk. **Traveline.** ☎ 0871/200–2233 ⊕ www.travelinescotland.com.

CAR
A car is the best way to see the northeast. If you are coming from the south, take the A90, continuing on from the M90 (from Edinburgh) or the M9/A9 (from Glasgow), which both stop at Perth. The coastal route, the A92, is a more leisurely alternative, with its interesting resorts and fishing villages. The most scenic route, however, is the A93 from Perth, north to Blairgowrie and into Glen Shee. The A93 then goes over the Cairnwell Pass, the highest main road in the United Kingdom. This route isn't recommended in winter, when snow can make driving difficult.

Around the northeast roads can be busy, with speeding and erratic driving a problem on the main A roads.

TRAIN
You can reach Aberdeen directly from Edinburgh (2½ hours), Inverness (2½ hours), and Glasgow (3 hours). ScotRail timetables have full details. There are

also London–Aberdeen routes that go through Edinburgh and the east-coast main line connecting Aberdeen to all corners of the United Kingdom.

CONTACTS ScotRail. ✉ *Aberdeen railway station, Guild St., Aberdeen* ☎ *0344/811–0141* ⊕ *www.scotrail.co.uk.*

Restaurants

As in much of the rest of Scotland, Aberdeen and the northeast have rediscovered the quality and versatility of the local produce. Juicy Aberdeen Angus steaks, lean lamb, and humanely reared pork appear on local menus, and there's a great choice of locally sourced seafood, from old-school fish-and-chips to dishes that fuse Mediterranean, Asian, and Latin influence. Traditional favorites like Cullen skink (a creamy smoked-fish soup) are on many menus.

Hotels

The northeast has some splendid country hotels with log fires and old Victorian furnishings, where you can also be sure of eating well. Many hotels in Aberdeen are in older buildings that have a baronial feel. The trend for serviced apartments has caught on here, with some extremely modish and good-value options for those who want a bit more privacy. This trend is now extending into Deeside, where it's been notoriously difficult to find good accommodations beyond some country-house hotels, even though it's a popular tourist spot.

Restaurant and hotel reviews have been shortened. For full information, visit Fodors.com. Restaurant prices are the average cost of a main course at dinner or, if dinner is not served, at lunch. Hotel prices are the lowest cost of a standard double room in high season, including 20% V.A.T.

WHAT IT COSTS in Pounds			
$	$$	$$$	$$$$
RESTAURANTS			
under £15	£15–£19	£20–£25	over £25
HOTELS			
under £125	£125–£200	£201–£300	over £300

Visitor Information

The tourist information center in Aberdeen supplies information on all of Scotland's northeast. There are also year-round tourist information offices in Braemar and Elgin. In summer, also look for tourist information centers in Alford, Ballater, Banchory, Braemar, Elgin, and Stonehaven.

CONTACT VisitScotland Aberdeen iCentre. ✉ *23 Union St., Aberdeen* ☎ *01224/900490* ⊕ *www.visitscotland. com, www.visitabdn.com.*

Aberdeen

As a gateway to Royal Deeside and the Malt Whisky Trail, Aberdeen attracts visitors, though many are eager to get out into the countryside. Today, though, the city's unique history is finally being recognized as more impressive than many Scots had previously realized, and Aberdeen is being rediscovered. Distinctive architecture, some fine museums, universities, and good restaurants, nightlife, and shopping add to the appeal of Scotland's third-largest city (population 217,000). Union Street is the heart of the city, but take time to explore the university and the pretty streets of Old Aberdeen.

In the 18th century local granite quarrying produced a durable silver stone that would be used boldly in the glittering blocks, spires, columns, and parapets of Victorian-era Aberdonian structures. The city remains one of the United Kingdom's most distinctive, although some would say it depends on the weather and the brightness of the day. The mica chips embedded in the rock look like a million mirrors in the sunshine. In rain (and there is a fair amount of driving rain from the North Sea) and heavy clouds, however, their sparkle is snuffed out.

The city lies between the Dee and Don rivers, with a working harbor that has access to the sea; it has been a major fishing port and is the main commercial port in northern Scotland. The North Sea has always been important to Aberdeen. In the 1850s the city was famed for its sleek, fast clippers that sailed to India for cargoes of tea. In the 1970s exploitation of newly discovered offshore oil and gas turned Aberdeen into a world energy capital. As reserves dwindle and the oil industry winds down, the city is seeking new ways to diversify its economy.

GETTING HERE AND AROUND
AIR
Stagecoach Bluebird Jet Service 727 operates between the airport terminal in Dyce and Union Square in the center of Aberdeen. Buses (£4) run frequently at peak times, less often at midday and in the evening; the journey time is approximately 30 minutes.

Dyce is on ScotRail's Inverness–Aberdeen route. The rail station is a short taxi ride from the terminal building (£16). Trains run approximately every two hours.

BUS
First Aberdeen has easy and reliable service within the city of Aberdeen. Timetables are available from the tourist information center in Union Street.

CONTACTS First Aberdeen. ☎ 0345/646–0707 ⊕ www.firstgroup.com.

CAR
Aberdeen is a compact city with good signage. Its center is Union Street, the main east–west thoroughfare, which tends to get crowded with traffic.

Anderson Drive is an efficient ring road on the city's west side; be extra careful on its many traffic circles. It's best to leave your car in one of the parking garages (arrive early to get a space) and walk around, or use the convenient park-and-ride stop at the Bridge of Don, north of the city. Street maps are available from the tourist information center, newsstands, and booksellers.

TAXI
You can find taxi stands throughout the center of Aberdeen: at the railway station and at Back Wynd, Chapel Street, Dee Street, and Hadden Street. The taxis have yellow plates, meters, and might be saloon cars (sedans) or black cabs. They are great ways to travel between neighborhoods.

TRAIN
Aberdeen has good ScotRail service.

◉ Sights

Aberdeen centers on Union Street, with its many fine survivors of the Victorian and Edwardian streetscape. Marischal College, dating from the late 16th century, is a city-center landmark, and has many grand buildings that are worth exploring.

Very much a separate area of the city, Old Aberdeen is north of the modern center, clustered around St. Machar's Cathedral and the many fine buildings of the University of Aberdeen. Take a stroll on College Bounds; handsome 18th- and 19th-century houses line this cobbled street in the oldest part of the city.

Aberdeen Art Gallery
ART MUSEUM | Northeast Scotland's most important art gallery now has seven exhibition spaces where over 1,000 of its treasures are displayed. There's also a penthouse gallery hosting three touring exhibitions each year. The collection contains excellent paintings, prints, drawings, sculptures, porcelain, costumes,

Perhaps Aberdeen's best museum, the Aberdeen Maritime Museum explores the city's history with the sea, from shipbuilding to fishing.

and more, from 18th-century art to major contemporary British works by Lucien Freud and Henry Moore. Scottish artists are well represented in the permanent collection and special exhibits. Local stone has been used in the interior walls, pillars, and the central fountain, all designed by the acclaimed British sculptor Barbara Hepworth. ⊠ *Schoolhill, Aberdeen* ☎ *03000/200293* ⊕ *www. aagm.co.uk* ⊠ *Free.*

★ Aberdeen Maritime Museum

HISTORY MUSEUM | FAMILY | This excellent museum, which incorporates the 1593 Provost Ross's House, tells the story of the city's relationship with the sea, from early inshore fisheries to tea clippers and the North Sea oil boom. The information-rich exhibits include the bridge of a fishing boat and the cabins of a clipper, in addition to models, paintings, and equipment associated with the fishing, shipbuilding, and oil and gas industries. The Gateway to the North gallery on the top floor is a lively introduction to the archaeology of the region, with

exhibits spanning the years 1136–1660. ⊠ *Ship Row, Aberdeen* ☎ *03000/200293* ⊕ *www.aagm.co.uk* ⊠ *Free* ☺ *Closed Mon. and Tues.*

Brig o'Balgownie

BRIDGE | Until 1827, the only northern route out of Aberdeen was over the River Don on this single-arch bridge. It dates from 1314 and is thought to have been built by Richard Cementarius, Aberdeen's first provost. ⊠ *Seaton Park, Aberdeen.*

Cruickshank Botanic Garden

CITY PARK | Built on land bequeathed by Miss Anne Cruickshank in memory of her beloved brother, Alexander, the 11-acre Cruickshank Botanic Garden at the heart of Old Aberdeen has a peaceful water garden and lush greens ideal for lounging—when the weather allows—and beautifully tended subtropical and alpine collections. Botanical tours are available. ⊠ *St. Machar Dr., at the Chanonry, Aberdeen* ☎ *01224/272000* ⊕ *www.abdn. ac.uk/botanic-garden* ⊠ *Free.*

Duthie Park

CITY PARK | FAMILY | These 44 acres were donated to the people of Aberdeen by a Miss Elizabeth Crombie Duthie in 1880. An excellent place to while away an afternoon, whether it be the sunniest or foulest day, it has a boating pond, a bandstand, playgrounds, and a popular conservatory café selling creamy ice cream. In the beautifully tended Winter Gardens (tropical and arid conservatories), you'll find fish ponds and free-flying birds among the luxuriant foliage and flowers. The park borders Aberdeen's other river, the Dee. ✉ *Polmuir Rd., Aberdeen* ✛ *About 1 mile south of city center* 🖼 *Free.*

King's College

COLLEGE | Founded in 1494, King's College is now part of the University of Aberdeen. Its chapel, built around 1500, has an unmistakable flying (or crown) spire. That it has survived at all was because of the zeal of the principal, who defended his church against the destructive fanaticism that swept through Scotland during the Reformation, when the building was less than a century old. Today the renovated chapel plays an important role in university life. Don't miss the tall oak screen that separates the nave from the choir, the ribbed wooden ceiling, and the stalls, as these constitute the finest medieval wood carvings found anywhere in Scotland. ✉ *25 High St., Aberdeen* ☏ *01224/272000* ⊕ *www.abdn.ac.uk* ⊙ *Closed weekends.*

King's Museum, Old Aberdeen Townhouse

HISTORY MUSEUM | Across from the archway leading to King's College Chapel, this plain but handsome Georgian building was the center of all trading activity in the city before it became a grammar school, a Masonic lodge, and then a library. Now housing the university's museum, it hosts constantly changing exhibitions. It presents some impressive and often strange curiosities from the university's collection, from prehistoric flints to a tiger's penis. ✉ *17 High St., Aberdeen* ☏ *01224/272000* ⊕ *www.abdn. ac.uk/kingsmuseum* 🖼 *Free* ⊙ *Closed Sun. and Mon.*

Marischal College

NOTABLE BUILDING | Founded in 1593 by the Earl Marischal (the keeper of the king's mares), Marischal College was a Protestant alternative to the Catholic King's College in Old Aberdeen. The two joined to form the University of Aberdeen in 1860. The spectacularly ornate work of the main university building is set off by the gilded flags, and this turn-of-the-20th-century creation is still one of the world's largest granite buildings. ✉ *Broad St., Aberdeen.*

Mercat Cross

OTHER ATTRACTION | Built in 1686 and restored in 1820, the Mercat Cross (the name stems from "marketplace"), always the symbolic center of a Scottish medieval burgh, stands just beyond King Street. Along its parapet are 12 portrait panels of the Stewart monarchs. ✉ *Justice and Marischal Sts., Aberdeen.*

Provost Skene's House

NOTABLE BUILDING | Built in 1545, this dignified medieval building is the oldest of Aberdeen's historic townhouses. Home to wealthy merchant and Provost (mayor) of Aberdeen, Sir George Skene from 1676 to 1685, it reopened after a lengthy refurbishment in 2021 as the city's newest attraction. Inside, the Hall of Heroes celebrates the achievements of local figures including artists, musicians, writers, and sporting legends. ✉ *Guestrow, off Broad St., Aberdeen* ☏ *03000/200293* ⊕ *www.aagm.co.uk* 🖼 *Free.*

Rosemount Viaduct

OTHER ATTRACTION | Three silvery, handsome buildings on this bridge are collectively known by all Aberdonians as Education, Salvation, and Damnation. The Central Library and St. Mark's Church date from the last decade of the 19th century, and His Majesty's Theatre

(1904–08) has been restored inside to its full Edwardian splendor. If you're taking photographs, you can choose an angle that includes the statue of Scotland's first freedom fighter, Sir William Wallace (1270–1305), in the foreground pointing majestically to Damnation. ✉ *Aberdeen.*

⭐ **St. Machar's Cathedral**

CHURCH | It's said that St. Machar was sent by St. Columba to build a church on a grassy platform near the sea, where a river flowed in the shape of a shepherd's crook. This beautiful spot, now the still-beating heart of Old Aberdeen, fits the bill. Although the cathedral was founded in AD 580, most of the existing building dates from the 15th and 16th centuries. Built as a fortified kirk, its twin towers and thick walls give it a sturdy standing. The former can be seen up close by climbing the spiral staircases to the upper floors, which also affords an admirable view of the "body of the kirk" inside and graveyard outside. It lost its status as a cathedral during the Reformation and has since been part of the Church of Scotland. The stained-glass windows depicting the martyrdom of the saints and handsome heraldic ceiling are worth noting. ✉ *Chanonry, Aberdeen* ☎ *01224/485988* ⊕ *www.stmachar.com.*

St. Nicholas Kirk

CHURCH | The original burgh church, the Mither Kirk, as this edifice is known, is not within the bounds of the early town settlement; that was to the east, near the end of present-day Union Street. During the 12th century, the port of Aberdeen flourished, and there wasn't room for the church within the settlement. Its earliest features are its pillars—supporting a tower built much later—and its clerestory windows: both date from the 12th century. The East Kirk is closed for renovation work, which has been extended due to the discovery of numerous skeletons, mainly children, that date back to the 12th century; the post-excavation work can be viewed from a large window in the Drum's Aisle. In the chapel, look for Shona McInnes's stained-glass window commemorating the victims of the 1989 Piper Alpha oil-rig disaster and a glass case containing two books. One lists the names of all those who've lost their lives in the pursuit of oil exploration in the North Sea; the second is empty, a testament to the many "unknown" workers whose deaths were never officially recorded. The church's congregation was dissolved in 2021 and it is no longer regularly used as a place of worship. ✉ *Union St., Aberdeen* ☎ *01224/643494.*

Tolbooth Museum

OTHER MUSEUM | **FAMILY** | The city was governed from this 17th-century building, which was also the burgh court and jail, for 200 years. Now a museum of crime and punishment, its highly entertaining tour guides take you around its cells and dungeons and bring life and death to the various instruments of torture—including the "Maiden," a decapitating machine—making it a must-see for older kids. ✉ *Castle St., Aberdeen* ☎ *01224/621167* ⊕ *www.aagm.co.uk* 🎟 *Free.*

Union Street

STREET | This great thoroughfare is to Aberdeen what Princes Street is to Edinburgh: the central pivot of the city plan and the product of a wave of enthusiasm to rebuild the city in a contemporary style in the early 19th century. ✉ *Aberdeen.*

Union Terrace

NEIGHBORHOOD | In the 19th-century development of Union Terrace stands a statue of Robert Burns (1759–96) addressing a daisy. Behind Burns are the Union Terrace Gardens. A £25.7 million development that aims to improve access to the gardens and make it a more attractive space for performances and corporate events is expected to be completed in summer 2022. ✉ *Aberdeen.*

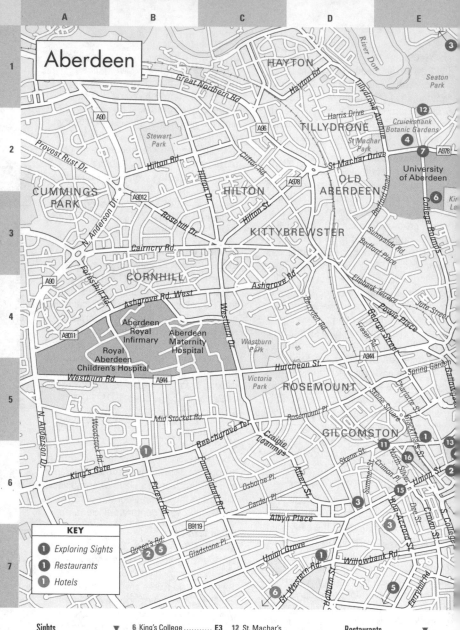

Aberdeen

NORTH
SEA

FERRY TO
KIRKWALL,
LERWICK

SEATON

King's Links
Golf Club

Nigg Bay
Golf Club

River Dee

Victoria
Bridge

🍴 Restaurants

Ashvale

$ | **BRITISH** | **FAMILY** | Ask anyone about this long-established place and the response will probably be overwhelmingly positive. Fish-and-chips is the specialty, and the secret-recipe batter is now the stuff of legend. **Known for:** free meals for those under age five; "The Whale," a giant 1-pound haddock fillet; tender locally sourced steaks. [$] *Average main: £14* ✉ *42–48 Great Western Rd., Aberdeen* ☎ *01224/575842* 🌐 *theashvale.co.uk.*

Café 52

$$ | **MODERN BRITISH** | This artsy café-restaurant has an innovative menu, an atmospheric dining room with open kitchen, and covered outdoor seating. The menu features veggie options such as mushroom falafel, grilled halloumi with crushed walnuts, and barley *fricassee*, as well as lots of imaginative Middle Eastern-fusion meat and seafood choices. **Known for:** cash-only policy; tagine-style slow-cooked beef casserole; oyster mushrooms with buttered barley, calvados, and lovage. [$] *Average main: £15* ✉ *52 The Green, Aberdeen* ☎ *01224/590094* 🌐 *www.cafe52onthegreen.co.uk* 💳 *No credit cards* ⏲ *Closed Sun.–Tues.*

Foodstory

$ | **VEGETARIAN** | **FAMILY** | A bright, breezy vegetarian and vegan café-eatery, Foodstory pulls in a loyal crowd to graze on its healthy, freshly made breakfasts, lunches, and wonderful cakes. Expect organic breakfast and brunch choices such as superfood porridge, scones, and filling dishes such as vegetarian hot pot. **Known for:** vegan breakfasts and lunches; vegan chilli with nachos, tzatziki, and sweet potato cheese; eco-friendly ethos. [$] *Average main: £7* ✉ *13–15 Thistle St., Aberdeen* ☎ 🌐 *www.foodstorycafe.co.uk.*

Moonfish

$$ | **BRITISH** | This elegant yet relaxed seafood restaurant can be found along a medieval lane next to St. Nicholas Kirk. Mains may include freshly caught sea trout, halibut, or hake served with imaginative accompaniments such as celeriac with seaweed. **Known for:** craft gin cocktails; baked scallops with parsnip, chorizo, and pine nuts; sophisticated atmosphere. [$] *Average main: £16* ✉ *9 Correction Wynd, Aberdeen* ☎ *01224/644166* 🌐 *www.moonfishcafe.co.uk* ⏲ *Closed Sun.-Mon.*

★ Silver Darling

$$$ | **SEAFOOD** | Huge windows overlook the harbor and beach at this quayside favorite in a former customhouse, long one of Aberdeen's most acclaimed restaurants. The French-inspired menu focuses on fish: try the crab bisque with samphire to start, then move on to a lavish seafood platter of scallops, mussels, langoustes, prawns, and cockles. **Known for:** steak fillet with king prawns in garlic butter; classic seafood platters; prawn and crab linguine. [$] *Average main: £25* ✉ *North Pier, Pocra Quay, Aberdeen* ☎ *01224/576229* 🌐 *thesilverdarling.co.uk* ⏲ *Closed Sun. No lunch Sat.*

🛏 Hotels

Atholl Hotel

$ | **HOTEL** | With its many turrets and gables, this granite hotel recalls a bygone era but has modern amenities that now include an elevator and two rooms specially designed for people with disabilities. **Pros:** private parking; family-run establishment; outdoor garden seating for sunny days. **Cons:** unexciting bar; popular with locals for wedding and funeral receptions; rooms are blandly decorated. [$] *Rooms from: £100* ✉ *54 Kings Gate, Aberdeen* ☎ *01224/323505* 🌐 *www.atholl-aberdeen.co.uk* 🛏 *34 rooms* 🍴 *Free Breakfast.*

★ Chester Hotel
$ | **HOTEL** | Contemporary style meets original 19th-century architectural detail within this gracious hotel. **Pros:** lively bar; fine dining at on-site restaurant; ultracomfortable accommodations. **Cons:** bar can get crowded and noisy on weekends; popular for meetings and events; gym is small and basic. [$] *Rooms from: £103* ✉ *59–63 Queen's Rd., Aberdeen* ☎ *01224/327777* 🌐 *www.chester-hotel.com* 🛏 *50 rooms* 🍴 *Free Breakfast.*

Craibstone Suites
$ | **HOTEL** | **FAMILY** | On one of Aberdeen's most attractive squares, these 18 modern and comfortable suites come with fully equipped kitchens. **Pros:** good self-catering facilities; great central location; feels more like an apartment than a hotel room. **Cons:** devoid of character; breakfast is pretty basic; executive suites are small—go for the grand or superior suites if you need elbow room. [$] *Rooms from: £62* ✉ *15 Bon Accord Sq., Aberdeen* ☎ *01224/857950* 🌐 *www.craibstone-suites.co.uk* 🛏 *18 suites* 🍴 *Free Breakfast.*

The Jays Guest House
$ | **B&B/INN** | Alice Jennings or her husband, George, will greet you at the front door of this granite house, a homey bed-and-breakfast they've run for more than 30 years. **Pros:** near Old Aberdeen and the university; immaculate rooms; expert advice on city's sights. **Cons:** not for those looking for a full-service hotel; popular, so book ahead; no public areas. [$] *Rooms from: £60* ✉ *422 King St., Aberdeen* ☎ *01224/612771* 🌐 *www.jaysguesthouse.co.uk* 🛏 *10 rooms* 🍴 *Free Breakfast.*

★ Malmaison
$ | **HOTEL** | Part of a British minichain, this boutique hotel with fabulously comfy rooms and suites—some with terraces from which you can watch the sunset—sets the standard by which all rivals in Aberdeen are judged. **Pros:** delightful staff; stylish rooms; excellent restaurant. **Cons:** meat-heavy restaurant could do more for vegetarians; no pool; not very central. [$] *Rooms from: £119* ✉ *45–93 Queen's Rd., Aberdeen* ☎ *01224/507097* 🌐 *www.malmaison.com/locations/aberdeen* 🛏 *77 rooms* 🍴 *Free Breakfast.*

Marcliffe Hotel and Spa
$$ | **HOTEL** | Offering a perfect combination of town and country outside the city center, this elegant hotel stands on 11 acres of wooded grounds and combines old and new to impressive effect. **Pros:** well-regarded restaurant; the wooded environs means a stunning dawn chorus of birds; big rooms. **Cons:** popular with wedding parties; a little out of town; if you struggle to sleep, the dawn chorus. [$] *Rooms from: £150* ✉ *N. Deeside Rd., Aberdeen* ☎ *01224/861000* 🌐 *www.marcliffe.com* 🛏 *39 rooms* 🍴 *Free Breakfast.*

🍸 Nightlife

Aberdeen has a fairly lively nightlife scene revolving around pubs and clubs. Theaters, concert halls, arts centers, and cinemas are also well represented. The principal newspapers—the *Press and Journal* and the *Evening Express* can fill you in on what's going on anywhere in the northeast.

Although it can't hold a candle to Edinburgh or Glasgow when it comes to sophisticated nightlife, Aberdeen has a very lively, even sometimes raucous, clubbing scene with numerous venues that are popular with students and other young locals but are less appealing to more mature visitors or anyone over 30. Belmont Street is a lively bar-hopping neighborhood with bars to suit all tastes. Pubs close at midnight on weekdays and 1 am on weekends; clubs go until 2 or 3 am.

The Blue Lamp
LIVE MUSIC | This is Aberdeen's coolest jazz venue, with brilliant acoustics and a laid-back atmosphere. The intimate vibe attracts all age groups with performances by world-class jazz talents and by local bands. On evenings when jazz is not

in the cards, there's often live comedy. ✉ *121 Gallowgate* ☎ *01244/647472* ⊕ *www.jazzatthebluelamp.com*.

BrewDog

BARS | Aberdeen's pioneering craft brewery–turned–global brand runs its flagship bar with suitable gusto and no lack of style. A bare-brick warehouse interior with lots of steel means there's lots of noise and chatter flying around the cavernous space, oiled by a choice of over 100 craft beers. ✉ *17 Gallowgate, Aberdeen* ☎ *01224/631223* ⊕ *www. brewdog.com*.

CASC Bar

BARS | A fine selection of malt whiskies and Cuban cigars (which can be smoked in the outside seating area) makes this one of Aberdeen's more sophisticated watering holes. CASC, which stands for cigars, ale, Scotch, and coffee, is popular for its craft beers (more than 150 of them) and cool industrial interior. It can seem a bit crowded and noisy on weekends. ✉ *7 Stirling St., Aberdeen* ☎ *01224/212373* ⊕ *www.cascnation. com*.

The Prince of Wales

PUBS | Dating from 1850, the Prince of Wales has retained its paneled walls and wooden tables. Still regarded as Aberdeen's most traditional pub, it's hardly regal, but good-quality food and reasonable prices draw the regulars back. ✉ *7 St. Nicholas La., Aberdeen* ☎ *01224/640597* ⊕ *www.belhavenpubs.co.uk*.

The Tippling House

BARS | Youthful Aberdonian *bon viveurs* have taken this subterranean and sophisticated (by Belmont Street standards) late-night drinking den to their hearts and stomachs. It's a great place to escape and mingle and offers casual dining, innovative cocktails, craft beers, and spirits. ✉ *4 Belmont St., Aberdeen* ☎ ⊕ *www. thetipplinghouse.com*.

🎭 Performing Arts

Aberdeen is a rich city, both financially and culturally.

ARTS CENTERS

Aberdeen Arts Centre

ARTS CENTERS | **FAMILY** | This midscale venue hosts plays, musicals, poetry readings, and exhibitions by professional, amateur, and youth companies. ✉ *33 King St., Aberdeen* ☎ *01224/635208* ⊕ *www.aberdeenartscentre.com*.

Lemon Tree

ARTS CENTERS | This intimate theater has an innovative and international program of dance, stand-up comedy, and puppet theater, as well as folk, jazz, and rock music. ✉ *5 W. North St., Aberdeen* ☎ *01224/641122* ⊕ *www.aberdeenperformingarts.com*.

Peacock Visual Arts

ARTS CENTERS | This gallery displays photographic, video, and slide exhibits of contemporary art and architecture. Entry is by appointment only. ✉ *21 Castle St., Aberdeen* ☎ *01224/639539* ⊕ *www. peacock.studio*.

CONCERT HALLS

His Majesty's Theatre

CONCERTS | The Edwardian His Majesty's Theatre hosts performances on par with those in some of the world's biggest cities. It's a regular venue for musicals and operas, as well as classical and modern dance. The restaurant, called 1906, is popular with audiences and cast members alike. ✉ *Rosemount Viaduct, Aberdeen* ☎ *01224/641122* ⊕ *www. aberdeenperformingarts.com*.

Music Hall

CONCERTS | The Scottish National Orchestra and the Scottish Chamber Orchestra are regulars here, as are shows with a vibrant mix of Scottish traditional, folk, jazz, and roots. ✉ *Union St., Aberdeen* ☎ *01224/641122* ⊕ *www. aberdeenperformingarts.com*.

FILM
The Belmont

FILM | Independent, foreign language, and classic films are screened at the Belmont. The basement café bar is a stylish place to hang out. ⊠ *49 Belmont St., Aberdeen* ☎ *01224/343500* ⊕ *www. belmontfilmhouse.com.*

Shopping

There's little to inspire visitors on Union Street, Aberdeen's main shopping thoroughfare or in Union Square and the bland Bon Accord & St. Nicholas Mall, where big British chain stores predominate, but Aberdeen does have a few good specialty shops. Rosemount Viaduct and Belmont Street are worth a meander.

Books and Beans

BOOKS | This independent bookshop has its own café with free Internet access and sells a good range of flavored coffees. You're welcome to browse, sip, and surf the web at the same time. ⊠ *22 Belmont St., Aberdeen* ☎ *01224/646438* ⊕ *www.booksandbeans.co.uk.*

Colin Wood Antiques

ANTIQUES & COLLECTIBLES | This shop is the place to go for small antiques, interesting prints, and regional maps. ⊠ *25 Rose St., Aberdeen* ☎ *01224/643019* ⊕ *www. colinwoodantiques.com.*

Activities

GOLF

With challenging dunes links swept by North Sea breezes, northeast Scotland is known for good golf.

You can expect to pay more than £100 for a round of world-class golf at courses in and around Aberdeen.

Murcar Links Golf Club

GOLF | Sea views and a variety of rugged terrain—from sand dunes to tinkling burns—are the highlights of this course, founded in 1909. It's most famous for breathtaking vistas at the 7th hole, appropriately called the Serpentine. Designer Archibald Simpson considered this course to be one of his finest. ⊠ *Bridge of Don, Aberdeen* ☎ *01224/704354* ⊕ *www.murcarlinks.com* 🏌 *£110 weekdays, £135 weekends* ⅄ *. 18 holes, 6314 yards, par 71.*

★ Royal Aberdeen Golf Club

GOLF | This venerable club, founded in 1780, is the archetypal Scottish links course: tumbling over uneven ground, with the frequently added hazard of sea breezes. Prickly gorse is inclined to close in and form an additional hurdle. The two courses are tucked behind the rough, grassy sand dunes, and there are surprisingly few views of the sea. One historical note: in 1783 this club originated the five-minute-search rule for a lost ball. A handicap certificate and letter of introduction are required. Visitors are allowed only on weekdays. ⊠ *Links Rd., Bridge of Don, Aberdeen* ☎ *01224/702571* ⊕ *www. royalaberdeengolf.com* 🏌 *Balgownie, £195; Silverburn, £70* ⅄ *. Balgownie: 18 holes, 6900 yards, par 71; Silverburn: 18 holes, 4021 yards, par 64.*

Stonehaven

15 miles south of Aberdeen.

Stonehaven's golden sands made this historic town near spectacular Dunnottar Castle a popular holiday destination, until Scots began vacationing in sunnier climates. The surrounding red-clay fields were made famous by Lewis Grassic Gibbon (real name James Leslie Mitchell), who attended school in the town and wrote the seminal Scottish trilogy *A Scots Quair,* about the people, the land, and the impact of World War I. Stonehaven is now famous for its Hogmanay (New Year's Eve) celebrations, where local men swing huge balls of fire on chains before tossing them into the harbor, and as the birthplace of a quirky Scots delicacy, the deep-fried Mars bar.

GETTING HERE AND AROUND

Most trains heading south from Aberdeen stop at Stonehaven; there's at least one per hour making the 15-minute trip. Stagecoach Bluebird runs bus services between Stonehaven and Aberdeen; the fastest, the X70, takes around 40 minutes. Drivers should take A90 south and turn off at A957.

Sights

★ Dunnottar Castle

CASTLE/PALACE | It's hard to beat the cinematic majesty of the magnificent cliff-top ruins of Dunnottar Castle, with its panoramic views of the North Sea. Building began in the 14th century, when Sir William Keith, Marischal of Scotland, decided to build a tower house to demonstrate his power. Subsequent generations added to the structure, and important visitors included Mary, Queen of Scots. The castle is most famous for holding out for eight months against Oliver Cromwell's army in 1651 and 1652, thereby saving the Scottish crown jewels, which had been stored here for safekeeping. Reach the castle via the A90; take the Stonehaven turnoff and follow the signs. Wear sensible shoes, and allow about two hours. ✉ *Off A92, Stonehaven* ☎ *01569/766320* 🌐 *www.dunnottarcastle.co.uk* 🎟 *£8.*

Stonehaven Tolbooth Museum

OTHER MUSEUM | Crime and punishment in days gone by are the central themes at this community-run museum in a 16th-century building that was once Stonehaven's jail and courthouse. Exhibits include the wooden stocks, where up to seven miscreants at a time could be publicly humiliated, and the crank, an appalling torture machine. There's also an eclectic collection of old farming tools and household utensils. ✉ *Old Pier, Stonehaven Harbour, Stonehaven* 🌐 *www.stonehaventolbooth.co.uk* 🎟 *Free* 🕒 *Closed weekdays.*

Restaurants

The Ship Inn

$$ | **SEAFOOD** | This former coaching inn is exactly where you want to take nourishment after a bracing walk from Dunnottar Castle. Refurbishment has taken away much of the history, but wood paneling and rattan chairs make it comfortable, and huge new windows provide views of the harbor. **Known for:** massive mixed grills; traditional Cullen skink; sweeping views of Stonehaven Bay. [$] *Average main: £16* ✉ *5 Shore Head, Stonehaven* ☎ *01569/762617* 🌐 *www.shipinnstonehaven.com.*

Hotels

Bayview B&B

$$ | **B&B/INN** | This contemporary bed-and-breakfast couldn't be in a more convenient location or have better views. **Pros:** fresh, modern design; spic-and-span rooms; right on the beach. **Cons:** not all rooms have sea views; narrow driveway not great for larger cars; standard rooms are smallish. [$] *Rooms from: £125* ✉ *Beachgate La., Stonehaven* ✥ *On the beach, down the lane from the town square* ☎ *07967/645684* 🌐 *www.bayviewbandb.co.uk* 🛏 *7 rooms* 🍴 *Free Breakfast.*

Shopping

Aunty Betty's

FOOD | **FAMILY** | Even if the weather is lousy, this coffee, sweets, and ice-cream shop confirms you are on your summer holidays. Grown-ups will love the gin-and-tonic or Champagne sorbets, kids the complimentary sprinkles. ✉ *The Promenade, Stonehaven* ☎ *01569/763656.*

Banchory

15 miles west of Stonehaven, 19 miles west of Aberdeen.

Banchory is an immaculate town filled with pinkish-granite buildings. It's usually bustling with ice-cream-eating strollers, out on a day trip from Aberdeen. Nearby are Crathes and Drum castles.

GETTING HERE AND AROUND

A car is by far the best way to get around the area; A93 is one of the main roads connecting the towns.

For those reliant on public transport, Stagecoach buses operate a number of services for towns along or just off A93 (Drum Castle, Banchory, Kincardine, Aboyne, Ballater, Balmoral, and Braemar).

Sights

★ Crathes Castle

CASTLE/PALACE | FAMILY | About 16 miles west of Aberdeen, Crathes Castle was once the home of the Burnett family and is one of the best-preserved castles in Britain. Keepers of the Forest of Drum for generations, the family acquired lands here by marriage and later built a castle, completed in 1596. The National Trust for Scotland cares for the castle, which is furnished with many original pieces and family portraits. The castle is open for guided tours only. Outside are grand yet lovingly tended gardens with calculated symmetry and flower-rich beds. There's an adventure park for kids, and the staff organizes activities that are fun and educational. ✉ *Off A93, Banchory* ☎ *01330/844525* 🌐 *www.nts.org.uk* 🎫 *£14.50* 🕒 *Closed Jan.-May and Tues. and Wed. in May–Oct.*

★ Drum Castle

CASTLE/PALACE | This foursquare tower has an evocative medieval chapel that dates from the 13th century; like many other castles, it also has later additions up to Victorian times. Note the tower's rounded corners, said to make battering-ram attacks more difficult. Nearby, fragments of the ancient Forest of Drum still stand, dating from the days when Scotland was covered by great stands of oak and pine. The Garden of Historic Roses, open from April to October, lays claim to some old-fashioned roses not commonly seen today. ✉ *Drumoak by Banchory, Banchory* ✥ *Off the A93, 8 miles east of Banchory and 11 miles west of Aberdeen* ☎ *01330/700334* 🌐 *www.nts.org.uk* 🎫 *£14.50* 🕒 *Closed Jan.–Apr., weekdays in May and Sept., and Tues.–Thurs. in June–Aug.*

Royal Deeside Railway

TRAIN/TRAIN STATION | FAMILY | Built for Queen Victoria, this historic station and its railway line now serve passengers using veteran steam and diesel locomotives to haul vintage carriages along a short scenic route; the journey takes only 15–20 minutes. ✉ *Milton of Crathes, Banchory* ☎ *01330/844416* 🌐 *www.deeside-railway.co.uk* 🎫 *Round-trip £7.50.*

Hotels

★ Banchory Lodge

$$ | HOTEL | Right on the River Dee, this Georgian lodge offers the lovely touches you expect at a luxury hotel, but at a moderate cost. **Pros:** excellent food and afternoon teas; a warm welcome; great bar. **Cons:** no elevators so might be an issue for those with mobility issues; room sizes vary; popular for weddings. [$] *Rooms from: £153* ✉ *Dee St., Banchory* ☎ *01330/822625* 🌐 *www.banchorylodge.com* 🛏 *28 rooms* 🍴 *Free Breakfast.*

Tor Na Coille Country House

$$ | HOTEL | Built as an Edwardian plutocrat's Highland retreat, this mock-baronial mansion hosted Charlie Chaplin and a clutch of small-time European bluebloods in its heyday. **Pros:** salmon fishing on the River Dee; very classy restaurant; incredibly good value at times. **Cons:** some way

The gardens and trails of Crathes Castle are home to a wide variety of plants and flowers, as well as buzzards, herons, and kingfishers.

from town center; sometimes overrun with wedding guests; slightly corporate feel. [$] *Rooms from: £165* ✉ *Inchmarlo Rd., Banchory* ☎ *01330/822242* 🌐 *www.tornacoille.com* 🛏 *25 rooms* 🍴 *Free Breakfast.*

Nightlife

★ Woodend Barn

GATHERING PLACES | Holding art exhibitions, film nights, and live performances, this arts venue packs a mean cultural punch for a renovated barn. ✉ *Burn O'Bennie, Banchory* ☎ *1330/825431 box office* 🌐 *www.thebarnarts.co.uk.*

Ballater

25 miles west of Banchory, 43 miles west of Aberdeen.

The handsome holiday resort of Ballater, once noted for the curative properties of its waters, has profited from the proximity of the royals nearby at Balmoral Castle. The Old Royal Station, purpose-built to pander to Victoria and her hangers-on, has been handsomely restored. You might be amused by the array of "by royal appointment" signs proudly hanging from many of its various shops (even monarchs need bakers and butchers).

The locals have long taken the town's royal connection in stride. To this day, the hundreds who line the road when the Queen and her family arrive for services at the family's parish church at Crathie are invariably visitors to Deeside—one of Balmoral's attractions for the monarch has always been the villagers' respect for royal privacy.

GETTING HERE AND AROUND

Stagecoach Bluebird Buses 201 and 202 operate hourly from Aberdeen to Ballater. However, unless you're on a tight budget, a car is the best way to visit Ballater and explore the nearby sights.

ESSENTIALS

VISITOR INFORMATION Ballater Visitor Information Centre. ✉ *Old Royal Station, Station Sq., Ballater* ☎ *01339/755306* 🌐 *www.visitscotland.com.*

Sights

★ Balmoral Castle

CASTLE/PALACE | The British royal family's favorite vacation spot is a fabulous fake-baronial pile, with emphasis on the "fake." Compared with Scotland's most authentic castles, Balmoral is a right royal upstart, designed in the 19th century by Queen Victoria's German-born consort, Prince Albert. That doesn't stop it being one of Scotland's most visited castles, though only the formal gardens, the ballroom, and the carriage hall, with their exhibitions of royal artifacts, commemorative china, and stuffed native wildlife, are on view.

When members of the royal family are in residence, usually from mid-August to the end of September, Balmoral is closed to visitors, including the grounds. You can take a guided tour in November and December; if the weather is crisp and bright, the estate is at its most dramatic and romantic. You're only allowed a peek inside, but the Royal Cottage is where Queen Victoria spent much of her time. You can see the table where she took breakfast and wrote her correspondence.

Around and about Balmoral are some notable spots—Cairn O'Mount, Cambus O'May, and the Cairngorms from the Linn of Dee—that are home to golden eagles, red squirrels, red deer, black and red grouse, snow bunting, and the United Kingdom's only free-roaming reindeer, some of which may be seen on the quintessentially royal Land Rover Safari Tour. Tempted by the setting? Balmoral Castle has a number of cottages (some very large) for rent by the week at certain times. These are atmospheric but can be spartan (which, believe it or not, is how the royal family likes its holidays to be). ✉ *A93, Ballater* ✣ *7 miles west of Ballater* ☎ *01339/742534* 🌐 *www.balmoralcastle.com* 🎟 *£15* ⏲ *Closed when royals are in residence.*

Loch Muick

TRAIL | A three- or four-hour walk takes you around glorious Loch Muick (Gaelic for "pig") and past Glas-alt Shiel, a favorite retreat of Queen Victoria's that you might recognize from the film *Mrs. Brown*. From Ballater, take the B976 over the River Dee before turning off at the sign for Glen Muick. Park at the Spittal of Loch Muick car park. The path around the loch is well signposted, although good boots are necessary for the stony beach at the far side of the loch. **■ TIP→ The native red deer are quite common throughout the Scottish Highlands, but here is one of the best places to see them.** ✉ *Ballater.*

Restaurants

★ The Rothesay Rooms

$$$$ | **BRITISH** | The Old Royal Station, built for Queen Victoria and restored after a disastrous fire in 2015, now houses the Rothesay Rooms (formerly the Carriage). The upscale restaurant serves a carefully curated menu with an emphasis on locally sourced game, meat, seafood, and vegetables. **Known for:** local regional produce; Lunan Bay asparagus; Wark Farm lamb and Hill of Gellen pheasant. [$] *Average main: £27* ✉ *Ballater Station, Station Square, Ballater* ☎ *01339/753816* 🌐 *www.rothesay-rooms.co.uk* ⏲ *Closed Mon.–Thurs. No dinner Sun.*

Hotels

Auld Kirk

$$ | **B&B/INN** | This simply renovated old church, with some interesting architectural features preserved in its public areas, is a comfortable enough base for a night or two in Ballater. **Pros:** family-friendly vibe; private lounge bar; pin-tidy bedrooms and public rooms. **Cons:**

Balmoral, Queen Victoria's Retreat 👁

Some credit Sir Walter Scott with having opened up Scotland for tourism through his poems and novels. But it was probably Queen Victoria (1819–1901) who gave Scottish tourism its real momentum when, in 1842, she first came to Scotland and when, in 1847—on orders of a doctor, who thought the relatively dry climate of upper Deeside would suit her—she bought Balmoral. The pretty little castle was knocked down to make room for a much grander house designed by her husband, Prince Albert (1819–61), in 1855. In full-blown Scottish baronial style, the new structure had a veritable rash of tartanitis. Before long the entire Deeside and the region north were dotted with country houses and mock-baronial châteaux.

"It seems like a dream to be here in our dear Highland Home again," Queen Victoria wrote. "Every year my heart becomes more fixed in this dear Paradise." Victoria loved Balmoral more for its setting than its house, so be sure to take in its pleasant gardens. Year by year Victoria and Albert added to the estate, taking over neighboring houses, securing the forest and moorland around it, and developing deer stalking and grouse shooting here.

In consequence, Balmoral is now a large property, with grounds that run 12 miles along the Deeside road. Its privacy is protected by belts of pinewood, and the only view of the castle from the A93 is a partial one, from a point near Inver, 2 miles west of the gates.

There's an excellent bird's-eye view of Balmoral from an old military road, now the A939, which climbs out of Crathie, northbound for Cockbridge and the Don Valley. This view embraces the summit of Lochnagar, in whose *corries* (hollows) the snow lies year-round and whose boulder fields the current Prince of Wales, Charles Windsor, so fondly and frequently treads.

not a full-service hotel; no restaurant; showers are small, and most rooms have no tub. $ *Rooms from: £140* ✉ *Braemar Rd., Ballater* ☎ *01339/755762* ⊕ *www.theauldkirk.com* ⇌ *7 rooms* ⏐◎⏐ *Free Breakfast.*

★ Hilton Grand Vacations at Craigendarroch Suites

$$ | **HOTEL** | **FAMILY** | This grand mansion has been turned into a resort with a luxury spa and country club, combining Victorian style with modern comforts. **Pros:** rooms and suites have kitchenettes; great pool and gym facilities; no smoking anywhere inside or out. **Cons:** a bit pricey for this area; incongruously corporate atmosphere; if there's a conference, non-attending guests can feel lost among the crowds. $ *Rooms from: £161* ✉ *Braemar Rd., Ballater* ☎ *01339/755558* ⊕ *www. hiltongrandvacations.com/scotland/ hgvc-craigendarroch-suites* ⇌ *51 suites* ⏐◎⏐ *Free Breakfast.*

No 45

$ | **B&B/INN** | With touches of period charm, this Victorian-era house offers old-fashioned hospitality and simple, understated comfort. **Pros:** unpretentious feel; good price; relaxing lounge. **Cons:** not for those seeking a full-service hotel; slightly garish decor; a few bedrooms on the small side. $ *Rooms from: £115* ✉ *45 Braemar Rd., Ballater* ☎ *01339/755420* ⊕ *www.no45.co.uk* ⇌ *8 rooms* ⏐◎⏐ *Free Breakfast.*

🛍 Shopping

Deeside Books

BOOKS | Beyond the gifts section, veer to the right and you will find an interesting collection of old, out-of-print, and hard-to-find books about Scotland, which make splendid gifts for lovers of all things Scottish. ⊠ *18–20 Bridge St., Ballater* ☎ *01339/754080* ⊕ *www.deesidebooks.com.*

McEwan Gallery

ART GALLERIES | A mile west of Ballater, the McEwan Gallery displays fine paintings, watercolors, prints, and books (many with a Scottish or golf theme) in an unusual house built by the Swiss artist Rudolphe Christen in 1902. ⊠ *A939, Ballater* ☎ *01339/755429* ⊕ *www.mcewangallery.com.*

Braemar

17 miles west of Ballater, 60 miles west of Aberdeen.

Synonymous with the British monarchy, due to its closeness to Balmoral, and with the famous Highland Games, this village is popular year-round as a base for walkers and climbers enjoying the Grampian Mountains.

GETTING HERE AND AROUND

The town is on A93; there's bus service here and to other towns on the road.

👁 Sights

Braemar Castle

CASTLE/PALACE | On the northern outskirts of town, Braemar Castle dates from the 17th century, although its defensive walls, in the shape of a pointed star, came later. At Braemar (the *braes*, or slopes, of the district of Mar), the standard, or rebel flag, was first raised at the start of the unsuccessful Jacobite rebellion of 1715. About 30 years later, during the last Jacobite rebellion,

Braemar Castle was strengthened and garrisoned by government troops. From the early 1800s the castle was the clan seat of the Farquharsons, who hold their clan reunion here every summer.

Thanks to the commitment of local volunteers, a remarkable 2008 renovation restored Braemar to the home it would have been in the early 20th century, complete with all the necessary comforts and family memorabilia. A dozen rooms are on view, including the laird's day room with a plush daybed and the kitchen. ⊠ *Off A93, Braemar* ☎ *01339/741219* ⊕ *www.braemarcastle.co.uk* 🎟 *£8* 🕙 *Closed Nov.–Easter and Mon. and Tues. in Apr.–June, Sept., and Oct.*

Braemar Highland Games Centre

OTHER ATTRACTION | This unabashedly royalist visitor attraction is devoted to the tartan heritage of the Braemar Royal Highland Society, the organizers of the original Highland Gathering. It also dedicates time to the British royal family's connection to the event and with Braemar from the days of Queen Victoria and Prince Albert through the 21st century. ⊠ *Duke of Rothesay Highland Games Pavilion, Princess Royal and Duke of Fife Memorial Park, Broombank Terr., Braemar* ⊕ *www.highlandgamescentre.org.*

Braemar Highland Gathering

OTHER ATTRACTION | FAMILY | The village of Braemar is associated with the Braemar Highland Gathering, held the first Saturday in September. Although there are many such gatherings celebrated throughout Scotland, this one is distinguished by the presence of the royal family. Competitions and events include hammer throwing, caber tossing, and bagpipe playing. If you plan to attend, book your accommodations months in advance and be sure to buy tickets and, if necessary, your car parking ticket about six months in advance, as they do sell out. ⊠ *Princess Royal and Duke of Fife Memorial Park, Broombank Terr., Braemar* ⊕ *www.braemargathering.org* 🎟 *£12 plus £3 booking fee.*

The Highland Games

They might not all be as royally attended as the Braemar Highland Gathering, but from spring to late summer across a wide swath of northern Scotland competitors gather to toss, pull, fling, and sing at various Highland events. No two games are the same, but many incorporate agricultural shows, sporting competitions, clan gatherings, or just beer in the sun. VisitScotland's website has a list of them.

Which one to attend? Braemar stands tall on ceremony and tradition, and the chance of seeing royalty up close means it attracts visitors from far and wide. Dufftown Games (🌐 *www.dufftownhighlandgames.com*) is the most competitive, with its race up the nearby Ben Rinnes, while the most picturesque is the Lochcarron Games (🌐 *www.lochcarrongames.org.uk*), which are played and danced out under the massif of the Torridon Hills.

Linn of Dee

VIEWPOINT | Although the main A93 slinks off to the south from Braemar, a little unmarked road will take you farther west into the hilly heartland. The road offers views over the winding River Dee and the blue hills before passing through the tiny hamlet of Inverey and crossing a bridge at the Linn of Dee. *Linn* is a Scots word meaning "rocky narrows," and the river's gash here is deep and roaring. Park beyond the bridge and walk back to admire the sylvan setting.

Hotels

★ The Fife Arms

$$$$ | **HOTEL** | This opulently quirky, art-filled boutique hotel is a much-needed addition to Braemar's rather thin lodging portfolio. **Pros:** great cocktails; fabulous, art-filled rooms; locally sourced game, salmon, and seafood on the dining menu. **Cons:** some may find taxidermied animals in rooms and public areas distasteful; overwhelmingly arty; very expensive. [$] *Rooms from: £393* ✉ *Mar Rd., Braemar* ☎ *01339/720200* 🌐 *www.thefifearms.com* 🔑 *46 rooms* 🍴 *Free Breakfast.*

Ivy Cottage

$ | **B&B/INN** | Everything at this 19th-century inn, from the silky bedding to the bright bathroom fittings, is of the highest standard and done with good taste. **Pros:** facilities for walkers and cyclists; relaxing rooms; owners who go out of their way to make you feel at home. **Cons:** two-night minimum stay; no check-in before 4 pm; no bar or restaurant. [$] *Rooms from: £88* ✉ *Cluniebank Rd., Braemar* ☎ *01339/741642* 🌐 *www.ivycottagebraemar.co.uk* 🔑 *5 rooms* 🍴 *Free Breakfast.*

Activities

Braemar Golf Course

GOLF | It's worth playing the tricky 18-hole Braemar Golf Course if only to say you've played the highest 18-hole course in Scotland. Founded in 1902, it is laden with foaming water hazards. ✉ *Cluny Bank Rd., Braemar* ☎ *01339/741618* 🌐 *www.braemargolfclub.co.uk* 🎟 *£35 weekdays, £40 weekends* ⛳ *18 holes, 4935 yards, par 65.*

Corgarff Castle

23 miles northeast of Braemar, 14 miles northwest of Ballater.

This castle has a striking setting on the moors and some rebuilt military features that recall its strategic importance.

GETTING HERE AND AROUND
By car, take A939 and then follow signs.

Sights

Castle Trail
SCENIC DRIVE | If you return east from Corgarff Castle to the A939/A944 junction and make a left onto the A944, the signs indicate that you're on the Castle Trail. The A944 meanders along the River Don to the village of Strathdon, where a great mound by the roadside turns out to be a *motte,* or the base of a wooden castle, built in the late 12th century. Although it takes considerable imagination to become enthusiastic about a grass-covered heap, surviving mottes have contributed greatly to the understanding of the history of Scottish castles. The A944 then joins the A97, and a few minutes later a sign points to **Glenbuchat Castle,** a plain Z-plan tower house. ⊕ *www.visitscotland.com/see-do/attractions/castles/scotland-castle-trail.*

Corgarff Castle
CASTLE/PALACE | Eighteenth-century soldiers paved a military highway north from Ballater to Corgarff Castle, an isolated tower house on the moorland with a star-shaped defensive wall that's a curious replica of Braemar Castle. Corgarff was built as a hunting lodge for the earls of Mar in the 16th century. After an eventful history that included the wife of a later laird being burned alive in a family dispute, the castle ended its career as a garrison for Hanoverian troops. The troops were responsible for preventing illegal whisky distilling. Reconstructed barracks show what the castle must have been like when the redcoats arrived in 1746. ⊠ *Off A939, Corgarff* ☎ *0131/668–8600* ⊕ *www.historicenvironment.scot* 🎫 *£6* ⊘ *Closed Oct.–Mar.*

Alford

28 miles west of Aberdeen, 41 miles northeast of Braemar.

A plain and sturdy settlement in the Howe (Hollow) of Alford, this town gives those who have grown somewhat weary of castle-hopping a break: it has a museum instead. Craigievar Castle and Castle Fraser are nearby, though.

GETTING HERE AND AROUND
The town is on A944.

⊙ Sights

Alford Heritage Museum
HISTORY MUSEUM | This award-winning, community-run museum, housed in an early 20th-century livestock auction mart, has a fascinating collection of local memorabilia and allows a glimpse into the history of Alford and the surrounding region. ⊠ *3 Mart Rd., Alford* ☎ *0195/562906* ⊕ *www.alfordheritagemuseum.com* 🎫 *£6* ⊘ *Closed Nov.– Mar. and Mon.–Wed.*

★ Castle Fraser
CASTLE/PALACE | The massive Castle Fraser is the ancestral home of the Frasers and one of the largest of the castles of Mar; it's certainly a contender as one of the grandest castles in the northeast. Although the well-furnished building shows a variety of styles reflecting the taste of its owners from the 15th through the 19th century, its design is typical of the cavalcade of castles in the region, and for good reason. This—along with many others, including Midmar, Craigievar, Crathes, and Glenbuchat—was designed by a family of master masons called Bell. There are plenty of family items, but don't miss the two Turret

Language and the Scots

Until quite recently, many Scots were made to feel uncomfortable—even within Scotland—about using their native regional dialects. After the Union of England and Scotland in 1707, Scotland's professional middle class, including its politicians, adopted an only mildly accented form of "standard English." Even today, the voices of the Scottish aristocracy—usually educated in elite English schools—are almost indistinguishable from those of their English counterparts. But in recent generations, Scots urban accents and rural dialects have become accepted once again. The creation of the post of Makar (first held by Edwin Morgan from 2004 to 2010, then by Jackie Kay, and since 2021 by Kathleen Jamie) signaled that Scots is once again to be taken seriously. Taking up the mantle of Robert Burns, whose poems drew on the *Lallans* (Lowlands) of his native southwest, contemporary authors such as Irvine Welsh and William McIlvanney and others write in the voices of working-class Scots city dwellers.

Lowland Scots

The Scots language (that is, Lowland Scots, not Gaelic), a northern form of Middle English influenced by Norse, Gaelic, French, and Dutch, was used in the court and in literature until the late 16th century. After the Scottish court moved to London in 1603 it declined as a literary or official language. But Scots survives in various forms, some of which—like the broadest urban accents of Dundee and Glasgow—are almost impenetrable to an ear used to "standard" English.

Some Scottish words are used and understood across the entire country (and world), such as *wee* (small), *aye* (yes), *lassie* (girl), and *bonny* (pretty). You may even find yourself exporting a few useful words, such as *dreich* (gloomy), *glaikit* (acting and looking foolish), or *dinna fash* (don't worry), all of which are much more expressive than their English equivalents. Doric, the regional dialect of Aberdeenshire, is the purest direct descendant of the old Scots tongue. It's loaded with borrowings from Norse, such as *quine* (a young woman) and *loon* (a young man), while "what" becomes "fit," "who" becomes "faa," and "which" becomes "fitna." The local version of "How do you do?" is "Fit like?" A country dweller might refer to an urban Aberdonian as a *toonser*; his city cousin might call him a *teuchter*. Neither term is entirely complimentary.

Gaelic

Scottish Gaelic—an entirely different language—is not, despite what many still think, Scotland's national tongue. This Celtic language is incomprehensible to 99% of Scots and spoken by fewer than 60,000 people. Most live in the Western Isles (*Eilean Siar* in Gaelic), with a handful in the Highlands and Argyll. All speak English as well as their mother tongue. Gaelic was frowned upon after the failure of the 1745 Jacobite rebellions, and numbers of Gaelic speakers have declined ever since, though the decline has slowed in recent years.

Rooms—one of which is the trophy room—and Major Smiley's Room. He married into the family but is famous for having been one of the escapees from Colditz (a high-security prisoner-of-war camp) during World War II. The walled garden includes a 19th-century knot garden, with colorful flower beds, box hedging, gravel paths, and splendid herbaceous borders. Have lunch in the tearoom or the picnic area. ⊠ *Off A944, Alford ✛ 8 miles southeast of Alford* ☎ *01330/833463* ⊕ *www.nts.org.uk* 🎫 *£12* ⊙ *Closed Nov.–Mar. and Tues.– Thurs. in Apr.–Oct.*

Craigievar Castle

CASTLE/PALACE | Pepper-pot turrets make Craigievar Castle an outstanding example of a tower house. Striking and well preserved, it has many family furnishings, and the lovely grounds are worth exploring, too. Craigievar was built in relatively peaceful times by William Forbes, a successful merchant in trade with the Baltic Sea ports (he was also known as Danzig Willie). ⊠ *A980, Alford ✛ 5 miles south of Alford* ☎ *01339/883635* ⊕ *www. nts.org.uk* 🎫 *£13* ⊙ *Closed Oct.-mid June, Mon.–Wed in mid-June–Aug., and weekdays in Sept.*

Grampian Transport Museum

OTHER MUSEUM | **FAMILY** | The entertaining and enthusiastically run Grampian Transport Museum specializes in road-based means of locomotion, backed up by archives and a library. Its collection of buses and trams is second to none, but the Craigievar Express, a steam-driven creation invented by the local postman to deliver mail more efficiently, is the most unusual. Look out for the Hillman Imp: if Scotland has a national car, this is it. There's a small café that offers tea, baked goods, and ice cream. ⊠ *Montgarrie Rd., Alford* ☎ *01975/562292* ⊕ *www.gtm.org. uk* 🎫 *£11* ⊙ *Closed Nov.–Mar.*

Dufftown

54 miles west of Aberdeen.

On one of the Spey tributaries, Dufftown was planned in 1817 by the Earl of Fife. Its simple cross layout with a square and a large clock tower (originally from Banff and now the site of the visitor center) is typical of a small Scottish town built in the 19th century. Its simplicity is made all the more stark by the brooding, heather-clad hills that rise around it. Dufftown is convenient to a number of distilleries.

GETTING HERE AND AROUND

To get here from Aberdeen, drive west on A96 and A920; then turn west at Huntly. It's not easy or quick, but you can take the train to Elgin or Keith and then the bus to Dufftown.

◉ Sights

Balvenie Castle

CASTLE/PALACE | On a mound just above the Glenfiddich Distillery is this grim, gray, and squat curtain-walled castle. This ruined fortress, which dates from the 13th century, once commanded the glens and passes toward Speyside and Elgin. ⊠ *Castle Road, Dufftown* ☎ *01340/820121* ⊕ *www.historicenvironment.scot* 🎫 *£6* ⊙ *Closed Oct.–Mar.*

Balvenie Distillery

DISTILLERY | As soon as you step into the old manager's office at Balvenie Distillery—now gently restored and fitted with knotted-elm furniture—you realize Balvenie wants to make sure that all visitors get to see, smell, and feel the magic of the making of this malt. Balvenie is unusual because it has its own cooperage with six coopers hard at work turning the barrels. Tours show the mashing, fermentation, and distillation process and end with a tasting. ⊠ *Balvenie St., Dufftown* ☎ *01340/822210* ⊕ *www.thebalvenie.com* 🎫 *£45* ⊙ *Closed weekends.*

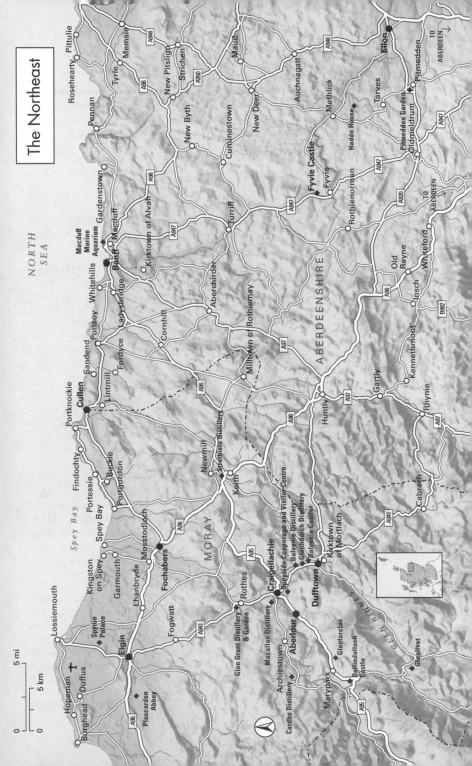

Whisky, the Water of Life

Conjured from an innocuous mix of malted barley, water, and yeast, malt whisky is for many synonymous with Scotland. Lowlanders and Highlanders produced whisky for hundreds of years before it emerged as Scotland's national drink and major export. Today those centuries of expertise result in a sublimely subtle drink with many different layers of flavor. Each distillery produces a malt with—to the expert—instantly identifiable, predominant notes peculiarly its own.

Whisky Types and Styles

There are two types of whisky: malt and grain. Malt whisky, generally acknowledged to have a more sophisticated bouquet and flavor, is made with malted barley—barley that is soaked in water until the grains germinate and then is dried to halt the germination, all of which adds extra flavor and a touch of sweetness to the brew. Grain whisky also contains malted barley, but with the addition of unmalted barley and maize.

Blended whiskies, which make up many of the leading brands, usually balance malt- and grain-whisky distillations; deluxe blends contain a higher percentage of malts. Blends that contain several malt whiskies are called "vatted malts." Whisky connoisseurs often prefer to taste the single malts: the unblended whisky from a single distillery.

In simple terms, malt whiskies may be classified into "eastern" and "western" in style, with the whisky made in the east of Scotland, for example in Speyside, being lighter and sweeter than the products of the Western Isles, which often have a taste of peat smoke or even iodine.

The production process is, by comparison, relatively straightforward: just malt your barley, mash it, ferment it, and distill it, then mature to perfection. To find out the details, join a distillery tour, and be rewarded with a dram. Check out ⊕ www.scotland-whisky.com for more information.

Tasting Whisky

When tasting whisky, follow these simple steps. First, pour a dram. Turn and tilt the glass to coat the sides. Smell the whisky, "nosing" to inhale the heady aromas. If you want, you can add a little water and turn the glass gently to watch it "marry" with the whisky, nosing as you go. Take a wee sip and swirl it over your tongue and sense what connoisseurs call the mouthfeel. Swallow and admire the finish. Repeat until convinced it's a good malt.

★ Glenfiddich Distillery

DISTILLERY | Many make Glenfiddich Distillery their first stop on the Malt Whisky Trail. The independent company of William Grant and Sons Limited was the first to realize the tourist potential of the distilling process. The company began offering tours around the typical pagoda-roofed malting buildings and subsequently built an entertaining visitor center. Besides a free 20-minute tour of the distillery there are various tours for more discerning visitors that include nosing and tasting sessions. Check out the Robbie Dhu bar for al fresco dining and tasy light meals with local flavor, and look out for viewings of the current Glenfiddich Distillery Artists in Residence's work. ⊠ A941, Dufftown ✛ ½ mile north *of Dufftown ☎ 01340/820373 🌐 www.glenfiddich.com 🎟 Tours from £10.*

Keith and Dufftown Railway

TRAIN/TRAIN STATION | FAMILY | Leaving from Dufftown three times a day on weekends then returning from Keith, this restored locomotive lets you return to the age when trains were exciting, chugging 11 miles through forests, fields, and across rivers. It passes Drummuir Castle on its way to Keith, home of the Strathisla Distillery. The Sidings Cafe at Dufftown Station serves breakfast, light lunches, snacks, and afternoon tea. ✉ *Dufftown Station, Station Rd., Dufftown ☎ 01340/821181 🌐 keith-dufftown-railway.co.uk 🎟 £7 ⏲ Closed Mon.–Thurs. and Oct.–July.*

Strathisla Distillery

DISTILLERY | Whisky lovers should take the B9014 11 miles northeast from Dufftown—or alternatively, ride the Keith Dufftown Railway—to see one of Scotland's most iconic distilleries, the Strathisla Distillery, with its cobblestone courtyard and famous double-pagoda roofs. Stretching over the picturesque River Isla, the Strathisla Distillery was built in 1786 and now produces the main component of the Chivas Regal blend. Guided tours, for those 18 and over only, take you to the mash house, tun room, and still house—all pretty much the same as they were when production began. The tour ends with a tasting session. ✉ *Seafield Ave., Keith ☎ 01542/783044 🌐 www.chivas.com 🎟 £30.*

Hotels

The Fife Arms Hotel

$ | B&B/INN | This 18th-century coaching inn offers a whiff of atmosphere and acceptable accommodations for a one-night stay (but for no longer) in motel-style rooms attached to an old-school pub popular with locals. **Pros:** very central; great full Scottish breakfast; off-street parking. **Cons:** basic amenities; unexciting decor; some noise from adjoining pub. [$] *Rooms from: £73 ✉ 2 The Square, Dufftown ☎ 01340/820220 🌐 www.fifearmsdufftown.co.uk 🛏 6 rooms 🍴 Free Breakfast.*

Craigellachie

4 miles northwest of Dufftown.

Renowned as an angling resort, Craigellachie, like so many settlements on the River Spey, is sometimes enveloped in the malty reek of the local industry. Glen Grant is one of the distilleries nearby. The Spey itself is crossed by a handsome suspension bridge, designed by noted engineer Thomas Telford (1757–1834) in 1814 and now bypassed by the modern road.

GETTING HERE AND AROUND

The town is on A491; it's best to drive here, as public transportation is infrequent and complicated.

Sights

★ Glen Grant Distillery & Garden

DISTILLERY | This historic distillery on the northern edge of Rothes has been producing award-winning single malts since 1840, and it's still going strong today. An impressive visitor center provides guided tours of the distillery, revealing its distinctive blend of centuries-old traditions and cutting-edge technology, as well as offering private tastings. There's a shop and café, too. But the biggest draw here is the stunning Victorian gardens; walk along the snaking path and pass pristine lawns, rare blooming flowers, gently flowing streams, and pretty pagodas. On your walk look out for a small cave and a locked safe; these were used to store founder Major Grant's private whisky collection, so he could share a dram with his walking companions. ✉ *A941, Rothes ✣ North of town, left at junction of A941 and B9015 ☎ 01340/832118 🌐 www.glengrant.com 🎟 £5 tour and tasting ⏲ Closed Sun.*

★ Macallan Distillery

DISTILLERY | Beneath a vast, undulating, turf-covered roof that mimics the outlines of the surrounding moorland, the Macallan Distillery and Visitor Centre is now an exciting tourism hub for Speyside. The Discovery Experience tour lasts 2 hours, 30 minutes and includes nosing and tasting of some of the distillery's distinctively sherry-tinctured malts. ✉ *Easter Elchies, Craigellachie* ✦ *About 1 mile west of Craigellachie, off B9102* ☎ *01304/318000* ⊕ *www.themacallan. com* ⊠ *£50* ◷ *Closed weekdays.*

Speyside Cooperage and Visitor Centre

FACTORY | Situated four miles south of Rothes, this working cooperage is the only place left in the U.K. where you can see coopers hard at work making wooden whisky casks. Since 1947, coopers here have been using American oak, along with traditional tools and methods, to create the casks for distilleries across Scotland and beyond. This visitor center gives you the chance to see the coopers at work and learn more about the life cycle of a cask, with tours throughout the working week. There's also a well-stocked gift shop and barrel-themed café. ✉ *Dufftown Rd., Craigellachie* ☎ *01340/871108* ⊕ *www.speysidecooperage.co.uk* ⊠ *£4* ◷ *Closed weekends.*

🍴 Restaurants

Copper Dog

$$ | **BRITISH** | With its reclaimed woodwork and mismatched wooden chairs, rows of malt whisky bottles, decorative oak barrel-ends, and walls hung with prints, the Craigellachie Hotel's bar-restaurant is an edgy blend of cozy and shabby chic. The menu is equally relaxed, with dishes such as locally produced gourmet sausages, rumbledethumps (a casserole of baked potato, cabbage, and onions), and an outstanding platter of Scottish cheeses with housemade chutney, all of which can be matched with regional craft beers. **Known for:**

local craft beers; whole grilled lobster; Speyside ribeye steak. $ *Average main: £17* ✉ *Craigellachie Hotel, Victoria St., Craigellachie* ☎ *01340/881204* ⊕ *www. craigellachiehotel.co.uk.*

🛏 Hotels

Craigellachie Hotel

$$ | **HOTEL** | Who would expect a rock-chic hideaway in the heart of sleepy Speyside? But that's what this stylish old town house has become. **Pros:** huge range of malt whiskies; stylish decor down to the details; perfectly pitched service. **Cons:** booked up months or years in advance; pretentious to a fault; popular for wedding parties. $ *Rooms from: £150* ✉ *Victoria St., Craigellachie* ☎ *01340/881204* ⊕ *www.craigellachiehotel.co.uk* ⇔ *26 rooms* ⦿ *Free Breakfast.*

Highlander Inn

$ | **B&B/INN** | This very-Scottish hotel prides itself on its whisky bar and its friendly welcome. **Pros:** great bar; simple and cozy accommodations; warm atmosphere. **Cons:** very whisky-focused, so might not be for everyone; could be rather too lively for some; uninspired decor. $ *Rooms from: £110* ✉ *Victoria St., Craigellachie* ☎ *01340/881446* ⊕ *www.whiskyinn.com* ⇔ *8 rooms* ⦿ *Free Breakfast.*

★ The Station Hotel

$$ | **HOTEL** | This historic yet contemporary hotel in the heart of Rothes is renowned for its luxury designer rooms and suites, its excellent café-restaurant serving hearty pub grub, and its enormous selection of world whiskies and gins, to be enjoyed in the comfort of the stunning Spirit Safe bar. **Pros:** free car parking; chic contemporary decor; incredible whisky selection. **Cons:** expensive for the area; no elevator; breakfast buffet a little sparse. $ *Rooms from: £200* ✉ *51 New St.* ☎ *01340/832200* ⊕ *www.stationhotelspeyside.com* ⇔ *15 rooms* ⦿ *Free Breakfast.*

Aberlour

2 miles southwest of Craigellachie.

Aberlour, often listed as Charlestown of Aberlour on maps, is a handsome little burgh, essentially Victorian in style, though actually founded in 1812 by the local landowner. The names of the noted local whisky stills are Cragganmore, Aberlour, and Glenfarclas; Glenlivet and Cardhu are also nearby. Also in Aberlour is Walkers, famous for producing shortbread, tins of buttery, crumbly goodness, since 1898.

GETTING HERE AND AROUND

Aberlour is on A95; public transportation here is infrequent.

 ## Sights

Ballindalloch Castle

CASTLE/PALACE | The family home of the Macpherson-Grants since 1546, Ballindalloch Castle is every visitor's idea of what a Scots laird's lair should look like. You can wander around the beautifully kept rooms and meticulously tended gardens at your leisure; you may even bump into the lord and lady of the manor, who live here all year. There's also a splendid tea shop offering large slices of cake. ⊠ *Off A95, Aberlour* ✛ *8 miles southwest of Craigellachie* ☎ *01807/500205* ⊕ *www. ballindallochcastle.co.uk* 🎟 *£12* ۞ *Closed Oct.–Easter.*

Cardhu Distillery

DISTILLERY | The striking outline of Cardhu Distillery, whose main product lies at the heart of Johnnie Walker blends, is set among the heather-clad Mannoch Hills. Established by John and Helen Cumming in 1811, it was officially founded in 1824 after distilling was made legal by the Excise Act of 1823. Guides take you to the mashing, fermenting, and distilling halls, and they explain the malting process, which now takes place on the coast at Burghead. ⊠ *B1902, Knockando* ✛ *10 miles north of Glenlivet and 7 miles west of Aberlour* ☎ *01340/875635* ⊕ *www.discovering-distilleries.com/cardhu/find-us* 🎟 *£15* ۞ *Closed Oct.–May.*

Glenfarclas

DISTILLERY | Glenfarclas is one of Scotland's few remaining family-owned distilleries, passed down from father to son since 1865. That link to the past is most visible among its low buildings, where the retired whisky-still sits outside: if you didn't know what it was, you could mistake it for part of a submarine. The tours end with tastings in the superlative Ship Room, the intact lounge of an ocean liner called the *Empress of Australia.* ⊠ *Off A95, Ballindalloch* ☎ *01807/500345* ⊕ *www.glenfarclas.com* 🎟 *£7.50; tasting tours from £40* ۞ *Closed weekends Oct.–June and Sun. July–Sept.*

Glenlivet

DISTILLERY | The famous Glenlivet was the first licensed distillery in the Highlands, founded in 1824 by George Smith. Today it produces one of the best-known 12-year-old single malts in the world. The 90-minute Original Tour offers an introduction to malt whisky making, explains the distillery's history, and includes a free dram; more in-depth tours are available. There's a coffee shop with baked goods and, of course, a whisky shop. Visitors must be 18 or over. ⊠ *Off B9008, Ballindalloch* ✛ *10 miles southwest of Aberlour via A95 and B9008.* ☎ *01340/821720* ⊕ *www.glenlivet.com* 🎟 *£15* ۞ *Closed mid-Dec.–July.*

 ## Hotels

Cardhu Country House

$$ | B&B/INN | This once-abandoned manse (minister's house) looks as if it has always been loved and lived in: huge bedrooms with wooden floors, antique fireplaces, and large beds dressed in Harris tweed throws are married to contemporary bathrooms. **Pros:** great breakfasts; period charm and modern comforts;

tasty meals on request. **Cons:** chintzy setting not for everyone; meals must be ordered in advance; popular with shooting parties. [$] *Rooms from: £125* ✉ *Off B9102, Knockando* ☎ *01340/810895* 🌐 *www.cardhucountryhouse.co.uk* 🛏 *6 rooms* 🍴 *Free Breakfast* ☞ *No children under eight.*

Mash Tun

$ | **B&B/INN** | Curvy yet sturdy, this former station hotel, now a smart bed-and-breakfast with a popular restaurant, is the social hub of the village. **Pros:** great atmosphere in the restaurant and bar; superb accommodations; tasty meals. **Cons:** on the more expensive side for this area; small bedrooms; often booked up in summer. [$] *Rooms from: £90* ✉ *8 Broomfield Sq., Aberlour* ☎ *01340/881771* 🌐 *www.mashtun-aberlour.com* 🛏 *5 rooms* 🍴 *Free Breakfast.*

Elgin

15 miles north of Craigellachie, 69 miles northwest of Aberdeen.

As the center of the fertile *Laigh* (low-lying lands) of Moray, Elgin has been of local importance for centuries. Sheltered by great hills to the south, the city lies between two major rivers, the Spey and the Findhorn. Beginning in the 13th century, Elgin became an important religious center, a cathedral city with a walled town growing up around the cathedral and adjacent to the original settlement.

Elgin prospered, and by the early 18th century it became a mini-Edinburgh of the north and a place where country gentlemen spent their winters. It even echoed Edinburgh in carrying out wide-scale reconstruction in the 18th century. Many fine neoclassical buildings survive today despite much misguided demolition in the late 20th century for better traffic flow. Nevertheless, the central main-street plan and some of the older little streets and *wynds* (alleyways) remain.

GETTING HERE AND AROUND

Elgin is on the A96 road from Aberdeen to Inverness. The A941 runs north from the distillery area to the city. There's a train stop here on the line that links Aberdeen and Inverness: Aberdeen is 90 minutes away.

ESSENTIALS

VISITOR INFORMATION Elgin Visitor Information Point. ✉ *Elgin Library, Cooper Park, Elgin* ☎ *01343/562608* 🌐 *www.morayspeyside.com.*

Sights

Elgin Cathedral

CHURCH | Cooper Park contains a magnificent ruin, the Elgin Cathedral, consecrated in 1224. Its eventful story included devastation by fire: a 1390 act of retaliation by warlord Alexander Stewart (circa 1343–1405), the Wolf of Badenoch. The illegitimate son of King David II (1324–71) had sought revenge for his excommunication by the bishop of Moray. The cathedral was rebuilt but finally fell into disuse after the Reformation in 1560. By 1567 the highest authority in the land, the regent earl of Moray, had stripped the lead from the roof to pay for his army. Thus ended the career of the religious seat known as the Lamp of the North. Some traces of the cathedral settlement survive—the gateway Pann's Port and the Bishop's Palace—although they've been drastically altered. ✉ *Cooper Park, Elgin* ☎ *01343/547171* 🌐 *www.historicenvironment.scot* 🎟 *£9; £12 with Spynie Palace.*

Pluscarden Abbey

RELIGIOUS BUILDING | Given the general destruction caused by the 16th-century upheaval of the Reformation, abbeys in Scotland tend to be ruinous and deserted, but at the 13th-century Pluscarden Abbey the ancient way of life continues. Monks from Prinknash Abbey near Gloucester, England, returned here in 1948, and the abbey is now a

Benedictine community. Daily mass is at 8 am (10 am on Sunday) and is sung by the monks using Gregorian chant. ✉ *Off B9010, Elgin* ✥ *6 miles southwest of Elgin* 🌐 *www.pluscardenabbey.org.*

Spynie Palace

CASTLE/PALACE | Just north of Elgin sits Spynie Palace, the impressive 15th-century former headquarters of the bishops of Moray. It has now fallen into ruin, though the top of the tower has good views over the Laigh of Moray. Find it by turning right off the Elgin–Lossiemouth road. ✉ *Off A941, Elgin* ☎ *01343/546358* 🌐 *www.historicenvironment.scot* 🎟 *£9, £12 with Elgin Cathedral* 🕓 *Closed Oct.–Mar.*

St. Giles Church

CHURCH | At the center of Elgin, the most conspicuous structure is St. Giles Church, which divides High Street. The grand foursquare building, constructed in 1828, exhibits the Greek Revival style: note the columns, the pilasters, and the top of the spire, surmounted by a representation of the Monument of Lysicrates. ✉ *High St., Elgin* 🌐 *www.elginstgileschurch.co.uk.*

Hotels

Mansefield Hotel

$$ | **HOTEL** | Four-poster beds add a touch of class to the very comfortable double rooms and suites in this modern hotel in the center of Elgin. **Pros:** good food and beverage options; comfortable rooms; free off-street parking. **Cons:** not much atmosphere; popular wedding and conference venue; bland decor. [$] *Rooms from: £140* ✉ *2 Mayne St., Elgin* ☎ *01343/540883* 🌐 *www.themansefield.com* 🔑 *42 rooms* 🍴 *Free Breakfast.*

Shopping

Gordon and MacPhail

WINE/SPIRITS | An outstanding delicatessen and wine merchant, Gordon and MacPhail also stocks rare malt whiskies. This is a good place to shop for gifts for your foodie friends. ✉ *58–60 South St., Elgin* ☎ *01343/545110* 🌐 *www.gordonandmacphail.com* 🕓 *Closed Sun.*

Johnstons of Elgin

CRAFTS | This woolen mill has a worldwide reputation for its luxury fabrics, especially cashmere. The large shop stocks not only the firm's own products, but also top-quality Scottish crafts. There's a coffee shop on the premises. ✉ *Heritage Centre, Newmill Rd., Elgin* ☎ *01343/554099* 🌐 *www.johnstonscashmere.com.*

Activities

GOLF

Moray Golf Club

GOLF | Discover the relatively mild microclimate of what vacationing Victorians dubbed the Moray Riviera, as Tom Morris did in 1889 when he was inspired by the lay of the natural links. Henry Cotton's New Course (1979) has tighter fairways and smaller greens. A handicap certificate is required for the Old Course. ✉ *Stotfield Rd., Lossiemouth* ☎ *01343/812018* 🌐 *www.moraygolf.co.uk* 🎟 *Old Course, £95; New Course, £50* ⛳ *Old Course: 18 holes, 6752 yards, par 71; New Course: 18 holes, 6068 yards, par 69.*

Fochabers

9 miles east of Elgin.

With its hanging baskets of fuchsia in summer and its perfectly mowed village square, Fochabers has a cared-for charm that makes you want to stop here, even just to stretch your legs. Lying just to the south of the River Spey, the former market town was founded in 1776 by the Duke of Gordon. The duke moved the village from its original site because it was too close to Gordon Castle. Famous today for being home to the Baxters brand of soups and jams, Fochabers is near some of the best berry fields: come and pick your own in the summer months.

GETTING HERE AND AROUND

Fochabers is not on the Inverness-to-Aberdeen train line, but there is an hourly bus service (Stagecoach Bluebird No. 10) from Fochabers to Elgin. It's near the junction of A98 and A96.

Sights

Fochabers Folk Museum & Heritage Centre
HISTORY MUSEUM | FAMILY | Once over the Spey Bridge and past the cricket ground (a very unusual sight in Scotland), you can find the symmetrical, 18th-century Fochabers village square. The old Pringle Church is now the home of the Fochabers Folk Museum, which boasts a fine collection of items relating to past life of all types of residents in the village and surrounding area. Exhibits include carts and carriages, farm implements, domestic labor-saving devices, and an exquisite collection of Victorian toys. ✉ *High St., Fochabers* ☎ *01343/821204* 🌐 *www.fochabers-heritage.co.uk* ⏲ *Closed Mon. and Oct.–mid-May.*

Gordon Chapel
CHURCH | One of the village's lesser-known treasures is the Gordon Chapel, which has an exceptional set of stained-glass windows by Pre-Raphaelite artist Sir Edward Burne-Jones. Look out for the Good Shepherd, carrying a newborn lamb around his neck. ✉ *Church of St. Elizabeth, 40 Castle St., Fochabers* ☎ *01542/882782* 🌐 *www.morayepiscopalchurch.scot.*

Restaurants

Gordon Castle Walled Garden Cafe
$$ | BRITISH | With light streaming through the large windows onto the wooden tables and rattan chairs, there is an airiness and freshness to this eatery. Fish landed just a few miles away on the Moray coast is a good bet, as are the long-aged steaks. **Known for:** pulled pork burgers; traditional Cullen skink; fresh summer fruit desserts. [$] *Average main: £15* ✉ *Fochabers* ✥ *Just off A96, Fochabers Bypass Rd.* ☎ *01343/612317* 🌐 *www.gordoncastlescotland.com.*

The Quaich
$ | BRITISH | The friendly Quaich is a local favorite, serving great cakes and other baked goods, outstanding full Scottish breakfasts, warming porridge, and a plethora of snacks and sandwiches. Unusual dishes include a salmon omelet and haggis panini. **Known for:** tempting cakes and pastries; imaginative omelets; stovies with pickled beets. [$] *Average main: £6* ✉ *85 High St., Fochabers* ☎ *01343/820981* ⏲ *Closed Mon.*

Shopping

Watt's Antiques
ANTIQUES & COLLECTIBLES | This shop has small collectibles, jewelry, ornaments, and china. ✉ *45 High St., Fochabers* ☎ *01343/820077* 🌐 *www.wattsantiques.com.*

Cullen

21 miles east of Elgin, 13 miles east of Fochabers.

Look for some wonderfully painted homes at Cullen, in the old fishing town below the railway viaduct. The real attractions of this charming little seaside resort, however, are its white-sand beach (the water is quite cold, though) and the fine view west toward the aptly named Bowfiddle Rock. In summer Cullen bustles with families carrying buckets and spades and eating ice cream and chips.

A stroll past the small but once busy harbor reveals numerous fishers' cottages, huddled together with small yards where they dried their nets. Beyond these the vast stretch of beach curves gently round the bay. Above are the disused Victorian viaduct—formerly the Peterhead train line—and the 18th-century town.

GETTING HERE AND AROUND

Cullen is on A98, on Cullen Bay.

Sights

Seafield Street

STREET | The town has a fine *mercat* (market) cross and one main street—Seafield Street—that splits the town. It holds numerous specialty shops—antiques and gift stores, an ironmonger, a baker, a pharmacy, and a locally famous ice-cream shop among them—as well as several cafés. ✉ *Cullen.*

Restaurants

Cullen Ice Cream Shop

$ | ICE CREAM | FAMILY | In summer it can seem as if everyone you see in Cullen is licking a cone from the Ice Cream Shop. There's only a handful of flavors but they are all made on-site. **Known for:** vintage Scottish candies; house-made vanilla ice cream; old-fashioned charm. [$] *Average main: £8* ✉ *40 Seafield St., Cullen* ☎ *01542/840484* 💳 *No credit cards.*

Linda's Fish & Chips

$ | SEAFOOD | FAMILY | This casual place serves the freshest fish, caught in nearby Buckie and cooked to crispy perfection (gluten-free batter is available, too). There's a seating area inside, but it's best for takeout. **Known for:** deep-fried squid rings; fish battered to perfection; surf and turf burgers. [$] *Average main: £10* ✉ *54 Seafield St., Cullen* ☎ *01542/840202.*

Rockpool

$ | SEAFOOD | This modish fish restaurant has remarkably reasonable prices for the quality of the food and size of the servings. Try the rich Cullen skink (a creamy smoked-haddock soup), a pint glass of fat prawns served with mayo and oat bread, or some freshly fried squid with a lime sauce, all beautifully presented on wooden boards. **Known for:** pan-fried herring in oatmeal; Cullen skink; smoked-fish platter. [$] *Average main: £10* ✉ *10 The Square, Cullen* ☎ *01542/841397* 🌐 *www.rockpool-cullen.co.uk* 🕒 *Closed Mon. No dinner.*

Hotels

Seafield Arms

$$ | HOTEL | Built in 1822, this gallant old coaching inn has retained much of its period character through its rebirth as a modern boutique hotel. **Pros:** casual bar and elegant dining room; local atmosphere; excellent value. **Cons:** popular with wedding parties; used for business meetings, so can feel a bit too businesslike; slightly pretentious. [$] *Rooms from: £150* ✉ *17–19 Seafield St., Cullen* ☎ *01542/841604* 🌐 *www.seafieldarmscullen.co.uk* 🛏 *16 rooms, 4 apartments* 🍴 *No Meals.*

🛍 Shopping

Cullen Antiques Centre

ANTIQUES & COLLECTIBLES | Housed in a former church, this is a treasure trove for anyone looking for quirky vintage trinkets, Victoriana items, movie memorabilia, antiquarian books, and Scottish-heritage bits and bobs such as vintage fishing tackle. ⊠ Seafield St., Cullen ☎ 07748/440725 ⊕ www.cullenantiquescentre.com.

Banff

36 miles east of Elgin, 47 miles north of Aberdeen.

Midway along the northeast coast, overlooking Moray Firth and the estuary of the River Deveron, Banff is a dour fishing town, huddled around a small harbor, with a bleak but sometimes lovely coastline of crags, cliffs, and sandy coves to either side. Sixteenth-century houses huddle around the harbor, while surprisingly grand Georgian streets are reminders of its glory years as a hub of the fishing industry.

GETTING HERE AND AROUND

Banff is on the A98 coastal road and at the end of the tree-lined A947 to Aberdeen. If you are relying on public transportation, Bus 325 from Aberdeen bus station takes two hours and gets you into Low Street, just five minutes from Duff House.

👁 Sights

★ Duff House

HISTORIC HOME | The jewel in Banff's crown is the grand mansion of Duff House, a splendid William Adam–designed (1689–1748) Georgian mansion. It's now an annex of the National Galleries, housing works by El Greco, Sir Henry Raeburn, and Thomas Gainsborough. A good tearoom and a gift shop are on the ground floor. ⊠ Off A98, Banff ☎ 01261/818181 ⊕ www.historicenvironment.scot ☞ £9 ⊙ Closed Mon.–Thurs. Oct.–Mar.

Macduff Marine Aquarium

AQUARIUM | FAMILY | Across the river in Banff's twin town, Macduff, on the shore east of the harbor, stands the conical Macduff Marine Aquarium. A 250,000-gallon central tank and many smaller display areas and touch pools show the sea life of the Moray Firth and North Atlantic. This place wouldn't be half as good without the staff, who are knowledgeable, inventive, and engaging, especially with children, and there's always some creature to admire—the stingrays cause the most excitement—or watch being fed by divers. ⊠ 11 High Shore, Banff ☎ 01261/833369 ⊕ www.macduff-aquarium.org.uk ☞ £7.90 ⊙ Closed Thurs. and Fri. in Nov.–Mar.

Activities

Duff House Royal Golf Club

GOLF | Just moments from the sea, this club combines a coastal course with a parkland setting. Close to the center of Banff, it's on the grounds of Duff House, a country-house art gallery in a William Adam–designed mansion. The club has inherited the ancient traditions of seaside play; golf records here go back to the 17th century. ⊠ The Barnyards, Off A98, Banff ☎ 01261/812075 ⊕ www.duffhouseroyal.com ☞ £70 🏌 18 holes, 6031 yards, par 68.

Fyvie Castle

18 miles south of Banff.

This castle mixes ancient construction with Edwardian splendor and includes excellent art. The grounds are also worth exploring.

GETTING HERE AND AROUND

If you're driving from Banff, take the A947 south for 20 minutes or so until you see the turnoff.

◉ Sights

★ Fyvie Castle

CASTLE/PALACE | In an area rich with castles, Fyvie Castle stands out as the most complex. Five great towers built by five successive powerful families turned a 13th-century foursquare castle into an opulent Edwardian statement of wealth. Some superb paintings are on view, including 12 works by Sir Henry Raeburn. There are myriad sumptuous interiors—the circular stone staircase is considered one of the best examples in the country—and delightfully laid-out gardens. A former lady of the house, Lillia Drummond, was apparently starved to death by her husband, who entombed her body inside the walls of a secret room. In the 1920s, when the bones were disrupted during renovations, a string of such terrible misfortunes followed that they were quickly returned and the room sealed off. Her name is carved into the windowsill of the Drummond Room. ✉ *Off A947, Turriff* ☎ *01651/819266* ⊕ *www.nts.org. uk* 🎟 *£14.50* ⊗ *Closed Nov.–Mar.*

Ellon

32 miles southeast of Banff, 14 miles north of Aberdeen.

Formerly a market center on what was then the lowest bridging point of the River Ythan, Ellon, a bedroom suburb of Aberdeen, is a small town at the center of a rural hinterland. It's also well placed for visiting Fyvie Castle and Haddo House.

GETTING HERE AND AROUND

To get to Ellon, take the A947 from Banff or the A90 from Aberdeen; both routes take half an hour.

◉ Sights

Haddo House

HISTORIC HOME | Built in 1732, this elegant mansion has a light and graceful Georgian design, with curving wings on either side of a harmonious, symmetrical facade. The interior is late-Victorian ornate, filled with magnificent paintings (including works by Pompeo Batoni and Sir Thomas Lawrence) and plenty of *objets d'art*. Pre-Raphaelite stained-glass windows by Sir Edward Burne-Jones grace the chapel. Outside is a terrace garden with a fountain, and a few yards farther is Haddo Country Park, which has walking trails leading to memorials about the Gordon family. ■**TIP→ Visits to the house are by prebooked tour only, which are held at 11 and 2.** ✉ *Off B999, Ellon* ⊕ *8 miles northwest of Ellon* ☎ *01651/851440* ⊕ *www.nts.org.uk* 🎟 *£14.50* ⊗ *Closed Nov.–May.*

Pitmedden Garden

GARDEN | Five miles west of Ellon, at Pitmedden Garden is an exquisite re-creation of a 17th-century garden. It is best visited in summer, from July onward, when annual bedding plants—framed by precision-cut box hedging—form intricate formal patterns. The 100-acre estate also has woodland and farmland walks, as well as the Museum of Farming Life. ✉ *Off A920, Pitmedden* ☎ *01651/843188* ⊕ *www.nts.org.uk* 🎟 *£9* ⊗ *Closed Nov.–Jun.*

📣 Performing Arts

Haddo House

ARTS CENTERS | Aristocratic Haddo House hosts a range of events in summer, from performances by the Haddo Choral and Operatic Society to opera, recitals, ballet, Shakespearean drama, and puppet shows on the grounds and in the salons of the mansion. The season runs from spring through fall. ⊠ *Off B999, Tarves ⊹ 8 miles northwest of Ellon* ☎ *01651/851440* ⊕ *www.nts.org.uk.*

🏃 Activities

GOLF

Cruden Bay Golf Club

GOLF | This historic golf course, sheltered among extensive sand dunes, offers a quintessential Scottish golf experience. Narrow channels and deep valleys on challenging fairways ensure plenty of excitement, making Cruden Bay one of the northeast's most outstanding courses. Be sure to book far in advance if you plan to play a round on a weekend. ⊠ *Aulton Rd., Cruden Bay* ☎ *01779/812285* ⊕ *www.crudenbay-golfclub.co.uk* 🏌 *Championship: £145; St. Olaf: weekdays £30, weekends £40* 🏌 *Championship: 18 holes, 6287 yards, par 70; St. Olaf: 9 holes, 2463 yards, par 32.*

Chapter 9

ARGYLL AND THE ISLES

Updated by
Robin Gauldie

👁 Sights	🍴 Restaurants	🛏 Hotels	🛍 Shopping	🍸 Nightlife
★★★★☆	★★☆☆☆	★★★☆☆	★☆☆☆☆	★☆☆☆☆

WELCOME TO ARGYLL AND THE ISLES

TOP REASONS TO GO

★ **Whisky:** With 14 distilleries—9 on Islay, 1 each on Jura and Mull, and just 3 on the mainland—the region has been nicknamed Scotland's whisky coast.

★ **Iona and its abbey:** Maybe it's the remoteness that creates the almost mystical sense of history on Iona. From this early center of Scottish Christianity, evangelists traveled throughout Europe from the 6th century onward. It was also the burial place of Scottish kings, including Macbeth.

★ **The great outdoors:** Salmon and trout fill the lochs and rivers, while even bigger trophy fish await farther out to sea. Golfers have more than two dozen courses to choose from, and cyclists and walkers will find every kind of terrain at hand.

★ **Castles:** Often poised on cliffs overlooking the sea, the region's castles tell the story of eight centuries of occupations, sieges, and conflicts between warring clan chiefs and nobles.

1 Oban. Argyll's gateway to the isles.

2 Appin. Remote, lovely, and steeped in clan history.

3 Loch Awe. Island-dotted and flanked by forested hills.

4 Inveraray. The storied seat of Campbell chieftains.

5 Crinan. A picturesque canalside village loved by yacht owners.

6 Kintyre Peninsula. A charming strip of land with beaches and wildlife.

7 Brodick. The largest town in Arran.

8 Lamlash. Arran's lively seaside resort.

9 Machrie. A Moorland village surrounded by ancient stone circles.

10 Lochranza. Home to a renowned distillery and a castle that sheltered Robert the Bruce.

11 Islay. A place of pilgrimage for whisky connoisseurs.

12 Jura. Rugged, hilly, and perfect for walkers and whisky lovers alike.

13 Isles of Mull and Iona. The Isle of Mull has great fishing, a spectacular castle, and the colorful village of Tobermory. Iona is a tranquil isle with a famed ancient abbey.

14 Tiree. Upscale island retreat famed for surf, sand, and a mellow microclimate.

15 Coll. A rarely visited isle where flocks of seabirds wheel above the shores.

16 Colonsay. A dazzlingly beautiful and utterly unspoiled isle.

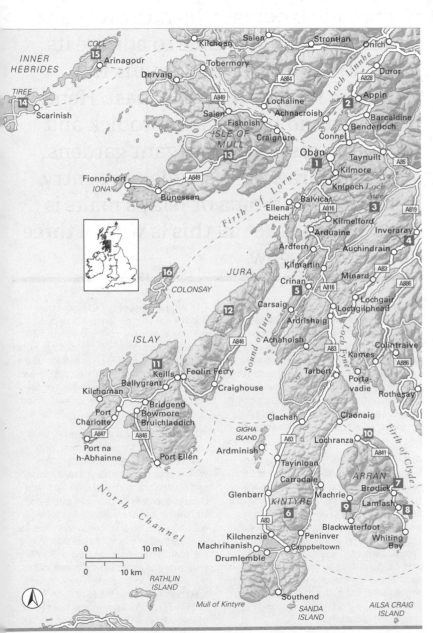

Argyll's rocky seaboard looks out onto islands that were once part of a single prehistoric landmass. Its narrow roads slow travel but give time to admire its lochs and woods, and the ruins that recall the region's dramatic past. Here, too, are grand houses like Brodick and Inveraray castles and elegant gardens such as Crarae. This is whisky country, too: the peaty aroma of Islay's malts is unmistakable. Yet all this is within three hours of Glasgow.

Western Scotland has a complicated, splintered coastline where you'll observe the interplay of sea, loch, and rugged green peninsula. The islands are breathtakingly beautiful, though they often catch the extremely wet weather arriving here from the Atlantic. It is common to experience four seasons in a day, as cliffs and woods suddenly and dramatically disappear in sea mists, then reappear just as suddenly.

Ancient castles like Dunstaffnage and the ruined towers on the islands of Loch Awe testify to the region's past importance. Prehistoric peoples left their mark here in the stone circles, carved stones, and Bronze and Iron Age burial mounds around Kilmartin and on Islay and Arran. The gardens of Inveraray and Brodick castles, nourished by the temperate west-coast climate, are the pride of Argyll, while the paths of Crarae's, south of Inveraray, wind through plantings of magnolias and azaleas.

The working people of Glasgow traditionally spent their family holidays on the Clyde estuary, taking day trips by steamer down the Firth, or making longer journeys to Rothesay on the Isle of Bute or to Arran and the Ayrshire coast. From Ardrossan, farther down the coast, ferries cruise to the prosperous and varied Isle of Arran.

Western Scotland's small islands have jagged cliffs or tongues of rock, long white-sand beaches, fertile pastures where sheep and cattle graze, fortresses, and shared memories of clan wars and mysterious beasts. Their cliff paths and lochside byways are a paradise for walkers and cyclists, and their whisky the ideal reward after a long day outside. While the islands' western coasts are dramatic, their more sheltered eastern seaboards are the location for pretty harbor towns like brightly painted Tobermory on Mull, or Port Ellen on Islay, with its neat rows of low whitewashed houses.

MAJOR REGIONS

Argyll. Topographical grandeur and rocky shores are what make Argyll special. Try to take to the water at least once, even if your time is limited. The sea and the sea lochs have played a vital role in the history of western Scotland since the time of the war galleys of the clans. Oban is the major ferry gateway and transport hub, with a main road leading south into the Kintyre Peninsula. The linked peninsulas of Knapdale and Kintyre—separated by the Crinan Canal at Tarbert—are areas of moorland and forest dotted with small lochs. From Inveraray at the head of Loch Fyne, you can take in Auchindrain's re-created fishing village on the way to the Arran ferry. Or turn west toward Crinan and the prehistoric sites around Kilmartin, then travel northward toward Loch Awe and its intriguing island ruins.

Arran. Touring this island will give you a glimpse in a day or two of the whole of Scotland in miniature. In the north the forbidding Goatfell (2,868 feet) is a challenge that draws walkers and climbers. The island's wilder west coast attracts bird-watchers and naturalists, while the fertile south of the island contains nine lovely golf courses, leisurely walks, and Brodick Castle. A temperate microclimate attracted ancient settlers whose stone circles still stand on the island. This weather also explains why it has long been a favorite getaway for Glaswegians, who come here to walk, climb Goatfell, or play golf.

Islay and Jura. The smell of peat that hangs in the air on Islay is bottled in its famous whiskies. Aside from distilleries, the island's historical sites evoke a past in which these islands were far less remote. The whitewashed cottages along the coast of Islay line clean and beautiful beaches, many of them visited by a variety of wildlife. Jura is wilder and more dramatic, its twin mountains (the Paps) dominating its infertile moorland.

Isle of Mull and Iona. The pretty harbor of Tobermory, with its painted houses, is a relaxing base from which to explore the varied and beautiful island of Mull. Along Mull's west coast, spectacular cliffs and rocky beaches look out onto the Atlantic. From Craignure the road crosses the sweeping green valleys of the Ross of Mull to Fionnphort and the ferry to the meditative island of Iona.

The Smaller Islands. The region's smaller islands, sometimes known as the Southern Hebrides, may seem quite remote but were once important centers of power and production. Successively depopulated by force or by emigration to Glasgow's industries or the promise of the Americas, the islands still survive on fishing, cattle and sheep raising, and tourism. Their populations remain small, though, and many residents are "incomers" from the mainland or from England. They are havens for birdlife, particularly Coll's giant dunes or the cliffs of Tiree. For the visitor the experience is one of open, often barely populated landscapes and a slightly brooding sense of history. Colonsay's Kiloran Bay is open to the Atlantic's breakers, while Tiree's waves draw surfers from around the world.

Planning

When to Go

This part of the mainland is close enough to Glasgow to make it accessible year-round. Oban is just over two hours from the city by car (three hours by bus), but getting to the isles via ferries takes longer, and the crossings are less frequent out of season. You can take advantage of quiet roads and plentiful accommodations in early spring and late autumn. The summer months of July and August can get very busy indeed; book accommodations and restaurants in advance during high season. In winter short daylight hours and winds can make island stays rather bleak, but add allure to the prospect of sipping malt whisky by a log fire. Birding enthusiasts can observe vast flocks of migrant Arctic wildfowl arriving and leaving Islay in autumn and spring. At any time come prepared with adequate clothing for fast-changing weather.

Getting Oriented

With long sea lochs carved into its hilly, wooded interior, Argyll is a beguiling interweaving of water and land. The Mull of Kintyre, a narrow finger of land, points south towards nearby Ireland, separating the Firth of Clyde and its islands from the Atlantic and the isles of the Inner Hebrides. Arran, largest of the Clyde isles, looms near the mouth of the Clyde, separated from Kintyre by Kilbrannan Sound. Ferry services allow all kinds of interisland tours and can shorten mainland trips as well.

Linking the region with Glasgow, the A82 runs along the west shore of Loch Lomond to connect with the A83. That road follows the north shore of Loch Fyne, a long fjordlike inlet known for some of Scotland's finest seafood, all the way to Campbeltown near the tip of Kintyre. Along the way is Kennacraig, departure point for ferries to Islay and Jura. Coming from the east, the A85 runs through equally spectacular scenery between Perth and Oban, the main port for ferries to Mull and other islands. From Oban the A828 runs north to Fort William and the Great Glen.

Planning Your Time

You could easily spend a week exploring the islands alone, so consider spending at least a few nights in this region. Argyll and some island excursions make pleasant and easy side trips from Glasgow and Loch Lomond. Driving anywhere

here takes a little longer than you'd think, so allow ample travel time. A leisurely day will take you to Inveraray, its castle, and the surrounding gardens (don't miss the folk museum at Auchindrain) before driving on to Kennacraig to take the ferry for Islay and Jura. Two or three days here will give you a sense of the history and varied landscapes of these stunning islands—and time for a distillery or two. If you have time to visit just one island, sail from Oban to Mull, returning the same day or the next to take in the Scottish Sea Life Sanctuary. If you can, drive around beautiful Loch Awe on your way back to Glasgow. If time is really tight, consider flying from Glasgow to Islay or Tiree.

Plan ahead: car ferries fill up in the summer months (there is usually no problem for foot passengers), and some of the smaller islands are served only once or twice a week. Bear in mind that it is not easy to find places to eat after 9 pm at any time of year—though you can usually find a place that will sell you a whisky until much later.

Getting Here and Around

AIR
The closest major airport to Argyll and the Isles is Glasgow. Hebridean Air Services flies from Oban to Islay, Coll, Colonsay, and Tiree.

CONTACTS Hebridean Air Services.
☎ 0845/805–7465 ⊕ www.hebrideanair. co.uk.

BOAT AND FERRY
Caledonian MacBrayne (CalMac) operates car-ferry and passenger services to and from the main islands. It is important to plan ahead when traveling to the islands in order to coordinate the connecting ferries; CalMac can advise you on this. Multiple-island tickets are available and can significantly reduce the cost of island-hopping.

CalMac ferries run from Oban to Mull, Lismore, Coll, and Tiree; from Kennacraig to Islay, Jura, and Gigha; from Ardrossan to Arran; and from Port Askaig on Islay to Feolin on Jura; as well as a number of shorter routes. Western Ferries operate between Dunoon, in Argyll, and Gourock, west of Glasgow. The ferry passage between Dunoon and Gourock is one frequented by locals; it saves a lot of time, and you can take your car across as well. Jura Passenger Ferry operates between Tayvallich (on the mainland) and Craighouse on Jura.

Ferry reservations are needed if you have a car; passengers traveling by foot do not need to make reservations.

CONTACTS Caledonian MacBrayne. (CalMac) ☎ 0800/066–5000 ⊕ www. calmac.co.uk. **Jura Passenger Ferry.** ☎ 07768/450000 ⊕ www.jurapassengerferry.com. **Western Ferries.** ✉ Dunoon ☎ 01369/704452 ⊕ www.western-ferries. co.uk.

BUS

You can travel throughout the region by bus, but service here tends to be less frequent than elsewhere in Scotland. Scottish Citylink runs daily service from Glasgow's Buchanan Street station to the mid-Argyll region and Kintyre; the trip to Oban takes about three hours. Several other companies provide local services within the region.

CONTACTS Garelochhead Coaches. ☎ 01436/810200 ⊕ www.garelochheadcoaches.co.uk. **Islay Coaches.** ☎ 01496/840273 ⊕ www.bmundell. co.uk. **Scottish Citylink.** ☎ 0871/266–3333 ⊕ www.citylink.co.uk. **Stagecoach West Scotland.** ☎ 0345/810000 ⊕ www. stagecoachbus.com. **West Coast Motors.** ☎ 01586/552319 ⊕ www.westcoastmotors.co.uk.

CAR

Negotiating this area is easy except in July and August, when the roads around Oban may be congested. A number of single-lane roads, especially on the east side of the Kintyre Peninsula and on the islands, require special care. Remember that white triangles indicate places where you can pass. You'll probably have to board a ferry at some point during your trip; nearly all ferries take cars as well as pedestrians.

From Glasgow take the A82 and the A85 to Oban, the main ferry terminal for Mull and the islands (about 2½ hours by car). From the A82 take the A83 at Arrochar; it rounds Loch Fyne to Inveraray. From there you can take the A819 from Inveraray around Loch Awe and rejoin the Glasgow–Oban road. Alternatively, you can stay on the A83 and head down Kintyre to Kennacraig, the ferry terminal for Islay. Farther down the A83 is Tayinloan, the ferry port for Gigha. You can reach Brodick on Arran by ferry from Ardrossan, on the Clyde coast (M8/A78 from Glasgow); in summer you can travel to Lochranza from Claonaig on the Kintyre Peninsula, but there are very few crossings.

TRAIN

Oban and Ardrossan are the main rail stations; it's a three-hour trip from Glasgow to Oban. For information call ScotRail. All trains connect with ferries.

CONTACTS ScotRail. ☎ 0871/200–2233 ⊕ www.scotrail.co.uk.

Restaurants

Argyll and the Isles have earned a reputation for excellent gastropubs and restaurants (many of which also offer accommodations) that use superb locally sourced produce, including luscious seafood, lamb, wild and farmed venison, and game of many kinds. Most hotels and many guesthouses offer evening meals, and it may often be your best option to look to hotel restaurants, though the quality can vary. Most restaurants and pubs stop serving food by 9 pm; lunch usually ends at 2:30.

Hotels

Accommodations in Argyll and on the Isles range from country-house hotels to private homes offering a bed and breakfast. Most small, traditional, provincial hotels in coastal resorts have been updated and modernized, while still retaining personalized service. And though hotels often have a restaurant offering evening meals, the norm is to offer breakfast only.

Restaurant and hotel reviews have been shortened. For full information, visit Fodors.com. Restaurant prices are the average cost of a main course at dinner or, if dinner is not served, at lunch. Hotel prices are the lowest cost of a standard double room in high season, including 20% V.A.T.

WHAT IT COSTS in Pounds			
$	$$	$$$	$$$$
RESTAURANTS			
under £15	£15–£19	£20–£25	over £25
HOTELS			
under £125	£125–£200	£201–£300	over £300

Tours

BOAT TOURS

Getting out on the water is a wonderful way to see the landscape of the islands and also sea life.

★ Sea Life Surveys

BOAT TOURS | FAMILY | Dolphins, seals, porpoises, and (if you're fortunate) minke whales and basking sharks are among the stars of the show on a Sea Life Surveys cruise from pretty Tobermory. Seabirds abound, too, and you may spot huge white-tailed eagles, once extinct here but reintroduced to this part of Scotland in recent years. Several cruises are offered: if time is short, choose the 90-minute Ecocruz. ✉ *A848, Tobermory* ⟴ *Cruises leave from floating pontoons opposite Mull Aquarium* ☎ *01688/302916* ⊕ *www.sealifesurveys.com* ✍ *From £20.*

Staffa Tours

BOAT TOURS | FAMILY | This company organizes a number of tours to the smaller islands, with the emphasis on wildlife. Tours run from Mull, Ardnamurchan on the mainland, or from Iona. The three-hour trip to uninhabited Staffa includes Fingal's Cave, commemorated by Mendelssohn in his famous overture. With luck you may encounter dolphins on the way. Staffa also runs tours to the Treshnish islands, famous for the puffin colonies on Lunga. ✉ *The Boat Shed, Iona, Iona* ☎ *07732/912370* ⊕ *www.staffatours.com* ✍ *From £30.*

Turus-Mara

BOAT TOURS | FAMILY | Based on the island of Mull, Turus-Mara runs trips to Staffa, Iona, and the Treshnish islands, with an emphasis on wildlife. There are puffins and guillemots through the summer, seals until late in the year, and sometimes even basking sharks. Tours depart from Ulva Ferry on the west coast of Mull, but there is a courtesy bus from Tobermory. ✉ *Penmore Mill, Dervaig* ☎ *01688/400242* ⊕ *www.turusmara.com* ✍ *From £35.*

BUS TOURS

Many of the bus companies in the area also arrange sightseeing tours, so check with them.

West Coast Tours

BUS TOURS | A range of bus tours and combined boat and bus tours in and around Oban are available through West Coast Tours. The company can also arrange combined bus and boat tours to Mull and Iona and boat trips to Staffa. ✉ *George St., Oban* ☎ *01631/552319* ⊕ *www.westcoast-tours.co.uk* ✍ *From £7.*

As Argyll's biggest town, Oban greets visitors to the region with its seaside charm.

Visitor Information

The only year-round visitor information offices are in Bowmore, Craignure, and Oban.

Oban

96 miles northwest of Glasgow, 125 miles northwest of Edinburgh, 50 miles south of Fort William, 118 miles southwest of Inverness.

It's almost impossible to avoid Oban when touring the west. Its waterfront has some character, but the town's main role is as a launch point for excursions into Argyll and for ferries to the islands. A traditional Scottish resort town, Oban has many music festivals, *ceilidhs* with Highland dancing, as well as all the usual tartan kitsch and late-night revelry in pubs and hotel bars. The Oban Distillery offers tours and a shop. Still, there are more exciting destinations just over the horizon, on the islands, and down into Kintyre.

GETTING HERE AND AROUND

From Glasgow the A82 along Loch Lomond meets the A85 at Crianlarich. Turn left and continue to Oban. In summer the center of Oban can become gridlocked with ferry traffic, so leave yourself time for the wait. Alternatively, the A816 from Lochgilphead enters Oban from the less-crowded south. Train services run from Glasgow to Oban (ScotRail); Scottish Citylink runs buses from Glasgow to Oban several times a day.

ESSENTIALS

VISITOR INFORMATION Oban Tourist Information Centre. ⊠ *3 North Pier, Oban* ☎ *01631/563122* ⊕ *www.oban.org.uk.*

👁 Sights

Dunstaffnage Castle

CASTLE/PALACE | Standing high atop volcanic rock, Dunstaffnage commands the hills and lochs that surround it. That is why this 13th-century castle was so strategic and contested by those battling for control of Argyll and the Isles.

Argyll
and Arran

From the walk along the walls you have outstanding views across the Sound of Mull and the Firth of Lorne. There are storyboards throughout the building that give you a sense of how it was used across the ages. In the woods is the ruined chapel of St. Cuthbert, built by the Macdougall clan at the same time as the castle. ✉ *Off A85, Oban* ☎ *01631/562465* 🌐 *www.historicenvironment.scot* 🎫 *£6* 🕒 *Closed Thurs. and Fri. Oct.–Mar.*

Oban Distillery

DISTILLERY | One of Scotland's oldest and smallest distilleries was founded in 1794, several years before the town where it now stands. It produces a well-known 14-year-old malt which, according to those who know, has a taste somewhere between the smoky Islay whiskies and the softer, sweeter Highland varieties—a distinctive West Highland flavor. ✉ *Stafford St., Oban* ✥ *Opposite North Pier* ☎ *01631/572004* 🌐 *www.obanwhisky.com* 🎫 *Basic tour £15* 🕒 *Closed weekends in Dec.*

Oban War and Peace Museum

HISTORY MUSEUM | **FAMILY** | This free museum recalls Oban's history through peace and war in photographs and other exhibits. Always a fishing harbor and a ferry port, during the Second World War the town became a key naval command center. ✉ *Old Oban Times Building, Corran Esplanade, Oban* ☎ *01631/570007* 🌐 *www.obanmuseum.org.uk* 🎫 *Free* 🕒 *Closed Nov.–Feb.*

Ocean Explorer Centre

SCIENCE MUSEUM | **FAMILY** | On the Firth of Lorn, this imaginative venture lets you get a look under the sea. Hands-on exhibits include microscopes where you can observe tiny algae and a live under-sea camera where you can see what's happening below the waves. Part of a scientific research center, it's educational but also accessible and fun. There is a bright little café and a shop with books on marine science and other topics. It's 2 miles from Oban—follow the signs for nearby Dunstaffnage Castle. ✉ *Kirk Rd., Oban* ☎ *01631/559123* 🌐 *www.ocean-explorercentre.org* 🎫 *Free* 🕒 *Closed weekends and late Dec.–early Jan.*

🍴 Restaurants

★ Ee-usk

$$$ | **SEAFOOD** | This clean-lined restaurant's name means "fish" in Gaelic, and it has earned quite a reputation for serving excellent dishes made with the freshest fish and shellfish delivered directly from Oban's harbor. The signature creations use appealingly simple sauces; try oven-baked wild halibut with creamed leeks or the full-scale seafood platter. **Known for:** island views; Mull scallops and Loch Linnhe oysters and langoustines; no children under 12 during dinnertime. [$] *Average main: £25* ✉ *North Pier, Oban* ☎ *01631/565666* 🌐 *www.eeusk.com.*

Hawthorn Restaurant

$ | **BRITISH** | Fish shares the menu here with local lamb, pork, and game. Although it's just a few miles from Oban (whence it sources its seafood), the setting is rural, surrounded by crofts that are still working farms. **Known for:** tasty steak pies; freshly caught haddock; Argyll lamb. [$] *Average main: £12* ✉ *Keil Crofts, Benderloch, Oban* ✥ *6 miles north of Oban off the main A816, after crossing the Connel Bridge* ☎ *07483/145534* 🕒 *Closed Mon. and Oct.–Mar.*

Oban Seafood Hut

$ | **SEAFOOD** | Serving arguably the best-value seafood in Oban, ex-fisherman John Ogden's quayside fish shack is a local legend. Look for a green-painted shed on the pier, then join the line of cognoscenti waiting for simply sautéed scallops, grilled langoustine and lobster, oysters, and mussels. **Known for:** only a few tables, so eating while standing a possibility; king prawn sandwiches and scallops in garlic butter; cash or debit card only. [$] *Average main: £8* ✉ *CalMac Pier, Oban* ☎ *07881/418565* 💳 *No credit cards* 🕒 *Closed Nov.–Apr.*

Hotels

Glenburnie House

$ | **B&B/INN** | At this typical seafront guesthouse in a Victorian building with fine views over Oban Bay, most rooms are spacious and comfortable, if slightly overdecorated in traditional style. **Pros:** lots of local atmosphere; centrally located; good sea views. **Cons:** only meal available is breakfast; no bar on-site; too many flowery fabrics for some tastes. [$] *Rooms from: £100* ✉ *Esplanade, Oban* ☎ *01631/562089* 🌐 *www.glenburnie.co.uk* ⏲ *Closed Dec.–Feb.* 🛏 *17 rooms* 🍴 *Free Breakfast.*

Kilchrenan House

$ | **B&B/INN** | Just a few minutes from the town center, this Victorian-era stone house has been transformed into a lovely bed-and-breakfast. **Pros:** cozy rooms; great sea views; tasteful attention to detail. **Cons:** credit cards not accepted for one-night stays; attic rooms have a slanting roof; some bedrooms may be too colorfully decorated for some tastes. [$] *Rooms from: £80* ✉ *Corran Esplanade, Oban* ☎ *01631/562663* 🌐 *www.kilchrenanhouse.co.uk* ⏲ *Closed Dec. and Jan* 🛏 *13 rooms* 🍴 *Free Breakfast.*

★ Manor House Hotel

$$ | **HOTEL** | On the coast near Oban, this 1780 stone house—once the home of the Duke of Argyll—has sea views and a convenient location. **Pros:** free off-street parking; excellent restaurant; harbour views. **Cons:** rooms on the small side; decor a bit old-fashioned for some; Wi-Fi could be better in bedrooms. [$] *Rooms from: £185* ✉ *Gallanach Rd., Oban* ☎ *01631/562087* 🌐 *www.manorhouse-oban.com* 🛏 *11 rooms* 🍴 *Free Breakfast.*

Activities

BICYCLING

Oban Cycles

BIKING | This shop rents bikes of various sorts starting at £28 for a full day. The area round Oban is good cycling country, and the staff is happy to advise you on routes. ✉ *89 George St., Oban* ☎ *01631/566033* 🌐 *www.obancycle-scotland.com.*

Appin

17 miles north of Oban.

The little peninsula of Appin, a 20-minute drive from Oban, is a charming, well-kept secret. Just 2 miles along a narrow road from the main Fort William route (A828), the bay opens to Lismore and the sea. Castle Stalker, a privately owned castle on the water, sits magnificently in the center of the picture, a symbol of ancient coastal Scotland. This is an excellent, uncrowded base for walking, fishing, water sports, and cycling.

GETTING HERE AND AROUND

From Oban follow the A828 around Loch Creran and take the left turn to Port Appin just beyond Tynribbie. Continue for just over 2 miles to the old pier. From the port the passenger ferry runs to the island of Lismore throughout the year. Steamers once plied the waters of Loch Linnhe, but today the largest boats here are those taking workers to the quarries of Kingairloch.

Restaurants

★ Pierhouse Hotel and Restaurant

$$$ | **SEAFOOD** | The round towers of the old pier mark the entrance to this restaurant, appealingly situated on the water's edge. The restaurant serves the freshest seafood; try its signature platter of lobster, scallops, mussels, and langoustines. **Known for:** rib-eye steak with langoustines; lively atmosphere; delicious lobster thermidor. [$] *Average main: £25* ✉ *Port Appin* ☎ *01631/730302* 🌐 *www.pierhousehotel.co.uk.*

While you can't actually visit Appin's Castle Stalker, it makes for a lovely backdrop to a sunset.

 Hotels

Airds Hotel and Restaurant

$$$$ | HOTEL | This luxurious small hotel (once a travelers' inn) has rooms with superb views. **Pros:** beautiful location; fabulous views from the breakfast room; lots of outdoor activities available. **Cons:** very expensive; rooms too small for some tastes; decor a bit too pretentious. $ *Rooms from: £378* ✉ *A828, Port Appin* ☎ *01631/730236* ⊕ *www.airds-hotel.com* ⊷ *11 rooms* ⦿ *Free Breakfast.*

★ Isle of Eriska

$$$$ | HOTEL | FAMILY | On one of Scotland's few private islands, this sybaritic enclave conceals luxury facilities like a spa, pool, gym, golf course, and a Michelin-starred restaurant behind a severe baronial facade. **Pros:** superb leisure facilities; exceptional food; gorgeous views. **Cons:** very popular with wedding parties; dining out not an easy option; usually booked out at least one year ahead in high season. $ *Rooms from: £380* ✉ *Off A828, Benderloch* ⚓ *Island* signposted from Benderloch village and connected to mainland by short bridge ☎ *01631/720371* ⊕ *www.eriska-hotel. co.uk* ⊷ *34 rooms* ⦿ *Free Breakfast.*

Loch Awe

18 miles east of Oban.

Measuring more than 25 miles long, Loch Awe is Scotland's longest stretch of freshwater. Its northwest shore is quiet; forest walks crisscross the Inverliever Forest here. At the loch's northern end, tiny islands, many with ruins, pepper the water. One, Inishail, is home to a 13th-century chapel.

GETTING HERE AND AROUND

From Oban the A85 will bring you to the head of Loch Awe and the small village of the same name. Turn onto the B845 at Taynuilt to reach the loch's northern shore, or continue through the forbidding Pass of Brander and turn onto the A819 to get to the southern shore. From here you can continue on to Inveraray, or drive along the loch on the B840.

◉ Sights

★ Bonawe Iron Furnace

FACTORY | FAMILY | Seemingly out of place in this near-wilderness setting, Bonawe is a fascinating relic from the dawn of Britain's Industrial Revolution. In the mid-18th century, Argyll's virgin forests attracted ironmasters from England, where such valuable fuel sources were harder to find. Business boomed when wars with France boosted demand for pig iron and cannonballs, and in its heyday Bonawe employed up to 600 unskilled local wood gatherers and skilled southern foundrymen. ☒ Off B845, Bonawe ☎ 01866/822432 ⊕ www. historicenvironment.scot ☷ £6 ⊘ Closed Sat.–Tues. and Oct.–Mar.

Cruachan

FACTORY | FAMILY | Like the lair of a classic James Bond villain, this triumph of 20th-century British technology lurks deep within a vast man-made cavern. Hidden 3,000 feet beneath the slopes of Ben Cruachan, the colossal water-driven turbines of this subterranean power station, completed in 1965, supply clean energy to much of Scotland. The ½-mile bus ride from the surface to the generating hall is a surreal experience, made all the more so by the subtropical plants that thrive under artificial light in the warm, humid atmosphere. ☒ A85, Dalmally ☎ 01866/822618 ⊕ www. visitcruachan.co.uk ☷ £7.50 ⊘ Closed weekends and Jan.

Duncan Ban Macintyre Monument

MONUMENT | The monument was erected in honor of this Gaelic poet (1724–1812), sometimes referred to as the Robert Burns of the Highlands. He fought at Culloden and wrote poetry and song in the language of the clans. The view from here is one of the finest in Argyll, taking in Ben Cruachan and the other peaks

nearby, as well as Loch Awe and its scattering of islands. To find the monument from Dalmally, just east of Loch Awe, follow an old road running southwest toward the banks of the loch. You can see the round, granite structure from the road's highest point, often called Monument Hill. ☒ Dalmally.

Kilchurn Castle

CASTLE/PALACE | This is one of Argyll's most evocative ruins, with its crumbling lochside towers and high ramparts. Built by the Campbells in the 15th century, Kilchurn was rebuilt as a government garrison after the troubles of the late 17th century. The castle was abandoned after peace came to the Highlands following the final defeat of the Jacobite cause in 1746. ☒ Lochawe, Dalmally ✛ 2½ miles west of Dalmally ⊕ www.historic-scotland.gov.uk/places ⊘ Closed Oct.–Mar.

Rest and Be Thankful

VIEWPOINT | This viewpoint at the highest point of the route from Loch Lomond to Inveraray is one of the few places where you can pull off the road to enjoy the spectacular panorama. It's an ideal place to take some selfies, and it's easy to imagine how it earned its name in the days when the only travelers on this trail went on foot or on horseback. ☒ A83 ✛ 10 miles northwest of Tarbert.

St. Conan's Kirk

CHURCH | St. Conan's may look medieval, but in fact, it's less than 100 years old. Built in 1930 from local boulders, it features modern stained glass and wood and stone carvings, including an effigy of Robert the Bruce. ☒ A85, Lochawe ✛ About 18 miles from Oban ⊕ www. stconanskirk.org.uk ☷ Free.

🛏 Hotels

★ Taychreggan Hotel

$$ | HOTEL | Peace and quiet are the big selling points of this lovely country-house hotel beside Loch Awe. Once a drovers' inn, the whitewashed building is surrounded by

lawns and wooded gardens. **Pros:** wonderful meals; magnificent and tranquil views; activities including fishing and kayaking. **Cons:** tiny bathrooms in standard rooms; limited restaurant menu; six miles from main road. $ *Rooms from: £125* ⊠ *Off B845, Kilchrenan* ☏ *01866/833211* ⊕ *www. taychregganhotel.co.uk* ⤳ *18 rooms* ⦿| *Free Breakfast.*

Inveraray

21 miles south of Loch Awe, 61 miles north of Glasgow, 29 miles west of Loch Lomond.

Inveraray's star attraction is the grandiose seat of the Campbell Dukes of Argyll, for centuries the most powerful magnates of the Highlands. It's a trim little township, planned and built in the mid-18th century at the behest of the third duke. There are fine views of Loch Fyne, and there are gardens and museums to see nearby.

GETTING HERE AND AROUND

Driving from Oban take the A85 and the A819 beyond Loch Awe (the village). From Glasgow take the A82, turn onto the A83 at Arrochar, and make the long drive around Loch Fyne.

◉ Sights

Ardkinglas Woodland Garden

GARDEN | Rambling over 12,000 acres, one of Britain's finest collections of conifers is set off by rhododendron blossoms in early summer. You can find the garden around the head of Loch Fyne, about 10 miles east of Inveraray. There's a wild woodland walk beyond the garden; both are open all year. The house, regarded as architect Sir Robert Lorimer's masterpiece, is open to visitors only on Fridays between April and October. ⊠ *Ardkinglas Estate, Cairndow* ☏ *01499/600261* ⊕ *www.ardkinglas.com* 🎫 *£5.*

★ Auchindrain Museum

MUSEUM VILLAGE | FAMILY | Step a few centuries back in time at this open-air museum, a rare surviving example of an 18th-century communal-tenancy farm. About 250 years ago, there were several thousand working communities like Auchindrain. Auchindrain was the last of them, its final tenant leaving in 1963. Today the bracken-thatch and iron-roof buildings, about 20 in all, give you a feel for early farming life in the Highland communities. Several houses are furnished and tell the story of their occupants. A tearoom is open morning to afternoon. ⊠ *Auchindrain, Inveraray* ⤋ *Off A83 about 6 miles south of Inveraray* ☏ *01499/500235* ⊕ *auchindrain.org.uk* 🎫 *£8* ⊗ *Closed Nov.–Mar.*

Crarae Garden

GARDEN | Exotic Himalayan plants flourish in the gentle microclimate of this 100-acre garden, where the Crarae Burn, a small stream, cascades through a rocky gorge. Rhododendrons, azaleas, and magnolias lend color, and native flowers and trees attract birds and butterflies. ⊠ *A83, Inveraray* ⤋ *10 miles southwest of Inveraray* ☏ *01546/886614* ⊕ *www.nts. org.uk* 🎫 *£8* ⊗ *Closed Nov.–Mar.*

Inveraray Castle

CASTLE/PALACE | The current seat of the Chief of the Clan Campbell is a smart, grayish-green turreted stone house with a self-satisfied air. Set among well-tended grounds, it contains displays of luxurious furnishings and interesting art, as well as a huge armory. Built between 1743 and 1789, the castle has spires on the four corner turrets that give it a vaguely French look. Tours of the castle follow the history of the powerful Campbell family and how it acquired its considerable wealth. There is a tearoom for snacks and light lunches. You can hike around the extensive estate grounds, but wear sturdy footwear. ⊠ *Off A83, Inveraray* ☏ *01499/302203* ⊕ *www. inveraray-castle.com* 🎫 *£13.50* ⊗ *Closed Nov.–Mar.*

Inveraray Jail

JAIL/PRISON | **FAMILY** | In this old jail, realistic courtroom scenes, carefully re-created cells, and other paraphernalia give you a glimpse of life behind bars in Victorian times—and today. Actors represent some of the jail's most famous occupants. The site includes a Scottish crafts shop. ✉ *Main St., Inveraray* ☎ *01499/302381* 🌐 *www.inverarayjail.co.uk* 🎟 *£11.50.*

🍴 Restaurants

★ Loch Fyne Oyster Bar and Restaurant

$$ | **SEAFOOD** | The legendary flagship of a chain of seafood restaurants that now stretches across the United Kingdom, this restaurant continues to please with its emphasis on ultrafresh, locally sourced seafood, simply prepared. Oysters, are, of course, a keynote, but the menu also features mussels, lobster, prawns, salmon, and much more from the sea, accompanied by perfect crunchy green vegetables such as peas, beans, and asparagus. **Known for:** seafood tapas; plump oysters perfectly prepared; meltingly tender smoked salmon. [$] *Average main: £19* ✉ *Clachan Farm, A83, Cairndow* ☎ *01499/600482* 🌐 *www.lochfyne.com.*

Samphire Seafood Restaurant

$$ | **SEAFOOD** | This small, cozy, unpretentious restaurant in the center of Inveraray has earned a reputation for excellently prepared seafood, though it also serves meat and vegetarian dishes. Favorites include the seafood pie, and the Taste of the Loch medley of shellfish and crustaceans is a special treat. **Known for:** roast cod loin; lavish seafood platters; hearty seafood pie. [$] *Average main: £18* ✉ *6A Arkland, Inveraray* ☎ *01499/302321* 🌐 *www.samphireseafood.com* 🕒 *Closed Sun. and Mon.*

🛏 Hotels

★ The George Hotel

$ | **HOTEL** | The George has been Inveraray's social hub since the 18th century, when it was a coaching inn, and it still exudes history. **Pros:** live music on weekends; excellent restaurant; atmospheric bars. **Cons:** live music makes some rooms noisy; extra charge for child beds; too much tartan for some. [$] *Rooms from: £90* ✉ *Main St. E, Inveraray* ☎ *01499/302111* 🌐 *www.thegeorgehotel.co.uk* 🛏 *25 rooms* 🍴 *Free Breakfast.*

Crinan

32 miles southwest of Inveraray.

Crinan is synonymous with its canal, the reason for this tiny community's existence and its mainstay. The narrow road beside the Crinan Hotel bustles with yachting types waiting to pass through the locks, bringing a surprisingly cosmopolitan feel to such an out-of-the-way corner of Scotland.

GETTING HERE AND AROUND

To reach Crinan, follow the A83 from Inveraray along the north shore of Loch Fyne through Lochgilphead, take the A816 Oban road north for about a mile, then turn left onto the B841 at Cairnbaan.

👁 Sights

Carnasserie Castle

CASTLE/PALACE | The tower house of Carnasserie Castle is all that remains of this Renaissance structure. It has the distinction of having belonged to the writer of the first book printed in Gaelic. John Carswell, Bishop of the Isles, translated a text by the Scottish reformer John Knox into Gaelic and published it in 1567. ✉ *Off A816, Crinan* ✥ *2 miles north of Kilmartin* 🌐 *www.historic-scotland.gov.uk* 🎟 *Free.*

The charming Crinan Canal has been popular with fishing vessels and royals alike; Queen Victoria took a trip up it in 1873.

Castle Sween

CASTLE/PALACE | The oldest stone castle on the Scottish mainland, this 12th-century structure sits on a rocky bit of coast about 12 miles south of Crinan. From the northwest tower, known as the Latrine Tower, you can enjoy the dramatic views of the Paps of Jura. ⊕ *www.historicenvironment.scot.*

Crinan Canal

OTHER ATTRACTION | This canal opened in 1801 to let fishing vessels reach Hebridean fishing grounds without making the long haul south around the Kintyre Peninsula. At its western end the canal drops to the sea in a series of locks, the last of which is beside the Crinan Hotel. Today it's popular with pleasure boats traveling to the west coast. ⊠ *Crinan.*

 ## Hotels

Crinan Hotel

$$$ | HOTEL | A dramatic location overlooking the Sound of Jura is this hotel's big selling point, along with bright, maritime-themed public areas and guest rooms. **Pros:** interesting art gallery; good dining; some rooms with private balconies. **Cons:** no satellite TV; popular for wedding receptions; not all rooms have showers. $ *Rooms from: £230* ⊠ *Off B841, Crinan* ☎ *01546/830261* ⊕ *www.crinanhotel.com* ⊗ *Closed Jan.–Mar.* ⤵ *20 rooms* ⫮◯⫮ *Free Breakfast.*

Kintyre Peninsula

57 miles south of Crinan.

Rivers and streams crisscross this long, narrow strip of green pasturelands and hills stretching south from Lochgilphead.

GETTING HERE AND AROUND

Continue south on the A83 (the road to Campbeltown) to Tarbert. Some 4 miles farther along the A83 is Kennacraig, where you catch the ferry to Islay. Beyond that is the pier at Tayinloan; CalMac ferries run from here to the Isle of Gigha. Loganair flies from Glasgow to Campbeltown.

ESSENTIALS

AIRPORTS Campbeltown Airport. ⊠ *Off A83, Campbeltown* ✈ *At Machrihanish, 3 miles west of Campbeltown* ☎ *01586/553797* ⊕ *www.hial.co.uk.*

👁 Sights

Achamore House Gardens

GARDEN | Visit Achamore House Gardens in late spring to see its azaleas and its prize collection of rhododendrons ablaze with color. The island's mellow microclimate fosters these lush shrubberies. ⊠ *Achamore House, Isle of Gigha* ☎ *01583/505390* ⊕ *www.gardens-of-argyll.co.uk* ⊠ *Free, donations welcome.*

Isle of Gigha

ISLAND | Barely 7 miles long, this sheltered island between Kintyre and Islay has sandy beaches and rich wildlife. Ferries make the 20-minute trip from Tayinloan on the mainland. ⊠ *Isle of Gigha* ☎ *01583/505390* ⊕ *www.gigha.org.uk.*

🏃 Activities

GOLF

Machrihanish Golf Club

GOLF | For many Scots golfers (and they should know) Machrihanish's out-of-the-way location makes it a place of pilgrimage. Laid out in 1876, it's an intimidatingly memorable links course by a sandy bay. There is also a 9-hole course, The Pans. The historic clubhouse, devastated by fire in December 2018, has been lovingly restored. ⊠ *Off B843, Machrihanish* ☎ *01586/810213* ⊕ *www. machgolf.com* ⊠ *£75 Apr.–Oct., £45 Nov.–Mar.* 🏌 *Championship Course: 18 holes, 6235 yards, par 70; The Pans: 9 holes (out), 2376 yards, par 34.*

Arran

Approaching Arran by sea, you'll first see forbidding Goatfell (2,868 feet) in the north, then the green fields of the south. These varied landscapes earn the island its sobriquet: "Scotland in Miniature." A temperate microclimate attracted ancient settlers whose stone circles still stand on the island. This weather also explains why it has long been a favorite getaway for Glaswegians, who come here to walk, climb Goatfell, or play golf.

GETTING HERE AND AROUND

Caledonian MacBrayne runs regular car and passenger ferries that cross the Firth of Clyde from Ardrossan (near Saltcoats) to Brodick throughout the year; crossing takes just under an hour. There is also a small ferry from Claonaig on the Kintyre Peninsula to Lochranza during the summer months.

Connecting trains run to the ferry at Ardrossan from Glasgow's Queen Street station. Stagecoach runs regular local bus services around the island. Exploring the island by car is easy, as the A841 road circles it.

Brodick

1 hour by ferry from Ardrossan.

Arran's largest village, Brodick, has a main street that is set back from the promenade and the lovely bay. Beyond that, it is really little more than a gateway to the rest of the island.

GETTING HERE AND AROUND

You can reach Brodick from Ardrossan by ferry. From Brodick the A841 circles the island; head south to reach Lamlash, north to reach Lochranza. The String Road crosses the island between Brodick and Machrie.

ESSENTIALS

The information center, opposite the landing point for the Ardrossan Ferry, has an accommodation desk as well as tourist information.

Sights

Brodick Castle and Country Park

CASTLE/PALACE | **FAMILY** | On the north side of Brodick Bay, this red-sandstone mansion with typical Scottish-baronial features was built in the 16th century and was the seat of the dukes of Hamilton, who added to it extensively throughout the 19th century. It reopened in 2019 after a £1.5 million renovation, and now features an adventure park and an exciting visitor experience where costumed performers bring the past to life. In summer the expansive gardens are ablaze with azalea and rhododendron blossoms.

The country park that surrounds the castle embraces Arran's most striking scenery, rising to the 2,867-foot summit of Goatfell, the island's highest peak. The beautiful upland landscape is more challenging to explore than it seems, so it's important to go prepared with sturdy footwear and waterproof clothing. From the summit there is a stunning panoramic view of the Firth, Kintyre, and the Ayrshire coast, and on a clear day you can just see Ireland. ✉ *Off A841, 1 mile north of Brodick Pier, Brodick* ☎ *01770/302202* 🌐 *www.nts.org.uk* 🎟 *£14.50* 🕓 *Castle closed Nov.–Apr.*

Isle of Arran Heritage Museum

HISTORY MUSEUM | A typical Arran cottage, a re-created 1940s schoolroom, and farm buildings filled with antiquated implements that were in use within living memory make this lively little museum a must-see for anyone interested in the island's social history. ✉ *Rosaburn, A841, Brodick* ☎ *01770/302636* 🌐 *www.arran-museum.co.uk* 🎟 *£5* 🕓 *Closed Nov.–Apr.*

Restaurants

Brodick Bar and Brasserie

$$$ | **BRITISH** | This lively bar and restaurant serves fixed-price lunch and dinner menus featuring popular if unadventurous seafood favorites such as monkfish, halibut, and scallops, and adds spice to the mix with an array of Asian-influenced dishes. Like many places in the west of Scotland, hours are restricted, so it is well worth booking ahead. **Known for:** Gigha halibut with roasted gnocchi; Sunday roast with all the trimmings; Brodick *bouillabaisse* of local langoustines and shellfish. [$] *Average main: £20* ✉ *Alma Rd., Brodick* ☎ *01770/302169* 🌐 *www.brodickbar.co.uk* 🕓 *Closed Sun.*

Hotels

★ Auchrannie Resort

$$ | **RESORT** | **FAMILY** | With outstanding indoor and outdoor leisure facilities (including two pools and a spa), well-designed modern rooms, and three restaurants and bars, Auchrannie is by far the best place to stay on Arran. **Pros:** excellent outdoor activities; indoor leisure facilities including spa and pool; good for families. **Cons:** not for anyone looking for peace and quiet; lacks character; could-be-anywhere atmosphere. [$] *Rooms from: £159* ✉ *Auchrannie Rd., Brodick* ☎ *01770/30234* 🌐 *www.auchrannie.co.uk* 🛏 *115 rooms* 🍴 *Free Breakfast.*

Shopping

Arran's shops are well stocked with locally produced goods. The Home Farm is a popular shopping area with several shops and a small restaurant.

Arran Aromatics

PERFUME | This is one of Scotland's best-known suppliers of scents, soaps, and perfumes of every kind. ✉ *Home Farm, A841, Brodick* ☎ *01770/303003* 🌐 *www.arran.com.*

Isle of Arran Cheese Company

FOOD | Arran is famous for its cheeses, especially its cheddar and its Arran blue; stop here to sample and buy handmade Scottish cheeses. ✉ *The Home Farm, A841, Brodick* ☎ *01770/302788* 🌐 *www.arranscheeseshop.co.uk.*

Activities

Arran Adventure at Auchrannie Resort

BIKING | Mountain biking, sea kayaking, hill and gorge walking, and climbing are among the activities offered by Arran Adventure. Segway tours and guided strolls along the coast and on the slopes of Goatfell are also on offer. ✉ *Shore Rd., Brodick* ☎ *01770/302244* 🌐 *auchrannie.co.uk* 🎟 *From £16* 🕒 *Closed Nov.–Mar.*

Lamlash

4 miles south of Brodick.

With views offshore to Holy Isle, which is now a Buddhist retreat, Lamlash has a breezy seaside-holiday atmosphere. To reach the highest point accessible by car, go through the village and turn right beside the bridge onto Ross Road, which climbs steeply from a thickly planted valley, Glen Scorrodale, and yields fine views of Lamlash Bay. From Lamlash you can explore the southern part of Arran: 4 miles to the southwest, Whiting Bay has a pleasant well-kept waterfront and a range of hotels and guesthouses. If you travel another 6 miles, you'll reach the little community of Lagg, which sits peacefully by the banks of the Kilmory Water.

GETTING HERE AND AROUND

You can reach Lamlash by driving south from Brodick on the A841. The town is also served by Stagecoach buses.

Hotels

Lagg Hotel

$$ | **B&B/INN** | Arran's oldest inn is an 18th-century lodge with fireplaces in the common rooms and 11 acres of gardens and grounds that meander down to the river. **Pros:** nice local feel; beautiful gardens; warming fireplaces. **Cons:** often fully booked months in advance; some rooms are small; floral designs everywhere. [$] *Rooms from: £125* ✉ *A841, Kilmory* ✣ *12 miles south of Lamlash* ☎ *01770/870255* 🌐 *www.lagghotel.com* 🛏 *13 rooms* 🍴 *Free Breakfast.*

Machrie

10 miles west of Brodick.

The area surrounding Machrie, home to a popular beach, is littered with prehistoric sites: chambered cairns, hut circles, and standing stones dating from the Bronze Age.

GETTING HERE AND AROUND

The quick route to Machrie is via the String Road (B880) from Brodick; turn off onto the Machrie Road 5 miles outside Brodick. A much longer but stunning journey will take you from Brodick, north to Lochranza, around the island to Machrie, and down the island's dramatic west coast, a distance of some 28 miles.

Sights

Machrie Moor Stone Circles

RUINS | Six ancient circles of boulders and head-high sandstone pillars are scattered across Machrie Moor. These relics of a prehistoric culture are as old as Egypt's pyramids, if not quite as impressive, and the site evokes a dim and distant past. ✣ *1½ miles north of Machrie* 🌐 *www.historicenvironment.scot.*

🍴 Restaurants

Cafe Thyme

$ | TURKISH | This bright and pleasant restaurant offers a combination of Scottish and Turkish flavors (an expression of the owners' backgrounds) as well as fine views out to sea. Look for meze as well as *pides* (Turkish pizza)—try the haggis-and-cheese or crayfish-and-olive combinations. **Known for:** Turkish-style haggis pizza; Mediterranean meze; unusual East–West fusion dishes. $ *Average main: £14 ✉ Machrie ✛ Next to Old Byre Visitor Centre ☎ 01770/840227 ⊕ www. oldbyre.co.uk/cafethyme.irs ⊘ No dinner.*

🛍 Shopping

Old Byre Showroom

CRAFTS | This shop sells sheepskin goods, hand-knit sweaters, leather goods, and rugs. *✉ Auchencar Farm, A841, Machrie ✛ 2 miles north of Machrie ☎ 01770/840227 ⊕ www.oldbyre.co.uk.*

Lochranza

13 miles north of Machrie, 14 miles north of Brodick.

Lochranza shows Arran's wilder northern side, with rocky seashores and sweeping slopes leading to the stark granite peaks of Goatfell and Caisteal Abahail (2,735 feet), which dominate the skyline.

The respected Isle of Arran Distillery nestles in the hills overlooking Lochranza Bay. Until recently, this was Arran's only distillery, but in 2019 it gained a baby sister, the Lagg Distillery at Kilmory, which began selling its own malts and offering tours and tastings in 2021.

GETTING HERE AND AROUND

Lochranza is north of Brodick via the A841.

👁 Sights

★ **Isle of Arran Lochranza Distillery**

DISTILLERY | The open aspect and closeness to the sea explain the taste of Arran's well-respected single malt, light and airy and with the scent of sea and fields. The round white building housing the distillery sits comfortably among fields and hills in the northernmost part of the island. The CASKS café-restaurant is a comfortable place for a long lunch. Tours and tastings are offered. *✉ Distillery Visitor Centre, Lochranza ☎ 01770/830264 ⊕ www.arranwhisky. com 🖛 Tastings and tours from £20.*

★ **Lochranza Castle**

CASTLE/PALACE | Perched above the bay, Lochranza is Arran's most picturesque ruin and occupies a special place in Scotland's history. It was here that Robert the Bruce, after years of dithering, returned from exile to commit himself to the war for Scotland's independence. *✉ Off A841, Lochranza ☎ 0131/668–8800 ⊕ www. historicenvironment.scot ⊘ Closed Oct.–Mar.*

🛏 Hotels

Butt Lodge

$ | B&B/INN | Set in 2 acres of private woods and gardens overlooking Kilbrannan Sound, this onetime Victorian shooting lodge offers a personalized welcome from owners who really make guests feel at home with hearty (but healthy) Scottish breakfasts and complimentary afternoon tea, served in a cozy lounge. **Pros:** great views; peace and quiet; luxurious rooms and suites. **Cons:** up a winding farm road that can be tough on cars; no bar; a little hard to find. $ *Rooms from: £105 ✉ Off Newton Rd., Lochranza ✛ ½ mile east of Lochranza ☎ 01770/830333 ⊕ www.buttlodge.co.uk 🛏 7 rooms ◉ Free Breakfast.*

Islay

Islay is an island of rolling fields and pastures, heather-covered uplands where red deer roam and rutting stags clash antlers in spring, and white-sand beaches that on a summer day can look as enticing as any Caribbean strand. Huge flocks of Arctic wildfowl migrate to Islay in fall, leaving again in spring, when their wings literally darken the sunset sky. This was the long-ago seat of the Macdonald Lords of the Isles, a mongrel Celtic-Norse dynasty that held sway over the southern Hebrides for almost three centuries. Some of their heritage can still be seen. But it's a different inheritance that draws many visitors, namely the smoky, peaty malt whisky produced here by eight world-famous distilleries. Upstart Ardnahoe joined their ranks in 2018, with the stated aim of producing its own take on the classic Islay malt, but you won't be able to sample its wares for some years yet.

Bowmore

11 miles north of Port Ellen.

Bowmore, Islay's capital, is a good base for touring because it's central to Islay's main routes. A tidy town, its grid pattern was laid out in 1768 by local landowner Daniel Campbell, of Shawfield. Main Street stretches from the pier head to the commanding parish church, built in 1767 in an unusual circular design—so the devil could not hide in a corner.

GETTING HERE AND AROUND

Loganair flights from Glasgow and Edinburgh to Islay Airport take 40–50 minutes; the airport is 5 miles north of Port Ellen. Hebridean Air links Islay with Colonsay and Oban. The trip by CalMac ferry from Kennacraig to Port Ellen takes about 2½ hours; ferries also travel less frequently to Port Askaig. From Port Ellen it is 10 miles on the A846 to reach Bowmore; drivers should use caution during the first mile out of Port Ellen, as the road is filled with sharp turns. The rest of the route is straight but bumpy, because the road is laid across peat bog.

Local bus services 450 and 451 connect the main island communities of Bowmore and Port Ellen with points around Islay. Timetables are available from the tourist information center.

ESSENTIALS

CONTACTS Islay Airport. ⊠ *A846, Glenegedale* ☎ *01496/302361* ⊕ *www.hial. co.uk.*

VISITOR INFORMATION

Bowmore Visitor Information Centre. ⊠ *The Square, Bowmore* ☎ *01496/305165* ⊕ *www.visitscotland.com.*

◉ Sights

★ Bowmore Distillery

DISTILLERY | Bowmore is the grand old lady of Islay's distilleries, and a tour is a must for any visitor. In business since 1779, the distillery, like all Islay whisky makers, stands by the sea. Standard tours include a walk around the malting areas and the stills, and connoisseurs can opt for in-depth tours that include tutored tastings. ⊠ *School St., Bowmore* ☎ *01496/810441* ⊕ *www.bowmore.com* 🎫 *From £10* ⊗ *Closed Sun. and Mon.*

Islay Woollen Mill

FACTORY | Gorgeous tweed, plaid, and tartan clothing, wraps, and throws—woven at this historic mill and dyed in subtle, traditional tones—are sold here. ⊠ *A846, Bowmore* ✛ *4 miles outside Bowmore on the A846* ☎ *01496/810563* ⊕ *www.islay-woollenmill.co.uk* 🎫 *Free* ⊗ *Closed Sun.*

🍴 Restaurants

★ Harbour Inn

$$$ | **SEAFOOD** | An adjunct of the Bowmore distillery, the Harbour Inn has a bar frequented by locals and a more upscale restaurant with a menu that emphasizes oysters, langoustines, mussels, and other local seafood. The elegant dining room looks out onto the water. **Known for:** seafood paired with malt whiskies; classic Islay oysters; North African–influenced vegetarian dishes. [$] *Average main: £20* ✉ *The Square, Bowmore* ☎ *01496/810330* 🌐 *www.bowmore.com/harbour-inn* 🕒 *Closed mid-Nov.–mid Feb.*

🛍 Shopping

Islay Whisky Shop

WINE/SPIRITS | If you don't have time to visit all of Islay's distilleries, let alone those elsewhere, you can do worse than visit this shop with its enormous collection of whiskies. ✉ *Shore St., Bowmore* ☎ *01496/810684* 🌐 *www.islaywhisky-shop.com.*

Port Charlotte

On Islay, 11 miles west of Bowmore.

Planned by a benevolent 19th-century laird (and named after his mom), Port Charlotte is an unusually (for Scotland) pretty village, with wild landscapes and sandy beaches nearby. South of the village, the A847 road leads to Portnahaven and Port Wemyss, where pleasing white cottages stand in a crescent around the headland.

GETTING HERE AND AROUND

To reach Port Charlotte from Bowmore, take the A846 via Bridgend and then the A847, Portnahaven Road. Local buses also connect Port Charlotte and Bowmore.

Islay's Whiskies 👁

With 3,500 inhabitants and eight working distilleries—with two more due by the 2020s—Islay claims more stills per person than anywhere in the world. Yet, considering the island's size, there's remarkable variety here. Malts from the southeast coast, like Laphroaig, Lagavulin, and Ardbeg, reek of peat and iodine. Peat is still the keynote of malts from the western distilleries, such as Bowmore, Bruichladdich, and Caol Ila, but old-school aging in sherry casks gives these a lighter, more floral nose.

👁 Sights

Museum of Islay Life

HISTORY MUSEUM | A converted church is home to this local museum, a loveable haphazard collection of local artifacts, photographs, and memorabilia. There is also a local history archive. ✉ *A847, Port Charlotte* ☎ *01496/850358* 🌐 *www.islay-museum.org* 🎟 *£5* 🕒 *Closed weekends and Nov.–Mar.*

Natural History Centre

OTHER MUSEUM | **FAMILY** | With its exhibits about the island's wildlife, the Natural History Centre has lots of hands-on activities for kids. It's a great stop on rainy days, and tickets are valid for a week. On Monday and Friday there are nature rambles, and family activities are offered throughout July and August. ✉ *Main St., Port Charlotte* ☎ *01496/850288* 🌐 *www.islaynaturalhistory.org* 🎟 *£5* 🕒 *Closed Oct.–Apr.*

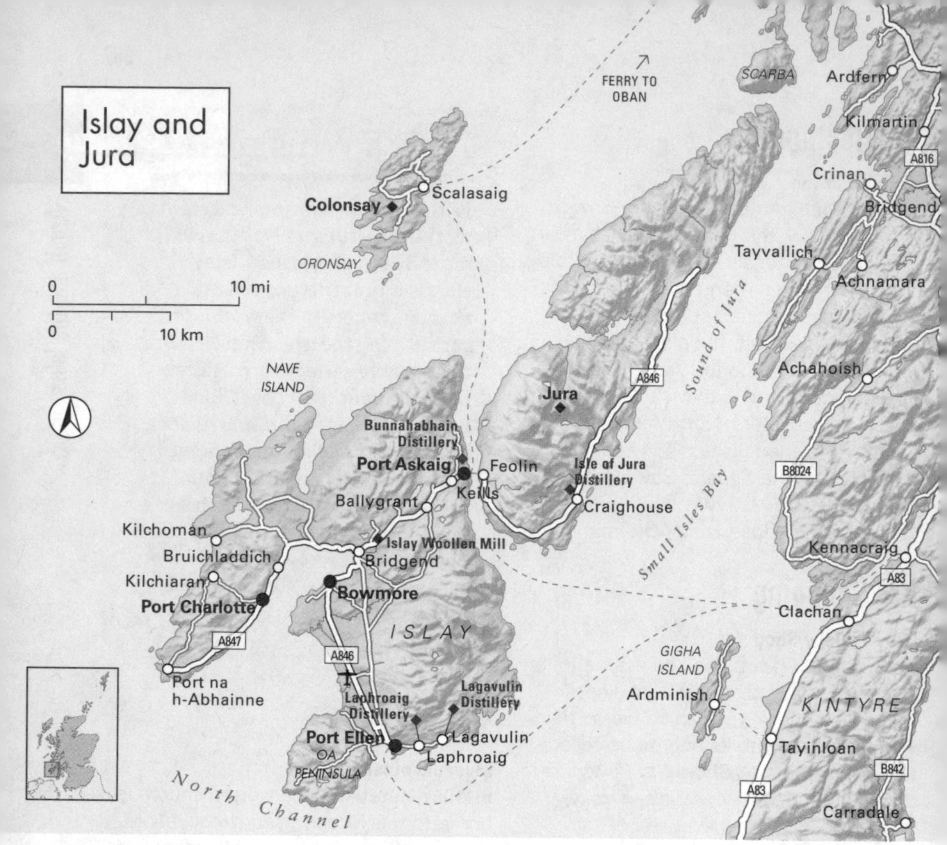

Hotels

★ Port Charlotte Hotel

$$$ | **HOTEL** | Once a row of fishermen's cottages and with views over a sandy beach, this whitewashed Victorian hotel has been lovingly restored. **Pros:** views over the water; beautiful location; lovely restaurant. **Cons:** not as luxurious as it claims; rooms are quite small; can be a little noisy from the bar. [$] *Rooms from: £260* ✉ *Main St., Port Charlotte* ☎ *01496/850360* 🌐 *www.portcharlottehotel.co.uk* 🛏 *10 rooms* 🍴 *Free Breakfast.*

Port Ellen

On Islay, 11 miles south of Bowmore.

Islay's sturdy community of Port Ellen was founded in the 1820s, and much of its architecture dates from the following decades. It has a harbor (ferries stop here), a few shops, and a handful of inns. The road traveling east from Port Ellen (the A846 to Ardbeg) passes three top distilleries and makes a pleasant afternoon's "whisky walk." All three distilleries offer tours, but you should call ahead for an appointment; there may be no tours on weekends at times. The last week in May, large numbers of whisky lovers descend on the island for the Islay Festival of Music and Malt, the heart of which is Port Ellen.

GETTING HERE AND AROUND

It is likely that Port Ellen will be your port of arrival on Islay. From here you can travel north to Bowmore, along the A846 before turning northwest towards Bridgend and Port Askaig.

Sights

Islay Festival of Music and Malt

OTHER ATTRACTION | The last week in May, large numbers of whisky lovers descend on the island for this festival, the heart of which is Port Ellen. Distilleries offer special events, and traditional music performances and ceilidhs take place all over Islay. Book lodgings and distillery tours at least six months ahead. ✉ *Port Ellen* ☎ *07914/675228* 🌐 *www.islayfestival.com.*

Kildalton Cross

RELIGIOUS BUILDING | Of interest only to anyone fascinated by Celtic heritage, this rock slab, engraved with elaborate 8th-century designs that meld pagan and early Christian motifs, stands in the kirkyard of a ruined medieval chapel. ✉ *Port Ellen* ✣ *About 8 miles northeast of Port Ellen* 🌐 *www.historicenvironment.scot.*

Lagavulin Distillery

DISTILLERY | Many malt whisky connoisseurs say the Lagavulin is the strongest nosed of all Islay's peaty malt whiskies. You can find out why, and how, with a distillery tour and tasting here. ✉ *A846, Port Ellen* ☎ *01496/302749* 🌐 *www.malts.com* 🎫 *Tours from £7.*

Laphroaig Distillery

DISTILLERY | Laphroaig (la-*froig*) is Islay's most distinctive malt, redolent of peat, seaweed, and iodine. You can take a tour of the distillery, then settle in for a spell of sipping at the whisky bar. ✉ *A846, Port Ellen* ☎ *01496/302418* 🌐 *www.laphroaig.com* 🎫 *From £60.*

Hotels

The Islay Hotel

$$$ | **HOTEL** | This charming hotel overlooking Port Ellen's harbor has large, bright rooms decorated in muted contemporary colors. **Pros:** good restaurant; central location; bright, welcoming interior. **Cons:** no lounge or sitting area; some noise at weekends from live music in bar; can get crowded. [$] *Rooms from: £250* ✉ *Charlotte St., Port Ellen* ☎ *01496/300109* 🌐 *www.theislayhotel.com* 🛏 *13 rooms* 🍴 *Free Breakfast.*

Port Askaig

On Islay, 11 miles northeast of Bowmore.

Serving as the ferry port for Jura and receiving ferries from Kennacraig, Port Askaig is a mere cluster of cottages. Uphill, just outside the village, a side road travels along the coast, giving impressive views of Jura on the way. There are distilleries near here, too; make appointments for tours.

GETTING HERE AND AROUND

Traveling from Bowmore, you can reach Port Askaig (where the road ends) via A846. The village is also served by local buses.

Sights

★ Bunnahabhain Distillery

DISTILLERY | Established in 1881, the Bunnahabhain (*Boon-a-ha*-bin) Distillery sits on the shore, with dramatic views across to the Paps of Jura. This is one of Scotland's most picturesque and evocative malt whisky distilleries, redolent of a preindustrialized era. ✉ *A846, Port Askaig* ☎ *01496/840557* 🌐 *www.bunnahabhain.com* 🎫 *From £7* 🕒 *Closed Nov.–Mar.*

Hotels

Kilmeny Country House
$$ | **B&B/INN** | This luxurious bed-and-breakfast is on a 300-acre farm, but the rooms are so elegantly furnished that the place feels more like a hotel. **Pros:** afternoon tea tray on arrival; elegant and quiet; great breakfast. **Cons:** hotel prices but without all hotel facilities; harsh cancellation policy; easy to miss. [$] *Rooms from: £160* ✉ *A846, Ballygrant* ✣ *Signposted off the A846 to Port Askaig, just before the village of Ballygrant* ☎ *01496/840668* 🌐 *www.kilmeny.co.uk* 🛏 *6 rooms* 🍴 *Free Breakfast.*

Jura

5 minutes by ferry from Port Askaig.

The rugged, mountainous landscape of the island of Jura—home to only about 200 people—looms immediately east of Port Askaig, across the Sound of Islay: a perfect landscape for walkers. Jura has only one single-track road (the A846), which begins at Feolin, the ferry pier. It climbs across moorland, providing scenic views of the island's most striking feature, the Paps of Jura, three breast-shaped rounded peaks. The ruined Claig Castle, on an island just offshore, was built by the Lords of the Isles to control the sound. The island has no cash machines, so plan ahead.

GETTING HERE AND AROUND

The Port Askaig–Feolin car ferry takes five minutes to cross the Sound of Islay, and there is a passenger-only ferry during the summer from Tayvallich on Argyll to Craighouse. Bus service is also available from Craighouse and Inverlussa.

Sights

Isle of Jura Distillery
DISTILLERY | The community of Craighouse has the island's only distillery, producing malt whisky since 1810. Tours must be booked in advance by phone or online. ✉ *Craighouse, Jura* ☎ *01496/820385* 🌐 *www.jurawhisky.com* 🎟 *Tours from £6* 🕒 *Closed mid-July–mid-Aug., weekends in Oct.–Mar., and Sun. in Mar.–Oct.*

Hotels

Jura Hotel
$$ | **HOTEL** | Jura's only hotel, next to the island's renowned distillery, has simple but cozy no-frills rooms, and its pleasant gardens are attractive on a summer day. **Pros:** lively bar; convenient location; good, unpretentious restaurant. **Cons:** the only hotel on the island, so almost always full; no in-room TVs; some shared bathrooms. [$] *Rooms from: £130* ✉ *A846, Craighouse* ☎ *01496/820243* 🌐 *www.jurahotel.co.uk* 🛏 *17 rooms* 🍴 *Free Breakfast.*

Isle of Mull and Iona

Mull is one of the most beguiling of Scotland's isles, and happily it's also one of the easiest to get to. The island's landscapes range from the pretty harbor of Tobermory and the gentle slopes around Dervaig to dramatic Atlantic beaches on the west. In the south the long road past the sweeping green slopes of the Ross of Mull leads to Iona, Scotland's holy island and a year-round attraction.

GETTING HERE AND AROUND

Ferries to Mull are run by the ubiquitous Caledonian MacBrayne. Its most frequent car-ferry route to Mull is from Oban to Craignure (45 minutes). Two shorter routes are from Lochaline on the

Home to the Maclean Clan, Duart Castle is one of the country's last privately owned clan castles.

Morvern Peninsula to Fishnish (15 minutes), or Kilchoan (on the Ardrnamurchan Peninsula) to Tobermory (15 minutes). The Kilchoan-Lochaline ferry is not bookable. West Coast Tours serves the east coast, running between Tobermory, Craignure, and Fionnphort (for the ferry to Iona).

Craignure

On Mull, a 40-minute ferry crossing from Oban, 15-minute ferry crossing to Fishnish (5 miles northwest of Craignure) from Lochaline.

Craignure, little more than a pier and some houses, is close to the well-known Duart Castle. Reservations for the year-round ferries that travel from Oban to Craignure are advisable in summer. The ferry from Lochaline to Fishnish, just northwest of Craignure, does not accept reservations and does not run on Sunday.

GETTING HERE AND AROUND

The arrival point for the 40-minute ferry crossing from Oban, Craignure is the starting point for further travel on Mull northwest toward Salen and Tobermory, or toward Fionnphort and the Iona ferry to the southwest.

VISITOR INFORMATION

Craignure Information Centre. ⊠ *The Pierhead, Craignure* ☎ *01680/812377* ⊕ *www.visitscotland.com.*

⊙ Sights

★ Duart Castle

CASTLE/PALACE | The 13th-century Duart Castle stands dramatically atop a cliff overlooking the Sound of Mull. The ancient seat of the Macleans, it was ruined by the Campbells, their archenemies, in 1691 but restored by Sir Fitzroy Maclean in 1911. Inside you can visit the dungeons and state rooms, then climb the keep for a view of the waterfront. Nearby stands the Millennium Wood, planted in 2000 with indigenous trees.

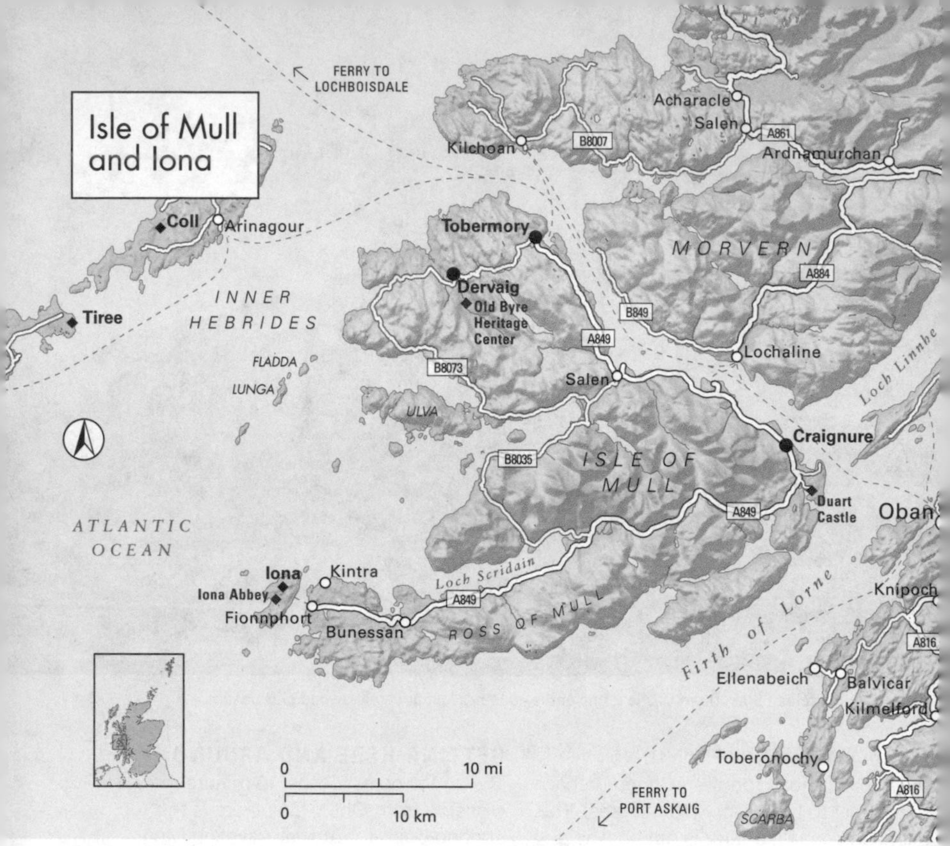

To reach Duart by car, take the A849 and turn left around the shore of Duart Bay. From Craignure's ferry port, there is a direct bus that takes you to the castle in about 10 minutes. ✉ *A849, Craignure* ⊕ *3 miles southeast of Craignure* ☎ *01680/812309* 🌐 *www.duartcastle.com* 🎫 *£8* 🕒 *Closed mid-Oct.–Mar.*

🛏 Hotels

Craignure Inn
$ | **B&B/INN** | Snug bedrooms with exposed beams, polished wood furniture, and views of the Sound of Mull make this 18th-century inn very appealing. **Pros:** expansive views; lively bar scene; hearty local food. **Cons:** rooms on the small size; bar can get very busy; live music can get loud. [$] *Rooms from: £95* ✉ *A849, Craignure* ⊕ *Near the ferry pier* ☎ *01680/812305* 🌐 *www.craignure-inn.co.uk* 🛏 *3 rooms* 🍴 *Free Breakfast.*

Dervaig

On Mull, 27 miles northwest of Craignure, 60 miles north of Fionnphort.

A pretty riverside village, Dervaig has a circular, pointed church tower that is reminiscent of the Irish-Celtic style of the 8th and 9th centuries. The Bellart is a good trout- and salmon-fishing river, and Calgary Bay, 5 miles away, has one of the best beaches on Mull.

GETTING HERE AND AROUND

You can reach Dervaig from Craignure via the A849. From Salen take the B8073, and from Tobermory take the B8073.

Sights

Old Byre Heritage Centre

HISTORY MUSEUM | At this museum, an audiovisual presentation on the history of the region is one of the highlights. The tearoom's wholesome fare, particularly the homemade soup, is a boon to travelers, as is the craft shop. You'll see signs for the center on the B8073, just before Dervaig. ✉ *Off B8073, Dervaig* ☎ *01688/400229* 🌐 *www.old-byre.co.uk* 🎫 *£4* 🕒 *Closed weekends and Nov.–Easter.*

Tobermory

On Mull, 5 miles northeast of Dervaig, 21 miles north of Craignure.

With its rainbow crescent of brightly painted harborside houses, Tobermory is the most photogenic village in the Isles and among the prettiest in all Scotland. Unsurprisingly, it's a lively tourist center and a popular base for exploring Mull, its smaller neighbors, and the sea-life-filled surrounding waters.

GETTING HERE AND AROUND

The most frequent service to Mull is via the Oban-Craignure ferry. Tobermory is 21 miles from Craignure along the A849/848 (via Salen).

VISITOR INFORMATION

Explore Mull Information Centre. ✉ *Ledaig Car Park, Tobermory* ☎ *01683/302875* 🌐 *www.isle-of-mull.net.*

Sights

Mull Eagle Watch

NATURE SIGHT | White-tailed sea eagles, extinct in Scotland since 1916, were reintroduced to the Hebrides in 1975. There are now around 80 breeding pairs, and on a Mull Eagle Watch trip you have an excellent chance of seeing these magnificent raptors on their nests and feeding their young at nesting sites around the island. Guides are paid directly in cash. From October to March, tours are by request only. ✉ *Tobermory* ✣ *Several different nest sites around Mull. Locations change each year* ☎ *01680/812556* 🌐 *www.mulleaglewatch.com.*

★ Tobermory Distillery

DISTILLERY | Tobermory's cute little distillery has been making distinctive malts (the peaty Ledaig and the unpeated, lighter-tasting Tobermory) since 1798, though there have been intervening decades when it was "silent" and produced no whisky. It was relaunched in 1993, and a tour here is a more personal experience than is offered by some bigger, better-known distilleries. Visitors can also sample the distillery's newest product: its own artisan gin. ✉ *Bad-Daraich House, Ledaig, Tobermory* ✣ *Off Main St. on south side of harbor* ☎ *01688/302647* 🌐 *www.tobermorydistillery.com* 🎫 *Tours from £8.*

Restaurants

★ Café Fish

$$$ | **SEAFOOD** | This restaurant's location has certainly contributed to its success—it's perched on the pier at the end of Tobermory. The owners pride themselves on the freshness of their fish; they have their own boat and bring in their own seafood each day. **Known for:** Mull lobster grilled with garlic butter; roast shellfish platters; Glengorm rib-eye steaks. [$] *Average main: £20* ✉ *The Pier, Tobermory* ☎ *01688/301253* 🌐 *www.thecafefish.com* 🕒 *Closed Jan.–mid-Mar.*

Hotels

Highland Cottage

$$ | **B&B/INN** | Set on the hill above the harbor, this family-run hotel prides itself on its elegant rooms and the imaginative dishes in its dining room. **Pros:** high-quality dining and a good wine list; comfortable rooms; attentive owners. **Cons:** not for those looking for full-service hotel amenities; a bit pricey for what you get; rooms are a bit small. [$] *Rooms from: £175* ✉ *Breadalbane St., Tobermory* ☎ *01688/302030* 🌐 *www.highlandcottage.co.uk* 🛏 *6 rooms* 🍴 *Free Breakfast.*

Tobermory Hotel
$$ | **HOTEL** | **FAMILY** | Made up of five former fishermen's cottages, this lodging on Tobermory's waterfront has a warm, intimate feel. **Pros:** very pet- and child-friendly; adorable cottage setting with fireplace; good restaurant. **Cons:** not all rooms have both shower and tub; tiny bathrooms; small rooms. [$] *Rooms from: £175* ✉ *Main St., Tobermory* ☎ *01688/302091* 🌐 *www.thetobermoryhotel.com* 🕒 *Closed Nov.–Mar* 🛏 *18 rooms* 🍴 *Free Breakfast.*

Western Isles Hotel
$$ | **HOTEL** | This grand hotel from the Victorian era looks down on Tobermory from its idyllic location overlooking the Sound of Mull. **Pros:** great food; brilliant views; spacious public rooms. **Cons:** overall lackluster atmosphere; rooms vary in size; some rooms look onto the car park. [$] *Rooms from: £198* ✉ *Off B882, Tobermory* ☎ *01688/302012* 🌐 *www.westernisleshotel.co.uk* 🛏 *26 rooms* 🍴 *Free Breakfast.*

Performing Arts

Mull Theatre
THEATER | The renowned Mull Theatre, founded in 1966, once prided itself on being the smallest theater in the United Kingdom. Today it has grown in size and in stature, and its productions tour not only the islands, but the whole of Scotland. It's wise to book ahead. ✉ *Druimfin, Salen Rd., Tobermory* ☎ *01688/302459* 🌐 *www.comar.co.uk/about/mull-theatre.*

Iona

5 minutes by ferry from Fionnphort (Mull), which is 36 miles west of Craignure.

The ruined abbey on Iona gives little hint that this was once one of the most important Christian religious centers in the land. The priceless *Book of Kells* (now in Dublin) was illustrated here, and it was the monks of Iona who spread Christian ideas across Scotland and the north. The abbey was founded in the year 563 by the fiery and argumentative Columba (circa 521–97) after his expulsion from Ireland. Until the 11th century, many of Scotland's kings and rulers were buried here, their tombstones still visible inside the abbey. Although few visitors venture beyond the pier and the abbey, there are several tranquil paths around the island.

GETTING HERE AND AROUND

Caledonian MacBrayne's ferry from Fionnphort departs at regular intervals throughout the year (£4.50 round-trip). Timetables are available on the Caledonian MacBrayne website. Note that cars are not permitted; there's a parking lot by the ferry at Fionnphort.

Sights

★ Iona Abbey
RELIGIOUS BUILDING | Overseen by St. Columba, who traveled here from Ireland, Iona was the birthplace of Christianity in Scotland in the 6th century. It survived repeated Norse sackings before falling into disuse around the time of the Reformation. Restoration work began at the beginning of the 20th century. Today the restored buildings serve as a spiritual center under the jurisdiction of the Church of Scotland.

Guided tours by the Iona Community, an ecumenical religious group, begin every half hour in summer and on demand in winter. ✉ *Iona* ☎ *01681/700404* ⊕ *www. iona.org.uk* 🎫 *£9.*

🛏 Hotels

St. Columba Hotel

$$ | HOTEL | As befits a religious retreat, rooms in this 1846 minister's home are simple to the point of being spartan, but those in the front make up for it with glorious views across the Sound of Iona to Mull. **Pros:** eco-friendly; impressive views; nice log fires. **Cons:** basic meals; few home comforts; pretty expensive for what is essentially a religious hostel. 💲 *Rooms from: £166* ✉ *Next to cathedral, Iona* ⊕ *About ¼ mile from the ferry pier* ☎ *01681/700304* ⊕ *www.stcolumba-hotel.co.uk* 🕐 *Closed Nov.–Mar.* 🛏 *27 rooms* 🍽 *Free Breakfast.*

Tiree

4-hour sail from Oban, via Coll.

Blue seas, white sands, a microclimate warmed by the Gulf Stream, and good surfing make this windy island popular in summer.

GETTING HERE AND AROUND

Caledonian MacBrayne runs ferries to Tiree via Coll, four times a week (Tuesday, Thursday, Saturday, and Sunday). You can also fly here from Glasgow on Loganair or from Oban on Hebridean Air Services. Tiree has a shared taxi service (☎ *01879/20419*), which you should book ahead of your arrival. An alternative is to rent a bike from Tiree Fitness (☎ *07867/304640*).

ESSENTIALS

CONTACTS Tiree Airport. ✉ *Off B8065, Tiree* ☎ *01879/220456* ⊕ *www.hial.co.uk.*

👁 Sights

Tiree

ISLAND | A fertile, low-lying island with its own microclimate, Tiree is windswept, but has long hours of sunshine in summer. Long, rolling Atlantic swells make it a favorite with surfers, and in summer, when an influx of wealthy visitors arrives, the posh accents of southern England sometimes drown out native voices. Among Tiree's several low-key archaeological sites are a large boulder near Vaul covered with more than 50 Bronze Age cup marks, and an excavated *broch* (stone tower) at Dun Mor Vaul. Tiree has two hotels and an assortment of self-catering accommodations, including a hostel with shared dorm rooms. The island is served by CalMac ferry from Oban.

Coll

3-hour sail from Oban.

Good birding and a number of ancient sites are among the attractions on Coll.

GETTING HERE AND AROUND

Caledonian MacBrayne runs ferries to Coll on Tuesday, Thursday, Saturday, and Sunday. You can also fly here from Oban on Hebridean Air Services. There is no public transportation or taxi service on Coll, but you can rent a bike at the post office (☎ *01879/230–3395*).

👁 Sights

Coll

ISLAND | Unlike their neighbors in nearby Tiree, Coll's residents were not forced to leave the island in the 19th century. Today half of the island's sparse population lives in its only village, Arinagour. Its coasts offer extraordinarily rich birdlife, particularly along the beautiful sandy beaches of its southwest. Coll is even lower lying than Tiree but also rockier and less fertile. There are prehistoric standing stones at

Totronald, a cairn at Annagour, and scant remains of several Iron Age forts around the island, though it takes some imagination to visualize what they must have looked like many centuries ago. ⊕ www.visitcoll.co.uk.

Colonsay

2½-hour sail from Oban.

Less bleak than Coll and Tiree, Colonsay is one of Scotland's quietest, most unspoiled, and least populated islands. It is partly wooded, with a fine 20-acre rhododendron garden surrounding Colonsay House, the private home of Baron Strathcona. The island also boasts a great variety of wildlife on land and in the surrounding waters.

GETTING HERE AND AROUND

CalMac ferries run to Colonsay on Monday, Wednesday, Friday, and Sunday. The island of Oronsay lies half a mile away and can be reached at certain times across a natural causeway. There is no public transport on Colonsay; bikes can be rented from Archie's Bike Hire (☎ 01951/200355) or Colonsay Bikes & Boards (☎ 07970/673942, ⊕ www.colonsaybikesandboards.co.uk).

◉ Sights

Colonsay

ISLAND | The beautiful beach at Kiloran Bay on Colonsay is an utterly peaceful place even at the height of summer. The standing stones at Kilchattan Farm are known as Fingal's Limpet Hammers. Fingal, or Finn, MacCool (Fionn mac Cumhaill) is a warrior of massive size and strength in Celtic mythology. Standing before the stones, you can imagine Fingal wielding them like hammers to cull equally large limpets from Scotland's rocky coast. The island's social life revolves around the bar at the 19th-century Colonsay Hotel, 100 yards from the ferry pier. The adjacent island of Oronsay with its ruined cloister can be reached at low tide via a 1½-mile wade across a sandy sound. ⊕ www.colonsay.org.uk.

Chapter 10

INVERNESS AND AROUND THE GREAT GLEN

Updated by
Joseph Reaney

👁 Sights	🍽 Restaurants	🛏 Hotels	🛍 Shopping	🍸 Nightlife
★★★★☆	★★☆☆☆	★★☆☆☆	★☆☆☆☆	★★☆☆☆

WELCOME TO INVERNESS AND AROUND THE GREAT GLEN

TOP REASONS TO GO

★ **Castles, fortresses, and battlefields:** Hear stories of the Highland people, learn about famous figures like Bonnie Prince Charlie, and absorb the atmosphere at local castles and battlefields, including Culloden Moor, Cawdor Castle, Fort George, and Glencoe.

★ **Outdoor activities:** The Great Glen is renowned for its hill walking, with some of the best routes around Glen Nevis, Glencoe, and on Ben Nevis, the highest mountain in Britain.

★ **Wild landscapes and rare wildlife:** Spot rare plants and beasts, including tiny least willow trees and golden eagles, in the near-arctic tundra of Cairngorms National Park.

★ **Whisky tours:** The two westernmost distilleries on the Malt Whisky Trail are in Forres. Benromach is the smallest distillery in Speyside and has excellent tours; Dallas Dhu is preserved as a museum.

If Inverness is the center point of a compass, the Great Glen spreads out to the east, south, and west. To the east, the A96 stretches along the Morayshire coast, which is populated with castles, beaches, and famous battlegrounds. Head southeast on the A9, and you pass Tomatin Distillery on the way to the Cairngorms National Park and other nature preserves. The A82 heads southwest from Inverness and hugs the western bank of Loch Ness, passing the contemplative ruins at Urquhart Castle and the interesting locks of the Caledonian Canal. Farther southwest, Fort William can be a good base for day trips to the foreboding and steep mountain pass of Glencoe. West from here on the A830 (Road to the Isles) lies Glenfinnan, Arisaig, and Mallaig.

1 Inverness. The biggest city in the Highlands and a popular base for the region.

2 Culloden Moor. The scene of one of Scotland's most famous battles.

3 Nairn. A former fishing village now famous for golfing and nearby Cawdor Castle.

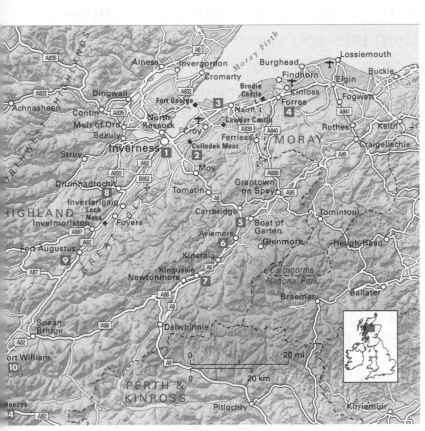

4 Forres. A perfect Scottish medieval town and a key stop on the Malt Whisky Trail.

5 Boat of Garten. A peaceful village home to a famous steam railway.

6 Aviemore. The gateway to Cairngorms National Park.

7 Kingussie. A pretty, more low-key base for the Cairngorms.

8 Drumnadrochit and Loch Ness. Nessie's stomping ground.

9 Fort Augustus. A good base to explore the lochs of the Caledonian Canal.

10 Fort William. Once a military outpost and now the gateway to the Great Glen.

11 Glenfinnan. Famous for its Jacobite history and photogenic viaduct.

12 Arisaig. A gateway to the smaller Scottish isles.

13 Mallaig. The gateway to Skye and the Knoydart Peninsula.

14 Glencoe. One of Scotland's most beautiful regions with plenty of Highlands history.

Defined by its striking topography, the Great Glen brings together mountains and myths, history and wild nature—then lets you wash it all down with a dram of the world's finest whisky. Inverness is the gateway to an area where the views from almost every twist and bend in the circuitous roads can take your breath away.

There's also plenty here for history buffs, including Culloden Moor, where the last battle fought on British soil ended the hopes of the tragically outgunned Jacobite rebels in 1746.

The Great Glen Fault runs diagonally through the Highlands of Scotland and was formed when two tectonic plates collided, shoving masses of the crust southwest toward the Atlantic Ocean. Over time the rift broadened into a glen, and a thin line of lochs now lies along its seam. The most famous of these is deep, murky Loch Ness, home to the elusive Loch Ness Monster.

The city of Inverness has a growing reputation for excellent restaurants, and from here nearly everything in the Great Glen is an easy day trip. To the east, the Morayshire coast offers a pastoral landscape. The 14th-century Cawdor Castle and its gardens have an opulent air, while nearby Brodie Castle has an awe-inspiring library and art collection. Impressive long, sandy beaches stretch along the coast from the towns of Nairn and Findhorn. Finally, the Malt Whisky Trail begins in Forres and follows the wide, fast River Spey south until it butts against the Cairngorms and the old Caledonian forests, with their diverse and rare wildlife.

Just south of the city, the ruins of the 13th-century Urquhart Castle sit on the shores of Loch Ness. In Fort Augustus, the Caledonian Canal joins Inverness to Fort William via a series of 29 locks. At the western end of the canal, Ben Nevis, Britain's highest mountain, rises sharply. The Nevis Range, like Cairngorms National Park to the east, is ideal for walking, climbing, and mountain biking amid hills and glens.

Fort William makes a good base for exploring Glencoe, an awe-inspiring region that was also the scene of another notorious episode in Scottish history: the Glencoe Massacre of 1692. It's an area where history seems to be imprinted on the landscape, which includes some of the steepest, most atmospheric hills in Scotland.

To the west of Fort William, the Road to the Isles offers impressive coastal views. The Small Isles of Rum and Eigg create a low rocky skyline across the water. Near the start of this road lies Glenfinnan, where, in 1745, Bonnie Prince Charlie rallied his Jacobite troops.

MAJOR REGIONS

Inverness. At the center of this region is Inverness, a small but appealing city that makes a useful gateway to the Great Glen. It has an increasingly strong range of restaurants and accommodations, but its cultural offerings remain more or less limited to what is happening at the Eden Court Theatre and the live music at a few good pubs. From Inverness just about anywhere in the Great Glen is a day trip.

Morayshire Coast. East of Inverness, the infamous Culloden Moor still looks desolate on most days, and you can easily imagine the fierce, brief, and bloody 1746 battle that ended in final, catastrophic defeat for the Jacobites. This thorny but colorful period of Scottish history is interwoven with landmarks throughout this entire area. The Morayshire coast also has many long beaches, some refined castles in Cawdor and Brodie, and the excellent Benromach distillery in Forres, a taste of what you can find farther south if you follow the Malt Whisky Trail into the heart of Speyside (part of the Aberdeen and the Northeast chapter).

The Cairngorms. Defining the eastern edge of the Great Glen, Cairngorms National Park provides sporty types with all the adventure they could ask for, including walking, kayaking, rock climbing, and even skiing, if the winter is cold enough. With craggy mountains, calm lochs, and swift rivers, the park has everything for lovers of the great outdoors. And while the towns and villages of the Cairngorms are nothing particularly special, they make great bases for heading out into nature.

Loch Ness. Have a go trying to spot Nessie from the banks of Loch Ness. Compared with other lochs, Ness is not known for its beauty—although it's hardly a stain on the landscape—but it draws global attention for its infamously shy monster. Heading south from Inverness, you can travel along the loch's quiet east side or the more touristy west side. A pleasant morning can be spent at Urquhart Castle, in the tiny town of Drumnadrochit, or a bit farther south in the pretty town of Fort Augustus, where the Caledonian Canal meets Loch Ness.

Fort William and Nearby. As you travel south and west, the landscape opens up and the Nevis Range comes into view. From Fort William you can visit the dark, cloud-laden mountains of Glencoe and the desolate stretch of moors and lochans at Rannoch Moor. Travelers drive through this region to experience the landscape, which changes at nearly every turn. It's a brooding, haunting area that's worth a visit in any season. If you dare, climb Britain's highest peak, Ben Nevis. The Road to the Isles, less romantically known as the A830, leads from Fort William to the coastal towns of Arisaig and Mallaig, with access to the Small Isles of Rum, Eigg, Canna, and Muck.

Planning

When to Go

Late spring to early autumn is the best time to visit the Great Glen. If you catch good weather in summer, the days can be glorious. Unfortunately, summer is also when you will encounter midges (tiny biting insects). Keep walking, as they can't move very fast. Winter can bring a damp chill, gusty winds, and snow-blocked roads, although many Scots value the open fires and warming whisky that make the off-season so appealing.

Planning Your Time

The Great Glen is an enormous area that can easily be broken into two separate trips. The first would be based in or near Inverness, allowing exploration of the Morayshire coast, including Cawdor and Brodie castles and perhaps a whisky distillery or two, as well as the Cairngorms.

The second involves traveling south along Loch Ness to Fort William, then either into the cloud-laden Glencoe (don't miss moody Rannoch Moor), or along the Road to the Isles. To do the whole area justice, you'll need at least five days.

For those with more time, a trip around the Great Glen could be combined with forays north into the Northern Highlands, east toward Aberdeen and the rest of the Malt Whisky Trail, southeastward to the Central Highlands, or south to Argyll.

Getting Here and Around

AIR

Inverness Airport has flights from London, Edinburgh, and Glasgow. Domestic flights covering the Highlands and islands are operated by Loganair. Fort William has good bus and train connections with Glasgow, so Glasgow Airport can be a good access point.

BUS

A long-distance Scottish Citylink service connects Glasgow and Fort William. Inverness is also well served from the central belt of Scotland. Discount carrier Megabus (book online to avoid phone charges) has service to Inverness from various U.K. cities.

Traveling around the Great Glen area without a car is very challenging and all but impossible in more rural areas. Stagecoach North Scotland serves the Great Glen and around Fort William.

BUS CONTACTS Megabus. ☎ *0900/160–0900* ⊕ *uk.megabus.com.* **Scottish Citylink.** ☎ *0871/266–3333* ⊕ *www.citylink.co.uk.* **Stagecoach North Scotland.** ☎ *01463/233371* ⊕ *www.stagecoachbus.com.*

CAR

As in all areas of rural Scotland, a car is a great asset for exploring the Great Glen, especially because the best of the area is away from the main roads. You can use the main A82 from Inverness to Fort William, or use the smaller B862/B852 roads to explore the much quieter east side of Loch Ness. Mallaig, west of Fort William, is reached via a new road, but there are still a few narrow and winding single-lane roads, which require slower speeds and greater concentration.

In the Great Glen, the best sights are often hidden from the main road, which is an excellent reason to favor peaceful rural byways and to avoid as much as possible the busy A96 and A9, which carry much of the traffic in the area.

TRAIN

ScotRail has connections from London to Inverness and Fort William (including an overnight sleeper service), as well as reliable links from Glasgow and Edinburgh. There's train service between Glasgow (Queen Street) and Inverness, via Aviemore, which gives access to the heart of Speyside.

Although there's no rail connection among towns within the Great Glen, this area has the West Highland Line, which links Fort William to Mallaig. This train, run by ScotRail, remains the most enjoyable way to experience the rugged hills and loch scenery between these two places. The Jacobite Steam Train is an exciting summer (late April to late October) option on the same route.

TRAIN CONTACTS Jacobite Steam Train. ☎ *0333/996–6720* ⊕ *westcoastrailways.co.uk.* **ScotRail.** ☎ *0344/811–0141* ⊕ *www.scotrail.co.uk.*

Restaurants

Inverness, Forres, Aviemore, and Fort William have plenty of cafés and restaurants in all price ranges. Inverness has particularly diverse dining options. Outside the towns there are many country-house hotels serving superb meals.

Hotels

In the Great Glen, town accommodations range from cozy inns to expansive hotels. Choices in more remote are usually limited to smaller establishments. Book as far in advance as you can: the area is very busy in the peak season, and the best places fill up early. In Inverness, you may find it more appealing to stay outside the city center or even in surrounding countryside.

Restaurant and hotel reviews have been shortened. For full information, visit Fodors.com. Restaurant prices are the average cost of a main course at dinner or, if dinner is not served, at lunch. Hotel prices are the lowest cost of a standard double room in high season, including 20% V.A.T.

WHAT IT COSTS in Pounds			
$	$$	$$$	$$$$
RESTAURANTS			
under £15	£15–£19	£20–£25	over £25
HOTELS			
under £125	£125–£200	£201–£300	over £300

Tours

Inverness Tours
GUIDED TOURS | This outfitter runs the occasional boat cruise and Inverness walking tour, but it's mainly known for high-quality Highlands bus tours led by expert guides and heritage enthusiasts. The price is per minibus, not per person, so while it's good value for parties of six or seven, it's less appealing for small groups. It may be possible to get single tickets if another group will sell its unused space. ✉ *High St., Inverness* ☎ *01667/455699* ⊕ *invernesstours.com* ✈ *From £320.*

J. A. Johnstone
DRIVING TOURS | At the more luxurious end of the scale, this company offers chauffeur-driven tours of the Highlands in air-conditioned Mercedes sedans. Excursions are completely tailored to what you want to see, and the guides have an encyclopedic knowledge of the region. The company also runs multiday tours of the Scottish regions and can help book accommodations along the way. ☎ *01463/798372* ⊕ *www.jajcd.com* ✈ *Prices on request.*

Inverness

176 miles north of Glasgow, 156 miles northwest of Edinburgh.

It's not the prettiest or the most charming Scottish city, but with a few attractions and some reliably good hotels and restaurants, Inverness makes a practical base for exploring a region that has a lot to offer. From here you can fan out in almost any direction for interesting day trips: east to Moray and the distilleries near Forres, southeast to the Cairngorms, and south to Loch Ness and Fort William. Throughout its past, the town was burned and ravaged by Highland clans competing for dominance.

GETTING HERE AND AROUND

You can easily fly into Inverness Airport, as there are daily flights from London, Bristol, Birmingham, Manchester, and Belfast. However, there are also easy train and bus connections from Glasgow Airport. Scottish Citylink has service here, and Megabus has long-distance bus service from Edinburgh and Glasgow. ScotRail runs trains from London, Edinburgh, Glasgow, and other cities.

Once you're here, you can explore much of the city on foot. A rental car makes exploring the surrounding area much easier. But if you don't have a car, there are bus and boat tours from the city center to a number of places in the Great Glen.

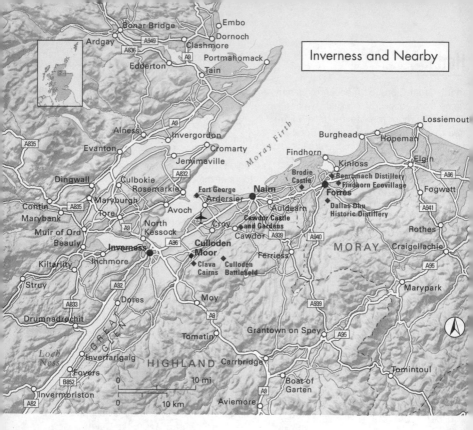

Inverness and Nearby

ESSENTIALS

AIRPORT CONTACTS Inverness Airport.
✉ *Dalcross, Inverness* ☎ *01667/464000*
⊕ *www.hial.co.uk/inverness-airport.*

BUS CONTACTS Inverness Bus Station. ✉ *Margaret St., Inverness*
☎ *01463/233371* ⊕ *www.stagecoachbus. com.*

VISITOR INFORMATION Visit Inverness Loch Ness. ✉ *Inverness* ⊕ *www. visitinvernesslochness.com.* **VisitScotland Inverness iCentre.** ✉ *36 High St., Inverness* ☎ *01463/252401* ⊕ *www.visitscotland.com.*

👁 Sights

Inverness Castle

CASTLE/PALACE | One of Inverness's few historic landmarks is reddish-sandstone Inverness Castle (now the local Sheriff Court), nestled above the river off Castle Road on Castle Hill. The current structure is Victorian, built after a former fort was blown up by the Jacobites in the 1745 campaign. The castle isn't open to the public, but you are free to wander the grounds. ✉ *Inverness.*

Inverness Museum and Art Gallery

HISTORY MUSEUM | **FAMILY** | The small but excellent Inverness Museum and Art Gallery covers archaeology, art, local history, and the natural environment in

The sandstone structure known as Inverness Castle stands guard over the small city of Inverness.

its lively displays. The museum is also home to the Highland Photographic Archive. ⊠ Castle Wynd, Inverness ☎ 01349/781730 ⊕ www.highlifehighland. com ⊙ Closed Sun.–Mon.

St. Andrew's Cathedral

RELIGIOUS BUILDING | This handsome Victorian cathedral, dating from 1869, has two unique claims to fame: in addition to being the northernmost cathedral in the British Isles, it was, more significantly, the first cathedral to be built in Britain after the Reformation. The twin-turreted exterior of the building is made from characteristically reddish local Tarradale stone. Inside, it follows a medieval layout, with the addition of an unusual patterned wooden floor. Check out the beautiful white marble font, carved in the shape of a seated angel. ⊠ Ardross St., Inverness ☎ 01463/225553 ⊕ inverness-cathedral.org.

🍴 Restaurants

★ Café 1

$$ | MODERN BRITISH | Consistently recommended by locals as one of the best restaurants in the area, Café 1 really practices what it preaches in terms of sustainable, local produce. Taking inspiration from such big names as Blue Hill in New York, the restaurant rears its own herds to provide the menu's Hebridean lamb and Highland beef, usually served with a simple order of chips (thick-cut fries) and rich garlic butter. **Known for:** ethically sourced ingredients; castle views; melt-in-your-mouth lamb. $ Average main: £19 ⊠ 75 Castle St., Inverness ☎ 01463/226200 ⊕ www.cafe1.net ⊙ Closed Sun.

The Dores Inn

$$ | BRITISH | Off a pretty country road on the eastern shore of Loch Ness, this low-slung, white-stone eatery is the perfect place to stop for lunch or dinner. The menu is a combination of well-prepared old favorites like fish-and-chips, together

with steaks, lamb, and seafood. **Known for:** gluten-free options; well-prepared Scottish classics; excellent range of whiskies. $ *Average main: £16* ✉ *B862, Dores* ☎ *01463/751203* ⊕ *www.the-doresinn.co.uk* ⊘ *Closed Mon.–Tue.*

Fig and Thistle Bistro

$$ | **BISTRO** | **FAMILY** | This intimate restaurant has been packing in the crowds nightly thanks to its modern bistro fare presented stylishly but without fuss. You could start with a delicious goat cheese and fig tart, for example, followed by a sumptuous steak with a red-wine-and-thyme sauce. **Known for:** reservations needed on weekends; seared local salmon infused with Thai flavors; tasty homemade desserts. $ *Average main: £18* ✉ *4A Stephens Brae, Inverness* ☎ *01463/712422* ⊕ *facebook. com/FigandThistleBistro* ⊘ *Closed Sun.– Mon. No lunch Tues.*

River House

$$$ | **SEAFOOD** | Head chef and owner Alfie Little draws heavily on local inspiration to shape the menu at this tiny riverside seafood restaurant, which has an interior as stylish as its appealing gray-and-white exterior. Start with mussels or oysters from the Scottish islands, then take your pick from mains based on native fish, such as Shetland halibut and Scrabster hake, and wash it all down with a local beer. **Known for:** riverside outdoor seating in summer; intimate atmosphere; fresh and sustainable local seafood. $ *Average main: £23* ✉ *1 Greig St., Inverness* ☎ *01463/222033* ⊕ *riverhouseinverness. co.uk* ⊘ *Closed Sun. and Mon. No lunch.*

★ Rocpool

$$$ | **BRASSERIE** | Another perennial favorite, the Rocpool has a frequently changing menu of modern bistro classics, with a few international twists. Local seafood from scallops to sea trout is a particular specialty, while meaty dishes range from Highland *côte de boeuf* steak to loin of Speyside venison. **Known for:** quality meat and seafood; outstanding wine selection; contemporary

twists on traditional dishes. $ *Average main: £22* ✉ *1 Ness Walk, Inverness* ☎ *01463/717274* ⊕ *www.rocpoolrestaurant.com* ⊘ *Closed Sun.*

★ Rocpool Reserve Hotel Restaurant

$$$ | **MODERN BRITISH** | The clean modern design is as sleek as the service at this restaurant in the Rocpool Reserve Hotel (not to be confused with the nearby Rocpool restaurant); think monochrome walls, straight lines, and a whole lot of upholstery in tasteful accent colors. As for the menu, expect creative, decadent dishes, from venison tartare to salmon risotto. **Known for:** a handful of lovely hotel rooms; inventive dishes and beautiful presentation; chic cocktail bar. $ *Average main: £24* ✉ *Rocpool Reserve Hotel, Culduthel Rd., Inverness* ☎ *01463/240089* ⊕ *www.rocpool.com.*

🛏 Hotels

Bluebell House

$ | **B&B/INN** | At this traditional Scottish guesthouse, sturdy oak furnishings are featured in each room, including a downstairs bedroom with a full-curtained four-poster bed and a curved chaise lounge. **Pros:** great hosts; large rooms; decadent furnishing. **Cons:** minimal technology; no windows in bathrooms; smallish bathrooms. $ *Rooms from: £120* ✉ *31 Kenneth St., Inverness* ☎ *01463/238201* ⊕ *www.bluebell-house. com* ⇄ *4 rooms* ⦿ *Free Breakfast.*

Bunchrew House Hotel

$$$ | **HOTEL** | This 17th-century baronial mansion, its turrets reflected in a glassy lake, looks like something from a Scottish fairy tale. **Pros:** good restaurant; beautiful setting; atmospheric building. **Cons:** a little out of town; quite expensive; some rooms could do with refurbishment. $ *Rooms from: £255* ✉ *Off A862, Inverness* ✛ *About 3 miles west of Inverness* ☎ *01463/234917* ⊕ *www. bunchrewhousehotel.com* ⇄ *16 rooms* ⦿ *Free Breakfast.*

Highland Apartments by Mansley

$$$ | APARTMENT | One of three Mansley properties in Scotland (the other two are in Edinburgh), Highland Apartments offers luxurious self-catering accommodations, many with delightful balcony views of the River Ness. **Pros:** secure parking available; chic modern apartments; great city center location. **Cons:** some may find entry by code impersonal; quite expensive; not all apartments have river views. $ *Rooms from: £225* ✉ *Bridge House, 21–23 Bridge St., Inverness* ☎ *0800/304–7160* ⊕ *bymansley. com* ⬅ *19 apartments* ⬤ *No Meals.*

★ Ness Walk

$$$ | HOTEL | This spot offers true five-star luxury in the form of spacious and stylish rooms, one of Inverness's best fine-dining restaurants (Torrish), and a verdant riverside location. **Pros:** lounge check-in with Champagne; beautiful riverside property; phenomenal afternoon tea. **Cons:** very expensive; superattentive service can be stifling; walk from the city center. $ *Rooms from: £295* ✉ *12 Ness Walk, Inverness* ☎ *01463/215215* ⊕ *www.nesswalk.com* ⬅ *47 rooms* ⬤ *Free Breakfast.*

Trafford Bank

$$ | B&B/INN | This former Bishop's home turned boutique B&B makes for a practical and stylish base, with owner Lorraine Freel's talent for interior design seen in the bespoke dining room chairs and handmade wallpaper—as well as in the eclectic array of art throughout. **Pros:** relaxing vibe; welcoming atmosphere; stylish rooms. **Cons:** a walk from the city center; early checkout time; some rooms on the small side. $ *Rooms from: £155* ✉ *96 Fairfield Rd., Inverness* ☎ *01463/241414* ⊕ *www.invernesshotelaccommodation.co.uk* ⬅ *5 rooms* ⬤ *Free Breakfast.*

🍸 Nightlife

★ Hootananny

PUBS | An odd but much-loved combination of Scottish pub, concert hall, and Thai restaurant, Hootananny is one of the best places in the region to hear live music. The excellent pub has a warm atmosphere and serves food that comes highly recommended by locals. Several bands play each Saturday evening and a few during the week, too—check the website for listings. ✉ *67 Church St., Inverness* ☎ *01463/233651* ⊕ *www.hootanannyinverness.co.uk.*

🎭 Performing Arts

★ Eden Court Theatre

ARTS CENTERS | The varied program at this excellent local filmhouse and theater includes movies, musical theater, comedy, ballet, and even pantomime. Check out the art gallery and the bright café, and take a walk around the magnificent Bishop's Palace. In summer, there's also regular live music on the lawn. ✉ *Bishops Rd., Inverness* ☎ *01463/234234* ⊕ *edencourt.co.uk.*

🛍 Shopping

Although Inverness has the usual indoor shopping malls and department stores, the most interesting goods are in the specialty outlets in and around town.

BOOKSTORES

★ Leakey's Bookshop

BOOKS | This shop claims to be Scotland's largest secondhand bookstore. When you get tired of leafing through the 100,000 or so titles, climb to the mezzanine café and study the cavernous church interior, complete with wood-burning fire. Antique prints and maps are housed on the balcony. ✉ *Greyfriars Hall, Church St., Inverness* ☎ *01463/239947* ⊕ *facebook. com/LeakeysBookshop* ⊘ *Closed Sun.*

CLOTHING

Chisholms Highland Dress

MEN'S CLOTHING | This shop specializes in kilts and tartans. Mail-order and made-to-measure services are available. ✉ *47–51 Castle St., Inverness* ☎ *01463/234599* ⊕ *www.kilts.co.uk* ⊘ *Closed Sun.*

GALLERIES

Castle Gallery

ART GALLERIES | The excellent Castle Gallery sells contemporary paintings, sculpture, prints, and crafts. It also hosts frequently changing exhibitions by up-and-coming artists. ✉ *43 Castle St., Inverness* ☎ *01463/729512* ⊕ *www. castlegallery.co.uk* ⊘ *Closed Sun.*

LOCAL SPECIALTIES

Inverness Coffee Roasting Co.

OTHER FOOD & DRINK | An ideal place to pick up a gift, this beautifully presented little coffee shop stocks a good selection of locally roasted beans to enjoy on the premises or take away with you. Indulgent handmade treats made in Inverness by luxury chocolatiers The Chocolate Place are also available here. ✉ *15 Chapel St., Inverness* ☎ *01463/242555* ⊕ *invernesscoffeeroasting.co.uk* ⊘ *Closed Sun. and Mon.*

SHOPPING CENTERS

The Victorian Market

MALL | Don't miss the colorful Victorian Market, built in 1870. The atmospheric indoor space houses more than 40 privately owned specialty shops, selling everything from fashion and jewelry to artisan chocolate. ✉ *Academy St., Inverness* ☎ *01463/710524* ⊕ *www.thevictorianmarket.com.*

⚡ Activities

★ Castle Stuart Golf Links

GOLF | Opened in 2009, this course overlooking the Moray Firth is already considered one of Scotland's finest—it's hosted the Scottish Open on four

---

Fishing in the Great Glen ⚡

The Great Glen is laced with rivers and lochs where you can fly-fish for salmon and trout. The fishing seasons are as follows: salmon and sea trout, from early February through September or even into October and November (depending on the area); brown trout, from mid-March through September; rainbow trout year-round. Sea angling from shore or boat is also possible. Tourist centers can provide information on locations, permits, and fishing rights.

---

occasions since. Expect undulating fairways and extensive bunkers that test your mettle. The 210-yard 17th hole provides perilous cliff-top play; the wind can defeat the canniest player. The art deco–inspired clubhouse offers stunning views of the water. ✉ *Off B9039, Inverness* ☎ *01463/796111* ⊕ *www.castlestuartgolf. com* 🏷 *£235* ⛳ *18 holes, 6553 yards, par 72* ⊘ *Closed mid-Nov.–mid.Mar.*

Inverness Golf Club

GOLF | Established in 1883, and partly designed by famous British Open champion and course designer James Braid, Inverness Golf Club welcomes visitors to its parkland course on the edge of the city. The tree-lined course overlooking the Beauly Firth presents some unique challenges to keep even experienced golfers on their toes. ✉ *Culcabock Rd., Inverness* ☎ *01463/239882* ⊕ *www.invernessgolfclub.co.uk* 🏷 *£69 May–Aug.; £50 Apr., Sept., and Oct.; £30 Nov.–Mar.* ⛳ *18 holes, 6094 yards, par 69.*

Bonnie Prince Charlie

His life became the stuff of legend. Charles Edward Louis John Casimir Silvester Severino Maria Stuart—better known as Bonnie Prince Charlie, or the Young Pretender—was born in Rome in 1720. The grandson of ousted King James II of England (King James VII of Scotland) and son of James Stuart, the Old Pretender, he was the focus of Jacobite hopes to reclaim the throne of Scotland. Charles was charming and attractive, and he enjoyed more than the occasional drink.

In 1745, Charles led a Scottish uprising to restore his father to the throne. He sailed to the Outer Hebrides with only a few men but with promised support from France. When that support failed to arrive, he sought help from the Jacobite supporters, many from the Highland clans, who were faithful to his family. With 6,000 men behind him, Charles saw victory in Prestonpans and Falkirk, but the tide turned when he lied to his men about additional Jacobite troops waiting south of the border. When these fictitious troops did not materialize, his army retreated to Culloden where, on April 16, 1746, they were massacred.

Charles escaped to the Isle of Benbecula, where he met and is rumored to have fallen in love with Flora MacDonald. After he had hidden there for a week, Flora dressed him as her maid and brought him to sympathizers on the Isle of Skye, who helped him escape to France.

Scotland endured harsh reprisals from the government after the rebellion. As for Charles, he spent the rest of his life in drunken exile, taking the title Count of Albany. In 1772, he married Princess Louise of Stolberg-Gedern, only to separate from her eight years later. He died a broken man in Rome in 1788.

Culloden Moor

6 miles east of Inverness.

Culloden Moor was the scene of the last battle fought on British soil—and to this day its name is enough to invoke raw and tragic feelings in Scotland. Austere and windswept, it is also a place of outstanding natural beauty.

GETTING HERE AND AROUND

Driving along the B9006 from Inverness is the easiest way to Culloden Battlefield, and there's a large car park to handle many visitors. Stagecoach North Scotland's Bus 2 also runs from Inverness to the battlefield.

◉ Sights

Clava Cairns

RUINS | Not far from Culloden Moor, on a narrow road southeast of the battlefield, are the Clava Cairns, dating from the Bronze Age. In a cluster among the trees, these stones and monuments form a large ring with underground passage graves that are reached via a tunnel. Helpful placards put everything into historical context. ✉ *Off B851, Culloden* ☎ *01667/460232.*

★ Culloden Battlefield

MILITARY SIGHT | Here, on a cold April day in 1746, the hopelessly outgunned Jacobite forces of Bonnie Prince Charlie were destroyed by King George II's army. The victorious commander, the Duke of Cumberland (George II's son), earned

Legend has it that Cawdor Castle was built around a thorn tree that can still be seen in the castle's dungeon.

the name of the Butcher of Cumberland for the bloody reprisals carried out by his men on Highland families, Jacobite or not, caught in the vicinity. In the battle itself, the duke's army—greatly outnumbering the Jacobites—killed up to 2,000 soldiers. The victors, by contrast, lost just 50 men. The National Trust for Scotland has re-created a slightly eerie version of the battlefield as it looked in 1746 that you can explore with a guided audio tour. An innovative visitor center enables you to get closer to the sights and sounds of the battle and to interact with the characters involved, while a viewing platform helps put things into perspective from on high (literally). Academic research and technology have helped recreate the Gaelic dialect, song, and music of the time. There's also a good on-site café. ⊠ Off B9006, Culloden ☎ 01463/796090 ⊕ www.nts.org.uk ⊠ £11.

Nairn

12 miles northeast of Culloden Moor.

This once-prosperous fishing village is now more likely to lure golfers than sailors, though its long sandy beach is great for a stroll. Nearby attractions include Cawdor Castle and Fort George.

GETTING HERE AND AROUND

From Inverness, you can reach Nairn by bus, train, or car: simply drive west along the A96. A car will give you the most flexibility to explore the area, though there are some local buses.

◉ Sights

★ Cawdor Castle and Gardens

CASTLE/PALACE | FAMILY | Shakespeare's Macbeth was the Thane of Cawdor (a local officer of the crown), but the sense of history that exists within the turreted walls of Cawdor Castle is certainly more than fictional. Cawdor is a lived-in castle, not an abandoned, decaying structure. The earliest part is the 14th-century central tower; the rooms contain family portraits, tapestries, fine furniture, and paraphernalia reflecting 600 years of history. Outside the walls are sheltered gardens and woodland walks. Children will have a ball exploring the lush and mysterious Big Wood, with its wildflowers and varied wildlife. There are lots of creepy stories and fantastic tales amid the dank dungeons and drawbridges. If the castle sounds appealing, keep in mind that the estate has cottages to rent. Cawdor Castle is 6 miles southwest of Nairn. ✉ *Off B9090, Cawdor* ☎ *01667/404401* 🌐 *www.cawdorcastle.com* 🎟 *Castle £13.50; grounds only £8* 🕒 *Closed Oct.–Apr.*

★ Fort George

MILITARY SIGHT | After the fateful Battle of Culloden, the nervous government in London ordered the construction of a large fort on a promontory reaching into the Moray Firth. Fort George was started in 1748 and completed some 20 years later. It's one of the best-preserved 18th-century military fortifications in Europe. At its height it housed 1,600 men and around 30,000 pounds of gunpowder; the on-site Highlanders Museum gives you a glimpse of the fort's history. The fort, 8½ miles west of Nairn, is also a great base for spotting dolphins and whales out at sea. ✉ *Old Military Rd., Ardersier* ✥ *Off B9006* ☎ *01667/460232* 🌐 *www.historicenvironment.scot* 🎟 *£9.*

Nairn Museum

HISTORY MUSEUM | **FAMILY** | The fishing boats have moved to larger ports, but Nairn's historical flavor has been preserved at the Nairn Museum, in a handsome Georgian building in the center of town. Exhibits emphasize artifacts, photographs, and model boats relating to the town's fishing past. A genealogy service is also offered. A library in the same building has a strong local-history section. ✉ *Viewfield Dr., Off A96, Nairn* ☎ *01667/456791* 🌐 *www.nairnmuseum.co.uk* 🎟 *£4* 🕒 *Closed Sun.*

Hotels

★ Boath House

$$$ | **B&B/INN** | Built in the 1820s and recently refurbished, this stunning Regency manor house offers elegant, spacious rooms (some with cast-iron bathtubs), a highly renowned fine-dining restaurant with local, ethically sourced ingredients, and a stunning setting within 20 acres of lovingly nurtured gardens. **Pros:** great package deals; excellent dining; gorgeous grounds and relaxed atmosphere. **Cons:** very pricey; no gym or spa facilities; some airplane noise. [$] *Rooms from: £250* ✉ *Off A96, Auldearn* ☎ *01667/454896* 🌐 *www.boath-house.com* 🛏 *9 rooms* 🍴 *Free Breakfast.*

Sandown House

$$ | **B&B/INN** | This former dairy-farm-turned-guesthouse offers a choice of accommodations: opt for one of the two charming sea-view guest rooms in the main 110-year-old building or for one of the more spacious, modern suites in the separate courtyard building. **Pros:** superb breakfast with lots of choice; easy access to Nairn Golf Club and beach; stylish rooms with spacious bathrooms. **Cons:** a 30-minute walk to the center of Nairn; no lunch or dinner available; main house rooms are smaller. [$] *Rooms from: £155* ✉ *Sandown Farm La., Nairn* ☎ *01667/451363* 🌐 *www.sandownhouse.com* 🛏 *6 rooms* 🍴 *Free Breakfast.*

★ Wendy Hoose

$ | **B&B/INN** | Located at the bottom of the Boath House Estate, the Wendy Hoose—named for owner Wendy Matheson, who runs the property with her husband, Don—is a charming B&B, where the historic exterior gives way to a thoroughly modern interior. **Pros:** easy access to dining at Boath House; informal and relaxed vibe; cozy contemporary decor. **Cons:** no guests under 18 allowed; two-night minimum in high season; accepts only cash or Bacs (U.K. payment system). Ⓢ *Rooms from: £120* ✉ *Boath House, Off A96, Auldearn* ☎ *07703/737530* ⊕ *www.thewendyhoose.com* ⇌ *2 rooms* �‖ *Free Breakfast.*

🛍 Shopping

Auldearn Antiques
ANTIQUES & COLLECTIBLES | It's easy to spend an hour wandering around this old church, 3½ miles southeast of Nairn. It's filled to the brim with furniture, fireplaces, architectural antiques, and linens, and the converted farmsteads also have tempting antique chinaware and textiles. ✉ *Dalmore Manse, Lethen Rd., Auldearn* ☎ *01667/453087* ⊕ *www.auldearnantiques.co.uk.*

🏃 Activities

BOATING
Phoenix Sea Adventures
BOATING | With one- and two-hour trips by boat from Nairn Harbour into the Moray Firth, Phoenix Sea Adventures offers you the chance to see seals, porpoises, and dolphins in their breeding areas. The daily departure times for the modern, ex-naval SWIFT vessels vary depending on the tides and the weather. Evening trips are offered on certain dates in summer. ✉ *Nairn Marina, Harbour St., Nairn* ☎ *01667/457175* ⊕ *www.phoenix-nairn.co.uk* ✉ *Tours from £20.*

GOLF
Nairn's courses are highly regarded by golfers and are very popular, so book far in advance.

Nairn Dunbar Golf Club
GOLF | Founded in 1899, the difficult Championship Links Course here features gorse-lined fairways and lovely sea views. ■**TIP→ Ask about the special-rate Nairn ticket, which allows you to play**

both this and the similarly named **Nairn Golf Club, for the bargain rate of £210 from April to October.** ✉ *Lochloy Rd., Nairn* ☎ *01667/452741* ⊕ *www.nairndunbar.com* ✉ *£70 (£50 after 2 pm) Apr. and Oct.; £100 (£70 after 3 pm) May–Sept.; £35 Nov.–Mar.* 🏌 *18 holes, 6721 yards, par 72.*

Nairn Golf Club
GOLF | Highly regarded in golfing circles, the Nairn Golf Club dates from 1887 and is the regular home of Scotland's Northern Open. Huge greens, aggressive gorse, a beach hazard for five of the holes, a steady prevailing wind, and distracting views across the Moray Firth make play on the Championship Course unforgettable. The adjoining nine-hole Cameron Course is ideal for a warm-up or a fun round for the family. ✉ *Seabank Rd., Nairn* ☎ *01667/453208* ⊕ *www.nairngolfclub.co.uk* ✉ *Championship Course: £190 (£160 off-peak) May–Sept.; £130 Apr. and Oct. Cameron Course: £20* 🏌 *Championship Course: 18 holes, 6832 yards, par 71; Cameron Course: 9 holes, 1634 yards, par 29.*

Forres

10 miles east of Nairn.

The burgh of Forres is everything a Scottish medieval town should be, with a handsome tolbooth (the former courthouse and prison) and impressive gardens as its centerpiece. It's remarkable how well the old buildings have adapted to their modern retail uses. With two distilleries—one still operating, the other preserved as a museum—Forres is a key point on the Malt Whisky Trail. Brodie Castle is also nearby. Just 5 miles north you'll find Findhorn Ecovillage, and a sandy beach stretches along the edge of the semi-enclosed Findhorn Bay, which is excellent bird-watching territory.

GETTING HERE AND AROUND

Forres is easy to reach by car or bus from Inverness (via Nairn) on the A96, while regular ScotRail trains run here from Inverness and Aberdeen.

👁 Sights

Benromach Distillery

DISTILLERY | The smallest distillery in Moray was founded in 1898. It's now owned by whisky specialist Gordon and MacPhail and produces an array of distinctive (often slightly peaty) malts, as well as its distinctive Red Door gin. An informative hourly tour will lead you through the facilities, including seeing the poignant signatures of distillery managers before and after a 15-year closure in the late 20th century. Tours end with a tutored nosing and tasting. ⊠ *Invererne Rd., Forres* ☎ *01309/675968* ⊕ *www. benromach.com* 🎫 *From £8.*

Brodie Castle

CASTLE/PALACE | A magnificent, medieval turreted fortification, Brodie Castle was rebuilt and extended in the 17th and 19th centuries. Consequently, there are fine examples of late-17th-century plasterwork preserved in the Dining Room and Blue Sitting Room, as well as a superb collection of artworks from the Old Masters up to the modern day. You'll also find an impressive library and beautiful gardens with more than 400 varieties of daffodils. The castle is around 4 miles west of Forres, on the road from Nairn. ⊠ *Off A96, Brodie, Forres* ☎ *01309/641371* ⊕ *www.nts.org. uk* 🎫 *Castle and gardens £15, castle only £11* ☉ *Closed Oct.–early Feb.*

Dallas Dhu Historic Distillery

DISTILLERY | The final port of call on the Malt Whisky Trail, the Dallas Dhu Historic Distillery was the last such facility built in the 19th century and was still in operation until the 1980s. Today, its distillery rooms—from the malt barn to the still house to the bonded warehouses—make up a fascinating exhibition that tells the story of Scotland's national drink. You'll be walked through the entire whisky-making process by an audio-tour guide, before eventually arriving in the bar to taste a dram and watch an entertainingly dated video. ⊠ *Mannachie Rd., Forres* ☎ *01309/676548* ⊕ *www.historicenvironment.scot* 🎫 *£6* ☉ *Closed Thurs.–Fri. in Oct.–Mar.*

Findhorn Ecovillage

TOWN | This fascinating, self-sufficient community project began in 1962 and is still going strong 60 years later. Dedicated to developing "new ways of living infused with spiritual values," the ecovillage draws its power from wind turbines, local farms, and gardens. You can wander around the village yourself for free, pick up a book for a self-guided tour (£7), or join a thought-provoking guided tour (£8, times and days vary by season so check the website) at the visitor center. The latter offers the most insight into the lives of the ultra-independent villagers, as well as a peek at some fascinating architectural quirks, from homes built out of whisky barrels to the Universal Hall, filled with beautiful engraved glass. Elsewhere, the Phoenix Shop sells organic foods and handmade crafts, and the Blue Angel Café serves organic and vegetarian fare. It's a short stroll from the ecovillage to Findhorn, with its pretty harbor and popular beach. ⊠ *The Park, Off B9011, Findhorn* ☎ *01309/690311* ⊕ *www.ecovillagefindhorn.com* 🎫 *Free; tours £7 or £8.*

Sueno's Stone

RUINS | At the eastern end of Forres stands Sueno's Stone, a 22-foot-tall pillar of stone carved with the ranks of soldiers from some long-forgotten battle. Nobody can quite agree on how old it is or what battle it marked, but its intricate Pictish carvings suggest it is from the early medieval period, probably erected between AD 600 and 1000. ⊠ *Findhorn Rd., Forres* ⊕ *www.historicenvironment.scot.*

🍴 Restaurants

Franklin's Restaurant

$$$$ | MODERN BRITISH | Set within the gorgeous front room of the Cluny Bank Hotel, this excellent but unfussy fine-dining restaurant is run by Lloyd Kenny, a passionate foodie who's spent decades honing his skills as a chef. Choose from a two-course (£38) or three-course (£48) menu, with each offering beautifully prepared dishes made from the very finest Scottish produce, from roe deer to guinea fowl and from scallops to sole. **Known for:** rooms available upstairs; relaxed fine dining; charming and chatty host. Ⓢ *Average main: £38* ✉ *69 St. Leonard's Rd., Forres* ☎ *01309/674304* ⊕ *clunybank-hotel.co.uk* ⊘ *Closed Sun. No lunch.*

🛏 Hotels

Knockomie Inn

$$ | HOTEL | Stylishly decorated bedrooms, consistently high quality dining, and an appealing whisky bar makes this one of the area's most upmarket accommodations. **Pros:** good value dinner-bed-and-breakfast deals; antique furnishings; delicious cooked breakfasts. **Cons:** a little out of town; showing signs of wear and tear; bathrooms small and lacking shelves. Ⓢ *Rooms from: £135* ✉ *Grantown Rd., Forres* ☎ *01309/673146* ⊕ *www.knockomie.co.uk* ⤳ *15 rooms* ⅋⏐ *No Meals.*

🛍 Shopping

★ Brodie Countryfare

MIXED CLOTHING | Visit Brodie Countryfare only if you're feeling flush: you may covet the unusual knitwear, quality designer clothing and shoes, gifts, and toys, but they are *not* cheap. The excellent restaurant, on the other hand, is quite inexpensive. In a rush? Pick up some delicious savory treats, like scotch eggs and sausage rolls, from the deli counter. ✉ *A96, Brodie, Forres* ☎ *01309/641555* ⊕ *www.brodiecountryfare.com.*

Boat of Garten

30 miles south of Forres.

In the peaceful village of Boat of Garten, the scent of pine trees mingles with an equally evocative smell—that of steam trains. The town is home to the historic Strathspey Steam Railway. Close to Cairngorms National Park, Boat of Garten has built a reputation as a great place to stay while exploring the region.

GETTING HERE AND AROUND

This charming town is an easy drive from Forres via the A940/A939, or Inverness via the A9. It's also serviced by local buses, and some people travel here on the Strathspey Steam Train.

👁 Sights

Landmark Forest Adventure Park

AMUSEMENT PARK/CARNIVAL | FAMILY | Situated 4 miles northwest of Boat of Garten, this park has a host of attractions, including nature trails, a heart-stopping parachute jump simulator, raft rides with varying degrees of wetness, a fire tower you can climb, and, best of all, the Wonder Wood, a place where visual tricks like forced perspective are used to befuddle your senses. You could easily spend half a day here. The park is open year-round, but most attractions close in winter (so prices are significantly lower). ✉ *B9153, Carrbridge* ☎ *01479/841613* ⊕ *www.landmarkpark.co.uk* 🎫 *Apr.–Oct. £24; Nov.–Mar. £10.*

RSPB Loch Garten Osprey Centre

NATURE PRESERVE | Set in the heart of Abernethy Forest, 3 miles east of Boat of Garten, the Loch Garten Osprey Centre offers a glimpse of the large fishing birds that come here to breed. The reserve, one of the last stands of ancient Scots pines in Scotland, attracts a host of other birds, too, including the bright crossbill and the crested tit. You might also spot the rarely seen red squirrel. The sanctuary is administered by the Royal Society for the Protection of

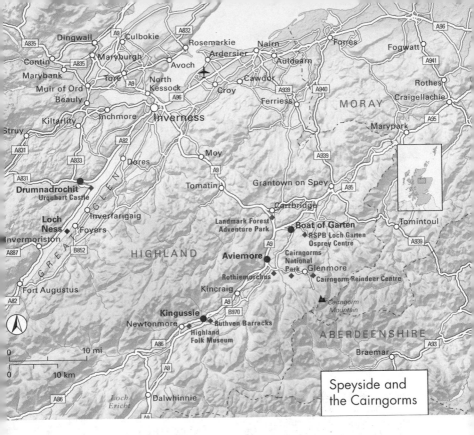

Speyside and the Cairngorms

Birds (RSPB). ⊠ *Off B970, Nethy Bridge* ☎ *01479/831476* ⊕ *www.rspb.org.uk* ⊠ *£5* ☉ *Closed early Sept.–Mar.*

Strathspey Steam Railway

TRAIN/TRAIN STATION | FAMILY | The oily scent of smoke and steam hangs faintly in the air near the authentically preserved train station in Boat of Garten. Travel in old-fashioned style and enjoy superb views of the high, often white domes of the Cairngorm Mountains. Breakfasts, lunches, and special dinners are served on board from March to October and in December. ■**TIP→ For the full experience, check the details carefully before you book, especially outside of the high season—less romantic diesel engines are used on certain days.** ⊠ *Boat of Garten station, Spey Ave., Boat of Garten* ☎ *01479/810725* ⊕ *www.strathspeyrailway.co.uk* ⊠ *£15.75 round-trip.*

★ Tomatin Distillery

DISTILLERY | Established in 1897 and once the largest malt distillery in Scotland, Tomatin is more of a large industrial complex than a typical pagoda-roofed Speyside distillery, yet the working nature of this place makes for a fascinating tour. Knowledgeable and playful guides take visitors through every step of the whisky-making process, with fun extras like a chance to stand inside a disused mash tun, and a photo opp with barrels dating back to the mid-1900s. Tours conclude with a tasting of three single malts, including the heavily peated Cu Bocan—worth the price of admission alone. Tomatin Distillery is located 13 miles northwest of Boat of Garten, on the road from Inverness. ⊠ *Off A9, Inverness* ☎ *01463/248144* ⊕ *www. tomatin.com* ⊠ *£10.*

Hotels

The Boat Country Inn
$$ | HOTEL | Great views of the Strathspey Steam Railway, welcoming traditional decor, and a wide variety of room types make this hotel much more than just a base for exploring the Cairngorms. **Pros:** garden access an option; good views; peaceful location. **Cons:** disappointing breakfast; some shared spaces need a lick of paint; not all rooms are family friendly. [$] *Rooms from: £140* ✉ *Deshar Rd., Boat of Garten* ☎ *01479/831258* 🌐 *www.boathotel.co.uk* 🛏 *34 rooms* 🍴 *Free Breakfast.*

Activities

★ **Boat of Garten Golf Club**
GOLF | This is one of Scotland's greatest "undiscovered" courses. The club, which dates from the late 19th century, was redesigned and extended by James Braid in 1932, and each of its 18 holes has a strong Highland feel. Some cut through birch wood and heathery rough, and most have long views to the Cairngorms. An unusual feature is the preserved steam railway that runs alongside part of the course. ✉ *Nethybridge Rd., Boat of Garten* ☎ *01479/831282* 🌐 *www.boatgolf.com* 🎟 *£75* ⛳ *18 holes, 5876 yards, par 70.*

Aviemore

6 miles southwest of Boat of Garten.

At the foot of the Cairngorms, once-quiet Aviemore now has all the brashness and boxiness of a year-round holiday resort. In summer, it's filled with walkers, cyclists, and rock climbers and is a convenient place for stocking up on supplies. Nevertheless, many of the smaller villages nearby are quieter places to stay. **■ TIP → Be forewarned: this region can get very cold above 3,000 feet, and weather conditions can change rapidly, even in the middle of summer.**

Boat of Garten's Ferry

A ferry that once linked both sides of the River Spey gave its name to Boat of Garten. The first official record of the ferry is in 1662, but the village itself did not appear until the coming of the railway in 1868, when cottages sprang up between the railway line and the ferry crossing. When it was time to pick a name, the ferry seemed like a good symbol. Not long after that, bridges were built across the River Spey, and demand for the little ferry disappeared. But the name stuck.

GETTING HERE AND AROUND

The A9, Scotland's major north–south artery, runs past Aviemore. From Boat of Garten take the A95 south. The town is serviced by regular trains and buses from Inverness, Edinburgh, and Glasgow.

ESSENTIALS

VISITOR INFORMATION VisitScotland Aviemore iCentre. ✉ *7 Grampian Rd., Aviemore* ☎ *01479/810930* 🌐 *www.visitscotland.com.*

Sights

★ **Cairngorms National Park**
NATIONAL PARK | This sprawling, rugged wilderness of mountains, moorlands, glens, and lochs covers nearly 1,750 square miles of countryside, making it Britain's largest national park. It is home to five of Scotland's nine 4,000-foot mountains, with 13 more over 3,000 feet. These rounded mountains, including Cairn Gorm (meaning "blue hill" in Gaelic) and Ben Macdui, the second highest in Britain at 4,295 feet, were formed at the end of the last ice age. The Lairig Ghru Pass, a stunning U-shaped glen, was carved by the retreating glacier.

Rugged Cairngorms National Park features many beaches and lochs, including rocky Loch Morlich.

A good place to start exploring the Cairngorms is the main visitor center in Aviemore. The staff can dispense maps, expert advice on the best trails, and information on guided walks and other activities. For hikers and cyclists, there are dozens of scenic trails centered around Loch Morlich. Because much of the park's best scenery—including ancient pine forests and open moorland—is off-road, a particularly good way to cover ground in the park is on a pony trek. The Rothiemurchus Estate leads treks for riders of all abilities.

The environment supports rare arctic-alpine and tundra plant and animal species (a full quarter of Britain's endangered species are found here), including flora such as the least willow and alpine blue-sow thistle and birds such as the ptarmigan, dotterel, and Scottish crossbill—the only bird completely unique to Britain. Lower down the slopes, terrain that was once filled with woodland is now characterized by heather, cotton grass, and sphagnum moss. This open expanse affords glimpses of animals such as the golden eagle, roe deer, or red deer. Fragments of the ancient Caledonian forest (largely Scots pine, birch, and rowan) remain and are ideal habitats for pine martens, red squirrels, and capercaillie (a large grouse). Studding these forests are dramatic glens and the rivers Spey, Don, and Dee, which are home to Atlantic salmon, otters, and freshwater pearl mussels.

Weather conditions in the park change abruptly, so bring cold-weather gear, particularly if you plan on hiking long distances. ✉ *Aviemore* ☎ *01479/873535* ⊕ *cairngorms.co.uk.*

Cairngorm Reindeer Centre

NATURE PRESERVE | FAMILY | On the high slopes of the Cairngorms, you may see the reindeer herd that was introduced here in the 1950s. The reindeer are docile creatures that seem to enjoy human company. Ranger-led visits to the 150-strong herd are offered at least once a day, weather permitting. In July and August you can also accompany rangers on gentle half-day treks through the mountains. From April through December a small herd of young reindeer is cared for at a paddock near the visitor center; you can visit (and pet them) for a small fee. Bring waterproof gear, as conditions can be wet and muddy. The Cairngorm Reindeer Centre lies 6 miles east of Aviemore. ✉ *Reindeer House, Glenmore, Aviemore* ☎ *01479/861228* 🌐 *www.cairngormreindeer.co.uk* 🎫 *£18.50; paddock £3.50.*

★ Rothiemurchus

NATURE PRESERVE | FAMILY | This excellent activity center has a host of organized outdoor diversions, including guided pony rides, mountain biking, fishing, gorge swimming, and white-water rafting. It also offers ranger-guided safaris to see the park's rare and endangered wildlife, including red squirrels and "hairy heilan coos" (Highland slang for Highland cattle—docile, yaklike creatures). The Rothiemurchus Centre is the best place to get oriented and book activities; it also has a handy restaurant and a well-stocked shop selling plenty of fresh produce from the estate. One of the most beautiful parts of the estate is a nature reserve called Loch an Eilein. There are great low-level paths around the tree-rimmed loch—perfect for bikes—or longer trails to Glen Einich. A converted cottage beside Loch an Eilein serves as a visitor center, art gallery, and craft store. ✉ *Rothiemurchus Centre, B970, Inverdruie* ☎ *01479/812345* 🌐 *rothiemurchus.net.*

🍴 Restaurants

Old Bridge Inn

$$ | MODERN BRITISH | This old-style bar and conservatory restaurant serves what many locals claim is the best pub food in Aviemore. The menu changes with the seasons, but you can always expect simple dishes built around quality ingredients such as local lamb chops or Angus beef, as well as a variety of fresh fish. **Known for:** warm and welcoming vibe; classic British fare; spirited live music. [$] *Average main: £17* ✉ *23 Dalfaber Rd., Aviemore* ☎ *01479/811137* 🌐 *www.oldbridgeinn.co.uk.*

Biking the Glen

A dedicated bicycle path, created by Scotland's National Cycle Networks, runs from Glasgow to Inverness, passing through Fort William and Kingussie. Additionally, a good network of back roads snakes around Inverness and toward Nairn. The B862 and B852, which run by the southern and eastern sides of Loch Ness, have little traffic and are good bets for cyclists. It's best to stay off the vehicle-heavy A9 on both sides of Aviemore, as well as the A82 main road along the northwest bank of Loch Ness via Drumnadrochit.

🛏 Hotels

Cairngorm Hotel

$ | HOTEL | The suit of armor standing guard at the entrance is a good indication of what awaits within this grand old house: acres of tartan carpet, chandeliers made from antlers, and a small museum's worth of distinctly Scottish decorative items (be sure to say hello to the taxidermy golden eagle on the stairs). **Pros:** family rooms offered; practical location; simple and traditional rooms. **Cons:** regular live bagpiper not for everyone; interior needs a refresh; not scenic. [$] *Rooms from: £110* ✉ *77 Grampian Rd., Aviemore* ☎ *01479/810233* 🌐 *cairngorm.com* 🛏 *32 rooms* 🍴 *Free Breakfast.*

★ Ravenscraig Guest House

$ | B&B/INN | Owned by Scottish-Swedish couple Scott and Helena, this charming little B&B offers a warm family welcome, modern rooms with bathrooms en suite, and a great location at the heart of Aviemore. **Pros:** free off-road parking; fantastic breakfast; smart TVs in the rooms. **Cons:** no dinner service; weak shower pressure; early checkout time. $ *Rooms from: £80* ✉ *141 Grampian Rd., Aviemore* ☎ *01479/810278* 🌐 *www.ravenscraighouse.co.uk* 🛏 *12 rooms* 🍴 *Free Breakfast.*

Activities

Glenmore Lodge

MOUNTAIN CLIMBING | In Cairngorms National Park, this is a good center for day and residential courses on rock and ice climbing, hiking, kayaking, ski touring, mountain biking, and more. Some classes are aimed at under-18s. There are superb facilities, such as an indoor climbing wall. Glenmore Lodge is about 7 miles east of Aviemore, just beyond Cairngorm Reindeer Centre. ✉ *Off B970, Glenmore, Aviemore* ☎ *01479/861256* 🌐 *www.glenmorelodge.org.uk.*

G2 Outdoor

WATER SPORTS | The wide range of adventures at G2 Outdoor includes white-water rafting, gorge walking, and rock climbing. The company offers a family float trip on the River Spey in summer, and in winter runs ski courses. ✉ *The Hatchery, Alvie Estate, Aviemore* ✥ *Off A9* ☎ *01540/651784* 🌐 *www.g2outdoor.co.uk.*

Mikes Bikes (Aviemore Bikes)

BIKING | This small bike shop stocks all the gear you might need to take advantage of the many paths around Aviemore. It also rents and repairs bikes. Prices start at £15 for three hours. ✉ *5A Myrtlefield Shopping Centre, Grampian Rd., Aviemore* ☎ *01479/810478* 🌐 *www.aviemorebikes.co.uk.*

Kingussie

12½ miles southwest of Aviemore.

Set in a wide glen, Kingussie is a pretty town east of the Monadhliath Mountains. With great distant views of the Cairngorms, it's perfect for those who would prefer to avoid the far more hectic town of Aviemore.

GETTING HERE AND AROUND

From Aviemore, Kingussie is easy to reach by car via the A9 (switch to the A86 for the last mile), although the slightly longer drive along the B9152 is generally quieter and more pleasant. There are also good bus and train services between the two towns.

Sights

★ Highland Folk Museum

HISTORY MUSEUM | **FAMILY** | Explore reconstructed Highland buildings, including a Victorian-era schoolhouse, at this open-air museum 2 miles west of Kingussie. You can also watch tailors, clock makers, and joiners demonstrating their trades. Walking paths (or old-fashioned buses) take you to the 18th-century township that was a setting for the hit TV show *Outlander* and includes a peat house made of turf and a weaver's house. Throughout the museum there are hands-on exhibits like a working quern stone for grinding grain. ✉ *Aultlarie Croft, Kingussie Rd., Newtonmore* ☎ *01349/781650* 🌐 *www.highlifehighland.com* 🎟 *Free* 🕒 *Closed Nov.–Mar.*

Ruthven Barracks

MILITARY SIGHT | Looking like a ruined castle on a mound, Ruthven Barracks is redolent with tales of "the '45," as the last Jacobite rebellion is often called. The defeated Jacobite forces rallied here after the Battle of Culloden, but they then abandoned and blew up the government outpost they had earlier captured. You'll see its crumbling, yet imposing, stone outline as you approach. Most come by car—there's a small car park across the road—but it's also walkable from Kingussie in about 20 minutes. ✉ *Off B970, Kingussie* 🌐 *www.historicenvironment.scot.*

🍴 Restaurants

★ The Cross at Kingussie

$$$$ | BRITISH | This former tweed mill, with a narrow river running alongside its stone walls, is a haven of wooden beams, whitewashed stone walls, and open fireplaces, all set within 4 acres of woodlands. The intimate dining room serves sumptuous Scottish produce, from duck and halibut to lamb and sea bass, each delicately prepared with an intimate knowledge of textures and flavors. **Known for:** gorgeous desserts like passion fruit cheesecake; perfectly curated set menus; stunning location. [$] *Average main: £55* ✉ *Tweedmill Brae, Ardbroilach Rd., Kingussie* ☎ *01540/661166* 🌐 *thecross.co.uk* ⏲ *Closed Jan. No dinner Sun. and Mon.*

🛏 Hotels

Coig Na Shee

$ | B&B/INN | This century-old Highland lodge has a warm and cozy atmosphere, and each of its spacious bedrooms is unique, with well-chosen furnishings and soothing color schemes. **Pros:** quiet location; great walks from house; plenty of privacy. **Cons:** hard to reach without a car; some rooms on the smaller side; 3½ miles outside Kingussie. [$] *Rooms from: £95* ✉ *Off Laggan Rd. (A86), Newtonmore* ☎ *01540/670109* 🌐 *www.coignashee.co.uk* 🔑 *5 rooms* 🍽 *Free Breakfast* ☞ *No children under 8.*

★ Sutherlands Guest House

$ | B&B/INN | Finding that sweet spot where contemporary meets cozy is no mean feat, but the husband-and-wife team behind this welcoming guesthouse make it look simple. **Pros:** great value; lovely spacious bedrooms; stunning lounge views. **Cons:** early checkout time; not licensed to sell alcohol; hilltop location best accessed by car. [$] *Rooms from: £115* ✉ *Old Distillery Rd., Kingussie* ☎ *01540/661155* 🌐 *www.sutherlandskingussie.co.uk* 🔑 *5 rooms* 🍽 *Free Breakfast.*

Drumnadrochit and Loch Ness

15 miles southwest of Inverness.

A tourist hub at the curve of the road, Drumnadrochit is not known for its style or culture, but it attracts plenty of people interested in searching for mythical monsters. There aren't many good restaurants, but there are some decent-enough hotels.

GETTING HERE AND AROUND

Drumnadrochit is an easy drive from Inverness (to the north) or Fort Augustus (to the south) on the A82. Buses run frequently, as this is a busy tourist destination.

👁 Sights

Loch Ness

BODY OF WATER | From the A82 you get some spectacular views of the formidable Loch Ness, which has a greater volume of water than any other British lake, a maximum depth of more than 800 feet, and—perhaps you've already heard?—a famous monster. Early travelers who passed this way included General Wade (1673–1748), who, prior to destroying much of Hadrian's Wall in England, came to dig a road up the loch's eastern shore; English lexicographer Dr. Samuel Johnson (1709–84), who remarked at the time about the poor condition of the population and the squalor of their homes;

"Nessie": The Loch Ness Monster

Tall tales involving some kind of beast inhabiting the dark waters of Loch Ness go all the way back to St. Columba in the 7th century AD—but, for the most part, the legend of "Nessie" is a disappointingly modern one. In 1933, two vacationing Londoners gave an intriguing account to a newspaper, describing a large, unidentifiable creature that slithered in front of their car before plunging into the loch. Later that year a local man, Hugh Gray, took the first purported photograph of the monster, and Nessie fever was born. The pictures kept coming—none of them *too* clear, of course—and before long the resident monster turned into a boon for the local tourism industry. Fortunately for them the age of camera phones has not dented Nessie's popularity: you don't have to search far on the Internet to find all sorts of photos of something—*anything*—that must surely be the monster, if you only squint a little. But does anybody seriously believe in it? Well ... no. But like all good legends, there is just enough doubt to keep the campfire tales alive. In 2006, declassified documents even revealed that, in the 1980s, Prime Minister Margaret Thatcher considered plans to declare the Loch Ness monster a protected species, as a safeguard against the hordes of bounty hunters she feared would descend should it ever be proven to exist.

and travel writer and naturalist Thomas Pennant (1726–98), who noted that the loch kept the locality frost-free in winter. None of these observant early travelers ever made mention of a monster. Clearly, they had not read the local guidebooks. ✉ *Drumnadrochit*.

Loch Ness Centre and Exhibition

OTHER MUSEUM | **FAMILY** | If you're in search of the infamous monster, the Loch Ness Centre and Exhibition walks you through the fuzzy photographs, the unexplained sonar readings, and the sincere testimony of eyewitnesses. It's an entertaining way to spend an hour, even if the boasts of "high tech" and "state-of-the-art" feel overly generous. It's said that the loch's huge volume of water has a warming effect on the local weather, making the loch conducive to mirages in still, warm conditions—but you'll have to make up your own mind about that explanation. ✉ *A82, Drumnadrochit* ☎ *01456/450573* ⊕ *www.lochness.com* 🎟 *£8.45*.

★ Urquhart Castle

CASTLE/PALACE | Located about 2 miles southeast of Drumnadrochit, this castle is a favorite Loch Ness monster-watching spot. This romantically broken-down fortress stands on a promontory overlooking the loch, as it has since the Middle Ages. Because of its central and strategic position in the Great Glen line of communication, the castle has a complex history involving military offense and defense, as well as its own destruction and renovation. The castle was begun in the 13th century and was destroyed before the end of the 17th century to prevent its use by the Jacobites. A visitor center gives an idea of what life was like here in medieval times. ✉ *Off A82, Drumnadrochit* ☎ *01456/450551* ⊕ *www.historicenvironment.scot* 🎟 *£12*.

Loch Ness, Fort William, and Nearby

Hotels

★ Loch Ness Lodge

$$$ | B&B/INN | Run by siblings Scott and Iona Sutherland, Loch Ness Lodge is an elegant and exclusive option offering a traditional Highland welcome; the formalities are kept to a minimum, but nice touches like the small decanter of sherry on arrival ensure you feel pampered. **Pros:** complimentary afternoon tea; superb views of Loch Ness; lovely rooms. **Cons:** easily confused with a (lesser) hotel of the same name in Drumnadrochit; no restaurant; near a busy road. $ *Rooms from: £250* ✉ *A82, Brachla* ☎ *01456/459469* ⊕ *lochnesslodge. cobbshotels.com* ⟿ *9 rooms* ⏍ *Free Breakfast.*

Shopping

An Talla

CRAFTS | This appealing retail destination en route from Inverness to Drumnadrochit sells traditional Scottish crafts, whisky, porcelain, and a whole host of other souvenirs. There's also a lovely little café; grab a takeout coffee, and stroll along Dochgarroch Loch. ✉ *Dochgarroch Loch, Drumnadrochit* ☎ *01463/572323* ⊕ *www. an-talla.co.uk.*

Activities

Jacobite Cruises

BOATING | FAMILY | The company runs morning and afternoon cruises on Loch Ness to Urquhart Castle and other destinations throughout the region. Tours depart from either Clansman Harbour, 5 miles northeast of Drumnadrochit, or Dochgarroch Loch farther up the A82. ✉ *Barckla Harbour, A82, Drumnadrochit* ☎ *01463/233999* ⊕ *www.jacobite.co.uk* ⟿ *Tours from £18.*

Fort Augustus

19 miles southwest of Drumnadrochit.

The best place to see the lochs of the Caledonian Canal is Fort Augustus, at the southern tip of Loch Ness. This bustling small town is a great place to begin walking and cycling excursions or to sit by the canal watching the loch fill and empty as boats sail between Loch Lochy, Loch Oich, and Loch Ness.

Fort Augustus itself was captured by the Jacobite clans during the 1745 rebellion. Later, the fort was rebuilt as a Benedictine abbey, but the monks no longer live here.

GETTING HERE AND AROUND

It's quick and easy to get here from Inverness via the A82, either by car or by local bus, and you'll pass Drumnadrochit on the way. A more leisurely alternative, however, is driving the B862 south from Inverness and along the east bank of Loch Ness. Take the opportunity to view the Fall of Foyers and the peaceful, reedy Loch Tarff along the way. Descend through forests and moorland until the road runs around the southern tip of Loch Ness. Parts of the route are remnants of the military road built by General Wade.

Sights

Caledonian Canal

OTHER ATTRACTION | The canal, which links the lochs of the Great Glen—Loch Lochy, Loch Oich, and Loch Ness—owes its origins to a combination of military and political pressures that emerged at the time of the Napoleonic Wars with France. In short: Britain needed a better and faster way to move naval vessels from one side of Scotland to the other. The great Scottish engineer Thomas Telford (1757–1834) surveyed the route in 1803, taking advantage of the three lochs that lie in the Great Glen and have a combined length of 45 miles, so that only 22 miles of canal had to be constructed to connect the lochs and complete the waterway from coast to coast. After 19 years, the canal, with its 29 locks and 42 gates, was open and ready for action. Travel along the canal today and stunning vistas open up: mountains, lochs, and glens, and to the south, the profile of Ben Nevis. At the visitor center in Fort Augustus, you can learn all about this historic engineering feat and take a picturesque walk along the towpath. ✉ *Caledonian Canal Centre, Canalside, Fort Augustus* ☎ *01463/725581* 🌐 *www.scottishcanals.co.uk.*

Hotels

Glengarry Castle Hotel
$$ | **HOTEL** | Tucked away in Invergarry, 7 miles south of Fort Augustus though still within reach of the Great Glen's most popular sights, this rambling baronial mansion offers alluringly old-fashioned rooms with traditional Victorian decor, some with superb views over Loch Oich. **Pros:** family rooms available; atmospheric building and gardens; good-value takeout lunches. **Cons:** some may find it old-fashioned; a little way from Loch Ness; no elevator. [$] *Rooms from: £180* ✉ *Off A82, Invergarry* ☎ *01809/501254* 🌐 *www.glengarry.net* 🕒 *Closed Nov.–Mar.* 🛏 *26 rooms* 🍴 *Free Breakfast.*

The Lovat
$$$ | **HOTEL** | The rooms in this charming Victorian hotel are tasteful and comfy, with some offering loch views, but the real highlights are the carefully furnished shared areas. **Pros:** some dog-friendly rooms; lovely lochside location; the region's best fine dining restaurant. **Cons:** expensive for the area; some corridors feel sterile; inconsistency in the quality of rooms. [$] *Rooms from: £225* ✉ *Off A82, Fort Augustus* ☎ *01456/490000* 🌐 *www.thelovat.com* 🛏 *28 rooms* 🍴 *Free Breakfast.*

Fort William

31 miles southwest of Fort Augustus.

As its name suggests, Fort William originated as a military outpost, established by Oliver Cromwell's General Monk in 1655 and refortified by George I (1660–1727) in 1715 to help combat an uprising by the turbulent Jacobite clans. It remains the southern gateway to the Great Glen and the far west. It's not Scotland's most charming or authentic town, but it's got several good hotels and makes a convenient base for exploring the surrounding countryside.

GETTING HERE AND AROUND

From Glasgow (to the south) and Inverness (to the north), the A82 takes you the entire way. From Edinburgh, take the M9 to the A84. This empties into the A85, which connects to the A82 that takes you to Fort William. Roads around Fort William are well maintained but mostly one lane in each direction. They can be very busy in summer.

A long-distance Scottish Citylink bus connects Glasgow and Fort William. ScotRail has trains from London, as well as connections from Glasgow and Edinburgh. It also operates a train service three times a day between Fort William and Mallaig. For those who like to combine travel and accommodations, the Caledonian Sleeper (🌐 *www.sleeper.scot*) leaves most days from London Euston late in the evening, arriving at Fort William midmorning the following day.

ESSENTIALS

VISITOR INFORMATION VisitScotland Fort William iCentre. ✉ *15 High St., Fort William* ☎ *01397/701801* 🌐 *www.visitfortwilliam.co.uk, www.visitscotland.com.*

The famous Jacobite Steam Train doubles as the Hogwarts Express in the Harry Potter films.

Sights

Ben Nevis

MOUNTAIN | The tallest mountain in the British Isles, 4,411-foot Ben Nevis looms over Fort William, less than 4 miles from Loch Linnhe. A trek to its summit is a rewarding experience, but you should be fit and well prepared—food and water, map and compass, first-aid kit, whistle, hat, gloves, and warm clothing (yes, even in summer), as well as insect spray for midges—as the unpredictable weather can make it a hazardous hike. Ask for advice at the local tourist office before you begin.

★ Jacobite Steam Train

TRAIN/TRAIN STATION | **FAMILY** | The most relaxing way to take in the wild, birch- and bracken-covered slopes is by rail, and the best ride is on the historic Jacobite Steam Train, a spectacularly scenic 84-mile round-trip that runs between Fort William and Mallaig. You'll see mountains, lochs, beaches, and islands along the way. There are two trips a day between late April and late October (though weekend trips are only in the height of summer). ⊠ *Fort William Travel Centre, MacFarlane Way, Fort William* ☎ *0844/850–4685* ⊕ *westcoastrailways. co.uk* ✉ *£69 round-trip* ⊘ *Closed late Oct.–late Apr.*

★ Nevis Range Mountain Experience

VIEWPOINT | Located 6 miles northeast of Fort William, this fantastic outdoor center offers a range of activities in all seasons, from downhill skiing and snowboarding to exhilarating mountain-biking trails, treetop adventure obstacle courses, and mountaintop paragliding. From June to early September, you can also take a gondola to the 2,000-foot summit of Aonach Mor, from which you can hike and explore more of the range (and enjoy stunning views of Ben Nevis). There are also two good dining options: try Pinemarten Café at the foot of the gondola for its rich macaroni and cheese and local craft beer selection. ⊠ *Off A82, Fort William* ☎ *01397/705825* ⊕ *www. nevisrange.co.uk* ✉ *Gondola £22.*

★ West Highland Museum

HISTORY MUSEUM | In the town center, the small but fascinating West Highland Museum explores the history of Prince Charles Edward Stuart and the 1745 rebellion. Included in the museum's folk exhibits are a costume and tartan display and an excellent collection of Jacobite relics. One of the most intriguing objects here is a tray decorated with a distorted image of Bonnie Prince Charlie that only becomes visible when reflected in a wine glass or goblet. This elaborate ruse enabled clandestine supporters among the nobility to raise a (treasonous) toast without fear of discovery. ✉ *Cameron Sq., Fort William* ☎ *01397/702169* 🌐 *www.westhighlandmuseum.org.uk* 🕓 *Closed Sat.–Mon.*

🍴 Restaurants

★ Crannog Seafood Restaurant

$$$ | **SEAFOOD** | With a reputation for quality and simplicity, this restaurant on the town pier serves outstanding seafood. Fishing boats draw up on the shores of Loch Linnhe and deliver their catch straight to the kitchen. **Known for:** offers seal-spotting cruises in summer; small but well-curated menu that includes delicious Cullen skink; idyllic lochside location. [$] *Average main: £22* ✉ *Town Pier, Fort William* ☎ *01397/705589* 🌐 *www.crannog.net.*

Lime Tree An Ealdhain

$$$ | **MODERN BRITISH** | One of Fort William's most upscale culinary spots, this restaurant is unfussy and modern inside, with low-hanging lamps, rich jewel-toned walls, and solid wood furniture. Expect filling dishes that, while not overly complex, are given an edge with embellishments such as fennel sauerkraut or marrowbone crumble. **Known for:** on-site art gallery; some of Fort William's most interesting food; inspired desserts. [$] *Average main: £21* ✉ *The Old Manse, Achintore Rd., Fort William* ☎ *01397/701806* 🌐 *www.limetreefortwilliam.co.uk* 🕓 *No lunch.*

🛏 Hotels

★ Ardrhu House

$$$ | **HOUSE** | Drive 10 miles south of Fort William, turn onto an unassuming country road, and you'll find this hidden gem of a guest house—a gorgeous old lochside manor with beautifully appointed bedrooms, a top-drawer restaurant, and even a small spa. **Pros:** outdoor whirlpool tub overlooking Loch Linnhe; Master Suite has its own steam room; exceptional dining. **Cons:** no TVs in the bedrooms; continental breakfast only; a 20-minute drive from Fort William. [$] *Rooms from: £240* ✉ *Off A82 near Onich, Fort William* ☎ *01855/821210* 🌐 *www.ardrhuhouse.com* 🔑 *6 rooms* 🍴 *Free Breakfast.*

★ Crolinnhe Guest House

$$ | **B&B/INN** | This beautiful old house with elegant suites and colorful gardens overlooks Loch Linnhe yet is only a 10-minute walk from town. **Pros:** comfortable rooms; stunning loch views; great breakfasts. **Cons:** grand decor not to everyone's tastes; short walk from town; late check-in and early check-out. [$] *Rooms from: £180* ✉ *Grange Rd., Fort William* ☎ *01397/703795* 🌐 *www.crolinnhe.com* 🕓 *Closed Nov.–Easter* 🔑 *3 suites* 🍴 *Free Breakfast.*

Inverlochy Castle Hotel

$$$$ | **HOTEL** | A red-granite mansion turned luxury boutique hotel, Inverlochy Castle stands on 50 acres of woodlands in the shadow of Ben Nevis, with striking scenery on every side. **Pros:** beautiful countryside location; gorgeous historic building; excellent restaurant. **Cons:** a little outside Fort William; strict dress code for dinner; extremely expensive. [$] *Rooms from: £515* ✉ *Off A82, Fort William* ☎ *01397/702177* 🌐 *www.inverlochycastlehotel.com* 🕓 *Closed mid-Jan.–mid-Feb.* 🔑 *17 rooms* 🍴 *Free Breakfast.*

Activities

GOLF

Fort William Golf Club

GOLF | This excellent course has spectacular views of Ben Nevis (indeed, it partly occupies its lower slope). The Highland course appeals to beginners and experts alike, drawn as much for the beautiful setting as the thoroughly reasonable green fees. Watch out for the treacherous 4th hole—it looks simple, but a fierce prevailing wind will test even the most practiced swing. ⊠ *North Rd., Torlundy, Fort William* ✛ *Off A82* ☎ *01397/704464* ⊕ *www.fortwilliamgolfclub.com* 💳 *£20* ⚑ *18 holes, 6217 yards, par 70.*

HIKING

This area—especially around Glen Nevis, Glencoe, and Ben Nevis—is popular with hikers. However, routes are not well marked, so contact the VisitScotland Fort William iCentre before you go. The center will provide you with expert advice based on your interests, level of fitness, and hiking experience.

★ Glen Nevis

HIKING & WALKING | For a walk in Glen Nevis, drive north from Fort William on the A82 toward Fort Augustus. On the outskirts of town, just before the bridge over the River Nevis, turn right up the road signposted Glen Nevis. About 6½ miles along this road is a parking lot (Upper Glen Nevis Car Park); from here, a footpath will lead you to a steel-cable bridge (1 mile) and then to Steall Waterfall. The ruined croft beside the boulder-strewn stream is a great picnic place. You can continue up the glen for some distance without any danger of becoming lost as long as you stay on the path and keep the river to your right. Watch your step going through the tree-lined gorge. The return route is simply back the way you came. ⊠ *Upper Glen Nevis Car Park.*

Glenfinnan

16 miles west of Fort William, 19 miles east of Arisaig.

Perhaps the most visitor-oriented stop on the route between Fort William and Mallaig, Glenfinnan has much to offer if you're interested in Scottish history. Here the National Trust for Scotland has capitalized on the romance surrounding the story of the Jacobites and their attempts to return a Stewart monarch and the Roman Catholic religion to a country that had become staunchly Protestant. It was at Glenfinnan that the rash adventurer Bonnie Prince Charlie gathered his meager forces for the final Jacobite rebellion of 1745–46.

GETTING HERE AND AROUND

If you're driving from Fort William, travel west via the A830. The same road continues to Arisaig and Mallaig. For great views, take a ride on the Jacobite Steam Train, which you can catch in Fort William.

◉ Sights

Glenfinnan Monument

MONUMENT | One of the most striking monuments in Britain, this 1815 tower overlooking Loch Shiel commemorates the place where Bonnie Prince Charlie raised his standard. Note, however, that the figure on the top is a Highlander, not the prince himself. The story of his ill-fated campaign is told in the nearby visitor center. ■ TIP➔ **The view down Loch Shiel from the Glenfinnan Monument is one of the most photographed in Scotland.** ⊠ *Off A830, Glenfinnan* ☎ *01397/722250* ⊕ *www.nts.org.uk.*

Glenfinnan Viaduct

BRIDGE | The 1,248-foot-long Glenfinnan Viaduct was a genuine wonder when it was built in 1897, and it remains so today. The railway's contractor, Robert MacAlpine (known among locals as "Concrete Bob"), pioneered the use of concrete for bridges when his company built the Mallaig extension, which opened in 1901. In more recent times the viaduct became famous for its appearance in the Harry Potter films. The viaduct can be seen on foot; about ½ mile west of the railway station in Glenfinnan, on the A380 road, is a small parking lot. Take the footpath from here; you'll reach the viaduct in about ½ mile. If you time it right, usually at 11 am, 3 pm, and 7:30 pm (confirm times at 🌐 *westcoastrailways.co.uk*), you'll see the iconic Jacobite Steam Train crossing the bridge. ✉ *Glenfinnan Viaduct Car Park, Off A380, Glenfinnan.*

🛏 Hotels

Glenfinnan House

$$ | **HOTEL** | This handsome hotel on the shores of Loch Shiel was built in the 18th century as the home of Alexander MacDonald VII of Glenaladale, who was wounded fighting for Bonnie Prince Charlie; it was transformed into an even grander mansion in the 19th century. **Pros:** beautiful views; fabulous setting; atmospheric dining experience. **Cons:** no air-conditioning; a bit fussy for some; can hear bar noise in some rooms. [$] *Rooms from: £150* ✉ *Off A830, Glenfinnan* ☎ *01397/722235* 🌐 *www.glenfinnan-house.com* 🕒 *Closed Nov.–mid-Mar.* 🔑 *15 rooms* 🍴 *Free Breakfast.*

Arisaig

18 miles west of Glenfinnan.

Considering its small size, Arisaig, gateway to the Small Isles, offers a surprising choice of high-quality options for dining and lodging. To the north of Arisaig, the road cuts across a headland to reach a stretch of coastline where silver sands glitter with the mica in the local rock. Clear water, blue sky, and white sand lend a tropical flavor to the beaches—when the sun is shining.

From Arisaig try to visit a couple of the Small Isles: Rum, Eigg, Muck, and Canna, each tiny and with few or no inhabitants. Rum serves as a wildlife reserve, while Eigg was the world's first community where electricity was produced off-grid, solely by wind, wave, and solar energy.

GETTING HERE AND AROUND

From Glenfinnan, you reach Arisaig on the A830, the only road leading west. The Fort William–Mallaig train also stops here.

🍴 Restaurants

The Old Library

$$ | **FRENCH** | On the waterfront, this 1722 barn has been converted into a lovely, reasonably priced restaurant. Expect simple but tasty plates of local fish and seafood—think haddock, monkfish, scampi, and salmon—prepared in a French-bistro style. **Known for:** local character; hearty meals; ultrafresh produce. [$] *Average main: £15* ✉ *B8008, Arisaig* ☎ *01687/450651* 🌐 *www.oldlibrary.co.uk.*

🛏 Hotels

Arisaig Hotel

$ | **B&B/INN** | A coaching inn built in 1720, this hotel is close to the water and has magnificent views of the Small Isles. **Pros:** lots of life and music in the bar; amazing views of the bay; good-value restaurant. **Cons:** the main bar is noisy for some; small restaurant portions; rooms comfy but lack style. [$] *Rooms from: £110* ✉ *B8008, Arisaig* ☎ *01687/450210* 🌐 *www.arisaighotel.co.uk* 🔑 *13 rooms* 🍴 *Free Breakfast.*

🏃 Activities

BOATING

Arisaig Marine

BOATING | **FAMILY** | Along with a host of wildlife excursions offering a chance to see minke whales, basking sharks, bottlenose dolphins, killer whales, porpoises, gray seals, and lots of sea birdlife (including cute puffins), Arisaig Marine runs a boat service from the harbor at Arisaig to the Small Isles from May to September. There's also a little tearoom and gift shop here. ✉ *Arisaig Harbour, Arisaig* ☎ *01687/450224* 🌐 *www.arisaig.co.uk* 🎫 *Eigg £18 round-trip.*

Mallaig

7½ miles north of Arisaig.

After the beautiful approach along the coast, the fishing port of Mallaig itself feels a little anticlimactic. It's pleasant enough, with some decent shops and cafes, but most jump straight on the ferry to the Isle of Skye, the largest island of the Inner Hebrides.

Mallaig is also the starting point for cruises up the Sound of Sleat, which separates Skye from the mainland. Daily ferries depart for Inverie on the Knoydart peninsula.

GETTING HERE AND AROUND

The train from Fort William, which stops at Arisaig on the way, is by far the best way to travel here, as you can relax and enjoy the stunning views along the way. Take the Jacobite Steam Train for a particularly memorable journey. Driving is a quick and easy alternative: simply head north from Arisaig on the A830.

Sights

★ Knoydart

NATURE PRESERVE | Often called mainland Britain's last wilderness, Knoydart is a peninsula off the west coast of Scotland that's only accessible by ferry from Mallaig—or by two-day trek from the already-remote village of Kinloch Hourn. Knoydart's main settlement of Inverie only has a population of 70, yet it boasts a post office, a tea room, and a small shop, as well as Britain's remotest pub, The Old Forge. Visitors come for many reasons: to hike the peninsula's four impressive *munros* (mountains over 3,000 feet), to stroll its sandy beaches, to spot wildlife from red deer to golden eagles, or to simply get away from it all. You can reach Inverie from Mallaig on the daily, year-round Western Isles Cruises ferry; check the seasonal timetables (🌐 *www.westernislescruises.co.uk*). ✉ *Inverie Ferry Terminal, Mallaig* 🌐 *www.visitknoydart.co.uk* 🎫 *Ferry £11 each way* ✍ *Ferry reservations required.*

Loch Morar

BODY OF WATER | This beautifully atmospheric loch, which starts 3½ miles southeast of Mallaig, is the deepest of all the Scottish lochs (more than 1,000 feet). In fact, the next deepest point is miles out into the Atlantic, beyond the continental shelf. Loch Morar is also said to have a resident monster, Morag, which undoubtedly gets less recognition than its famous cousin, Nessie. Whether that means you have more chance of getting her to appear for a photo, we can't say. You can drive part way along the northern edge of the loch on a small, unnamed side road; to get there, turn off the main A830 road onto the B8008 just south of Morar, then turn right again. ✉ *Loch Morar, Off A830, Mallaig.*

Hotels

★ Sandaig B&B

$ | **B&B/INN** | If you're looking for a bonafide get-away-from-it-all stay, this remote B&B on the western reaches of the Knoydart peninsula is hard to beat. **Pros:** delicious raclette cooked by Swiss hosts; historic building with rustic charm; stunning bay views. **Cons:** a 90-minute walk from Inverie; no TV or Wi-Fi but games galore; clean and comfy rather than all-out luxury. [$] *Rooms from: £70* ✉ *Mallaig* ☎ *07826/707697* 🌐 *www.sandaig.ch/en* 💳 *No credit cards* 🕒 *Closed Nov.–mid-Mar.* 🛏 *5 rooms* 🍴 *Free Breakfast.*

The Glencoe Massacre

In 1692, Glencoe was the site of a brutal and bloody massacre, still remembered in the Highlands for the treachery with which soldiers of the Campbell clan (acting as a government militia) treated their hosts, the MacDonalds. According to Highland code, in his own home a clansman should give shelter even to his sworn enemy. In the face of bitter weather, the Campbells were accepted as guests by the MacDonalds. But apparently acting on orders from the British Crown, the Campbells turned on their hosts and murdered them. The Massacre of Glencoe has gained an unlikely resurgence of fame in recent years, since it was revealed to be the historical basis for the infamous "Red Wedding" in George R. R. Martin's popular books (and even more popular HBO series) *Game of Thrones*.

Glencoe

16 miles south of Fort William.

Glencoe is both a small town and a region of stunning grandeur, with high peaks and secluded glens. Dramatic scenery is the main attraction here: it's as awesomely beautiful for a drive as it is for a hike. The A82—the main route through Glencoe—can get surprisingly crowded in high season, but it's one of the great scenic drives in Scotland. This area, where wild, craggy buttresses loom darkly over the road, has a special place in the folk memory of Scotland, as it was the site of an infamous 17th-century massacre.

GETTING HERE AND AROUND

Glencoe is easily accessed by car via the A82. Regional buses arrive from most of Scotland's major cities.

👁 Sights

Glencoe Visitor Centre

VISITOR CENTER | This impressive visitor center, 1 mile south of Glencoe village, tells the life story of the region, from its volcanic origins to the MacDonald massacre to its current wildlife maintenance projects. There are fascinating exhibitions on Glencoe's landscape and people, as well as great hiking trails leaving from the center (you can get expert advice on longer hikes, too). There's also an excellent café and shop. ⊠ *Off A82, Glencoe* 📞 *01855/811307* ⊕ *www.nts.org.uk* 🅿 *Parking £4* ⊗ *Closed Jan.–Apr.*

🛏 Hotels

★ Glencoe House

$$$$ | B&B/INN | Peaceful surroundings, arresting views, and the friendliest of welcomes await you at this former Victorian hunting lodge. **Pros:** lovely hosts; beautiful landscape; superb restoration. **Cons:** breakfast a little underwhelming; limited facilities; very expensive. 💲 *Rooms from: £605* ⊠ *Glencoe Lochan, Glencoe* 📞 *01855/811179* ⊕ *www.glencoe-house. com* 🛏 *14 suites* 🍴 *Free Breakfast.*

🏃 Activities

★ Woodlands Glencoe

LOCAL SPORTS | FAMILY | This popular outdoor center, 3½ miles west of Glencoe village, offers a long list of fun activities, from archery and laser clay shooting to golf and whisky tasting. Guided Segway tours (£39.50) last 45 minutes and take you through some spectacular scenery, with stunning mountain views and even a trail along a stretch of Loch Leven. ⊠ *Woodlands, Off A828, Glencoe* 📞 *01855/413201* ⊕ *www.woodlands.scot.*

THE NORTHERN HIGHLANDS AND THE WESTERN ISLES

11

Updated by
Joseph Reaney

⊙ Sights	🍴 Restaurants	🛏 Hotels	🛍 Shopping	🍸 Nightlife
★★★★☆	★★★☆☆	★★★☆☆	★★☆☆☆	★☆☆☆☆

WELCOME TO THE NORTHERN HIGHLANDS AND THE WESTERN ISLES

TOP REASONS TO GO

★ **Isle of Skye:** Scotland in miniature, the landscape here ranges from the lush, undulating hills and coastal tracks of Sleat to the deep glens and saw-toothed peaks of the Cuillin Mountains to geological features like the Old Man of Storr and Kilt Rock.

★ **Seafood:** Sample fresh Bracadale crab, Dunvegan Bay langoustines, or Sconser king scallops, as well as smoked salmon, lobster, and oysters.

★ **Coastal walks:** Enjoy an invigorating coastal walk on the islands of the Uists, Lewis, and Harris, where vast swaths of golden sand contrast with blue bays, and giant waves often crash against the rocks.

★ **Wildlife viewing:** The region is rife with seals, deer, otters, dolphins, and birdlife. Don't miss a boating foray to the Handa Island bird reserve off Scourie. Feeling extra adventurous? Visit the remote peninsula of St. Kilda, surrounded by marine life and home to a seabird colony and unique species of field mice, wren, and sheep.

1 Dingwall. A pleasant first stop when heading north.

2 Dornoch. Known for its legendary links golf course.

3 Helmsdale. A fishing village shaped by Vikings.

4 Wick. Famed for its silver (herring) and gold (whisky).

5 John O'Groats. Britain's northeastern tip.

6 Thurso. The north coast's biggest town.

7 Tongue. Home to a dramatic ruined castle.

8 Durness. A village surrounded by nature.

9 Scourie. An ideal base for visiting Handa Island.

10 Kylesku. A fishing hamlet close to Britain's highest waterfall.

11 Lochinver. A pretty shoreside community.

12 Ullapool. A big town with ferries to Lewis and Harris.

13 Gairloch. Peaceful, pretty, and pleasantly warm.

14 Shieldaig. A lovely lochside village.

15 Kyle of Lochalsh. The gateway to Skye.

16 Broadford. One of Skye's main towns.

17 Armadale. The ferry gateway to Sleat, Skye's southernmost peninsula.

18 Portree. Skye's main town with a pretty harbor.

19 Trotternish Peninsula. Skye's dramatic north, with Quiraing, Kilt Rock, and the Old Man of Storr.

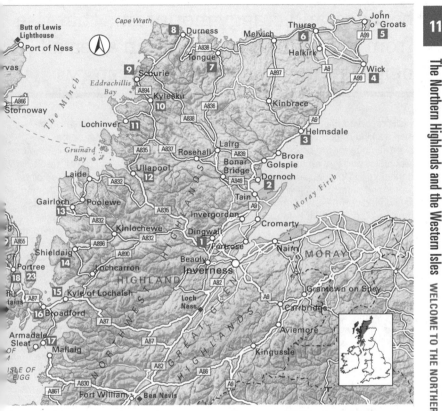

20 Waternish Peninsula. Off Skye's northwest, home to crofting communities and coastal views.

21 Glendale. A rocky coastline with dramatic castles and Skye's best restaurant.

22 Glen Brittle and the Cuillin Mountains. An impossibly green valley.

23 Isle of Raasay. Skye's little brother with striking scenery and great whisky.

24 Isle of Lewis. Bronze Age standing stones, Iron Age towers, and Victorian blackhouses.

25 Isle of Harris. Known for spectacular beaches and handwoven tweed.

26 St. Kilda. A unique day trip to see colossal cliffs and swooping seabirds.

27 North Uist. A hidden gem with remarkable birdlife and historic ruins.

28 South Uist. An island steeped in royal history.

Wild and remote, the Northern Highlands and the Western Isles have a timeless grandeur. Dramatic cliffs, long beaches, and craggy mountains that rise from moorland like islands in a sea all heighten the romance and mystery.

Well-preserved Eilean Donan Castle marks a kind of gateway to the Isle of Skye, famous for the brooding Cuillin Mountains and forever associated with Bonnie Prince Charlie. Jurassic-era sites, prehistoric ruins, crumbling castles, and abandoned crofts (small farms) compress the whole span of history in the islands.

The Northern Highlands is a region where roads hug the coast, dipping down toward beaches and back up for stunning views over the clear ocean, across to the dramatic mountains or along stunning heather moorland. These twisted, undulating roads—many of them single-track—demand that you shift down a gear, pause to let others pass, and take the time to do less and experience more of the rough-hewn beauty. If you're lucky, you may see a puffin fishing below the cliffs, an eagle swooping for a hare, or perhaps even a pod of dolphins or whales swimming off the coast. Adorable Highland *coos* (cows) are sure to make an appearance, too.

Sutherland, a historic county that stretched from Dornoch up to Durness and the northwest coast, was once the southern land belonging to the Vikings, and some names reflect this. Cape Wrath got its name from the Viking word *hvarth*, meaning "turning point," and Suilven translates as "pillar." The Isle of Skye and the Outer Hebrides are referred to as the Western Isles, and remain the stronghold of the Gaelic language. Skye is often called Scotland in miniature because the terrain shifts from lush valleys in the south to the rugged girdle of the Cuillin Mountains and then to the steep cliffs that define the northern coast. A short ferry journey away, the moody islands of Lewis and Harris lay claim to the brilliant golden sands of Luskentyre and incredible prehistoric sites, from the lunar-aligned Calanais Standing Stones to the Iron Age Doune Broch.

Depending on the weather, a trip to the Northern Highlands and the Western Isles can feel like a tropical getaway or a blustery, rain-drenched holiday. Just remember: "There's no such thing as bad weather, just inappropriate clothing."

MAJOR REGIONS

The Northern Landscapes. The northernmost part of Scotland, from Inverness all the way up to John O'Groats in the east and Cape Wrath in the west, has some of the most distinctive mountain profiles and coastal stretches in all of Scotland. The rim roads around the wilds of Durness overlook rocky shores, and the long beaches are as dramatic as the awe-inspiring and desolate cross-country routes like Destitution Road in Wester Ross. And then there's Glen Torridon, with its brooding peaks, mirrorlike lochs, and tantalizing glimpses across to the Isle of Skye.

To explore these landscapes most thoroughly, you should travel by car. You'll want to explore Stoer Point Lighthouse, the beaches north of Lochinver, and spectacular islandlike hills such as Suilven. Follow the North Coast 500 loop from Inverness to see the very best of the region. If you head counterclockwise up the east coast, along the north coast, and down the west coast, the spectacular landscape gets more and more dramatic at every turn. Travel clockwise, and you might find the east coast down from John O'Groats feels a bit anticlimactic.

Isle of Skye. Scotland's most famous island is home to the 11 peaks of the Cuillin Mountains, the quiet gardens of Sleat, and the dramatic peninsulas of Waternish and Trotternish. You can take a day trip to Skye, but try to spend a few days exploring its shores.

The Outer Hebrides. The Outer Hebrides—the Western Isles in common parlance—stretch about 130 miles from end to end and lie roughly 50 miles from the Scottish mainland. This splintered archipelago extends from the Butt of Lewis (no giggling) south to Barra Head, whose lighthouse has the greatest arc of visibility in the world. In the Hebrides, clouds cling to the hills, and rain comes in squalls. Any trip here requires protection from the weather and a conviction that a great holiday does not require constant sunshine.

It may contain two areas called isles, but it is just one single island that makes up the isles of Lewis and Harris. The island is the third largest in the United Kingdom, in fact, after Britain and Ireland. Lewis and Harris is the term to describe the island as a whole, but people also talk about the isles individually. Lewis by itself refers to the northern two-thirds of the island, while Harris represents the southern third. The only major town, Stornoway, is on a nearly landlocked harbor on the east coast of Lewis and is the most convenient starting point for a driving tour of Lewis and Harris (assuming you arrive, like most visitors, by ferry from the mainland). The island has some fine historic attractions, including the Calanais Standing Stones—which offer a truly magical glimpse of an ancient civilization—as well as an abundance of natural beauty. It's also the jumping-off point for a day trip to the unique isolated archipelago of St. Kilda.

Just south of the Sound of Harris is the Isle of North Uist, rich in monoliths, chambered cairns, and other reminders of a prehistoric past. Benbecula, sandwiched between North and South Uist, is in fact less bare and neglected-looking than its bigger neighbors to the north. The Isle of South Uist, once a refuge of the old Catholic faith, is dotted with ruined forts and chapels; in summer its wild gardens burst with alpine and rock plants. Eriskay Island and a scattering of islets almost block the 6-mile strait between South Uist and Barra, an island you can walk across in an hour. Harris tweed is available at many outlets on the islands, including some of the weavers' homes; keep an eye out for signs directing you to workshops. Sunday on the islands is observed as a day of rest, and nearly all shops and visitor attractions are closed. This includes most restaurants, with the exception of those in some island hotels, so make dinner plans in advance.

Planning

When to Go

The Northern Highlands and islands, as this region is sometimes called, are best seen from May to September. The earlier in the spring or later in the fall you go, the greater the chances of your encountering the elements in their extreme form, and the fewer attractions and accommodations you will find open (even Skye closes down almost completely by the end of October). Then again, you'll also find fewer tourists. Winter is best avoided altogether, unless taking a ferry in a relentless gale is your idea of fun.

Planning Your Time

The rough landscape of the Highlands and islands means these aren't place you can rush through. It could take eight busy days to do a coastal loop and also see some islands. Single-lane roadways, undulating terrain, and eye-popping views will slow you down. You can base yourself in a town like Ullapool or Portree, or choose a B&B or hotel (of which there are many) tucked into the hills or sitting at the edge of a sea loch. If you have only a couple of days, head directly to the Skye and the other islands. Although they attract hordes of tourists (for good reason), you don't have to walk far to find yourself in the wilderness. Sunday is a day of minimal activity here; restaurants, bars, and shops are closed, as are many sites.

You could combine a trip to the Northern Highlands with forays into the Great Glen (including Inverness and Loch Ness) or up to Orkney (there are day trips from John O'Groats) and the Shetland Islands.

Getting Here and Around

AIR

On a map this area may seem far from major urban centers, but it's easy to reach. Inverness has an airport with direct links to London, Dublin, and Amsterdam.

The main airport for the Northern Highlands is Inverness. Loganair has direct air service from Belfast, Birmingham, and Manchester. You can fly from London Gatwick, London Luton, or Bristol to Inverness on one of the daily easyJet flights. British Airways also has a service from London Heathrow. Loganair

operates flights to and among the islands of Benbecula and Lewis and Harris in the Outer Hebrides.

AIRPORT CONTACTS Inverness Airport. ⊠ *Dalcross* ☎ *01667/464000* ⊕ *www.hial. co.uk/inverness-airport.*

BOAT AND FERRY

Ferry services are generally reliable, weather permitting. Car and passenger vessels run from Ullapool to Stornoway (Lewis and Harris), Oban to Castlebay (Barra), Mallaig to Lochboisdale (South Uist), and Uig (Skye) to Tarbert (Lewis and Harris) and Lochmaddy (North Uist). The Hopscotch route tickets offered by Caledonian MacBrayne (known locally as CalMac) give considerable reductions on interisland fares. Call ahead and ask for the best route plan.

BOAT AND FERRY CONTACTS Caledonian MacBrayne. (*CalMac*) ⊠ *Ullapool* ☎ *0800/066–5000* ⊕ *www.calmac.co.uk.*

BUS

Scottish Citylink runs two main routes in the Northern Highlands: one heading west from Inverness to Ullapool and the other up the east coast to Scrabster (via Dornoch, Wick, and Thurso). It also has a route across the Isle of Skye to Uig. These buses can be a good way to see the region, but they don't run frequently.

Once you're in the Northern Highlands, Stagecoach has some routes up the east coast of the mainland to Brora. It also has regular services on Skye. In the Outer Hebrides, several small operators run regular routes to most towns and villages. Traveline Scotland, a handy website, provides timetables and a journey planner to help you navigate around Scotland. There's an app, too.

BUS CONTACTS Scottish Citylink. ⊠ *Inverness* ☎ *0871/266–3333* ⊕ *www.citylink. co.uk.* **Stagecoach.** ☎ *01463/233371* ⊕ *www.stagecoachbus.com.* **Traveline Scotland.** ⊠ *Inverness* ☎ *0871/200–2233* ⊕ *www.travelinescotland.com.*

CAR

Because of infrequent bus and train services, a car is by far the best way to explore this region. You can reach Inverness (the natural starting point for an exploration of the Northern Highlands) in 3½ hours from Edinburgh or Glasgow; it's around 4½ hours to Skye. Note that in this sparsely populated area distances between gas stations can be considerable, so it is wise to fill your tank when you see one.

Drivers always wave, as a courtesy and as a genuine greeting. The winding single-lane roads demand a degree of driving dexterity, however. Local rules of the road require that when two cars meet, whichever driver is the first to reach a passing place (a pullout, or extra patch of pavement to the side of the lane, often marked by a diamond-shaped sign) must stop and allow the oncoming car to continue. This may entail a bit of backing up. You can also pull into passing places to allow traffic behind you to pass. Never park in passing places.

Cars driving uphill have priority, and small cars tend to yield to large commercial vehicles. On bad days you can encounter trucks at the most awkward of spots, but on good days single-track driving can be relaxing, with a lovely pace of stopping, waving, moving on.

TRAIN

The main railway station in this area is Inverness, with lines running north to Thurso (with connections to Wick). There's direct service from London to Inverness and connecting service from Edinburgh and Glasgow. On the west coast, you will find stations at Kyle of Lochalsh (for Skye) and Oban (for ferries to Barra and the Uists).

TRAIN CONTACTS National Rail. ✉ *Inverness* ☏ *03457/484950* ⊕ *www.nationalrail.co.uk.* **ScotRail.** ✉ *Inverness* ☏ *0344/811–0141* ⊕ *www.scotrail.co.uk.*

Restaurants

Northern Scotland has many fine restaurants, where talented chefs use locally grown produce. Most country-house inns and pubs serve reliable, hearty seafood and tasty meat-and-potatoes meals. The Isle of Skye has the most—and the most expensive—restaurants, many of them exceptionally good, but you can find good meals almost everywhere. In remote regions, you may just have to drive some distance to find them. Remember that locals eat early, so most restaurants stop serving dinner at 9.

Hotels

Charming B&Bs, inexpensive inns, and a few excellent luxury hotels are all here to welcome you after a day touring the Highlands. Most accommodations book up far in advance in high season, when some require a minimum two-day stay.

In the more remote parts of Scotland, your best lodging option may be to rent a cottage or house. Besides allowing you to make your own meals and to come and go as you please, it can also be less expensive. VisitScotland (⊕ *www.visitscotland.com*), the official tourism agency, lists many cottages and even rates them with stars, just like hotels.

Restaurant and hotel reviews have been shortened. For full information, visit Fodors.com. Restaurant prices are the average cost of a main course at dinner or, if dinner is not served, at lunch. Hotel prices are the lowest cost of a standard double room in high season, including 20% V.A.T.

WHAT IT COSTS in Pounds

	$	$$	$$$	$$$$
RESTAURANTS				
	under £15	£15–£19	£20–£25	over £25
HOTELS				
	under £125	£125–£200	£201–£300	over £300

Tours

There are fascinating boat tours from a number of places around the coast, including seal- and bird-watching trips. Inland bus tours of castles, distilleries, fishing lochs, and hill-walking routes are available locally.

Rabbie's

BUS TOURS | This popular tour operator organizes tours of various lengths throughout the Highlands, from half-day trips to 17-day epics. Tours start from Edinburgh, Glasgow, Aberdeen, or Inverness, and travel is in comfortable 16-seat minibuses. ✉ *Inverness* ☎ *0131/226–3133* ⊕ *www.rabbies.com* ✄ *From £39.*

Visitor Information

The number of VisitScotland iCentres in the Northern Highlands and the Western Isles has dwindled to just four: in Inverness and Ullapool (Northern Highlands), Portree (Skye), and Stornoway (Lewis). They're open daily in July and August but closed the rest of the year. Some towns in the region also have independently run visitor centers.

CONTACTS VisitScotland Inverness iCentre. ✉ *36 High St., Inverness* ☎ *01463/252401* ⊕ *www.visitscotland.com.*

Dingwall

12 miles northwest of Inverness, 180 miles north of Glasgow.

This pretty market town and royal burgh (a Scottish town granted a royal charter) is a very pleasant stop if you're heading north from Inverness. Although it may not have the headline-grabbing attractions of some other Northern Highland towns, it has an excellent museum and a historic center that's replete with alluring architecture, charming cafés, and quaint little shops. What's more, it's a convenient place to stock up on fuel and supplies before venturing farther up the east coast; opportunities become scarcer after this point.

GETTING HERE AND AROUND

From Inverness take the A9 north to Dingwall, turning off onto the A835 at Tore.

◉ Sights

Dingwall Museum

HISTORY MUSEUM | Set inside the old town council building, topped by the pretty Townhouse Tower, this small museum offers real insight into local life throughout the 20th century. Exhibits include reproductions of a 1920s kitchen and a local *smiddy* (blacksmiths), a section on military life in the town, and details of historical crimes and punishments. Upstairs has a re-creation of a town council meeting with information on the walls, though the creepy mannequins around the table may make you wary of turning your back. ✉ *Town House, 65 High St., Inverness* ☎ *01349/865366* ⊕ *www.dingwallmuseum.info* ✄ *Free (donations welcome)* ⊗ *Closed Oct.–mid-May.*

The Northern Highlands

🛏 Hotels

Coul House Hotel

$$$ | HOTEL | Situated in the countryside 8 miles west of Dingwall, this magnificent Georgian manor offers stylish rooms with mountain views, comfortable lounges with log fireplaces, and an excellent restaurant that's open all day. **Pros:** outdoor dining when sunny; family-run and family-friendly; free golf practice court. **Cons:** expensive in high season; a little off the beaten path; hunting portraits not to all tastes. $ *Rooms from: £215* ✉ *Off A835, Contin* ☎ *01997/421487* ⊕ *coulhousehotel.com* 🛏 *21 rooms* ❑ *Free Breakfast*.

Tulloch Castle Hotel

$$$ | HOTEL | For hundreds of years, Tulloch Castle has watched over the town of Dingwall and the Cromarty Firth, first as the home of the Bain family and Clan Davidson, now as a grand, historic hotel. **Pros:** good breakfasts; characterful accommodations; comfy beds and armchairs. **Cons:** very expensive; thin walls and creaking floorboards; a whiff of faded glory. $ *Rooms from: £230* ✉ *Tulloch Castle Dr., Dingwall* ☎ *01349/861325* ⊕ *bespokehotels.com/tullochcastlehotel* 🛏 *22 rooms* ❑ *Free Breakfast*.

Dornoch

33 miles northeast of Dingwall.

A town of sandstone houses, tiny rose-filled gardens, and a 13th-century cathedral with stunning traditional and modern stained-glass windows, Dornoch is well worth a visit. It's noted for golf (you may hear it referred to as the "St. Andrews of the North"), but because of the town's location, the golf courses here are delightfully uncrowded. Royal Dornoch is the jewel in its crown, praised by the world's top golfers.

GETTING HERE AND AROUND

From Dingwall (or Inverness), take the A9 north to Dornoch. Note that this stretch of the road can get busy with ferry traffic.

ESSENTIALS

VISITOR INFORMATION Dornoch

Visitors Centre. ✉ *Argyle St., Dornoch* ☎ *07341/284405* ⊕ *www.visitdornoch.com*.

👁 Sights

Dunrobin Castle

CASTLE/PALACE | FAMILY | Situated 12 miles north of Dornoch, flamboyant Dunrobin Castle is an ancient seat that became the home of the dukes of Sutherland, at which point it was transformed into the 19th-century white-turreted behemoth you see today. As well as its grand palatial facade and lavish interiors, the property also has falconry demonstrations and Versailles-inspired gardens. Head upstairs in the house for fine views over the garden and out to sea. The first duke, who was fascinated by trains, built his own railroad in the park and staffed it with his servants. Yet for all this frivolity, the duke has a controversial legacy: he was responsible for the Sutherland Clearances of 1810 to 1820, when people were forcibly removed from their farms to make room for sheep to graze. ✉ *Off A9, Golspie* ☎ *01408/633177* ⊕ *www.dunrobincastle.co.uk* 🎫 *£12.50* ⊘ *Closed Nov.–Apr.*

★ Glenmorangie Distillery

DISTILLERY | The light color and delicate floral taste of the Speyside whiskies is exemplified in Glenmorangie, one of the best known of the Highland whiskies. The picturesque distillery in Tain, 8 miles south of town across Dornoch Forth, offers fascinating tastings that reveal how the taste is achieved (the secret's in the exceedingly tall stills). The Classic Tasting (£15) includes three drams, and the Innovator Tasting (£40) offers a chance to sample four of their most prized bottles. ✉ *Off A9, Tain* ☎ *01862/892477* ⊕ *www.glenmorangie.com* 🎫 *Tours from £8.50*.

One of the most treasured properties in the Highlands, Glenmorangie House sits grandly amid expansive manicured grounds.

Restaurants

Sutherland House

$ | **BRITISH** | Just off Dornoch's main square, Sutherland House restaurant has a feeling of intimacy in its two separate rooms—a feeling that's reinforced by the enthusiastic reception and the delicious food. The menu is imaginative, with some unusual combinations dreamed up by the chef. **Known for:** friendly service; imaginative seafood; chicken in Glenmorangie sauce. *Average main: £14* *Argyle St., Dornoch* *01862/811023* *www.sutherland-house.net.*

Hotels

★ Glenmorangie House

$$$$ | **RESORT** | Situated 8½ miles southeast from the distillery, Glenmorangie House offers luxurious but casual stays in a spectacular 17th-century country home. **Pros:** extensive whisky collection; wonderfully rural location; superb service. **Cons:** extremely expensive; need a car to get here; puny showers take a while to heat up. *Rooms from: £370* *Fearn by Tain, Tain* *01862/871671* *www.theglenmorangiehouse.com* *9 rooms* *Free Breakfast.*

Royal Golf Hotel Dornoch

$$$ | **HOTEL** | Set on the edge of the town's famous golf course but run independently, this historic Highland hotel offers comfortable and modern rooms, an excellent restaurant with golf course views, and a cozy bar lounge with an open log fire (and nonstop golf on the TV). **Pros:** great dining (try the sticky toffee pudding); historic property; many rooms have golf course views. **Cons:** no elevator; public lounges showing some wear and tear; single rooms are quite small. *Rooms from: £219* *The First Tee, Dornoch* *01862/810283* *www.royalgolfhoteldornoch.com* *14 rooms* *Free Breakfast.*

🛍 Shopping

Jail Dornoch

MIXED CLOTHING | It's rare for people to voluntarily walk into jail, but this place is the exception: it's an old prison that has been converted into a popular fashion store. The one-time cells now contain a range of elegant clothes and accessories, toiletries, housewares, and interesting gifts. It's so popular that there's now a second outlet at Inverness Airport. ✉ Castle St., Dornoch ☎ 01862/810555 ⊕ jail-dornoch.com.

🏃 Activities

GOLF

★ Royal Dornoch Golf Club

GOLF | The legendary Championship Course, laid out by Tom Morris in 1886, is still regularly voted one of the world's best golf courses. It challenges even the most skilled golfers with its fast, raised greens, while inspiring them with views of white sandy beaches and tall mountains carpeted in wild yellow gorse each spring. The Struie Course provides even more sea views and demanding golf for players of every level. ✉ Golf Rd., Dornoch ☎ 01862/810219 ⊕ royaldornoch.com 💳 Championship: £210 Apr.–Oct., £115 Nov.–Mar.; Struie: £50 Apr.–Oct., £35 Nov.–Mar. 🏌 Championship: 18 holes, 6754 yards, par 70; Struie: 18 holes, 6265 yards, par 71.

Helmsdale

28 miles northeast of Dornoch.

Helmsdale is a fascinating fishing village with a checkered past. It was once a busy Viking settlement, later became the scene of an aristocratic poisoning plot, and then was transformed into a Victorian village, used to house some of the poor souls removed from their land to make way for sheep. These "clearances," perpetrated by the Duke of Sutherland, were among the Highlands' most inhumane.

GETTING HERE AND AROUND

Helmsdale is one of the few towns on this part of the coast that has direct train services from Inverness (four a day). But a car will allow you to see more in the surrounding area. Get here via the coastal A9 from Dornoch.

👁 Sights

Timespan

HISTORY MUSEUM | FAMILY | This thought-provoking mix of displays, artifacts, and audiovisual materials portrays the history of the area, from the Stone Age to the 1869 gold rush in the Strath of Kildonan. There's a geology exhibit in the garden and a tour of the Kildonan gold-rush site. The complex also includes a café and an art gallery that often hosts visiting artists and changing exhibitions. ✉ Dunrobin St., Helmsdale ☎ 01431/821327 ⊕ timespan.org.uk 💳 £4 ◷ Closed Mon.–Fri. in Nov.–mid-Mar.

Wick

35 miles northeast of Helmsdale.

Wick is a substantial town that was built on its fishing industry. The town itself is not especially noteworthy, but it does have a handful of worthwhile sights.

GETTING HERE AND AROUND

From Helmsdale follow the A9 north, then stay on the A99.

👁 Sights

Castle Sinclair Girnigoe

CASTLE/PALACE | Dramatically perched on the edge of the cliff, this ruined castle— or rather, castles—is a spectacular sight. Situated 3 miles north of Wick, this site comprises the remains of the 15th-century Castle Girnigoe and the 17th-century

Castle Sinclair, set among stunning scenery. The precipitous location, with old walls teetering inches from the cliff edge, means it has a limited lifespan, so go take a look while you can. ⊠ *Wick.*

Grey Cairns of Camster

RUINS | The remarkable Grey Cairns of Camster, two Neolithic chambers made of rough stones, were built more than 5,000 years ago and are among the best preserved in Britain. **Camster Round Cairn** is 20 yards in diameter and 13 yards high, while **Camster Long Cairn** stretches an extraordinary 77 yards. Some 19th-century excavations revealed skeletons, pottery, and flint tools in the round cairn's internal chamber. They are in an isolated location, around 8 miles southwest of Wick and without a visitor center in sight, so if you feel adventurous and don't mind dirty knees, you can crawl into the chambers (the metal grills over the entrances mean they appear locked, but they aren't). To get here, you'll need to drive 5 miles along the unnamed road from Occumster to Watten; when you're just beyond Lybster on the A99, look out for the brown signposts pointing the way. ⊠ *Off A99, Wick* ⊕ *www.historicenvironment.scot.*

★ Pulteney Distillery

DISTILLERY | Unusually for a distillery, Pulteney is situated very close to the town center, and it has been for almost 200 years. The spirit produced here, known as "gold," was once in the shadow of the town's other big "silver" industry—herring fishing. But, despite a hairy period of prohibition, it has easily outlasted its competition. The brooding brick distillery is open for tours and tastings, so join the standard one-hour tour (£10) for a behind-the-scenes look at the facilities and a taste of the award-winning 12-year-old Old Pulteney—famed for its smooth, faintly briny character with a lingering, butterscotch-sweet finish. Or, for £25, experience all this plus additional tastings of three older expressions. ⊠ *Huddart St., Wick* ☏ *01955/602371* ⊕ *www.oldpulteney.com* 🎫 *Tours from £10* ⊘ *Closed weekends.*

Wick Heritage Museum

HISTORY MUSEUM | The locals who run this lovely town museum are real enthusiasts, and they will take you through Wick's history from its founding by the Vikings to its heyday in the 1860s as a leading herring port. The collection includes everything from ancient fossils and a 19th-century cooperage to the Johnston Photographic Collection, a set of 40,000 images that show more than a century of life in Wick through one local family's eyes. There's also an art gallery and lovely terraced gardens that overlook the town. ⊠ *18–27 Bank Row, Wick* ☏ *01955/605393* ⊕ *www.wick-heritage.org* 🎫 *£4* ⊘ *Closed Sun. and Nov.–Easter.*

John O'Groats

16 miles north of Wick.

The windswept little outpost of John O'Groats is usually taken to be the northernmost point on the Scottish mainland, though that is not strictly true, as a short drive to Dunnet Head will reveal. From the harbor you can take a boat to see the dolphins and seals that live beneath the coastal cliffs—or head farther afield with a ferry to Orkney. The little town's charms include a row of colorful wooden houses, a small brewery, and a crafts center with high-quality shops selling knitwear, candles, and other gifts. In between these, however, are some very tacky tourist stores. Note that parking here costs £2.

GETTING HERE AND AROUND

From Wick, head north on the coast-hugging A99.

TOURS
John O'Groats Ferries

BOAT TOURS | Sailing from John O'Groats Harbor, this company offers 90-minute wildlife cruises past spectacular cliff scenery and birdlife into the Pentland Firth, to Duncansby Stacks, and to the island of Stroma. Trips cost £20 and are available daily at 2:30 between June and August. The company also offers a day tour of Orkney between May and September. It leaves at 8:45 am and costs £79. ⊠ *John O'Groats* ☎ *01955/611353* ⊕ *www.jogferry.co.uk* ⤳ *Tours from £20.*

 ## Sights

Duncansby Head

LIGHTHOUSE | Head to this lighthouse for spectacular views of cliffs and sea stacks, as well as seabirds like guillemots and (if you're lucky) puffins. It's on the coastal road east of town. There are a few parking spaces here, or you can walk (about 30 minutes) from the main road. ⊠ *John O'Groats* ⊕ *www.nlb.org.uk/lighthouses/duncansby-head.*

Hotels

★ John O'Groats by Together Travel

$$ | APARTMENT | Local landmarks in their own right, the brightly colored lodges here are the region's best self-catering accommodations—not to mention the most photogenic—and they provide stunning views out to sea (on a clear day, all the way to Orkney). **Pros:** natural light all day long; very comfy beds; good Wi-Fi (a rarity here). **Cons:** a little expensive; some lodges are two nights minimum in high season; can feel understaffed. $ *Rooms from: £150* ⊠ *John O'Groats* ☎ *01625/416430* ⊕ *www.togethertravel.co.uk* ⤳ *23 lodges* ⦿ *No Meals.*

Performing Arts

Lyth Arts Centre

ARTS CENTERS | Housed in a Victorian-era school building with a modern interior, the Lyth Arts Centre serves as a cultural hub for the region. From April to November, professional music and theater companies fill the schedule, and locals fill the seats. There are also exhibitions of contemporary fine art. Lyth is 11 miles southwest of John O'Groats. ⊠ *Lyth* ☎ *01955/641434* ⊕ *lytharts.org.uk.*

Thurso

19 miles west of John O'Groats.

The town of Thurso is quite substantial for a community so far north. In-town attractions include Old St. Peter's Kirk, which dates from the 12th century; nearby attractions include the fine Dunnet Bay beach and great seabird-spotting at Dunnet Head.

GETTING HERE AND AROUND

From John O'Groats simply follow the A836 west. Local buses travel the same route but take twice as long as driving yourself.

Sights

★ Dunnet Bay Distillery

DISTILLERY | This small north coast distillery proves that Scotland's craft-spirits boom has stretched to the very edges of the mainland. Run by husband and wife team Martin and Claire Murray, Dunnet Bay Distillery has gained plaudits and prizes galore for its Rock Rose gin—notable for its use of sea buckthorn, rhodiola rosea (the eponymous "rock rose"), and other coastal botanicals. The distillery also produces a superb vodka called Holy Grass. As well as selling the spirits neat, there are also fun, seasonal cocktail releases, from the gingerbread espresso martini to the winter-spiced negroni.

You can tour the "wee" distillery all year round, including taking a stroll around the herb garden and greenhouse (lean down to sniff the deliciously citrusy lemon verbena). ■ **TIP→ Children younger than 18 are allowed to visit and are admitted on the tour free of charge with an accompanying adult.** ✉ *Off A836, Thurso* ☎ *01847/851287* 🌐 *www.dunnetbaydistillers.co.uk* 🎟 *Tours £15* ⏲ *Closed Sun.*

Dunnet Head

VIEWPOINT | Most people make the trip to Dunnet Head to stand at the northernmost point of mainland Britain. But it's also worth a visit for the pretty Dunnet Head Lighthouse (built 1831), the dramatic sea cliffs, and the fine views over the water to Orkney. The Royal Society for the Protection of Birds also runs a nature reserve here, due to the number of seabirds nesting in the cliffs. ✉ *Thurso.*

Old St. Peter's Kirk

RELIGIOUS BUILDING | This roofless, ruined parish church on the banks of the River Thurso was once the principal place of worship in northeast Scotland. Dating from (at least) the early 1100s, the church is known for its decorative window carved from a single slab of stone, as well as its atmospheric graveyard. Look for headstone emblems that represent the trade of the person buried beneath. ✉ *Back Shore St., Thurso.*

Hotels

★ Forss House

$$$ | B&B/INN | This historic country house, 5 miles west of Thurso, offers a mix of beautiful bedrooms in the main building and super-luxurious suite-apartments on the expansive grounds—treat yourself with a stay in the spectacular Mill House. **Pros:** lots of outdoor activities; large guest rooms and stunning suites; the best restaurant for miles. **Cons:** expensive option; short outdoor walk from suites to the restaurant; creaky floorboards and squeaky old doors. [$] *Rooms from: £215* ✉ *Forss, Thurso* ☎ *01847/861201* 🌐 *www.forsshousehotel.co.uk* 🛏 *14 rooms* 🍴 *Free Breakfast.*

Activities

The Bike Shop

BIKING | This cycle-repair shop has a friendly staff and a handful of hybrid bikes to rent. You can also get advice on the best local routes. ✉ *35 High St., Thurso* ☎ *01847/895385* 🌐 *facebook.com/thebikeshopthurso* ⏲ *Closed Sun. and Mon.*

Tongue

43 miles west of Thurso.

A popular pit stop between Thurso and Durness, Tongue has some worthwhile sights and good accommodation options.

GETTING HERE AND AROUND

From Thurso, simply head west along the A836, which turns into A838 just before you reach Tongue.

Sights

★ Castle Varrich

CASTLE/PALACE | Standing on a high rocky outcrop, overlooking both the town and the Kyle of Tongue, Castle Varrich (or Bharrich) was built by Clan Mackay in the 14th century—but possibly not from scratch. It's believed an old Norse fort may have previously occupied the site. Today, a steel staircase and viewing platform make it easily accessible to visitors, who can walk from Tongue and back in less than an hour. The clearly signposted path gets a little steep in parts, but the climb is worth it for the spectacular views. ✉ *Tongue.*

Beaches

★ Coldbackie Beach

BEACH | This windswept bay, 3 miles north of Tongue just off the road from Thurso, is a well-kept secret, offering powder-white sands, spectacular island views, and perfect peace and quiet—so long as you don't arrive when surf's up. To get here simply park in Coldbackie and walk. **Amenities:** parking (no fee); water sports. **Best for:** solitude; surfing; walking. ✉ *Coldbackie, Tongue* ✥ *Off A836.*

Hotels

Garvault House

$$ | **HOTEL** | Billed as mainland Britain's most remote hotel (Tongue, its nearest town, is 28 miles and an hour's drive away), the charmingly rustic and almost entirely off-grid Garvault House offers a classic countryside escape in the heart of the Highlands. **Pros:** fishing and hill walking galore; beautiful panoramas; communal meals around a mahogany table. **Cons:** no amenities for miles; limited Wi-Fi and phone signal; a little fusty in places. [$] *Rooms from: £130* ✉ *Off B871* ☎ *07596/202171* 🌐 *garvaulthouse.uk* 🕒 *Closed Dec.–Mar.* 🛏 *8 rooms* 🍴 *Free Breakfast.*

The Tongue Hotel

$$ | **HOTEL** | With open fireplaces, tartan rugs, and floral wallpaper, this traditional Highland hotel is a great base for exploring the northern coast of the Scottish mainland. **Pros:** deliciously creamy porridge at breakfast; warm and friendly staff; beautiful location with stunning views. **Cons:** food is hit and miss; TV sets from the '80s; Wi-Fi only in public areas. [$] *Rooms from: £120* ✉ *A838, Tongue* ☎ *01847/611206* 🌐 *tonguehotel.co.uk* 🕒 *Closed late Dec.–mid-Feb.* 🛏 *19 rooms* 🍴 *Free Breakfast.*

Durness

29 miles west of Tongue.

The sudden patches of green surrounding the village of Durness, on the north coast, are caused by the richer limestone outcrops among the acidic moorlands. The town is the jumping-off point for several natural highlights, from a beautiful sandy beach to the country's highest cliff.

GETTING HERE AND AROUND

From Tongue, simply head west along the A838.

Sights

Balnakeil Craft Village

MARKET | Artisans sell pottery, leather, weavings, paintings, chocolate, and more from their studios at Balnakeil Craft Village. It's a charmingly odd place consisting of rows of shabby former military buildings located on an unnamed road running northwest from Durness and framed by dramatic views of Balnakeil Bay. The village is open during the summer, with most shops open daily from 10 to 5. ✉ *Craft Village, Balnakeil, Durness* ☎ *01971/511713 Nicola Poole's Wee Gallery* 🌐 *balnakeilcraftvillage.weebly.com.*

Cape Wrath

VIEWPOINT | If you've made it this far north, you'll probably want to go all the way to Cape Wrath, a rugged headland at the northwest tip of Scotland. The white-sand beaches, impressive dunes covered in marram grass, and crashing seas of nearby Balnakeil Bay make it an exhilarating place to visit. As this land is owned by the Ministry of Defence (it is listed as an area for air force training), you can't drive your own vehicle. From May through September, a small boat ferries people here from Keoldale, 2 miles outside Durness. En route, look out for Clo Mor: at 920 feet, they're the highest sea cliffs in mainland Britain. Once you're across the sea inlet, a minibus will

The dramatic Smoo Cave has one of the largest entrances to any sea cave in Britain.

take you to the lighthouse. Call ahead or check departure times on the board at the jetty. ☎ *01971/511284* ⊕ *www. visitcapewrath.com* ✉ *£20.50 boat/bus round-trip* 🕑 *No boat mid-Oct.–mid-Apr.*

Lotte Glob Sculpture Croft

ART GALLERY | This odd garden of delights provokes a double-take from most drivers traveling along the A838, thanks to its incongruous ceramic-topped gates. Park opposite, and stroll down into Danish artist Lotte Glob's pottery wonderland, where ceramic and metal sculptures are scattered across the gardens. Several paths lead down to the coast, and there are hundreds of pieces, including a library of ceramic books, en route. Her work reflects and adds to the landscape, using natural shapes and forms and building patterns into the rocks themselves. End your visit with a trip to the studio and pottery shop. ✉ *105 Laid, Durness* ☎ *01971/511727* ⊕ *www.lotteglob.co.uk* 🕑 *Only open by appointment Oct.–mid-May.*

★ Smoo Cave

CAVE | This atmospheric cavern, hollowed out of the limestone by rushing water, feels like something from a fantasy novel. Located a mile east of Durness, the combined sea-and-fresh-water cave, complete with gushing waterfall, can be reached via a steep cliff stairway from the Smoo Cave parking lot. But don't start your descent before reading the explanatory boards at the top of the stairs: they tell the history of those who lived and used the caves in much earlier times. From April through October, 20-minute boat trips (£10) into the cave's inner chamber are available. Once you've climbed back up to the parking area, cross the road for a view down into the cavern from atop the waterfall. ✉ *Off A838, Durness.*

Beaches

Ciannabeine Beach

BEACH | Situated 10 miles east of Durness, between Rispond and Sangobeg, Ciannabeine is one of Scotland's most achingly beautiful beaches, a spectacular sweep of sand caught in the embrace of 10,000-year-old rocks. There is a car park opposite and a path down to the beach itself. You will recognize it by the white house just beyond, once the village school. **Amenities:** parking (no fee). **Best for:** swimming; walking. ✉ *Off A838, Durness.*

★ Sandwood Bay

BEACH | Sandwood Bay is one of Scotland's most spectacular—and most isolated—beaches. The only way to reach it is to walk 4 miles each way across sheep fields and sand dunes. It's a lovely, fairly easy walk, and while it's not quite the hidden gem it once was, leave early and you're still likely to have the long, sandy beach, with its dramatic sea stack Am Buachaille, all to yourself. To get here turn off the A838 onto the B801 at Rhiconich (14 miles southwest of Durness), then turn off at Kinlochbervie to Balchrick. Just before you reach the latter, look for a tiny white sign to "Sandwood," then follow this single-track lane to its end, where you can park and start walking. Plan for a four-hour trip in all, including a good amount of time on the beach. **Amenities:** parking (no fee). **Best for:** solitude; walking. ✉ *Durness.*

Restaurants

Cocoa Mountain

$ | **CAFÉ** | A must for those with a sweet tooth, this "chocolate bar" within the Balnakeil Craft Village serves world-class truffles and stunningly rich hot chocolate made in its specialist "chocolate factory," which sources the beans from around the world. There are also sandwiches, cakes, and coffee available. **Known for:** friendly service; sublime chocolate truffles; homemade hot chocolate. [$] *Average main: £5* ✉ *Balnakeil Craft Village, Balnakeil, Durness* ☎ *01971/511233* 🌐 *www.cocoamountain.co.uk.*

Scourie

25 miles southwest of Durness.

Scourie is a small coastal settlement catering to visitors—particularly fisherfolk—with a good range of accommodations. The bayside town makes a good base for a trip to the bird sanctuary on Handa Island.

GETTING HERE AND AROUND

From Durness, head south on the A838, continuing onto the A894 just after Laxford Bridge.

Sights

★ Handa Island

NATURE PRESERVE | **FAMILY** | Just off the coast of Scourie is Handa Island, a sanctuary that shelters huge seabird colonies, especially impressive at nesting time. On the dramatic cliffs you can gaze at more than 200,000 nesting birds, including guillemots, razorbills, great skuas, kittiwakes, and, of course, crowd-pleasingly colorful puffins. Sturdy boots, a waterproof jacket, and a degree of fitness are needed to walk the path around the island. This remarkable reserve, administered by the Scottish Wildlife Trust, is open only in spring and summer. Get there on the Handa Ferry (🌐 *www.handa-ferry.com*)—in reality, a small open boat—from Tarbet, 3 miles north of Scourie. It runs Monday to Saturday and costs £20 per person. 🌐 *scottishwildlifetrust.org.uk* ⏲ *Closed Oct.–Mar.*

🍴 Restaurants

★ Shorehouse Restaurant
$$ | **SEAFOOD** | If you're feeling peckish after a trip to Handa Island, stop at this exceptional restaurant overlooking Tarbet Harbor. It serves freshly caught seafood specialties, from hand-dived scallops and hot smoked mackerel to whole lobsters, in a quaint, maritime-themed setting. **Known for:** friendly and attentive service; spectacular seafood; gorgeous views. *[$] Average main: £17 ✉ Tigh Na Mara, Tarbet, Scourie ☎ 01971/502251 🌐 www.shorehousetarbet.co.uk ⏲ Closed Sun. and Oct.–Easter.*

🛏 Hotels

★ Eddrachilles Hotel
$$ | **B&B/INN** | With one of the most spectacular vistas—out toward the picturesque islands of Badcall Bay—of any hotel in Scotland, Eddrachilles sits on a huge plot of private moorland just south of the Handa Island bird sanctuary. **Pros:** close to bird sanctuary; attractive garden; stunning shoreline nearby. **Cons:** set menus only; Wi-Fi limited to public areas; needs a lick of paint. *[$] Rooms from: £145 ✉ Off A894, Scourie ☎ 01971/502080 🌐 www.eddrachilles.com ⏲ Closed Nov.–Mar. 🛏 10 rooms 🍴 Free Breakfast.*

Kylesku

10 miles southeast of Scourie.

This tiny settlement once served as a ferry crossing, before being usurped by the (incredibly photogenic) Kylesku Bridge. Today, it's a lovely stop for lunch, a boat trip along Loch Glendhu and Loch Glencoul, or even an overnight stay.

GETTING HERE AND AROUND

From Scourie, simply head south on the A894.

👁 Sights

★ Drumbeg Loop
SCENIC DRIVE | Bold souls journeying from Kylesku to Lochinver may enjoy taking the interesting, single-track B869 Drumbeg Loop. It has several challenging hairpin turns along with breathtaking coastal views. Head 2 miles south of Kylesku on the A894, and hang a right when you see the brown sign to "An Druim Beag." Although it's only 20 miles to Lochinver, it will take at least an hour without stops—but plan on longer, because you'll definitely want to stop. Highlights include the stunning sweep of sand at Clashnessie Bay, the beautiful Stoer Point Lighthouse, and the red-sandstone sea stack known as the Old Man of Stoer (not to be confused with the Old Man of Storr on Skye). The latter two are just off the Drumbeg Loop; turn right onto the small, signposted road between Clashnessie and Stoer. If you're an energetic walker, you can hike across the short turf and heather along the cliff-top for fine views west toward Lewis and Harris.

Eas a' Chual Aluinn Waterfall
WATERFALL | With a drop of 685 feet, this is the longest waterfall in the United Kingdom. A rugged hike leads to the falls, which are at the head of Loch Glencoul. Start from the parking area off the A894, on the bend of the road 4 miles south of Kylesku, just before you reach Loch na Gainmhich. *✉ Off A894, Lochinver.*

🛏 Hotels

Kylesku Hotel
$$$ | **HOTEL** | This charming hotel, looking out over Loch Glendhu and toward Eas a' Chual Aluinn (Scotland's highest waterfall), has great service, a warm and relaxed atmosphere, and the region's best restaurant. **Pros:** excellent restaurant (try the fresh oysters and lobster); stunning loch views; stylish and understated decor. **Cons:** expensive for the area;

two tiny (but cheap) attic rooms; some old-building quirks. [$] *Rooms from: £230* ✉ *Off A894, Scourie* ☎ *01971/502231* 🌐 *www.kyleskuhotel.co.uk* 🛏 *11 rooms* 🍴 *Free Breakfast.*

Lochinver

18 miles southwest of Kylesku.

Lochinver is a pretty, quiet, shoreside community of whitewashed cottages overlooked by soaring Suilven Mountain. There are lovely beaches to the north, a harbor used by the west-coast fishing fleet, and some good dining and lodging options, making it an ideal base for exploring Sutherland.

GETTING HERE AND AROUND

To get to Lochinver from Kylesku in roughly 30 minutes, head south on the A894, then turn west onto the A837. If you prefer to take your time, opt for the scenic B869 (known as the "Drumbeg Loop") instead—the journey takes around 75 minutes.

Sights

Ardvreck Castle

CASTLE/PALACE | Beside Loch Assynt, 11 miles east of Lochinver on the fast road to Ullapool, stands the striking Ardvreck Castle. A onetime Clan MacLeod stronghold built in the late 1500s, this atmospheric ruin sits on an outcrop with perfect views the length of the loch in both directions. You'll find a parking area directly opposite the ruins. From there, you can take the muddy path down to a stony beach and then walk along to the castle. ✉ *Off A837, Lochinver* 🌐 *www.undiscoveredscotland.co.uk.*

★ Assynt and Coigach

NATURE SIGHT | To the east and south of Lochinver lies a different kind of landscape: a vast region of brooding mountains and languid lochs, where peaks punch their way out of heathered terrain and appear to constantly shift positions. Even their names have a more mysterious air than those of the *bens* (mountain peaks or hills) elsewhere: Cul Mor, Cul Beag, Stac Pollaidh, Canisp, Suilven. Some hark back to Norse rather than to Gaelic—a reminder that Vikings used to sail this northern shore. The highlight of the region is the eerily pretty Loch Assynt, peppered with tiny wooded isles, but the Coigach Peninsula northwest of Ullapool is equally dramatic.

Beaches

Achmelvich Bay

BEACH | This beautiful white-sand beach, 4 miles northwest of Lochinver, is a popular summer spot with water babies, from kayakers to windsurfers, as well as landlubbers who delight in the surrounding hiking trails and climbing opportunities. It's also a favorite of fishers, dog walkers, and "rockpoolers." In summer, expect a bit of a traffic jam to reach the beach, then a fight for a parking space. The beach is considerably quieter outside of peak season. **Amenities:** parking (no fee); water sports. **Best for:** walking; windsurfing ✉ *Off B869, Lochinver.*

Restaurants

An Cala Café

$ | **BRITISH** | An abandoned fishermen's mission (a place where fishermen stayed while in port), situated at the far end of town near the harbor, now houses this pleasant café serving lunch, soup, sandwiches, and house baking. The specials often include fish freshly delivered from the harbor. **Known for:** cozy 14-bed bunkhouse on site; delicious house-made soup; great fish-and-chips. [$] *Average main: £9* ✉ *Culag Park, Lochinver* ☎ *01571/844598* 🌐 *www.ancalacafeandbunkhouse.co.uk* 🕓 *Closed Sun.–Tues.*

Hotels

Inver Lodge Hotel
$$$ | HOTEL | In a commanding location on a hillside above Lochinver, this modern luxury hotel has stunning views of the coast, as well as smart guest rooms that are decorated in contemporary colors and have traditional mahogany furniture. **Pros:** great fishing nearby; cozy public room with a fireplace; refreshing sauna. **Cons:** expensive for the area; not good for families with children; slightly drab exterior. $ *Rooms from: £300* ⊠ *Iolaire Rd., Lochinver* ☎ *01571/844496* ⊕ *www. inverlodge.com* ☣ *Closed Nov.–Mar.* ☞ *21 rooms* ❍ *Free Breakfast.*

Tigh Na Sith
$$ | B&B/INN | Set just above the bay at Lochinver, this family-run B&B wins rave reviews for its warm welcome. **Pros:** delicious breakfast; welcoming hosts; fantastic views. **Cons:** small TVs in rooms; beds can be creaky; Munro room has no view. $ *Rooms from: £140* ⊠ *Off A837, Lochinver* ☎ *01571/844588* ⊕ *www.tighnasith. com* ☞ *3 rooms* ❍ *Free Breakfast.*

● Shopping

Highland Stoneware
CERAMICS | The huge sofa and television composed entirely of broken crockery are a witty introduction to the beautiful ceramic works of art made at Highland Stoneware. The potters and decorators busy themselves in a studio behind the shop, and visitors are encouraged to watch as they create pieces incorporating Highland themes. If you miss this one, there's a second Highland Stoneware store in Ullapool. ⊠ *Baddidarroch, Lochinver* ☎ *01571/844376* ⊕ *www. highlandstoneware.com.*

Ullapool

30 miles south of Lochinver, 58 miles northwest of Inverness.

Ullapool is an ideal base for hiking throughout Sutherland and taking wildlife and nature cruises, especially to the Summer Isles. By the shores of salty Loch Broom, the town was founded in 1788 as a fishing station to exploit the local herring stocks. There's still a smattering of fishing vessels, as well as visiting yachts and foreign ships. When their crews fill the pubs, Ullapool has a surprisingly cosmopolitan feel. The harbor area comes to life when the Lewis and Harris ferry arrives and departs.

GETTING HERE AND AROUND
To reach Ullapool from Lochinver, either head east on the A837 along Loch Assynt then south on the A835 (1 hour), or head directly south on the windier A837 via Stac Pollaidh (1 hour 15 minutes). From Inverness, a desolate but well-maintained stretch of the A835 takes you to Ullapool via the Falls of Measach.

ESSENTIALS
VISITOR INFORMATION VisitScotland Ullapool iCentre. ⊠ *Argyle St., Ullapool* ☎ *01854/612486* ⊕ *www.visitscotland.com.*

◉ Sights

The Ceilidh Place
ARTS CENTER | Ullapool's cultural focal point is an excellent venue for concerts and other events all through the year (*ceilidh* is a Scottish social gathering with traditional music and dance). It started out as a small café, but, over the years, it has added space for local performers, an excellent bookshop specializing in Scottish writing, and a handful of comfortable rooms (as well as a basic bunkhouse) for those who want to spend the night. It's a great

place for afternoon coffee or a wee dram in the evening. ✉ *14 W. Argyle St., Ullapool* ☎ *01854/612103* 🌐 *www.theceilidhplace.com.*

Corrieshalloch Gorge

WATERFALL | For a thrilling touch of vertigo, don't miss Corrieshalloch Gorge, 12 miles south of Ullapool, just off the A835. Draining the high moors, the Falls of Measach plunge into a 200-foot-deep, thickly wooded gorge. There's a suspension-bridge viewpoint and a heady atmosphere of romantic grandeur, like an old Scottish print come to life. A short walk leads from a parking area to the viewpoint. 🌐 *www.nts.org.uk.*

Ullapool Museum

HISTORY MUSEUM | Films, photographs, and audiovisual displays tell the story of Ullapool and the local area, from the Ice Age to modern times. There's a particularly fascinating display on the the "klondyking" period between 1970 and 1990, when foreign boats, mainly from the Eastern Bloc, filled the loch to fish the mackerel. The historic church building that houses the museum was designed by Thomas Telford and dates from the early 19th century. ✉ *7–8 W. Argyle St., Ullapool* ☎ *01854/612987* 🌐 *www.ullapoolmuseum.co.uk* 🎟 *£5* 🕓 *Closed Sun. and Nov.–Mar.*

🍴 Restaurants

The Arch Inn

$ | **BRITISH** | This restaurant's simple pub-style menu of sausages-and-mash and fish-and-chips hardly pushes the envelope, but its use of local ingredients, its pretty presentation of dishes, and its appealing waterside seating make it a favorite dining spot among locals. Book in advance if you can, especially if you're visiting on a weekend. **Known for:** always busy; fresh and tasty pub grub; waterside seating. [$] *Average main: £14* ✉ *10–11 W. Shore St., Ullapool* ☎ *01854/612454* 🌐 *www.thearchinn.co.uk.*

★ West Coast Delicatessen

$ | **CAFÉ** | This charming family-run deli serves delicious housemade sandwiches, pies, soups, salads, and hummus to a long line of locals and tourists. It also has great cakes and baked goods. **Known for:** an array of artisanal products; deliciously warming soups; excellent coffee. [$] *Average main: £8* ✉ *5 Argyle St., Ullapool* ☎ *01854/613450* 🌐 *www.westcoastdeli.co.uk* 🕓 *Closed Sun. No dinner.*

🛏 Hotels

★ The Dipping Lugger

$$$$ | **HOTEL** | This pretty whitewashed house on Ullapool's waterfront, dating from the late 1700s, is home to the town's most luxurious boutique hotel—and perhaps its finest restaurant, too. **Pros:** appealing lounge area; lavish rooms with Loch Broom views; delicious dinner included in room rate. **Cons:** very expensive for Ullapool; bedroom windows only open part way; only open Thurs.-Sun. [$] *Rooms from: £390* ✉ *4 W. Shore St., Ullapool* ☎ *01854/613344* 🌐 *thedippinglugger.co.uk* 🕓 *Closed Mon.–Wed.* 🛏 *3 rooms* 🍴 *All-Inclusive.*

Tanglewood House

$ | **B&B/INN** | Sitting on a headland above a rocky beach, with spectacular views across Loch Broom toward Ullapool, one of Scotland's most unique and appealing B&Bs feels wonderfully remote while only being a short drive (or even a walk) into town. **Pros:** fast and reliable Wi-Fi; truly unique property; beautiful setting. **Cons:** a little remote; some fusty decor; steep drive down to the house. [$] *Rooms from: £99* ✉ *Off A835, Ullapool* ☎ *01854/612059* 🌐 *www.tanglewoodhouse.co.uk* 🛏 *3 rooms* 🍴 *Free Breakfast.*

★ Westlea House

$ | **B&B/INN** | This quaint, quirky boutique B&B is one of Ullapool's undoubted gems, with bedrooms themed around different natural features and cozy common rooms stuffed with comfy armchairs, colorful cushions, and off-the-wall artworks. **Pros:** great location; wonderfully whimsical decor; superfriendly owners. **Cons:** some low ceilings; sea views limited; TVs are small. [$] *Rooms from: £120* ✉ *2 Market St., Ullapool* ☎ *01854/612594* 🌐 *www.westlea-ullapool.co.uk* 🛏 *5 rooms* 🍴 *Free Breakfast.*

Shopping

Highland Liquor Co.
WINE/SPIRITS | This small bottle shop sells the up-and-coming local producer's signature Seven Crofts gin, along with limited edition bottlings like the Ullapool Gin. You'll also find hand-picked craft beers, wines, and soft drinks for sale. ✉ *26 W. Argyle St., Ullapool* 🌐 *facebook.com/HLCBottleShop.*

Activities

Stac Pollaidh
HIKING & WALKING | For a great afternoon of walking, ascend the dramatic hill of Stac Pollaidh (pronounced "stack polly"), about 14 miles north of Ullapool. The clearly marked path climbs for a bit and then curves around to the right and takes you on a loop with incredible views over Sutherland, north to Suilven, and west to the Summer Isles. About halfway around the hill, a steeper path takes you to the start of the ridge; only very experienced rock climbers should continue from here, as the route requires rock climbing in very exposed conditions. To get to Stac Pollaidh, take the A835 to Drumrunie, then a minor road off to the west (there's a sign for "Achiltibuie"). Five miles along the road on the left is a parking area; start your walk from here. ✉ *Off A835, Dornie.*

Fishing in the Highlands

The possibilities for fishing are endless in Sutherland, as a glance at the loch-covered map suggests. Brown trout and salmon are abundant. You can fish from the banks of Loch Garve, 33 miles southeast of Ullapool, or Loch Assynt, 6 miles east of Lochinver, from March to October. Boat fishing is popular on Loch Maree, southeast of Gairloch and north of Poolewe, from May to October. Fishing permits are available at local post offices and shops; some hotels have their own fishing rights but most will arrange permits for you.

Gairloch

55 miles southwest of Ullapool.

Aside from its restaurants and lodgings, peaceful Gairloch has one further advantage: it often escapes the rain clouds that can cling to the high summits. You can enjoy a round of golf here and perhaps stay dry, even when the nearby Torridon Hills are deluged.

GETTING HERE AND AROUND

From Ullapool, head south down the A835 for around 12 miles. From there, signs for "Corrieshalloch Gorge" lead you west onto the winding A832—also known as "Destitution Road".

Sights

Destitution Road
SCENIC DRIVE | The road south between Corrieshalloch Gorge and Gairloch passes through wild woodlands around Dundonnell and Loch Broom, then takes in stunning coastal scenery with views

of Gruinard Bay and its white beaches. Look out for the toothed ramparts of the mountain An Teallach (pronounced tyel-lack), visible on the horizon for miles. The moorland route you travel is officially called the A832 but is better (and more chillingly) known as Destitution Road; a holdover from the terrible potato famines of the 1840s.

★ Inverewe Garden

GARDEN | FAMILY | A highlight of the area, Inverewe Garden has lush plantings tucked away behind a dense barrier of trees and shrubs. This is all thanks to the warm North Atlantic Drift, which takes the edge off winter frosts. Inverewe is sometimes described as subtropical, but this inaccuracy irritates the head gardener; do not expect coconuts and palm trees here. Instead, look for rarities like the blue Himalayan poppy. The garden, located 6 miles north of Gairloch, is also a haven for wildlife, with Scotland's Big 5 (the red squirrel, red deer, otter, seal, and golden eagle) all found around here. ⊠ Off A832, Poolewe ☎ 01445/712952 ⊕ www.nts.org.uk ⊠ £13 ⊘ Closed Nov.–Mar.

★ Loch Maree

BODY OF WATER | Southeast of Gairloch stretches one of Scotland's most scenic lochs, Loch Maree. Its harmonious setting, with tall Scots pines and the mountain Slioch looming as a backdrop, is regularly visited by red deer, as well as the endangered pine marten (a member of the weasel family)—though they're just as likely to be hanging around the trash cans as in the trees. There are few official parking places along the loch, but these are nestled between the trees with limited views, so be prepared to park and climb to a better vantage point. ⊠ Gairloch.

🛏 Hotels

★ Shieldaig Lodge

$$$ | HOTEL | Located 4 miles southwest of Gairloch in the tiny hamlet of Shieldaig (not to be confused with the relative metropolis just down the coast), this spectacular Victorian hunting-lodge-turned-luxury hotel sits on a gorgeous, secluded bay. **Pros:** top-drawer restaurant; activities include on-site falconry; remote location with bay views. **Cons:** heavy curtains require some wrangling; poor Wi-Fi; dining is expensive (but worth it). $ Rooms from: £215 ⊠ Badachro, Gairloch ☎ 01445/741333 ⊕ www.shieldaiglodge.com ⇄ 12 rooms ⊚ Free Breakfast.

🏃 Activities

GOLF
Gairloch Golf Club

GOLF | This lovely nine-hole course is one of the few to be found on this stretch of coast, but it is the coastal location that gives it its charm—as well as its challenges. There has been a golf club here since 1898, and local records show that putters of more than a century ago played on the golden sand dunes (which have long since been replaced by rolling greens). While you are waiting for your turn at the tee, take a moment to drink in fine views of the Minch and Skye. ⊠ Off A832, Gairloch ☎ 01445/712407 ⊕ gairlochgolfclub.co.uk ⊠ £15 for 9 holes, £25 for 18 holes ⅄ 9 holes, 2137 yards, par 31.

Shieldaig

36 miles south of Gairloch.

Just west of the southern coast of Upper Loch Torridon is Shieldaig, a village that sits in an attractive crescent overlooking a namesake loch of its own. For an atmospheric evening foray, walk north toward Loch Torridon, at the northern end of the village by the church. The path—fairly well made, though hiking shoes are recommended—leads to exquisite views and tiny, rocky beaches.

GETTING HERE AND AROUND

From Gairloch, head southeast on the A832, then turn southwest onto the A896 at Kinlochewe. Shieldaig is around 16½ miles along this road.

Sights

★ Applecross

SCENIC DRIVE | The most exciting way to reach this small community facing Skye is by a twisting, turning coastal road, which leaves the A896 just a few miles south of Shieldaig; simply follow the brown sign marked "Wester Ross Coastal Trail." A series of hairpin bends corkscrews up the steep wall at the head of a corrie (a glacier-cut mountain valley) and over the Bealach na Ba (Pass of the Cattle). There are spectacular views of Raasay and Skye from the bare plateau on top, and you can brag afterward that you've been on what is probably Scotland's highest drivable road.

★ Glen Torridon

SCENIC DRIVE | The scenic spectacle of Glen Torridon lies east of Shieldaig; if you're following the A896 from Kinlochewe to Shieldaig, you pass right through it. Some say that Glen Torridon has the finest mountain scenery in Scotland. It consists mainly of the long, gray, quartzite flanks of Beinn Eighe and Liathach, with its distinct ridge profile that looks like the keel of an upturned boat.

Restaurants

The Bealach Cafe and Gallery

$ | **CAFÉ** | At the eastern edge of the Bealach na Ba, the steepest road ascent in Britain, this lovely café offers sandwiches, soups, and fine house baking against a stunning mountain backdrop. Enjoy the view through the café's large windows or from the outside deck, if weather allows. **Known for:** views to die for; lovely house-baked cakes; friendly hosts. [$] *Average main: £9* ✉ *A896, Lochcarron* ☎ *01520/733436* 🌐 *www.thebealach.co.uk* ⏲ *Closed Mon. and Tues. No dinner.*

Hotels

The Torridon

$$$$ | **HOTEL** | The Victorian Gothic turrets of this former hunting lodge promise atmosphere and grandeur—and, with its log fires, handsome plasterwork ceilings, mounted stag heads, and antique mahogany furniture, The Torridon doesn't disappoint. **Pros:** two restaurants and a bar with more than 300 malts; wonderful countryside location; center for outdoor activities. **Cons:** activities must be booked in advance; 6 miles out of town; very pricey. [$] *Rooms from: £595* ✉ *Off A896, Shieldaig* ☎ *01445/791242* 🌐 *www.thetorridon.com* 🛏 *18 rooms* 🍴 *Free Breakfast.*

Shopping

Lochcarron Weavers

MIXED CLOTHING | Watch a weaver producing pure-wool tartans that can be bought here or at the company's other outlets in the area. There's also a nice little café. The store is 16½ miles southeast of Shieldaig; follow the A896 to Lochcarron, then turn south onto Church Street. ✉ *Lochcarron* ☎ *01520/722212* 🌐 *www.lochcarron.co.uk* ⏲ *Closed Sun.*

Kyle of Lochalsh

38 miles south of Shieldaig, 78 miles west of Inverness, 180 miles northwest of Glasgow.

The little town of Kyle of Lochalsh is the mainland gateway to Skye. Opened in 1995, the bridge here transformed not only travel to Skye but the very seascape itself. The area's most notable (and most photographed) attraction, Eilean Donan Castle, is 8 miles east of town.

GETTING HERE AND AROUND
From Shieldaig, head south on the A896, then join the A890 arriving from Inverness. There are also four direct trains a day from Inverness. From the south, you'll arrive by the A87.

Sights

Attadale Gardens
GARDEN | FAMILY | A little over halfway between Shieldaig and Kyle of Lochalsh, this 20-acre estate centered around a striking 18th-century house makes for an energizing break. Highlights here include the historic Sunken Garden, the atmospheric Old Wood, and the peaceful Japanese Garden. Kids will also enjoy following the sculpture trail, with a range of eclectic animal figures by artists from around the world; look out for the distinctive wild-cat pointer on the sundial. Climb the steps up from the Old Rhododendron Walk for stunning views of the estate and beyond—on a clear day you can see the Cuillin Hills of Skye—then grab a drink and snack in the DIY tearoom. You can also reach Attadale by train from Kyle of Lochalsh or Inverness; the station is just outside. ⊠ *Off A890, Attadale, Kyle of Lochalsh* ☎ *01520/722603* ⊕ *www. attadalegardens.com* ⏁ *£10* ⊗ *Closed Nov.–Mar.*

★ Eilean Donan Castle
CASTLE/PALACE | Guarding the confluence of lochs Long, Alsh, and Duich stands the most picturesque of all Scottish fortifications. Eilean Donan Castle, perched on an islet connected to the mainland by a stone-arched bridge, dates from the 14th century and has all the dramatic stone walls, timber ceilings, and winding stairs you could possibly desire. Empty and neglected for years after being bombarded by frigates of the Royal Navy during an abortive Spanish-Jacobite landing in 1719, this romantic Scottish icon was almost entirely rebuilt from a ruin in the early 20th century. The kitchen re-creates the busy scene before a grand banquet, and the upper floors show how the castle was transformed into a grand house. The picturesque cover of a thousand travel brochures, Eilean Donan has also appeared in a number of Hollywood movies and TV shows, from *The Wicker Man* to *Highlander*. There's a gift shop and a coffeehouse for the many visitors. The castle lies 8½ miles east of Kyle Lochalsh; you'll pass it if you're coming from the south. ⊠ *Off A87, Dornie* ☎ *01599/555202* ⊕ *www.eileandonancastle.com* ⏁ *£10* ⊗ *Closed Jan.–Feb.*

Plockton
TOWN | Once a fishing and crofting center, Plockton today attracts visitors for its natural beauty and its warm microclimate, which allows palms to grow all along the main Harbour Street. Situated just 6 miles northeast of Kyle of Lochalsh, its natural bay is an ideal space for the small yachts that make their leisurely way to the coast and beyond, where gray seals can often be seen. Park at the car park at the entrance to the village and stroll along the main street, ideally with an ice cream as your companion. ⊠ *Kyle of Lochalsh.*

Restaurants

★ All the Goodness
$ | CAFÉ | This excellent little bakery–café serves house-made cakes, tray bakes, and pastries, along with artisan coffee and an array of tempting foodie gifts and souvenirs—all to be enjoyed with a stunning vista of Eilean Donan Castle. In summer, the café also displays evocative works by local artist Lorraine Tolmie.
Known for: unbeatable castle views; delicious baked goods; superior tea and coffee. ⑂ *Average main: £5* ⊠ *Off A87, Kyle of Lochalsh* ☎ *01599/555221* ⊕ *www.allthegoodness.co.uk* ⊗ *Closed Mon. and Tues. No dinner.*

Just a glimpse at Eilean Donan Castle from a distance makes it clear why this is one of the most photographed castles in all of Scotland.

🛏 Hotels

★ Duncraig Castle

$$$ | **HOTEL** | Built high on a cliff-top overlooking Plockton, this striking 19th-century castle recently opened as a hotel—and instantly became the region's go-to luxury retreat. **Pros:** free kids sweets and dog treats; beautiful rooms with modern bathrooms; spectacular views over Loch Carron. **Cons:** access road is rough and potholed; taxidermy animals—including a polar bear—will repel some; no meals except breakfast. [$] *Rooms from: £275* ✉ *Plockton, Kyle of Lochalsh* ☎ *0599/544295* 🌐 *duncraigcastle.co.uk* 🕒 *Closed Oct.–Mar.* 🛏 *12 rooms* 🍴 *Free Breakfast.*

Isle of Skye

The misty Isle of Skye is awash with romance and myth, lush green gardens, and steep, magnetic mountains. Its extraordinary natural beauty and royal connections see it rank highly on most must-see lists, and its proximity to the mainland makes it one of Scotland's most accessible islands.

Adding to Skye's scenic drama are sunsets that linger brilliantly until late at night, and otherworldly mists that roll gently through valleys. Much photographed are the old crofts, one or two of which are still inhabited. The island also has an impressive range of accommodations, as well as restaurants that showcase the best local produce and culinary talent.

To reach Skye, cross the bridge over the narrow channel of Kyleakin from Kyle of Lochalsh on the mainland. Or, if you're visiting in the summer, take a romantic boat trip between Mallaig and Armadale or Glenelg and Kylerhea. You can tour the island readily in two or three days but staying a bit longer will afford time to hike or sea kayak.

Orientation is easy: in the north, follow the roads that loop around the peninsulas of Waternish and Trotternish; in the

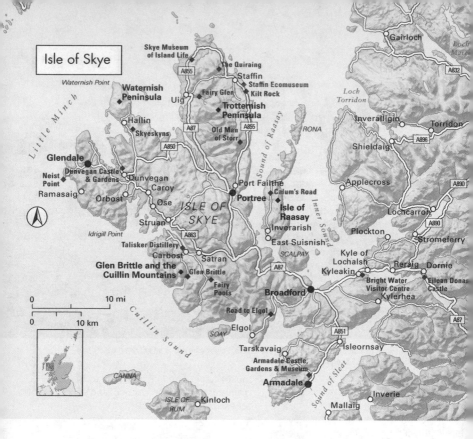

south, enjoy the road running the length of the Sleat Peninsula. There are some single-lane stretches, but, for careful drivers, these shouldn't pose a problem.

Broadford

8½ miles west of Kyle of Lochalsh via Skye Bridge.

One of the larger of Skye's settlements, Broadford lies along the shore of Broadford Bay, which has been known to welcome whales to its sheltered waters.

GETTING HERE AND AROUND

Broadford is on the A87, the main road from Kyle of Lochalsh up to Portree and beyond.

TOURS
★ Misty Isle Boat Trips

BOAT TOURS | FAMILY | Explore some of the most remote corners of Skye's Cuillin Mountains with a boat trip to Loch Coruisk. The scenery around here is some of the most expansive in Scotland, and the wildlife is equally spectacular: look out for seals, basking sharks, red deer, golden eagles, and more. Round-trip journeys depart from the town of Elgol, 15 miles southwest of Broadford, and booking ahead is essential. Wildlife tours to the Small Isles are also available. ⊠ *Elgol jetty, Sealladh na Mara, Elgol* ☎ *01471/866288* ⊕ *www.mistyisleboat-trips.co.uk* ✉ *From £28* ⊗ *Closed Sun. and Nov.–Mar.*

Sights

Bright Water Visitor Centre

VISITOR CENTER | FAMILY | Discover *Ring of Bright Water*, Gavin Maxwell's much-loved account of his work with otters on the island of Eilean Ban, at this center just across the bridge from Kyle of Lochalsh, 8 miles east of Broadford. There's an interesting exhibit illustrating Maxwell's work, as well as displays on local history—including, most obviously, a 70-foot-tall, 165-year-old lighthouse designed by Robert Louis Stevenson's father. The center also offers wildlife tours that promise otters, seals, and birdlife. ✉ *The Pier, Kyleakin* ☎ *01599/530040* 🌐 *www.eileanban.org* 🕒 *Closed Oct.–Easter and weekends.*

Road to Elgol

SCENIC DRIVE | The B8083 leads from Broadford to one of the finest vistas anywhere in Scotland. This road passes by Strath Suardal and little Loch Cill Chriosd (Kilchrist), and it takes in breathtaking views of the mountain Bla Bheinn en route. As you near Elgol, look out for a gathering of traditional crofts that descends to a pier, and then admire the heart-stopping profile of the Cuillin peaks from the shore. Seek out the path, around halfway down the hill, that leads across rough grasslands into the mountains. ✉ *Elgol.*

Restaurants

Deli Gasta

$ | CAFÉ | This rustic little deli-café, in an old mill on the edge of Broadford, serves delicious coffee, cakes, and savory snacks ranging from toasted sandwiches and baked potatoes to soups and salads. Come early for the Eggs Royale made with locally smoked Scottish salmon. **Known for:** delicious coffee from an artisan roastery; tasty sandwiches and bagels; charming stone-wall interior. [$] *Average main: £6* ✉ *The Old Mill, Broadford* ☎ *01471/822646* 🌐 *www.deligasta.co.uk* 🕒 *No dinner.*

Hotels

Broadford Hotel

$$ | HOTEL | Watch over Broadford Bay in comfort and style with a stay at this well-appointed hotel, which takes pride in being the place where Drambuie was invented. **Pros:** Drambuie-colored tartan; quintessentially Scottish; convenient location. **Cons:** breakfast underwhelming; poorly lit public areas; no elevator. [$] *Rooms from: £195* ✉ *Torrin Rd., Broadford* ☎ *01471/822204* 🌐 *www.broadfordhotel.co.uk* 🛏 *11 rooms* 🍴 *Free Breakfast.*

Armadale

5 miles southeast of Broadford, 5 miles (ferry crossing) west of Mallaig.

Rolling moorlands, scattered with rivers and lochans, give way to enchanting hidden coves and scattered waterside communities. Welcome to Sleat, Skye's spectacular southernmost peninsula.

GETTING HERE AND AROUND

From Broadford, the A851 heads south down the Sleat Peninsula, following its stunning coast to Armadale (smaller roads continue even farther south). You can also arrive directly into Sleat on the Mallaig-Armadale ferry.

Sights

Armadale Castle, Gardens & Museum

CASTLE/PALACE | As the name suggests, this attraction has three distinct strings to its bow: a romantic, ruined castle; a lush, flower-filled estate; and a fascinating museum of local island history. The castle is a windswept 17th-century mansion house built by the influential Clan Donald, while the extensive gardens cover 40 acres, offering magnificent views across the Sound of Sleat to Knoydart and the Mallaig Peninsula. The highlight, however, is the fascinating museum, which tells the story of the clan and its proud title, the Lords of the Isles, with the help of an excellent audiovisual presentation. There's a gift shop, restaurant, library, and center for genealogy research. Also on the grounds are high-quality accommodations in the form of seven cottages, complete with kitchen facilities. Access is from Armadale Pier, where signs indicate the different forest walks that are available. ✉ *Off A851, Armadale* ☎ *01471/844305* 🌐 *www.armadalecastle.com* 🎟 *£9* ⏲ *Closed Nov.–Mar.*

★ Torabhaig Distillery
DISTILLERY | Opened in 2017 as Skye's second-ever licensed distillery, Torabhaig debuted its single malt four years later. And just like those from Skye's first distillery, Talisker, the whisky is smooth, rich, and wonderfully peaty. Come for a tasting in the comfort of the beautiful courtyard, flanked by the old stone farmhouses where the magic happens. You can also join a guided tour of the distillery, though note that it's a small operation; don't expect photo ops in barrel-filled warehouses. If you have time, stroll from the distillery down to the pretty, ruined Knock Castle, a former stronghold of the Macdonalds. ✉ *Off A851, Teangue, Armadale* ☎ *01471/833447* 🌐 *www.torabhaig.com* 🎟 *£10* ⏲ *Closed weekends and Jan.–Mar.*

🛏 Hotels

Duisdale House Hotel
$$$$ | **HOTEL** | Sea views and a lovely hillside location amid 35 acres of mature woodlands and gardens are highlights of this former mansion, which is boutique chic at its very best. **Pros:** expansive views; finely furnished rooms and lodges; delicious cooked breakfasts. **Cons:** very expensive in summer; three-course dinner is pricey; unappealing carpets in many rooms. [$] *Rooms from: £329* ✉ *Off A851, Isleornsay* ☎ *01471/833202* 🌐 *skyehotel.co.uk/duisdale* 🔑 *21 rooms* 🍴 *Free Breakfast.*

★ Kinloch Lodge
$$$$ | **HOTEL** | An upscale hotel with an excellent restaurant, Kinloch Lodge peacefully overlooks the tidal Loch na Dal. The buildings date from the 17th century, although the best views are from the newer South House, which was built from the ground up with comfort and relaxation in mind. **Pros:** historic and characterful property; beautiful lochside setting; top-drawer dining. **Cons:** far from amenities; noisy bathroom fans; expensive stay. [$] *Rooms from: £420* ✉ *Off A851, Isleornsay* ☎ *01471/833333* 🌐 *kinloch-lodge.co.uk* 🔑 *19 rooms* 🍴 *Free Breakfast.*

🛍 Shopping

★ Ragamuffin
MIXED CLOTHING | This well-stocked shop specializes in designer knitwear and has some of the nicest staff you could hope to meet. On cold winter days, they might make you coffee while you browse, then mail your purchases back home for you. ✉ *Armadale Pier, Off A851, Armadale* ☎ *01471/844217* 🌐 *www.ragamuffin-store.com.*

Portree

30 miles northwest of Sleat Peninsula.

Portree, the population center of the island, is a pleasant place clustered around a small and sheltered bay. Although not overburdened by historical features, it's a fine touring base with a number of good shops.

GETTING HERE AND AROUND

From the Sleat Peninsula, follow the A851 north to join the A87, which continues up to Portree. As the biggest town on Skye, Portree is also reachable by local buses from Broadford or Kyle of Lochalsh.

Clans and Tartans

The Scottish clans have a long and varied history. Some claim Norman roots and later married into Celtic society; others were of Norse origin, the product of Viking raids on Scotland; while still others may have been descended from Pictish tribes. Whatever their origins, by the 13th century, the clans were at the heart of Gaelic tribal culture. By the 15th century, clan chiefs of the Scottish Highlands were even a threat to the authority of the Stewart monarchs. The word *clann* means "family" or "children" in Gaelic, and it was customary for clan chiefs to board out their sons among nearby families, a practice that helped to bond the clan unit and create strong allegiances.

The Clan System

Gradually, by the 18th century, increasing knowledge of Lowland agricultural improvements and better roads into the Highlands that improved communication of ideas and "southern" ways, began to weaken the clan system. The Battle of Culloden marked the death of the clan system, as the victorious English armies banned the kilt and the pipes and claimed the land of the rebellious clan chiefs. And when the new landowners introduced the hardy Cheviot breed of sheep and changed farming activity, the Highlands were transformed forever. Many Highlanders, and especially islanders, began to emigrate in the 1750s. By the 1820s, landowners were paying people to leave.

Tartan Revival

Tartan's own origins as a part of the clan system are disputed; the Gaelic word for striped cloth is *breacan*—piebald or spotted—so even the word itself is not Highland. Nevertheless, when cloth was locally spun, woven, and dyed using plant derivatives, each neighborhood would use different colorings. In this way combinations of colors and favorite patterns of the local weavers could become associated with an area and therefore its dominant clans. Between 1746 and 1782 the wearing of tartan was generally prohibited, and by the time the ban was lifted, many recipes for dyes and weaving patterns had been forgotten.

It took the influence of Sir Walter Scott, with his romantic (and fashionable) view of Highland history, to create the "modern myth" of clans and tartan. Sir Walter engineered George IV's visit to Scotland in 1822, which turned into a tartan extravaganza. The idea of one tartan or group of tartans "belonging" to one particular clan was created at this time—literally created, with new patterns dreamed up and "assigned" to particular clans.

11

The Northern Highlands and the Western Isles ISLE OF SKYE

VISITOR INFORMATION
VisitScotland Portree iCentre. ✉ Bayfield House, Bayfield Rd., Portree ☎ 01478/612992 ⊕ www.visitscotland.com.

◉ Sights

Aros
ARTS CENTER | On the outskirts of town, Aros is a community center that screens films, exhibits artworks, and hosts live music, dance, and theater productions. It's the cultural hub of the Isle of Skye.

✉ *Viewfield Rd., Portree* ☎ *01478/613649* 🌐 *www.aros.co.uk.*

🍴 Restaurants

Café Arriba

$ | **BRITISH** | Up a steep flight of stairs, this laid-back café has window seats with great views over Portree Harbour. It uses only local produce (whatever is "fresh, local, and available") and is a good no-frills option for hearty breakfasts, as well as lunchtime favorites—from locally caught scallops to creamy summer risotto. **Known for:** expect long lines; delicious house-made cakes; mildly treacherous stairs. [$] *Average main: £9* ✉ *Quay Brae, Quay St., Portree* ☎ *01478/611830* 🌐 *www.cafearriba.co.uk* 🕒 *Closed Mon.*

Scorrybreac Restaurant

$$$$ | **BRITISH** | It may be tiny, but this upscale, 20-seater restaurant is packed every night of the week. The vibe is relaxed and informal, while the cooking is imaginative and varied, with unexpected marriages such as coffee-crusted venison or hake with coconut. **Known for:** very expensive for Portree; inventive dishes; gorgeous bay views. [$] *Average main: £75* ✉ *7 Bosville Terr., Portree* ☎ *01478/612069* 🌐 *www.scorrybreac.com* 🕒 *Closed Sun. and Mon. No lunch.*

🛏 Hotels

Cuillin Hills Hotel

$$$ | **HOTEL** | This delightful Victorian-era hunting lodge looks down on Portree and the brightly painted houses around the harbor. **Pros:** attentive service; a short stroll from Portree; good breakfast menu. **Cons:** no elevator; restaurant can be full; rooms at back overpriced. [$] *Rooms from: £295* ✉ *Off A855, Portree* ☎ *01478/612003* 🌐 *www.cuillinhills-hotel-skye.co.uk* 🔑 *34 rooms* 🍽 *Free Breakfast.*

The Skye Inn

$$ | **B&B/INN** | Clean and comfortable rooms, a quiet but convenient location, and a wonderful communal space makes this a popular base for exploring Portree and the Trotternish Peninsula. **Pros:** appealing lounge area with roaring fire; friendly above-and-beyond service; free parking. **Cons:** not as good value in high-season; may be too "dog-friendly" for some; food could be better. [$] *Rooms from: £175* ✉ *Springfield Rd., Portree* ☎ *01478/612282* 🌐 *theskyeinn.com* 🔑 *24 rooms* 🍽 *No Meals.*

🛍 Shopping

Isle of Skye Soap Company

COSMETICS | This charming little shop handcrafts its own soaps, aromatherapy oils, candles, and other pleasingly fragranced gifts. Founder (and soap maker-in-chief) Fiona is an aromatherapist. ✉ *Somerled Sq., Portree* ☎ *01478/611350* 🌐 *www.skye-soap.co.uk* 🕒 *Closed Sun.*

Trotternish Peninsula

5 miles north of Portree.

Travel north from Portree on the A855 and you'll see cliffs rising to the left. These are the closest edge of an ancient lava flow, set back from the road and running the length of the peninsula. Fossilized dinosaur bones have been uncovered at the base of these cliffs, while overhead you might just spot a sea eagle, identifiable by the flash of its white tail.

GETTING HERE AND AROUND

From Portree, take the twisting, undulating A855 up the east coast. If you want head back to Portree a different way, or continue straight on to the Waternish Peninsula, follow the A87 on the west coast.

Sights

Fairy Glen

NATURE SIGHT | What was once a hidden gem is now just another stop on the ever-expanding Skye tourist trail. Still, if you come early or late and avoid the crowds, the Fairy Glen remains magical—an enchanting, otherworldly valley of strange green hillocks, eerily still pools, crumbling cottages, and roaming sheep. To get here, take a small road just south of Uig signed "Sheader and Balnaknock" and drive for a little over a mile.

Kilt Rock

VIEWPOINT | No drive between Portree and Staffin is complete without a sojourn to Skye's most famous sea cliff. Named for the shape of its sheer rock face, which is ridged like a pleated kilt and swoops out to sea at the "hem," soaring Kilt Rock (and its gushing waterfall) can be seen from a specially built viewing platform. ⊠ *Off A855, Staffin* ⊕ *1½ miles south of Staffin.*

Old Man of Storr

NATURE SIGHT | Along the dramatic road around the Trotternish Peninsula, a gate beside a parking area marks the beginning of the climb to the Old Man of Storr, one of Skye's most iconic landmarks. At 2,000 feet, this volcanic pinnacle is the highest point on the peninsula. Give yourself at least three hours to explore and enjoy the spectacular views from the top. ■TIP→ **The weather here changes very quickly, so be prepared.** ⊠ *Off A855.*

★ The Quiraing

MOUNTAIN | A spectacular geological formation of rocky crags and towering stacks, Quiraing dominates the horizon of the Trotternish Peninsula. It's about 5 miles beyond Kilt Rock, so for a closer look, make a left onto a small road at Brogaig by Staffin Bay. There's a parking lot near the point where this road breaches the ever-present cliff line. The road is very narrow and rough, so drive cautiously. The rambler's trail is on uneven, stony ground, and it's a steep scramble up to the rock formations. In ages past, stolen cattle were hidden deep within the Quiraing's rocky jaws. ⊠ *Quiraing Car Park.*

Skye Ecomuseum

MUSEUM VILLAGE | **FAMILY** | Billed as "a museum without walls," this collection of 13 open-air, geological and social exhibits dots the landscape of the peninsula. . Follow the map along the coastal route, and you will discover dinosaur footprints, a healing well, a deserted village, and more. ⊠ *Staffin Community Trust, 3 Ellishadder, Staffin* ☎ *01470/562464* ⊕ *skyeecomuseum.com.*

Skye Museum of Island Life

HISTORY MUSEUM | **FAMILY** | Discover the old crofting ways of the local population at this museum close to the tip of the Trotternish Peninsula. Informative displays and exhibits, from reconstructed interiors with traditional implements to historical photographs and documents, show life as it was on the island merely a century ago. ⊠ *Off A855, Kilmuir* ☎ *01470/552206* ⊕ *www.skyemuseum.co.uk* ⊠ *£5* ⊗ *Closed Sun. and Oct.–Easter.*

Staffin Dinosaur Museum

OTHER MUSEUM | **FAMILY** | Built on the foundations of an 1840s schoolhouse, this single-room museum is a labor of love of builder Dugald Ross, who first saw the fossilized dinosaur prints as a boy and as an adult saved them from rough seas. You'll also find objects saved from shipwrecks, agricultural implements, and some old photographs. It is highly individual and perhaps slightly eccentric, but fascinating. ⊠ *6 Ellishadder, Staffin* ☎ *01470/562321* ⊕ *www.staffindinosaurmuseum.com* ⊠ *£4* ⊗ *Closed weekends.*

Hotels

The Flodigarry Hotel
$$$ | **HOTEL** | With spectacular coastal views and antique furnishings throughout, the Flodigarry retains the feel of a grand country manor. **Pros:** great seafood restaurant; spectacular views; a good base for walking. **Cons:** a long way from anywhere; expensive rooms; steep road down. [$] *Rooms from: £240* ✉ *Off A855, Staffin* ☎ *01470/552203* 🌐 *www.hotelintheskye.co.uk* 🛏 *18 rooms* 🍴 *Free Breakfast.*

Skeabost House Hotel
$$$$ | **HOTEL** | Set at the foot of Loch Snizort, this 19th-century hunting-lodge-turned-luxury hotel offers charming, traditionally furnished rooms; a pleasant lounge with a roaring fire; a cozy little cocktail bar; and a conservatory restaurant that's one of the area's best, with Scottish specialties such as smoked salmon, spiced monkfish, and 28-day-aged prime fillet steak. **Pros:** free-to-use 9-hole golf course; modern and accessible Garden rooms; beautiful lochside setting. **Cons:** expensive option; service is hit and miss; not close to any one particular attraction. [$] *Rooms from: £350* ✉ *Skeabost Bridge, Portree* ☎ *01470/532202* 🌐 *skyehotel.co.uk/skeabost* 🛏 *20 rooms* 🍴 *Free Breakfast.*

Waternish Peninsula

17 miles west of Trotternish.

Jutting like a beckoning finger from the northwest of Skye, the Waternish Peninsula has scattered crofting communities and magnificent coastal views. In the Hallin area, look westward for a sea loch with small cliffs rising from the water like miniature models of full-size islands.

GETTING HERE AND AROUND
From the Trotternish Peninsula, head west on the A850 from Borve (around 4 miles northwest of Portree). Then, after 14 miles, turn right onto the B886, which travels up the west coast of the Waternish Peninsula.

Sights

Skyeskyns
FACTORY | A 15-minute tour of this working tannery gives visitors excellent insight into the process of salting, washing, and preparing sheepskins. You'll learn the source of such phrases as "on tenterhooks" and "stretched to the limits," and you can buy sheepskins from the on-site shop (there's another outlet in Portree). In summer, there's also a lovely little yurt café around the back. ✉ *17 Lochbay, Waternish* ☎ *01470/592237* 🌐 *www.skyeskyns.co.uk* 🎟 *Tour £5.*

Restaurants

★ Loch Bay Restaurant
$$$$ | **SEAFOOD** | Situated right on the waterfront, this distinctive black-and-white restaurant, where the island's top chefs come to unwind on their nights off, is a Skye foodie favorite. The seafood is freshly caught and simply prepared by renowned chef Michael Smith, with the aim of enhancing the natural flavors of the ingredients rather than overwhelming them with superfluous sauces. **Known for:** impeccable service; sublime yet simple seafood; beautiful bay views. [$] *Average main: £110* ✉ *1 Macleods Terr., Stein* ☎ *01470/592235* 🌐 *www.lochbay-restaurant.co.uk* 🕒 *Closed Sun.–Tues. and Jan.–Mar. No lunch.*

Shopping

Edinbane Pottery
CERAMICS | Specializing in quirky handmade ceramics and watercolors of local wildlife, this is a great place to pick up a distinctive souvenir from your time on Skye. ✉ *Off A850, Edinbane* ☎ *01470/582234* 🌐 *www.edinbane-pottery.co.uk* 🕒 *Closed weekends.*

Glendale

14 miles southwest of Waternish.

Glendale is a region rich in flora and fauna: otters, seals, and dolphins can be spotted off its rocky coast, while white-tailed sea eagles soar overhead. Dunvegan Castle lies just across the water from the region's eastern edge.

GETTING HERE AND AROUND

From the Waternish Peninsula, take the A850 southwest to Dunvegan. From here, turn left onto the A863, then right onto the twisty, turny B884, which runs west along the coast. It can feel rather isolated in bad weather or after dark.

◉ Sights

Dunvegan Castle & Gardens

CASTLE/PALACE | In a commanding position over a sea loch, Dunvegan Castle has been the seat of the chiefs of Clan MacLeod for more than 700 years. Today, it's a popular (if overpriced) tourist attraction. Step inside and into the clan's illustrious past through plush interiors, fascinating photos, and, most notably, the Fairy Flag—a silk banner, thought to be originally from Rhodes or Syria, which is credited with protecting the clan from danger. And make time to explore the gardens, with their water features, fern house, walled garden, and various viewing points. There's a café beside the parking lot. Boat trips from the castle to the nearby seal colony run April through September. The castle lies a mile north of the A850/A863 junction between Waternish and Glendale. ⊠ *Dunvegan* ☎ *01470/521206* ⊕ *www.dunvegan-castle.com* 🎟 *Castle and gardens £14; gardens only £12; seal trips £10* 🕙 *Closed mid-Oct.–Mar.*

Neist Point

LIGHTHOUSE | Skye's westernmost point is famed for its steep sea cliffs and picturesque, early-20th century lighthouse, designed by David Alan Stevenson (cousin of *Treasure Island* author Robert Louis Stevenson). The Neist Point Trail begins at the cliff-top parking area, from which it's a short but steep walk down to the lighthouse. ⊠ *Neist Point Car Park, Waterstein, Colbost* ⊕ *Turn west off the B884 between Borrodale and Milovaig, following the signs to Waterstein.*

🍴 Restaurants

★ Three Chimneys

$$$$ | MODERN BRITISH | Perhaps the Isle of Skye's biggest culinary draw, this old stone-walled restaurant on the banks of Loch Dunvegan serves consistently daring, well-crafted food. Head chef Scott Davies's belief in quality Scottish ingredients is evident in every dish, from the locally sourced game to the sublime Scottish seafood, with most dishes available as part of a multicourse meal or à la carte. **Known for:** faultless service; inventive seafood dishes; delicious oysters and sublime scallops. Ⓢ *Average main: £32* ⊠ *B884, Colbost* ☎ *01470/511258* ⊕ *www.threechimneys.co.uk* 🕙 *Closed mid-Dec.–mid-Jan.* ☞ *No children under eight at dinner.*

🛏 Hotels

★ Carter's Rest

$$ | B&B/INN | This brilliant little B&B offers three large, comfortable rooms with modern bathrooms and a host of thoughtful extras, like mini fridges with water and snacks, pod coffee machines, and US two-pin plug sockets. **Pros:** stunning coastal views; modern and spacious bathrooms; walkable to Neist Point. **Cons:** minimum two-night stay; showers a little slow to heat up; no alcohol license so BYOB. Ⓢ *Rooms from: £180* ⊠ *8–9 Upper Milovaig, Colbost* ☎ *01470/517143* ⊕ *www.cartersrestskye.co.uk* 🛏 *2 rooms* ⦿ *Free Breakfast.*

The Isle of Skye's most magical walk is to the Fairy Pools, rock pools of spring water fed by waterfalls from the Cuillin Mountains.

🧳 Shopping

Skye Silver

JEWELRY & WATCHES | Distinctive gold and silver jewelry with Celtic themes is the bread and butter of Skye Silver. From pendants to rings, bracelets to earrings, the unique pieces here are inspired by the surrounding landscapes of sea and countryside, with motifs of island wildlife. ⊠ *The Old School, B884, Colbost* ☎ *01470/511263* ⊕ *skyesilver.com.*

Glen Brittle and the Cuillin Mountains

32 miles southeast of Glendale.

The gentle slopes of this valley are a gateway to the dramatic peaks and ridges of the Cuillin Mountains. Glen Brittle's lower slopes are fine for walkers and weekend climbers, but the higher ridges are strictly for serious (and well-equipped) mountaineers.

GETTING HERE AND AROUND

From Glendale, follow the B884 east to Lonmore, turn south onto the A863, then, after 16 miles (at the junction with the scarecrow sculpture), head west on the B8009. Glen Brittle extends from here to cover the southwest corner of the island.

👁 Sights

★ Fairy Pools

BODY OF WATER | One of the most magical sights in Scotland, the Fairy Pools are a spectacularly beautiful collection of waterfalls and plunge pools in the midst of Glen Brittle. The rocky gray landscape contrasts with the vivid blue-green of the pools, the colorful plant life, and visiting wildlife (including, occasionally, red deer) to give the environment a fairy-tale feel. You can walk to the pools from a parking lot 20 minutes away. Come at sunrise or sunset for smaller crowds and the opportunity for a truly enchanting swim— just don't expect the water to be warm. If you're willing to climb to the upper pools, you can even find some seclusion at peak hours. ✉ *Fairy Pools Car Park, Glenbrittle* 🎟 *Free; parking £5 a day.*

Glen Brittle

MOUNTAIN | Enjoy spectacular mountain scenery in Glen Brittle, including some unforgettable views of the Cuillin Mountains. Note: these are not for the casual walker, due to steep and dangerous cliff faces. The drive from Carbost along a single-track road (follow signs off the B8009) is one of the most dramatic in Scotland and draws outdoorsy types from across the globe. At the southern end of the glen, around 4 miles beyond the Fairy Pools, is one of Britain's most scenic campsites, overlooking a beautiful, dog-friendly beach and flanked by gentle foothills that were made for strolling. ✉ *Off A863 and B8009.*

Talisker Distillery

DISTILLERY | It may no longer be the only distillery on the Isle of Skye (since the opening of Torabhaig Distillery in 2017), but it remains one of the best in Scotland. Talisker produces a sweet, light, single malt that has the distinctive peaty aroma of island whiskies, yet with less intensity—making it a great introductory dram for newcomers to Scotch. Robert Louis Stevenson called Talisker "the king of drinks," and the inhabitants of Skye are very proud of it. Classic tours here take about 45 minutes, while tasting tours (available weekdays) take between 90 and 120 minutes. Book ahead, as tours are very popular. ✉ *B8009, Carbost* ☎ *01478/614308* 🌐 *www.malts.com* 🎟 *Tours from £10.*

Isle of Raasay

17 miles northeast of Glenbrittle.

This beautiful and rugged isle lies a few miles off Skye's east coast and offers a pleasant escape from its tourist hordes. Although only 10 miles long, it's home to some fine coastal walks, a brooding castle ruin, and an up-and-coming distillery.

GETTING HERE AND AROUND

There are regular ferries to Raasay from Sconser on Skye (on the A87, roughly halfway between Broadford and Portree) every day of the week, all year-round.

👁 Sights

Calum's Road

STREET | An extraordinary feat of human endeavor, this single-track, 2-mile road was conceived and constructed by one man—local crofter Calum MacLeod. Following several failed petitions to the local council, requesting them to improve access to northern Raasay by transforming a narrow footpath into a usable road, MacLeod decided to take matters into his own hands. Using only a pick-axe, shovel, and wheelbarrow, he began laying the road in 1964. Ten years later it was finally complete. The road would later be officially adopted and surfaced by the council and named "Calum's Road" in MacLeod's honor. It begins just beyond the atmospheric, 16th-century ruins of Brochel Castle on the northeast coast of Raasay, and it ends at Arnish. ✉ *Near Brochel, Isle of Raasay.*

🛏 Hotels

★ Isle of Raasay Distillery

$$$ | **HOTEL** | As well as being Raasay's first legal distillery, which released its first single-malt Scotch in 2021, this stunning building—a modern glass-and-steel structure wrapped around a Victorian-era villa—also happens to be the island's most luxurious place to stay. **Pros:** breathtaking views of Skye; chic minimalist design; comfy lounge with honesty bar. **Cons:** a little pricey in summer; some rooms are small; no dinner (try nearby Raasay House). [$] *Rooms from: £225* ✉ *Borodale House, Isle of Raasay* ☎ *01478/470178* 🌐 *raasaydistillery.com* 🕒 *Closed Nov.–Feb.* 🛏 *6 rooms* 🍴 *Free Breakfast.*

The Outer Hebrides

ATLANTIC OCEAN

FLANNAN ISLES

0   20 mi

0   20 km

Butt of Lewis Lighthouse

Port of Ness

Barvas

The Blackhouse
Gearrannan
Blackhouse Village

Arnol

Carloway and Callanish

Dalbeg

Dun Carloway Broch

Aird Uig

Breaclete

Timsgarry

A866

Carnish

Calanais
Standing Stones

Stornoway

Giosla

Archmore

ISLE OF LEWIS

Baile Ailein

The Minch

FERRY TO ULLAPOOL

Aribruach

Cliasmol

Traig Luskentyre

Tarbert

Losgdintir

Seilebost

ISLE OF HARRIS

← **St. Kilda**

Seallam! Visitor Centre
and Co Leis Thu Genealogical Research Centre

Northton

Leverburgh

Roghadal

Brusda

St. Clement's Church

Dun an
Sticar

Eilean Siar

Balranald
Nature Reserve

Lochmaddy

Staffin

Waternish Point

North Uist

Uig

A855

Cairinis

Taigh
Chearsabhagh

Barpa
Langass

Hallin

MONACH ISLANDS

A87

BENBECULA

Dunvegan

ISLE OF RAASAY

RONA

Ardmore

Ramasaig

Caroy

ISLE OF SKYE

Portree

Applecross

Our Lady
of the Isles

Struan

Inner Sound

South Uist

Idrigill Point

A87

Kildonan Museum

Broadford

Daliburgh

Lochbaghasdail

Sea of the Hebrides

Elgol

Isleornsay

Eriskay

CANNA

Cuillin Sound

Tarskavaig

ERISKAY

Armadale

Borve

BARRA

Castlebay

ISLE OF RUM

SANDRAY

PEBBAY

MINGULAY

BERNERAY

FERRY TO
OBAN

Little Minch

Ferry

Isle of Lewis

50 miles from Ullapool via ferry.

The history of Lewis stretches back 5,000 years, as archaeological sites scattered across the island attest. Here, the Highland past persists in the Gaelic that is spoken everywhere, and most of its inhabitants still bear clan names. The main town on Lewis is Stornoway.

GETTING HERE AND AROUND

Three main routes radiate from Stornoway to give access to the rest of the island. The A859 leads south all the way to Harris; the A857 leads north to Port of Ness, the island's northernmost point (an early diversion onto the B895 takes you to stunning Traigh Mhòr beach); and the A858 leads west, looping up and round to meet the A857 near Brue.

Stornoway

2¾-hour ferry trip from Ullapool.

The port capital for the Outer Hebrides is Stornoway, the only major town on Lewis. As the island's cultural center, it has a few interesting attractions and makes a good base for exploring. Watch for seals bobbing about in the harbor.

GETTING HERE AND AROUND

The ferry docks at Stornoway terminal, and there's an airport within easy reach of the center. It's best to have a car to explore the island, but there are also infrequent local buses to attractions including the Calanais Standing Stones and the Blackhouse at Arnol.

AIRPORT CONTACTS

Stornoway Airport. ⊠ *A866, Stornoway* ☎ *01851/702256* ⊕ *www.hial.co.uk.*

VISITOR INFORMATION

VisitScotland Stornoway iCentre
⊠ *26 Cromwell St., Stornoway* ☎ *01851/703088* ⊕ *www.visitscotland. com.*

◉ Sights

An Lanntair

ARTS CENTER | This fabulous arts center hosts exhibitions of contemporary and traditional art and frequent traditional musical and theatrical events in the impressive auditorium. There's also a cinema, a gift shop, and a café-bar serving coffee and snacks alongside fine international and Scottish fare. ⊠ *Kenneth St., Stornoway* ☎ *01851/708480* ⊕ *lanntair. com* ☉ *Closed Sun. and Mon.*

Lews Castle

CASTLE/PALACE | This Victorian-era castle—well, neo-Gothic country house—houses the free Museum nan Eilean, with fascinating exhibitions on life in the Outer Hebrides, from the landscape to the language. It also displays six of the famous Lewis Chessmen, intricate 12th-century chess pieces carved from walrus ivory (the rest are in Edinburgh's National Museum of Scotland and London's British Museum). Take a stroll around the castle grounds, with its pleasant mix of woodland, parkland, and gardens overlooking Stornoway harbor. ⊠ *Stornoway* ☎ *01625/416430* ⊕ *www.lews-castle. co.uk* ☉ *Museum closed Sun.*

🛏 Hotels

Broad Bay House

$$$ | B&B/INN | It may be a little out of town, but the view alone makes Broad Bay House a worthwhile detour—and it's a bonus that the hotel is also meticulously designed and constructed. **Pros:** close to beautiful Traigh Mhòr beach; stunning sea views; delicious evening meals (when available). **Cons:** expensive for the area; 7 miles outside Stornoway; no kids under 12. $ *Rooms from: £205* ⊠ *B895, Stornoway* ☎ *01851/820390* ⊕ *www. broadbayhouse.co.uk* ☉ *Closed Nov.–Mar.* ⤴ *4 rooms* ᵀᵒ¹ *Free Breakfast.*

Port of Ness

27 miles north of Stornoway.

The stark, windswept community of Port of Ness cradles a small harbor squeezed in among the rocks.

GETTING HERE AND AROUND

From Stornoway, simply drive up the A857 or take bus W1.

 Sights

Butt of Lewis Lighthouse

LIGHTHOUSE | At the northernmost point of Lewis, 3 miles northwest of Port of Ness, stands the Butt of Lewis Lighthouse, which was first illuminated in 1862. Designed by David and Thomas Stevenson, it's one of many Scottish lighthouses built by the prominent Stevenson engineering family, whose best-known member was not an engineer at all but novelist Robert Louis Stevenson. The adjacent cliffs provide a good vantage point for viewing seabirds, whales, and porpoises. ⊠ *Off A857, Port of Ness* ⊕ *www.nlb.org.uk.*

💼 Shopping

★ Borgh Pottery

CERAMICS | Pick up a range of attractive ceramics, including lamps, vases, and bowls, all hand-thrown on the premises by studio potter Sue Blair. There's also a lovely little garden for visitors to enjoy. Borgh Pottery is 9 miles southwest of Port of Ness, on the road from Stornoway. ⊠ *Fivepenny House, Off A857, Borve* ☎ *01851/850345* ⊕ *www.borghpottery.co.uk* ⊗ *Closed Sun. and Mon.*

Carloway and Callanish

16 miles west of Stornoway.

The old crofting town of Carloway is surrounded by historic sights that give real insight into island life, including the mysterious arrangement of ancient stones at Callanish, the island's top attraction.

GETTING HERE AND AROUND

Travel west on the A858 and then Pentland Road to reach Carloway directly. To get here via Callanish, follow the A858 all the way. You can also include Arnol by taking the A858 all the way to Barvas, then joining the A857 south back to Stornoway. The W2 bus from Stornoway does the full loop (both directions) with stops at Carloway, Callanish, and Arnol.

👁 Sights

★ The Blackhouse

MUSEUM VILLAGE | In the small community of Arnol, the Blackhouse is a well-preserved example of an increasingly rare type of traditional Hebridean home. Common throughout the islands as recently as the mid-20th century, these dwellings were built without mortar and thatched on a timber framework without eaves. Other characteristic features include an open central peat hearth and the absence of a chimney (hence "blackhouse," from all the soot). Inside, you'll find half the house designated for family life, complete with many original furnishings, and the other half a stable for animals. Opposite is the White House, built later when houses were no longer allowed to accommodate humans and animals together. ⊠ *Off A858, Arnol* ☎ *01851/710395* ⊕ *www.historicenvironment.scot* ⊠ *£6* ⊗ *Closed Sun. Also closed Wed. in Oct.–Mar.*

★ Calanais Standing Stones

(*Callanish Stones*)

RUINS | The west coast of Lewis is rich in prehistoric sites, and the most famous of these is the Calanais Standing Stones. Believed to have been positioned in several stages between 3000 BC and 1500 BC, this arrangement consists of an avenue of 19 monoliths extending northward from a circle of 13 stones, with other rows leading south, east, and

At Gearrannan Blackhouse Village, you can experience traditional Scottish crofting life via the many blackhouses scattered throughout the living museum.

west. Ruins of a cairn sit within the circle on the east side. Researchers believe they may have been used for astronomical observations, but you're free to cook up your own theories. The visitor center has an interesting exhibit on the stones, a very pleasant tearoom, and a gift shop. ⊠ *Callanish* ☎ *01851/621422* ⊕ *www.historicenvironment.scot.*

Dun Carloway Broch (*Doune Broch*) **RUINS** | Discover one of the country's best-preserved Iron Age *brochs* (circular stone towers). These fortified residences are exclusive to Scotland, and Dun Carloway Broch dominates the scattered community of the same name. The mysterious tower was probably built around 2,000 years ago as protection against seaborne raiders. The nearby visitor center explains all about the broch, its history, and its setting. ⊠ *Off A858, Carloway* ⊕ *www.historicenvironment.scot.*

Gearrannan Blackhouse Village (*Garenin*) **MUSEUM VILLAGE** | Situated at the end of a side road north from Carloway, Gearrannan is an old coastal crofting village

that has been brought back to life as a living museum with excellent guided tours evoking its past. You can stay in one of the restored blackhouses here if you want a unique (if no-frills) stay; it's £20 a night for a hostel bunk or £65 for a family room. There is also a small gift shop and café. ⊠ *5a Gearrannan, Carloway* ☎ *01851/643416* ⊕ *www.gearrannan.com.*

Isle of Harris

16 miles southwest of Stornoway.

For most people, Harris is forever linked to tweed. The fabric woven here and on nearby islands has colors that echo the tones of the landscape. The dramatic mountains of the northern part of Harris give way in the south to *machairs*, grassy plains typical of this region, and a series of spectacular sandy beaches.

GETTING HERE AND AROUND
The A859 heads south from Stornoway and becomes the main artery through Harris. From Tarbert, follow the A859

south to Leverburgh (21 miles), where you can take a boat to St. Kilda or a ferry to North Uist. The single-track road down the east coast of South Harris is known as the Golden Road.

Tarbert

45 miles south of Carloway, 36 miles southwest of Stornoway.

The main port of Harris has some good shops and a few worthwhile sights. Traigh Luskentyre, roughly 5 miles southwest of Tarbert, is a spectacular example of a Harris beach—2 miles of pristine white sand flanked by dunes. Across the bay lies another beautiful beach, Traigh Seilebost; both of these would be crowded with vacationers if in warmer climes. The narrow Golden Road, which runs along the east coast of South Harris, offers some glorious views of a rocky, otherworldly landscape.

GETTING HERE AND AROUND

The ferry from Uig on the Isle of Skye arrives at Tarbert once or twice daily. Having a car makes travel on Harris much easier, but with careful planning and plenty of patience, it's possible to see the area with local buses.

Sights

★ Isle of Harris Distillery

DISTILLERY | Opened in 2015, this island distillery rapidly gained a reputation for its distinctive gin, infused with coastal botanicals including sugar kelp. Its first malt whisky, called The Hearach (the Gaelic term for an inhabitant of Harris), is currently maturing in bourbon barrels. The distillery conducts guided tours (£10) every weekday from March to October—call to book in advance. ✉ *Tarbert* ☎ *01859/502212* 🌐 *harrisdistillery.com* 🎟 *Free; tours £10.*

Beaches

★ Traigh Luskentyre

BEACH | One of Scotland's most spectacular beaches, Traigh Luskentyre is flanked by rolling sand dunes on one side and the shimmering sea on the other. Add in the distant peaks, the lush grassland, and the rocky islets, and there are few better places on Lewis and Harris for a windswept walk. To reach the beach, drive 8 miles south of Tarbert on the A859, then turn right at the sign to "Losgaintir" (Gaelic for Luskentyre). **Amenities:** parking (no fee); toilets. **Best for:** solitude; sunset; walking. ✉ *Off A859, Tarbert.*

Restaurants

Skoon Art Café

$ | **CAFÉ** | This renovated croft house café, which is tucked just off the twisting Golden Road running south from Tarbert to Leverburgh, has a simple, delicious menu that changes daily. It serves everything from filling house-made soups to sumptuous smoked salmon to mouthwatering cakes. **Known for:** wonderfully remote; simple but delicious fare; good tea and coffee. [$] *Average main: £8* ✉ *4 Geocrab Tarbert* ☎ *01859/530268* 🌐 *www.skoon.com* 💳 *No credit cards* 🕒 *Closed Sun. and Mon. No dinner.*

Hotels

Hotel Hebrides

$$ | **HOTEL** | A welcoming hotel with lovely gardens and views across the loch and harbor, Hotel Hebrides is an oasis of luxury in unassuming Tarbert. **Pros:** parking on the street right outside; wonderful location; comfortable bedrooms. **Cons:** noise from the bar can drift up; sea view not guaranteed; some rooms are small. [$] *Rooms from: £180* ✉ *Pier Rd., Tarbert* ☎ *01859/502364* 🌐 *www.hotel-hebrides.com* 🔑 *21 rooms* 🍴 *Free Breakfast.*

The Isle of Harris is home to many spectacular landscapes, like this one with St. Clement's Church in the distance.

Scarista House
$$$ | **HOTEL** | This lovingly converted Georgian manse (minister's residence) offers large and comfortable bedrooms; a peaceful location with spectacular views over a pristine, 3-mile, sandy beach; and a dining experience that's unmatched on Harris. **Pros:** friendly and attentive service; magnificent setting and views; delicious food (try the *tarte tatin*). **Cons:** very expensive for Harris; some oppressively floral wallpaper; minimum two-night stay. *Rooms from: £245* ✉ *Off A859, Borve* ☎ *01859/550238* 🌐 *scaristahouse.com* *6 rooms* 🍴 *Free Breakfast.*

Shopping

Essence of Harris
COSMETICS | This popular pierside store specializes in candles, bath products, and reed diffusers with wonderful fragrances inspired by the island. The black pomegranate Seilebost hand and body lotion is particularly popular. ✉ *The Pier, Tarbert* ☎ *01859/502768* 🌐 *essenceofharris.co.uk* *Closed Sun.–Tues.*

Leverburgh

18 miles southwest of Tarbert.

Named after Lord Leverhulme, who bought Lewis and Harris in 1917 with an eye to developing its local industries, Leverburgh is now the departure and arrival port for North Uist ferries, as well as day-tripping boats to St. Kilda. Nearby Northton and Rodel have several attractions, with St. Clement's Church a particular highlight.

GETTING HERE AND AROUND

From Tarbert, simply take the A859 south around the west coast. Or, for a longer and more dramatic drive, follow the Golden Road down the east coast.

Sights

Seallam! Visitor Centre and Co Leis Thu Genealogical Research Centre
VISITOR CENTER | Learn more about life in the Western Isles and trace your Hebridean ancestry at this informative

visitor center. Photographs and interpretive signs reveal the long and turbulent history of Harris and its residents, with the owners organizing guided walks and cultural evenings every week between May and September. ✉ *Off A859, Northton* 🕾 *01859/520258* ⊕ *www.hebridespeople.com* 🎫 *£3* ⊘ *Closed weekends in summer and Sat.–Tues. in winter.*

★ **St. Clement's Church** (*Eaglais Roghadail*)
RELIGIOUS BUILDING | At the southernmost point of Harris, in the village of Rodel 3 miles southeast of Leverburgh, lies St. Clement's Church—the most impressive pre-Reformation House of God in the Outer Hebrides. The large cruciform church, which sits atop a small hillock, was built around 1500. Head inside to see the magnificently sculpted 16th-century wall tomb of the church's builder, clan chief Alasdair Crotach MacLeod of Dunvegan Castle. ✉ *A859, Rodel* ⊕ *www.historicenvironment.scot.*

🍴 Restaurants

Anchorage Restaurant
$$ | **MODERN BRITISH** | Along the southern coast of Harris, looking across the Sea of Hebrides toward North Uist, this lively restaurant is a great place to grab a bite before hopping aboard the ferry. It's open unusually late for the islands, which makes it something of a refuge, and its menu ranges from burgers, sandwiches, and fish-and-chips to quality local seafood. **Known for:** handy harborside location; cheap and tasty dishes; open until fairly late. 💲 *Average main: £18* ✉ *The Pier, Ferry Rd., Leverburgh* 🕾 *01859/520225* ⊕ *www.anchoragerestaurant.co.uk* ⊘ *Closed Sun. and Mon.*

St. Kilda

57 miles west of Leverburgh.

The most distant corner of the British Isles, this archipelago of five islands has double World Heritage status, recognized for both its natural and cultural significance. The natural highlights are immediately obvious, with Eiffel Tower–sized cliffs, colossal sea stacks, and soaring seabirds in abundance. Make the most of main island Hirta's natural highlights with a hike to Ruival in the south of the island, or to Conachair (the island's highest point) in the north. The human impact is more subtle yet equally captivating, with hillside *cleits* (stone storage huts) and a 19th-century village offering insight into the lives of the people who, until recently, called this inhospitable environment home.

GETTING HERE AND AROUND
You can get to Hirta, St. Kilda's main island, on a private tour boat from Leverburgh on Harris or from Stein on Skye. Tours are operated by Kilda Cruises (⊕ *www.kildacruises.co.uk*) and Sea Harris (⊕ *www.seaharris.com*) from Harris, and by Go to St. Kilda (⊕ *www.gotostkilda.co.uk*) from Skye.

TOURS
Kilda Cruises
BOAT TOURS | This popular tour operator organizes day trips to St. Kilda on Monday, Wednesday, and Friday; the days in between are standbys, in case of bad weather. Tours leave from Leverburgh on Harris and include 4½ hours ashore on Hirta island, as well as a cruise around the archipelago's dizzyingly high cliffs and sea stacks. ✉ *Pier Rd., Tarbert* 🕾 *01859/502060* ⊕ *www.kildacruises.co.uk* 🎫 *£245* ⊘ *No sailing Sun.*

Sights

★ St. Kilda Village

TOWN | This crumbling, wind-ravaged village is the last remnant of the community that lived on Hirta for thousands of years. For most of that time, the St. Kildans lived in utter isolation, with the abundant birdlife providing the bulk of their diet. But, in the 1830s, visiting missionary Reverend Neil Mackenzie decided to improve living conditions on the island and raised funds for the construction of this street of Hebridean blackhouses, along with a church, manse (minister's residence), and school. Today, visitors to St. Kilda can walk in and around the village buildings, with one house containing an informative museum telling the incredible story of island life through pottery, textiles, and photographs. ⊕ *www.nts.org.uk.*

North Uist

7 miles southwest of Leverburgh.

Stunning coastal scenery and ancient ruins are the main draws on North Uist. There are lochs everywhere you look, and a surprising number of public artworks, too—from the ends of roads, to the top of hills, to the edge of the coast.

GETTING HERE AND AROUND

You can get to North Uist by ferry from Leverburgh on Harris and from Uig on the Isle of Skye, or you can drive from South Uist and Benbecula on the A865. Public transport is infrequent, so a car (or a bike) is the most reliable way to get around.

Sights

Balranald Nature Reserve

NATURE PRESERVE | Run by the Royal Society for the Protection of Birds (RSPB), the Balranald Nature Reserve shelters large numbers of waders and seabirds that inhabit the rock foreshore and marshland.

Listen for corncrakes, whose distinctive rasping cry sounds not unlike a plastic drink lid being unscrewed. ⊠ *RSPB Balranald, Hougharry* ☎ *01876/560422* ⊕ *www.rspb.org.uk.*

Barpa Langass

RUINS | Dating back around 5,000 years, Barpa Langass is a chambered cairn (a Neolithic burial monument), the only one in the Western Isles to retain a fully intact inner chamber. You can peek inside, but don't venture too far without a light. You'll find Barpa Langass just off the A867, two-thirds of the way between Lochmaddy and Clachan. ⊠ *Off A687, Lochmaddy.*

Dun an Sticir

RUINS | Near Port nan Long in the very north of North Uist stands the remains of Dun an Sticir, reputed to have been the last inhabited broch on the island. This defensive tower, reached by a causeway over the loch, was built in the Iron Age but abandoned when the Vikings arrived in the 9th century. In 1602, it was reoccupied by Hugh Macdonald, a descendant of Macdonald of Sleat, but since he reached an unpleasant end (starved to death in a castle dungeon on the Isle of Skye), it has been slowly crumbling into the sea. ⊠ *Off B893.*

Taigh Chearsabhagh

ARTS CENTER | Set right on the shore in Lochmaddy, the well-run Taigh Chears-abhagh is an informative museum and arts center, complete with two exhibition spaces, a working printshop, and a permanent exhibition that reveals what life is really like on North Uist. The café serves a selection of cakes and soup, as well as excellent French-press coffee. ⊠ *Lochmaddy* ☎ *01870/603970* ⊕ *www. taigh-chearsabhagh.org* 🖃 *£3 museum; galleries free* ⊗ *Closed Sun.*

South Uist

*12 miles south of Carinish (on North
Uist) via Grimsay, Benbecula, and three
causeways.*

Carpets of wildflowers in spring and early
summer, superb deserted beaches, and
historical connections to Flora Macdonald
and Bonnie Prince Charlie head the list of
reasons to visit this island.

GETTING HERE AND AROUND

You can travel the length of South Uist
along the A865; most of the main attractions are on (or very close to) this main
road. At Lochboisdale in the southeast of
South Uist, you can catch ferries to Barra,
the southernmost of the Outer Hebrides'
main islands, or to Oban on the mainland.

◉ Sights

Kildonan Museum

HISTORY MUSEUM | This small museum
has a number of interesting artifacts
related to the Uists and their people. The
small details, like how locals filled their
mattresses or the names for the tools
they used in their houses, are what make
this place interesting. There is also a craft
shop and an excellent café renowned for
its filled baked potatoes and house-made
cakes. ⊠ *A865, Kildonan* ☎ *01878/710343*
⊕ *kildonanmuseum.co.uk* ⊠ *£3* ⊗ *Closed
Nov.–Mar.*

Our Lady of the Isles

PUBLIC ART | This 30-foot-high granite stat-
ue of the Madonna and child is a symbol
of island resistance. In the 1950s, the
Ministry of Defense proposed building a
missile-testing facility on South Uist, but
islanders opposed the plans, fearing it
would destroy their way of life, culture,
and language. So they raised the funds
for this ambitious work of art and erected
it on land earmarked for development by
the MOD. Today, it is a listed monument,
making any future building proposals
even less likely to succeed. ⊠ *Off A865.*

🛏 Hotels

Polochar Inn

$ | **B&B/INN** | Set within a 300-year-old
property, this secluded inn at the southern end of South Uist offers basic but
pleasant rooms with sea views, as well
as a good seafood restaurant. **Pros:** free
and reliable Wi-Fi; reasonable rates; good
food and drink. **Cons:** a little old-fashioned; remote location; some small
rooms. Ⓢ *Rooms from: £99* ⊠ *Off B888,
Lochboisdale* ☎ *01878/700215* ⊕ *www.
polocharinn.com* ⤴ *11 rooms* ❘⊙❘ *Free
Breakfast.*

🛍 Shopping

Hebridean Jewellery

JEWELRY & WATCHES | Handcrafted,
Celtic-influenced, silver or gold earrings,
brooches, and pendants are the order of
the day at Hebridean Jewellery. Come
for a tour of the workshop, and stay for
an espresso and cake in the on-site café.
⊠ *Bualadubh, Iochdar* ☎ *01870/610288*
⊕ *www.hebrideanjewellery.co.uk*
⊗ *Closed Sun.*

Chapter 12

ORKNEY AND SHETLAND ISLANDS

12

Updated by
Robin Gauldie

⊙ Sights	🍴 Restaurants	🛏 Hotels	🛍 Shopping	🍸 Nightlife
★★★☆☆	★☆☆☆☆	★★☆☆☆	★★☆☆☆	★☆☆☆☆

WELCOME TO ORKNEY AND SHETLAND ISLANDS

TOP REASONS TO GO

★ **Ancient sites:** Among the many Neolithic treasures in Orkney are the Ring of Brodgar, a 3,000-year old circle of standing stones, and Skara Brae, the remarkable remains of a village uncovered on the grounds of delightful Skaill House.

★ **Music and arts festivals:** The Shetland Folk Festival in late April–early May is a fiddling shindig that attracts musicians and revelers from around the world. Orkney's St. Magnus International Festival is a more highbrow celebration of classical music, poetry, and performance.

★ **Seabirds, seals, and more:** These islands have some of the planet's most important colonies of seabirds, with millions clinging to colossal cliffs. You're guaranteed to see seals and may spot dolphins, orcas, or porpoises.

★ **Outdoor activities:** The rugged terrain, beautiful beaches, and unspoiled waters make a perfect backdrop for invigorating strolls, sea fishing, diving, or exploring the coastline and sea lochs by boat.

Ten miles from Caithness in Scotland, Orkney is made up of 70 islands, of which 10 are inhabited. A number of ferries travel to ports on the Mainland, the main island of Orkney, including its administrative center, Kirkwall, where an airport serves Scotland's larger cities. The primary road is essentially a loop that passes near the key historic sites. The Mainland is linked to the southern island of South Ronaldsay by way of the Barricades.

About 125 miles north of Orkney lies the spiny outline of Shetland, comprising 100 islands. Sumburgh has the main airport, and 25 miles north is Lerwick, the island's "capital" and a port linking the island to Scotland and Orkney. South Mainland, half an hour from Lerwick, has prehistoric sites. Less than an hour north of Lerwick are dramatic landscapes such as Eshaness. Ferries go beyond the Mainland to Yell and Unst, the latter Britain's most northerly point.

1 Stromness and the Neolithic Sites. Home to some important and very ancient sites.

2 Birsay. A tiny village with Iron Age, Norse, and Pictish ruins.

3 Kirkwall. Orkney's charming capital.

4 Scapa Flow Visitor Centre. Where you can explore the role of this area in two world wars.

5 Lerwick. A handsome Shetland harbor town.

6 The South Mainland. A region of Shetland littered with prehistoric treasures.

7 Scalloway. The original capital of Shetland.

8 Weisdale. A tiny hamlet with an interesting art gallery.

9 Brae. A thriving modern village surrounded by rugged landscapes.

10 Yell. A peaceful isle covered with boggy moorland.

11 Unst. Scotland's most northerly inhabited island.

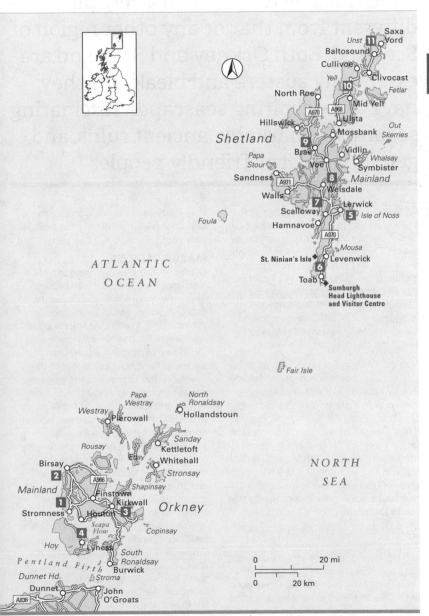

Saxa
Vord
Unst **11**
Baltosound
Cullivoe
Clivocast
Yell **10** *Fetlar*
North Roe
A970
A968
Mid Yell
Hillswick
Ulsta
*Out
Skerries*
Shetland
Mossbank
9
Brae
Vidlin
Whalsay
*Papa
Stour*
Voe
Symbister
Sandness
A971
8
Mainland
Walls
Weisdale
7
Lerwick
Foula
Scalloway
5 *Isle of Noss*
Hamnavoe
A970
Mousa
St. Ninian's Isle ◆
Levenwick
6
Toab
**Sumburgh
Head Lighthouse
and Visitor Centre**

**ATLANTIC
OCEAN**

⌖ *Fair Isle*

*Papa
Westray*
*North
Ronaldsay*
Westray
Pierowall
Hollandstoun
Rousay
Sanday
Kettletoft
Eday
Whitehall
Stronsay
Birsay
**NORTH

SEA**
2
A966
Shapinsay
Mainland
Finstown
Stromness
1
Houton
Kirkwall
Orkney
3
*Scapa
Flow*
Copinsay
4
Hoy
Lyness
*South
Ronaldsay*
Pentland Firth
Burwick
Dunnet Hd.
Stroma
Dunnet
A836
John
O'Groats

0 ———————— 20 mi
0 ———————— 20 km

A Scandinavian heritage gives the 170 islets that make up Orkney and Shetland a history and an atmosphere different from that of any other region of Scotland. Both Orkney and Shetland are essentially austere and bleak, but they have awe-inspiring seascapes, fascinating seabirds, remarkable ancient ruins, and genuinely warm, friendly people.

An Orcadian has been defined as a crofter (farmer) with a boat, whereas a Shetlander has been called a fisherman with a croft. Orkney, the southern archipelago, is greener and is rich with artifacts that testify to the many centuries of continuous settlement here: stone circles, burial chambers, ancient settlements, and fortifications. UNESCO has recognized the key remains as a World Heritage site called the Heart of Neolithic Orkney.

North of Orkney, Shetland, with its ocean views and sparse landscapes—trees are a rarity because of ever-present wind—seems even more remote. But don't let Shetland's desolate countryside fool you: it has a wealth of historic interest and is far from being a backwater. Oil money from local mineral resources and its position as a crossroads in the northern seas for centuries have helped make Shetland a busy, thriving community that wants for little.

For mainland Scots, visiting these islands is a little like traveling abroad without having to worry about a different language or currency. Neither has yet been overrun by tourism, but the people of Orkney and Shetland will be delighted that you have come so far to see their islands and learn a little of their extraordinary past.

MAJOR REGIONS

Orkney. If you're touring the north of Scotland, the short boat trip to Orkney offers the chance to step outside the Scottish history you've experienced on the mainland. Prehistoric sites such as the Ring of Brodgar, and the remnants of Orkney's Viking-influenced past, are in dramatic contrast to that of the mainland. The Orkney Islands may have a population of just 20,000, but a visit reveals the islands' cultural richness. In addition Orkney's continued reliance on farming and fishing reminds you how some things can stay the same despite technological advances. At Maeshowe, for example, it becomes evident that graffiti is not solely an expression of today's youths: the Vikings left their marks here way back in the 12th century. The towns of Stromness and Kirkwall have sights and museums testifying to Orkney's rich past, including Kirkwall's Norman St. Magnus Cathedral. For many people though, they're a prelude to impressive Neolithic sites around the Mainland: Maeshowe, Skara Brae, the

Ring of Brodgar, and others. Beyond the Mainland, explore sights such as the Scapa Flow Visitor Centre on Hoy, which reveals the strategic role of the islands in both world wars.

■ TIP→ **You can purchase the Historic Scotland Orkney Explorer Pass joint-entry ticket (£18) at the first site you visit; the ticket costs less than paying separately for entry into each site.**

Shetland. A descent at Sumburgh's airport provides stunning views of a shining white lighthouse, bird-crammed cliffs, and golden bays. The Shetland coastline is an incredible 900 miles because of the rugged geology and many inlets; there isn't a point on the islands farther than 3 miles from the sea. Lerwick is the prima-ry town, but the population of 22,000 is scattered across the 15 inhabited islands. Lerwick has the excellent Shetland Museum, and nearby on the South Main-land are the prehistoric sites of Jarlshof, Old Scatness, and Mousa Broch. Worth exploring to the north are the lunarlike Ronas Hill and wave-lashed Eshaness. Unst, the island farthest north, is worth the journey for wide-open ocean views and superb bird-watching at Hermaness National Nature Reserve. Wherever your interest, you'll see and hear an island that buzzes with music, life, and history.

Planning

When to Go

Although shivering, wind-flattened visitors braving Orkney and Shetland's winter are not unheard of, the travel season doesn't really start until May, and it runs until September. June is one of the most popular months for both islands. The bird colonies are at their liveliest in early summer, which is also when the long northern daylight hours allow you plenty of sightseeing time.

Shetland's northerly position means that it has only four or five hours of darkness around the summer solstice, and on a clear night it doesn't seem to get dark at all. Beware the changeable weather even in summer: it could be 75°F one day and then hail the next. Many sights close in September, and by October wilder gales will be mixed with snow flurries one min-ute and glorious sunshine the next. If you are determined to brave the elements, take into account that there are only six hours of daylight in winter months. More important, there can be thick mist and high winds at Sumburgh and Kirkwall airports even in July, meaning flights can-not take off for days, although they will put you on the Northlink boat if there's space. Bear this in mind when planning flight connections.

Shetland's festival of fire, Up Helly Aa, is held the last Tuesday of each January. The spectacle of Lerwick overrun by Vikings, with torches aflame and a huge Viking longship, is wildly popular. Book at least a year in advance if you want to get a bed for the night.

FESTIVALS
Orkney Blues
MUSIC FESTIVALS | This eclectic three-day festival normally held around the last weekend in September is billed as the most northerly blues event in the United Kingdom, attracting leading rhythm and blues performers from all over the world. It takes place in hotel bars and pubs around Stromness, and all the concerts, except the grand finale event, are free. ✉ *Stromness* ⊕ *www.orkneyblues.co.uk.*

Orkney Folk Festival
MUSIC FESTIVALS | This four-day festival held in and around Stromness in late May attracts musicians of all ages from Ork-ney's own vibrant folk music scene and from as far away as Canada, Latin Amer-ica, Africa, and the Caribbean. ✉ *Ferry Terminal, Stromness* ☎ *01856/851331* ⊕ *www.orkneyfolkfestival.com.*

Shetland Accordion and Fiddle Festival

MUSIC FESTIVALS | This busy five-day event in early October is one of the biggest fixtures on Shetland's cultural calendar, with concerts by celebrated local fiddlers, squeezebox players, and visiting musicians at venues all over the islands. ✉ *Shetland Accordion and Fiddle Club, 21 Twageos Rd., Lerwick* ☎ *01595/693162* ⊕ *www.shetlandaccordionandfiddle.com.*

Shetland Folk Festival

MUSIC FESTIVALS | Shetland fiddlers are legends in the folk music world, keeping the musical traditions of the islands alive when such folkways had all but died out in the rest of Scotland. Musicians and music fans from all over the world gather for four days and nights of foot-tapping tunes at venues in Lerwick and all over Shetland, normally during the last weekend in April. ✉ *Islesburgh Community Centre, King Harald St., Lerwick* ☎ *01595/694757* ⊕ *www.shetlandfolkfestival.com.*

★ St. Magnus International Festival

FESTIVALS | Usually held in the third week of June, Kirkwall's St. Magnus International Festival is a world-class celebration of classical music, opera, chamber music, ensemble and solo performances, dance, and drama, performed in inspiring venues including St. Magnus Cathedral. ☎ *01856/871445* ⊕ *www.stmagnusfestival.com.*

Up Helly Aa Festival

FESTIVALS | On the last Tuesday in January, Shetlanders celebrate their Norse heritage by dressing as Vikings, parading through the streets with flaming torches, and then burning a replica of a Viking galley. This is naturally followed by extensive feasting, carousing, and dancing. ✉ *The Galley Shed, St. Sunniva St., Lerwick* ⊕ *www.uphellyaa.org.*

Planning Your Time

Orkney and Shetland require at least a couple of days each if you're to do more than just scratch the surface. The isles generate their own laid-back approach to life, and once here, you may want to take it slowly.

A good clutch of the key sights of Mainland Orkney can be seen in a day, if you have a car and are disciplined, but to really get the most out of them, take two days. You can do the Kirkwall sights in a morning before heading to the Italian Chapel on South Ronaldsay in the afternoon. This allows a whole day for Stomness, a town caught in the most poignant of time warps, and the archaeological sites of Maeshowe, the Ring of Brodgar, Skara Brae and Skaill House, and Gurness Broch. To include Birsay, plan your day round the tides.

Since getting to Shetland isn't easy, you may want to spend three or four days here. The sights on the South Mainland—Jarlshof, Old Scatness, the Shetland Crofthouse Museum, St. Ninian's Isle, and Mousa Broch—take the best part of a day, although sailing times for Mousa must be factored into your schedule. Lerwick, with its lanes and spectacular museum, is a good day, and can be supplemented with a trip to the Bonhoga Gallery in Weisdale. It's a good idea to take a whole day to explore the north of the islands, including Eshaness and Tangwick Haa, although a car or a guide who drives will be necessary. Ferry times allow for a mad dash round the northern islands of Yell and Unst, but you will see more if you book an overnight stay.

Getting Here and Around

AIR

Loganair flies to Sumburgh in Shetland and to Kirkwall in Orkney from Edinburgh, Glasgow, Aberdeen, Inverness, and Manchester. Tickets are very expensive. Loganair also flies to the outer islands of Eday, North Ronaldsay, Sanday, Stronsay, Westray, and Papa Westray. The flight between Westray and Papa Westray, which takes two minutes, is claimed to be the world's shortest scheduled passenger flight. Airtask flies to Fair Isle, Foula, the Outer Skerries, and Papa Stour from Lerwick.

AIRLINE CONTACTS Airtask.
☎ 01595/840246 ⊕ www.airtask.com. **Loganair.** ☎ 0344/800–2855 ⊕ www. loganair.co.uk.

BOAT AND FERRY

For those willing to travel the slow way, Northlink operates ferries—locally known as "the boat"—from Aberdeen to Kirkwall in Orkney and Lerwick in Shetland. These leave Aberdeen Harbor each evening (or every second night for Kirkwall), arriving at Kirkwall at 11 pm and Lerwick at 7:30 am the next day. These services have reclining seats for the budget traveler, pods for those wanting more comfort, and clean, compact cabins in single, double, or four-berth combinations. There's a shop, a cinema, two bars, and two restaurants (one self-service and one table service) on each boat.

If you're arriving in Aberdeen on Sunday morning and plan on meeting a train, note that the station does not open until 8 am. Northlink allows you to stay in your cabin or the restaurant until 9:30 am.

An alternate way of reaching Orkney is the Northlink ferry from Scrabster to Stromness. There is also a ferry from John O'Groats to Burwick, operated by John O'Groats Ferries, with up to three daily departures May through September. The fastest and smoothest sail is by

catamaran from Gills Bay, Caithness, to St. Margaret's Hope on Orkney. Operated by Pentland Ferries, it has three daily departures.

In both Orkney and Shetland, the local council runs the interisland ferry networks (Orkney Ferries and Shetland Island Ferries) to the outer islands. Northlink Ferries has service between Lerwick on Shetland and Kirkwall on Orkney.

■ TIP→ These are lifeline services, so not just for visitors; always book ferry tickets in advance.

FERRY CONTACTS John O'Groats Ferries.
☎ 01955/611353 ⊕ www.jogferry.co.uk. **Northlink Ferries.** ☎ 0845/600–0449 ⊕ www.northlinkferries.co.uk. **Orkney Ferries.** ☎ 01856/872044 ⊕ www.orkneyferries.co.uk. **Pentland Ferries.** ☎ 0800/688–8998 ⊕ www.pentlandferries.co.uk. **Shetland Island Ferries.** ☎ 01595/745804 for Unst, Fetlar, Yell, Whalsay, Skerries, and Papa Stour, 01595/760363 for Fair Isle ⊕ www.shetland.gov.uk/ferries.

BUS

John O'Groats Ferries operates the Orkney Bus, a direct express coach from Inverness to Kirkwall (via ferry) that runs daily from June to early September, making a day trip to Orkney a definite—if hurried—possibility.

The main bus service on Orkney is operated by Stagecoach and on Shetland by ZetTrans (although buses are run by small operators).

BUS CONTACTS John O'Groats Ferries.
☎ 01955/611353 ⊕ www.jogferry. co.uk. **Stagecoach.** ☎ 01856/878014 ⊕ www.stagecoachbus.com. **ZetTrans.** ☎ 01595/744868 ⊕ www.zettrans.org.uk.

CAR

The most convenient way of getting around these islands is by car, especially if your time is limited. Roads are well maintained and traffic is nearly nonexistent, although speeding cars can be a problem. Orkney has causeways—the

Barricades—connecting some of the islands, but in some cases these roads take fairly roundabout routes.

You can transport your rental car from Aberdeen, but for fewer than five days it's usually cheaper to rent a car from one of Shetland and Orkney's agencies. Most are based in Lerwick, Shetland, and Kirkwall, Orkney, but airport pickups are easily arranged.

LOCAL CAR RENTAL CONTACTS Bolts Car and Minibus Hire. ✉ *26 North Rd., Lerwick* ☎ *01595/693636* ⊕ *www.boltscarhire. co.uk.* **Orkney Car Hire.** ✉ *Junction Rd., Kirkwall* ☎ *01856/872866* ⊕ *www.orkney-carhire.co.uk.* **Star Rent-a-Car.** ✉ *22 Commercial Rd., Lerwick* ☎ *01595/692075 Lerwick, 01950/460444 Sumburgh Airport* ⊕ *www.starrentacar.co.uk.* **W. R. Tullock.** ✉ *Castle Garage, Castle St., Kirkwall* ☎ *01856/875500* ⊕ *www.wrtullock. com.*

TRAIN
There are no trains on Orkney or Shetland, but you can take the train to Aberdeen or Thurso and then take a ferry to the islands.

TRAIN CONTACTS ScotRail. ☎ *0871/2002233* ⊕ *www.scotrail.co.uk.*

Restaurants

Kirkwall has an increasing number of good cafés and restaurants, as does Lerwick, but both islands now have memorable spots beyond the main towns, from cafés and fish-and-chips spots to some fancier restaurants. Orkney and Shetland have first-class seafood, and in pastoral Orkney the beef is lauded and in Shetland the heather- or seaweed-fed lamb. Orkney is famous for its cheese and its fudge; a glug of its Highland Park malt whisky or some Skull Splitter Ale is also worth trying. Shetlanders are also now brewing their own and make much of their natural edible resources of seaweed-fed lamb and mussels, while

making ice cream and smoking fish in a variety of ways. Some bakeries create their own version of bannocks—a scone-type baked item you eat with salt beef, mutton, or jam—but Johnson and Wood (otherwise known as the Voe bakery), available in shops across the islands, takes the biscuit.

Hotels

Accommodations in Orkney and Shetland are on par with mainland Scotland, with a growing range of stylish bed-and-breakfasts that might suit some travelers better than the bigger hotels that rely on, and therefore focus on, business customers, which in Shetland—with the oil and the building of a major gas plant—are many. Although standards are improving, the islands still do not offer luxury accommodations. To experience a simpler stay, check out the unique "camping *böds*" in Shetland—old cottages providing inexpensive, basic lodging (log fires, cold water, and sometimes no electricity). For details, contact the Shetland Tourist Information Centre.

Restaurant and hotel reviews have been shortened. For full information, visit Fodors.com. Restaurant prices are the average cost of a main course at dinner or, if dinner is not served, at lunch. Hotel prices are the lowest cost of a standard double room in high season, including 20% V.A.T.

WHAT IT COSTS in Pounds			
$	$$	$$$	$$$$
RESTAURANTS			
under £15	£15–£19	£20–£25	over £25
HOTELS			
under £125	£125–£200	£201–£300	over £300

Tours

★ Island Trails

GUIDED TOURS | Local tour guide and crofter James Tait offers tours steeped in the social history of Shetland, giving you a lively account, and no doubt many an introduction, to Shetland and its people. Opt for a guided tour around St. Ninian's Isle or a bespoke day's tour of the island. ☎ *01950/950228* ⊕ *www.island-trails. co.uk* ✉ *From £25.*

Shetland Nature

SPECIAL-INTEREST TOURS | Here you'll find richly informed tours that cover a lot of ground while quietly tracking Shetland's otters, birds, and the unique wildflowers of the islands. Photographers are specially catered to. ☎ *01595/760212* ⊕ *www. shetlandnature.net* ✉ *From £120.*

Wildabout Orkney

GUIDED TOURS | Well-organized and informative tours, including Treasures of Orkney and Megalithic Masterpieces, run daily April to September. ☎ *01856/877737* ⊕ *www.wildaboutorkney.com* ✉ *From £59.*

Visitor Information

The official Visit Scotland visitor information centers in Kirkwall and Lerwick are open year-round. The visitor information websites, provided by the Orkney Islands Council and Shetland Islands Council, are helpful online sources.

CONTACTS Visit Orkney. ✉ *W. Castle St.* ☎ *01856/872856* ⊕ *www.orkney.com.* **Visit Shetland.** ☎ *01595/693434* ⊕ *www. shetland.org.*

Stromness and the Neolithic Sites

1¾ hrs north of Thurso on Scotland's mainland, via ferry from Scrabster.

On the southwest of the Mainland, on the shore of the old Norse anchorage Hamnavoe, is Stromness, a remarkably attractive fishing town seemingly so unsullied by modernity that it evokes an uncomplicated way of life long gone. Walk past the old-fashioned shops and austere cottages that line the main street and you'll understand why local poet and novelist George Mackay Brown (1921–96) was inspired and moved by its sober beauty.

With its ferry connection to Scrabster in Caithness, Stromness makes a good base for visiting the western parts of Orkney, and the town holds several points of interest. It was once a key trading port for the Hudson's Bay Company, and the Stromness Museum displays artifacts from those days. Nearby are three spectacular ancient sites, the Ring of Brodgar, Maeshowe, and Skara Brae at Skaill House.

GETTING HERE AND AROUND

Stromness is at the end of the A965 and can be reached by one of the many buses from Kirkwall.

Stagecoach Buses 7 and 8S link Kirkwall, the Ring of Brodgar, and Skara Brae and Skaill House with Kirkwall. Altogether there are three bus services there and three back per day except Sunday, so plan accordingly.

👁 Sights

Maeshowe

RUINS | The huge burial mound of Maeshowe, circa 2500 BC, measures 115 feet in diameter and contains an enormous burial chamber. It was raided by Vikings in the 12th century, and Norse crusaders found shelter here, leaving a rich collection of runic inscriptions. Outside you see a large, grassy mound; the stunning interior of the chambered tomb has remarkably sophisticated stonework. This site is 6 miles northeast of Stromness and 1 mile from the Ring of Brodgar. The site is open for guided tours only, which start at the visitor center at Stenness. Due to COVID-19 restrictions, the chambered tomb may remain closed through 2023; call ahead or check the website before visiting to confirm. ✉ *A965, Stromness* ☎ *01856/851266* ⊕ *www.historicenvironment.scot* 🎫 *£9.*

★ Pier Arts Centre

ARTS CENTER | At the striking Pier Arts Centre, a gallery in a former merchant's house and adjoining buildings, huge sheets of glass offer tranquil harborside views and combine with space-maximizing design to make the best use of every shard of natural light and inch of wall to display the superb permanent collection. The more than 100 20th- and 21st-century paintings and sculptures include works by Barbara Hepworth and Douglas Gordon, and edgy temporary exhibitions showcase international contemporary artists such as Damien Hirst. A chic shop sells design products and art books. ✉ *28–30 Victoria St., Stromness* ☎ *01856/850209* ⊕ *www.pierartscentre. com* 🎫 *Free* ⊘ *Closed Sun. and Mon.*

★ Ring of Brodgar

RUINS | About 5 miles northeast of Stromness, the Ring of Brodgar is a magnificent circle of 36 Neolithic standing stones (originally 60) surrounded by a henge, or deep ditch. When the fog descends over the stones—a frequent occurrence—their looming shapes seem to come alive. The site dates to between 2500 and 2000 BC. Though the original use of the circle is uncertain, it's not hard to imagine strange rituals taking place here in the misty past. The stones stand between Loch of Harray and Loch of Stenness. ✉ *B9055, Stromness* ☎ *01856/841815* ⊕ *www.historicenvironment.scot* 🎫 *Free.*

★ Skara Brae and Skaill House

RUINS | After a fierce storm in 1850, the laird of Breckness, William Graham Watt, discovered this cluster of Neolithic houses at the bottom of his garden. The houses, first occupied around 3000 BC and containing stone beds, fireplaces, dressers, and cupboards, are the most extensive of their kind in northern Europe and provide real insight into this ancient civilization. A reconstruction of one house can be seen in the visitor center, which displays artifacts from the site and hosts an excellent café. Skara Brae stands on the grounds of **Skaill House,** a splendid, intriguing mansion built by the Bishop of Orkney in the 1600s. His descendants, the lairds of Breckness, along with the various ladies of the manor, added to the house and to the eclectic furnishings. These sites offer a joint ticket in summer months that's well worth the price: the juxtaposition of different societies thousands of years apart that shared the same corner of Orkney makes a fascinating visit. ✉ *B9056, Sandwick, Stromness* ✛ *8 miles north of Stromness* ☎ *01856/841815* ⊕ *www.historicenvironment.scot* 🎫 *Skara Brae £7, Skara Brae and Skaill House £9* ⊘ *Skaill House closed Nov.–Mar.*

★ Stromness Museum

HISTORY MUSEUM | **FAMILY** | The enchanting Stromness Museum has the feel of some grand Victorian's private collection but has, in fact, been community owned since it opened in 1837. Its crammed but utterly fascinating exhibits on fishing, shipping, and whaling are full of interesting trinkets

The stone circles that make up the Ring of Brodgar are part of the Heart of Neolithic Orkney, a UNESCO World Heritage Site.

from all over the world that found their way to this small Orcadian town because of its connections with the Hudson's Bay Shipping Company. The company recruited workers in Stromness between the late 18th and 19th century as they were considered more sober and therefore more reliable than other Scots. Also here are model ships and displays on the German fleet that was scuttled on Scapa Flow in 1919. Upstairs don't miss the beguiling, traditionally presented collection of birds and butterflies native to the British Isles. ✉ *52 Alfred St., Stromness* ☎ *01856/850025* 🌐 *www.stromnessmuseum.org.uk* 🎟 *£5 (allows as many visits as you like within a week)* 🕒 *Closed Sun. Nov.–Mar.*

🍴 Restaurants

★ Julia's Café Bistro

$ | **CAFÉ** | Right on the quayside, this casual spot serves the cakes that make you forget about calories. Expect huge slices of lemon drizzle, coffee layer, raspberry cream, and other cakes, as well as scones and traybakes (cakes baked in pans and cut up). **Known for:** vibrant decor and sunny harbor views; Orkney crab sandwiches; full Scottish breakfasts. [$] *Average main: £8* ✉ *20 Ferry Rd., Stromness* ☎ *01856/850484* 🌐 *www.juliascafe.co.uk* 🕒 *No dinner.*

🛏 Hotels

Ferry Inn

$ | **HOTEL** | This traditional inn with rooms and a restaurant is handy for the ferry and other transport links for Orkney's sights. **Pros:** handy location for ferry; good restaurant; friendly pub. **Cons:** uninspired decor; can get very busy; no elevator. [$] *Rooms from: £110* ✉ *10 John St., Stromness* ☎ *01856/850280* 🌐 *www.ferryinn.com* 🕒 *Closed Nov.–Apr.* 🛏 *20 rooms* 🍽 *Free Breakfast.*

Merkister Hotel

$$ | **HOTEL** | Popular with anglers, this family-run hotel overlooks the gentle lap of Loch Harray—its experienced *ghillies* (guides) know the choicest spots and provide instruction for novices.

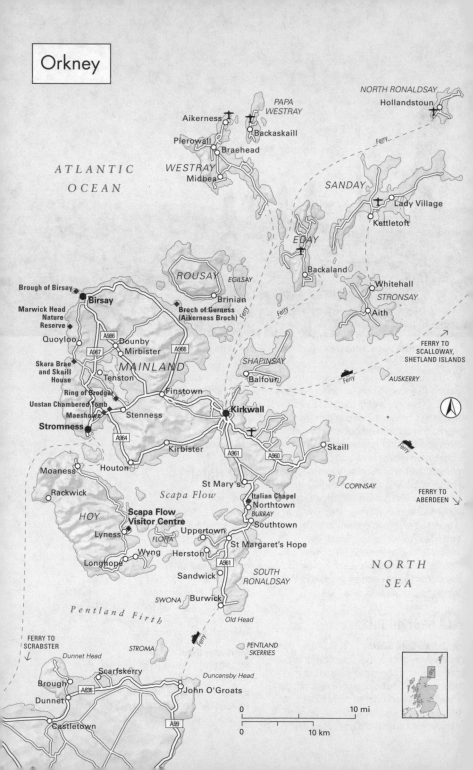

Pros: fishing experts; endless coffee in the lounge and library; notable restaurant. **Cons:** bar can get crowded; dated decor; some small rooms. $ *Rooms from: £140* ✉ *A965, Harray, Birsay* ☎ *01856/771366* ⊕ *www.merkister.com* ⇌ *16 rooms* �‖ *Free Breakfast.*

★ **Mill of Eyrland**

$ | **B&B/INN** | White-painted stone walls, country antiques, and the rippling sound of a stream running beneath the windows make for an evocative stay at this former mill dating from 1861. **Pros:** notable breakfasts and packed lunches; the old grinding stones are a stunning focal point in the lounge; beautiful views out to Scapa Flow. **Cons:** 25% nonrefundable deposit required for all bookings; breakfast is served at one big table, so be prepared to socialize; difficult to find. $ *Rooms from: £90* ✉ *Off A964, Stenness* ☎ *01856/850136* ⊕ *www.millofeyrland.co.uk* ⇌ *4 rooms* �‖ *Free Breakfast.*

🏃 Activities

The cool, clear waters of Scapa Flow and eight sunken ships that were part of Germany's fleet during World War I make for an unparalleled diving experience. Several companies organize trips to Scapa Flow—including shore and offshore dives among the Churchill Barriers—and other nearby dive sites.

Birsay

12 miles north of Stromness, 25 miles northwest of Kirkwall.

Birsay itself is a small collection of houses, but some interesting historic and natural sights are nearby.

GETTING HERE AND AROUND

The village is on A966; a car is the easiest way to see the nearby sights.

👁 Sights

Broch of Gurness (Aikerness Broch)

RUINS | An Iron Age tower built between 500 BC and 200 BC, the Broch of Gurness stands more than 10 feet high and is surrounded by stone huts, indicating that this was a village. The tower's foundations and dimensions suggest that it was one of the biggest brochs in Scotland, and the remains of the surrounding houses are well preserved. ✉ *A966, Birsay* ⊹ *8 miles east of Birsay* ☎ *01856/751414* ⊕ *www.historicenvironment.scot* ✉ *Free* ⊗ *Closed Oct.–Mar.*

Brough of Birsay

RUINS | A Romanesque church can be seen at the Brough of Birsay, a tidal island with the remains of an early Pictish and then Norse settlement. (*Brough* is another word for "fort.") The collection of roofless stone structures on the tiny island, close to Birsay, is accessible only at low tide by means of a concrete path that winds across the seaweed-strewn bay. The path is slippery, so boots are essential. To ensure you won't be swept away, check the tides with the tourism office in Kirkwall or Stromness before setting out. ■**TIP**➔ **The cliffs at the far side of the island are stunning but be very careful as you look for puffins.** ✉ *A966, Birsay* ☎ *01856/841815* ⊕ *www.historicenvironment.scot* ✉ *£6* ⊗ *Closed Oct.–mid-Jun.*

Marwick Head Nature Reserve

NATURE PRESERVE | The Royal Society for the Protection of Birds tends the remote Marwick Head Nature Reserve, where in spring and summer the cliffs are draped in wildflowers such as campion and thrift, and resound with thousands of nesting seabirds including cormorants, kittiwakes, and guillemots. The Kitchener Memorial, recalling the 1916 sinking of the cruiser HMS *Hampshire* with Lord Kitchener aboard, sits atop a cliff. Access to the reserve, which is unstaffed, is along a path north from Marwick Bay.

✉ Off B9056, Birsay ✈ 4 miles south of Birsay ☎ 01856/850176 ⊕ www.rspb.org.uk ✆ Free, donations welcome.

Kirkwall

16 miles east of Stromness.

In bustling Kirkwall, the main town on Orkney, there's plenty to see in the narrow, winding streets extending from the harbor. The cathedral and some museums are highlights.

GETTING HERE AND AROUND

Kirkwall is a ferry port and also near Orkney's main airport. Its sights are all near one another, though visitors to the Highland Park Distillery might want to hop on the T11 Kirkwall Circular or get a taxi (about £7).

CRUISE

The larger cruise ships drop anchor at the Hatston Pier just outside Kirkwall and passengers are bused into town. Smaller cruise ships come alongside Kirkwall Pier or Stromness, both of which are within walking distance of the town centers.

The cruise-ship operators organize bus tours for their passengers, but you can go it alone and join one of Wildabout Orkney's tours specifically designed for passengers coming ashore: its Treasures of Orkney tour is an excellent all-rounder.

Alternatively, you can hire a small car for a day and easily see the main Neolithic, megalithic, and wartime sites. A rental car costs approximately £50 for the day, plus fuel, making it an affordable option.

ESSENTIALS

VISITOR INFORMATION Kirkwall Visitor Information Centre. ✉ *Travel Centre, W. Castle St., Kirkwall* ☎ *01856/872856* ⊕ *www.visitscotland.com.*

◉ Sights

Bishop's and Earl's Palaces

CASTLE/PALACE | The Bishop's Palace dates to the 12th century when St. Magnus Cathedral was built. In 1253 this was the site of King Hakon IV of Norway's death, marking the end of Norwegian rule over Sudreyjar (the Southern Hebrides). It was rebuilt in the late 15th century, and a round tower was added in the 16th century. The nearby Earl's Palace was built in 1607 for Earl Patrick Stewart, the much despised Earl of Orkney and Shetland who bound the people of both into terrible, inescapable poverty. While his name is still mud, his Orcadian residence is considered one of the finest examples of Renaissance architecture in Scotland. The great hall with its magnificent fireplace may be a ruin, but it evokes the splendor of its age. ✉ *Palace Rd., Kirkwall* ☎ *01856/871918* ⊕ *www.historicenvironment.scot* ✆ *£6* ⊗ *Closed Oct.–Mar.*

★ Highland Park Distillery

DISTILLERY | Having come this far, you'll have earned a dram of the local single malt at one of Scotland's northernmost distilleries. It was founded around the turn of the 19th century by Magnus Eunson, a church officer who dabbled in illicit stilling. The Viking Soul tour is highly recommended and takes you through the essential aspects of this near-sacred process, from the ingredients to the hand-turning of the malt, the peating in the peat kilns, the mashing, and finally the maturation in oak casks. This smoky, peaty malt can be purchased all over Orkney, as well as from the distillery's austere shop. ✉ *Holm Rd., Kirkwall* ☎ *01856/885604* ⊕ *www.highlandpark-whisky.com* ✆ *Tours from £30* ⊗ *Closed weekends Oct.–Mar.*

★ Italian Chapel

CHURCH | During World War II, 550 Italian prisoners of war were captured in North Africa and sent to Orkney to assist with the building of the Churchill Barriers, four causeways that blocked entry into Scapa Flow, Orkney's great natural harbor. Using two corrugated-iron Nissan huts, the prisoners, led by Domenico Chiocchetti, a painter-decorator from the Dolomites, constructed this beautiful and inspiring chapel in memory of their homeland. The elaborate interior frescoes were adorned with whatever came to hand, including bits of metal, colorful stones, and leftover paints. ⊠ *A961, Kirkwall ✦ 7 miles south of Kirkwall* ☎ *01856/781580* ⊕ *www.facebook.com/ italianchapelorkney* 🎫 *£3.50.*

Orkney Museum

HISTORY MUSEUM | FAMILY | With artifacts from the Picts, the Vikings, and other ancient peoples, this museum—the former townhouse of the prosperous Bakie family of Tankerness—has the entire history of Orkney crammed into a rabbit warren of rooms. It's not easily accessible for those with disabilities, but with the help of staff, can be done. The setup may be old-fashioned, but some artifacts—especially those from everyday Orcadian life in the 19th century—are riveting. Lovely gardens around the back provide a spot to recoup after a history lesson. ⊠ *Broad St., Kirkwall* ☎ *01856/873191* ⊕ *www.orkney.gov.uk* 🎫 *Free* ⊘ *Closed Sun.*

Orkney Wireless Museum

OTHER MUSEUM | Vintage radio buffs will find this oddball museum fascinating. Amassed by the late Jim MacDonald, a radio operator during World War II, it tells the story of wartime communications at Scapa Flow, where thousands of service members were stationed; they used the equipment displayed to protect the Home Fleet. Run by volunteers, the museum also contains many handsome 1930s wireless radios and examples of the handicrafts produced by Italian prisoners of war. ⊠ *Kiln Corner, Junction Rd., Kirkwall* ☎ *01856/871400* ⊕ *www.gb2owm.org.uk* 🎫 *£3* ⊘ *Closed Oct.–Mar.*

St. Magnus Cathedral

CHURCH | Founded by the Norse earl Jarl Rognvald in 1137 and named for his uncle, this grand red-and-yellow-sandstone cathedral was mostly finished by 1200, although more work was carried out during the following 300 years. The cathedral is still in use and contains some fine examples of Norman architecture, although traces of later styles are found here and there. The ornamentation on some of the tombstones in the church is particularly striking. At the far end to the left is the tomb of the tragically discredited Dr. John Rae, the Victorian-era Orcadian adventurer and unsung hero who discovered the final section of the Northwest Passage in Canada but was decried for his reporting that the British men of the Franklin expedition, overwhelmed by starvation, had resorted to cannibalism: an assertion that has since been proved true. ⊠ *Broad St., Kirkwall* ☎ *01856/873312* ⊕ *www.stmagnus.org* 🎫 *Free* ⊘ *Closed Fri. and Sat. Oct.–Mar.*

Unstan Chambered Tomb

RUINS | This intriguing burial chamber lies within a 5,000-year-old cairn. Excavations here uncovered a collection of similarly designed pottery bowls, subsequently found in other Orcadian Neolithic tombs. Access to the tomb by trolley can be awkward for those with mobility problems. ⊠ *A964, Kirkwall ✦ 7½ miles west of Kirkwall* ☎ *01856/841815* ⊕ *www. historicenvironment.scot* 🎫 *Free.*

🍴 Restaurants

★ Lucano

$$ | ITALIAN | FAMILY | This modern trattoria-style Italian restaurant has been taken to the heart of Orcadians, and rightly so, as it delivers an abundant menu of good Italian food. From pizza to classic pasta dishes—with fulsomely meaty carbonara and Bolognese and very tasty vegetarian *burro e salvia* (butter and sage) and pesto—to excellent *secondi piatti* such as chicken in rosemary, it's got something for every appetite. **Known for:** ice-cream pudding for dessert; healthy choice of classic Italian dishes; pizza Lucano with tomato, mushrooms, olives, peppers, and Parma ham. $ *Average main: £17* ✉ *31–33 Victoria St., Kirkwall* ☎ *01856/875687* ⊕ *www.lucanokirkwall.co.uk.*

🛏 Hotels

Ayre Hotel
$$$ | HOTEL | This large, functional hotel by the harbor offers ample accommodation choices—including a wing of nine spacious, self-catering apartments—plus a good bar-restaurant. **Pros:** location near the harbor; great for families and groups; some rooms have great sea views. **Cons:** used by tour groups often; feels like a chain hotel; uninspiring parking lot views from some rooms. $ *Rooms from: £245* ✉ *Ayre Rd., Kirkwall* ☎ *01856/873001* ⊕ *www.ayrehotel.co.uk* ⮑ *60 rooms* ⦿ *Free Breakfast.*

Foveran Hotel
$$ | HOTEL | About 34 acres of grounds surround this modern, ranch-style hotel overlooking Scapa Flow, about 3 miles southwest of Kirkwall. **Pros:** food that's cooked to perfection; great views across Scapa Flow; super helpful management. **Cons:** simple decor; you must book the popular restaurant ahead of time; minimal staffing during the day. $ *Rooms from: £130* ✉ *Off A964, Kirkwall* ☎ *01856/872389* ⊕ *www.thefoveran.com* ⮑ *8 rooms* ⦿ *Free Breakfast.*

West End Hotel
$ | B&B/INN | Built in 1824 by a retired sea captain, the West End Hotel once served as Kirkwall's first hospital and is now a small, affably run hotel. **Pros:** on-site restaurant and beer garden; great location; friendly owners. **Cons:** basic furnishings; some rooms are small; no tubs, just showers. $ *Rooms from: £120* ✉ *Main St., Kirkwall* ☎ *01856/872368* ⊕ *www.westendkirkwall.co.uk* ⮑ *10 rooms* ⦿ *Free Breakfast.*

🛍 Shopping

Beyond its famed silversmiths, Orkney's others crafts, from textiles to furniture making to ceramics, have been given a boost by the Orkney Craft Trail (⊕ *www.orkneydesignercrafts.com*), which encourages customers with an interest in these crafts to go straight to the makers, visit their workshops, and buy direct. If you don't have time to do the trail, some of these wares can be found in Kirkwall shops, along with specialty foods and books particular to Orkney and its history.

Judith Glue
CRAFTS | Not only can you purchase designer knitwear with traditional patterns, as well as handmade crafts and hampers of local produce at Judith Glue, the shop is also home to the Orkney Real Food Café. ✉ *25 Broad St., Kirkwall* ☎ *01856/874225* ⊕ *www.judithglue.com.*

The Longship
JEWELRY & WATCHES | Don't miss this eclectic shop, open since the 19th century, which sells a huge array of Ola Gorrie's original designs in gold and silver jewelry with Celtic and Norse themes. It also stocks knitwear, under-the-radar designer clothes labels, and quirky housewares. Its wineshop in the courtyard has a large selection, plus locally brewed craft beers and quality deli staples from Italy. ✉ *11 Broad St., Kirkwall* ☎ *01856/888790* ⊕ *www.thelongship.co.uk.*

🏃 Activities

Largely flat and with lovely stretches of quiet road, Orkney is the perfect place for cycling, so long as you pack waterproof gear and can deal with the wind in your face as well as your hair. The Visit Orkney tourist information office has information on interesting routes. The brown-trout-filled lochs of Orkney have all the makings of a spectacular day's fishing. Visit ⊕ *www.orkneytroutfishing.co.uk* for the lowdown on the lochs and how to fish them.

BIKING
Cycle Orkney
BIKING | For £25 a day bicycles can be rented from Cycle Orkney, which is open year-round. For less energetic visitors, Cycle Orkney also rents e-bikes for £35 a day. ✉ *Tankerness La., Kirkwall* ☎ *01856/875777* ⊕ *www.cycleorkney.com.*

FISHING
Merkister Hotel
FISHING | The Merkister Hotel, on Loch Harray, arranges fishing trips. All your equipment, including boats, is available to rent, and ghillies provide instruction. ✉ *A965, Harray, Birsay* ☎ *01856/771366* ⊕ *www.merkister.com.*

Scapa Flow Visitor Centre

On Hoy, 14 miles southwest of Kirkwall, 6 miles south of Stromness.

On the beautiful island of Hoy, Scapa Flow Visitor Centre explores the strategic and dramatic role that this sheltered anchorage played in two world wars.

GETTING HERE AND AROUND
The car ferry from Houton (7 miles east of Stromness) takes 25 minutes to reach Lyness on Hoy and the visitor center. The ferry costs around £28 round-trip for a regular-size car and £8.80 round-trip per passenger.

ESSENTIALS
FERRY CONTACTS Orkney Ferries.
☎ *01856/872044* ⊕ *www.orkneyferries.co.uk.*

◉ Sights
Scapa Flow Visitor Centre
VISITOR CENTER | Military history buffs will appreciate the Scapa Flow Visitor Centre, which displays military vehicles and guns from both world wars. You'll also find equipment salvaged from the German boats scuttled off the coast. In the plain but poignant graveyard here, British and German personnel both rest in peace. If you want to take your car over to Hoy, book well in advance with Orkney Ferries, as this is a popular route. The visitor center is a short walk from the ferry terminal on the island of Hoy. ✉ *Off B9047, Lyness* ☎ *01856/791300* ⊕ *www.scapaflow.co.uk* 🎫 *Free* ⊗ *Closed Nov.–Feb. and weekends in Mar., Apr., and Oct.*

Lerwick

14 hrs by ferry from Aberdeen.

Founded by Dutch fishermen in the 17th century, Lerwick today is a busy town and administrative center. Handsome stone buildings—known as lodberries—line the old harbor; they provided loading bays for goods, some of them illegal. The town's twisting flagstone lanes once heaved with activity, and Lerwick is still an active port today. This is also where most visitors to Shetland dock, spilling out of cruise ships to walk around the town.

GETTING HERE AND AROUND
The town center of Lerwick is 1 mile south of Holmsgarth, the terminal for the ferry from Aberdeen. You can take a bus from Holmsgarth to the center or to the bus station for travel to Sumburgh or Scalloway. Car rentals can be arranged to meet you at the ferry terminal. Lerwick is small and compact, and the bus network, overseen by ZetTrans, offers hourly bus service around town.

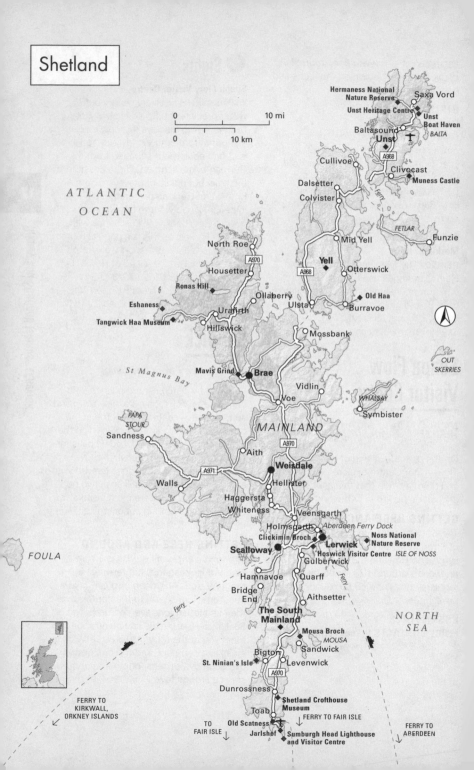

Shetland

ATLANTIC OCEAN

Hermaness National Nature Reserve
Saxa Vord
Unst Heritage Centre
Unst Boat Haven
Baltasound
Unst
BALTA
A968
Clivocast
Muness Castle
Cullivoe
Dalsetter
Colvister
FETLAR
Mid Yell
Funzie
Yell
A968
Otterswick
North Roe
A970
Housetter
Ronas Hill
Ollaberry
Ulsta
Old Haa
Eshaness
Urafirth
Burravoe
Tangwick Haa Museum
Hillswick
Mossbank
Mavis Grind
Brae
St Magnus Bay
Vidlin
Voe
WHALSAY
PAPA STOUR
MAINLAND
Symbister
OUT SKERRIES
Sandness
Aith
A970
Weisdale
Walls
Hellister
Haggersta
Whiteness
Veensgarth
FOULA
Holmsgarth
Aberdeen Ferry Dock
Clickimin Broch
Noss National Nature Reserve
Scalloway
Lerwick
Hoswick Visitor Centre
ISLE OF NOSS
Gulberwick
Hamnavoe
Quarff
Bridge End
Aithsetter
NORTH SEA
The South Mainland
Mousa Broch
MOUSA
Bigton
Sandwick
St. Ninian's Isle
Levenwick
A970
Dunrossness
Shetland Crofthouse Museum
FERRY TO KIRKWALL, ORKNEY ISLANDS
Toab
Old Scatness
FERRY TO FAIR ISLE
TO FAIR ISLE
Jarlshof
Sumburgh Head Lighthouse and Visitor Centre
FERRY TO ABERDEEN

0   10 mi
0   10 km

CRUISE

Larger cruise ships moor in Bressay Sound with a tender bringing passengers ashore to Victoria Pier. Although this pier is occupied by oil industry accommodation barges, smaller ships moor at Holmsgarth, the Ferry Terminal, a 15-minute walk or short bus ride to Lerwick center.

The cruise-ship operators organize bus tours for their passengers, but the more independently minded can prearrange a tour guide, such as Island Tours or Shetland Nature. They will pick you up and take you to the places you want to see. Prices are around £250 for a bespoke daylong tour for two persons, but check websites for available places on day tours (prices from £60 per person).

Alternatively, you can jump on the Airport Bus and head straight to Jarlshof (45 minutes, every 90 minutes, £2.90 each way) or rent a small car for a day, which costs approximately £55 plus fuel, making it an affordable option.

ESSENTIALS

TRANSPORTATION CONTACTS Boddam Cabs. ☎ *01950/460111* ⊕ *www.boddam-cabs.co.uk.*

VISITOR INFORMATION Lerwick Visitor iCentre. ⊠ *Market Cross, Lerwick* ☎ *01595/693434* ⊕ *www.shetland.org.*

◉ Sights

★ Clickimin Broch

MILITARY SIGHT | A stone tower on the site of what was originally an Iron Age fortification, Clickimin Broch makes a good introduction to these mysterious buildings. It was possibly intended as a place of retreat and protection in the event of attack. South of the broch are vivid views of the cliffs at the south end of the island of Bressay, which shelters Lerwick Harbor. ⊠ *Off A970, Lerwick* ✛ *1 mile south of Lerwick* ⊕ *www.historicenvironment.scot* ☞ *Free.*

Fort Charlotte

MILITARY SIGHT | This artillery fort was built in 1665 to protect the Sound of Bressay from the invading Dutch. They seized it in 1673 and razed the fort to the ground. They were soon chased out of Shetland and the fort was rebuilt in 1781. ⊠ *Market St., Lerwick* ⊕ *www.historicenvironment.scot* ☞ *Free.*

★ Mareel

ARTS CENTER | Next to the Shetland Museum, the bold and beautiful—although somewhat brutal around the back—Mareel is Shetland's adventurous and ambitious arts center. It has a live performance space attracting national and international musicians, two cinemas showing art-house and mainstream films, and a café and bar area that showcases local crafts, acoustic musicians, and some very drinkable Shetland beers. ⊠ *North Ness, Lerwick* ☎ *01595/745500* ⊕ *www.mareel.org.*

Noss National Nature Reserve

NATURE PRESERVE | The island of Noss (which means "nose" in old Norse) rises to a point called the Noup. The smell and noise of the birds that live on the vertiginous cliffs can assault the senses. Residents nest in orderly fashion: black-and-white guillemots (45,000 pairs) and razorbills at the bottom; gulls, gannets, cormorants, and kittiwake in the middle; fulmars and puffins at the top. If you get too close to their chicks, some will dive-bomb from above. To get here, take a ferry from Lerwick to Bressay, then (weather permitting) an inflatable boat to Noss. It's a four- to five-hour walk around the reserve, so allow plenty of time if the walk is the draw. Mid-May to mid-July is the best time to view breeding birds. No matter when you visit, be sure to wear waterproof clothing and sensible shoes. ⊠ *Noss* ☎ *01595/693345* ⊕ *www.nature.scot* ☞ *Free* ☉ *Visitor center and inflatable ferry closed Sept.–Apr.*

★ Shetland Museum

HISTORY MUSEUM | FAMILY | On the last remaining stretch of the old waterfront at the restored Hay's Dock, the striking Shetland Museum, with its sail-like tower, is the area's cultural hub and a stimulating introduction to local history. The two-story space is filled with displays about archaeology, textiles, and contemporary arts. Standout exhibits include depictions of the minutiae of everyday Shetland life across the centuries, the last remaining *sixareen* (a kind of fishing boat), and the collection of lace shawls donated by Shetland families. Its informal spaces make this a wonderful place to hang out; look for vintage vessels moored in the dock and seals that pop up to observe everyone at the glass-fronted café-restaurant terrace. The museum shop is a must-visit, with a beautiful selection of nicely priced postcards and useful things inspired by the museum's collection. ✉ *Hay's Dock, Commercial Rd., Lerwick* ☎ *01595/695057* 🌐 *www.shetlandmuseumandarchives.org.uk* 🎫 *Free.*

🍴 Restaurants

★ Fjarå

$$ | CAFÉ | Sitting on rocks on the ebb (or *fjara* in Faroese) of Brewick Bay, the views from this large wood-and-glass house allow you to look at otters and seals between courses. The menu is very simple: big breakfasts, coffees, and cake—including an array of gluten-free items—soup and huge salads, as well as Shetland mussels or fish-and-chips for lunch. **Known for:** handmade burgers; delicious local lamb; gorgeous views. [$] *Average main: £16* ✉ *Sea Rd., Lerwick* ☎ *01595/697388* 🌐 *www.fjaracoffee.com.*

★ The Peerie Shop Cafe

$ | CAFÉ | Who would believe you could get such good cappuccino at 60 degrees north? In back of the popular Lerwick knitwear shop is a modish, consistently good café that sells filled sponge cakes, lip-smackingly good soups, and, yes, the best coffee on the islands. **Known for:** crowds of locals; excellent coffee; full Scottish breakfast. [$] *Average main: £6* ✉ *Esplanade, Lerwick* ☎ *01595/692817* 🌐 *www.peerieshop.co.uk* 🕒 *Closed Sun. No dinner.*

🛏 Hotels

Alder Lodge Guest House

$ | B&B/INN | Occupying a bank building dating from the 1830s, this family-run guesthouse sits on a quiet street within easy reach of Lerwick's shops, pubs, and harbor. **Pros:** charming patio; comfortable beds; superb location. **Cons:** bedrooms rather basic; dull motel-style exterior; booked solid in the summer months. [$] *Rooms from: £80* ✉ *8 Clairmont Pl., Lerwick* ☎ *01595/695705* 🔑 *10 rooms* 🍽 *Free Breakfast.*

Kveldsro House Hotel

$$ | B&B/INN | Tucked away behind the town's main thoroughfare is this unfussy small hotel with comfortable, if rather expensive, rooms. **Pros:** excellent staff; minutes from the city center; cheery bar. **Cons:** expensive for what it offers; noise from the bar in some rooms; slightly pretentious decor scheme. [$] *Rooms from: £185* ✉ *Greenfield Pl., Lerwick* ✥ *Off Commercial St.* ☎ *01595/692195* 🌐 *www.shetlandhotels.com* 🔑 *17 rooms* 🍽 *Free Breakfast.*

🛍 Shopping

Shetland's tradition of knitting and knitted lace is still going strong. You can still buy the traditional Fair Isle knitwear, but also look out for the new wave of Shetland knitters. The Shetland Museum shop is perhaps one of the best in the islands for cards, books, and souvenirs, but there are a number of other independent sellers who stock interesting knitwear, gifts, and books. The island's artisans have, like Orkney, opened their studios to visitors and are selling their work directly:

look on the Shetland Craft Trail (⊕ www.shetlandartsandcrafts.co.uk and, as you tour the island, fit in a visit to a craftsman who takes your fancy. Appointments are generally required.

Anderson & Co.

CRAFTS | On Commercial Street, Anderson & Co. carries hand-knitted cardigans, jumpers, Shetland lace scarves, sheepskin slippers, and woven throws. ✉ 60–62 Commercial St., Lerwick ☎ 01595/693714 ⊕ www.shetlandknitwear.com ⊗ Closed Sun.

Ninian

MIXED CLOTHING | Tempting 21st-century interpretations of traditional Fair Isle clothing, scarves, and throws as well as ceramics, gifts, and beautiful children's toys are found at Ninian. ✉ 80 Commercial St., Lerwick ☎ 01595/696655 ⊕ www.ninianshetland.co.uk.

★ Peerie Shop

CRAFTS | The Peerie (Shetland for small) Shop sells a colorful mix of knitwear, cards, ceramics, and interesting—and, yes, small—miscellanea. ✉ Esplanade, Lerwick ☎ 01595/692816 ⊕ www.peerieshop.co.uk.

The South Mainland

14 to 25 miles south of Lerwick.

The narrow 3- or 4-mile-wide stretch of land that reaches south from Lerwick to Sumburgh Head has a number of fascinating ancient sites (and an airport) as well as farmland, wild landscapes, and dramatic ocean views.

GETTING HERE AND AROUND

Arriving in Sumburgh by plane offers stunning views of Sumburgh Head and its golden sands. A fairly regular bus makes the hour-long trip between the airport and Lerwick, and it's also easy to

Shetland Ponies ⊙

The squat and shaggy Shetland pony has been a common sight for more than 12 centuries. Roaming wild over the hills, the pony evolved its long mane and dense winter coat. The animals stand between 28 and 42 inches tall, which made them ideal for working in cramped coal-mine tunnels in the 1850s, when child labor was restricted. They became a popular pet for the aristocracy in the late 19th century; many believe this helped save the breed. Today you'll see ponies at equine events and all over the island, chomping the grass.

drive here if you're based in Lerwick. You can rent a car from the airport or take a taxi. Jarlshof and Scatness are both within walking distance of the terminal.

⊙ Sights

Hoswick Visitor Centre

VISITOR CENTER | This café has an unmanned museum space that heaves with an impressive collection of vintage radios (hugely important to an island community), knitting, spinning, and fishing paraphernalia. The café is popular with locals and visitors alike and sells cakes and soups while trading in knitted and crafty keepsakes made by entrepreneurial Shetlanders. In the mezzanine room is an interesting exhibition on the historic Hoswick whale case, when in 1888 the local fishermen took on an oppressive laird (estate owner) and won. ✉ Hoswick ☎ 01950/431406 ⊕ www.hoswickvisitorcentre.com ▣ Free ⊗ Closed Oct.–May.

The stone tower of Mousa Broch dates back 2,000 years and is impressively preserved.

★ Jarlshof

RUINS | FAMILY | In 1897 a huge storm blew away 4,000 years of sand to expose the multilayered remains of Bronze Age, Iron Age, Pictish, and Viking buildings; prehistoric wheelhouses; and earth houses that represented thousands of years of continuous settlement. It's a large and complex site, and you can roam—and photograph—the remains freely. The small visitor center is packed with details of the lives of former residents and illustrates Jarlshof's more recent history as a medieval farmstead and home of the 16th-century Earl of Orkney and Shetland, "cruel" Patrick Stewart, who enslaved the men of Scalloway to build Scalloway Castle. ✉ Sumburgh Head, Virkie ✛ Off A970 ☎ 0131/668–8600 ⊕ www.historicenvironment.scot ☒ £6 ⊙ Closed Oct.–Mar.

★ Mousa Broch

RUINS | Sandsayre Pier in Sandwick is the departure point for the passenger ferry to the tiny isle of Mousa, where you can see Mousa Broch, a fortified Iron Age stone tower rising about 40 feet high.

The massive walls give a real sense of security, which must have been reassuring for islanders subject to attacks from ship-borne raiders. Exploring this beautifully preserved, curved-stone structure, standing on what feels like an untouched island, makes you feel as if you're back in 100 BC. From April to September, the ferry (£16 round-trip) departs for the island once or twice each afternoon. From May to July there are dusk boat trips (£25 round-trip) to catch the tiny storm petrels as they return from their day feeding at sea to their nests in the walls of the broch. The sight—and feel—of them swarming in the half-light is something you'll never forget. Note that you must pay in cash for the ferry rides and boat trips. ✉ Sandsayre Pier, Sandwick ✛ Off A970, 14 miles south of Lerwick ☎ 07901/872339 ferry ⊕ www.mousa.co.uk ⊙ Closed Oct.–Mar.

Old Scatness

RUINS | FAMILY | This ongoing excavation of an Iron Age village is a worthwhile stop. Enthusiastic and entertaining guides, most in costume, tell stories that breathe life into the stones and the middens, showing how its former residents made their clothes and cooked their food, including their staple dish: the ghastly seaweed porridge. ✉ *Off A970, Virkie* ☎ *01595/694688* ⊕ *www.shetlandamenity.org* ✆ *£6* ⊘ *Closed Sat.–Mon. and Sept.–mid-May.*

★ Shetland Crofthouse Museum

HISTORY MUSEUM | FAMILY | Nine miles south of Sandwick, this 19th-century thatched house reveals the way of life of rural Shetlanders, which the traditionally attired attendant will be delighted to discuss with you. The peat fire casts a glow on the box bed, the resting chair, and the wealth of domestic implements, including a hand mill for preparing meal and a straw "keshie" for carrying peat. One building made from an upturned boat was used for storing and drying fish and mutton; huts like this inspired the design of the new Scottish Parliament. ✉ *East of A970, South Voe, Dunrossness* ☎ *01590/460557* ⊕ *www.shetlandheritageassociation.com* ✆ *Free (donations welcome)* ⊘ *Closed Oct.–Apr.*

★ St. Ninian's Isle

ISLAND | It was on St. Ninian's Isle that a schoolboy helping archaeologists excavate the ruins of a 12th-century church discovered the St. Ninian treasure, a collection of 28 silver objects dating from the 8th century. This Celtic silver is housed in the Museum of Scotland in Edinburgh (a point of controversy), but good replicas are in the Shetland Museum in Lerwick. Although you can't see the silver, walking over the causeway of golden sand (called a tombolo or *ayre*) that joins St. Ninian's Isle to the Mainland is an unforgettable experience. From Sumburgh head 8 miles north on A970 and B9122, then turn left at Skelberry.

Puffins and More ◉

Every summer more than a million birds alight on the cliff faces in Shetland to nest. Bird-watchers can spot more than 20 species, from tiny storm petrels to gannets with 6-foot wingspans. Popular with visitors are the puffins, with their short necks, striped beaks, and orange feet. Look for them on the cliffs at Sumburgh Head near the lighthouse, 2 miles south of Sumburgh Airport. The visitor center has information about nesting sites, as well as live puffin cams during breeding season.

★ Sumburgh Head Lighthouse and Visitor Centre

LIGHTHOUSE | FAMILY | Perhaps one of northern Europe's most stunning locations, this Robert Stevenson—grandfather of the writer Robert Louis—designed lighthouse, built in 1821, was the first lighthouse in Shetland. Sir Walter Scott was very taken with the location and based his novel *The Pirate* on the nearby landmarks of Jarlshof and Fitful Head. The stories of the Old Radar Hut—crucial during WWII—and the engine room with its deep booming foghorn are brought back to life here, while a Marine Life Centre has excellent displays on the birds, fish, and sea mammals found around the cliffs. If you walk round the dry-stone dikes, you will hear and probably see puffins, guillemots, and fulmars breeding, feeding, and fighting on the rocks, but if it's wet and wild, the circular café and Education Suite with its jaw-dropping panorama will provide enough drama. ✉ *Sumburgh Head, Sumburgh* ☎ *01595/694688* ⊕ *www.sumburghhead.com* ✆ *£6* ⊘ *Closed Oct.–Mar.*

🛏 Hotels

★ Hayhoull B&B

$ | B&B/INN | FAMILY | This lively bed-and-breakfast offers the chance to slip into the life of the buzzing Shetland community of Bigton. **Pros:** beautiful views; in friendly village next to the magical St. Ninian's Isle; children welcomed warmly. **Cons:** expensive meals; 4 miles to the nearest pub or restaurant; shared bathroom in two rooms. $ *Rooms from: £90* ✉ *Off B9122, Bigton* ☎ *01950/422206* ⊕ *www.hayhoull.co.uk* ▬ *No credit cards* 🛏 *4 rooms* ◎ *Free Breakfast.*

🛍 Shopping

★ Nielanell

CRAFTS | The designs here are rich in texture, color, and shape, but it's the philosophy behind the knitwear—she makes it for the day you feel your worst—that makes it so desirable. Most of the pieces are made to be worn in multiple ways, meaning you get three pieces for the price of one. ✉ *Hoswick* ☎ *01950/431516* ⊕ *www.nielanell.com.*

Scalloway

6 miles west of Lerwick, 21 miles north of St. Ninian's Isle.

On the west coast of Mainland Island is Scalloway, which preceded Lerwick as the capital of the region. During World War II Scalloway was the port for the "Shetland Bus," a secret fleet of boats that carried British agents to Norway to perform acts of sabotage against the Germans, who were occupying the country. On the return trips, the boats would carry refugees back to Shetland. As you approach the town from the A970, look for the information board, which overlooks the settlement and its castle.

GETTING HERE AND AROUND

The town is 10 minutes by car from Lerwick, or you can get one of the fairly regular buses or even a taxi (£12).

👁 Sights

Scalloway Castle

CASTLE/PALACE | This waterfront fortress was built in 1600 by Patrick Stewart, Earl of Orkney and Shetland. He was hanged in 1615 for his cruelty and misdeeds, and the castle was never used again. To enter, retrieve the key from the Scalloway Museum. You may explore these handsome ruins to your heart's content. ✉ *A970, Scalloway* ☎ *01856/841815* ⊕ *www.historicenvironment.scot* 🎫 *Free* ◷ *Closed Oct.–mid-Apr.*

Scalloway Museum

HISTORY MUSEUM | This modern museum tells some fascinating stories about Scalloway and its well-traveled locals. There is a section dedicated to the exploits of the Shetland Bus, the WWII resistance movement that operated between Norway and Shetland, and cabinet upon cabinet of maritime artifacts and *proil* (sailors' booty) donated by locals. ✉ *Castle St., Scalloway* ☎ *01595/880734* ⊕ *www.scallowaymuseum.org* 🎫 *£3* ◷ *Closed Oct.–mid-Apr.*

🍴 Restaurants

The Cornerstone

$ | CAFÉ | The unfussy menu here features dishes such as soups, quiche, and sandwiches by day or steaks and lasagna by night. It isn't fancy, but it is made and served with great enthusiasm and generosity. **Known for:** friendly, welcoming atmosphere; mammoth scones; tasty quiches. $ *Average main: £12* ✉ *Burn Beach, Main St., Scalloway* ☎ *01595/880346* ⊕ *www.thecornerstonebandb.com* ◷ *No dinner Sun.–Thurs.*

Weisdale

9 miles north of Lerwick.

This tiny place is less a village than a group of houses, but it does have a worthwhile gallery.

GETTING HERE AND AROUND
Take A971 from Lerwick. The No. 9 bus runs three times a day weekdays; the trip from Lerwick is 20 minutes.

⊙ Sights

Bonhoga Gallery
ART GALLERY | Built in 1855 using stones from the Kergord estate's "cleared" (forcibly evicted) crofts, Weisdale Mill is now the Bonhoga Gallery, a contemporary art space showing quirky exhibitions by local, national, and international artists. Downstairs is a small but cake-laden café that looks over the Weisdale burn. An excellent shop sells artist-made housewares. ⊠ *B9075, Weisdale* ☎ *01595/745750* ⊕ *www.shetlandarts. org.*

⬤ Shopping

Shetland Jewellery
JEWELRY & WATCHES | This shop sells gold and silver Nordic- and Celtic-inspired jewelry, desk knives, and belt buckles made in the on-site workshop. ⊠ *Sound Side, Weisdale* ☎ *01595/830275* ⊕ *www. shetlandjewellery.co.uk.*

Brae

15 miles north of Weisdale, 24 miles north of Lerwick.

A thriving community, Brae is where you can see the spoils of Shetland's oil money. The rugged moorland and tranquil *voes* (inlets) of Brae are the home of Busta House, one of the best hotels on the island.

GETTING HERE AND AROUND
There are buses from Lerwick to Brae, but the spread-out sights make it impossible to really see this area without a car. A970 is the main road, and B9078 will take you through Hillswick and to Eshaness.

⊙ Sights

Eshaness and Ronas Hill
VIEWPOINT | About 15 miles north of Brae are the rugged, forbidding cliffs around **Eshaness**; drive north and then turn left onto B9078. On the way, look for the defiant Drongs, striking sandstone stacks or pillars battered into shape by thousands of years of crashing seas. Then return to join the A970 at Hillswick, but before reaching Ura Firth, turn left toward the old crofting community of Heylor on Ronas Voe, beautifully documented by the pioneer filmmaker Jenny Gilbertson in the 1930s. Providing a front-on vista of rounded, red **Ronas Hill,** the highest hill in Shetland, Heylor's delightful sandy beach is known as the Blade. Beware: arctic terns—which Shetlanders call Tirricks—nest among the pebbles in May and June.

★ Tangwick Haa Museum
HISTORY MUSEUM | After viewing the cliffs at Eshaness, call in at Tangwick Haa Museum, the 17th-century home of the Cheynes, now packed full with photographs, household items, and knitting, farming, and fishing equipment from the 18th to early 20th century. Upstairs is the Laird's Room—a traditional sitting room of the 19th century and a room of curiosities, including whale eardrums. Downstairs—next to the help-yourself café—there are rows of folders; ask one of the staff to let you hear what's in them and you will be rewarded with the soft, gentle voices of local elders telling you of life lived in Shetland. ⊠ *Off B9078, Tangwick* ☎ *01806/503389* ⊕ *www. tangwickhaa.org.uk* ⬛ *Free* ⊙ *Closed. Oct.–Mar.*

🏖 Beaches

Mavis Grind

BEACH | North of Brae the A970 meanders past Mavis Grind, a strip of land so narrow you can throw a stone—if you're strong—from the Atlantic, in one inlet, to the North Sea, in another. Keep an eye out for sea otters, which sometimes cross here.

🍴 Restaurants

Braewick Café

$ | BRITISH | With a stunning position overlooking the Drongs (rocky columns standing in the sea), this eatery serves famously large portions popular with visitors and Shetlanders alike. Browse the local crafts in the shop while waiting for a crispy battered-fish supper, or just sit back on the sofas by the huge picture window and watch the dramatic sea and sky. **Known for:** wonderful ocean view; Shetland roast lamb; lovely cakes. $ *Average main: £10* ✉ *Off B9078, Eshaness* ☎ *01806/503345* ⊕ *www.eshaness.moonfruit.com* ⊗ *No dinner.*

★ Frankie's Fish & Chips

$ | SEAFOOD | Proudly claiming to be the northernmost fish-and-chips shop in Britain, this "chipper" is also the best of its kind on the islands. The combination of superfresh seafood—skate wings, squid, and crab legs—and light and crispy batter (including a gluten-free option) means Frankie's is everything a chip shop could be. **Known for:** early closing at 8 pm; Shetland mussels; king scallops in garlic butter. $ *Average main: £11* ✉ *A970, Brae* ☎ *01806/522700* ⊕ *www.frankies-fishandchips.com.*

🛏 Hotels

★ Busta House

$$ | HOTEL | Dating from the 16th century, Busta House—built by the well-heeled but ill-fated Gifford family—is one of the few grand houses of Shetland. **Pros:** truly haunting atmosphere; charming public rooms; lovely grounds. **Cons:** popular with wedding parties; some rooms are a tight fit; noisy plumbing. $ *Rooms from: £125* ✉ *Off A970, Brae* ☎ *01806/522506* ⊕ *www.bustahouse.com* ⇋ *22 rooms* ❯ *Free Breakfast.*

Yell

11 miles northeast of Brae, 31 miles north of Lerwick.

A desolate-looking blanket bog cloaks two-thirds of the island of Yell, creating an atmospheric landscape to pass through on the way to Unst to the north.

GETTING HERE AND AROUND

Although you will see the odd walker or cyclist, a car is needed to explore the northern isles. To get to Yell, take A970 or B9076 and catch the ferry from Toft to Ulsta. On Yell, B9081 runs through Burravoe and up the east side and joins the A968, which leads to Gutcher and the ferry to Unst.

👁 Sights

Old Haa

HISTORIC SIGHT | The oldest building on the island, Burravoe's Old Haa is known for its crowstepped gables (the stepped effect on the ends of the roofs), typical of an early-18th-century Shetland merchant's house. There's an earnest memorial to Bobby Tulloch, the great Shetland naturalist and champion of Shetland's bird population (1929–96), and the displays in the upstairs museum tell the story of the wrecking of the German ship, the *Bohus,* in 1924. A copy of the ship's figurehead is displayed outside the building. The Old Haa serves light meals with home-baked bannocks, cakes, and other goodies and also acts as a kind of unofficial information center. A crafts shop is on the premises, too. ✉ *Burravoe* ☎ *01957/722339* ⊕ *www.oldhaa.com* ⊠ *Free* ⊗ *Closed Fri. and Oct.–June.*

Unst

49 miles north of Lerwick.

Unst is the northernmost inhabited island in Scotland, a remote and special place, especially for nature lovers and those who want to experience a community on the edge of faraway. On a long summer evening, views north to Muckle Flugga, with only the ocean beyond, are incomparable. If you're a bird-watcher, head to the Hermaness and Keen of Hamar nature reserves.

GETTING HERE AND AROUND

A ferry (take the A968 at the village of Mid Yell to Gutcher) crosses the Bluemull Sound to Unst. A car is best for exploring, though there is limited bus service, including from Lerwick; taxis are an option.

◉ Sights

Hermaness National Nature Reserve

NATURE PRESERVE | A bleak moorland ending in rocky cliffs, the Hermaness National Nature Reserve is prime bird-watching territory. About half the world's population (6,000 pairs) of great skuas, called "bonxies" by locals, are found here. These sky pirates attack anything that strays near their nests, including humans, so keep to the paths. Thousands of other seabirds, including more than 50,000 puffins, nest on the cliffs, about an hour's walk from the reserve entrance. Gray seals haul out at the foot of the cliffs in fall, and offshore, dolphins and occasionally whales (including orcas) can be seen on calm days.

A path meanders across moorland and climbs up a gentle hill, from which you can see, to the north, a series of tilting offshore rocks; the largest of these sea-battered protrusions is **Muckle Flugga,** meaning "big, steep-sided island," on which stands a lighthouse. The lighthouse was built by engineer Thomas Stevenson, whose son, the great Scottish writer Robert Louis Stevenson, used the outline of Unst for his map of Treasure Island. Muckle Flugga is the northernmost point in Scotland.

Mid-May to mid-July is the best time to visit. To get here from Haroldswick, follow the B9086 around the head of Burrafirth to the signposted car park. ⊠ *B9086, Burrafirth* ☎ *01957/693345* ⊕ *www.nature.scot* ⊠ *Free.*

Muness Castle

CASTLE/PALACE | Scotland's northernmost castle was built in 1598 by Laurence Bruce of Cultmalindie, uncle of "cruel" Patrick Stewart. Despite being a ruin it is rather fetching, with circular corner towers and a scale-and-platt (that is, not circular but straight on) staircase. ⊠ *B9084, Uyeasound* ⊕ *www.historicenvironment.scot* ⊠ *Free.*

Unst Boat Haven

OTHER MUSEUM | Reflecting Shetland's intimacy with the sea, Unst Boat Haven displays a beautiful collection of traditional small fishing and sailing boats. ⊠ *Beach Rd., Haroldswick* ☎ *01957/711528* ⊕ *www.unstheritage.com* ⊠ *£3, includes Unst Heritage Centre* ⊗ *Closed Oct.–Apr.*

Unst Heritage Centre

HISTORY MUSEUM | The unique and colorful history of the people of Unst is told in this fascinating assemblage of artifacts, tools, photographs, and reconstructions, including a classroom and a *ben* or "good" end (sitting room) of a croft house. It will leave you with an enduring visual memory of the ways in which the locals learned, crofted, knitted, fished, and worshipped through the last two centuries. ⊠ *Haroldswick* ☎ *01957/711528* ⊕ *www.unstheritage.com* ⊠ *£3, includes Unst Boat Haven* ⊗ *Closed Oct.–Apr.*

🍴 Restaurants

Victoria's Vintage Tea Rooms

$ | CAFÉ | FAMILY | Run by a Devon girl who knows a thing or two about cream teas, this vintage-style café does a roaring trade right on the water at Haroldswick. The Shetland smoked salmon on Skibhoul (the local baker) bread is a sandwich worth getting excited about, as are the cakes, especially the Victoria Sponge and scones. **Known for:** seal and otter spotting; Devon cream teas; great coffee. $ *Average main: £6* ⊠ *Old Haroldswick Shop, Haroldswick* ☎ *01957/711885* ⊕ *victoriasvintagetearooms.co.uk* ⊗ *Closed Mon. No dinner.*

🛏 Hotels

Gardiesfauld Hostel

$ | B&B/INN | With options limited for an overnighter in Unst, this quiet and spacious youth hostel will appeal to travelers who want more than a quick day trip and take an interest in others who end up in the same remote location. **Pros:** family rooms en suite available; perfect for travelers on a shoestring; quiet (especially outside school holidays). **Cons:** private rooms must be booked well in advance; you can't guarantee silence; communal facilities. $ *Rooms from: £32* ⊠ *B9084, Uyeasound* ☎ *01957/755279* ⊕ *www.unst.org* ⊟ *No credit cards* ⊗ *Oct.–Mar. by arrangement only* ⤴ *6 rooms* ⦿ *No Meals.*

🛍 Shopping

Skibhoul Stores and Bakery

FOOD | The bread from Skibhoul is so popular that large shipments of it head south to the rest of the Isles on Thursdays. It's also famous for the Oceanic sea-salt oatcakes and Balta biscuits that are perfect for picnics. There's a small self-serve café so you can taste the wares. ⊠ *Northside* ☎ *01957/711444.*

Index

Photo Credits

Front Cover: Lingxiao Xie/GettyImages [Glenfinnan railway viaduct and Jacobite steam train, Lochaber, Highland, Scotland, UK. It goes by the route Fort William to Mallaig only 2-4 times a day]. **Back cover, from left to right:** Martin M303/Shutterstock, f11photo/Shutterstock, Nataliya Hora/ Shutterstock. **Spine:** Shaiith/ Dreamstime. **Interior, from left to right:** Buccleuch Estate (1). Paul Tomkins/VisitScotland (2-3). **Chapter 1: Experience Scotland:** Heartland Arts/ Shutterstock (8-9). W. McKelvie 2005 (10-11). Kenny Lam/VisitScotland (11). Tomas Rebro/Shutterstock (11). John A Cameron/Shutterstock (12). Jaime Pharr/Shutterstock (12). A. Karnholz/Shutterstock (12). Nabil Imran/Shutterstock (12). Paul Tomkins/VisitScotland (13). Kenny Lam/VisitScotland (13). Hufton Crow/V&A Dundee (14). Kenny Lam/VisitScotland (14). Kawhia/Shutterstock (14). Jimmcdowall/iStockphoto (14). Kenny Lam/VisitScotland (15). Kenny Lam/VisitScotland (16). Kenny Lam/VisitScotland (16). Ben Queenborough/Shutterstock (16). Kenny Lam/VisitScotland (16). Ian Rutherford/VisitScotland (17). Essevu/Shutterstock (17). Monkey Business Images/ Shutterstock (18). MTBjorn/Shutterstock (18). Kenny Lam/ VisitScotland (18). Kenny Lam/VisitScotland (19). Apostolis Giontzis/Shutterstock (19). Vertmedia/iStockphoto (26). Tana888/Shutterstock (26). Jag_cz/iStockphoto (26). Yingko/Shutterstock (27). Joerg Beuge/Shutterstock (27). Paolo Gallo/Shutterstock (28). Courtesy_The Quaich Company (29). Jeff Whyte/Shutterstock (30). Anton_Ivanov/Shutterstock (30). CSG CIC Glasgow Museums Collection (30). Elinor Staniforth (30). Alaistair Ramsay/Scottish Fisheries Museum (31). Timawe/Dreamstime (31). Hufton Crow (31). James McDowall/Shutterstock (31). Kenny Lam/VisitScotland (32). Kenny Lam/VisitScotland (32). Kenny Lam/VisitScotland (32). Klodien/Dreamstime (32). Kenny Lam/VisitScotland (32). Craig Duncanson/Shutterstock (33). Targn Pleiades/Shutterstock (33). Damian Shields/North East 250/VisitScotland (33). Kenny Lam/VisitScotland (33). Simon Taylor/Dreamstime (33). TreasureGalore/Shutterstock (34). Heartland Arts/Shutterstock (34). JeniFoto/Shutterstock (34). Kenny Lam/VisitScotland (34). Kenny Lam/VisitScotland (34). Paul Tomkins/VisitScotland (35). Moomusician/Shutterstock (35). Paul Tomkins/VisitScotland (35). Kenny Lam/VisitScotland (35). Kenny Lam/VisitScotland (35). Jasper Image/Shutterstock (36). Damian Shields/North East 250/VisitScotland (36). Glen Grant (36). 13threephotography/Shutterstock (36). Søren Solkær/Highland Park (36). Tyler W. Stipp/Shutterstock (37). 13threephotography/Shutterstock (37). John Paul/The Glenmorangie Company (37). Christian Jordi/Dreamstime (37). Robert Porter/Dreamstime (37). **Chapter 3: Edinburgh and the Lothians:** Kenny Lam/VisitScotland (65). Kenny Lam/VisitScotland (70). Kenny Lam/VisitScotland (83). Matteo Provendola/ Shutterstock (85). Anton_Ivanov/Shutterstock (87). Harald Lueder/Shutterstock (88). Lou Armor/Shutterstock (115). Alexey Fedorenko/Shutterstock (119). Serge Bertasius Photography/ Shutterstock (122). PhotoFires/Shutterstock (124). **Chapter 4: Glasgow:** Kenny Lam/VisitScotland (131). Leonid Andronov/Shutterstock (145). Cornfield/Shutterstock (146). Anton_Ivanov/Shutterstock (158). Roman Babakin/Shutterstock (163). Stefano_Valeri/Shutterstock (177). Ulmus Media/Shutterstock (189). **Chapter 5: The Borders and the Southwest:** David Bostock/Shutterstock (191). WApted/Shutterstock (205). Keith K/Shutterstock (221). **Chapter 6: Fife and Angus:** HuftonCrow (229). Juliet Photography/Shutterstock (237). James McDowall/Shutterstock (251). HuftonCrow (252). MagSpace/Shutterstock (265). **Chapter 7: Stirling and the Central Highlands:** Kenny Lam/VisitScotland (267). HeroToZero/Shutterstock (281). Khirman Vladimir/Shutterstock (287). Cornfield/Shutterstock (303). **Chapter 8: Aberdeen and the Northeast:** Paul Tomkins/ VisitScotland (305). Kenny Lam/VisitScotland (313). Francesco Dazzi/Shutterstock (325). **Chapter 9: Argyll and the Isles:** Lukasz Pajor/Shutterstock (345). Lukassek/Shutterstock (353). Nick Fox/Shutterstock (357). Dmitry Naumov/Shutterstock (361). Joost van Uffelen/Shutterstock (371). **Chapter 10: Inverness and Around the Great Glen:** George KUZ/Shutterstock (377). Lowsun/Shutterstock (385). Chbaum/Shutterstock (390). Johnbraid/Shutterstock (397). Samot/Shutterstock (405). **Chapter 11: The Northern Highlands and the Western Isles:** Helen Hotson/Shutterstock (411). John Paul/The Glenmorangie Company (421). Boris Edelmann/Shutterstock (427). Lukassek/Shutterstock (437). EyesTravelling/Shutterstock (446). M. Vinuesa/Shutterstock (451). Helen Hotson/Shutterstock (453). **Chapter 12: Orkney and Shetland Islands:** Kenny Lam/VisitScotland (457). Colin Keldie/VisitScotland (467). Marcin Kadziolka/Shutterstock (478). **About Our Writers:** All photos are courtesy of the writers.

*Every effort has been made to trace the copyright holders, and we apologize in advance for any accidental errors. We would be happy to apply the corrections in the following edition of this publication.

Fodor's ESSENTIAL SCOTLAND

Publisher: Stephen Horowitz, *General Manager*

Editorial: Douglas Stallings, *Editorial Director*; Jill Fergus, Amanda Sadlowski, Caroline Trefler, *Senior Editors*; Kayla Becker, Alexis Kelly, *Editors*; Angelique Kennedy-Chavannes, *Assistant Editor*

Design: Tina Malaney, *Director of Design and Production*; Jessica Gonzalez, *Graphic Designer*

Production: Jennifer DePrima, *Editorial Production Manager*; Elyse Rozelle, *Senior Production Editor*; Monica White, *Production Editor*

Maps: Rebecca Baer, *Senior Map Editor*; Mark Stroud (Moon Street Cartography), *Cartographer*

Photography: Viviane Teles, *Senior Photo Editor*; Namrata Aggarwal, Payal Gupta, Ashok Kumar, *Photo Editors*; Eddie Aldrete, *Photo Production Intern*

Business and Operations: Chuck Hoover, *Chief Marketing Officer*; Robert Ames, *Group General Manager*; Devin Duckworth, *Director of Print Publishing*

Public Relations and Marketing: Joe Ewaskiw, *Senior Director of Communications and Public Relations*

Fodors.com: Jeremy Tarr, *Editorial Director*; Rachael Levitt, *Managing Editor*

Technology: Jon Atkinson, *Director of Technology*; Rudresh Teotia, *Lead Developer*; Jacob Ashpis, *Content Operations Manager*

Writers: Nick Bruno, Robin Gauldie, Mike Gonzalez, Joseph Reaney

Editors: Amanda Sadlowski, Laura Kidder

Production Editor: Monica White

3rd Edition

ISBN 978-1-64097-496-8

ISSN 2574-0636

SPECIAL SALES
This book is available at special discounts for bulk purchases for sales promotions or premiums. For more information, e-mail SpecialMarkets@fodors.com.

PRINTED IN CANADA

10 9 8 7 6 5 4 3 2 1

About Our Writers

Based in Dundee, **Nick Bruno** is a travel writer, journalist, and a Fodor's contributor for over a decade. He has authored many books and features about both Italy and Scotland, and also works for the BBC. An interest in history has led to a project researching the lives of Italians—including his paternal family—before, during, and after Il Ventennio Fascista. For this edition, he updated the Experience Scotland, Travel Smart, and Fife and Angus chapters.

Robin Gauldie was born in Dundee and studied history at Edinburgh University before training as journalist on local newspapers in Tayside. Since 1990 he has been a freelance journalist specializing in travel and the tourism industry, and is the author of more than 30 travel guidebooks to destinations in Europe, Asia, Africa, and South America. When not traveling he divides his time between his home in Edinburgh's New Town and a village house in Languedoc, southern France. This edition, Robin updated Aberdeen and the Northeast, Argyll and the Isles, and Orkney and Shetland Islands.

Mike Gonzalez is emeritus professor of Latin American Studies at Glasgow University and also writes regularly for the *Herald* and other publications on politics and culture. This edition, Mike updated the Borders and the Southwest and Stirling and the Central Highlands chapters. His travels have taken him to places familiar and less familiar, including exploring a tiny island on Islay whose houses were once an imperial center and walking in a hidden sculpture park in the hills near Dumfries.

Originally from Aberdeen, **Tara Hepburn** is a Glasgow-based writer and journalist. She works as the Glasgow arts and culture editor of *The Skinny*, writing about new places in the city. She updated the Glasgow chapter this edition.

Joseph Reaney is an experienced travel writer and editor based part-time in Scotland and part-time in the Czech Republic—and regularly writes about both. He contributes to *Lonely Planet*, *National Geographic*, and *Forbes Travel Guide*, among others, and runs his own travel content writing agency, World Words. When he has the time, he also writes and directs short films and comedy sketches. He updated three chapters for this edition: Edinburgh and the Lothians, Inverness and Around the Great Glen, and the Northern Highlands and the Western Isles.